WORLD POLITICS DEBATED

A READER IN CONTEMPORARY ISSUES

WORLD POLITICS DEBATED

A Reader in Contemporary Issues

FOURTH EDITION

Herbert M. Levine

McGraw-Hill, Inc.

New York St. Louis San Francisco Auckland Bogotá Caracas
Lisbon London Madrid Mexico Milan Montreal New Delhi
Paris San Juan Singapore Sydney Tokyo Toronto

This book was set in Times Roman by General Graphic Services, Inc.
The editors were Bert Lummus and John M. Morriss;
the production supervisor was Friederich W. Schulte.
The cover was designed by Carla Bauer.
Project supervision was done by The Total Book.
R. R. Donnelley & Sons Company was printer and binder.

WORLD POLITICS DEBATED
A Reader in Contemporary Issues

3 4 5 6 7 8 9 0   DOHDOH   9 0 9 8 7 6 5 4 3

ISBN 0-07-037512-7

Library of Congress Cataloging-in-Publication Data

World politics debated: a reader in contemporary issues / [selected
  by] Herbert M. Levine.—4th ed.
       p.   cm.
   Includes bibliographical references.
   ISBN 0-07-037512-7
   1. World politics—1989-   I. Levine, Herbert M.
D860..W67   1992
327′.09′04—dc20   91-15942

ABOUT
THE EDITOR

HERBERT M. LEVINE is a political scientist, who taught at the University of Southwestern Louisiana for twenty years. He is the author or editor of several debate books in political science. His recent books include *What If the American Political System Were Different?* (M. E. Sharpe) and *Point-Counterpoint: Readings in American Government* (St. Martin's Press). He is currently a writer based in Chevy Chase, Maryland.

To Bob and Pushpa Schwartz

CONTENTS

LIST OF CONTRIBUTORS

ADEOYE A. AKINSANYA is professor of government and public administration at the University of Ilorin in Nigeria. He is the author of *The Expropriation of Multinational Property in the Third World (1980)*.

ARMS CONTROL ASSOCIATION is a public-interest group in Washington, D.C.

BRUCE BARTLETT is deputy assistant secretary for economic policy at the Department of the Treasury. He is the author of *Reaganomics: Supply Side Economics in Action* (1981).

PETER T. BAUER is professor emeritus, London School of Economics, fellow of Caius College, Cambridge, and fellow of the British Academy. He is the author of *Reality and Rhetoric: Studies in the Economics of Development (1984)* and *Equality, the Third World, and Economic Delusion (1981)*.

WILLIAM O. BEEMAN, associate professor of anthropology at Brown University and associate editor of Pacific News Service, San Francisco, has conducted research in the Middle East since 1967. He has served as adviser to the U.S. State Department and has testified before Congress on Middle Eastern affairs.

ROBERT H. BORK is the John M. Olin Scholar in Legal Studies at the American Enterprise Institute, Washington, D.C.

FIDEL CASTRO is president of Cuba.

CHEN JIABAO is a writer for *Beijing Review*.

MIDGE DECTER, a member of the Heritage Foundation's Board of Trustees, is a writer. She served as executive director of the Committee for the Free World.

DEFENSE MONITOR is a publication of the Center for Defense Information, Washington, D.C.

LEWIS A. DUNN led the U.S. delegation to the 1985 Nuclear Nonproliferation Treaty Review Conference and is now assistant vice-president of Science Applications International Corporation in McLean, Virginia.

JAMES EAYRS is Eric Dennis Memorial Professor of Government and Political Science at Dalhousie University in Halifax, Canada.

ANNE H. EHRLICH is a senior research associate in biological sciences at Stanford University. She is the coauthor of *Earth* (1987), *Extinction: The Causes and Consequences of the Disappearance of Species* (1981), and *The End of Affluence: A Blueprint for Your Future* (1974).

PAUL R. EHRLICH is Bing Professor of Population Studies and a professor of biological sciences at Stanford University. He is the author of *The Population Bomb* (1968).

MARK FALCOFF is a resident fellow at the American Enterprise Institute, Washington, D.C.

GREGORY A. FOSSEDAL is John M. Olin Media Fellow at the Hoover Institution of War, Revolution and Peace and a columnist for Copley News Service.

FRANK J. GAFFNEY, JR., is director of the Center for Security Policy and a former staff member of the U.S. Senate.

MEG GREENFIELD is editorial page editor of the *Washington Post* and a columnist for *Newsweek*.

HENRY GRUNWALD, former editor-in-chief of Time Inc., is U.S. ambassador to Austria.

FERRY HOOGENDIJK is the editor of *European Affairs*, a quarterly magazine. He served for twenty-two years as editor-in-chief of *Elsevier*, the leading Dutch news magazine.

MICHAEL HOWARD is professor of history at Yale University. He is the author of *Causes of War and Other Essays* (1983).

ISHIHARA SHINTARŌ is a member of the Liberal Democratic party serving in Japan's House of Representatives. He was director general of Japan's Environment Agency and minister of transport. He is also a novelist.

JOSEF JOFFE is foreign editor of *Süddeutsche Zeitung* (Munich).

ASHOK KAPUR is professor of political science at the University of Waterloo, Ontario, and the author of *Pakistan's Nuclear Development* (1987).

ALAN L. KEYES, president of Citizens against Government Waste, served as assistant secretary of state for U.N. affairs from 1985 to 1987.

STANLEY KOBER is an adjunct scholar at the Cato Institute, Washington, D.C.

MELVYN B. KRAUSS is professor of economics at New York University and a senior fellow at the Hoover Institution of War, Revolution and Peace.

CHARLES KRAUTHAMMER is a syndicated columnist.

MICHAEL LERNER is editor and publisher of *Tikkun*, a bimonthly Jewish critique of politics.

ROBERT McGEEHAN is department head of international relations, United States International University—Europe in Watford, England,

JAMES MAYALL is reader in international relations at the London School of Economics.

TADEUSZ MAZOWIECKI was prime minister of Poland from September 1989 to January 1991. He is the leader of the Democratic Union party.

JOHN J. MEARSHEIMER is chair of the Political Science Department at the University of Chicago. He is the author of *Liddell Hart and the Weight of History* (1988) and *Conventional Deterrence* (1983).

The late HANS J. MORGENTHAU was a political scientist who taught for many years at the University of Chicago.

JOHN MUELLER is a professor of political science and director of the Watson Center for the Study of International Peace and Cooperation at the University of Rochester.

NAKANISHI TERUMASA is a professor at Shizuoka Prefectural University in Japan.

JOHN A. PERKINS is legal counsel at Palmer and Dodge, Boston. A former president of the Boston Bar Association and a member of the International Law and Probate sections, he is the author of *The Prudent Peace: Law as Foreign Policy* (1981).

VLADIMIR F. PETROVKSKY is deputy minister for foreign affairs of the Soviet Union.

ANDREW M. SCOTT is professor of political science at the University of North Carolina.

GEORGE SHULTZ served as secretary of state in the administration of Ronald Reagan. He is currently a professor of economics at Stanford University.

EPHRAIM SNEH, Israeli brigadier general (reserve), was the head of the Civil Administration on the West Bank, 1985–1987. He is currently director general of the Golda Meir Association, which teaches democratic values to Israeli high school students.

JOHN SPANIER is professor of political science at the University of Florida in Gainesville. Among his many books is *American Foreign Policy since World War II* (1991).

KENNETH W. THOMPSON is Director of the Miller Center of Public Affairs at the University of Virginia. He is the author of *Political Realism and the Crisis of World Politics* (1960).

MICHAEL WIDLANSKI, former Middle East correspondent for the Cox Newspaper Group, was editor and project coordinator of *Can Israel Survive a Palestinian State?* (1990) published by the Institute for Advanced Strategic and Political Studies.

YI DING is a writer for *Beijing Review*.

ZHANG ZHEN is president of the China National Defence University.

KARL ZINSMEISTER is a Washington-based writer and an adjunct fellow at the American Enterprise Institute, Washington, D.C.

PREFACE

I continue to be gratified by the response to *World Politics Debated* from students and teachers alike. Instructors have made two central comments about the book. First, they have noted that the focus on major contemporary issues of world politics has made the book a success in supplementing their standard textbooks. Second, they found the debate format to be a pedagogical device that is well suited to engaging student interest and provoking lively discussion in class.

The fourth edition of *World Politics Debated* is significantly different from the third edition, reflecting issues that have emerged in the post–cold war era. There are new topics and new articles; other material has been updated, and the book has been reorganized. New topics include the future of the third world, communist ideology, Germany, a united Europe, a Palestinian state, U.S.-Japan relations, the future of war between developed countries, chemical weapons, and U.S. military commitments abroad. In addition, every effort was made to select current readings, and more than 70 percent of the articles are new to this edition. Chapter introductions, Questions for Discussion, and Suggested Readings have been updated.

The revisions have retained the book's basic focus on the changing character of power in the international arena. Some of the debate questions of the third edition, such as those dealing with the decline of the nation-state, interdependence, and economic sanctions, have been retained because of their continuing interest. As with the first three editions, the editor has attempted to present strong arguments for each contending viewpoint so that readers may carefully analyze issues of world politics.

ACKNOWLEDGMENTS

McGraw-Hill and the author wish to express their appreciation to the many people who were helpful in the preparation of this book. Editorial consultants made valuable criticisms and suggestions for change. These consultants were Gary Buckley, Northern Arizona State University, R. Carter, Texas Christian University; David T. Jervis, Washburn University of Topeka; John Kroll, Dartmouth College; Howard Lenter, CUNY Bernard Baruch; Timothy Lomperis, Duke University; Donald Megnin, Slippery Rock University; Frederic S. Pearson, Wayne State University; Martin Rochester, University of Missouri; Margaret Scranton, University of Arkansas–Little Rock; and Primo Vanicelli, University of Massachusetts–Boston.

As in the past, I received editorial support from my editors at McGraw-Hill. I am indebted to Bert Lummus, the political science editor, who guided the development of the book; and to Annette Bodzin, the project supervisor, who managed its production. Ann Hofstra Grogg copyedited the manuscript with extraordinary attention to detail and with a magnificent command of the rules governing grammar and style.

Herbert M. Levine

INTRODUCTION

Power is central to politics. It is also an ambiguous concept. A standard definition of power—and the one used in this book—is the ability to make someone do what he or she may not want to do.

This book deals with the changing nature of power in world politics since the end of World War II. It pays special attention to issues of the post–cold war era. It is organized into sections, discussing the international system, beliefs, regional issues, instruments of power, constraints on war, and the future world order.

Each chapter begins with an introduction describing the significant power relationships since 1945. Relevant issues are highlighted, and for each there is an Affirmative and a Negative position. The readings are taken from diverse sources, including magazines, newspapers, government documents, and books. They reflect a variety of ideological and national viewpoints and are selected because of their value in a debate framework. Questions for Discussion and Suggested Readings follow each debate to encourage further thought and study.

The purpose of the debate format is to stimulate interest in the subject matter of world politics. Debate is a pedagogical device that encourages critical thinking. But it also presents some problems. Of necessity, it restricts focus on a single issue from only two sides. When evaluating an issue, consequently, readers should keep in mind that there may be no clear Yes or No answer. Often each of the two views presented has some merit, and readers must decide for themselves what to accept and what to reject.

Another problem of the debate format is that the question asked may seem to imply that it is the only issue worthy of consideration for that topic. To counter this impression, the introductory essay in each chapter often suggests other questions requiring examination, although space limitations of the book prevent them from being examined.

Moreover, the debate format may seem to imply that the arguments presented for saying Yes or No on an issue are always those given in the readings. In reality, on many issues entirely different positions are sometimes taken that reject the arguments made on both sides presented here. In other words, there is often a much wider variety of views than the debate format can accommodate.

In spite of these problems, the debate format offers opportunities for critical investigation. A useful way to evaluate a debate is first to discover the specific differences between the two viewpoints and then to analyze the differences by answering the following questions:

1. Do the contending authors disagree about the facts?
2. Is there a disagreement about the consequences of certain actions?
3. Does the disagreement arise because the backgrounds of the authors differ, so that each author perceives events from a different perspective?
4. Are the disagreements related to the different ideological orientations of the authors?
5. Are there ways of looking at the issues involved other than those presented in the readings?

These five questions do not constitute the only ones that may be considered. They do, however, offer a framework for evaluating the readings and reaching informed opinions about the questions raised.

WORLD POLITICS DEBATED

A READER IN CONTEMPORARY ISSUES

CHAPTER 1

The Nature of the International System

Few observers in the West imagined at the beginning of the 1980s that the world would be a very different place by the end of the decade. Conservatives regarded the Soviet Union as a mighty power, building up its nuclear and conventional armaments to unnecessarily high levels and causing trouble in third world countries by undermining pro-Western or neutral governments. Liberals saw the arms race as out of control and criticized both the communist and noncommunist world for perpetuating the distrust that fueled it.

These views were based on a number of assumptions: (1) The cold war—with its lack of trust between the Soviet Union and its allies on the one side and the United States and its allies on the other—would continue. (2) Germany would continue divided between the Federal Republic of Germany, allied with the West, and the German Democratic Republic, allied with the East. (3) The nuclear arms race would continue, albeit with occasional arms control agreements.

But the emergence of Mikhail Gorbachev to power in 1985 heralded large changes in the Soviet Union's domestic and foreign policies. Gorbachev instituted policies of *perestroika* (restructuring), which sought to change the Soviet economic system so that it would be more productive, and *glasnost* (openness), which relaxed the political controls restricting freedom. Gradually the Soviet Union moved toward a market economy and political democracy.

Five years later, the Soviet empire began to collapse. Gorbachev brought Soviet troops back from Afghanistan where they had been fighting for nearly a decade. Moreover, he supported democratic forces challenging communist rule in friendly Eastern European countries. He moved to reduce the number of Soviet conventional forces in the German Democratic Republic and the rest of Eastern Europe and entered into a series of arms control agreements with the United States. Partly as a result of his policies, the power of the Communist party of the U.S.S.R. was in decline.

These changes were received in the Soviet Union and abroad with uncertainty; many observers believed that Soviet foreign policy and domestic politics could easily revert to older ways. Soviet troops moved into Lithuania to repress that republic's efforts at independence. Economic reform slowed down. The Soviet media came back under government control. Some Soviet dissidents accused Gorbachev of trying to become a dictator, and there was increasing speculation that he would be removed from power. And with the igniting of ethnic tensions, there was even a prospect that the Soviet Union would be dismembered.

In the view of most observers, the cold war was clearly over, and the world was now moving into a new age—the post–cold war era. Optimists hoped that political and military cooperation would replace conflict and distrust. In their view, economic development, human rights, and environmental protection would now be at the center of the global arena. International institutions would help the world adjust to military, economic, and environmental insecurity.

To some extent the optimism of the post–cold war world was like that expressed in the aftermath of World War II, although the political, military, and economic conditions were different. Even before World War II came to an end, political observers had looked with hope to the establishment of new institutions to cope with the problems facing the postwar world. That war had produced horrendous destruction of life and property in Europe, Asia, and Africa. The economies of many countries—whether victorious or vanquished—had been shattered by military devastation or the distorted priorities of war. Colonial rule in Africa and Asia was already being challenged by the war itself as well as by the rise of nationalism among the peoples of these continents, the decline of the West's economic power, and the influence of ideologies committed to ending colonialism.

Political observers offered a variety of predictions about the character of world politics in the postwar world. Some believed that the system of independent states would survive the war and that power considerations should be based on this reality. Others looked to the creation or strengthening of international organizations—both public and private—to transform world politics so that the problems of war and economic development could be solved. The more idealistic hoped for a world government to emerge as the principal actor in the global arena. Any observer creating a view of the future had to consider who would be the principal actors and what would be the structure of power in world politics. This chapter presents issues dealing with both actors and structure in the global arena since 1945 and into the post–cold war era.

ACTORS

In the more than four and one-half decades since the end of World War II, the participants in world politics have been diverse in character. The changes these principal actors experienced reflect the political, military, economic, and social forces that have shaped the postwar world.

The principal actors in the postwar period have been states, private groups, and international governmental organizations. These actors are not new to world politics; some have been in existence for four hundred years. Private groups have had an even older history, and international governmental organizations (IGOs) antedate the Congress of Vienna, which assembled in 1814.

States are defined as political institutions that are characterized by territory, population, government, and sovereignty. By the end of World War II, there were about fifty states in the world. By late 1945 two states stood out as superpowers—the United States and the Soviet Union. Because the United States possessed vast economic resources and had not been attacked on its mainland during the war, it emerged as the strongest country in the world. It had preeminence in military power in part because it possessed a rich economy that could sustain a strong defense establishment and in part because it was a master of military technology, most notably in its leadership in producing the atomic bomb. The Soviet Union had the strongest army in Europe. Although it experienced the most destruction of life and property of any Allied Power, it emerged from the war as strong relative to other states. France and Great Britain were recovering from the economic problems of the war. On the Axis side, Germany was wrecked by the war and divided into occupation zones. Both Italy and Japan coped with severe human and economic hardships.

By the early 1990s the character of the state system had changed significantly. Rather than wither away to be replaced by a world government, states grew in number and diversity. By 1991 the number of states had risen to about 170. Most of the new states had been under colonial rule and had achieved their independence either through war or voluntary agreement by the colonial powers. The emergence of these independent states—many of them in Africa and Asia—had a profound impact on world politics as power shifted to them. Because of their strategic locations, vital resources, military strength, and diplomatic leverage, these new states made demands on the world community—particularly in areas such as economic development, redistribution of the world's income, arms transfers, and disarmament.

A prominent feature of post–World War II states was nationalism, the feeling of a strong attachment to a state. Not only did the countries under colonial rule seek independence, but national communities within the newly independent states in turn also sought self-rule. The unsuccessful attempt by Biafra to achieve independence from Nigeria in 1967–1970 and the successful effort by Bangladesh to secede from Pakistan in 1971 are two cases in point. In general, new states have sought to prevent their secessionist groups from forming additional states.

More recently, every Soviet republic has had a strong movement seeking to secede from the U.S.S.R. and form an independent state. And secessionist groups have sought independence in other countries, including Czechoslovakia, Yugoslavia, and Canada.

States have not been the only prominent actors in the international arena in the postwar period. Private groups have also played an important role in shaping world politics. Some of these have exercised their primary influence within states rather than across state boundary lines. Economic groups have sought to promote their interests through influencing such matters as tariffs, immigration, governmental subsidies to domestic producers, and export assistance. Ethnic, religious, and racial groups have attempted to get government help to achieve their objectives on matters such as immigration laws and foreign policy support for kindred groups around the world.

Private groups have also acted in the international arena. The most prominent new economic groups are the multinational corporations (MNCs), or transnational corporations as they are sometimes called. These corporations are organizations with personnel and offices located in more than one country and whose commercial interests are global in nature. Although the MNCs have received considerable attention in the past decade, international economic groups have existed for many centuries. The most prominent early economic groups were the great trading companies of the seventeenth and eighteenth centuries, such as the East India Company, the Hudson's Bay Company, and La Compagnie des Indes. In the more recent past the United Fruit Company, a private U.S. firm, held enormous economic investments in Latin America. International Telephone and Telegraph (ITT) was operating internationally even before World War II. Nevertheless, the MNCs have grown in importance in the postwar period. Their influence in directing the flow of capital, building factories, and employing a labor force has become an important feature in the economic plans of developing nations.

Private groups continue to play a role in other areas, such as in religious and ethnic matters. The Roman Catholic church, for example, is one international religious institution with political interests in every continent. As was the case in 1945, the Roman Catholic church is today involved in many matters not necessarily religious. The church played an important role in the 1980s in mediating between government and the trade unions in the management of the Polish economy, for example.

In 1945 ethnic groups generally acted domestically to wield influence by getting their governments to support their policies. In the past decades, however, they have been more likely to act across national lines. A notable example is the Palestine Liberation Organization (PLO), which has sought an independent Arab Palestine.

In addition to states and private groups, international governmental organizations have been formed to play a role in the conduct of world politics. These associations include economic organizations, cartels, military alliances, regional asociations, and general international organizations.

During World War II, the Allied Powers prepared for the postwar period through the establishment of international organizations such as the International Monetary Fund (IMF) and the International Bank for Reconstruction and Development (now known as the World Bank). The IMF was created to act as a clearing agency and monitor of monetary transactions among states. The World Bank was established to aid postwar recovery, and its work later encompassed aid for economic development in the third world. Since 1945 other international economic institutions, such as the European Economic Community (EC) and the Organization for Economic Cooperation and Development (OECD), have been established.

International governmental cartels in essential commodities were nonexistent in 1945. A cartel is an organization of suppliers that controls the production and price of scarce items. The most successful governmental cartel of the postwar period is the Organization of Petroleum Exporting Countries (OPEC), which was formed in 1960 by five states and now consists of thirteen states. Other international organizations have been formed to strengthen the producers' position with respect to such products as bauxite, tin, iron ore, coffee, and bananas. None has met with the success of OPEC, however, which raised prices more than ten times the 1973 level in less than a decade. Even OPEC's power declined in the 1980s, as non-OPEC states have increased production of oil and other sources of energy (most notably nuclear energy and coal) and energy demands have declined with greater conservation efforts and a world economic recession. Although the price of oil rose sharply after Iraq invaded Kuwait in 1990, the price rise was caused by speculation driven more by the fear of war than by the power of OPEC. The price of oil declined to low levels as soon as a UN coalition led by the United States defeated Iraq in 1991.

Military alliances have existed as long as the state system itself. There were military alliances even in ancient Greece. In 1945, however, the grand alliance that defeated Germany in World War II came to an end as the Soviet Union and the United States became bitter foes. In the 1940s and 1950s military alliances became widespread. The North Atlantic Treaty Organization (NATO) was born in 1949 and continues to the present day. When the Federal Republic of Germany joined NATO in 1955, the Soviet Union established the Warsaw Pact of seven communist countries. Military alliances such as these formed institutions that transcended state boundaries. With the end of the cold war by 1990, the future of NATO is uncertain. In 1991, the Warsaw Pact was formally disbanded.

Some regional associations were in existence in 1945 but became more institutionalized in the following decades. The International Union of American Republics, which was established in 1890, evolved into the Organization of American States (OAS) in 1948. New regional organizations were also formed, such as the Organization of African Unity (OAU) and the Association of Southeast Asian Nations (ASEAN). They played important political and economic roles in world politics.

The people who drafted the United Nations Charter had no vision that they were creating a world government. Rather they set up an organization that would be effective provided the big powers—principally the United States and the Soviet Union—maintained the degree of unity they had shown during World War II. At first the United States, with its preeminence over its allies in Latin America and Europe, dominated the United Nations. The subsequent history of the United Nations records both the decline of U.S. power in that organization and the rise of the new states of Africa and Asia that joined on their independence. Since the 1950s, smaller powers in Latin America, Asia, and Africa have played an important role in the United Nations. Yet in 1990–1991, U.S. leadership in marshaling U.N. support of economic and military measures to reverse Iraq's conquest of Kuwait suggests that U.S. influence in the United Nations is increasing. In addition, the new harmony between the superpowers has led to a resurgent interest in the United Nations. The smaller states have mixed feelings about this newfound vitality, however, fearing a superpower condominium that would shape the United Nations to its own interests.

THE STRUCTURE OF POWER

World War II unleashed forces of political, military, and economic change that transformed power relationships in the global arena. Just as the defeat of Napoleon in 1815 and the defeat of the Central Powers in Europe in 1918 produced new regimes and a new map of the world, so, too, did the conquest of the Axis Powers in 1945. As indicated earlier, the most significant features of the international system after World War II were the emergence of the two superpowers, the United States and the Soviet

Union; the independence of colonies from their imperial rulers; and the rise of IGOs and MNCs. The changing political, military, and economic relationships in the international system in the postwar period have been widely studied, with much attention directed to the impact of these developments on the balance of power and the interdependence of nations.

The term ''balance of power'' has been used in many ways, and there is no consensus about its definition. It can mean a state of equality or preponderance in power, stability or instability in a political system, and peace or war. The concept has its modern origin in the period following the Treaty of Westphalia in 1648, which ended the devastating Thirty Years' War. Here we will define a ''balance-of-power system'' as a system characterized by several powerful states in which no one is dominant. In such a system, states seek to maintain their security by preventing any one state from becoming too powerful.

In the European balance-of-power system of the period between 1648 and the late eighteenth century, there were several powerful states, no one of which was dominant. The leaders of the European countries shared a common cultural heritage, and many were linked through family ties. They also shared a concern for territorial security and took measures to strengthen that security. These measures included acquiring territory, strengthening armed forces, and making alliances with other countries.

When in the late seventeenth and early eighteenth centuries, Louis XIV sought to expand the power of France to a degree that the other powers found dangerous, they united to put down that French monarch. The system also worked to defeat Napoleon's armies, which had gone to war against most of Europe in the late eighteenth and early nineteenth centuries. Although the balance-of-power system continued after the defeat of Napoleon, new forces undermined it. These forces included ideologies, democracy, the industrial revolution, and military technology.

The classic balance-of-power system required that the political leaders make foreign policy decisions based on security considerations. The appearance of new ideologies— most notably nationalism but also liberalism and socialism—often restrained leaders from acting according to security considerations and redrawing boundary lines. Groups committed to aiding liberal or socialist causes in foreign countries influenced state behavior by urging governments to base foreign policy on considerations of human rights or class solidarity.

Democratic institutions further limited the actions of policymakers. Ethnic, economic, religious, and racial groups influenced foreign policy, although their views were at times contrary to the state's security interests. Moreover, the industrial revolution created new classes—business and labor—that played important foreign policy roles. Pressures on governments to promote trade, secure cheap sources of raw materials, and collect debts were powerful forces in the nineteenth and twentieth centuries. At the same time, industrialization and military technology produced more destructive weapons. These weapons affected the civilian population, whose popular support for foreign policy became increasingly important. Such support became necessary since civilians were recruited in large numbers to fight in war and civilian population centers were chosen as military targets.

Although the classic balance of power was influenced by these new forces, it was not until after World War II that these forces became global. Before the twentieth century the balance of power was primarily a European system. This is not to say that non-European countries, such as the United States and Japan, played no role, but rather that the major players of the balancing game were European.

In the post–World War II period, the balance-of-power system took a different form. The new system was characterized by two superpowers whose military strength was so overwhelming that no other state could become their rival. The system was also marked by the increase in the number of states resulting from the independence of countries from colonial rule. These new states—principally in Africa and Asia—often affected the balance-of-power system through their efforts in the nonaligned movement, which was committed to neither superpower. As the number of states grew, the United Nations came more to reflect the interests of the new member states.

Another factor influencing the balance of power was the existence of nuclear weapons so powerful and swift as to make the destruction of earth and its civilization a possibility. Nuclear weapons in the arsenals of both superpowers increased enormously, so that each side developed the capacity to annihilate the other. Not only did the superpowers increase their nuclear arsenals (vertical proliferation), but more countries became nuclear powers (horizontal proliferation). France, Great Britain, and the People's Republic of China are nuclear-weapons states. In 1974 India detonated a nuclear device, which it labeled a peaceful nuclear explosion. Israel is reported to possess many of these weapons, although it may not have tested them. Some reports assert that South Africa may have the bomb and that Pakistan is on the verge of producing it. Iraq sought to manufacture nuclear weapons, but its efforts were set back by the bombing of suspected nuclear sites by coalition forces in 1991. Many more countries could have these weapons in the decades ahead.

The rise of the superpowers, the increase in the number of states playing important global roles, and the appearance and proliferation of nuclear weapons have all had an impact on the character of the balance of power. In addition, the increasing interdependence of states suggests possible changes in the international system. The interdependence of states in military, economic, political, social, and ecological matters has led some observers to use expressions like ''global village,'' ''spaceship earth,'' and ''the politics of the planet earth'' to describe central features of world politics since the end of World War II. ''Interdependence,'' like ''balance of power'' and ''imperialism,'' lacks precise meaning, but we shall use it here to signify a situation in which the entire world is tightly linked in an unprecedented way in such matters as military security, trade, monetary exchange, economic investment, political matters, communications, and ecology. Such ties may influence the willingness and ability of states to act.

In military matters, the invention, development, and production of nuclear weapons constitute one form of interdependence. Nuclear weapons are so powerful that nearly every state is concerned with their possible use either by the superpowers or by other countries. The mere above-ground testing of these weapons produces stratospheric fallout containing Strontium 90 and Cesium 137, which can cause cancer, especially leukemia, locally and in distant nations. Countries that are nonnuclear-weapons states, consequently, are as much concerned with regulating nuclear tests as are the nuclear-weapons states. The world became keenly aware of the potential global dangers of nuclear war in 1986 when a Soviet nuclear reactor exploded in Chernobyl, causing not only death and personal injury in the immediate area but environmental damage most prominently in countries of Eastern and Western Europe.

It is perhaps in economic matters that interdependence is most clearly seen. Since the end of World War II, trade and capital transfers across state lines have increased. Some countries, such as Japan and Great Britain, have been heavily dependent on foreign trade. In contrast the United States has had only a small percentage of its gross national product directed to foreign trade. Even the United States, however, has been dependent on other countries for essential resources, such as oil, copper, and uranium—a dependency that has made it vulnerable to political events throughout the world.

The rise in the power of OPEC in the 1970s highlights the importance of oil and the economic interdependence of states. When Israel and some Arab states went to war in October 1973, the Arab members of OPEC announced an embargo of oil exports to the West. That action and subsequent steep rises in the price of OPEC oil generated inflation and unemployment in the Western economies and severely impeded the economies of third world countries that lacked their own oil resources. Moreover, the importance of maintaining a flow of oil to the West and keeping oil prices low was a major factor in the involvement of the United States and other countries in the war to liberate Kuwait from Iraqi occupation in 1991.

The post–World War II period also featured an increase in capital transfers across state boundary lines. These transfers, in the form of aid, business investments, and loans, made some countries dependent on others. The increase in the number and influence of MNCs, moreover, is a reflection of the transnational character of economic interdependence. As indicated above, new institutions, particularly in the economic realm, were established to cope with the many problems that states could not deal with by themselves. The IMF and the World Bank were two of the most important.

Politically, many alliances among states and meetings among diplomats reflected the new reality of interdependence. NATO and OAS are examples of the political interaction. The OAU serves as a vehicle for third world African states to discuss and resolve their common political problems.

Political leaders met in various international arenas. The United Nations provided a forum for continuous negotiations among diplomats. Summit conferences of heads of government became periodic events, facilitated by the jet age. Communication networks linked to satellites in space provided immediate means for discussion among diplomats and political leaders.

Moreover, there has been an increasing flow of people from one country to another. Refugees seeking political freedom or economic opportunities flocked to countries that would receive them. Immediately after World War II the flow originated in Europe. Later there were major refugee exoduses from India, Vietnam, Cuba, and Haiti. Tourists used jet aircraft to vacation outside of their own countries. Even communist countries that had been closed to most Westerners were opened up largely because of a need for hard currency.

Ecological interdependence in a world becoming more economically developed has taken many forms. Pollution of the oceans endangers fishing interests and creates a need for international control. Infectious diseases respect no territorial limits.

Few would argue with the fact of interdependence in many areas. What is in dispute, however, is the significance of this interdependence to the character of world politics. The debates in Chapter 1 consider both the actors in world politics and the structure of the international system. Issues include the significance of states, the effectiveness of the United Nations, the effects of MNCs, the nature of interdependence, and the future of the third world.

STATES

The growth in the number of states in the postwar period has produced questions about their role in world politics. More than 90 of the U.N. General Assembly's 159 members came into being after World War II. Secessionist movements in many countries, most notably in Eastern Europe, may lead to a further increase in the number of states.

Some people wonder whether the existence of the state system encourages wars. Still others ask whether states are the political institutions best organized for promoting security and prosperity and whether economic groups rather than governments are the real manipulators of power.

Debate 1 centers on the power of states as actors in contemporary world politics. Although states have grown in numbers since 1945, this development may not reflect an increase in the power of states. Is the state declining in significance as an actor in the post–cold war era? James Eayrs, professor of Political Science at Dalhousie University in Halifax, Canada, argues that it is. He contends: (1) No state can truthfully promise military security and economic well-being for its people. (2) States continue to exist because political elites prefer the existing state system, the appeal of patriotism to citizens in every stratum of society is strong, and viable alternatives seem not to exist. (3) Current trends point to polyarchy—a system in which there are a variety of actors and no dominant structure for managing cooperation and conflict.

This view of the decline of the state is challenged by James Mayall of the London School of Economics. He contends: (1) Even when states cooperate in international organizations, that cooperation is based on a prior recognition of the sovereignty principle. (2) The sovereignty principle asserts noninterference in the domestic affairs of other states, consent on the basis of international law, and diplomatic immunity—the legal protection accorded to diplomats of states. (3) New principles of international society, such as the restriction on the legitimate use of force and the duty of states to recognize the political, social, economic, and cultural rights of their people, have not undermined the importance of the state. (4) The nation-state remains the basic political unit of world politics.

UNITED NATIONS

The United Nations was formed in 1945 in the universal hope that the existence of a general international organization would make a contribution to the peaceful settlement of disputes. At the time of its creation the organization contained 51 members. By 1990 it had grown to 159 members.

For the United Nations to succeed, the major powers that had vanquished Germany and Japan in World War II (most notably the United States and the Soviet Union) would have to cooperate. Such unity was dictated constitutionally by a U.N. Charter provision allowing each permanent member of the U.N. Security Council (China, France, the Soviet Union, the United Kingdom, and the United States) to exercise a veto on important matters.

That unity was a casualty of the cold war between the United States and the Soviet Union, and the United Nations became a political battlefield for the superpowers. The Security Council, the unit within the organization most responsible for security issues, was unable to act in most cases because of big-power disunity. With the growth of membership brought on by the independence of states formerly under Western colonial rule, the General Assembly became the dominant political institution. As votes in the General Assembly are based on the principle of one-state–one-vote, assembly resolutions and recommendations increasingly reflected the wishes of the developing countries.

In the 1980s, it was fashionable to regard the United Nations as ineffectual in the major matters of war and peace. The improved relations between the United States and Soviet Union in the post–cold war era, however, have given hope to advocates of the international organization that the United Nations would become the important actor its founders advocated. And when the Security Council passed resolutions condemning Iraq for its invasion of Kuwait in 1990 and successfully instituted economic sanctions against Iraq, it seemed as if the United Nations was revitalized. Certainly the statements by U.S. president George Bush and Soviet president Mikhail Gorbachev calling for greater reliance on the United Nations in this and other matters offered further evidence of a new U.N. significance in world affairs.

Will the United Nations become an important actor in the post–cold war era? Soviet diplomat Vladimir F. Petrovsky argues the affirmative. He contends: (1) U.S.–Soviet cooperation in international relations and at the United Nations will help promote a new international order. (2) Since the preservation of security, development of the global economy, and concerns for the environment and human rights require cooperation, the United Nations will become increasingly important. (3) The United Nations is now promoting cooperation rather than engaging in polemics. (4) The United Nations and its system have now become the only important institution for interaction among states that exercises a real influence on their external and internal behavior.

Alan L. Keyes, a former U.S. assistant secretary of state for U.N. affairs, argues that the United Nations will not become more important in dealing with problems of peace and security. Recognizing that U.N. action in dealing with the Iraqi invasion of Kuwait demonstrates an assertive role for the international organization, he nonetheless does not see the role as prominent. He contends: (1) The United Nations has still not overcome its inherent structural and political deficiencies. (2) The assertiveness of the United Nations is really a reflection of the preeminence of U.S.—and not U.N.—power. (3) The current effectiveness of the United Nations is based on the self-interest of most Arab states and the weakness of the Soviet Union, factors that are subject to change. (4) The United States may find itself opposed to U.N. action in the future.

MULTINATIONAL CORPORATIONS

Because of their vast wealth, multinational corporations exercise enormous influence. The leading MNCs have economic resources transcending the gross national product of most states. Such is the wealth of MNCs that some observers argue they have more power than states themselves.

The economic activity of MNCs is concentrated in advanced industrial societies. Since most of these societies are located in northern latitudes, they are categorized as the ''North.'' But MNCs also play a major role in the economies of developing countries. Since most developing countries are located in southern latitudes, they are called the ''South.'' The relationship between the North and the South is a subject of controversy among analysts of economic development. Do MNCs exploit developing countries? Political scientist Adeoye A. Akinsanya argues that they do. He contends: (1) By and large MNCs provide vehicles through which capital resources are transferred from capital-poor countries to capital-rich countries. (2) MNCs destroy jobs. (3) The technology transferred from MNCs to developing countries is inappropriate to the needs of the latter. (4) MNCs encourage inappropriate consumption patterns. (5) MNCs contribute to the widening of the economic gap between the elite and the masses in the host states. (6) MNCs stifle local development by making the third world dependent on them for technology.

Economist Melvyn B. Krauss defends MNCs. He makes his case by attacking the Brandt Commission study of developing nations, named after Willy Brandt, the former chancellor of the Federal Republic of Germany. Specifically Krauss contends: (1) MNCs bring the prosperity of industrialized countries to developing countries by transferring technology and capital and by promoting trade. (2) To the extent that MNCs are not restricted by third world countries, they stimulate economic development for the people of those countries. (3) Labor in third world countries benefits from MNC investment. (4) MNCs will provide the greatest benefit to developing nations to the extent that international flows of private capital are not restricted. (5) MNCs pay higher wages to workers in developing countries than do local firms in those countries. (6) MNCs act in an ethical manner. (7) MNCs charge a fair price for the technology, and they transfer appropriate technology to the third world. (8) MNCs are often unfairly blamed for inefficient policies when the blame should go to the policies of third world governments.

INTERDEPENDENCE

Analysts of world politics note the interdependence of states. Although recognizing that interdependence exists, they differ in evaluating its consequences. Is interdependence among states changing the character of world politics? Political scientist Andrew M. Scott argues that it is. His main points are: (1) The world is becoming more interdependent. (2) As the global system evolves, national interest is progressively defined less in state-centered terms and more in system-centered (that is, global) terms. (3) Interdependence does not necessarily lead to a utopia in which conflict is eliminated.

There will be conflicts between state-centered interests, between various system-centered interests, and between state-centered and system-centered interests. (4) Formulation of an adequate, informed definition of the national interest will become increasingly difficult in an interdependent world.

Political scientist John Spanier is critical of the view that interdependence is transforming the international system. He argues: (1) The major global problems require national solutions. (2) Security, and not welfare, remains the highest priority of states. (3) The degree of interdependence among states varies. (4) Some states retain great choice of policies they can pursue. (5) Political considerations dominate economic considerations in state behavior. (6) Interdependence holds little appeal to the third world, where the idea is viewed as a way to harm developing countries. (7) Global economic issues have underscored the primacy of old-fashioned national security goals. (8) Much of the discussion of interdependence is prescriptive rather than descriptive.

THIRD WORLD

The third world includes the poorer states of Africa, Asia, and Latin America. The use of the term "third" derives from the historical period of economic development. Thus the first world to achieve the industrial revolution was the West; the second world to achieve it was Eastern Europe. The third world is the last of the world's regions to move toward industrialization.

The rise of the third world came mostly in the period following World War II, when colonies under Western rule achieved their independence. Third world countries demonstrated their increasing influence by their voices and votes in the United Nations and by the assertive role that they played in world affairs. Most third world countries adopted a policy of nonalignment, positioning themselves in neither the U.S. nor the Soviet camp. Many sought to influence the superpowers by playing one off against the other. For their part the superpowers tried to extend their influence on third world countries by economic and military assistance as well as by political support where possible.

The third world and the nonaligned movement were never entirely in sync. Some third world countries allied with the United States, and others with the Soviet Union. Some leaned toward one or the other bloc but did not enter into formal alliances. Nor was the third world monolithic. Third world countries differed among themselves and sometimes fought wars with each other. Still, nonalignment was the principal foreign policy of third world countries. Their agenda also included economic development, foreign aid, and anti-imperialism.

Will the third world play an increasingly important role in world politics? Chen Jiabao contends that it does. He argues: (1) Third world countries participated in resolving significant geopolitical issues, easing regional tensions, and actively opposing outside interference by the superpowers. (2) Third world influence is increasing at the United Nations. (3) Third world influence was shown at the summit meetings of nonaligned nations.

Latin American specialist Mark Falcoff sees the third world in decline. He argues:

(1) With no cold war, there can be no third world and no nonaligned movement since third world countries will have no political leverage over the superpowers. (2) Conflict in the third world will increase. (3) Third world countries will find it difficult to extract concessions and resources from Western governments. (4) Many third world countries will be unable to develop economically because of their planned economies or political instability. (5) Third world countries can advance if they embrace free markets and democracy, but they will not be subsidized by developed countries if they do not.

1 Is the State Declining in Significance as an Actor in World Politics?

YES

James Eayrs

The Outlook for Statehood

NO

James Mayall

Nationalism and International Society

The Outlook for Statehood

James Eayrs

"Are your rulers—the Council of Ministers, I think you said—are they what you call a 'Parliament'?"

"By no means," the guide said, "But they are responsible to the national parliaments."

"Oh, I see. You still have nations here. How quaint. You certainly spare no expense. But I suppose you have a parliament of Europe, if only to control your army and your foreign policy?"

"I'm afraid not," the guide said. "We have a European assembly, of sorts, but no army and precious little foreign policy."

"In that case," said the Man from Mars, "I'm off. I always thought Europe was a safe place . . . . Well, good luck. I hope you survive."

And with that he was gone, leaving his vapour trail behind.

Pangloss, a pseudonymous piece in *The Times* (London), January 6, 1986

This fictive interrogation of a spokesman for the European Community by an extraterrestrial visitor to Planet Earth is among the more recent entries to a long tradition of commentaries upon the extraordinary way in which the family of man has chosen, or, rather, allowed itself to become organized so as to do its chores and commit its crimes. An allegation of "absurdity" is common to them all. A pioneering treatise on international politics invokes the conceit of "the man in the Moon" who, gazing at Earth through a miraculous telescope, is astounded to discover that all its inhabitants are subjects of "a large number of states," each of which has "full power

over all . . . it shelters."[1] Another pioneering study asserts that "nothing but the sluggish pace of man's evolution can justify the citizens of a particular nation in considering themselves as privileged exclusively to control a government whose activities react on other countries with almost as much effect, if not more, than in their own."[2] In 1959 an American practitioner and historian of diplomacy denounces as "absurd" the world's division "into several dozens of secular societies, each devoted to the cultivation of the myth of its own overriding importance and virtue.[3] And in 1962 a Canadian *philosophe* flatly proclaims: "The very idea of . . . nation-state is absurd. The concept of the nation-state has managed to cripple the advance of civilization."[4]

Absurdity of Statehood

A case for the absurdity of statehood has become stronger and more easily made since this bevy of prosecutors rested theirs. The "several dozens of secular societies" about which George F. Kennan complained nearly three decades ago has tripled: sovereign entities have multiplied so that a United Nations designed on the best political advice for a potential maximum of eighty occupants now is host to twice that number. The disproportionality among the parts of this universe is even more grotesque than their number. Five and one-tenth million is not the population of a medium-sized state; it is the population of the census force required to ascertain how many people lived in the world's most populated state. China's are a million times more numerous than Vatican City's; yet both belong to the same species, as do a St. Bernard and a Chihauhua rather

[1] Raymond Leslie Buell, *International Relations* (New York, 1925), pp. 3–4.

[2] Salvador de Madariaga, *Disarmament* (New York, 1929), p. viii.

[3] George F. Kennan, "History and Diplomacy as Viewed by a Diplomatist," in Stephen D. Kertesz and M. A. Fitzsimons (eds.), *Diplomacy in a Changing World* (Notre Dame, Ind., 1959), p. 102.

[4] Pierre Elliott Trudeau, *Federalism and the French Canadians* (Toronto, 1968), pp. 158–159.

Source: James Eayrs, "The Outlook for Statehood," *International Perspectives: The Canadian Journal of International Affairs* (Ottawa), (Mar./Apr. 1987), pp. 3–7. Reprinted by permission.

than being a kind of buffalo and a kind of rat. The four most populous states comprise a million times as many square miles as do the four least territoried states. Yet all share a common statehood; all play by the same rules.

The doctrine of the formal equality of states was assailed by Prime Minister Mackenzie King at conferences where he argued that postwar international institutions should not treat Canada as they might El Salvador. But that system had no special place for middle powers. The special place for great powers is hardly worth occupying in a toothless Security Council. Only in the International Monetary Fund, that unloved "policeman of capitalism," is there provision for weighted voting; and the price for speaking out is putting up.

The majority of states are small states, ministates, micro-states, atoll-states, sand-spit states, dockyard-states, casino-states, company-states. If these anomalies amused themselves demurely in the far-flung corners of their playground, there would be no need to worry. But their behaviour is far from orderly. They are forever feuding and fighting, falling out and falling apart.

Small, Not Harmless

It might be argued that, for all the statelets' quarrelling, their shenanigans are harmless. So why not let their leaders fill their puny local arenas with sound and fury that signify nothing on the wider state? Here are some reasons why not.

First, because they occupy that wider stage. At the General Assembly of the United Nations their tribunes cobble windy and unenforcible manifestos on the rights of their states and the duties of others. Antigua and Barbuda argues for renegotiation of, of all things, the Antarctic regime. An energetic representative persuades Assembly members to devote more debate to the security of the Seychelles than to the Iran-Iraq war and the plight of Poland combined. This is absurd, this is "out of harmony with reason or propriety."

Besides the capacity to distract, small states possess the capacity to destroy. Theirs is the power of the weak, the power of the pyromaniac in a fireworks factory. Just by being there Serbia toppled the proud tower of Europe across what became its killing ground. Libya could do the same, as could Lebanon, as could any of Lebanon's murderous cantons. Wagers of *jihad* cannot be deterred.

FAILED STATE SYSTEMS

If statehood is allegedly absurd, it has become patently inadequate, out of harmony with necessity, along with reason and propriety. Statehood no longer delivers the goods, rises to the occasion. Playing by statehood's ridiculous rules, posturing in its ineffectual forums, states no longer meet human needs.

One of the first to see statehood's inadequacy and proclaim it to be so was, of all people, an American politician. In 1941 Wendell Willkie (who had lost a run at the presidency the year before) flew 31,000 miles to more than a dozen countries. An Ulyssean voyage for those days, it left upon the traveller an indelible impression. "Peace must be planned on a world basis," Willkie wrote on his return. "I mean quite literally that it must embrace the earth. Continents and oceans are plainly only parts of a whole, seen, as I have seen them, from the air."[5] Whence came the title for his journal, *One World*—precursor of such later catch phrases as "Spaceship Earth," "Earth Politics," "Global Village," "the common heritage of mankind."

The ideal of a family of man sharing the earth as its common home is as old as literate humanity itself. Ancient scripture lauds it. Thinkers down the ages propound it—utopians who would somehow banish power and conflict from human affairs (a process requiring us, as Jonathan Schell has provocatively conceded, "to reinvent politics"),[6] realists who argue for better command and control.

The cosmopolitan cause has been helped by footage. Televised space probes make us all men on the

---

[5] Wendell L. Willkie, *One World* (New York, 1943), p. 203.
[6] Jonathan Schell, *The Fate of the Earth* (New York, 1982), p. 226.

Moon. We see our Earth through the spacecraft's porthole, caught by NASA's [National Aeronautics and Space Administration] Hasselblad, and what we see is not the patchwork of Mercator's political quilting but an amethyst sphere wreathed by cloud. We see a small and vulnerable planet which astronauts and cosmonauts orbit in fewer minutes than it took Walter Cronkite to shower, shave, dress, drive to the studio and make up, to tell us of their splash-down.

Images of mushroom clouds ought to have been even more compelling; to a few they were. But even before newsreels of Japan's nuclear apocalypses were being shown at the Translux in New York City, L. B. Pearson became convinced that the system of sovereign states needed to be changed as radically as the atomic bomb had changed weapons and war. Pearson assessed the destroyers of Hiroshima and Nagasaki as forerunners of "ever more devastating bombs . . . which will be to the present bomb as a machine gun to the breech-loader." It seemed obvious to him that "any constructive solution of this problem of the war-use of atomic energy must be international." Pearson meant "supranational," for he went on to propose that the three governments then privy to atomic bomb production—the U.S., Britain, his own—trade "the knowledge of invention and manufacture they alone possess at present, for renunciation by all nations of the right of production or use."[7]

Learning Too Slowly

Such a deal could not be made. The Truman administration, intent on keeping to itself what it wrongly supposed to be an ultimate weapon conferring ultimate power, bargained in bad faith, insisting upon intrusive inspection procedures it knew the regime of the *gulag* could never accept. Stalin, intent on breaking the U.S. atomic weapons monopoly with the aid of his spies, likewise bargained in bad faith, insisting

that the United States should then and there destroy its stockpile.

In 1949, the Soviets exploded an atomic bomb. George Kennan turned to Ottawa for support for his unpopular proposal that the West return to the table with less rigid demands on inspection. The Canadian civil servant who then advised on such matters turned thumbs down. "The strategic use of the atomic weapon," George Ignatieff argued, "is an essential element [of Western defence]."[8] Here, we now see, was a decisive turning point. What might the self-styled "peacemonger" now not give to arrive at it again? But History is chary with her second chances.

Protection of citizens against armed attack has been the state's basic *raison d'être*, the bottom line of loyalty. Not its guarantee of survival to the last man, woman, child and suckling, but of a reasonable assurance of coming through alive. Today no government can truthfully promise protection in that sense. Swiss officials claim that "if any society in Europe is still functioning after a general nuclear war, Switzerland will be functioning."[9] Swiss may find that comforting, but it leaves the rest of us cold. Widespread nuclear neurosis, a kind of atomic *angst*, persists as a result. Cannily detecting it, perhaps cruelly exploiting it as well, is President Reagan's assurance to his people that they will be able, with due effort made by science and technology, to "live secure in the knowledge . . . that we could intercept and destroy strategic ballistic missiles before they reached our own soil."[10]

If states can no longer protect their peoples, neither can they keep many of them gainfully employed. Communist party states claim to fulfill this basic human need. Perhaps they do; but only by draconian measures that are unacceptable in free societies and create malingering in theirs—a cure (as

[7] Quoted in J. A. Munro and A. I. Inglis, "The Atomic Conference 1945 and the Pearson Memoirs," *International Journal*, no. 1 (Winter 1973–74), p. 96.

[8] Quoted in James Eayrs, "Apocalypse Then: Aspects of Nuclear Weapons-Acquisition Policy Thirty Years Ago," *Dalhousie Review*, 59, no. 4 (Winter 1979–80), p. 647.

[9] Freeman Dyson, *Weapons and Hope* (New York, 1984), p. 87.

[10] Quoted in *Survival* (May–June 1983), p. 130.

shown by the demand to emigrate) worse than the disease. In First World states the disease is debilitating, and worsening. Our country is becoming the homeland of what the Royal Commission on the Economic Union and Development Prospects for Canada calls ''a lost generation of 'walk-arounds'.'' In much of Africa and Latin America, where third world states have slid unexpectedly into a fourth world of absolute poverty, the Samaritans are foreigners. No one eats *uhuru*.

RESIDUAL ATTRACTIONS OF STATE SYSTEMS

Why—why on Earth—do states continue to be created? Why does the system of states, for all the allegations of its preposterousness and for all the demonstrations of its inadequacies, continue to endure? All states, the late Barbara Ward wrote more than fifteen years ago,

> lack ultimate sovereignty. The dollar cannot dictate world policies for liquidity. Four times overkill cannot guarantee even superpowers full security. Capitalist markets use Communist gold. Communist stomachs need capitalist wheat. The ever-tightening, thickening web of complete interdependence draws all the sovereignties great and small, kicking and screaming, into a single planetary system. But the institutions to express this unity are so frail, so dependent upon sovereign vetoes of unsovereign states that they give little more than the tribute of hypocrisy which vice pays to virtue, recognizing its necessity but giving it the widest berth.[11]

States, as Harold Isaacs has memorably put it, are ''the idols of our tribes,'' and they are ''here to stay, . . . granitelike in their power to survive, mobile and vital in their power to reproduce themselves, to be reborn, to evolve. They preside over all our altars. . . . Despite occasional impulses and even

efforts in a number of cultures to see if it could be otherwise, this remains the essential order of human existence.''[12] But why?

The culture of statehood enables its elites to enjoy the international style—that life of seemingly purposeful activity and assuredly frenetic pace, lavished upon them uniquely by the protocol of sovereignty. Here is a heartfelt testimonial to its allure:

> How wonderful international life is. It suffices to recall our visits; airports, greetings, cascades of flowers, embraces, orchestras, every moment polished by protocol, and then limousines, parties, toasts written out and translated, galas and brilliance, praise, confidential conversations, global themes, etiquette, splendour, presents, suites, and finally tiredness, but how magnificent and relaxing, how refined and honoured, how dignified and proper, how—exactly—international.[13]

Where a former prime minister of Canada was ready to abandon a mission to discuss Soviet espionage with the president of the United States on learning that it would involve the rerouting of his railway car for which taxpayers would incur a charge of $300, the present prime minister of Canada is ready to defend an expenditure of $2.6 million for a day's entertainment of the Reagan entourage. ''Lines of limousines for a conference in Paris, a separate airplane for the Prime Minister's television lighting and his podium, suites . . . that would make a Saudi sheikh blush.''[14] Such is the international style, and those who experience it are loath to relinquish it.

What, and Give Up Candy!

The international style offers more than jet-setting and the Mercedes at the door. It offers a role upon the world stage and in all its myriad sets. A head of state

---

[11] Barbara Ward, ''The First International Nation,'' in William Kilbourn (ed.), *Canada: A Guide to the Peaceable Kingdom* (Toronto, 1970), p. 45.

[12] Harold R. Isaacs, *Idols of the Tribe: Group Identity and Political Change* (New York, 1975), p. 205.

[13] Quoted in Ryszard Kapuscinski, *The Emperor: Downfall of an Autocrat* (New York, 1984), p. 88.

[14] Hugh Winsor, ''Slide for Mulroney Never Seemed to End,'' *Globe and Mail*, 27 December 1986.

thus describes that role and what it means to him:

> We have found our self-confidence in the international community, and other countries have come to respect us for what we are. If this were not so, would our Ambassador to the U.N. have been accepted as Chairman of the Afro-Asian Committee? Would our special envoy to the OAU Conference of Ministers. . .have been elected Secretary? Would you have thought that my recent Policy speech at the U.N. Assembly would have received the hundred percent support of all Member States? . . . I personally have been received and honoured in many countries. . . . During my recent visit to the U.S. I had important discussions with high ranking officials of Government, corporations and banking institutions. . . . I have received an invitation to pay a state visit to Israel . . . and . . . a similar visit to Canada. . . . I shall also want to pay a visit to the Holy See and a courtesy call on the Italian prime minister.[15]

That is what the international style does for Lesotho and its president, for scores of other states and heads of state.

The affinity of elites for the international style is readily understood. But whence derives support for statehood by the masses—ordinary folk for whom no Mercedeses idle, no colour guards await?

Fear of statelessness is foremost. To be a stateless person in the terrible twentieth century is to live life before Leviathan, life "solitary, poor, nasty, brutish and short." So oppressed nationalism seeks out statehood. For an Armenian, a Kurd, a Palestinian, a Sikh, a Tamil, nationality is insufficiently protective. Only citizenship offers the prospect of security.

Safely set up in a state of one's own, fear subsides and pride swells in its place. Displacement of fear by pride is most evident in Israel. "A Jew, whenever he came to a country, checked the exits," a rabbi in Jerusalem remarks. Now, in Israel, "a new generation has grown up. . . . They can't stand an obsequious nation. They hate it. Dignity. You hear them all the time saying, 'Why can't you stand up to the world?' "[16] These Israelis want to feel good about their state, as do other peoples. To feel good about your state, and about yourself for being its citizen, is to experience the appeal of patriotism. Elites have more reasons to be turned on by their country, but the patriotic high lifts lesser mortals, too. There is a Yiddish folk saying: "Why is the Land of Israel so stony? Because every Jew who arrives casts off a stone from his heart."

Elusive Alternatives

A third clue to the persistence of statehood, besides the affinity of elites for the international style and the appeal of patriotism to citizens in every stratum, is a dearth of viable alternatives.

The city once served splendidly to let people (who were not slaves) live life full and well. Pericles's tribute to Athens—"Our city. . .is an education to Greece"—still reminds us of what we have a right to hope for our country. And there are those who argue that the city could so serve again, and should. During the 1960s, when small allegedly was beautiful, Leopold Kohr became a minor cult figure for insisting that the world would be safer and more humane if existing states were fractioned into city-states. But he did not tell us how.

Jane Jacobs wants states and empires to break up not for the virtue of smallness, but because she believes that cities are engines for development, while hinterlands are agents for decline. Cut cities free from their debilitating surrounds, she argues, free them from crippling—because irrational—jurisdictions, and councillors will be enabled by improved feedback (such as the market value of city currencies) to make sounder decisions. Look at Hong Kong. Look at Singapore. But where else to look? Elsewhere cities are in thrall to faulty feedback and political pressure to provide capital for "transactions

---

[15] Quoted in J. D. B. Miller, *Survey of Commonwealth Affairs: Problems of Expansion and Attrition, 1953–1969* (London, 1974), pp. 15–16.

[16] Quoted in David K. Shipler, "A Divided Israel," *New York Times*, 7 July 1984.

of decline''—military expenditure and regional subsidies. Jacobs does not expect a revival for the city-state on an extensive scale, but some experimentation is to be expected ''since it seems that sooner or later human beings get around to trying everything within their capacities.''[17] She will have noted with interest the efforts of Atlanta and Syracuse, among other U.S. cities, to conduct urban foreign policy by sending missions abroad to drum up trade and investment. ''In the past, we never looked beyond our own borders,'' the mayor of Syracuse explains. ''We were dependent on the umbilical cords that linked us to our capitals.''[18]

Ubiquitous Corporations

The firm is another contender for our allegiance. There are countries whose policies and qualities of life are shaped not so much by their governments as by the decisions of head offices and plant managers, ''company states'' such as Firestone's Liberia, United Fruit's El Salvador, Gulf and Western's Dominican Republic. (Canada has been held to differ from these only in the number and diversity of the U.S. branch plants accused of dominating all aspects of our society.) It is claimed that the multinational corporation drains many states of their autonomy. And some say a good thing too, because (as Henry Kissinger maintains) ''in the developing countries there is often no substitute for [the multinational company's] ability to marshal capital, management skills, technology and initiative.''[19]

The global reach of firms, whether constructive or—as is most commonly assumed—retardant—is probably overestimated. As a species, the free-wheeling corporate buccaneer, *pace* Adnan Khashoggi, is endangered. Host governments monitor, regulate, shut down, take over (sometimes without compensation) foreign operations. These are even hassled by their own government: the ''sovereign state of ITT [International Telephone and Telegraph]'' was hauled before the Senate, its documents subpoenaed, its CEO [chief executive officer] cross-examined, its executives fined and jailed. ''Merely to ask which institution one expects to be around 100 years from now, France or General Motors,'' one commentator observes, ''shows the nature of the problem.'' He bets on France, as do I. It is pardonable not to want to bet on either. ''It is only because we do not know how to organize large masses of people to perform those tasks essential for society,'' the U.S. economist Robert Heilbroner laments, ''that we have to depend on the nation-state with its vicious force and shameful irrationality and the corporation with its bureaucratic hierarchies and carefully inculcated dissatisfaction.''[20]

EVOLVING GLOBAL REGIMES

There being plague at both these houses, let us visit a third—the global regime, which may develop in three modes: by conquest, by consent, and by evolution.

There have always been those who crave to rule the world (or as much of it as was known to them), and some—like Emperor Augustus after Rome's defeat of Carthage—who believed they did. Had Hitler not wasted resources on exterminating Jews, had he pressed development of the atomic bomb, his bloated ambition—''Today Germany, Tomorrow the World''—might have been achieved. At present only the men in the Kremlin are thought by some (including, as of 1981, President Reagan)[21] to harbour a design for a world state under their control. Even if that were their intent, it is hard to see its execution now that one government or more can destroy any would-be conqueror and all his works in a barrage of thirty minutes' duration.

---

[17] Jane Jacobs, *Cities and the Wealth of Nations* (New York, 1984), p. 220.
[18] Quoted in William Robbins, ''Cities Going Where the Business Is,'' *New York Times*, 24 June 1984.
[19] ''Secretary Kissinger's Address to U.N. General Assembly,'' *New York Times*, 24 September 1974.

[20] Robert L. Heilbroner, ''The Multinational Corporation and the Nation-State,'' *New York Review of Books*, 11 February 1971.
[21] ''Text of President Reagan's Press Conference,'' *New York Times*, 24 January 1981.

More likely than a global regime by conquest is a global regime by consent. In *The World Set Free*, H. G. Wells foresaw in 1913 the development of nuclear power and its application to warfare. Major cities are laid waste by atomic attack. "From this point on the book gets utopian," comments the scientist Leo Szilard. "With the world in shambles, a conference is called in which a world government is set up."[22] But with the world in shambles a world government would not be utopian: if anyone were spared to govern and be governed, one would probably be formed. One of the late Herman Kahn's most plausible scenarios invites us to imagine the aftermath of an atomic war that breaks out inadvertently when the superpower leaderships lose control of escalation. What happens on the morning after? "There are many things that might happen," Kahn speculates,

> but one thing almost certainly would not happen. Neither of the principal antagonists would announce that since the war was over, they would now return to the old deterrence policy with accident-prone forces. . . .
> There is a well-known book . . . , *World Peace through World Law*.[23] . . . The President of the United States might send a copy of this book to the Chairman of the Council of Ministers, saying, "There is no point in your reading this book; you will not like it any more than I did. I merely suggest you sign it, right after my signature. . . . If we are to have a settlement, we must have it now, before the dead are buried.

"I can even imagine," Kahn concludes, "the Chairman accepting the offer, and signing."[24] Stranger things have almost happened—most recently at Reykjavik.

Welcome Polyarchy

Some years ago, the late Hedley Bull dismissed the notion that "the states system may be giving place to a secular reincarnation of the system of overlapping or segmented authority that characterized medieval Christendom."[25] That notion posited an evolved global regime that would have as its outcome not a single central authority created by design but rather a set of authorities, competing and overlapping, under whose several jurisdictions the human family had allowed itself to be placed as it pursued its myriad concerns. Now there is evidence that the world *is* coming to be governed neomedievally. Where there were kings, feudal lords, the Church and the guilds, there are now states, international organizations, industrial associations, unions, banks and insurers, all rule-makers for economic operators. "And now," a leading student of international political economy points out, "as in medieval Europe, there are extensive and significant areas of anarchy in which little or no authority is exercised."[26] Behaviour and habitat worldwide are more and more subject to non-state pressures and procedures.

Such a hodgepodge of jurisdictions alongside *laissez faire* might seem to promise even more chaotic anarchy than we endure at present, rather than anything resembling a global regime. Yet, as a U.S. student of the process has noted, "not anarchy but *polyarchy* is the more appropriate term for describing and understanding the emerging patterns in the world polity. In a polyarchic system, there is no dominant structure for managing cooperation and conflict." While a polyarchy may relapse into anarchy, it may also be nudged in the direction of world order. "The 'statesmen' of the polyarchic system," Seyom Brown has told us (in a passage whose opacity is for once in political science literature justified

[22] Quoted in Spencer R. Weart and Gertrude Weiss Szilard (eds.), *Leo Szilard: His Version of the Facts* (Cambridge, Mass., 1978), p. 16.

[23] Grenville Clark and Louis B. Sohn, *World Peace through World Law*, 2d ed. (Cambridge, Mass., 1960).

[24] Herman Kahn, *Thinking about the Unthinkable* (New York, 1962), pp. 155–156.

[25] Hedley Bull, *The Anarchical Society: A Study of Order in World Politics* (London, 1977), p. 264.

[26] Susan Strange, "The Study of Transnational Relations," *International Affairs*, 52, no. 3 (July 1976), pp. 333–334.

by the daring of the leap of intellect required to compose it),

> can seek to transform the fragmented polyarchic pattern into worldwide and regional communities in which the complex interdependencies are matched by political and legal processes and institutions. . . .
>
> The model for such a world system is the modern, ethnically diverse greater metropolitan areas. . . . These megalopolises comprise numerous municipal and special-purpose jurisdictions, many of which overlap, but they lack a strong central government for the whole. The polyarchic "global city" could exhibit an analogous structure.[27]

The contours of that analogous structure are already visible. Regimes to protect wildlife, to track weather, to regulate telemetry, to select sites for geostationary satellite transmitters, to limit the emission of ozone-destroying chemicals, to monitor, under non-governmental auspices, seismic events in the interests of arms control—such regimes, whether in place or proposed, are manifestations of a trend towards global coordinated polyarchy. "It is still possible to imagine new systems of power, new pluralisms in which human beings may be able to live with one another in some more satisfying and mutually satisfactory way" than is allowed by statehood as of old,[28] so even a moderately pessimistic American was able to hope more than a decade ago. The odds on that possibility have since improved.

---

[27] Seyom Brown, "The World Polity and the Nation-State System: An Updated Analysis," *International Journal*, 39 (Summer 1984), pp. 509–528.

[28] Isaacs, *Idols of the Tribe*, p. 219.

Nationalism and International Society

James Mayall

The two central claims of this book can be briefly stated. First, the primacy of the national idea amongst contemporary political principles has modified the traditional conception of an international society but has not replaced it. Second, there is no immediate prospect of transcending the national idea, either as the principle of legitimisation or as the basis of political organisation for the modern state. Hence, for the time being, international society cannot develop in ways which are inconsistent with the continued existence of separate national states. Islands of supra-national authority may arise here and there, but the principle of popular sovereignty will not easily translate into supra-nationalism in general.

To summarise the argument which supports these claims let us return to. . .three questions. . . . What is meant by international society? On what normative principles is the idea of international society based? How has nationalist doctrine, and more broadly the national idea, influenced its evolution? I shall consider each briefly in turn.

The original conception of international society has survived into the modern world with its basic structure intact. It is a conception of a society of states which recognise each other's sovereignty, engage in regular diplomatic relations with one another and uphold international law. The theoretical alternatives to this scheme have not materialised. These are some form of world empire or dominion, or the evolution of political arrangements designed with reference to a community of mankind, rather than separate national communities. The separate state has shown an equally stubborn resistance to withering away, as Marx and his immediate followers hoped it would, as it has to retreating to the parsimonious but universal Republican form favoured by Kantian liberals.

International cooperation is always and everywhere dependent on the prior recognition of the sovereignty principle. When modern states collectively endorse a solidarist ideology—as the new African states did with Pan-Africanism in the 1960s—they define it in a way which reasserts the primacy of the state in the event of a conflict between the national interest and any wider obligation. And when the government of a single state elects to ignore the conventions of international society and to base its foreign policy on a unilateral interpretation of either a common ideology or its own rights, it finds it correspondingly difficult to solicit international support. This is the fundamental explanation of Libya's diplomatic isolation within the Arab world and Africa, as it is of post-revolutionary Iran's in international society as a whole. It is also the reason why irredentist states find it difficult to attract allies.

It may reasonably be objected that the sovereignty principle provides weak states with scant protection against the predatory interventions of the powerful. Both the United States and the Soviet Union have not hesitated to equate their own interests with some universal imperative—the defence of the "free world" in the one case, of the socialist commonwealth in the other—when it suited them to do so. Nor have lesser states been much more scrupulous in the exercise of self-restraint when they have found themselves involved in international disputes.

This is a forceful objection, but from the standpoint of international society, it needs to be placed in context. In the original conception, the balance of power was generally acknowledged to be one of the institutions of international society. Indeed, in the view of many realists it was the primary institution which provided the minimum of

Source: James Mayall, Nationalism and International Society (Cambridge, England: Cambridge University Press, 1990), pp. 145–152. Copyright © 1990 by Cambridge University Press. Reprinted with the permission of Cambridge University Press and James Mayall.

order on which the whole edifice rested. Admittedly, one result of the attempt—enshrined in the United Nations Charter—to confine the legitimate use of force to self-defence, has been to remove war from its place as an institution of international society. Instead it is regarded as the primary evidence of its breakdown. Nonetheless, this is an area in which state practice sadly lags behind the development of international law. Although great as well as small powers must these days resort to moral justification for the use of force, there is little doubt that they still consider themselves as enjoying special rights to match their ultimate responsibility for world order.

If the waging of war is one aspect of the idea of international society which has been modified in the twentieth century, the arrangements for the conduct of peaceful relations amongst states is another. The original conception envisaged a society of sovereigns who held certain principles and practices in common. They saw no need for an institutional infrastructure in the modern sense. Indeed, both their interpretation of sovereignty to include the right to wage war as an act of policy, and the two economic strategies open to them—mercantilism and classical liberalism—precluded such an infrastructure. By contrast, twentieth-century experience of war and peace not only brought about modifications in the traditional idea of international society but ensured that an attempt would be made to operationalise the idea by giving it a permanent institutional form.

The attempt to create a new multilateral system of collective security, although unsuccessful, nonetheless expanded the conception of international society to include multilateralism in general. The United Nations Organization, and its affiliates, continued the process of institutionalisation begun under the League: since 1945, very few issues in international relations, particularly in the economic and social fields, have escaped multilateral debate and negotiation. To the idea of an international society of states has been added the notion of an international agenda, a set of problems which it is their collective duty to keep under review, and eventually to resolve.

So much for the idea of international society. What of the principles on which it is based and which

are embedded within it? Those on which the original conception was based have already been alluded to since they are all derivations of the sovereignty principle. A society of sovereigns came into being when they acknowledged each other's political supremacy, including the right to determine the beliefs of their respective subjects. This right has been formally abandoned in the light of one of the major modifications to the idea of international society. I shall return shortly to this modification—the entrenchment of human rights on the international agenda. Here the point is that *cuius regio eius religio*, the original principle, bears a strong family resemblance to its contemporary successor, the principle of non-interference in the domestic affairs of other states.

Two other principles underpin contemporary international society, as they did the original conception. The first is the principle of consent as the basis of international law. This body of law has expanded continuously to keep pace with the enormously increased volume and scope of international interactions, but the sovereignty principle continues to set limits to the legal sanctions that can be imposed to uphold it. International law thus continues to depend on the binding status which governments accord to treaties, on the fear of reciprocal reprisals, and on self-policing.

The second principle which has survived the modification of international society is diplomatic immunity. Modern diplomats are in many respects indistinguishable from other servants of the state. Their day to day work is increasingly concerned with the administration of complex economic or military programmes and the resolution of conflicts of interest through negotiation. But, when they serve abroad, their privileges and immunities still derive from their symbolic not their functional role, i.e. from the fact that they are the representatives of a sovereign state. In practice more attention is no doubt paid to the plenipotentiaries of the United States, the Soviet Union or China than to those of Mexico, Bulgaria or Thailand. But, in a formal sense, in any capital of the world, they are all the representatives of sovereign powers in a society of equals.

The modifications and additions to the original conception of international society stem from the acceptance of new principles. These are all derived, in the first instance, from liberal theory. Since the idea of international society is not exclusively the preserve of liberals, it is important to emphasise that the derivation is *intellectual* not practical or political. The claim is that certain Enlightenment principles have become so firmly embedded in modern consciousness that, as Ortega Y Gasset argued, they establish the language of political argument—and its idiom—even for those who might wish to repudiate them. Not all allegedly liberal principles have achieved this bipartisan, a-political, international status. The attempt to transform international society by means of multilateral diplomacy, into a kind of surrogate welfare state, has conspicuously failed.

The liberal principles which have been universally endorsed, at least at the international level, are all concerned with the idea of human rights. From the egalitarian conception of a humanity, commonly endowed with natural rights to life, liberty and the pursuit of happiness, derives the necessity, only grudgingly and partially admitted by states, that individual human beings are the ultimate source of political authority, and that, therefore, their rights must be publicly acknowledged within international society. It is still a society of states but the states now belong to the people. Governments which torture some of the people for their political or religious beliefs, or blatantly exploit them for the narrow advantage of an unrepresentative political clique, must be accountable for their actions. However far short of this ideal state practice falls, it is the logic behind the United Nations human rights regime. It is also a logic that no one is prepared to deny. The crucial document is appropriately entitled *The Universal Declaration of Human Rights.*

Two other principles, also derived from the same Enlightenment seed-bed, have been grafted onto the idea of international society. These are the restriction on the legitimate use of force, and the duty of states to recognise the social, economic and cultural rights of their people in addition to the original list of civil and political rights. Arguably neither is as firmly enthroned in the contemporary conception of international society as the other principles we have discussed. The attempt to constrain governments in their use of force continues to fall foul, as we have seen, of the appeal of the balance of power as an enabling concept in the foreign policies of the strongest states. More generally, it has been repeatedly undermined by the impossibility of reaching an uncontested definition of the concept of aggression. The idea of social and economic rights is seriously weakened by the impossibility of specifying how these rights are to be delivered, and by whom, in circumstances which often lie beyond the control of governments or even of international society as a whole. Nonetheless the fact that no government will admit that its foreign policy is aimed at military aggrandisement and that they all acknowledge the need for economic cooperation strongly supports the inclusion of these principles in our account of the modified idea of an international society.

We come finally to nationalism. How has the national idea influenced the evolution of international society? While the influence of nationalism has been enormously extensive, touching, at some point, most aspects of international life, the modern history of international society is neither subsumed within, nor exhausted by, the history of nationalism. The idea crystallised before the nationalist era, and its subsequent evolution has been influenced by ideas which are, at least, partially independent on the national idea. The principles of the Enlightenment were originally conceived in a universal, not a national, form. Similarly, the idea of a complex international division of labour serving a world market, was a response to the logic of industrial capitalism rather than to nationalism. Such ideas have led to efforts to create international standards and to establish structures for international cooperation.

Yet, despite the influence of these and other ideas, my argument is that the modification of the traditional conception of international society arose primarily from its confrontation with the national idea. In support of this claim let us review three themes which run through the book. These deal respectively with the national principle of international legitimacy; the way in which national identity is taken for granted in liberal (and for that matter socialist) ideology; and the national basis of political organisation in the modern state.

The most important impact has undoubtedly been the substitution of a popular for the prescriptive principle of sovereignty on which the original conception of international society was based. Conceivably, a principle of popular sovereignty could have been advanced without tying it to the nation—it could have been expressed, for example, by a common imperial citizenship. However, the way in which the principles of the French Revolution were exported by Napoleon ensured that this did not happen in Europe. And the policies of the liberal imperialist powers in Asia and Africa ensured that it would not happen there also. The concept of a people was tied historically to the concept of nation, even where national consciousness was embryonic or even non-existent.

Once the principle of national self-determination had done its work in extinguishing the concept of empire as an acceptable political form, its continuing function in international society became largely mythic. Nations were deemed to have created states in their own image. No further creations were in order. Domestication of the concept has allowed it to support the sovereignty of existing states rather than subvert it. However, it still has enormous subversive appeal to all those actual and potential secessionists who remain convinced that their fundamental rights have been denied.

It is difficult to see the lineaments of some more satisfactory principle of state legitimisation emerging in the future. If government is to belong to the people (and to whom else?) then it cannot belong to mankind, which is, from an organisational point of view, a mere abstraction. Since communities do not exist within natural boundaries, there seems little alternative but to define the principle of popular sovereignty by reference to historical communities, or those whose collective identity is being created within frontiers handed down to them in the more recent past. Certainly the strength of national sentiment should not be underestimated. The Soviet Union, one of the few major states whose government claims to derive its legitimacy from an alternative source to the nation, has found that *perestroika*, the process of domestic reform, has revived national political demands in the Baltic republics and in the trans-Caucasus. Even limited schemes of liberal integration such as the United States–Canada Free Trade Agreement may be perceived by their opponents as an unwarranted attack on national identity. This does not mean that the national idea must frustrate all schemes for international cooperation, merely that those which ignore it, or confront it directly, are likely to meet with heavy and sustained resistance. The subversive appeal of national self-determination is not confined to third world secessionists.

In origin the idea of self-determination (i.e. the free development of individual potential) is impeccably liberal. Liberal thought is generally conceived of in terms of its opposition to nationalism. On this view, liberalism places the individual at the centre of the argument, nationalism the collective. The idea of national self-determination is not logically derived from the idea of an autonomous individual, it is a perversion of it. On one level this view is obviously correct. The argument of this book, however, is that this traditional opposition conceals the extent to which liberal international theory was explicitly statist and implicitly nationalist. This second theme was explored mainly with reference to the economic aspects of sovereignty, since national liberalism most clearly revealed itself in this area. The explicit statism stemmed from those legitimate state functions (defence, the maintenance of law and order and the stability of the currency) which liberal theorists reserved from their attack on the mercantilist system. The implicit nationalism derived partly from their acceptance of existing cultural communities as effectively "natural" (and, therefore, invisible) and partly from the refinement of their argument to accommodate the principle of popular sovereignty. Liberal nationalism broke into the open after 1945 with the elaboration of the idea of the welfare state.

Not all nationalists are liberals. Indeed, in the popular imagination, the typical nationalist is likely to be portrayed as a romantic enthusiast, fundamentally opposed to the bloodless cosmopolitanism of liberal rationality. During the twentieth century the cult of national irrationalism has repeatedly savaged the liberal conception of international society, most infamously in the Nazi onslaught, but also more recently in Kampuchea and in innumerable communal massacres. These only appear to be less terrible because, from the outside, they seem to lack the purposeless, pre-meditated anti-morality of the holocaust.

After 1945 a deliberate attempt was made to create an international framework of political and economic cooperation which would channel the irrational and destructive potential of the national idea into a relatively benign liberal mould. This effort has not been wholly successful. It was, no doubt, compromised from the start by the cultural myopia of the victors of the Second World War, and the age-old tendency of the powerful to behave arrogantly towards the weak. But it created more possibilities for international cooperation and conflict resolution than had ever previously existed.

Ultimately, international society is an historical not a theoretical construct. Its moral order is neither functionally built-in nor guaranteed by the rationality of human nature. If the argument of this book is accepted, therefore, we should not look for our salvation to some miraculous or mechanical supersession of the national idea. The final theme is that nationalism has become structurally embodied, in all parts of the world, as the basis of the modern state. The implication is not that the nation-state is an eternal category or that some less deadly basis of political organisation and international solidarity may eventually emerge. It is that there is little sensible that we can say about these possibilities: on this issue, if no other, we lack a reliable guide to the future.

The nation-state (or the would-be nation-state) remains the basic political unit. It continues to define the primary space in which political argument takes place. The competing ideas, of a world market dominated by multi-national corporations to whom we owe loyalty, or international proletarian solidarity, are equally implausible. In relation to other states and peoples the nation-state also defines the context in which real, as opposed to fantastical, moral choices must be faced. We must live in the world we have made. Our task is not god-like: we cannot hope to transform the world, if we are very lucky we might just improve it.

QUESTIONS FOR DISCUSSION

1. What information is needed to determine whether states are declining as actors in the international arena?
2. What are the strengths and weaknesses of each of the alternatives to the state in solving the problems of military security, economic well-being, and environmental protection?
3. What lessons can be applied to world politics from the experience of the United States in which, over two centuries, many states united into one country?
4. How effective are international organizations in dealing with global problems?
5. What will the international system look like in the year 2050? What are the reasons for your answer?

SUGGESTED READINGS

Adam-Schwaetzer, Irmgard. "Transformation of National Sovereignty." *European Affairs* (Amsterdam), **3** (Winter 1989), pp. 47–52.

Alter, Peter. *Nationalism*. Trans. Stuart McKinnon-Evans. London: Edward Arnold, 1989.

Caporaso, James A. (ed.). *The Elusive State: International and Comparative Perspectives*. Newbury Park, Calif.: Sage Publications, 1989.

Claude, Inis L., Jr. "Myths about the State." *Review of International Studies*, **12** (Jan. 1986), pp. 1–11.

Elshtain, Jean Bethke. "Nationalism Is as Deadly as Ever." *Wall Street Journal*, Oct. 11, 1989, p. A18.

Frankel, Glenn. "Nation-State: An Idea under Siege." *Washington Post*, Nov. 11, 1990, pp. A1, A28.

Gablentz, Otto van der. "Those Who Are Afraid for Their Little Kingdoms." *European Affairs* (Amsterdam), **4** (Spring 1990), pp. 113–116.

"Goodbye to the Nation State?" *Economist* (London), **315** (June 23, 1990), pp. 11–12.

Hinsley, F. H. *Sovereignty*, 2d ed. Cambridge, England: Cambridge Univ. Press, 1986.

Holsti, K. J. "The Necrologists of International Relations." *Canadian Journal of Political Science*, **18** (Dec. 1985), pp. 675–695.

Mann, Michael. *The Rise and Decline of the Nation State.* Oxford, England: Blackwell, 1990.

Shtromas, Alexander. "Grievances around the World." *Wall Street Journal*, Oct. 11, 1989, p. A18.

Soroos, Marvin S. *Beyond Sovereignty: The Challenge of Global Policy.* Columbia, S.C.: Univ. of South Carolina Press, 1986.

Waltz, Kenneth. "The Myth of National Interdependence." In Charles P. Kindleberger (ed.). *The International Corporation*, pp. 205–223, Cambridge, Mass.: MIT Press, 1970.

2 Will the United Nations Become an Important Actor in the Post–Cold War Era?

YES

Vladimir F. Petrovsky

Multifaceted Cooperation: A Post-Confrontational Perspective for the United Nations

NO

Alan L. Keyes

The U.N.: A Wobbly House of Cards

Multifaceted Cooperation: A Post-Confrontational Perspective for the United Nations

Vladimir F. Petrovsky

At the beginning of a new year—indeed a new decade—it is of benefit to review the results of the one that has just ended. Looking back as interested parties over the mosaic of the United Nations' recent achievements, we single out the day 15 November 1989. It was on that day that the General Assembly, on an initiative of the Union of Soviet Socialist Republics and the United States of America, adopted by consensus resolution 44/21, entitled "Enhancing international peace, security and international co-operation in all its aspects in accordance with the Charter of the United Nations."

Wherein lies the significance of the Soviet-American initiative? For the first time in the history of the United Nations, the Soviet Union and the United States acted in concert to support this unique Organization. Drawn up on the basis of the efforts of two great Powers, the resolution became their joint contribution to the strengthening of the United Nations, and thus a joint success. The manner in which the resolution was adopted is also important. Although the draft resolution was originally proposed by the Soviet Union and the United States, participation in it was, from the outset, open to other countries. Another 41 Member States joined in sponsoring it, and it was supported by the entire world community. In substance, the draft resolution affirms the cardinal Charter concept of collective action by Members of

the Organization in the interest of maintaining and enhancing international peace and security.

Let us emphasize right away that it would be utterly wrong to regard this resolution as some "covert" understanding between the Soviet Union and the United States in which only their interests are represented. The very fact that the proposal was made—and it may have been something of a surprise to many—illustrates, indeed, that the USSR and the United States have renounced such an approach. Accordingly the significance of the joint action lies in the fact that it symbolizes the beginning of a new and different phase in the activities of the USSR and the United States at the United Nations, a phase in which they work together in parallel: now, instead of maintaining a separate Soviet-American dialogue, they are incorporating it into the international debate.

No less important is the content of the resolution adopted. Action of this type puts an end to the cold war and confrontation at the United Nations. The habitual tendency to make proclamatory statements in United Nations proceedings, with propaganda battles and the cultivation of political intolerance, is becoming a thing of the past. The stereotyped behaviour whereby one side automatically, so to speak, rejected the other side's proposals is ceasing. The United Nations is entering the post-confrontational era, in which a new international order will be established, based on mutual understanding and active cooperation. It is no accident that at the most recent session of the General Assembly a number of other resolutions were also adopted by consensus, including two important international conventions of a humanitarian character: on the rights of the child and against the use of mercenaries.

The changes in the material and spiritual life of civilization which are taking place before the eyes of the present generation are of an unprecedented character. The rapid scientific and technological progress of recent years, the takeoff of computer technology and the transformation of the world into a single information space, the trend towards interacting economic mechanisms and integration on a regional and global scale, and the growing gap between the levels of development of individual countries: all of these

Source: Vladimir F. Petrovsky, "Multifaceted Co-operation: A Post-Confrontational Perspective for the United Nations," *Disarmament: A Periodic Review by the United Nations* 13, no. 2 (1990), pp. 267–285. Reprinted with permission.

developments turn upside down the conventional wisdom about the present and the future. Transformations of a political character are also accelerating. Ideas of freedom and democracy, the supremacy of law, freedom of choice, and responsible behaviour on the part of States are uppermost in people's minds. Peoples, nations and countries are becoming politically more active, and an international community in the full meaning of that term is taking shape. Not finding convincing answers to the contemporary challenges which affect the very foundations of human existence, in the economic, political, humanitarian or any other sphere, means being left on the sidelines of world civilization.

Thus, what is at issue is not simply security, but security in all its aspects and forms. Resolution 44/21 properly reflects this requirement. It is apparent from its text that peace, security and co-operation are inseparable. The combining of these three concepts is no accident; it embodies the essential characteristic of the kind of international relations now taking shape.

The maintenance of international peace and security is the central aim of the United Nations Charter. Today it is particularly important to understand the two-in-one, complex nature of authentic security. Such security is characterized not simply by the absence of war, but also by the presence of reliable and positive guarantees of the non-use of force and the establishment of comprehensive conditions for peaceful development. With the recognition of this complex and diverse character of security it can be seen that a multifaceted, comprehensive approach to the achievement of security is called for.

It also follows from resolution 44/21 that, in the new conditions, co-operation is the only possible course of action for States. Co-operation affords, for the first time, an opportunity—at the current level of world civilization and with the United Nations Charter as a basis—to set the development of international relations on an evolving course that would allow the turbulent natural changes occurring in the world to be set within a framework of stability, so as not to break up existing structures or endanger peace and security. Co-operation, previously a sporadic

phenomenon, is becoming the central principle of active joint creation and co-development. It is the proper response to the needs of an emerging peaceful era in international relations. It is characterized by positive, rather than negative, interaction by States in their efforts to ensure optimal external conditions for their development.

Precisely for this reason, the aim of the joint resolution is to mobilize Member States for the expansion of practical efforts to guarantee peace and security. The search for lasting security through power rivalry is unthinkable today. The States Members of the United Nations have spoken up unequivocally in favour of ensuring security in tomorrow's world through political means alone, that is to say, through consultations and co-operation within the framework of the United Nations, in all its bodies without exception.

Lastly, it follows from the resolution that peace, security and co-operation are regarded as a *single system*, based on the United Nations Charter. This constitutes a recognition of observable trends in today's world, which for all its diversity is increasingly becoming an indivisible and interdependent whole. Our civilization is a functioning system the component parts of which cannot be disturbed without causing harm to the working of the entire mechanism. In other words, peace cannot be maintained on a selective basis, in a particular region, without regard to peace in other parts of the world. The organic bond between national and international security is becoming increasingly apparent: when the diminished security of any country becomes unfavourable for other countries, this leads to a destabilization of the overall situation, and hence it is only within the framework of global security that the security of an individual State can be reliably ensured. It is becoming obvious that, in an interdependent system, progress in a given society which is separated from other societies by artificial boundaries and ideological limits is in fact impossible.

It follows from resolution 44/21 that the system of peace, security and co-operation must be backed by the authority and capabilities of the United Nations. In the past, when the work of the United Nations was greatly distorted, the Organization served first and foremost as a forum for States to express their own—uncompromising—viewpoints. Today, however, the United Nations is becoming a forum of a different kind. In it, the representatives of the Member States speak, not to engage in polemics or make accusatory statements, but to promote co-operation among all States and ensure that decisions have a practical orientation. As the Secretary-General, Javier Pérez de Cuéllar, observed in his most recent annual report on the work of the Organization,[1] "the assistance of the world Organization is being sought as never before in its history." It is impossible not to share the Secretary-General's gratification at the "renewal of confidence in multilateralism and its agents."

Pacta sunt servanda. As far as the United Nations is concerned, the full and universal implementation of the United Nations Charter is today a doubly important goal. These are not simply words, but a deeply meaningful and significant statement. In the past, States not infrequently singled out some provisions of the Charter and ignored its other constituent parts. In the new, post-confrontational world, all the provisions of the United Nations Charter must be observed in letter and in spirit, and the Charter must be the corner-stone of all international action by States.

Such a corner-stone is now more necessary than ever. In a world that is changing so fast and at times so unpredictably, it cannot be dispensed with. (Some politicians say, not without foundation, that at the time of the cold war they felt more at ease because, however paradoxical it may seem, peace, although tottering on the brink of a "hot" war, appeared more reliable and more stable.) Today changes may occur in any region. Resolution 44/21 is therefore aimed at promoting, through the United Nations, the stability of an international system undergoing change.

The Soviet Union and the United States, together with all the States Members of the United Nations, chose to act at a critically important and decisive moment. They reached the unanimous view that the basis of action should be unconditional respect for the Charter of the United Nations and the purposes and principles enshrined in it. This means closely following the course set as a result of carefully weighing the interests of all the countries which worked on framing the Charter at a time when there was real co-operation as the war against fascism ended. In addition, the United Nations itself must be developed, and relations must be renewed between the participants in its proceedings.

The direct joint search for solutions to quite specific and tangible issues on the agenda, at all levels of international interaction, is now becoming a decisive factor.

In the military-political sphere, a real breakthrough was achieved with the Treaty between the United States and the Soviet Union on the Elimination of Their Intermediate-Range and Shorter-Range Missiles. This was the first agreement to affirm the organic nature of comprehensive security through the elimination of two classes of nuclear weapons.

The new security order can and must be established, not by the build-up of arms, but by their elimination. The results of the meeting in Malta between the leaders of the Soviet Union and the United States justify the hope that, by the next stage of their dialogue—in the second half of June 1990—the basic elements of a treaty on a 50 per cent reduction in strategic offensive arms will be agreed on. Following that, in the course of the next few months, the treaty could be prepared for signature. In the course of this year, 1990, understandings are likely to be reached at the Vienna talks on the reduction of conventional weapons and armed forces. Work on a convention for the prohibition and destruction of chemical weapons is nearing completion at Geneva.

New basic categories are emerging in the concept of disarmament. Accompanying conditions such as verification and openness are assuming particular significance. The strictest and most reliable verification is needed in order to ensure the full confidence of all parties to the agreements. With the progressive introduction and refinement of multilat-

---

[1] United Nations document A/44/1.

eral procedures and the necessary extension of inspections to foreign military bases in the territories of third countries, the role of international verification, particularly under the auspices of the United Nations, will be enhanced.

Meanwhile, openness and *glasnost* will serve as the "philosopher's stone" of disarmament, facilitating an ordered transformation of military confrontation into arrangements to end such confrontation. Publication of the military doctrines and military budgets of States, their comparison and the establishment of agreed standards for the greatest possible transparency in military activity are becoming particularly topical issues. The Soviet Union is to take an active part in the work on this subject that is to be started by the United Nations Disarmament Commission in 1990. We believe that the new world order should be based, not on military—including nuclear—restraint, but on restraint grounded in policy, law, transparency and verification, supported by the authority and facilities of the United Nations.

The winding down of military capabilities lends substance to the economic dimension of disarmament, and gives real content to the principle of disarmament for development. On the international level, we must ensure that resources are indeed released as a result of the reduction of military programmes and that a share of them is used to assist the poorest countries and to solve global problems. This process will certainly be facilitated now that the United Nations has begun to examine the problem of converting military production, covering both international scientific research and the exchange of relevant experience.

We are convinced that development is a decisive factor in shaping the construction of a new kind of world. From the political, moral and economic points of view, the general transition to reasonable sufficiency for defence purposes is capable of giving an enormous boost to positive processes in all other spheres of human existence. However, every aspect of security is increasingly being affected by non-military factors, such as the creation of a healthy environment, stable economic development, the defence of human rights, and freedom of information.

The list could be continued: more and more new transnational problems are appearing on the agenda of the United Nations.

Just as important as the banning of war will be the prevention of an ecological crisis. Everyone is by now aware that a nuclear conflict would mean the immediate annihilation of mankind. A recent analysis of "nuclear winter" by the Secretary-General of the United Nations[2] provided further scientific evidence of that fact. Nevertheless, the approaching ecological catastrophe could produce similar results. The only difference is that they would be gradual. It is therefore becoming increasingly evident that there is a vital and urgent need for special measures to conserve nature in every part of the planet, in order not only to save mankind from suffering irreparable losses but also to protect humanity against new destabilizing factors in the development of international relations.

There is growing understanding that the field of humanitarian co-operation, with primary emphasis on the defence of human rights, must be free from confrontation. Democratic society as a whole has in common the same objectives as those enshrined in the Universal Declaration of Human Rights and the related International Covenants, and the task of bringing the internal practices of each country up to the level of recognized international standards is one that has to be assumed by all. Efforts in the new and delicate sphere of information have also been raised to a new level.

Problems which used to be considered as relating to the purely "internal" jurisdiction of States are now moving into the forefront of international discussions. The special session of the United Nations General Assembly on the campaign against narcotic drugs and the Assembly's adoption of a resolution stating the commitment of the United Nations to the prevention of international terrorism show that world society is not indifferent to these threats.

There is now a pressing need for efforts to deal

---

[2] *Study on the Climatic and Other Effects of Nuclear War* (United Nations publication, Sales No. 89.IX.1).

with every aspect of international security. This is the most important facet of the comprehensive approach. What we need is not to establish linkages and aggregate problems, but to solve them simultaneously and in a co-ordinated manner in each specific sphere. This approach is consistent with the need to harmonize international relations and to strengthen the links between States in their search for world stability, including their quest for social and other types of change on a basis of widely diverse systems of development.

The point at which the new thinking that has emerged in the Soviet Union was incorporated into United Nations activities may be said to have been four years ago, when the Soviet Union and certain other States proposed the establishment of a comprehensive system of international security, a proposal which was later consolidated and developed by Mikhail Gorbachev in his messages to the United Nations in 1987 and 1988. The Soviet Union unequivocally pronounced itself in favour of building a new world order, to be supported by the authority and facilities of the United Nations.

As may be seen, these initiatives have achieved their objective, which was, first and foremost, to usher in a broad democratic dialogue on the methods and principles whereby comprehensive security could be established, to enhance the role of the United Nations and eventually to lead the dialogue towards some sort of common denominator. This was done in a period of less than four years. Considering that the cold war lasted for over 40 years, this period is really quite short.

If we compare the proposal on comprehensive security with resolution 44/21, differences in wording immediately leap to the eye. But their essential meaning and basic provisions are entirely consistent. Previously, the primary emphasis was on the need to unite the efforts of States with a view to establishing comprehensive security; the resolution also addresses the need to strengthen the system of peace and security. Previously, the idea of a comprehensive approach was given prominence; now another—possibly more precise—expression is to be found: "multifaceted approaches." In other words, the essential meaning remains the same, but language has been found which suits all States Members of the United Nations.

In the course of discussions it proved possible to identify a number of areas of agreement, which now provide a clear framework for the immediate trends in the activization of multilateralism. These are to strengthen the principal organs of the United Nations, to enhance the possibilities for the conduct of United Nations peace-keeping operations, to strengthen the role of international law and actively involve the International Court of Justice in this process. The essential purpose of these measures is to promote the collective search for ways and means to increase the effectiveness of the United Nations through the full and non-selective implementation of the provisions of its Charter and the active utilization of its mechanisms and procedures. Further ahead lies the genuine possibility of proceeding to concentrate the efforts of the United Nations on preventive diplomacy and developing its ability to take effective measures to prevent differences of opinion from growing into conflicts.

As a result, the United Nations is now witnessing its own renaissance. This is being noted by all Member States, as well as by the Secretary-General. It may be said, without exaggeration, that the Organization has now begun—for the first time since 1945—once again to operate under external conditions comparable to those which were seen as a premise underlying its structure by its founder Members. The trend towards dialogue and the solution of problems by means of negotiations—in other words, multilateralism and the rule of law and order—must prevail over approaches based on military methods and the use of force and over reliance on unilateral action. The United Nations, having entered with vigour into the world-wide processes of renewal, is now to some extent becoming their catalyst and a powerful force for their acceleration.

A universal instrument has also emerged: the solution of problems by political methods and by means of co-operation, together with a determination to ensure that interests are balanced. In the efforts to harmonize interests, the patterns of parliamentary diplomacy are now assuming particular significance. Parliamentary diplomacy involves refusing to think in terms of outdated stereotypes, engaging in civilized dialogue from the speakers' rostrum and searching persistently behind the scenes for solutions to disagreements. In the case of the United Nations, it is essential that preliminary consultations should be held in each and every body that has a bearing on the balance of interests.

We are convinced that the world, in breaking with the philosophy of hostility and confrontation, is becoming more balanced, mature and wise. No longer is it an obligation to endure manifestations of national egocentricity, high-handed ways or any kind of *idée fixe*. It is now in the interests of all that policies should always be designed to strengthen the international community and to promote its survival and development.

In order to ensure the transition to political approaches using negotiating mechanisms and law, military prescriptions must be rejected, and ways of thinking generally demilitarized.

While in the last century it was the practice to describe political subjects in terms of the theatre (the international scene, the actors and performers on the stage, the curtain), the twentieth century has seen the general adoption of concepts borrowed from military theory, such as those of an offensive, a front, a breakthrough. The need is now urgently felt—and *perestroika* has clearly illustrated this—for a fresh new language of diplomacy which both reflects the creative values shared by all and operates in accordance with the interests of nations and States.

The principle of universal membership in the United Nations and related international organizations is also viewed today in a new light. The United Nations and its system have now become the only ramified mechanism for interaction between States which exercises a real influence on the external and internal political practice of any given country. Full-fledged participation in United Nations activities not only meets the interests of the world community as a whole in identifying multifaceted approaches to a strengthening of the system of peace, security and co-operation but also fulfils the long-term interests of each participant in the maintenance of international contacts."To practise tolerance and live together in peace with one another as good neighbours": that phrase from the preamble of the Charter serves as a logical prelude to the provision whereby membership in the Organization is open to all peace-loving States. The task ahead—that of ensuring a prolonged period of peaceful development for mankind—is more than ever inseparable from realizing in practice the principle of universality of the United Nations and erasing the heritage of the cold war and of colonial and racist oppression.

There is also a need to ensure the active participation in the United Nations of all the basic groups of States. The Movement of Non-Aligned Countries is an important force in the Organization, and its voice should be heard to the full, not only in the General Assembly but also in the Security Council. A special role is now played by public, non-governmental organizations, which must work in close contact with the United Nations, keeping open a permanent channel of communication with the broadest masses of the population in different countries.

A commitment to reaching consensus on the greatest number of problems under consideration is the most effective way to further the progressive development of international organizations. The positive results of the forty-fourth session of the General Assembly confirm this. It is no coincidence that at that session more resolutions were adopted by merging separate draft resolutions submitted initially by different sponsors. In other words, the general ethos of conducting international affairs is entering an entirely new phase; and there is a growing readiness to consider the arguments put forward by the other side and to take them into account in refining one's position.

Of course, politicians are still faced with the task of reaching a sort of "consensus about consensus." But it is already clear to us now that a consensus, by its legal status, occupies a special place among the various means at the disposal of multilateral forums. By virtue of its effectiveness it differs from recommendations and is similar to binding decisions, in view of the moral authority of the world community on which it is based. For precisely this reason, it is important always to apply the rule of consensus during both the period of drafting a document and the stage of implementing its provisions once it is adopted. We see consensus as a means to promote responsible behaviour by States and a guarantee that the interests of all will be considered, which opens up the possibility of the participation of each and every party in the taking of major decisions. The right of veto of the five permanent members of the Security Council also appears in a different light through the prism of consensus—the veto here exerts a positive influence and forces the permanent members of the Council to reach agreement among themselves.

This dramatic breakthrough is, of course, not easy to achieve; there are still many difficulties to be overcome in revitalizing the United Nations. We cannot rid ourselves of the past immediately. There are still instances of reversion to power politics and a bipolar view of the world, and this influences the actions of many States within and outside the United Nations.

A critical re-evaluation of past experience is needed to overcome outmoded stereotypes, and create the conditions necessary to prevent a repetition of past mistakes. Since April 1985 in the Soviet Union we have been evaluating the history of our activities in the United Nations from this standpoint. We see that we sometimes used a position of strength in a way that reduced the effectiveness of the Organization. We believe that the urgent task of diplomacy now is to consider objectively the prevailing attitudes in the United Nations, to initiate a dialogue involving the entire spectrum of the world's political forces, and to realize that in solving problems affecting all mankind we do not have and cannot have opponents, only allies and partners.

But we do not claim a monopoly with regard to the need for self-criticism. All States, and particularly the nuclear powers that are permanent members of the Security Council, must take a critical look at their past policies, correct them where necessary and focus this analysis on the future. Ignoring the will of the United Nations is today, as in the past, inadmissible.

The ability and readiness to undertake self-criticism is perhaps only one of the elements of a truly up-to-date policy. The efforts of all are needed to consolidate a radical breakthrough in world affairs and create guarantees ensuring the irreversibility of positive changes. The cumulative effect of joint action by peoples, States, their blocs and groups—East and West, North and South—is necessary.

It is important to bring about also a change of style in relations between States. One-sided approaches and the posturing of a schoolmaster lecturing others have little effect today. If accompanied by pressure involving the use of force, then such actions are unacceptable and dangerous. No, a mature and wise civilization requires, not instructions from one side, but rather collective efforts, in the spirit of a ''new internationalism,'' which is responsible and devoid of double standards.

The post-confrontational era requires as never before the intelligent management of world affairs. The period of joint creation and development is precisely what constitutes, in our view, a real challenge for politicians and diplomats. Finding a multifaceted approach leading to a comprehensive solution of the problems confronting mankind is an extremely complicated task, one which is in no way comparable to the simplistic pattern of relations during the cold-war period. It demands of those participating in the task constant work, creative initiative and a good deal of common sense. The ultimate common goal—bringing about a marked change in the overall picture of the world through co-operation—cannot be compared in terms of its importance with the selfish interests of individual countries and blocs that prevailed earlier.

The path to achieving this goal is a long one, since adapting to new realities is never an easy matter. It is encouraging, however, to note that dialogue has already made it possible to single out a number of common connecting elements in a comprehensive approach to security. These include the demilitarization of the thinking and behaviour of States, the democratization and humanization of international relations, and the elimination of ideology from relations between States.

The vulnerability of the contemporary world faced with man-made means of destruction has focused attention on the urgent need to demilitarize by gradually reducing arms and moving towards the elimination of weapons of mass destruction. Mankind must once and for all reject war as a means for resolving political and economic differences and ideological disputes between States.

The democratization of international life requires the elimination of exclusive clubs, including the nuclear club, and the participation of one and all in working out solutions. It is closely linked to the task of humanizing international relations, since the human dimension is now becoming particularly important as a goal and a means of achieving a safe world. A non-nuclear and non-violent world would tend also to be a more just world. One of the functions of the human factor in formulating policy is to strengthen the moral basis of the policy. Our new thinking holds that man deserves a better fate than being the hostage of nuclear weapons. His living conditions and political position are increasingly determining the direction in which international relations will develop and the way in which the problems that arise in them are solved.

Eliminating ideological barriers from such relations has become a prerequisite for improving co-operation along new lines. The primacy of law, respect for human rights, and the progress of society as a whole are essential to eliminating ideology from relations between States and the rejection by States of claims to knowledge of the ''absolute truth.'' Of course, this does not entail abandoning one's views and convictions. The fundamental right of peoples to choose their own path of development is unquestionable. The human right to freedom of conscience, belief and opinion, enshrined in universally recog-

nized international instruments, is just as inalienable. This involves the inadmissibility of making the clash of ideological views into a battlefield between States. General moral principles must be put into practice by means of one's own example and the methods used by countries in their foreign and domestic policies.

Eliminating ideology from multilateral interaction requires the deliberate rejection of ideological attitudes towards machinery for co-operation; it is necessary to overcome the artificial politicization of the activities of the United Nations and its specialized agencies, focus their attention on carrying out specific tasks in accordance with their mandates, and raise the professional level of their activities.

A multifaceted and comprehensive approach requires that greater attention should be given also to the question of administering the Organization itself, an issue which has become acutely political in nature. The task is to make optimum use of the United Nations financial and material resources, co-ordinate and rationalize the activities of international organizations, and eliminate duplication and overlapping.

The post-confrontational period requires practical steps. Only convergent unilateral, bilateral and multilateral actions can give assurance that the system of peace, security and co-operation laid down in the Charter of the United Nations will become an effective barrier preventing a return to confrontation and provide an assurance that the twenty-first century will be marked by a new approach to developing our civilization as a unified whole by combining all the finest achievements of mankind.

Yes, the model social system of the third millennium will be characterized first of all by a synthesis of positive experience and the United Nations will become the forum for this process. This synthesis is creating progressive norms that can be used in all countries in order to establish constitutionally governed States and civil societies. The synthesis represents the new culture of a united and interdependent world which, on the one hand, rejects rapacious behaviour, condemns such ''breaches'' of civilization as fascism and racism, and repudiates oppression and violence; and on the other hand, creates a culture based on tolerance, diversity and recognition of the right of different ideological and political viewpoints to exist regardless of whether they are supported at any given time by a majority or a minority.

The 1990s, undoubtedly, must be a time of change, a time for entering a peaceful era. They must also be a period in which the world community makes determined efforts to create guarantees for ensuring stability and making positive changes irreversible. Not everything is easy in the world and not everything is clear-cut in the discussions conducted in the United Nations. Much work remains to be done in order to ensure that General Assembly resolution 44/21 shall be implemented in all fields of activity of the United Nations. The adoption of this resolution was not a goal in itself. It is designed to promote the further expansion of dialogue, co-operation through specific measures and greater co-ordination of concrete actions by States.

The main thing, in our view, is to ensure that the resolution on enhancing international peace, security and co-operation represents a further stage in the dialogue about a fundamentally new, post-confrontational world order based on the Charter of the United Nations.

The U.N.:
A Wobbly House of Cards

Alan L. Keyes

In the days since Iraq invaded Kuwait, the United Nations has acted with greater promptitude and cohesion that at any time since the Korean War. Within 48 hours the U.N. Security Council issued a resolution condemning the invasion, demanding that Iraq withdraw, and invoking comprehensive Chapter VII sanctions. Even more striking is the most recent resolution authorizing member states to use minimal force to enforce the sanctions. Even rogue states like Libya, Syria and Iran have supported the U.N. actions and declared that they will respect them. Armed with this universal solidarity, the U.N. secretary general will meet with Iraq's foreign minister today, leading some to hope that the U.N. will provide an escape route from war.

It is probably fair to say that the U.N. has never before in its history looked more like the peacekeeping, order-preserving institution it is supposed to be. Many observers ascribe this to the apparent end of the Cold War. There has certainly been an unprecedented degree of Soviet cooperation with the Security Council's actions. But the superpower conflict hasn't been the only, or, in many cases, the main, obstacle to an effective U.N. response to regional threats to peace.

In fact, the Korean War is a good example of a tough U.N. response against the wishes of the Soviet Union. Of course, at the time the U.S. dominated the world scene. This nation's relative power combined with the strong support of Western Europe and the

Latin American countries to give us an almost automatic majority in the U.N. bodies. In the Korean case this led to circumstances in which we could even circumvent the Soviet veto on the Security Council.

A LOOK AT THE NUMBERS

As Europe's colonial empires in Africa and Asia collapsed, however, U.S. domination of the U.N. gave way to domination by a new majority composed mainly of developing countries—the so-called Third World. This majority has since determined the issues that dominated the U.N.'s political agenda. Two components of the majority, the Africans and the Arab states, proved most effective at promoting their preoccupations, South Africa and Israel, to the top of the U.N. agenda. Beyond these regionally determined priorities, an anti-colonial and leftist ideological thrust superficially united the Third World majority. This gave the Soviets some advantage in advancing their anti-Western agenda through U.N. institutions.

To see how destructively this arrangement has worked, it helps to look at the numbers. A Heritage Foundation review of voting patterns during the U.N.'s 44th General Assembly (September–December 1989) shows that the rest of the world voted the same way the U.S. did an average of only 17 percent of the time. The average overall coincidence of voting with the Soviet Union for these countries was by contrast 95 percent. On Middle East questions, the rate was about the same. Some 94 percent of U.N. members supported resolutions 44/40 A and 44/42, which condemned Israel for being "terrorist" and "aggressive" and called for Israeli withdrawal from "occupied territories."

Long before last fall, once it became clear that we could no longer dominate its decisions, the U.S. ceased to take the U.N.'s politics seriously. It seemed easier for us to use our great power unilaterally, or to take advantage of the superiority in bilateral relations that our global economic dominance made possible.

As a result, the U.N. ceased to be a viable instru-

Source: Alan L. Keyes, "The U.N.: A Wobbly House of Cards," *Wall Street Journal*, Aug. 30, 1990, p. A8. Reprinted with permission.

ment for pursuing U.S. policy goals. Yet the Third World majority that dominated its decisions had no effective power to translate decision into action outside the U.N. In this sense the great-power veto on the Security Council merely reflects reality. Without involvement and support from the great powers, the U.N. can't do much more than talk. The necessary but not sufficient condition of its effectiveness is the support, indeed the leadership, of a nation powerful enough to add meaningful economic and political muscle to its actions. The Third World majority can provide the chassis for the U.N. vehicle. The great powers, and especially the U.S., must provide the engine.

The U.N.'s remarkably cohesive response to Iraq's aggression reflects a set of circumstances that have at least temporarily pushed aside the factors that have rendered the U.N. impotent. In the context of the Soviet Union's apparent collapse in the Cold War competition, the U.S. has, for the moment, emerged again in a position of undisputed global preeminence.

Iraq's invasion of Kuwait posed an immediate threat to Saudi Arabia, whose wealth and quiet political skills have made it a very influential player among Arab countries. Other traditional or more moderate Arab regimes (Egypt and Morocco, for example) also feel the shadow of this threat, while the leaders of the radical states (such as Libya and Syria) don't want to see Saddam Hussein achieve the Nasserite position of dominance in Arab politics that will result if his bold move against Kuwait succeeds. Given Iraq's regional military dominance, and the Soviet Union's current weakness, the U.S. represented the only power with the wherewithal to respond to Iraq's move in time to forestall an Iraqi takeover of Saudi Arabia.

A combination of regional self-interest and U.S. readiness have created an opportunity to fashion a coalition of support for prompt, and even forceful, U.N. action. The Soviets are in no position to oppose this coalition (which has some of the same elements as the one that repeatedly secured passage of resolutions in the General Assembly against the Soviet invasion of Afghanistan). In fact, since a prolonged

crisis in the Gulf will increase U.S. eagerness for continued good relations, the Soviets have an interest in encouraging international action—with the U.S. in the lead-role. Given the importance of Middle Eastern oil to their economies, the Europeans and the Japanese clearly have an important stake in making sure that supplies are not disrupted, or permanently controlled, by an Arab power less susceptible to their influence than the Arab monarchies.

It would be a mistake to believe that the U.N.'s ability to deal with the Gulf situation means that the organization itself has suddenly overcome its inherent structural and political deficiencies. The organization is not a catalyst or agent of events, it is more like a barometer. Its present role reflects a certain state of existing interests and power relations in the world. At the moment, those interests and relations have allowed the U.S. to reassert the strong leadership role that allowed the U.N. to take decisive action in the early years of its existence. What we are witnessing therefore tells us more about the current pre-eminence of the U.S. than it does about the U.N.

Even with that insight, we should be wary of concluding that the U.N. has now become a routinely reliable instrument for U.S. policy. The self-interest of certain Arab states combined with our readiness and Soviet weakness have made the current moment possible. The key factor, in U.N. terms, is majority support in the Arab bloc. Even in the present crisis it is not hard to envisage a change in that support over time. If Saddam Hussein can foment anti-American, anti-Western feeling among the Arab masses, this might weaken the resolve of the vulnerable moderate and traditional governments that are the core of the coalition that supports our presence and forceful action in the region. Weakness at the Arab core would give rise to European vacillation and doubtless affect the Soviets' calculations about the wisdom of being too positive in their cooperation with the international effort built around U.S. power.

HIGHLY POLITICIZED

We should also bear in mind that at some point this situation may become the precedent for actions less consonant with U.S. interests than at present. Will we someday find ourselves called upon to acquiesce in an effort built around Soviet military power (which still exists, by the way, despite current Soviet preoccupations that discourage its use), aimed at South Africa or Israel, with an African or more radical Arab majority at its core? The U.N. remains a highly politicized arena, in which—for the moment—global and regional circumstances favor our leadership. Circumstances can change, however. Rather than betting on naive theories about a fundamental reform of the U.N.'s weak character, we should constantly remember that there can be no substitute for our own prudence, diplomacy and decisiveness.

QUESTIONS FOR DISCUSSION

1. Had there been no United Nations in existence from 1945 to the present, how would the course of international relations have been affected? What are the reasons for your answer?
2. Had the cold war never existed, how would the United Nations have developed? What are the reasons for your answer?
3. What effect does the end of the cold war have on the behavior of third world countries in the United Nations?
4. What criteria should be used in evaluating the success or failure of the United Nations?
5. What states benefit most from the United Nations at the present time? Why? Which ones benefit the least? Why?

6. What reforms should be made in the structure of the United Nations to meet the criticisms that have been leveled at it?

SUGGESTED READINGS

Childers, Erskine B. "The Future of the United Nations: The Challenges of the 1990s." *Bulletin of Peace Proposals*, **21** (June 1990), pp. 143–152.

Cousins, Norman. "The Gulf Crisis as Teacher." *Christian Science Monitor*, Sept. 18, 1990, p. 18.

Franz, Mark A. "U.N. Peace: Euphoria vs. Reality." *World and I*, **5** (Apr. 1990), pp. 126–131.

Hottelet, Richard C. "U.N. Growing Muscle in a Multipolar World." *Los Angeles Times*, Mar. 12, 1989, sec. V, p. 2.

Karns, Margaret P., and Karen A. Mingst. "Peacekeeping Efforts: Some Fly, Some Flop." *Bulletin of the Atomic Scientists*, **46** (May 1990), pp. 43–47.

Lewis, Paul. "The United Nations Comes of Age, Causing Some Anxiety." *New York Times*, Aug. 5, 1990, sec. IV, p. 3.

Mowat, Lucia. "UN's Post–Cold War Stature Grows." *Christian Science Monitor*, Sept. 7, 1990, p. 3.

Moynihan, Daniel Patrick, with Suzanne Weaver. *A Dangerous Place*. Boston: Little, Brown, 1978.

Renninger, John P. (ed.). *The Future Role of the United Nations in an Interdependent World*. Dordrecht, The Netherlands: Martinus Nijhoff, 1989.

Urquhart, Brian. "The United Nations and Its Discontents." *New York Review of Books*, **37** (Mar. 15, 1990), pp. 11–16.

3 Do Multinational Corporations Exploit Developing Countries?

YES

Adeoye A. Akinsanya

Multinationals in a Changing Environment

NO

Melvyn B. Krauss

The Multinational Corporation

Multinationals in a Changing Environment

Adeoye A. Akinsanya

Economic nationalism in developing countries is often characterized by the desire to increase control over their economies; it is also often characterized by the desire to secure greater control over alien-owned enterprises that play a very key role in the economy and the development of these countries. The position of many governments in less-developed countries is that the political gains from regulating or controlling the activities of alien-owned enterprises, particularly local subsidiaries of MNCs [multinational corporations], will outweigh any economic costs in terms of creating new employment opportunities; local expenditure on goods and services; contribution to government revenues, gross domestic product, and foreign exchange reserves; and transfer of technology. Many of these countries emerged from colonial domination in the 1960s only to discover, to their chagrin, that political independence was not synonymous with economic independence. Put differently, many of these countries emerged from colonial domination in the 1960s only to discover, most painfully, that political independence was often accompanied by a more subtle form of economic dependence that could be as binding as more formal political links. However, concern about economic dependence is not limited to the emergent states of Africa, Asia, and the Caribbean. There is an increasing concern as well in countries such as those in Latin America, which achieved political independence more than a

century ago but see themselves as having remained in a dependent economic relation to developed market economies, particularly the United States. In any event, regardless of when political independence was gained, this concern has focused increasingly around the role of MNCs in the economies of these countries.

In the main, these business entities have been the vehicles through which the natural resources of developing countries have been developed: bauxite in Guyana and Jamaica, . . . has been identified with Alcan, Reynolds, and Revere, while copper in Chile has meant Anaconda and Kennecott. More significant, the majority of the imports of developing countries, particularly intermediate and capital goods, originate with MNCs while a large proportion of their exports, directly or indirectly, pass through them (i.e., MNCs). To be sure, "intrafirm" or "related-party trade" forms an important proportion of the total trade undertaken by MNCs. In 1970 alone, half of the manufactured goods exported by U.S.-based MNCs seemed to have been traded on an intrafirm basis between parents and majority-owned subsidiaries, while 32 percent of U.S. imports from developing countries in 1973 were intrafirm deliveries from majority-owned subsidiaries. Additionally, 32 percent of U.S. imports in 1975 were intrafirm deliveries from majority-owned subsidiaries, while 13 percent were related-party deliveries from minority-owned affiliates, namely, companies in which U.S.-based MNCs own between 5 and 49 percent of the voting stock. In fact, no less than 88 percent of U.S. bauxite imports, 80 percent of rubber imports, 68 percent of cotton imports, and 67 percent of banana imports are related-party deliveries.[1]

The MNCs control many of the most important export commodities of developing countries, and a high proportion is exported on an intrafirm basis. Thus, the mining affiliates of U.S. MNCs in Latin America and the Caribbean export up to 80 percent

---

Source: Adeoye A. Akinsanya, *Multinationals in a Changing Environment: A Study of Business-Government Relations in the Third World* (New York: Praeger, 1984), pp. 21–27, 319–332. Reprinted by permission of Greenwood Publishing Group, Inc., Westport, CT.

---

[1] Garret Fitzgerald, *Unequal Partners* (New York: United Nations, 1979), p. 11.

of their total sales to their parent companies. More important, available data suggest that the bulk of world production and processing of a number of export commodities is controlled by very few MNCs: while three multinationals share 70 percent of the world's production, marketing, and distribution of bananas, six multinationals control 60 percent of bauxite production capacity as well as 70 percent of aluminum production capacity; additionally, fewer than ten MNCs share the world's production and processing of copper, iron ore, lead, nickel, tea, tin, tobacco, and zinc. In some cases, such as the Dominican Republic and Haiti, the whole of a country's output (i.e., bauxite) is exported on an intrafirm basis.[2]

The role of MNCs in the manufacturing sector has been more important in relation to the imports of developing countries than their exports. For example, imports by subsidiaries of MNCs into the six newly industrialized countries in Latin America exceed that of exports by a ratio of 3 to 1; in Mexico alone, the imports of MNCs are more than double those of nationalized (state-owned) enterprises. However, as far as manufactured goods are concerned, the bulk of the exports of developing countries consists of labor-intensive products, although a rapidly increasing proportion consists of machinery, transport equipment, and miscellaneous light manufactured goods. Indeed, a significant proportion of these exports is manufactured by subsidiaries of foreign-based MNCs, and in 1976 a large proportion of these products in Brazil, Argentina, Mexico, and India were intrafirm deliveries from majority-owned subsidiaries of German-based MNCs.[3]

Critics of the role of multinationals in developing countries have commented on the effect of direct foreign investment on local competition and entrepreneurship. In the introduction to his classic study on the role of the International Petroleum Company in Peruvian development, Adalberto Pinelo lamented on the impact of U.S.-based MNCs on the ownership patterns in Latin America.[4] Specifically, there are two aspects to this issue. The first is the effect on the entry of foreign-owned enterprises on existing or potential local enterprises in the same business, while the second concerns the effect of the marketing practices of foreign enterprises in shaping or "distorting" local tastes and creating a form of cultural dependency. For example, Isaiah Frank comments on "how local entrepreneurs are smothered when multinationals, with their tremendous technological and financial resources, establish subsidiaries in developing countries."[5] He adds:

> Existing firms may be forced out of business or may decide to sell out to the multinationals. Moreover, barriers are created to the entry of new, indigenous entrepreneurs as a consequence of the advertising, promotion, and product-differentiation practices of multinationals.[6]

According to Garret Fitzgerald, "a survey of 396 transnationals operating in developing countries showed that close to 60 percent of 2,904 subsidiaries existing in the late 1960s had been set up by acquisition rather than by new investment."[7] While the marketing practices of multinationals place barriers on the entry of new, local businessmen, such practices often lead to another "dimension of the third world's concern: the stimulation by multinationals of a demand for types of products too sophisticated for,

[2] Ibid., pp. 11–12.
[3] Ibid.

[4] Adalberto J. Pinelo, *The Multinational Corporation as a Force in Latin American Politics: A Case Study of the International Petroleum Company in Peru* (New York: Praeger, 1973), p. x. The International Petroleum Company, until its expropriation by the Velasco regime in Octber 1968, is a wholly owned subsidiary (99.5 percent) of Standard Oil Company (New Jersey), the world's largest industrial corporation, with annual sales of $103.1 billion according to the August 1981 *Fortune List* of the world's 50 largest industrial corporations.
[5] Isaiah Frank, *Foreign Enterprise in Developing Countries* (Baltimore, Md.: Johns Hopkins University Press, 1980), p. 43.
[6] Ibid.
[7] Fitzgerald, *Unequal Partners*, p. 12.

or otherwise inappropriate to, a poor country's stage of development."[8] Thus, the marketing practices of the multinationals are therefore "seen as suppressing local entrepreneurs not only by direct competition but also by capitalizing on and reinforcing a strong prejudice in favor of foreign products. . . . This is regarded as objectionable not only in economic terms but also because it perpetuates a form of sociocultural dependence rooted in the colonial experience from which the developing countries seek emancipation."[9]

Multinationals control many of the most important export commodities of developing countries, and a large proportion of these exports are intrafirm deliveries from majority-owned subsidiaries. However, the market power of MNCs is reinforced by collective or cartel agreements with other firms, particularly with other multinationals operating in similar markets. According to Fitzgerald, studies in the United Kingdom and the Federal Republic of Germany indicate that MNCs "participated in approximately 70 percent of all export cartels" in both countries. These cartel agreements, declared Fitzgerald, "include provisions for the allocation of export and import markets as well as quotas for production, frequently including price-fixing, collective actions such as boycotts to deter new entrants, and notification clauses to enable members of the cartel to engage in collusive tenderings in regard to imports."[10]

Finally, "spheres of influence" are not only evident in the exports of MNCs in small developing countries, meaning that these countries must pay more for imports of manufactured goods (such as machinery, chemicals, and steel) than are paid for comparable imports by larger developing countries; "spheres of influence" are also evident in the location of manufacturing subsidiaries as well as the percentage of direct foreign investments in the third world. Data show that in 12 former British colonies

in Africa, five in Asia, one in the Middle East (South Yemen and Aden) and one in the Western Hemisphere (British Honduras), over half (in a majority of cases, well over three-quarters) of direct foreign investment at the end of 1967 was British;[11] at the same time, over two-thirds of direct foreign investments in 14 former French colonies in Africa, one in Asia (French Polynesia), and two in the Western Hemisphere (French Antilles and French Guyana) represented French investments,[12] while between 85 and 88 percent of direct foreign investments in Burundi, Ruanda, and Zaire was Belgian.[13] A similar degree of dominance by the United States was evident in a large number of Latin American countries as well as certain countries in the Middle East, Asia, and Africa although the distribution of direct foreign investments in some of these countries is changing.[14] For example, at the end of 1967, the percentage of the United States share of direct foreign investments in Argentina, Brazil, Colombia, Mexico, South Korea, Thailand, and the Philippines stood at 55.8, 35.6, 86.2, 76.4, 92.3, 20.1, and 92.3, respectively; however, the percentage of the United States share of direct foreign investments in the years indicated stood at 39.5 (1971), 32.2 (1976), 48.1 (1975), 68.7 (1975), 14.0 (1975), and 47.9 (1976), respectively.[15] Finally, in South Korea and Thailand, the percentage of the Japanese share of direct foreign investments in 1975 stood at 66.5 and 41.0, respectively, while the percentage of Japanese share of direct foreign investments in Indonesia in 1976 stood at 36.9.[16] To be sure, 70 percent of Japanese subsidiaries in the late 1960s and early 1970s were to be found in Asia and Oceania. Undoubtedly, the concentration of British investments in the former British colonies or the concentration of U.S. investments in Latin America and Asia or the dominance of Japanese investments

---

[8] Frank, *Foreign Enterprise*, p. 43.
[9] Ibid., p. 44.
[10] Fitzgerald, *Unequal Partners*, p. 13.

---

[11] United Nations, *Multinational Corporations in World Development*, Publication no. E.73II, A.11, 1973, pp. 182–85.
[12] Ibid.
[13] Ibid., pp. 182–83.
[14] Ibid., pp. 182–85.
[15] Frank, *Foreign Enterprise*, pp. 14–15.
[16] Ibid., p. 15.

in Asia reflects past colonial or semicolonial relationships.

Certainly, these are some of the features of the activities of MNCs that have given rise to a number of proposals that their activities be regulated, controlled, or monitored to ensure that their operations are not at variance with the interests and goals of developing countries. Consequently, we have witnessed in the past two decades or so a rash of "creeping expropriations," expropriations of the assets of MNCs without "prompt, adequate, and effective" compensation, or unilateral termination of concession agreements or state's contracts (with aliens). These measures are symptomatic of a changing balance of power between MNCs and host countries. The home countries of these business entities which are subject to "expropriatory" measures increasingly find themselves inhibited from the kind of interventionalism which they have resorted to in the 1950s. But they have devised elegant measures aimed at protecting and defending their nationals' investments abroad.

As a consequence, then, of the new economic nationalism that has characterized the politics of developing countries since the late 1960s as well as the changing circumstances governing the relationship between MNCs and host countries on the one hand and between developing countries and developed market economies on the other, we can expect a continuation, indeed an intensification, of the conflicts between the North and South, and above all between the nation-state and the MNC. Yet, an effective collaboration between governments and business is a sine qua non for dealing with most of the major problems facing the international community today. For many, it appears self-evident that MNCs jeopardize the sovereignty and independence of nation-states. Thus, the publication of the *ITT Papers* on the purported subversive activities of the International Telephone and Telegraph Company in Chile created much sensation not only in Chile but elsewhere in the world. There are several instances when assets of alien-owned enterprises whose annual revenues sometimes exceed the total outputs of the host countries have been nationalized by the host govern-

ments without a moment's hesitation. More significant, while the AFL-CIO [American Federation of Labor-Congress of Industrial Organizations] and the sponsors of the Burke-Hartke Bill claim that U.S.-based MNCs export jobs and capital from the United States,[17] leaders and radical intellectuals of developing countries maintain that MNCs exploit their [developing countries'] irreplaceable natural resources for the benefit of their [MNCs'] home countries. Certainly, all these propositions cannot be simultaneously true, if only because MNCs cannot at the same time be exporting benefits from the home countries and from host countries. Thus, "the benefits in question have to end in one geographical area or the other."[18] . . .

CONCLUSIONS

Economic nationalism in several third world countries is often characterized by the desire to exercise control over their economies. It is often characterized by the desire to exercise greater control over foreign-owned enterprises, particularly local MNC subsidiaries. Several claims have been made on behalf of MNCs. First, it has been argued that MNCs operating in the third world contribute resources that are generally not available or insufficiently available, namely, capital, technology, and marketing skills. Second, it has also been claimed that MNCs create jobs and, through import-substitution industrialization, alleviate balance-of-payments deficits in their host states. On the other hand, critics of MNC operations in the third world have three general complaints. The first is that MNC operations generally have had an adverse impact on their host states. Second, multinationals have been accused of engaging in illegal political activity and offering bribes

---

[17] See Dana T. Ackerly, "The Multinational Corporation and World Economic Development," *American Journal of International Law* **66** (1972): 14–22.

[18] Patrick M. Boarman and Hans Schollhammer, "Preface," in *Multinational Corporations and Governments: Business-Government Relations in an International Context* (New York: Praeger, 1975), p. vi.

in order to circumvent local regulations. Third, MNCs are beyond national control; they constitute *imperium in imperio* and thus undermine the territorial nation-state.

From this study emerges the following general conclusions. First, while it may be true to say that MNCs transfer capital resources from a capital-rich country to a capital-poor country, by and large, MNCs are vehicles through which capital resources are transferred from capital-poor countries to capital-rich countries through such devices as transfer pricing, sharp accounting practices, overinvoicing imports, and underinvoicing exports as well as overpricing technology.[19]

Second, MNCs may well have created jobs; on the balance, and when compared with domestic enterprises, MNCs do in fact destroy jobs because they employ capital-intensive technologies which are inconsistent and inappropriate with the factor endowments of third world countries.[20]

Third, while it is not denied that MNCs transfer technology to DCs [developing countries], the technology so transferred is inappropriate, obsolete, overpriced, and inconsistent with the factor endowments of host states. More fundamental, extractive MNCs create enclave economies, namely, they have few backward and forward linkages with the host economy.[21]

Fourth, MNCs encourage inappropriate consumption patterns through product differentiation (or innovation) and/or marketing and advertising techniques, although some of the undesirable consumption patterns may well be a reflection of an existing uneven distribution of national income rather than the effects of MNC operations.[22]

Fifth, because MNCs generally pay their employees higher salaries and provide generous fringe benefits than do domestic enterprises, MNCs may have, albeit unwittingly, contributed to the widening of the elite-mass gap and polarization of social forces in the host states.[23]

Sixth, one of the costs of MNC operations in the third world is technological dependence. A major danger posed by the state of technological dependence of most third world countries is that it impedes and stifles local development. Not only does the easy access of foreign technology prevent domestic or state-owned enterprises from investing in research and development [R and D]. As Sanjaya Lall puts it, it makes DCs "biased against using what innovations are produced locally. The effect is cumulative, since R and D generates considerable 'learning by doing' over time; the less research developing countries do, the less experience they gather to do it in the future."[24]

As a result of new economic nationalism in the 1960s and 1970s, several DCs have taken measures against foreign-owned enterprises ranging from nationalization and majority equity participation in local MNC subsidiaries to indigenization of certain sectors of the economy.

Because it is the duty of a state to protect the person and property of its nationals abroad, investor states have responded in many forms to the waves of economic nationalism. In general, expropriations of foreign assets have not been questioned unless they are arbitrary, discriminatory, and are not accompanied by some compensation. Some investor states

---

[19] David Colman and Frederick Nixson, *Economics of Change in Less Developed Countries* (Oxford, Eng.: Philip Alan, 1978), pp. 224–34; Ronald E. Muller, "The Multinational Corporation and the Underdevelopment of the Third World," *The Political Economy of Development and Underdevelopment*, Charles K. Wilber (ed.) (New York: Random House, 1973), pp. 136–46.

[20] Colman and Nixson, *Economics of Change*, pp. 231–33; Muller, "The Multinational Corporation," pp. 132–36.

[21] Frank, *Foreign Enterprise*, pp. 73–93; Thomas J. Biersteker, *Distortion or Development?* (Cambridge, Mass.: MIT Press, 1978), pp. 119–29.

[22] Biersteker, *Distortion*, pp. 129–35; Colman and Nixson, *Economics of Change*, pp. 231–33.

[23] Biersteker, *Distortion*, pp. 137–54.

[24] Sanjaya Lall, *Developing Countries and Multinational Corporations* (London: Commonwealth Secretariat, 1976), p. 28. On dependence, see, generally Sanjaya Lall, "Is 'Dependence' a Useful Concept in Analysing Underdevelopment?" *World Development* 3 (1975): 799–810; Theotonio Dos Santos, "The Structure of Dependence" in *The Political Economy of Development and Underdevelopment*, pp. 100–17.

have intervened on behalf of their nationals by making diplomatic representations to the taking states; others have threatened foreign-aid sanctions against countries taking their nationals' investments without discharging their obligations under customary international law; and still others have intervened directly or indirectly and ousted the nationalist regimes, thus restoring the status quo ante. Because investor states have often intervened on behalf of their nationals through covert or overt operations and because the gap between the industrialized countries of the North and the agrarian countries of the South continues to yawn largely through MNC operations,[25] many third world countries have used the instrumentalities of the United Nations to demand a new international economic order.[26] But as we noted in a study with Arthur Davies, it is impossible to have a new international economic order without a new *national* economic order.[27] This means that third world countries will have to depend much more on their own resources and rarely on MNCs. They will have to develop their own technologies either through industrial spying and/or massive investment in education as well as R and D. More fundamental, they will need to undergo radical structural transformation so as to smash local allies of MNCs. All these measures can only be successfully implemented within the framework of a centrally planned (socialist) economy.

---

[25] See Adeoye A. Akinsanya, "The United Nations Charter of Economic Rights and Duties of States," *Annual of the Nigerian Society of International Law* **3** (forthcoming).

[26] Ibid.

[27] Adeoye Akinsanya and Arthur Davies, "Third World Quest for a New International Economic Order: An Overview," *International and Comparative Law Quarterly* **33** (1984): 208–17.

The Multinational Corporation

Melvyn B. Krauss

The key institution in the world economy facilitating the transfer of prosperity from the industrialized countries to the developing ones is the multinational corporation. The multinationals transfer technology to the LDCs [less-developed countries] that then can be used to produce exports; they transfer capital to the LDCs that provides employment for LDC labor, and they also are a vehicle through which a considerable amount of North-South trade takes place.

The multinationals, in other words, integrate the world economy. Otherwise fragmented labor markets, commodity markets and capital markets in the South are unified with their northern counterparts by the multinationals to provide truly *world* markets for products and factors of production. This is without doubt the most important consequence of the multinational corporation.

This crucial virtue, however, often has been misrepresented by the critics of multinationals. Critics do not dispute that multinationals transfer technology and capital to the LDCs. But they claim that the technology transferred is inappropriate to the LDCs, and that foreign direct investment by the multinationals goes into the wrong industries. They also criticize the multinationals for undermining the tax base of third world countries.

MULTINATIONALS AND THE CONTROL OF GOVERNMENT

On the theory that the best way to determine what's right about the multinational corporations is to find out what the social democrats are saying is wrong with them, the following quotes from the Brandt Report are instructive.

> Much of the international trade which multinational corporations conduct goes on within their own organizations. . . . In all such transactions, transfer prices may be settled which are different from the price which would have been the case between independent parties operating at arm's length. Such differences may reflect the legitimate business concerns of the companies but are also capable of being used in order to shift profits from high to low tax countries or to get around exchange or price controls or customs duties. The ability of multinationals to manipulate financial flows by the use of artificial transfer prices is bound to be a matter of concern to government.[1]

One baffling implication of this quote is why shifting profits from high- to low-tax countries and getting around exchange and price controls, as well as customs duties, somehow are not considered to be "legitimate business concerns" of private companies. The Brandt Commission needs to be reminded that the first obligation of the directors and managers of a private corporation is to its stockholders, and this obligation would not be legitimately discharged if they did not take full advantage of any and all legal means to minimize taxes and avoid profit-reducing interferences with proper commerce. The ability of private concerns and individuals to avoid the burdens that governments attempt to impose upon them long has been a source of frustration and irritation to social democrats.

The Brandt quote raises the essential question of whether or not the "legitimate business concerns" of the multinationals are in harmony with the legitimate concerns of society: in other words, whether shifting taxes from high to low countries, and getting around controls of various kinds, are in the social as well as private interest.

The first point to be made (which the social

Source: Melvyn B. Krauss, *Development without Aid: Growth, Poverty and Government* (New York: McGraw-Hill, 1983), pp. 126–138. Reprinted by permission.

---

[1] *North-South: A Programme for Survival* (London: Pan Books, Ltd., 1980), pp. 188–89.

democrats never have understood) is that the interests of government and those of society do not come to the same thing. High taxes and controls on private initiative may be in the interests of some governments. But are high taxes in the interests of society when they create scarcities and induce corruption? Are exchange controls that permit inflation-prone governments to continue to inflate beneficial for the economy? And is it wrong to avoid customs duties which serve to promote inefficiency in domestic resource allocation and rob the consumer by increasing prices? The answer to these three questions must be negative unless, like the Brandt Report, one identifies the society's interest with that of the government.

The public should applaud the flexibility of multinationals that allows them to avoid the burdens government attempts to impose. For example, the ability of multinationals to shift profits from high-tax to low-tax countries puts needed and socially beneficial pressure on governments to be reasonable in their tax policies. The Brandt Commission not only is aware of the capacity of multinationals to put governments into competition with one another to lower taxes, but seeks to suppress it by proposing

> the *harmonization* of fiscal and other incentives to avoid *the undermining of the tax base* and competitive positions of host countries.[2]

What Willy Brandt's "harmonization" means, of course, is cartel; governments collude with one another to prevent anyone from undercutting a competitor in seeking the business of the multinationals. Harmonization is precisely analogous to the attempt by vendors to suppress competition amongst themselves by fixing industry-wide "fair" prices. It is typical of the Brandt Report's double-think that the suppression of competition between governments should be championed on the grounds that it prevents "the undermining of the competitive positions of host countries."

The Brandt Report claims that

underlying many of the fears about multinational corporations is the concern that they have been able to race ahead in global operations and out of reach of effective controls by nation-states or international organizations.[3]

But the Brandt Report has got it backwards. In the modern world, it is government—not the multinational corporation—that is out of control. To the extent that the multinationals help control governments by inducing competition between them, they render the public a valuable service.

One area in which multinationals help control governments is social welfare programs. The ability of multinationals to transfer capital from one country to another puts useful pressure on governments to have reasonable social welfare policies. In both North and South, minimum wages, employer-financed social insurance, minority employment policies and regulatory burdens on business all are moderated to some degree by the multinationals' ability to transfer capital elsewhere.

Protection of northern labor is also moderated. Tariffs on imports of labor-intensive goods raise wages in the advanced countries. If domestic capital responds to the higher wages by going abroad, the tariff's beneficial effects for advanced-country labor are neutralized. It makes little difference to capital-abundant countries like the United States whether they export capital-intensive goods and import labor-intensive ones, or export capital and import labor-intensive goods with the proceeds of capital export.[4] Both patterns of international exchange keep labor's

---

[2] Ibid., pp. 192–93.

[3] Ibid., p. 189.

[4] The equivalence—or potential equivalence—of various forms of international exchange has been the subject of several papers in the international literature. The most important of these is R. A. Mundell, "International Trade and Factor Mobility," *American Economic Review*, **47**, June 1957, pp. 321–35. See also F. Flatter's "Commodity Price Equalization: A Note on Factor Mobility and Trade," *American Economic Review*, **62**, June 1972, pp. 473–76; and Melvyn B. Krauss, "Commodity Trade and Factor Mobility," *American Economic Review*, **64**, September 1974, pp. 797–801.

domestic price in line with its international price by enabling the advanced country to economize on labor—its relatively scarce factor of production. If one way of effectuating the competition between foreign and domestic labor is blocked, the job is done the other way.

JOB EXPORTING

The demand in the industrialized countries that private capital outflow by multinationals be restrained because of so-called job exporting to foreign countries is analogous to, and as protectionist as, the demand that tariffs be placed on imports of labor-intensive goods. Both import tariffs and capital outflow restrictions violate the law of comparative advantage by causing the labor-scarce countries to overuse labor; and both artificially increase the wages of workers in the North. Thus, while the halt to job exporting by the multinationals would be good for advanced-country labor, it would be bad for everyone else, North and South alike. The issue of job exporting is nothing more than old-fashioned protectionism of labor dressed up in modern clothes.

Moreover, when northern social democrats criticize multinationals because they ''export'' jobs, they are not only arguing against the law of comparative advantage, for which in truth they have shown little past appreciation, but against the interest of poor workers in the third world countries. Free trade can be expected to benefit labor in the third world because it would increase the demand for labor there; that is, free trade causes the LDCs to economize on their scarce-factor capital rather than labor. Restrictions on capital export from the industrialized countries damage the cause of workers in the third world precisely because they cause the LDC economies to economize on labor.

The above highlights an important contradiction in the position of social democrats toward multinationals. On the one hand, social democrats criticize multinationals because they export jobs to the LDCs. On the other, they criticize multinationals because they don't provide enough jobs for poor people in the third world. The multinationals are damned if they do and damned if they don't.

TAXING FOREIGN CAPITAL

Restricting international flows of private capital for reasons of domestic income redistribution is not the monopoly of northern protectionists—southern protectionists do it also. Inflows of private capital into less-developed countries are subject to taxation by LDC governments as well as northern ones. If third world governments impose a tax on capital imports, for whatever reason, the implication for income distribution within the LDC economy will be that domestic capitalists gain at the expense of other groups in the economy. Needless to add, the internal redistribution effects of taxes on capital imports may be their prime motivation.

Why do domestic capitalists gain when government places a tax on capital imports? The reason is that the import tax on capital creates imbalances in domestic capital markets that can be resolved only by an increase in the rate-of-return to capital. An import tax on capital lowers the rate-of-return that foreign investors in the tax-imposing country receive by comparison with the rate-of-return they receive elsewhere. This means that they will withdraw their capital from the tax-imposing country and put it to work elsewhere, i.e., in other countries, until capital's rate-of-return in the tax-imposing country rises to the extent necessary to equalize with its return elsewhere. That is, because foreign investors pay a differential tax on income produced by capital in the LDC, the rate-of-return in the LDC must cover the tax, or else investors will not employ their capital there. Of course, the very act of foreigners withdrawing their capital from the tax-imposing LDC serves to make capital more scarce there and thus raises its rate-of-return.

The irony of a policy of taxing the import of capital (or foreign capital) is that while to the public's eye the tax appears to be paid by foreign capitalists, it is the *domestic* users of capital who suffer, because they must pay a higher price for capital.

Indeed, ultimately, domestic firms may be able to shift the tax backwards onto domestic labor if labor is not sufficiently mobile to escape the tax's burden. In this case, a tax that appears to be on foreign capitalists winds up affecting a purely internal income transfer from domestic workers to domestic capitalists. True, lawyers can point out, the tax legally is imposed on foreign capital. But economists can counter that because of the tax, foreign (and domestic) capital make a higher rate-of-return. Hence, after the tax is paid, foreign capital is no worse off than it was before the tax was imposed. Domestic capitalists, on the other hand, are pure gainers, since they also receive a higher rate-of-return and do not have to pay the tax.

No wonder foreigners often are made scapegoats. They provide the perfect subterfuge behind which purely internal income transfers can be effectuated.

International flows of private capital provide a convenient vehicle for protectionist groups in both the North and South to pursue their invested interests at the expense of the economic growth of the world community. Northern protectionists, representing the interests of labor in the developed world, want to restrict capital flows from North to South to artificially raise wages. Southern protectionists, representing the interests of capitalists in the less-developed world, also want to restrict North-South capital flows to artificially raise capital's rate-of-return in the third world. Protectionists in both parts of the globe, therefore, have a harmony of interests in pursuing their own separate and distinct vested interests by restricting the international flow of private capital from North to South. Unfortunately, the prosperity of the world economy suffers: first, because artificially high wages threaten the northern "engine for growth," and, second, because whatever growth does take place in the North may not get transmitted to the South.

EXPLOITATIVE WAGES

In their litany of charges against multinational corporations, leftists allege that multinationals "ex-

ploit" third world workers by paying them substandard wages. "Exploitative wages," of course, is not a very scientific term. The International Labor Organization (ILO), for example, has shown that multinationals pay higher wages than do local firms for similarly skilled labor in the third world. If this is exploitation, poor people may want all they can get.

Of course, third world wages are not the same as wages paid in the industrialized countries. One would expect wages in labor-abundant economies to be lower than wages in labor-scarce ones. But this is the law of supply and demand, not exploitation. Moreover, lower wages in the third world benefit people there because it attracts jobs to the area. If multinationals had to pay the same wages in the South as they do in the North, the international transfer of prosperity would not take place.

Multinationals also are attacked by the Left on the grounds that they exploit child labor in the third world. To the extent that multinationals do use child labor, the criticism of this practice by northern leftists reflects a sort of "cultural imperialism"—that third world countries adopt cultural standards appropriate to the industrialized countries but inappropriate to their own situations. If child labor is considered a social evil by a third world country, it can always legislate against it. In the absence of child labor laws, the multinationals cannot be blamed for hiring children. Indeed, the earnings of children can be an important factor in keeping families together; hence the multinationals do a social good rather than evil.

ETHICS AND MULTINATIONALS

Multinational corporations have been heavily criticised for unethical political and commercial activities. The attempt to bring down the Allende regime in Chile; the illegal payments of oil companies to governments in different parts of the world; such cases have exposed the corporation to scrutiny and criticism in the United Nations and elsewhere.[5]

---

[5] *North-South: A Programme for Survival*, p. 189.

Whether or not it is a sign of disrepute to be criticized in the United Nations, the Brandt Commission fails to explain why attempting "to bring down the Allende regime in Chile" may be judged "unethical." After all, the Allende regime was a brutal Communist government that had brought inflation in Chile to a rate of 1,000 percent per annum, transformed economic life into a circus and enraged, in particular, such groups as housewives and transport workers. Multinationals operating in Chile and elsewhere had, and have, a legitimate interest in the economic health of the country in which they operate, just as domestic residents do. That the multinationals were able to use their legal influence to rid Chile of a government that had brought untold economic misery to the country is to their credit. Undoubtedly, if the multinationals had used their influence the other way, and supported Allende, the Brandt Commission would have been more approving—not because the Brandt Commission is pro-Communist, but because it is progovernment. The social democrats dearly resent checks placed on government power by private economic groups. But it is precisely by providing an effective counterweight to governments that multinationals play a useful function in the world economy.

TECHNOLOGY TRANSFER AND PROTECTIONISM

Ronald Findlay points out that in earlier days the transfer of technology between lands was accomplished for the most part by migration. Today, multinational corporations have replaced the migrant as the prime diffusor of technical knowledge. At the outset, the preeminent role of the multinationals in the transfer of technology was not controversial. But in recent years this has ceased to be the case. The multinationals have been attached on *terms of trade* grounds—that they charge the LDCs too high a price for technology—as well as on the grounds that they transfer "inappropriate" technology to the third world.

The Brandt Report states:

Earlier enthusiasm for the unqualified transfer of technology from the industrialized to the developing countries and optimism and faith in its beneficial effects have given way to increasing skepticism and criticism. There has been vigorous questioning of the "appropriateness" of the technology and critical scrutiny of the various costs associated with the transfer . . . only the developing countries themselves can decide which machines and systems will suit their own local needs. . . . The multinational corporations and other commercial firms which control most technological developments are unlikely, of their own accord, to direct their research into areas which do not promise high returns to themselves. There is an urgent need to provide new incentives to develop appropriate technologies and, almost equally important, to make them known to everyone.[6]

The Brandt Commission makes it clear that the essence of the so-called " 'appropriateness' of the technology" issue is *where the technology is produced*, and that they favor LDCs producing technology themselves rather than having it produced in the North and then importing it. The appropriateness-of-technology issue, therefore, has strong protectionist overtones since the North, not the South, has a comparative advantage in the production of technology. The Brandt Report justifies its protectionist intent by arguing that the foreign producers of technology cannot satisfy third world consumers. To wit, "only the developing countries themselves can decide which machines and systems will suit their own local needs."[7] But it is unclear whether the Brandt Report means that northern producers of technology cannot satisfy southern consumers of technology as they, the consumers, see their needs, or merely as the Brandt Commission sees them.

Behind the appropriateness-of-technology issue lie two obvious facts: first, that the Brandt Commission, probably reflecting a social democratic consen-

---

[6] Ibid., p. 195.
[7] Ibid., p. 196.

sus, does not like the type of technology that is being produced in the North; and second, that the Commission does not like the multinational corporation, a private economic actor, being the principal vehicle for the diffusion of this technology to the LDCs.

The Brandt Commission, for example, is concerned with "the major technological breakthrough in micro-electronics which may not only reduce the demand for labor in the North, but also deprive the South of its comparative advantage in low wage goods."[8] It also is concerned that "51 percent of research and development in industrialized countries is devoted to defense, atomic and space research," and concludes "the importance of disarming as a possible means of promoting development is nowhere more evident than in the field of research."[9]

Both arguments appear to be smoke screens for northern rather than southern concerns. It is difficult to see, for example, how the LDCs would benefit from reduced research on defense and aerospace technology in the North. But presumably the détente that Willy Brandt so favors would. After having made his name by fighting Communists as mayor of Berlin, Brandt now apparently is willing to tarnish it by caving in to present Communist demands.

Northern social democrats obviously are disturbed that business in the North has found a way—by labor-saving technical innovations—to adjust to the exaggerated wages that the social democrats have imposed upon them by their one-sided pro-labor policies. If the social democrats don't like labor-saving technical progress, they shouldn't provoke it.

For its part, the Brandt Commission would like to use technology to turn back the clock, "to defend and improve the market competitiveness of those raw materials mainly produced in the developing countries, including rubber, jute, cotton and hard fibres, most of which are threatened by synthetic substitutes."[10] This is a most concrete example of the protectionist use of technology that the Brandt Report advocates. Naturally, to achieve this, control over technology must be taken away from profit-seeking private groups, such as multinational corporations, and given to governments and international organizations. Hence, the attack on multinationals on the grounds that they transfer inappropriate technology to the South.

The Brandt Report's contention that "the multinational corporations . . . are unlikely, of their own accord, to direct their research into areas which do not promise high returns to themselves"[11] reflects the assumption that the pursuit of private interest by the multinationals will not promote the public or general interest. But why would profit-seeking business organizations transfer inappropriate technology to the South when, almost by definition, the inappropriate technology would reduce profits compared to what they would have been had the appropriate technology instead been transferred. It is only in cases where prices are distorted by government intervention that the multinationals would transfer technology that is appropriate to the natural or underlying economy, but [in]appropriate to the distorted one. Here, however, the inappropriateness of technology would be the fault of the government distortions of the economy, not the multinationals.

Indeed, the multinationals often get blamed for the mistakes made by big government. Government subsidies are a further example. The industrial sector in many labor-abundant LDCs consists of two distinct parts: the highly subsidized, capital-intensive and usually inefficient protected part; and the unprotected labor-intensive, highly competitive and dynamic part. The modern part often is dominated by multinationals and the argument made that the multinationals bring inefficiency to the LDCs rather than prosperity. But why would profit-seeking private firms on their own invest in inefficient activities?

---

[8] Ibid., p. 197.
[9] Ibid., p. 197–98.

[10] Ibid., p. 197.
[11] Ibid., p. 196.

The answer, of course, is that they are enticed to do so by government subsidies. Without the subsidies, the modern inefficient sector would not exist.

An example in the oil industry is the trend to refine crude oil in the nation where the crude oil is found rather than in the industrial nations where the oil products are consumed. The economics of oil dictate that the refining be done in the industrial countries. Yet the oil-rich countries and the oil refineries within their borders are willing to subsidize the refineries to this effect. Experience has shown that the multinationals on their own would not refine oil in the oil-rich countries without a subsidy. Clearly it is the subsidy that is to blame for the inefficiency, not the multinationals.

Or consider the case of import substitution policies in the third world. Writing about Japanese foreign investment, Ozawa claims that "there are two basic motives for this geographical transplant of Japan's manufacturing activities: one is to circumvent the import substitution policy of the host country; the other is to set up a production base to utilize the manufacturing costs overseas."[12]

These two motives reflect the different sides of the multinational coil. The multinationals contribute to the transfer of prosperity when they participate in the export of labor-intensive industries from capital-abundant to labor-abundant economies. This is the positive side of the coin. But circumventing the import substitution policies of LDCs by capital export is another matter. Clearly it is to the benefit of the industrialized capital exporter to be protected, rather than be kept out of the protected market by the import substitution policies of the LDCs. But the LDCs suffer from these policies nonetheless; local markets continue to be served by high-cost domestic enterprises (whether owned by foreigners or not) rather than low-cost foreign ones. The basic elements in the protectionist equation are not changed by the fact that the multinationals and not purely national firms are protected from foreign competi-

tion by tariffs and quotas. Consumers may pay higher prices for the protected goods in either case, and resources are diverted to import substitutes that best could be employed elsewhere in the economy.

Would the multinational invest in an essentially inefficient industry in the LDC were it not for the protection offered by the host government? Not if it were interested in profits, which we safely can assume it is. It is the import substitution policies of big government that bring the multinationals into the LDC, and it is these policies—and the big government that is responsible for them—that must bear the burden of blame for the waste of the LDC's resources.

QUESTIONS FOR DISCUSSION

1. What criteria should be used in evaluating whether MNCs are exploiting third world countries?
2. What alternatives to MNCs do third world governments possess to raise capital and attract technology? Are these alternatives better or worse than MNCs?
3. What political leverage do host countries have on regulating MNCs?
4. What political leverage do MNCs have over host countries in avoiding such regulation?
5. What effect do MNCs have on the autonomy of states?

SUGGESTED READINGS

Ahiakpor, James C. W. *Multinationals and Economic Development: An Integration of Competing Theories.* London: Routledge, 1990.

Bornschier, Volker, and Christopher Chase-Dunn. *Transnational Corporations and Underdevelopment.* New York: Praeger, 1985.

Buckley, Peter J., and Jeremy Clegg (eds.). *Multinational Enterprises in Less Developed Countries.* New York: St. Martin's Press, 1991.

Dixon, C. J., D. Drakakis-Smith, and H. D. Watts (eds.). *Multinational Corporations and the Third World.* Boulder, Colo.: Westview, 1986.

Krasner, Stephen D. *Structural Conflict: The Third World against Global Liberalism.* Berkeley, Calif.: Univ. of California Press, 1985.

---

[12] Terutomo Ozawa, *Multinationalism, Japanese Style* (Princeton: Princeton University Press, 1980), p. 186.

Livingstone, J. M. *Internationalization of Business.* New York: St. Martin's Press, 1989.

Martinussen, John. *Transnational Corporations in a Developing Country: The Indian Experience.* Newbury Park, Calif.: Sage Publications, 1988.

Marton, Katherin. *Multinationals, Technology, and Industrialization: Implications and Impact in Third World Countries.* Lexington, Mass.: Lexington Books, 1986.

Moran, Theodore H. (ed.). *Multinational Corporations: The Political Economy of Foreign Direct Investment.* Lexington, Mass.: Lexington Books, 1985.

Rothgeb, John M., Jr. *Myths and Realities of Foreign Investment in Poor Countries: The Modern Leviathan in the Third World.* New York: Praeger, 1989.

Samuels, Barbara C. *Managing Risk in Developing Countries: National Demands and Multinational Response.* Princeton, N.J.: Princeton University Press, 1990.

4 Is Interdependence among States Changing the Character of World Politics?

YES

Andrew M. Scott

Interdependence and National Interests

NO

John Spanier

Evaluation of Interdependence: "New" Cooperation or "Old" Strife?

Interdependence and National Interests

Andrew M. Scott

THE REDEFINITION OF INTERESTS

The ''national interest'' is a familiar notion, one that underpins decisions on public policy and that has informed a great deal of scholarly analysis. What has not always been made clear, however, is that national interests should be perceived as relative to the circumstances of the nation involved. If the general principle is that interests must be situationally defined, then a change in the circumstances of a nation should lead to a reexamination, and possible redefinition, of its interests.

Its circumstances might change because of internal or external developments, and the latter, in turn, will be affected by factors both related to and unrelated to the global system. Whether a given line of activity would be in the interest of a nation might, therefore, depend on the state of the global system and the relationship of that nation to the system. If the global system has changed significantly from one era to another, the interest definitions of the earlier period will almost certainly be inappropriate for the later. With movement along the interaction/technology continuum, the global system has undergone remarkable change since the end of World War II, and it follows, therefore, that the national interests of major actors will have to be reexamined.

Many of the prevailing ideas about the interests of the United States, for example, emerged in an era in which nations were less interdependent than they now are, and those ideas are now suffering from

Source: Andrew M. Scott, *The Dynamics of Interdependence* (Chapel Hill, N.C.: Univ. of North Carolina Press, 1982), pp. 129–142. Copyright © 1982 by Univ. of North Carolina Press. Reprinted by permission.

obsolescence. They have not evolved as rapidly as have the conditions to which they are being applied. Since the United States has become closely linked to the operation of the global system, its interests cannot be defined save with constant reference to that linkage. If, as seems likely, it continues to become progressively more involved, its interests will have to be defined progressively more in terms of system concerns.

This [discussion] will examine some of the implications of this line of argument. For purposes of exposition, these implications will be presented in the form of a set of linked propositions. The points made will apply to other great powers as well, but illustrative material will be drawn largely from the experience of the United States.

Proposition 1:
>   *The interests of a nation should be defined situationally.*

Proposition 2:
>   *When there is substantial change in the functioning of the global system, or in the relationship of a nation to that system, national interests will need to be reassessed.*

Proposition 3:
>   *As a nation becomes progressively more involved with the global system, it will normally define its geographic national interests in progressively broader terms.*

If a nation were completely isolated and in no way dependent on the global system, it could define its national interests in purely domestic terms. As a practical matter, however, interdependence is now so pervasive that few nations can pursue the experiment of trying to operate as isolates or semiisolates.

When a major actor becomes involved in a geographical area new to it, it will begin to have preferences about what happens there. Before long, it will incorporate those preferences into a definition of its national interest as related to that area. ''Interests'' follow involvement. Therefore, as the geographic involvement of an actor expands, other things being equal, so will its definition of its national interest.

The point can be illustrated with reference to the experience of the United States. The expansion of its geographic interests began shortly after the colonies achieved independence in 1783 and has continued to the present. Even if one omits commercial treaties and the acquisition of military bases and small islands, the pattern is still impressive. In the two centuries since independence, the geographic interests of the United States have expanded so as to be virtually global in extent. A partial list of U.S. geographic interests follows:

1800—Louisiana Purchase

1810–13—West Florida occupied

1821—East Florida purchased from Spain

1823—Monroe Doctrine

1845—Texas annexed

1848—New Mexico, Utah, and Upper California annexed; Polk's corollary to the Monroe Doctrine; formation of Oregon Territory

1849—Hawaii made a protectorate

1854—Gadsden Purchase

1867—Alaska annexed

1871—United States secures perpetual free navigation of the St. Lawrence River

1898—Puerto Rico, Philippine Islands, Guam ceded by Spain; Hawaii annexed

1901—Platt Amendment concerning Cuba

1903—Panama Canal Zone leased

1917—World War I and the assertion of a vital U.S. interest in western Europe

1941—World War II and the assertion of vital U.S. interests in the Far East

After World War II other geographical interests were quickly made evident with the Truman Doctrine, the Marshall Plan, NATO [North Atlantic Treaty Organization], the U.S. response in Korea in 1950, the U.S.-Japanese Mutual Defense Treaty, SEATO [South East Asia Treaty Organization], and so on.

Proposition 4:

> As the global system evolves and becomes more interactive and as technology develops, a national actor must define its interests more broadly and consider system-centered interests in addition to state-centered interests.

A preoccupation with state-centered interests is appropriate in a preinterdependent world. An increased concern with system-centered interests, however, is appropriate in an era of interdependence. State-centered interests, which may be political, economic, strategic, social, or cultural, are characteristically defined without reference to the impact their pursuit may have upon the global system and, because of feedback, upon the broader and more enduring interests of the nation. System-centered interests, on the other hand, will be defined with an eye to the way the parts of the system relate to the whole and are affected by the whole.

System-centered national interests may be related to global processes and may involve physical linkages, as with pollution processes or inadvertent manmade climatic changes, or may involve coordination and collaboration, as with efforts to maintain peace or achieve international economic stability. Finally, they may involve the positing of broad goals such as the achievement of universal human rights, an improved position for women, or rapid economic development.[1] The category of system-centered national interests includes regional phenomena, such as

---

[1] System-centered interests may involve "collective goods" but need not. The aspiration to universalize human rights is not a collective good. It is not a good, such as clean air, which, once supplied (1) can be consumed by anyone irrespective of his or her contribution to its provision and (2) the use of which by one actor does not diminish the amount available to another. In the case of human rights, your not achieving them does not prevent me from achieving them, and my achieving them does not automatically make them available to you. Human rights would be a collective good only in the sense that they can be achieved broadly only if they are pursued collectively. For a discussion of collective goods, see Mancur Olson, *The Logic of Collective Action: Public Goods and the Theory of Groups* (Cambridge, Mass.: Harvard University Press, 1965); and John Gerard Ruggie, "Collective Goods and Future International Collaboration," *American Political Science Review*, **66**, no. 3 (Sept. 1972), pp. 874–93.

support of the EEC [European Economic Community] by its members. A regional arrangement fashioned and held together solely by a dominant actor would not, of course, qualify. That would remain an expression of state-centered national interest. The proposition might be restated, then, to take advantage of this distinction: As the global system evolves, national interest needs to be defined progressively less in state-centered terms and progressively more in system-centered terms. Such changes in definition can be seen even in connection with something as manifestly state-centered as the definition of ''*national* security.'' Prior to World War II it was defined primarily in military terms. Now there is wide recognition that ''national security'' must be understood as involving far more.

Proposition 5:
> *System-centered interests are often pursued by means different from those used in the pursuit of state-centered interests.*

State-centered interests may be advanced by the unaided efforts of an individual nation-state, but system-centered interests, if they are to be pursued effectively, must usually be pursued collectively. Global inflation, for example, cannot be dealt with effectively if it is defined as a purely domestic issue. The same holds for problems involving population, the environment, resources, or the global economy.

Proposition 6:
> *Because of the evolution of the global system, system-centered national interests have been increasing in number.*

This point, too, can be illustrated from the experiences of the United States. In the wake of World War I the United States played an important part in bringing the League of Nations into existence, even though the Senate ultimately rejected American participation. After World War II the United States, by degrees, assumed a role of international leadership, which is to say that it perceived a national interest in

connection with a number of system-related issues. It was instrumental in bringing the United Nations into existence, recognizing that its interests in a variety of important goals could best be advanced by collective means. The initiatives taken by the United States in connection with the Bretton Woods institutions reflected an awareness that the national interest lay in trying to regularize international trade and payments and in trying to foster international development. The United States has given expression to system-related interests in connection with arms control, nuclear nonproliferation, world population problems, human rights, the role of women, pollution of the atmosphere, pollution of the seas, the military uses of space, humankind's impact on climate, global telecommunications, the exploitation of ocean resources, nonrenewable resources, and the future of energy resources, to mention a few.

State-centered interests of the United States have grown over a period of two hundred years, but system-centered interests did not begin to expand in a significant way until the twentieth century. The explanation for that is, of course, that most system-centered interests are associated with the growth of interaction and/or the advance of technology. Since movement along the interaction/technology continuum did not become notable until World War I and did not achieve great momentum until World War II and after, the development of system-centered interests was correspondingly delayed. Pollution of the atmosphere and the seas, for example, did not emerge as a serious global problem until the growth of the global economy following World War II.

Proposition 7:
> *For major nations new system-related national interests will be created with increasing rapidity in the future.*

The emergence of national interests is a continuing process. If an effort had been made a few years ago to develop an exhaustive inventory of the system-centered interests of the United States, preservation of the ozone layer would not have been included, nor maintenance of the oxygen-producing capacity of the oceans, nor the holding of man-induced climatic change within narrow limits. A few years hence system-centered interests will doubtless have come into being that are not yet imagined. Since movement along the interaction/technology continuum is accelerating, the accumulation of such interests must also accelerate.

State-centered interests of the United States are close to their geographical limits (although not necessarily their numerical limits), which is to say the limits of the planet itself. New system-centered interests, on the other hand, will continue to multiply as long as the global system continues to evolve along the continuum and produce new conditions.

Proposition 8:

> As the system-centered interests of a nation increase, so does its dependence on the system. To the extent that a nation has such interests, it will be vulnerable.

Major nations, accustomed to a degree of freedom of action, have tended to view dependence on other nations as a threat to national security and have sought to find ways to reduce it and the vulnerability flowing from it. The United States, for example, formulated programs designed to reduce its dependence on the OPEC [Organization of Petroleum Exporting Countries] nations and their oil and, appropriately, dubbed the effort Project Independence. In an interdependent world, however, a developed nation will have so many dependencies and vulnerabilities that the numbers will pose an insoluble problem. It may be able to reduce a few dependencies, at great cost and effort, but many others will remain. Actors have inadvertently created a global system in which a great power can no longer hope to be sole master of its own affairs or its destiny. It is no longer feasible, therefore, for a major developed nation to attempt to define its national interest in terms of freedom from dependency and vulnerability. Instead,

it must learn to live with its vulnerability, as smaller nations have long had to do.

Proposition 9:

> As the system-centered interests of a nation are defined in broader terms, they will increasingly overlap the broadening interests of other nations.

Expansion of the realm of shared interests makes it harder to find clear-cut enemies. In a highly interactive world one's enemy is also apt to be one's partner. The government of the Soviet Union, for example, is ambivalent about treating the United States as an enemy, since it also wants to have the United States as a trading partner and a source of high technology.

If the area of overlapping national interests continues to increase, may not the interests of one nation, eventually, become virtually identical with those of another? No. Interests and interest conflicts do not disappear in a highly interactive world; they are only modified and transformed. A natural harmony of interests will not emerge out of interdependence and advanced technology. Utopia is not to be found farther along the interaction/technology continuum. The realm of shared interests may broaden, but significant situational differences, as well as differences in values and priorities, will guarantee the survival of interest conflicts.

Proposition 10:

> As national interests increase in number, conflicts between various interests must also increase.

There will be conflicts between various state-centered interests, between various system-centered interests, and between state-centered and system-centered interests. In those circumstances it may be taken for granted that no combination of policies can simultaneously advance all interests. Decisions on trade-offs must be made continuously, and wisdom will lie in emphasizing the more important rather than the less important interests.

Proposition 11:

An increasingly common, and important, form of interest conflict will be that between state-centered and system-centered national interests.

Analysts have been intrigued by the way in which a hard-nosed pursuit of narrow self-interest can sometimes be self-defeating. They have looked closely at the ''prisoner's dilemma.'' This involves a two-person non-zero-sum game that illustrates how ''rational'' considerations, combined with a lack of mutual trust, can lead to outcomes that are bad for both players.[2]

In one form or another, the prisoner's dilemma has long been with us. The account by Thucydides of the wars in the Peloponnesus can be interpreted in terms of the prisoner's dilemma. Individual city-states pursued a narrow definition of their interests and were unwilling to help one another. Because of their lack of confidence in one another, they could not achieve a collective solution to the problem and so suffered from a succession of wars destructive to all. They were dependent on one another but did not perceive the policy implications of their interdependence.

A contemporary variation of the problem, reminiscent of the story of the goose that laid golden eggs, appears in connection with ''common pool'' resources. When there exists a finite, common pool of resources, such as ocean fisheries, from which many actors may draw, the stage is set for another showing of the ''tragedy of the commons.'' A narrow national-interest calculus dictates that an actor try to get as much of the common resource as possible in as short a time as possible, for what it does not get will be lost to it forever. When a multitude of actors all follow this policy, the resource will soon be exhausted and all will be losers in the long run, including those that got the largest share of the resource before it disappeared. Following this logic, eager national operators are busily over-fishing the oceans with the result that total yield is now dropping despite an increase in effort devoted to fishing.

The conflict between system-centered and state-centered interests will raise difficult ethical problems for American foreign policymakers. What should be the American stance on matters relating to resource use, the redistribution of global resources, the amount of foreign aid, the proper handling of U.S. food exports, and so on? To date, American policymakers are inclined to rely on a narrow national-interest calculus that undervalues concern for system-centered interests. This is understandable, for most individuals are more accustomed to thinking in terms of state-centered than system-centered interests. A systematic bias is, therefore, built into their calculations. State-centered considerations do not have to fight for recognition and are automatically assigned a high priority while system-centered interests, such as those having to do with the environment, are just as automatically assigned a lower priority.

The policy consequences of this bias were not extremely costly prior to World War II because important system-centered interests were far fewer in number. Now, because the proportion of system-centered interests in the mix of total national interests has increased, that bias leads to serious distortion of policy priorities. System-centered interests are habitually undervalued. As the web of interaction becomes more tightly woven and the dimensions of the globe shrink under the pressure of technology, interaction of every kind acquires an increasingly social aspect.

Perhaps in time, in response to events such as the energy shortage, this shift will be reflected more fully in the amount of attention devoted to system-centered interests by the foreign policy establishment of the United States. Reassessment of priorities is not something that comes easily to complex bu-

---

[2] See, for example, Anatol Rapoport, *Fights, Games, and Debates* (Ann Arbor: Univ. of Michigan Press, 1960), pp. 173–74, and Thomas C. Schelling, *Micromotives and Macrobehavior* (New York: W. W. Norton, 1978), pp. 218 ff.

reaucracies, however. Established conceptions of the national interest become embodied in entrenched bureaucratic structures while spokesmen for emergent interests, lacking effective organizational support, are at a disadvantage in the struggle for funding and attention. No invisible hand guarantees that the organizational potency of support for a given interest must tally closely with the intrinsic importance of that interest. Because of the lag involved in the recognition of new national interests and in finding ways to give them effective expression, national resources must always be misallocated to some extent and trade-offs among those interests will not reflect the policy priorities that should be in effect.

For a government faced with a concrete situation, the problem may not be so much that of understanding the situation and the need for a collective solution as it is the political problem of making and justifying a decision that will be unpopular. A government must sometimes choose between a tangible short-term interest defended by voluble, angry, and well-organized supporters, and a long-term interest not supported by delegations from the future, the costs and benefits of which are somewhat uncertain. It may have to choose between a limited national interest, which will do some damage to the global community, and the interests of the global community, which will do some damage to short-term national interests. In an era of interdependence questions such as the following must come up again and again:

- Should the United States protect domestic industries threatened by competition from abroad? On the one side, there are the imperatives of jobs and politics and, on the other, the U.S. commitment to liberal economic principles and global economic development and well-being.

- Should the United States discourage private investment abroad on the grounds that such investment represents the exportation of American jobs? If it does so, may it not slow the development of the poorer countries and work against its own long-term interests?

- Should the United States oppose demands for a New International Economic Order on the grounds that they are designed to change the rules of the game in favor of the developing nations and must, therefore, adversely affect U.S. interests? Or might such opposition reduce opportunities for change that could improve the long-term stability of the international economic system and thus benefit the United States?

- More concretely, should the United States oppose the efforts of developing nations to get a larger share of world industrial production? Or should the United States support those efforts in the name of justice, the development of the poorer nations, and the long-term economic and political stability of the international system?

- Should the United States continue to seek high rates of economic growth in the name of national interest and national security? Or should the United States, considering the impact of high growth rates on the consumption of scarce resources, start moving in the direction of zero growth?

- Spokesmen of developing nations sometimes charge that the United States, because of governmental policy and the activities of corporations based in the United States, has altogether too much influence over global communications and is, as a consequence, engaged in cultural imperialism on a near-global scale. Should the United States, acknowledging the communications asymmetry and deferring to the increasing sensitivity of the developing nations on communications issues, seek to be more restrained? Or should it, in the name of national interest and freedom of communications, continue to play as prominent a role in global communications as its talents and energies will permit?

Other nations encounter the same kinds of interest conflict. Some OPEC nations appear to be torn between the desire to maximize short-term benefits, on the one hand, and a fear of bankrupting their customers and throwing the world economy into a tailspin, on the other. Should the Japanese, in the name of the national interest, continue to eat whale meat, or should the survival of endangered species be an overriding concern? Should Japan continue to maintain a very strong payments position, in the national interest? Or is it in the interest of Japan to ease the payments pressure on other countries by increasing its imports?

Proposition 12:

The pursuit of the "national interest," even when it is enlightened and broadly defined, will not be an adquate guide to national policy; a sense of obligation must also come into play.

National interests must be defined more broadly: under what circumstances, if any, should a nation rein in its interests?

The basis on which the global system is organized—nation-states plus the principle of national sovereignty—does not obligate a nation to ever rein in its interests. Since it is a sovereign entity, it is not obligated, either legally or morally, to sacrifice its own state-centered interests in favor of the interests of the global system. In a highly interdependent, high-technology world, that approach is no longer viable, as can be illustrated with reference to resource policy and the position of the United States.

The ideas about resources that have long been controlling were developed during a period of plenty, a time in which global constraints did not seem to fit tightly around humankind. In recent decades those pre-scarcity assumptions and ideas have begun to encounter the reality of a planet that is finite and nonrenewable resources that are limited. At present high rates of consumption, the global system can move quickly from a situation in which there is no apparent availability problem for a given resource to one in which a critical shortage is imminent.

As nations begin to realize that resources are indeed finite, the question of who gets how much of what will become more central. As long as the pie was thought to be unlimited in size, distributional issues did not seem vital. In conditions of scarcity, however, with a pie that is finite in size, the more that goes to Y the less there is for X. Before long, therefore, questions must arise concerning the basis on which global resources should be allocated under conditions of scarcity.

Any system of allocation will be based on a set of assumptions, principles, and ethical values, even though they may never have been explicitly stated. Certainly that holds for present arrangements, which are based on "supply and demand," the "market system," and the principle of "equal access" to resources for all nations. What could be more fair and natural, Americans might be inclined to ask, than that resources should go to those who can pay for them? Economic principles are seldom neutral, however. They represent choices of a kind, and they have serious political, moral, and distributional implications.

The doctrine of "equal access" favors the rich. Although all nations may have equal legal access to natural resources, the rich will be able to buy and consume them to a greater extent than will the poor. The "free play of market forces" has had potent distributional consequences. Economists from developing countries have pointed out that the free play of market fores contributed to the magnification of inequalities of wealth among nations. Continued adherence to that principle can be counted on to work strongly in the direction of perpetuating those inequalities.

The United States, with 6 percent of the world's population, accounts for 30 percent of the world's annual consumption of energy and selected minerals. That is quite in accord with the principle of equal access. Suppose, however, to explore the issue, U.S. consumption of key global resources rose to 50 percent or 70 percent. Is there still no problem? Does ability to pay confer a right to consume that is without limit? Is it altogether appropriate that scarce resources should flow to the low-priority, or even frivolous, needs of a highly affluent society rather than to the high-priority needs of a less wealthy society? Can one not sense a lack of congruence between the reality of global scarcities, on the one hand, and a principle of allocation, on the other, that allows unlimited consumption by the rich? Might it not be argued that the doctrine of ''equal access'' to natural resources should, in an era of scarcity, be viewed as a doctrine that legitimizes raids on the commons by wealthy nations? A principle that allocates resources to those who can pay simultaneously denies resources to those who cannot pay. Energy and mineral resources that now flow to the United States in such abundance will never be available to developing nations. May not the present use of scarce resources to maintain American affluence be effectively denying the possibility of economic growth to less wealthy nations?

More than any other nation the United States has benefited from the era of plenty. It cannot fail, therefore, to be heavily affected by the consequences of an era of scarcity. If demands should emerge that the United States restrict its resource use, should the United States refuse, on the grounds that to do so would be contrary to its national interest? Or, should it take the position that, in the event of conflict between the national interest and the human interest, a nation is under obligation to defer to the broader interest unless vital national interests are clearly at stake?

The issue has not yet been raised in a pointed way, but it may be before long. The principle of equity in the use of global resources has the potential for becoming the standard against which present resource use could be measured and found wanting. . . .

Proposition 13:
When important actors do not defer to broader system needs but act in accord with narrow state-centered interests, the costs are likely to be heavy and to be borne by all.

The more important an actor is in the global system, the more important it will be to others that its actions be characterized by knowledge and responsibility. Because the global system is becoming increasingly vulnerable to disruption, its tolerance for

irresponsible behavior is declining. A small nation may raid the commons, for example, and do relatively little damage, but when a superpower raids the commons—as the Soviet Union does with its giant fishing fleets—the impact will be felt by scores of others. By the same token, when the United States behaves irresponsibly by running successive massive-payments deficits or by failing to restrain energy use, the impact is felt globally.

The record of the United States in this respect leaves much to be desired. Since World War II, however, the United States has made significant progress in accepting the realities of interdependence. The Soviet leadership, on the other hand, has been slow to perceive that country's involvement in global interdependence, perhaps because that involvement has been less striking than in the case of the United States and perhaps, in part, because of ideological obstacles to perception. Classical Marxist-Leninist formulations say nothing about increasing interdependence, and, indeed, the implications of interdependence are at odds with Leninist notions about the imperialist thrust of capitalist nations and the necessity for hostility between imperialist and ''socialist'' nations.

How will the Soviet Union react when it begins to discover interdependence? Will it be made uncertain and truculent by the irrelevance of much of its ideology to emerging world conditions, or will it move slowly toward an appreciation that, although system membership dues are heavy for a superpower, they must nevertheless be paid?

Proposition 14:
As awareness of system needs becomes more common, greater attention will probably be given to the question of who should make what decisions affecting the global system and on what basis.

Logic will suggest that decisions affecting the global community should not be viewed as legitimate unless there is broad participation in their making. If, for example, certain resources are finite and all of humankind must draw on that limited common pool, does not equity suggest that principles governing their use should reflect global needs? And if the allocation of global resources is everyone's business, might not entitlement to those resources be based more reasonably on need and the ability to put them to good use rather than on the ability of one nation to outbid others in paying for them? If the direction of global development is a matter of common interest, why should investment decisions totaling hundreds of billions annually remain in the hands of private banks and multinational corporations? Is corporate well-being the proper basis on which global investment decisions should be made, or should basic investment decisions increasingly reflect collective judgments about needs?

Proposition 15:

> *Formulation of an adequate, informed definition of the national interest will become increasingly difficult.*

For one thing, a major nation will have multitudinous interests and they will criss cross and conflict in complex and baffling ways. For another, the content of the definition of national interest must evolve with the changing involvement of a nation in the global system and with the evolution of the global system itself. The content now given to the "national interest" would have seemed absurd twenty-five years ago.

An analyst must also weigh long-term interests against immediate interests and that, in turn, is complicated by the difficulty of discerning the distant consequences of present options. One would need to be able to perceive tensions between state-centered interests and system-centered interests and weigh one against the other judiciously. That, too, would be complicated by the problem of distant consequences. If an actor cannot know the more distant results of a set of actions, it might unknowingly, and with the best intentions in the world, endanger the common good. However, even if one *had* complete knowledge, one might still have to weigh a narrow national interest against the obligation of a nation to defer to the broader good.

Evaluation of Interdependence: "New" Cooperation or "Old" Strife?

John Spanier

PRIORITY OF NATIONAL SOLUTIONS OVER GLOBAL SOLUTIONS

In evaluating interdependence, Robert Paarlberg raised a fundamental issue when he questioned the emphasis on managing national welfare at the global level. He stressed instead that the prerequisite for prosperity is improvement in domestic policy leadership. It may sound convincing to say that global problems require global solutions, but fertility, for example, is hardly amenable to agreement among states. The problem of rapidly growing populations is still primarily a national responsibility. What can foreign governments do in the absence of a domestic will to manage this issue? Similarly, emergency food shipments or worldwide food reserves are no substitute for national policies emphasizing agricultural development. These problems require greater national commitments and shifts of internal priorities and resources than most LDCs [less-developed countries] have been willing to make in the past; for many, painful and difficult structural reforms in landowning patterns also will be necessary. "[G]lobal welfare cannot be properly managed abroad until it has been tolerably managed at home. Without a prior exercise of domestic political authority, the global welfare crisis will not admit to efficient interstate control."[1] States remain the most effective means for resolving nations' internal problems. Like charity, global welfare management must begin at home.

Indeed, we may add to Paarlberg's comment that, when the distinction between foreign and domestic policies has been blurred, weak domestic efforts to encourage economic growth and promote prosperity may lead to corresponding tendencies to pin the blame for domestic problems on other nations. This appeal to nationalism and the search for foreign devil figures increase tensions among the states whose alleged interdependence is supposed to create more harmonious relations. The incentive to externalize domestic failure will surely be very strong if the LDCs do not modernize fairly rapidly. And such failure is very likely to produce more activist, radical, authoritarian governments that will be more disposed to confrontation than to conciliation. Beleaguered governments, struggling with massive domestic dissatisfaction, may well adopt intensely nationalistic and aggressive policies out of desperation.

CONTINUING EMPHASIS ON SECURITY

Another issue is that, although there can be little doubt that welfare concerns have become prominent on the international agenda, it is an overstatement to assert that they have achieved priority because security can be taken virtually for granted. The threat of global war has not vanished just because the nuclear balance has so far guaranteed the peace. Both superpowers still use the threat of force and from time to time have confronted one another in crises that could have escalated. Miscalculation in future crises remains a distinct possibility. And there is always the possibility that a limited war might escalate. But most of all, technological innovations in offensive or defensive weapons that lead to asymmetry might yet undermine the strategic balance, which is the main reason interdependence theorists argue that security can be taken for granted and primary attention paid to economic issues. Projecting mutual deterrence into the distant future and assuming that the issue of security is no longer relevant, or at least no longer of principal importance, may be a bit premature.

Source: John Spanier, *Games Nations Play*, 6th ed. (Washington, D.C.: CQ Press, 1987), pp. 661–669. Reprinted by permission.

[1] Robert L. Paarlberg, "Domesticating Global Management," *Foreign Affairs* (April 1976): 571.

TABLE 1

CLAIMED DISTINCTIONS BETWEEN POWER POLITICS AND INTERDEPENDENCE

	Power Politics	Interdependence
Issues	High politics: security, balance of power, spheres of influence	Low politics: natural resources, energy, food and population, environment
Actors	States (primarily in the First and Second Worlds)	States (primarily in the First and Third Worlds), multinational corporations
State relationships	Conflicting "national interests"	Interdependence, common interests, and transnational cooperation
Rule	Conflict: "What you gain I lose" (balance of power)	Cooperation: "We gain or lose together" (community building)
Management	Bilateral	Multilateral
Role of power	Coercion	Rewards
Role of force	High	Low, if not obsolete
Organization	Hierarchical (bipolar or multipolar)	More nearly egalitarian
Future	Basic continuity	Radical change

More fundamental, however, is that the security game is not some antique remnant from the Dark Ages, which is now best forgotten; the socioeconomic game may be more worthwhile, but it is not the only game being played. The superpowers still give priority to their relations with one another. China pays a great deal of attention to the Soviet Union and to Asian security in general. Western Europe must focus on its relations with the Soviet Union and the question of Atlantic security. Even in the third world's preoccupation with regional security, competition for leadership, maintenance of military strength, and alignments with extraregional powers typify international politics. The socioeconomic game is, in fact, played within the larger framework of the security game. Instead of economic interdependence generating a new kind of international order that weakens traditional reliance on forcible means of conflict resolution, the historical and ever-present security problems are more likely to continue conditioning the character of interdependence.

For example, it was American postwar security policy, with its focus on alliances with Europe and Japan, that established the conditions for the high degree of interdependence that exists today within the European Economic Community (EEC) and be-

tween its members and the United States and Japan. Multiple public and private links in trade, investment, and currency bind these highly industrialized states together. But for the U.S.-Soviet security conflict, U.S. protection of Europe, and the European integration movement, the present measure of interdependence would probably not have come to exist. Symbolically, the chiefs of governments of the major nations of the Atlantic community (which includes Japan) have met regularly at economic summit conferences for years. It may well be, therefore, that

> [i]f major conflagration between the superpowers is avoided, if lesser conflicts are kept from spreading, if indeed governments are able to devote their energies to solving those planet-wide economic, social, and ecological problems which undeniably call for universal cooperation, it will be *because* of successful management of the strategic relationships between the superpowers.[2]

---

[2] John J. Weltman, "On the Obsolescence of War," *International Studies Quarterly* (December 1974): 413–414. It needs to be noted that even among these interdependent states, the recession has produced increasing economic nationalism and political quarrels.

VARYING DEGREES OF INTERDEPENDENCE

A third issue is that the degree of interdependence among states varies. The United States is in some ways the least vulnerable of the Western states. Militarily, it provides security for its allies around the world: thus, they are dependent upon the United States. On economic issues, the United States is comparatively invulnerable, except for oil. It produces abundant food and feeds much of the world. The United States also remains a major producer of raw materials and, thanks to superior technology, has a significant capacity for making substitutions for those raw materials it lacks. Even in energy, it has enormous coal reserves and the technology to develop other sources. But Europe and Japan are less secure in regard to resources. In short, some states are more vulnerable than other states. There is nothing new about that; some states have always been able to use another state's vulnerabilities to influence its behavior. Even if it were granted that military power is less useful today than in the past, the substitution of economic means to achieve the same purpose is surely not an argument that the fundamental nature of international politics has been transformed.

A CHOICE OF POLICIES

A fourth issue is that states, while interdependent, may not be equally vulnerable. This means that states have a choice of policies to pursue. During the 1970s the United States pursued a deliberate strategy of *increasing* interdependence with the Soviet Union on trade and arms control. The United States also sought to strengthen its ties with Saudi Arabia by helping it to modernize and by supplying it with arms. Conversely, states can also pursue a policy of *decreasing* interdependence, such as the various programs proposed by the administrations of Richard Nixon, Gerald Ford, Jimmy Carter, and Ronald Reagan to make the United States more self-reliant in energy. During the 1970s also many LDCs became increasingly concerned about their dependence on the United States for food and began to emphasize

their agricultural development programs, which previously had been regarded as less important than industrialization.

The prospects of too much interdependence may provide the incentive for a state to make itself *less* dependent! Few states, if any, seem ready to accept any radical infringement of their freedom of choice and action. There is no available evidence, for instance, that Soviet leaders have given much thought to the problem of interdependence and the allegedly obvious conclusion that their stake in a peaceful and orderly international system is growing. Indeed, the Soviet economy, rich in resources, is less dependent on the rest of the world than are most Western economies. Given the nature of the Soviet regime, it will undoubtedly try to limit the political consequences of importing Western technology and food. Nor did countries like Iran, Libya, Algeria, or Iraq during the 1970s appear very concerned about the effects of their constant push for higher oil prices on the world economy.

THE PRIMACY OF POLITICS

A fifth issue, as the above examples show, is that political considerations remain primary in international politics. Events in Iran since the shah's overthrow suggest that interdependence among nations is more than simply a matter of mutually beneficial exchanges and the internationalization of production and services. It is also a matter of compatible political regimes. Ayatollah Ruhollah Khomeini of Iran clearly considers his regime less "interdependent" with the West, especially with the United States, than did the pro-Western shah. Khomeini was convinced that the United States, and even more Western Europe and Japan, were *dependent* on Iranian oil. American actions confirmed this conviction. Before the Iranians seized the American hostages in late 1979, the United States did everything it could to avoid arousing the ayatollah's wrath and causing a break in oil shipments. For example, Washington refused to let the shah settle in the United States after he left Iran. These efforts notwithstanding, Khomeini encouraged the fanatical Muslim "students'' in their invasion of the American Embassy and their holding of its personnel as hostages. Only as Iran's war with Iraq continued did Khomeini become concerned with markets for his oil because he needed the money to pay for the war.

Is it accidental that the highest degree of interdependence is among the Common Market countries and between them and the United States and Canada—that is, among primarily industrialized and democratic countries with closely linked political and security interests? Is it surprising that interdependence between the United States and the Soviet Union is much less likely to occur except on arms control issues? The Soviet Union has rejected all U.S. attempts to create economic links that would make it more dependent on the United States. And is it really amazing that governments in conflict with the United States and the West should reject claims of interdependence as attempts to prevent them from advancing their national purpose? Was interdependence from the 1970s not actually the cry of the vulnerable?

INTERDEPENDENCE AS A WESTERN CONSTRUCT

Indeed, interdependence, a Western and especially American intellectual construct, holds little appeal in the third world, even though those nations presumably would be the principal beneficiaries of a global redistribution of weath. Indeed, the LDCs are very suspicious of Western ideas about interdependence. When it is suggested that a major problem is overpopulation in the LDCs, the latter reply that birth control is tantamount to genocide. Allegedly the West is seeking to maintain a favorable ratio of white to nonwhite peoples and to preserve its own high standard of living, which is purportedly based on the exploitation of the LDCs' resources. More people in the third world would mean the LDCs would keep these resources for themselves, thus interfering with Western patterns of consumption. Or when it is proposed that all nations show more concern for the environment, the LDCs reply that such concern would prevent them from indus-

trializing. After decades of polluting the land, sea, and air freely, the hypocritical West now seeks to persuade the LDCs to remain simply raw-material suppliers. In addition, suggestions that nuclear diffusion is dangerous to all states are countered with arguments that efforts to limit proliferation of nuclear arms hinder the LDCs' development of nuclear energy for peaceful purposes—even while the nuclear powers continue to build up their arsenals. In short, these arguments show that Western suggestions as to how the LDCs might develop more quickly are not viewed by the LDCs as well-intended, helpful proposals, but as a means of holding them down.

ECONOMICS AN ENCOURAGEMENT TO CONFLICT

A seventh point is that not only is the issue of security far from old-fashioned and outdated, but also that it is likely that economic issues will underscore and reemphasize the essentially Hobbesian character of international politics. The reaction to the oil crisis of the 1970s vividly demonstrated the continued stress on national interest, even if close allies and friends were hurt. The United States sought greater energy independence; Canada decided to keep more of its oil and not send it to the United States; and the various European states scrambled to make their own oil deals with OPEC [Organization of Petroleum Exporting Countries] countries, including offers of trading technical expertise in nuclear engineering for oil. Cooperation fell victim to a me-first policy among the Western industrial countries.

Other nations were hardly wiser or more virtuous, least of all the OPEC countries, which regularly raised oil prices. Indeed, OPEC's more radical anti-Western members—whose declarations of policy were generally filled with denunciations of ''imperialism'' and sympathy for the lot of the poor deprived masses in the underdeveloped world—were frequently in the vanguard of the price hawks seeking to maximize their earnings. They ''beggared'' all their neighbors, Western and non-Western; when oil supplies exceeded demand (which should have lowered oil prices), they cut supplies to keep prices high. In both security and economic terms, nations, by and large, continued to fear that another state's advantage was their disadvantage; one state's increase in security and/or wealth was perceived as a loss of security and/or wealth for themselves.

The downfall of OPEC in the 1980s is further testimony to the priority nations give to their specific national interests. Had each OPEC member accepted the production quotas allotted, all would have earned far more than at present. But to enhance earnings, individual countries ignored their quotas, produced more oil, and created an oil glut. The collapse of oil prices was the result. OPEC's experience is not unique. Economic conflicts are severe even among the Western industrial countries, where a genuine interdependence exists. The growth of the new mercantilism is but one symptom of this trend.

PRESCRIPTION RATHER THAN DESCRIPTION

An eighth point is that much of the discussion in favor of interdependence is *prescriptive*. The emphasis is on a strategy of increasing the degree of interdependence among nation-states; the more links there are, the more cooperation will be required, and the greater will be the restraints on states' freedom of action. This point is really the crux of interdependence thesis: that by *placing contraints on the national egotism and assertiveness of states by catching them in a "web of interdependence" in which they will become so deeply enmeshed, states will be unable to extricate themselves without suffering great harm and will be compelled therefore to cooperate for the "good of humanity."* An argument supposedly based on description of the facts of interdependence, whether in security or in economics, thus shifts almost imperceptibly to advocacy of a course of policy intended to suppress conflict in the state system in favor of a focus on the welfare of all people. Says Seyom Brown, "At issue is whether we can grasp the nature and dimensions of the emerging threats to our well-being, whether we can create an integrated world economy and a workable world order, and whether we can render global priorities so that the quality of life will improve rather than deteriorate."[3]

For those who are not optimistic about the feasibility of supranational integration and a possible new world order, but who despair of the ability of states to solve their security problems in the nuclear age and achieve the welfare of their people in an age of overpopulation, scarcity of food, and environmental pollution, interdependence becomes an argument for a world without borders, a unified global society, a halfway house. In short, the advocacy of interdependence frequently tends to become a plea for a world beyond the contemporary nation-state. It is a plea for changing international behavior and building a better, more cooperative, and more harmonious world order, for subordinating power politics to welfare politics and national interests to planetary interests, for recognizing before it is too late that humanity shares a common destiny. *Advocacy of interdependence is essentially a normative, rather than a functional, argument for a revolutionary shift to a new world order from the current state system in which asymmetrical interdependence equals the capacity to coerce.*

It may be that appeals to global solidarity, moral imperatives, and humanitarian motives are more favorably received today than in the past and that images of a "global village" and "planetary humanism" have been increasingly reflected in world conferences on the environment, population, food, the new international economic order, and women's rights. But this receptivity does not constitute an

effective consensus on global redistribution of income or wealth, or global guarantees of minimum human needs, or on global equality of opportunity. Those precepts have scarcely achieved a solid footing domestically, even in the most advanced societies, where democratic voting pushes governmental policies toward egalitarianism. At the international level, no

---

[3] Seyom Brown, *New Forces in World Politics* (Washington, D.C.: Brookings, 1974), 12.

corresponding political structure is either in hand or in prospect.[4]

Today there may be more interaction in more areas linking humanity than ever before, but it is questionable whether these will create the necessary internal consensus or community upon which common institutions and rules can be built.

It is probably for this reason that the facts of interdependence so often, and almost unnoticed, become a plea for a better and less conflict-prone "world politics" which, while acknowledging the continued existence of states, will produce a behavior among them as if they had already been abolished. In short, the *process* of collective cooperation and problem solving will overcome the defects of the state system's decentralized *structure*—a dubious proposition.

AND BEWARE OF REGIMES

It is for this reason, among others, that the word *regime* is so inappropriate to describe the cooperation of states in specific issue areas. Why was the term introduced at all? After all, state cooperation on issues of common interest is not a new phenomenon. Admittedly, there are more states today and low-politics issues have gained a new prominence. But is that reason enough for labeling such interstate cooperation *regimes?* And why was that particular word chosen? Not only is it commonly used to describe left- or right-wing dictatorships of which most people disapprove, but the word clearly denotes government and authority. Yet, as Susan Strange in her devastating critique of regimes has noted, the state system is basically characterized

not by discipline and authority, but by the absence of government, by the precariousness of peace and order, by the dispersion not the concentration of authority, by

the weakness of law, and by the large number of unresolved conflicts over what should be done, how it should be done, and who should do it.

Above all, a single, recognized focus of power over time is the one attribute that the international system conspicuously lacks.[5]

That the word *regime* is used in these circumstances suggests the special meaning with which the term has been invested: the collective management by the "international community" in the absence of world government of what is now commonly called the transnational or global agenda (population, food, resources, ocean management, and so forth). Regimes composed of the agreements, treaties plus associated international machinery, are viewed as an essential ingredient of a spreading "global political process" or expanding "politics of global problem solving."[6] Susan Strange comments as follows:

All these international arrangements dignified by the label *regimes* are only too easily upset when either the balance of bargaining power or the perception of national interests (or both together) change among those states who negotiated them. In general, moreover, *all the areas in which regimes in a national context exercise the central attributes of political discipline are precisely those in which corresponding international arrangements that might conceivably be dignified with the title are conspicuous by their absence.* (Emphasis added.)[7]

QUESTIONS FOR DISCUSSION

1. What measures can states take to reduce their vulnerability to economic, political, and military forces outside of their borders? Is it desirable that states do so?
2. What effect does increased interdependence have on conflict?
3. What criteria should be used in evaluating whether the world is becoming more interdependent?

---

[4] David H. Blake and Robert S. Walters, *The Politics of Global Economic Relations*, 2d ed. (Englewood Cliffs, N.J.: Prentice-Hall, 1982), 35.

[5] Susan Strange, "Cave! hic dragones: A Critique of Regime Analyses," *International Organization*, Spring 1982, 487.

[6] Frederic S. Pearson and J. Martin Rochester, *International Relations* (Reading, Mass.: Addison-Wesley, 1984), part IV, 395.

[7] Strange, "Cave! hic dragones," 487.

4. What effect does increasing interdependence have on the power of actors, such as states, multinational corporations, and international governmental organizations, in world politics?

5. What are the economic, political, and military features of countries that are most likely to be interdependent?

SUGGESTED READINGS

Cooper, Richard N. *Economic Policy in an Interdependent World*. Cambridge, Mass.: MIT Press, 1986.

Eastby, John. *Functionalism and Interdependence*. Lanham, Md.: University Press of America, 1985.

Falk, Richard. *A Global Approach to National Policy*. Cambridge, Mass.: Harvard Univ. Press, 1975.

Ferguson, Yale H., and Richard W. Mansbach. *The State, Conceptual Chaos, and the Future of International Relations Theory*. Boulder, Colo.: Lynne Rienner Publishers, 1989.

Fromkin, David. *The Independence of Nations*. New York: Praeger, 1981.

Jones, R. J. Barry, and Peter Willetts (eds.). *Interdependence on Trial: Studies in the Theory and Reality of Contemporary Interdependence*. New York: St. Martin's Press, 1984.

Keohane, Robert O., and Joseph Nye, Jr. (eds.). *Transnational Relations and World Politics*. Cambridge, Mass.: Harvard Univ. Press, 1972.

Mansbach, Richard W., Yale H. Ferguson, and Donald E. Lampert. *The Web of World Politics: Non-State Actors in the Global System*. Englewood Cliffs, N.J.: Prentice-Hall, 1976.

Morse, Edward. *Modernization and the Transformation of International Relations*. New York: Free Press, 1976.

Rosecrance, R. A., A. Alexandroff, W. Koehler, J. Kroll, S. Laqueur, and J. Stocker. "Whither Interdependence?" *International Organization*, **31** (Summer 1977), pp. 425–471.

Rosenau, James S. *The Study of Global Interdependence: Essays on the Transnationalization of World Affairs*. New York: Nichols, 1980.

5 Will the Third World Play an Increasingly Important Role in World Politics?

YES

Chen Jiabao

Third World's Role in International Affairs

NO

Mark Falcoff

First World, Third World, Which World?

━━━━━━━━━━━━━━━━━━━━━━━━

Third World's Role in International Affairs

Chen Jiabao

The increasingly important role played by the third world in international affairs was one of the most notable developments of the 1980s. Third world countries participated in resolving significant geopolitical issues, easing regional tensions and actively opposing outside interference by the superpowers. In doing so they have defended world peace.

Gone forever is the domination of the world by the superpowers, therefore giving third world countries more room to speak out about international affairs.

At the United Nations, third world influence is increasing. In this influential international organization with 159 members, third world representatives form an overwhelming majority. This majority is a strong force in maintaining peace and upholding justice, thereby preventing the superpowers and hegemonistic countries from doing whatever they please as they have done in the past.

The U.N. agenda in the 1980s included discussions on the problems creating regional tensions, such as those concerning Afghanistan, Kampuchea, Lebanon, the Arab-Israeli conflict, South Africa's apartheid policy, the Palestinian issue, Namibian independence and the long time North-South debt issue. In many cases, resolutions were passed in favour of the oppressed nations.

Development and expansion of the non-aligned movement in the 1980s showed that the role of the third world in international political struggles was increasing.

Source: Chen Jiabao, ''Third World's Role in International Affairs,'' *Beijing Review*, 33 (Jan. 22, 1990), pp. 10–12. Reprinted by permission.

The non-aligned movement, at its nine summit meetings and during many sessions of the U.N. General Assembly as well as other international conferences, forwarded many resolutions in favour of the national security, independence and economic development of third world countries, thereby fighting for justice as well as their interests and rights.

For instance, at the recent 44th U.N. General Assembly some countries in the non-aligned movement successfully drafted resolutions regarding aid by the international community to third world countries hoping to improve the social environment, enhance North-South dialogue and coordinate drug-deterrence measures. Although these resolutions were opposed by a certain superpower or by several developed countries, they were finally passed with an overwhelming majority because they reflected the wishes of the third world countries.

Because the non-aligned movement reflects the wishes of the developing countries on many international issues, its membership has grown to 102 in the 1980s from 25 in the 1960s, when it was founded. Now, it boasts two-thirds representation of all the countries and two-fifths of the total population in the world. Some developed countries, who in the past paid little attention to the non-aligned movement, began to send observers to its summit meetings in the 1980s.

Any third world countries, even those that are weak or small in size, now have the support of other third world nations when they have been invaded by superpowers or powers that seek regional hegemony. Therefore, power politics leading to injustice, aggression and interference will be thwarted.

Since the Soviet invasion of Afghanistan in 1979, the United Nations, urged by third world countries, passed numerous resolutions demanding an immediate pullout of Soviet troops.

The non-aligned movement and the Organization of the Islamic Conference also passed similar resolutions supporting the Afghan people's struggle and the mediation by the United Nations. Finally, an agreement was reached and the Soviet Union withdrew all its troops from Afghanistan in February 1989.

After Viet Nam invaded Kampuchea in 1978, the United Nations with an overwhelming majority passed many resolutions demanding Vietnamese troop withdrawal.

In December, the United States invaded Panama, provoking strong condemnation from the third world. The reaction from Latin American countries was particularly strong, with some nations recalling their ambassadors from the United States and others offering material and humanitarian aid to the Panamanian people. The U.N. Security Council held an emergency session to discuss the U.S. invasion.

What is worth mentioning is that some Western countries, backed by the United States, proposed a resolution on "freedom of speech and peaceful assembly" during a U.N. special committee meeting in November 1989. The resolution, designed to interfere in the internal affairs of third world countries, was strongly opposed by many third world countries. They proposed amendments to the resolution. The Western countries then attempted to kill the amendments through a voting procedure, but only managed to look bad when the amendments were confirmed by a vote of 85 to 30.

Third world countries have been serving as mediators more frequently. They have helped resolve regional disputes by preventing interference by the superpowers.

In the 1980s, frequent disputes arose among third world countries because of old border and ethnic squabbles. In settling those disputes, regional organizations set up by third world countries played an active role through mediation.

The Arab League, consisting of more than 20 member states, met often during the 1980s and did much towards mediating the Iran-Iraq war. Working with the United Nations, the league finally succeeded in bringing an end to the decade-old Persian Gulf war. The Arab organization is continuing to act as mediator in negotiations towards a final settlement of disputes between the two countries.

The Organization of African Unity is also working towards settlements in the Chad-Libya border dispute and in other border conflicts in Africa. It campaigned continuously at the United Nations for the independence of Namibia. As well, it continues the fight against apartheid in South Africa.

Since its establishment in 1963, the Organization of African Unity has helped nearly 20 African countries break from colonial rule, develop national economies and maintain independence.

Meanwhile, the Contadora Group, composed of Mexico, Panama, Colombia and Venezuela, has made great efforts in easing tensions in Central America. In recent years Latin American leaders have consulted frequently on regional issues and called on the superpowers to stop interfering in the internal affairs of Nicaragua and El Salvador.

Hindsight has revealed that third world countries, which became politically mature in the 1980s, played an increasingly important role in defusing world tension and safeguarding world peace.

However, sources of world tension and turbulence still exist. The superpowers' arms race is still going on; hegemony and power politics are still causing problems in third world countries; regional conflicts continue; and external interference and internal problems are an ever-present irritant in long-standing "hot-spots" in third world countries.

In Afghanistan, the civil war is growing fiercer after the Soviet troop withdrawal; in Kampuchea, war continues unabated because Viet Nam lacks sincerity in resolving the Kampuchean problem; the Israeli expansionism with superpower backing is still blocking independence for the Palestinian people; Lebanon is still in the throes of civil war; many unstable factors exist in southern Africa, especially the Pretoria regime's apartheid system; the American invasion of Panama took place a mere two months after a failed coup attempt.

The world political situation remains unstable in some third world countries in Central America, South America, the Middle East, Africa and Asia.

Difficulties facing the third world countries are particularly serious in economics. By the end of 1989, the developing countries owed the developed countries U.S.$ 1.3 trillion. North-South debt negotiations are now in stalemate. Meanwhile, more and more capital has flown out of third world countries to developed countries.

The general trend as the world enters the 1990s is towards peace and dialogue. But that doesn't mean peace prevails throughout the world. The arduous task of establishing a new international political and economic order lies ahead. And third world countries will play an even greater role as they expand and strengthen their forces.

First World, Third World, Which World?

Mark Falcoff

Nineteen eighty-nine, the most pivotal year since World War II, marked a drastic, radical shift in the world's political and military geography. The only date in recent history to which it is comparable is 1945, which saw the destruction of the German and Japanese empires, the emergence of the United States and the Soviet Union as the global superpowers, and the end of the colonial era in Africa and Asia. In some ways, in fact, 1989 closed the cycle begun in 1945. It marked the end of the Cold War: the collapse of the Soviet empire in Eastern Europe, the virtual dissolution of the Warsaw Pact, and the devastation of the Marxist idea, both as a political faith and an economic doctrine.

What many people have failed to notice, however, is that 1989 signified the end of the postcolonial era as well. For with no Cold War, there can be no "Third World," or rather, no "Third Worldism." And with no alignment—no sharp bipolarity within the international system—there can be no nonalignment, either. The countries are still there, of course—some 77 non-Western nations, including most of the Latin American republics. But their value as pieces on the strategic and ideological chessboard has significantly depreciated. What will these regimes use in place of the "double blackmail" (a term from the French magazine *L'Express*) by which they have obtained political leverage and resources from both East and West for 40 years or more? The answer is, probably nothing.

Source: Mark Falcoff, "First World, Third World, Which World?" *American Enterprise Magazine* (July 1990), pp. 13–14. Copyright 1990, Mark Falcoff. Reprinted with permission from *The American Enterprise Magazine.*

Of course, there will be some sort of relationship between the former Third World and the erstwhile First and Second, but it will be very different from the past. First, because the fundamental centers of power will be more concerned with devising methods of cooperation than competing for dubious foreign clients, the capacity of peripheral societies to disrupt the system as a whole will be greatly diminished. This means no more Sarajevos, no more Vietnams—and no more Lebanons, either.

There will still be disorder in such places; in fact, conflict is likely to persist or even grow in much of the non-Western world, as it often has in the past when colonial or tutelary forces have been withdrawn. Wars will continue to occur between countries (Iran and Iraq, Ethiopia and Somalia) or within societies (the Sendero Luminoso guerrilla movement in Peru, the civil strife in El Salvador, the divided island of Cyprus). But without the larger framework of the East-West struggle, the causes at issue—religious and ethnic conflict, millenarian ideologies, irredentism—will seem strange and irrelevant to the United States, Europe, the Soviet Union, and Japan and the outcome therefore virtually meaningless. John P. Roche, former dean of the Fletcher School at Tufts University and former adviser to President Lyndon Johnson, provides pithy counsel for the regional influentials of the future: "Never get mixed up in the religious wars of other people's churches." He adds, "We simply have to realize that while we can blow up the world, we simply can't persuade Azerbaijanis to be lovable toward Armenians or vice versa."

Second, these countries will find it increasingly difficult to extract concessions and resources from Western governments. Now that political influence in the former Third World is no longer a commodity worth bidding for, it will be possible to admit publicly something economists have known all along—that the majority of "developing countries" (a United Nations' euphemism) are not developing at all and never have been. In fact, those non-Western countries that have succeeded in getting on the escalator of growth (the so-called NICs, newly industrializing countries—Korea, Taiwan, Malaysia,

Singapore) have done so without massive foreign economic assistance from us or anyone else.

Even if this were not the case, the prospects for Africa, Latin America, and parts of South Asia would not be particularly good—Western European governments will be preoccupied with budget decisions on aid to East Germany, Poland, Hungary, and Czechoslovakia, and in the long term, perhaps the Baltic republics and even the Soviet Union. The U.S. foreign-assistance budget (now estimated at $14.5 billion, most of it to five or six countries) will have to survive competing pressures to reduce the deficit or to reallocate defense resources to social spending (the "peace dividend"). The truth is that foreign aid has never been popular with the American people, who believe—repeated polls show—that you can't buy friends; Americans also think (not wrongly) that little foreign aid reaches the people for whom it is intended. Nothing less than a life-and-death struggle with the Soviet Union these past 40 years could have overruled these sentiments; now that the war is over, however, our principal clients will compete for benefits with the very people who pay the bills. The outcome is not difficult to predict. As Congressman David Obey (D-Wisc.) recently put it, "The country is not going to get very excited about aid to anywhere if it comes at the expense of job training, health care, and other things at home."

Third, we can expect that many non-Western societies will simply drop out of the race for economic development because their own domestic political environment renders impossible the implementation of market-oriented economic reforms, or because they do not have the requisite stability, or both. Lacking minimal public order in some of their cities and provinces, and unable to obtain even short lines of commercial credit, such countries will probably have to establish trading entrepôts at their ports or in heavily fortified air and rail termini and deal by barter or for cash. (This has already happened in Iran and Iraq and will probably happen soon in Peru.) The major Western countries and Japan will probably find it necessary to devise a kind of international economic triage, offering credit to only those countries whose policies render them likely to succeed (Chile, Costa Rica) and dispensing outright charity (called charity, not "development assistance") to the most tragic cases of failure (Ethiopia).

RICH WORLD?

Leaders of the former Third World have no reason to accept this analysis of the future, and in fact many of them are struggling to resist it. As Venezuelan President Carlos Andreás Pérez put it recently, the Latin American countries "own more-or-less half the planet's resources. It would be crazy if the industrialized world forgot us." Ivory Coast President Houphouet-Boigny put it even more categorically: "If the Western Europeans were to allow themselves to abandon Africa, they would inflict enormous damage to themselves." He too mentioned "formidable resources of raw materials"—as though these could not be purchased for ready money rather than as part of a complicated political and economic relationship.

What these leaders fail to grasp is that the United States is no longer living in the nineteenth century when raw materials and abundant inexpensive labor were the principal factors of national wealth. Modern economies depend on technology, research, organizational skills, education, and social mobility, which define the developed world and by their absence establish the boundaries of the underdeveloped world as well. Even from a military point of view, the major powers no longer require, as they did 50 or 100 years ago, an extensive network of overseas bases to project their presence abroad. What most industrial countries will need in the future will not be bases or constabulary facilities but effective airlift capability and elite small-infantry units to periodically rescue beleaguered nationals from disorder in remote or inhospitable foreign locales.

The non-Western world can, of course, threaten to disrupt the order of the center—in fact, it is already doing so with the specter of drugs, uncontrolled immigration, damage to the environment, even nuclear weapons. But what this points to is not a massive program of resource transfer but, as Suzan George of the Transnational Institute recently remarked, an eventual "*cordon sanitaire . . . around* the North, while the South, forgotten, will sink into poverty and instability.'' There is no reason why Western countries and Japan cannot restrict the entry of drugs and illegal immigration if they decide to do so; the problem is merely one of political will. As for nuclear weapons, while some non-Western societies are apparently close to nuclear capability (or, like India, already possess it), they are far from having adequate delivery systems. They may develop them, of course—but what better argument could there be for continued work on our own Strategic Defense Initiative?

There is a solution to the problems of what used to be called the Third World. It has already been offered by Brazilian Senator Roberto Campos: ''The time has arrived for us to reach a choice for wealth— preferring to be the last member of the Jockey Club instead of the first member of the dance hall''—in other words, to choose to be a winner, not a loser. To be winners, these countries must embrace free markets and democracy, the very things that have made what used to be called the First World what it is. One hopes that many countries will make this choice, and to the extent that they do, their societies will be better, safer places. But thanks to the geopolitical changes of 1989, nobody is going to make that choice for them—or even want to try—much less subsidize failure if they do not.

QUESTIONS FOR DISCUSSION

1. What role did third world countries play during the cold war?
2. What were the political, military, and economic conditions that allowed them to play that role?
3. What are the sources of strength of third world countries in the post–cold war era?
4. What are the sources of weakness of third world countries in the post–cold war era?
5. How can third world countries maximize their power in world politics? What are the reasons for your answer?

SUGGESTED READINGS

Ayoob, Mohammed. ''The Third World in the System of States: Acute Schizophrenia or Growing Pains?'' *International Studies Quarterly*, **33** (Mar. 1989), pp. 67–79.

Bissell, Richard E. ''Who Killed the Third World?'' *Washington Quarterly*, **13** (Autumn 1990), pp. 23–32.

Brands, H. W. *The Specter of Neutralism: The United States and the Emergence of the Third World, 1947–1960*. New York: Columbia Univ. Press, 1989.

Conable, Barber. ''Third World Must Overcome 1980s.'' *Bulletin of the Atomic Scientists*, **46** (Jan./Feb. 1990), pp. 11–12.

Copulos, Milton R. ''The Coming North-South Conflict.'' *World and I*, **4** (June 1989), pp. 22–31.

David, Steven R. ''Why the Third World Matters.'' *International Security*, **14** (Summer 1989), pp. 50–85.

Ghosh, Bimal. ''1992: Third World in the Margin.'' *European Affairs* (Amsterdam), **3** (Winter 1989), pp. 117–119, 122–126.

Holm, Hans-Henrik. ''The End of the Third World?'' *Journal of Peace Research*, **27** (Feb. 1990), pp. 1–7.

Klare, Michael T. ''Who's Arming Who? The Arms Trade in the 1990s.'' *Technology Review*, **93** (May/June 1990), pp. 42–50.

Lewis, Flora. ''Nonaligned Nations in Crisis.'' *New York Times*, Sept. 5, 1989, p. A19.

''Non-sequitur.'' *Economist* (London), **312** (Sept. 9, 1989), pp. 44–45.

Radu, Michael. ''The Third World: Proceed with Caution.'' *World and I*, **5** (Jan. 1990), pp. 133–139.

Samuelson, Robert J. ''End of the Third World.'' *Washington Post*, July 18, 1990, p. A23.

Wolpin, Miles D. ''Third World Non-Alignment: Does It Make a Difference?'' *Bulletin of Peace Proposals*, **20** (Mar. 1989), pp. 99–112.

CHAPTER 2

Beliefs

Observers of world politics differ about the conduct of foreign policy. Some explain foreign policy by reference to fixed features of the global system, while others argue that policymakers have a far greater choice in deciding how to act and have, in fact, pursued policies based on strongly held beliefs.

One group asserting that foreign policy is determined by fixed features is the geopoliticians, who hold that geography is the single most important factor of world politics. Although differing among themselves about specifics, Halford Mackinder, Alfred Thayer Mahan, and Nicholas Spykman reflect this assumption in their works. Other writers who explain foreign policy in fixed terms argue that war is caused by capitalism, for example, or dictatorship, the sovereign state system, or simply human nature.

Another group of observers argues that the conduct of foreign policy involves a large measure of choice. In such a view, foreign policy can be based on the beliefs of a people or the judgment of government leaders. Foreign policy is seen not as a mechanistic response to given conditions but rather as philosophical and ethical judgments about the relations of states and peoples or about the methods that should be used in resolving conflict.

The debates in Chapter 2 consider these matters in different contexts. Issues include the wisdom of promoting human rights in the conduct of foreign policy, the relevancy of communism as an ideological force in the post–cold war era, and realism versus idealism in international relations.

HUMAN RIGHTS

Two ideologies that have played important roles in world politics since World War II are liberalism and communism. Debate 6 focuses on human rights, a central tenet of liberalism.

Classical liberalism, which developed in the late eighteenth and nineteenth centuries and retains support in the twentieth century, is based on the notion that certain rights should be accorded to people everywhere. These rights are said to include primarily political rights, many of which are articulated in the Bill of Rights of the U.S. Constitution as well as in the Constitution itself. Such rights include freedom of speech, press, and assembly; the rights of individuals accused of committing crimes; and the right to hold free and fair elections.

Liberals are clear about the need to promote human rights at home, but in considering the promotion of human rights abroad they often perceive a conflict between human rights and the needs of national security. In practical terms, they have to answer a difficult question: Should a country that adheres to liberal democratic values promote those values even when such action undermines the bonds between it and a friendly country that happens to be violating the human rights of its own people?

From the earliest days of the republic, the United States has wrestled with this issue. When the French Revolution broke out in 1789, many Americans thought that the United States should side with the French revolutionaries in their initial quest for liberty, equality, and fraternity, but that would have meant getting involved in a European war. During World War II, the United States allied with the Soviet Union, which under Josef Stalin was one of the most brutal dictatorships in the world. But since Nazi Germany was at war with both the United States and the Soviet Union, most Americans believed that they had to ally with the Soviets against a greater evil.

Despite such alliances of necessity, the United States has also often sought to promote democracy and freedom throughout the world. President Woodrow Wilson's Fourteen Points epitomized these ideals.

In the post–World War II period the liberal creed of human rights has been advocated frequently by every successive president. In 1947 Harry Truman set the tone when he announced the Truman Doctrine, which called for the United States "to support free peoples who are resisting attempted subjugation by armed minorities or by outside pressures." John F. Kennedy's inaugural address of 1961 had a similar theme: "Let every nation know, whether it wishes us well or ill, that we shall pay any price, bear any burden, meet any hardship, support any friend, oppose any foe to assure the survival and success of liberty."[1]

The Carter and Reagan administrations made human rights an important part of the political agenda. Jimmy Carter announced in his inaugural address in 1977 that the United States would promote human rights abroad. Ronald Reagan recognized the importance of human rights but indicated that the United States would not undermine friendly governments even when those governments violated human rights.

In 1989, George Bush had to reconcile human rights with national security in devising a response to the Chinese government's brutal suppression of China's democracy movement. In the summer of that year the Chinese army massacred hundreds (and maybe thousands) of protesters in Beijing's Tiananmen Square and harshly treated

---

[1] "Text of President Truman's Speech on New Foreign Policy," *New York Times*, Mar. 13, 1947, p. 2; "Text of Kennedy's Inaugural Outlining Policies on World Peace and Freedom," *New York Times*, Jan. 21, 1961, p. 8.

those who challenged government authority. Bush considered withdrawing most-favored-nation status from China—a preferential tariff treatment for Chinese products entering the United States—because many Americans objected to "business as usual" with the Chinese. But he decided that quiet diplomacy might be more effective in ultimately bringing about democratic change. He therefore downplayed Chinese violations of human rights and sent emissaries to China to repair deteriorating relations between the United States and China.

Should human rights be a goal of foreign policy? U.S. writer Meg Greenfield argues the Affirmative. She contends: (1) Dissidents supporting human rights in dictatorships have succeeded in toppling autocratic regimes. (2) The United States should be consistent in supporting democratic regimes. (3) Such support will improve the plight of dissidents. (4) The United States can still assert its support of human rights with a friendly government in a manner that will not upset its relationships with that government.

Yi Ding, a writer for the *Beijing Review*, argues against interfering in the internal affairs of a country on human rights matters. The author contends: (1) There are no universal and abstract human rights. (2) Human rights are a matter of domestic law. (3) International documents relating to human rights do not supersede the laws of any country.

COMMUNISM

Cataclysmic economic and political events can undermine existing ideologies and propel new ones. The Great Depression, which began in 1929 and continued through the 1930s, seriously shook confidence in capitalism—a system in which market forces, with no or little government interference, determine the economy. With production throughout the Western democracies in decay and large numbers of workers unemployed, many hailed the ideology of communism as capable of ushering in an era of unprecedented prosperity and universal peace.

Communism is a political ideology based principally on the writings of the nineteenth-century theorists Karl Marx and Friedrich Engels and of the twentieth-century theorist and political leader V. I. Lenin. Marxism-Leninism, as communism is sometimes called, was implanted in the old state of Russia in 1917, was extended to Eastern Europe and China after World II, and has had an enormous impact on ideas and political developments on every continent.

Marxism was first devised as a response to the industrial conditions of the nineteenth century. Marx depicted economic forces as fundamental to historical development. According to his view, history unfolds from one stage to the next as naturally as day follows night. The key to moving history forward is the class struggle—the war between the haves and have-nots, or those who own or control the means of production and those who do not. Marx saw that feudalism, based on an agricultural economy, had given way to capitalism, structured on an industrial economy. But capitalism, he argued, had created the seeds of its own destruction. The instrument of its destruction would be the proletariat—the industrial workers. Capitalists create conditions that they cannot control—such as overproduction and unemployment—and eventually an unemployed proletariat would rise up to destroy the capitalist order.

Marx did not provide a blueprint describing what would follow capitalism. But Marxist writings mention that a classless society will emerge. There is scarcely any discussion in Marx's writings about the way in which the political and economic system would function once capitalism had been destroyed, however.

From the point of view of world politics, Marxism explained wars as resulting from economic pressures and the class struggle, not from nationalism or ethnic tensions, which Marx considered irrelevant to the forces of history. When capitalism was toppled, there would be no further need for nation-states or for ethnic solidarity. Since a classless society would be formed, there would be no further need for war either.

The writings of Marx are often contradictory since he and Engels wrote over many years and modified their views from time to time. And so those who followed Marx went off on different paths in interpreting his writings. For example, at times Marx regarded democracy as a sham, nothing more than a mechanism for capitalist control. At other times he said that the proletariat could make great gains by using democratic processes.

After the death of Marx, his followers divided into two principal factions—the social democrats and the communists. Social democrats believed that capitalism should be controlled and limited and a welfare state should be adopted but also advocated political democracy as applied in modern liberal states, with their principles of majority rule and free elections and their regard for basic human rights.

The other faction, the communists, was led by Lenin, a revolutionary in czarist Russia. As a young revolutionary, Lenin had to operate in secret lest the czarist government suppress him. Leninism, as his theory was called, is based on the notion that revolutions do not happen automatically, as Marx had predicted. Instead, they can be created by a small conspiratorial organization, the Communist party. This small, effective party could bring communism to a country even before capitalism was instituted there. Consequently, stages could be skipped, with the Communist party the instrument of revolution and the architect of an industrial society.

Lenin came to power in Russia in 1917. He believed that a world revolution was imminent. That revolution, however, did not occur. And so a largely agrarian country on the eve of an industrial take-off became the first communist country and looked to export its communist ideology. To this end, Lenin established the Comintern, or Communist International, in 1919. He attempted to make all socialist parties more loyal to Soviet leadership than to their own countries. This pressure precipitated a split with the social democrats, who objected to the dictatorial features of communism as well as the call for them to be traitors to their homelands.

Communism made its greatest initial gains as a result of Soviet military action in World War II against the Germans. As Soviet armies liberated the occupied countries in Eastern Europe, they implanted communist regimes. Later communism became the basis for the political systems of some Asian countries, such as China and Vietnam. Communist parties in noncommunist countries sought political power through legal and sometimes illegal means. The ideology had a continuing appeal to some Western intellectuals, especially during the Great Depression.

In turn, communism itself was discredited by events, including the 1939 Nonaggression Pact between the Soviet Union and Nazi Germany and by Soviet leader Nikita Khrushchev's revelation in 1956 of the crimes of the Stalin era. But the events of 1989 and 1990 caused a convulsion for the proponents of communism by revealing how thoroughly communist governments ruined the economies of their states and how heavy a toll they took in the destruction of freedom, human rights, and human life.

In 1989 and 1990, democratic governments were established in most Eastern European countries previously under communist rule, and the new governments sought to jettison the command economies that had been so inefficient and to introduce, instead, a heavy dose of capitalism. Communism became discredited in many places it had been imposed—most notably in the Soviet Union itself. Only Cuba, China, and Vietnam tenaciously retained their communist ideology. As noted above, the Chinese government ruthlessly crushed a democratic movement in 1989 and renewed its ideological adherence to Marxism-Leninism.

Is communism a dead ideology, now likely to have little further impact on world events? Henry Grunwald, former editor-in-chief of *Time* magazine, argues that it is. He contends: (1) The phenomenon known as Gorbachev signifies the dismal failure of Marxism as an economic, political, and social system. (2) After seventy years of communist rule, the Soviet Union remains an underdeveloped country that cannot feed its own people. (3) The Marxist view of man is false. (4) Even in the third world Marxism is not a realistic means to bring about development. (5) The West must offer alternatives to Marxism—most notably political democracy, a free market, and support of countries that lack the infrastructure, education, and social values that the free market requires.

Zhang Zhen, president of the China National Defence University, argues that Marxism-Leninism is a valid theory of our times. He contends: (1) Although capitalism has demonstrated flexibility in responding to economic crises, eventually it will collapse because of fundamental contradictions, as Marx and Lenin said. (2) The failures of communist countries have come about not because of the failure of Marxism-Leninism but rather because those countries violated the scientific tenets of Marxism-Leninism. (3) Marxism-Leninism has been beneficial to China. (4) Advocates of pluralism are only serving the interests of the bourgeoisie and are undermining the government.

REALISM

A subject of continuing controversy in analyzing world politics is the utility of the concept of realism (or *realpolitik*, as it is sometimes called). In the United States realism emerged as a viewpoint mostly after World War II. Its principal early proponents were Walter Lippmann, Hans J. Morgenthau, and George F. Kennan, and it has continued to attract later generations of scholars and policymakers, whose viewpoint is sometimes referred to as ''neorealism.'' The early realist writings were a reaction to what realists regarded as a legalistic-moralistic tradition in thinking about foreign policy. Realists emphasize the state-centric model of international relations, the concept of power, and the balance of power.

Is the realist model an accurate description of world politics? Political scientists Hans J. Morgenthau and Kenneth W. Thompson argue that it is. They present six fundamental principles of political realism: (1) Political realism believes that politics, like society in general, is governed by objective laws that have their roots in human nature. (2) The central signpost of political realism in international politics is the concept of interest defined in terms of power. (3) The concept of interest defined as power is not fixed once and for all but depends upon the political and cultural context within which foreign policy is formulated. (4) Political realism is aware of the moral significance of political action. It also recognizes the tension between morality and the requirements of successful political action. (5) Political realism refuses to identify the moral aspirations of a particular nation with the moral laws that govern the universe. (6) Political realism has profound differences with other schools of thought.

Stanley Kober, a scholar at the Cato Institute, argues that idealism is an alternative to the realist analysis. According to Kober, idealism is based on the notion that the foreign policy of a state is an outgrowth of the values embodied in its institutions. In such a view, dictatorships are more likely to be expansionist than democracies, since the latter must be accountable to their people.

Kober contends: (1) Realism cannot explain some important developments in world politics, such as the U.S.-Canadian relationship and the outbreak of World War II. (2) Idealist analysis provides criteria for assessing whether a military buildup is the result of perceptions of insecurity or the product of a drive for military supremacy to achieve political objectives by the threat or use of arms. (3) Idealism accepts the need for a balance of power but rejects the idea that international peace is solely the product of a balance of power. (4) Idealism is careful not to exaggerate military or economic threats. (5) Idealism recognizes that imperialism is an unstable basis for continuing economic growth. (6) Realists have oversimplified the concept of power and misunderstood the lessons of history. (7) Idealists believe that the spread of freedom will ultimately eliminate the need for a balance of power. (8) Idealism is not naive utopianism but a rigorous approach to foreign policy.

6 Should Human Rights Be a Goal of Foreign Policy?

YES

Meg Greenfield

Beware of Geobaloney

NO

Yi Ding

Opposing Interference in Other Countries' Internal Affairs through Human Rights

Beware of Geobaloney

Meg Greenfield

I've never understood why the phrase "human rights" always seems to end up in the et cetera category of policy concerns. And I've never understood exactly how those in government who make a habit of relegating the human-rights atrocities of other governments to some lower order of priority than a lot of other high-sounding matters (to which they invariably append the pretentious and meaningless prefix "geo") get away with their terrible, beaming condescension to those of us who protest their values—excuse me: to those of us who protest their geostrategic, geopolitical geovalues.

You will have guessed that I have China on my mind. It is just like all the other familiar episodes of its kind in recent history. A government somewhere commits acts of fearful brutality against its own citizens whose crime is espousing democratic purposes, and our own government refuses to jar its relationship with the offending government. Smugly and with ostentatious forbearance it tells us there are larger considerations to be taken into account and that Papa knows best and/or that we are so cute and so understandable, but so terribly wrong, when we are mad. "You'll see," they say; "it's the geo thing, the big geo. Hush now . . . you wouldn't understand. Just trust us."

So what *have* we seen? We have seen a worldwide honor roll of brave, unyielding political dissidents and troublemakers upend superior force, stare down brutish captors and often bring down governments or bring them to the bargaining table or at a minimum outlast them and live to see vin-

dication. Andrei Sakharov, Natan Sharansky, Aleksandr Solzhenitsyn, Lech Walesa, Armando Valladares, Vaclav Havel, Walter Sisulu, Nelson Mandela, Benigno Aquino, Fang Lizhi—each is or was different and each achieved a different measure of success; but surely they and the hundreds of thousands of honorable, democratic resisters of totalitarian and authoritarian tyranny around the world they symbolize represent a force with which we should openly and robustly identify, as distinct from one to which we should merely pay our stiff, formal and unconvincing respects as a kind of noble afterthought to our practical policy considerations.

What are the reasons offered for our usual skittishness about taking up their cause? Sometimes they are the need to stand by a friend (such as, God help us, Ferdinand Marcos); sometimes they are the need not to antagonize a foe with whom we are trying to do other business (such as old Mr. Stagnation, Leonid Brezhnev). Generally we are inconsistent and selective in our application of our standards in these matters. American administrations that go all pious and self-righteous about not interfering in the internal affairs of a friendly thug will seek funds to help those who are resisting one we don't like.

Two main arguments persist. One is that the American government's intervention only makes things worse for the dissident himself. This is interesting. I have heard the position argued by members of every kind of administration. I have *never* heard it espoused or even accepted by one of those foreign human-rights disturbers of the peace for whose sake our solicitous government always thought it was keeping quiet. No matter what horrors they have endured and still face, invariably in my experience they will argue for—beg for—overt, conspicuous, noisy, wholehearted American governmental endorsement.

The other main argument made against such involvement is that it will get in the way of our larger and more critical business with the government in question. I concede that there are times and issues and circumstances that dictate cozying up to or at least humoring repressive governments for the sake of achieving other necessary goals. And I don't think

Source: Meg Greenfield, "Beware of Geobaloney," *Newsweek*, 94 (Dec. 25, 1989), p. 84. Reprinted by permission.

we should saw off relationships with governments that offend on human rights and thereby yield up whatever chance we have to affect them or to do other business that is also essential. But this, despite what the administration says, was not the choice in the China case, and it rarely is. The question was one of negotiating, of letting the Chinese know how our president and our government felt about the horrible onslaught on the demonstrators of Tiananmen last spring, of showing that this actually mattered to us, of keeping faith with the pro-democracy forces there (and in hiding or taking refuge abroad).

DOUBLE STANDARD

The Bush administration has from the beginning seemed reluctant to do this. It has never found its true voice or authority in protesting what happened, rather, sounding uncertain and even unconvinced of the case against the Chinese government and nervous about making it. To some extent this may just be endemic to the institution: governments tend to like other governments, even those they classify as enemies, better than they like a mob. Governments understand each other and sympathize with each other on some level inaccessible to the rest of us— they drive off in the big black car together after coordinating their arrival statements and that sort of thing. They are often more comfortable with each other than they are with the unpredictable troublemakers protesting outside their doorways or refusing to eat in prison or otherwise disturbing the natural hierarchic order of things.

And then there is also the much commented upon, if unaccountable, double standard that has long prevailed in some parts of the American political establishment concerning Chinese repressiveness. The Chinese have always been able to get away with murder, literally, in this quarter. And they will again unless more than some showy action providing relief for, say, Fang or a couple of other prominent dissidents is forthcoming. Such limited gestures could actually provide cover for their continuing assault on the thousands of endangered foot soldiers of the uprising. Is that kind of cynical cover all our government asks? Unless the Scowcroft mission to Beijing demanded and expects to get relief for those young people being hunted down, imprisoned, tortured and executed, then I think in a terrible way we will have broken faith with them, with our traditions and, yes, with our own best interests in whatever terms the heavy thinkers choose to define them. Human rights are not an add-on, a frill, an extra sentence in a realpolitik speech. They are what the fight was about. Look at Eastern Europe, if you don't think so.

Opposing Interference in Other Countries' Internal Affairs through Human Rights

Yi Ding

In the turn of spring and summer this year, turmoil and then a counter-revolutionary rebellion in Beijing attempted to overthrow the leadership of the Chinese Communist Party and subvert the government of the socialist People's Republic of China. At first, the Chinese government imposed martial law in some sections of Beijing in accordance with the Constitution. Only later did it take drastic measures to crush the counter-revolutionary rebellion.

These actions were the proper, rational and lawful actions of a sovereign nation and have been understood and supported by most countries in the world. However, some foreign forces made unwarranted charges and wantonly interfered with this country's internal affairs. This, of course, sparked great indignation and opposition from the Chinese people. Consequently, these foreign forces explained they were only showing their concern for human rights, and that human rights have no boundaries. They maintained that concern for human rights in other countries does not constitute interference in those countries' internal affairs. This opinion is utterly unjustified.

NO ABSTRACT HUMAN RIGHTS EXIST

First, there are no universal and abstract human rights. Countries with different ideologies and social systems and at different stages of development have different understandings of the basic concept of human rights.

The traditional Western view is that human rights are natural, inborn and inalienable, But from the Marxist standpoint, all rights emerge historically and are based on economic relations in society. Accepted "human rights" are only those which have been recognized in law by the dominant class of a country.

As for the scope of human rights, the West's traditional view is to stress the individual. Rights are defined as an individual's political and civil rights which are protected under law. But this view obviously does not consider different levels of economic development or political conditions in different countries. The third world countries, given their national conditions, stress collective rights. They regard collective human rights as the foundation of individual rights and the precondition for individuals to enjoy all rights and freedoms. They also consider that economic, social and cultural rights cannot be separated from civil and political rights. These two aspects are equally important—full economic rights and guarantees are material conditions for realizing the civil and political rights.

Some Western scholars also recognize differences in the theory and concept of human rights. Hedley Bull, for example, contends, "We should remember how slender is the consensus that unites the governments of the world today in the matter of human rights," and that "the reluctance evident in the international community even to experiment with the conception of a right of humanitarian intervention reflects not only an unwillingness to jeopardize the rules of sovereignty and non-intervention by conceding such a right to individual states, but also the lack of any agreed doctrine as to what human rights are."

Second, there are, fundamentally, no universal human rights that override the laws of various countries.

The human rights we talk about today exist not only in theory, but also in the concrete form of specific laws. In the international community, most countries outline the citizen's basic rights and free-

Source: Yi Ding, "Opposing Interference in Other Countries' Internal Affairs through Human Rights," *Beijing Review*, 32 (Nov. 6, 1989), pp. 14–16. Reprinted by permission.

doms through internal legislation, especially through their constitutions or related documents. These internal laws are the legal basis for the enjoyment and realization of human rights. Without these specific laws, the individual's rights and freedoms cannot be said to exist and individuals cannot ask for guarantees of their rights and freedoms.

Different concepts of human rights are evident in the way various countries draft their laws indeed. These laws are unique to each country and sometimes contradict the legislation of another nation.

According to the Western view, the right of property is an important component of human rights. For example, the idea that private property is sacred and inviolable appears in similar form in the constitutions of the United States, France, Japan and the Netherlands. Property rights—as one aspect of human rights—are essential to maintain the capitalist system.

This principle is quite different from those of countries that pursue a socialist policy of public ownership. For example, in the constitutions of China, the Soviet Union and Romania, the system of public and collective ownership is stressed. Public property is sacred and inviolable, while private property is protected according to the laws.

Given these differences in human rights legislation, where is the legal justification for saying there are no national boundaries for human rights?

Third, international documents relating to human rights do not supersede the laws of any country. Human rights documents adopted by the United Nations, such as the Universal Declaration of Human Rights, International Covenant on Civil and Political Rights and International Covenant on Economic, Social and Cultural Rights, have played a great role in promoting and encouraging respect for human rights and for fundamental freedoms. However, they have failed to create specific and common laws about human rights. The reasons are:

1. Sovereign countries played a leading role in drawing up these international documents. Without their involvement and agreement, these documents would not exist.

2. International documents about human rights only state some general principles. The power of explaining and practising these principles is in the hands of sovereign countries. In fact, each country practises these principles according to its unique situation. For example, British Chancellor Lord Denning said that the International Covenant on Civil and Political Rights "is so wide as to be incapable of practical application. So it is much better for us to stick to our own statutes and principles and only look to the convention in case of doubt."

3. International declarations on human rights must be implemented through the legislative, judicial and administrative measures of each signatory. For example, the International Covenant on Civil and Political Rights stipulates that each signatory is permitted "to adopt such legislative or other measures as may be necessary to give effect to the rights recognized in the present Covenant."

The fact that many countries have reservations about international conventions on human rights also proves there is no such thing as rights that completely transcend national boundaries and legal limits. As a matter of fact, not a single international convention or agreement passed by the United Nations has been accepted without reservation by member states.

In the case of the two most important international documents on human rights—the International Covenant on Civil and Political Rights and the International Covenant on Economic, Social and Cultural Rights—more than 30 countries have reservations about the former and more than 20 countries about the latter.

The United States' attitude towards these international covenants is typical. In a report advising the U.S. government not to approve some covenants on human rights, the American Bar Association pointed out that human rights are within domestic jurisdiction and that ratification would open the door to intervention by the United Nations in the field of human rights. In considering these two covenants, the U.S. Congress recommended a reservation, understanding or declaration wherever a provision is in conflict with United States law. To date the U.S. Congress still hasn't ratified the covenants.

PRETEXT FOR MEDDLING IN OTHER COUNTRIES' INTERNAL AFFAIRS

The theory that human rights know no national boundary is not only theoretically wrong, legally groundless but also very harmful politically and practically. The preachers of this theory say that they are merely concerned about human rights and do not intend to interfere in other countries' internal affairs. This runs counter to the facts. A certain country has used its embassy to provide shelter for a criminal wanted by the host country, intervening in the host's normal judicial activities; allowed wanted criminals to conduct activities aimed at subverting another government; discussed the internal affairs of another country in its own Congress and imposed economic sanctions on that country just because they share different values; and even set as a precondition for improving bilateral relations the lifting of martial law. Does this represent gross interference in another country's internal affairs?

On December 9, 1981, U.N. Resolution 36/103 adopted a Declaration on the Inadmissibility of Intervention and Interference in the Internal Affairs of States. The declaration stated, "No State or group of States has the right to intervene or interfere in any form or for any reason whatsoever in the internal and external affairs of other States." It further added, "The duty of a State (is) to refrain from the exploitation and the distortion of human rights issues as a means of interference in the internal affairs of States, of exerting pressure on other States or creating distrust and disorder within and among States or groups of States."

Though favourable to peace and development, the world situation today is still complicated. Any attempt to impose one's values, political beliefs and social systems on others will lead only to friction and

tension in international relations. Only the Five Principles of Peaceful Coexistence, including the principle of non-interference in each other's internal affairs, provide a healthy guide for international relations.

The Chinese government has repeatedly stated that China will continue its independent foreign policy of peace and the policy of reform and openness. We believe that on the basis of the Five Principles of Peaceful Coexistence, the friendly and cooperative ties between China and other countries will be further strengthened and developed.

QUESTIONS FOR DISCUSSION

1. What are human rights?
2. What criteria should be used in evaluating the best means to promote human rights in foreign countries?
3. Is the promotion of human rights by a Western country against a third world country nothing more than a form of cultural imperialism? What are the reasons for your answer?
4. What effect does the promotion of human rights by a country from abroad have on the actual human rights policies of a country that is a serious violator of those rights?
5. What is the relationship between the promotion of human rights and security interests?

SUGGESTED READINGS

Best, Geoffrey. "Whatever Happened to Human Rights?" *Review of International Studies* (Cambridge, England), **16** (Jan. 1990), pp. 3–18.

Forsythe, David P. *Human Rights and World Politics*, 2nd ed. Lincoln, Nebr.: University of Nebraska Press, 1989.

Hehir, J. Bryan. "Morality and Foreign Policy: A Sketch of the Issues." *America*, **156** (Jan. 31, 1987), pp. 64–68.

"Human Rights around the World." *Annals of the American Academy of Political and Social Science*, **506** (Nov. 1989), entire issue.

Kristol, Irving. "Human Rights: The Hidden Agenda." *National Interest*, no. 6 (Winter 1986–87), pp. 1–11.

Novak, Michael. *Human Rights and the New Realism:*

Strategic Thinking in a New Age. New York: Freedom House, 1986.

Renstein, Alison Dundes. "The Unanswered Challenge of Relativism and the Consequences for Human Rights." *Human Rights Quarterly*, **7** (Nov. 1985), pp. 514–540.

Roberts, Brad. "Human Rights and International Security." *Washington Quarterly*, **13** (Spring 1990), pp. 65–75.

Vincent, R. J. (ed.) *Foreign Policy and Human Rights.* Cambridge, England: Cambridge Univ. Press, 1986.

———. *Human Rights and International Relations.* Cambridge, England: Cambridge Univ. Press, 1986.

7 Is Communism a Dead Ideology?

YES

Henry Grunwald

Sorry, Comrades—You're in History's Dustbin Now

NO

Zhang Zhen

Marxism-Leninism Is the Banner of Our Times

Sorry, Comrades—You're In History's Dustbin Now

Henry Grunwald

Henry Luce, the founder of the *Time* and *Life* publishing concern and the man who before World War II called this the "American Century," made a speech in the 1950s in which he said that America must win the cold war. I was present at the speech and I thought the goal was unrealistic. But in a sense, America and its allies have now indeed won the cold war.

We are witnessing the dismal failure of Marxism as an economic, political and social system. That is the true meaning of the phenomenon known as Gorbachev. The failure of Marxism has not happened suddenly; we cannot point to a single date or a single event as marking the change. All we can say is this: Throughout this century, Marxism was a major force in the world, desperately fought against and fought for; today it is simply no longer that important.

This is a major change in the balance of power of ideas. As the world's leading democratic, anti-communist country, America is entitled to take some satisfaction from this, and to expect some benefits. But those benefits will not come automatically, unless we can substitute for a failed Marxism the continuing success and expanding relevance of our own system.

What is the evidence for the failure of Marxism? First of all, the Soviet Union. Seventy years after the Russian Revolution and after innumerable reform programs and several rules of very different styles, the Soviet Union remains an underdeveloped country that cannot feed its own people.

The facts and figures to illustrate this are endless. An estimated one out of three Russian families lives near or below the poverty line. The amount of time Soviet citizens spend in queues equals the yearly labor of 35 million people working a 40-hour week. The Soviet Union ranks 50th in infant mortality, just behind Barbados. In the life expectancy of women, it ranks 38th, of men 51st. And so forth. All this shows how wrong we are in casually talking about the "two super-powers." Except for its military capacity, the Soviet Union simply does not rate that label.

Gorbachev claims he can repair and revitalize Marxism. He blames "deformations" of Marxism for the disaster, blames bureaucracy, overcentralized management, corruption, the cult of personality, Stalin, Brezhnev. But the phenomena and individuals now being condemned were themselves the product—I would say the inevitable product—of Marxism and its mistaken view of man.

The doctrine that sought to explain all of history through economic forces did not understand that economics is at bottom psychology: a matter of what motivates people. Marxism tried to organize industrial society by combining the social principle of an egalitarian commune and the command principle of an army—two principles that are contradictory and incompatible. The egalitarian proved a sham and the command system ineffective.

Alexander Yakovlev, a Politburo member who is reputed to be Gorbachev's close ideological ally, has explained that *perestroika* must "instill a sense of ownership. . . . If he has a stake in something, a person will move moountains; if he does not, he will be indifferent. . . . The market [is] a natural self-regulating mechanism for uncovering existing needs and meeting them."

Vadim Medvedev, the new chief ideologue in the Politburo, spoke of a likely convergence of capitalism and socialism, extolled free enterprise and favored the expression of opinions divergent from the party (although he still insisted on party supremacy).

But as they try to introduce market forces and incentives, Gorbachev's men are finding that these are not gadgets that can be bolted onto a flawed

---

Source: Henry Grunwald, "Sorry, Comrades—You're in History's Dustbin Now," *Washington Post,* Nov. 27, 1988, pp. D1, D2. Reprinted by permission.

machine to make it run better. They are incompatible with the machine—the system. The market is not merely an economic arrangement: It is a philosophy. Nor is pricing just an economic system: It is a social force. And it is no accident that Gorbachev has postponed price reform, although it is the essential reform on which all others depend.

The reformers often argue that it is not necessary or possible to import western-style capitalism or democracy intact. That may be true, and one can construct all kinds of intermediate systems— in theory. The Chinese, who have undertaken far more radical reforms than Gorbachev so far, seem bent on removing the party and the government from economic management and making private enterprise coexist with a communist political system. They may have a greater talent than the Soviets for reconciling opposites. But despite their spectacular success in agriculture, it is doubtful that they can succeed in industry and the economy as a whole. In fact they have recently applied the brakes.

Possibly Gorbachev can build a mixed system and improve the Soviet economy to a degree, given persistence and patience—his persistence and the people's patience. He certainly seems to have consolidated his power as against the opposition. But it seems virtually impossible for him to do what he says he wants: to turn the Soviet Union into a modern industrial society that can successfully compete in world markets.

The notion that the West should ''help'' him is somewhat naive. We should certainly not seek to obstruct him; we have an important stake in his success. But we must be realistic. Economic cooperation should depend not only on improvement in human rights but on Soviet progress in economic reform. Credit should be extended at commercial rates, for sensible projects and with a reasonable prospect of repayment. Western bankers—and those western governments which offer credit guarantees—should draw on the lessons learned from the debt crisis in both the third world and in Eastern Europe.

It is increasingly clear that the circle cannot be squared, that an efficient economy is not compatible with Marxism and the party's monopoly of power. Democratic communism or pluralistic communism are contradictions in terms. The transformation required in the Soviet Union and other Marxist countries is deeper than anything yet projected by Gorbachev. What is needed is a perestroika of the mind: radical changes in the habits of thought and the system of value among populations which for decades have known only regulation, dependence and supposed security as opposed to initiative, risk-taking and individualism.

What are the consequences of all this in world affairs? To a large extent, the consequences have been obscured by Gorbachev. Such is his brilliance as a leader and public-relations man that he has come close to turning failure into a political advance, to turning retreat into a psychological offensive, to which the West often reacts uncertainly.

Soviet foreign policy is currently dominated by a single effort: to present the Soviet Union as a changed country, dedicated not only to greater efficiency but to democracy and more freedom. But we need to remember that *glasnost* is relatively easy; unlike economic and deep political reforms, it largely involves the removal of some restrictions and the right signals to the intellectual elite. When Gorbachev speaks of democracy and freedom, he still uses the words quite differently from the way we do; glasnost is still severely limited, still—as was the case with enlightened monarchs—a gift from the rulers rather than an irrevocable right of the people.

Despite Russia's new flexibility, the rivalry between the United States and the Soviet Union—and the larger rivalry between the free western societies and totalitarian societies—is not over. That is especially clear from the fairly obvious Soviet attempts to divide NATO and to denuclearize Europe. Indeed the failure of Marxism, which is also the failure of what used to be known as ''world revolution,'' and the failure of military action, as in Afghanistan, have prompted the Soviets to try to spread their influence in more conventional ways. A more benign, pragmatic and less ideologically driven Russia may actually present a greater challenge than the old, heavyhanded, crusading power which frightened people and often was its own worst enemy.

In the third world we should welcome the apparent Soviet recognition that it has been overextended and that heavy support for Marxist regimes and insurgencies is too costly for what the failing Russian economy can bear. We must work hard to hold the Soviets to their new realism, displayed in Angola and Afghanistan, and press them to apply it elsewhere, for instance in Central America.

Regardless of Soviet policies, in parts of the third world—in Latin America, for instance—Marxism still has a hold on people's imagination and remains highly troublesome. Where social change is badly needed, Marxism retains considerable appeal as a revolutionary tool, a way of gaining power and punishing the ruling elites.

But it is increasingly plain even in the third world that Marxism is simply not a realistic means to bring about development. Neither are the policies of non-Marxist regimes with their usual mixture of statism, central planning, uneconomic subsidies and protectionism. We in the West must try even harder to make this clear, and to offer alternatives. The alternatives must be built around democracy, which has made encouraging progress in Asia and Latin America, and around market economics. At the same time we must recognize that market solutions are extremely hard to apply in countries that lack the infrastructure, the education and the social values that the free market requires. The often frightening and harsh side effects of the market in such societies will have to be cushioned.

Finally, the failure of Marxism has important echoes in the advanced industrial countries. For decades, in Western Europe and parts of Asia, the dominant conflict was between communism and the free society. Today, the public debate has moved to the center; it is concerned with different forms and degrees of the free society. The American economist John Kenneth Galbraith said not long ago: "The so-called welfare revolution today is stuck in about the same difficulties as the Soviet revolution."

Democratic socialism has recognized the need for market forces, incentives, enterprise, decentralization, the lessening of bureaucracy. Socialist politicians increasingly speak of pragmatism. They are recognizing that if wealth is to be redistributed, wealth must first be created, and continuously. That is the task before us in a post-Marxist world.

We are not playing a zero-sum game. The failure of Marxism does not automatically assure our success. Our great challenge is to fill the void left by Marxism, and it can only be done by capitalism with a human face. We should not forget what gave rise to Marxism in the first place. It was not only a rebellion against the misery caused by the Industrial Revolution, but against the lack of spirituality and common humanity in early capitalism. The free market, efficiency, the creation of wealth—by themselves— will not satisfy people in the long run unless their nonmaterial yearning, their spiritual needs are also served. That cannot be done by governments and their bureaucracies, but must be accomplished by our churches, our community institutions, by the marshaling of all our spiritual resources. Unless we also succeed in this dimension, the failure of Marxism will not ultimately benefit our side.

Marxism-Leninism Is the Banner of Our Times

Zhang Zhen

I

At the First Session of the First National People's Congress of the People's Republic of China 35 years ago, Mao Zedong solemnly declared in his opening address, "The force at the core leading our cause forward is the Chinese Communist Party and the theoretical basis guiding our thinking is Marxism-Leninism." This aphoristic language is not only the summation of China's experience gained in several decades of revolution but is also the fundamental principle guiding the nation's work.

In recent years, however, because of the unrestrained spread of bourgeois liberal trend of thought, Marxism-Leninism has been so seriously denounced and attacked that some people have questioned whether it can continue to be the theoretical basis guiding our thinking. Therefore, to refute the fallacies mouthed by exponents of bourgeois liberalization on this fundamental issue and to clarify what is right and wrong theoretically is an important task confronting us.

The common argument used by those favouring bourgeois liberalization to negate Marxism-Leninism is none other than "outdated theory." Taking advantage of changes in human history of the past decades they arbitrarily assert, "Marxism-Leninism belongs to a certain past, cultural period. Like clothes showing signs of wear, it should be changed."

Is that how things stand? No.

It is known to all that Marxism-Leninism is the revolutionary theory born in the struggle between the international working class and the international bourgeoisie in the 19th century.

After summing up the practical experience of the struggle for liberation of the international working class and critically adopting the best ideology of their time, Marx and Engels founded the materialist conception of history, an act of epoch-making significance in the history of science. Where bourgeois scholars could only see the motives of the people, Marx and Engels perceived the historical causes which lay hidden behind the motives; where bourgeois scholars could only perceive isolated historical events, Marx and Engels could see the law of history running through these historical events.

With materialist conception of history as the weapon, Marx and Engels dissected the capitalist society and discovered the capitalists' secret of exploiting the workers which lay hidden in the creation of the surplus value. As a special commodity, the labour force carries in itself the unique property of being a source of value. After the "equal" exchange of commodities, in the process of the use of labour, labour force creates the value of its own, it also creates a surplus sum which exceeds its own value. The increment of the value was called by Marx and Engels surplus value. The discovery of surplus value was a revolution in the political economy and illuminated a field in which classical economists had long been groping in the dark. The uncompromising contradiction between the bourgeoisie and working class was laid bare all at once.

Because of the founding of materialist conception of history and the theory of the surplus value, socialism was transformed from a utopian theory into a scientific one. As Lenin confirmed, Marx's conclusion that the capitalist society will inevitably be changed into the socialist society, was made solely on the basis of the law governing economic movement in modern society. Since the capitalist class and the working class are two diametrically opposed classes with regard to their fundamental interests, the conflicts originate in capitalism's private ownership

Source: Zhang Zhen, "Marxism-Leninism Is the Banner of Our Times, *Beijing Review* 32, (November 27, 1989), pp. 17–19; (December 4, 1989), pp. 27–28; and (Dec. 11, 1989), pp. 27–29. Reprinted with permission.

and its system of wage labour. Since this economic system has seriously hampered the growth of the productive forces, capitalism would itself prepare the material conditions and class forces necessary for the new social revolution; the new social revolution in which the "expropriators will be expropriated" will be unavoidable.

It is thus clear that Marxism brought to light the general trend and the general law of the great epoch that mankind would move from capitalism to socialism and then, to communism and, so long as the great epoch is in process, Marxism will forever be the theoretical banner for the development of this epoch. Because its fundamental interests keep in step with the general trend and the general law of the development of the epoch, the proletariat has become the leading class in the epoch. The historical mission incumbent upon it is to complete the great task of abolishing capitalism and building socialism and communism. Marxism, on its part, is the theoretical expression of the proletariat's fundamental interests and is the guiding theory of the great historical mission of the proletariat. So long as the proletariat exists and its epochal task has not been completed, the proletariat will forever hold high the banner of Marxism to forge ahead courageously.

Already, Marxism has a 100-year history. During this time, and especially after World War II, great changes have taken place throughout the world and many new situations and problems have developed. There have been the relative stability and prosperity of capitalism and the errors and twists and turns in the development of socialism. These changes, however, have not altered the fundamental contradiction, essential content and the developmental trend of the great epoch, but are, instead, minor happenings.

The relative stability of the fundamental contradiction, essential content and developmental trend of the great epoch in the transition from capitalism to socialism and communism is the historical basis for our adherence to the basic theory of Marxism. Constant changes in the relatively stable world situation are the historical requirement for the development of Marxism. The vitality of Marxism lies in the fact that it develops along with the advance of practice, and this is the inherent basis on which Marxism is the banner of the epoch.

Mao Zedong made an incisive exposition when speaking on the "process of all things." He said,

> The fundamental contradiction in the process of development of a thing and the essence of the process determined by this fundamental contradiction will not disappear until the process is completed; but in a lengthy process, the conditions usually differ at each stage. The reason is that, although the nature of the fundamental contradiction in the process of development of a thing and the essence of the process remain unchanged, the fundamental contradiction becomes more and more intensified as it passes from one stage to another in the lengthy process. In addition, among the numerous major and minor contradictions which are determined or influenced by the fundamental contradiction, some become intensified, some are temporarily or partially resolved or mitigated, and some new ones emerge; hence the process is marked by stages. (*On Contradiction*)

The mistake made by advocates of the "outdatedness" theory lies in their ignorance of the Marxist theory on the process of development of things.

In the eyes of Marxists and Leninists, the relative prosperity which has emerged in the capitalist countries in the last decades has been shaped by certain historical conditions and has something to do with the various reform measures pursued by capitalist countries after World War II, with the breakthrough in the development of science and technology and with their exploitation of third world countries. It has not changed the essence of capitalism and abolished the contradictions inherent in capitalism. Capitalism is still capitalism and the relationship between the capitalists and workers is still one of the exploiting and the exploited classes. Although, along with the changes of the industrial structure, the ranks of the working class have changed and the number of the "white-collar" workers is still on the increase, both the "white-collar" and "blue-collar" workers are still exploited by capitalists. Surplus value is still the excess value of the labour force itself, created by the labour of all the workers, ''white-collar'' workers included. Although workers' wages have increased by a big margin, it shows only that, along with the development of the capitalist society, the reproduction conditions and expenses of the labour force have also changed. In no way does it indicate that the exploitative relationship has changed.

The relative prosperity of capitalism involves profound social contradictions. The capitalist society has always been plagued with inextricable economic stagflation, the sluggish growth of labour productivity, the serious unemployment, the endless strikes, the increasing number of criminal cases and plots hatched by the international monopoly capitalists against each other. No one, including the many representatives of the capitalist class can deny this fact. Currently, although no revolutionary situation exists in capitalist countries, what merits our attention is that workers' parties in some developed countries are exploring new paths to emancipation in accordance with the new situation. They live in a developed capitalist society, but they don't believe that capitalism has entered a stage without class conflicts. Conversely, they still view capitalist society as a society full of contradictions and evils, one which should undergo revolutionary reform in accordance with the direction charted by Marxism-Leninism.

Marxists and Leninists do not view the twists and turns, errors and setbacks and the consequential reforms emerging in socialist practice as a proof of Marxism-Leninism being ''outdated.'' On the contrary, it proves that Marxism-Leninism is the inviolable, objective truth. Let's leave aside the fact for the moment that, in history, one social formation replacing another must undergo prolonged, tortuous and repeated struggle, and that the substitution of socialism for capitalism is the most profound social change in human history. As far as setbacks and errors are concerned, they did not result from our adherence to but, instead, from our violation of certain scientific tenets of Marxism-Leninism. When socialist states adopted the model of a certain country in their economic construction and thus formed

an ossified economic structure, it was not because they adhered to but instead ran counter to the principle that a country must be based on its specific features in taking the socialist road, an idea repeatedly emphasized by Marx, Engels and Lenin. When leaders in some socialist countries formerly practised the cult of personality, which harmed the socialist democracy and the legal system, it was not because they upheld but instead violated the historical materialism of Marxism-Leninism on mutual relations between leaders, political parties, classes and the masses. In the past, impatient for success, we made blind and premature advances and practised the ''great leap forward'' in our socialist construction. It was not because we adhered to but rather went against Marxist-Leninist theory of seeking truth from facts and respecting the objective law.

Currently, many socialist countries are carrying out reforms on the basis of summing up their experience and lessons. Reforms are a means of self-perfection and self-development of the socialist system under the guidance of Marxism-Leninism. The great historic turn of a decade ago in China was attained under the guidance of the principle of Marxism-Leninism and Mao Zedong Thought on seeking truth from facts. The great achievements made in China's construction, reform and opening up in the past decade are great victories for Marxism-Leninism and Mao Zedong Thought. The facts fully prove that Marxism-Leninism is the victorious banner guiding our advance.

All in all, the world today is developing along the general direction charted by Marxism-Leninism. It remains the banner of our time; this is the common understanding of Marxists and Leninists the world over, as well as the conclusion of some serious Western scholars. A noted U.S. scholar said in 1980 that Marx's works could still have such an impact after one century. Clearly, he pointed out, it is because of Marx's method of social analysis which made him unique in social theory. Those who explore the motivation of social development and those who are engaged in social critical studies must learn from Marx.

II

Some people who stick to their bourgeois liberalization stand have also advanced the theory that Marxism-Leninism is harmful. They say that Marxism-Leninism is not suitable to China's national conditions and is the source for China's prolonged backwardness.

This is but an abuse of truth and distortion of history. China's history over the past 100 years has proved that reactionary theory completely wrong.

In China's modern history, countless revolutionary people witnessed the misery of their country and sought a way to save it and the Chinese people from outside China. But what was the result?

Hong Xiuquan, leader of a peasant uprising in the mid-19th century, learned from Western Christianity and, combining it with the demands of Chinese peasants, founded the Society for Worshipping God. He dreamed of a Heavenly Kingdom of Peace where everybody shared everything. However, his rebellion, though reaching some momentous heights, failed in the end. The conclusion was that neither Western Christianity nor egalitarianism could save China.

The "Hundred Days" reformists in 1898 imported the theory of evolution from the West and rested their hope of introducing a new set of laws for China on a wise emperor. They even dreamed of relying on several imperialist countries to help promote their reform programme. However, the movement was crushed in its early stages by feudal diehards and imperialists. History has concluded that neither vulgar evolutionism nor a "wise emperor" nor imperialist "assistance" could save China.

Bourgeois revolutionaries led by Sun Yat-sen sought another road of saving China by advancing their own democratic doctrine and revolutionary goals and establishing their own revolutionary organization. They borrowed the Western bourgeois theory of "natural human rights" and formulated a plan for building a bourgeois republic. They organized revolutionary armies, determined to eliminate feudalism, founded a republic and tried to distribute all the land equally. However, several decades of hard struggle and sacrifices still failed to rescue China. The 1911 armed uprising ended feudal ruling that had lasted for more than 2,000 years and implanted the idea of democracy and republic in the people, but China was still reduced to a semi-feudal, semi-colonial society. History again proved that neither the "natural human rights" theory nor the bourgeois republic formula could deliver China.

Then how could China find a way out?

"The salvoes of the October Revolution brought us Marxism-Leninism," said the late Chairman Mao Zedong. Henceforce, the Chinese revolution presented a new set of characters.

It was the introduction of Marxism-Leninism to China and the subsequent integration of the theory and the workers' movement that gave birth to the Communist Party of China. Thus the Chinese people's revolutionary struggle had the leadership of an advanced political party, strictly organized, guided by a scientific theory and fighting for the interests of the working-class and all the people of China.

It was the introduction of Marxism-Leninism that helped the Chinese people develop a scientific world outlook and methodology and their correct approach towards the destiny of China. With Marxism-Leninism, the Party analysed China's historical situation at that time, and class relationships in China and the international context. Accordingly, it formulated a programme for the democratic revolution against imperialism and feudalism, and answered many basic questions concerning the task, targets, incentives, nature, development phase and the future of the Chinese revolution. Therefore the Party formed an extensive united front including the working-class, peasantry, urban petty bourgeoisie and national bourgeoisie, realizing a powerful political unity that had never before been witnessed in China.

It was only after Marxism-Leninism was introduced to China that the Chinese people came to understand that both the criticism by weapons and the weapon of criticism were indispensable to the success of the Chinese revolution. It was utterly necessary for the Party to organize an innovative type of army that was closely linked to the people like blood and flesh. Without it, there would be no liberation of the Chinese people or China's independence. The Chinese revolution should be won through prolonged armed struggle, which is both the characteristic and the strong point of the Chinese revolution. There would be no way out otherwise.

After Marxism-Leninism spread throughout China, the revolutionary struggle of the Chinese people won one victory after another. The Chinese people finally overthrew imperialism, feudalism and bureaucractic capitalism and established the People's Republic of China in 1949 in which the people were masters, ending more than 100 years of misery. China's economy and culture have greatly developed from extremely backward beginnings and through very difficult conditions.

The Chinese nation now stands among world nations. China has the right to speak on the world arena and the Chinese people feel proud and stand tall. Millions of descendants of the Yan Di and Huang Di (the Yellow Emperor), who are living abroad, feel great pride at being Chinese.

History has shown that Marxism has not harmed China, but has saved it.

The great historical role of Marxism-Leninism in China is embodied in Mao Zedong Thought. Mao Zedong Thought is the product of the combination of the general principles of Marxism-Leninism and the specific Chinese revolutionary practice. The fundamental principle of Marxism-Leninism is the integration of practice and theory. Out of all the schools of thought, only Marxism-Leninism can save China. Of all the schools of Marxism, after it was introduced to China, only Mao Zedong Thought—Marxism-Leninism combined with Chinese conditions—can save China.

Old China was a semi-colonial and semi-feudal country in the East. As China carried out its revolution, it faced many special and complicated issues. All these issues could not be resolved by reciting the general principles of Marxism-Leninism and copying the experiences of foreign countries. In the history of the Chinese revolution led by the Chinese Communist Party, there were times when Marxism-Leninism became dogma and the resolutions of the Communist International and the Soviet experience

were sacrosanct, damaging the cause of the Chinese revolution.

Mao Zedong firmly dismissed the way of dogmatism. Using conditions in China as a starting point, he studied the characteristics and law of the Chinese revolution. He enriched and developed Marxism-Leninism, being embodied in the programme and line he formulated for democratic revolution, the policies and tactics of the People's Army, and the principle guiding Party building, ideological and political and cultural work, socialist transformation and construction. These constituted the basic points of Mao Zedong Thought. It is based on seeking truth from facts, relying on the masses, independence, hard struggle and plain living, diligence, self-reliance and serving the people wholeheartedly.

Running through all these are the stand, viewpoints and method of Marxism-Leninism; they fully embody the features of Marxist-Leninist practice, class struggle and revolution. At the same time, they are Marxism-Leninism with Chinese characteristics.

True, Mao Zedong committed serious mistakes in his later years, but this cannot be an excuse to negate Mao Zedong Thought. These mistakes were not the result of following Mao Zedong Thought. On the contrary, they went against Mao Zedong Thought. People should distinguish the mistakes of his later years from Mao Zedong Thought, which has been jointly created by the old proletarian revolutionaries represented by Mao Zedong and all the comrades of the Party, based on their revolutionary experience.

Those who stubbornly adhere to bourgeois liberalization have denied Mao Zedong Thought, not because they are entirely ignorant, but because in the final analysis, they have opposed the Chinese people, revolution and history. Their stand is mistaken, so they have come to completely different conclusions.

III

Those advocating bourgeois liberalization have put forward the idea that the so-called "pluralism" is the guiding ideology and asserted that Marxism-Leninism is only one of many schools of thought; it should not and cannot, they assert, become the guiding ideology by simply placing itself above other schools of thought. If Marxism-Leninism must treat other sciences with an equal attitude, respect the independent developmental laws of each science, constantly absorb theoretical nourishment from the development of other sciences to enrich and develop itself, and refrain from playing the part of the all-inclusive "science of the sciences," then classical writers of Marxism-Leninism would be in agreement for they have always held this view. The Communist Party of China, as well, has always maintained such a stance. That is not where the divergence with the preachers of "pluralism" lies. The point of divergence lies, instead, in the question whether Marxism-Leninism will be used as the fundamental ideology guiding our work.

Those who propagate that "pluralism" should be the guiding ideology have ignored the basic common sense that in a society where classes exist, the ruling ideology of any country will naturally be the thought of the ruling class. In countries where slavery existed, the ruling ideology was the thought of the slave-owner class. In feudal countries, the ruling ideology was the thought of the feudal land-owning class. In capitalist countries, the ruling ideology is the thought of the bourgeoisie. In socialist countries, the ruling thought is naturally the thought of the proletariat, that is, of Marxism-Leninism. The reason for this is clear to all. The class holding the dominant position in the socio-economic structure will naturally set up an ideology to protect its economic base. In other words, different ruling thoughts in different countries are the reflection and extension of the economic base of the country into the ideological realm. Marx and Engels pointed out in the *Manifesto of the Communist Party*: "The ruling ideas of each age have ever been the ideas of its ruling class."

The bourgeoisie has always hypocritically concealed the class character of the ruling idea and depicted capitalist society as a paradise in which any ideology can freely develop. Actually, the capitalist society has its clear guiding ideology. This ideology is the social and political theory of the bourgeoisie which has gradually taken shape along with the growth of the capitalist commodity economy and which has been fully implemented in the constitutions and laws of the capitalist countries. The bourgeoisie has always adopted an attitude of rejection of any ideology that may endanger the capitalist domination. When the ideology of scientific communism came into being, the bourgeoisie regarded it as a dreadful "spectre" and tried its best to destroy it. Early in the 20th century, the bourgeoisie took further steps to formulate a global strategy for dealing with the "communist pestilence" and vowed to "terminate the terrible threat enshrouding the world."

Thus, it can be seen that the "ideological freedom" of the bourgeoisie has its rigid demarcation line. Given such a situation, is it fair and equitable to require that socialist countries allow bourgeois ideology to have "an equal footing" with Marxism-Leninism and to permit every hue of Western ideologies to overflow society?

The guiding position of Marxism-Leninism, however, is determined not only by its class character but also by its fundamental nature. Like other sciences, Marxism-Leninism cannot dissociate itself from the concrete problems of the times. Its focus of attention is the general law of nature, of social and ideological development, the general trend and law of development of the times and the fundamental method by which the proletariat can fulfil its historical mission; it is concerned with a global, society, state, class and revolutionary outlook. Compared with other scientific research aspects, these matters are of a fundamental nature.

This trait mandates that Marxism-Leninism should be of universal guiding significance. In man's multiple social and economic structures, a world outlook and methodology cover all of their aspects. There is no scientific research or any other kind of work that is not under the guidance of world outlook and methodology. The point is whether it is the scientific world outlook and methodology or non-scientific ones that give guidance.

In the field of social research, apart from world outlook and methodology, the outlook of the society, the state, class and revolution also penetrates all structural aspects and so every step in scientific research and in other kinds of work should be subject to the fundamental viewpoints mentioned above. The question, again, is whether it is controlled by the scientific viewpoint or by the non-scientific one. In research of natural sciences, for example, so long as the researcher is a member of the class society, his research work will be affected by the outlook of the society, the state, class and revolution. Marxism-Leninism, on the other hand, assimilated and reformed all useful aspects of mankind's ideological and cultural development of the past several thousand years, founded the world outlook and methodology of dialectical materialism (the scientific outlook of the society, the state, class and revolution), and tested and verified, over a long period of time, the truth of such methods in social practice.

Those who advocate "pluralism" do not really intend to practise pluralistic guidance. Their real aim is to undermine our theoretical base and let the bourgeois ideology occupy the leading position. To attain their goal, they have adopted the trick of "hanging up a sheep's head and selling dog meat," flaunting the banner of "developing Marxism-Leninism" in order to negate it. Fang Lizhi, one representative of bourgeois liberalization, once said, "Leaders have said that Marxism should be developed, and I have made use of this phrase." He also asserted, "The form can be retained, but the content should be changed. Protestants opposed Catholicism and carried out religious reform. However, they still used the same Bible. We can follow suit in China and hang up a sheep's head and sell dog meat."

Marxism-Leninism does need to be developed. This is, first of all, required in its practice. The theory came into existence by its being put into practice and, likewise, is developed by its ongoing practice. Its vitality lies in its constant analysis and study of new situations and new problems which arise in practice, the ability to enrich and develop itself by the formulation of new theory as well as its ability to give guidance to its ongoing practice. Second, this is the essential developmental demand. An important mark that distinguishes Marxism-Leninism from other ideological systems is the former's disavowal of an ultimate truth for all time; and it is, in nature,

revolutionary and critical. Marx, Engels and Lenin criticized those thinkers who frequently regarded their theories as the "ultimate truth." Lenin openly declared that if socialists were truly unwilling to lag behind the real life, they had to push science forward in all aspects. Third, the development of Marxism-Leninism requires the defence of Marxism-Leninism. It is currently being defamed and attacked, a situation to which no Marxist should remain indifferent. For this defence, however, we must continue its development. If we rigidly adhere to every sentence and word of Marxism and reject the theory's practical development, we will suffocate its vitality and create an ossified dogma. This, in itself, will provide an excuse for those who attack it. Only by developing Marxism-Leninism, enriching this scientific system with new theories and thus enabling it to have a clear and practical guiding significance, can we effectively answer those who defame and attack it on the pretext that the situation has changed.

However, developing Marxism-Leninism does not mean an excuse for discarding Marxism-Leninism; it means, on the contrary, a more strict adherence to its guiding role. While speaking of its development, we also mean adherence to it for without adhering to it, its development will be out of the question. Likewise, without its development, adherence will lose its real sense. Therein exists the conflict between the two views on development. Proceeding from reality, Marxists respect the dialectical law of cognition and regard the truth as a process; they not only oppose the absolutes of man's cognition of a certain period, but also oppose the view that the cognition of mankind's truth is a thing passing in a flash. That is to say, adherence and development are integrated in a dialectical way and unified on a practical basis.

The opposite view of development, proceeding from a subjective supposition, is that its representatives negate the linked chain of mankind's cognition and deny the fact that truth is itself a process. They substitute relativism for dialectics and fall into a quagmire by negating the objective truth. With regard to those who advocate bourgeois liberalization, as far as the source of their theory of knowledge is concerned, they treat Marxism-Leninism precisely with the developmental view based on relativism. Of course, to negate the guiding position of Marxism-Leninism in excuse of "developing Marxism-Leninism" is, first of all, not a problem of cognition, but of politics.

Advocating "substitution" in the name of "development" is a new form of struggle between us and the exponents of bourgeois liberalization. In recent years, they have peddled a great deal of mistaken ideas to the youth and to society as a whole by the appeal of such channels as the "multi-party system" in politics, "private ownership" in the economy and the "theory of pluralism" in guiding ideology. To rebut such ideas, we must sum up the law of class struggle which takes special forms during the socialist period, enhance our ability to discern bourgeois liberalization and raise our level of struggle.

To sum up, Marxism-Leninism is the theoretical basis guiding our thinking. This is our firm and unshakable principle. The "outdatedness theory," the "theory of harmfulness" and the "theory of pluralism" spread by those who advocate bourgeois liberalization are aimed at demolishing this theoretical base. In order to thoroughly foil their plot to undermine socialism, we must carry out the study, publicity and research into the basic theories of Marxism-Leninism among the cadres and young people in a down-to-earth manner. Only by comparison can one distinguish. Truth also needs to be compared. Only if we study with a practical eye the works of Marx, Engels and Lenin while at the same time grasping their profound meaning, can we clearly perceive the insignificance of some currently fashionable "theories" of the West.

QUESTIONS FOR DISCUSSION

1. Is communism a dead ideology, or will it come back into vogue? What are the reasons for your answer?
2. What will be the dominant political ideologies in the next decade? What are the reasons for your answer?
3. What relevance did Marxist-Leninist theory have on the foreign policy behavior of communist states?
4. What were the factors that contributed to the decline of communism?
5. What relevance does Marxism-Leninism have to the study of world politics?

SUGGESTED READINGS

Brzezinski, Zbigniew. *The Grand Failure: The Birth and Death of Communism in the Twentieth Century.* New York: Charles Scribner's Sons, 1989.

Crozier, Brian. "The Enduring Soviet Global Threat." *Global Affairs*, 5 (Summer/Fall 1990), pp. 1–18.

Etzioni-Halevy, Eva. "How Western Marxism Is Attempting to Survive the Collapse of Communism in Eastern Europe." *Society*, 28 (Nov./Dec. 1990), pp. 85–87.

Fox, Robin. "Marxism's Obit Is Premature." *Nation*, 250 (May 14, 1990), pp. 664, 666.

Gueye, Semou Pathe. "The 'Crisis of Marxism': Myth and Reality." *World Marxist Review*, 32 (Feb. 1989), pp. 60–64.

Hamerow, Theodore S. *From the Finland Station: The Graying of the Revolution in the Twentieth Century.* New York: Basic Books, 1990.

Kinsley, Michael. "Who Killed Communism?" *New Republic*, 201 (Dec. 4, 1989), p. 4.

Selbourne, David. "Marx Is Not Quite Dead." *World Press Review*, 36 (Oct. 1989), pp. 20, 23.

Sweezy, Paul M. "Is This Then the End of Socialism?" *Nation*, 250 (Feb. 26, 1990), pp. 257, 276, 278.

Vilas, Carlos M. "Is Socialism Still an Alternative for the Third World?" *Monthly Review*, 42 (July/Aug. 1990), pp. 93–109.

8   Is the Realist Model an Accurate Description of World Politics?

YES

Hans J. Morgenthau and Kenneth W. Thompson

A Realist Theory of International Politics

NO

Stanley Kober

Idealpolitik

A Realist Theory of International Politics

Hans J. Morgenthau and Kenneth W. Thompson

This book purports to present a theory of international politics. The test by which such a theory must be judged is not *a priori* and abstract but empirical and pragmatic. The theory, in other words, must be judged not by some preconceived abstract principle or concept unrelated to reality, but by its purpose: to bring order and meaning to a mass of phenomena which without it would remain disconnected and unintelligible. It must meet a dual test, an empirical and a logical one: Do the facts as they actually are lend themselves to the interpretation the theory has put upon them, and do the conclusions at which the theory arrives follow with logical necessity from its premises? In short, is the theory consistent with the facts and within itself?

The issue this theory raises concerns the nature of all politics. The history of modern political thought is the story of a contest between two schools that differ fundamentally in their conceptions of the nature of man, society, and politics. One believes that a rational and moral political order, derived from universally valid abstract principles, can be achieved here and now. It assumes the essential goodness and infinite malleability of human nature, and blames the failure of the social order to measure up to the rational standards on lack of knowledge and understanding, obsolescent social institutions, or the depravity of certain isolated individuals or groups. It trusts in education, reform, and the sporadic use of force to remedy these defects.

Source: Hans J. Morgenthau and Kenneth W. Thompson, *Politics among Nations: The Struggle for Power and Peace*, 6th ed. (New York: Knopf, 1985), pp. 3–14. Reprinted by permission of McGraw-Hill, Inc.

The other school believes that the world, imperfect as it is from the rational point of view, is the result of forces inherent in human nature. To improve the world one must work with those forces, not against them. This being inherently a world of opposing interests and of conflict among them, moral principles can never be fully realized, but must at best be approximated through the ever temporary balancing of interests and the ever precarious settlement of conflicts. This school, then, sees in a system of checks and balances a universal principle for all pluralist societies. It appeals to historic precedent rather than to abstract principles, and aims at the realization of the lesser evil rather than of the absolute good.

This theoretical concern with human nature as it actually is, and with the historic processes as they actually take place, has earned for the theory presented here the name of realism. What are the tenets of political realism? No systematic exposition of the philosophy of political realism can be attempted here; it will suffice to single out six fundamental principles, which have frequently been misunderstood.

SIX PRINCIPLES OF POLITICAL REALISM

1. *Political realism believes that politics, like society in general, is governed by objective laws that have their roots in human nature.*

In order to improve society it is first necessary to understand the laws by which society lives. The operation of these laws being impervious to our preferences, men will challenge them only at the risk of failure.

Realism, believing as it does in the objectivity of the laws of politics, must also believe in the possibility of developing a rational theory that reflects, however imperfectly and one-sidedly, these objective laws. It believes also, then, in the possibility of distinguishing in politics between truth and opinion—between what is true objectively and rationally, supported by evidence and illuminated by reason, and what is only a subjective judgment, divorced from the facts as they are and informed by prejudice and wishful thinking.

Human nature, in which the laws of politics have their roots, has not changed since the classical philosophies of China, India, and Greece endeavored to discover these laws. Hence, novelty is not necessarily a virtue in political theory, nor is old age a defect. The fact that a theory of politics, if there be such a theory, has never been heard of before tends to create a presumption against, rather than in favor of, its soundness. Conversely, the fact that a theory of politics was developed hundreds or even thousands of years ago—as was the theory of the balance of power—does not create a presumption that it must be outmoded and obsolete. A theory of politics must be subjected to the dual test of reason and experience. To dismiss such a theory because it had its flowering in centuries past is to present not a rational argument but a modernistic prejudice that takes for granted the superiority of the present over the past. To dispose of the revival of such a theory as a ''fashion'' or ''fad'' is tantamount to assuming that in matters political we can have opinions but no truths.

For realism, theory consists of ascertaining facts and giving them meaning through reason. It assumes that the character of a foreign policy can be ascertained only through the examination of the political acts performed and of the foreseeable consequences of these acts. Thus we can find out what statesmen have actually done, and from the foreseeable consequences of their acts we can surmise what their objectives might have been.

Yet examination of the facts is not enough. To give meaning to the factual raw material of foreign policy, we must approach political reality with a kind of rational outline, a map that suggests to us the possible meanings of foreign policy. In other words, we put ourselves in the position of a statesman who must meet a certain problem of foreign policy under certain circumstances, and we ask ourselves what the rational alternatives are from which a statesman may choose who must meet this problem under these circumstances (presuming always that he acts in a rational manner), and which of these rational alternatives this particular statesman, acting under these circumstances, is likely to choose. It is the testing of this rational hypothesis against the actual facts and their consequences that gives theoretical meaning to the facts of international politics.

2. *The main signpost that helps political realism to find its way through the landscape of international politics is the concept of interest defined in terms of power.*

This concept provides the link between reason trying to understand international politics and the facts to be understood. It sets politics as an autonomous sphere of action and understanding apart from other spheres, such as economics (understood in terms of interest defined as wealth), ethics, aesthetics, or religion. Without such a concept a theory of politics, international or domestic, would be altogether impossible, for without it we could not distinguish between political and nonpolitical facts, nor could we bring at least a measure of systemic order to the political sphere.

We assume that statesmen think and act in terms of interest defined as power, and the evidence of history bears that assumption out. That assumption allows us to retrace and anticipate, as it were, the steps a statesman—past, present, or future—has taken or will take on the political scene. We look over his shoulder when he writes his dispatches; we listen in on his conversation with other statesmen; we read and anticipate his very thoughts. Thinking in terms of interest defined as power, we think as he does, and as disinterested observers we understand his thoughts and actions perhaps better than he, the actor on the political scene, does himself.

The concept of interest defined as power imposes intellectual discipline upon the observer, infuses rational order into the subject matter of politics, and thus makes the theoretical understanding of politics possible. On the side of the actor, it provides for rational discipline in action and creates that astounding continuity in foreign policy which makes American, British, or Russian foreign policy appear as in intelligible, rational continuum, by and large consistent within itself, regardless of the different motives, preferences, and intellectual and moral qualities of successive statesmen. A realist theory of international politics, then, will guard against two popular fallacies: the concern with motives and the concern with ideological preferences.

To search for the clue to foreign policy exclusively in the motives of statesmen is both futile and deceptive. It is futile because motives are the most illusive of psychological data, distorted as they are, frequently beyond recognition, by the interests and emotions of actor and observer alike. Do we really know what our own motives are? And what do we know of the motives of others?

Yet even if we had access to the real motives of statesmen, that knowledge would help us little in understanding foreign policies, and might well lead us astray. It is true that the knowledge of the statesman's motives may give us one among many clues as to what the direction of his foreign policy might be. It cannot give us, however, the one clue by which to predict his foreign policies. History shows no exact and necessary correlation between the quality of motives and the quality of foreign policy. This is true in both moral and political terms.

We cannot conclude from the good intentions of a statesman that his foreign policies will be either morally praiseworthy or politically successful. Judging his motives, we can say that he will not intentionally pursue policies that are morally wrong, but we can say nothing about the probability of their success. If we want to know the moral and political qualities of his actions, we must know them, not his motives. How often have statesmen been motivated by the desire to improve the world, and ended by making it worse? And how often have they sought one goal, and ended by achieving something they neither expected nor desired?

Neville Chamberlain's politics of appeasement were, as far as we can judge, inspired by good motives; he was probably less motivated by considerations of personal power than were many other British prime ministers, and he sought to preserve peace and to assure the happiness of all concerned. Yet his policies helped to make the Second World War inevitable, and to bring untold miseries to millions of people. Sir Winston Churchill's motives, on the other hand, were much less universal in scope and much more narrowly directed toward personal and national power, yet the foreign policies that sprang from these inferior motives were certainly superior in moral and political quality to those pursued by his predecessor. Judged by his motives, Robespierre was one of the most virtuous men who ever lived. Yet it was the utopian radicalism of that very virtue that made him kill those less virtuous than himself, brought him to the scaffold, and destroyed the revolution of which he was a leader.

Good motives give assurance against deliberately bad policies; they do not guarantee the moral goodness and political success of the policies they inspire. What is important to know, if one wants to understand foreign policy, is not primarily the motives of a statesman, but his intellectual ability to comprehend the essentials of foreign policy, as well as his political ability to translate what he has comprehended into successful political action. It follows that while ethics in the abstract judges the moral qualities of motives, political theory must judge the political qualities of intellect, will, and action.

A realist theory of international politics will also avoid the other popular fallacy of equating the foreign policies of a statesman with his philosophic or political sympathies, and of deducing the former from the latter. Statesmen, especially under contemporary conditions, may well make a habit of presenting their foreign policies in terms of their philosophic and political sympathies in order to gain popular support for them. Yet they will distinguish with Lincoln between their "*official* duty," which is to think and act in terms of the national interest, and their "*personal* wish," which is to see their own moral values and political principles realized throughout the world. Political realism does not require, nor does it condone, indifference to political ideals and moral principles, but it requires indeed a sharp distinction between the desirable and the possible—between what is desirable everywhere and at all times and what is possible under the concrete circumstances of time and place.

It stands to reason that not all foreign policies have always followed so rational, objective, and unemotional a course. The contingent elements of personality, prejudice, and subjective preference, and of all the weaknesses of intellect and will which flesh is heir to, are bound to deflect foreign policies from their rational course. Especially where foreign policy is conducted under the conditions of democratic control, the need to marshal popular emotions to the support of foreign policy cannot fail to impair the rationality of foreign policy itself. Yet a theory of foreign policy which aims at rationality must for the time being, as it were, abstract from these irrational elements and seek to paint a picture of foreign policy which presents the rational essence to be found in experience, without the contingent deviations from rationality which are also found in experience.

Deviations from rationality which are not the result of the personal whim or the personal psychopathology of the policy maker may appear contingent only from the vantage point of rationality, but may themselves be elements in a coherent system of irrationality. The possibility of constructing, as it were, a counter-theory of irrational politics is worth exploring.

When one reflects upon the development of American thinking on foreign policy, one is struck by the persistence of mistaken attitudes that have survived—under whatever guises—both intellectual argument and political experience. Once that wonder, in true Aristotelian fashion, has been transformed into the quest for rational understanding, the quest yields a conclusion both comforting and disturbing: we are here in the presence of intellectual defects shared by all of us in different ways and degrees. Together they provide the outline of a kind of pathology of international politics. When the human mind approaches reality with the purpose of taking action, of which the political encounter is one of the outstanding instances, it is often led astray by any of four common mental phenomena: residues of formerly adequate modes of thought and action now rendered obsolete by a new social reality; demonological interpretations of reality which substitute a fictitious reality—peopled by evil persons rather than seemingly intractable issues—for the actual one; refusal to come to terms with a threatening

state of affairs by denying it through illusory verbalization; reliance upon the infinite malleability of a seemingly obstreperous reality.

Man responds to social situations with repetitive patterns. The same situation, recognized in its identity with previous situations, evokes the same response. The mind, as it were, holds in readiness a number of patterns appropriate for different situations; it then requires only the identification of a particular case to apply to it the preformed pattern appropriate to it. Thus the human mind follows the principle of economy of effort, obviating an examination *de novo* of each individual situation and the pattern of thought and action appropriate to it. Yet when matters are subject to dynamic change, traditional patterns are no longer appropriate: they must be replaced by new ones reflecting such change. Otherwise a gap will open between traditional patterns and new realities, and thought and action will be misguided.

On the international plane it is no exaggeration to say that the very structure of international relations—as reflected in political institutions, diplomatic procedures, and legal arrangements—has tended to become at variance with, and in large measure irrelevant to, the reality of international politics. While the former assumes the "sovereign equality" of all nations, the latter is dominated by an extreme inequality of nations, two of which are called superpowers because they hold in their hands the unprecedented power of total destruction, and many of which are called "ministates" because their power is minuscule even compared with that of the traditional nation states. It is this contrast and incompatibility between the reality of international politics and the concepts, institutions, and procedures designed to make intelligible and control the former, which has caused, at least below the great-power level, the unmanageability of international relations which borders on anarchy. International terrorism and the different government reactions to it, the involvement of foreign governments in the Lebanese civil war, the military operations of the United States in Southeast Asia, and the military intervention of the Soviet Union in Eastern Europe cannot be explained or justified by reference to traditional concepts, institutions, and procedures.

All these situations have one characteristic in common. The modern fact of interdependence requires a political order which takes that fact into account, while in reality the legal and institutional superstructure, harking back to the nineteenth century, assumes the existence of a multiplicity of self-sufficient, impenetrable, sovereign nation states. These residues of an obsolescent legal and institutional order not only stand in the way of a rational transformation of international relations in light of the inequality of power and the interdependence of interests, but they also render precarious, if not impossible, more rational policies within the defective framework of such a system.

It is a characteristic of primitive thinking to personalize social problems. That tendency is particularly strong when the problem appears not to be susceptible to rational understanding and successful manipulation. When a particular person or group of persons is identified with the recalcitrant difficulty, that may seem to render the problem both intellectually accessible and susceptible of solution. Thus belief in Satan as the source of evil makes us "understand" the nature of evil by focusing the search for its origin and control upon a particular person whose physical existence we assume. The complexity of political conflict precludes such simple solutions. Natural catastrophes will not be prevented by burning witches; the threat of a powerful Germany to establish hegemony over Europe will not be averted by getting rid of a succession of German leaders. But by identifying the issue with certain persons over whom we have—or hope to have—control we reduce the problem, both intellectually and pragmatically, to manageable proportions. Once we have identified certain individuals and groups of individuals as the source of evil, we appear to have understood the causal nexus that leads from the individuals to the social problem; that apparent understanding suggests the apparent solution: Eliminate the individuals "responsible" for it, and you have solved the problem.

Superstition still holds sway over our relations within society. The demonological pattern of thought and action has now been transferred to other fields of human action closed to the kind of rational enquiry and action that have driven superstition from our relations with nature. As William Graham Sumner put it, "The amount of superstition is not much changed, but it now attaches to politics, not to religion."[1] The numerous failures of the United States to recognize and respond to the polycentric nature of Communism is a prime example of this defect. The corollary of this indiscriminate opposition to Communism is the indiscriminate support of governments and movements that profess and practice anti-Communism. American policies in Asia and Latin America have derived from this simplistic position. The Vietnam War and our inability to come to terms with mainland China find here their rationale. So do the theory and practice of counterinsurgency, including large-scale assassinations under the Phoenix program in Vietnam and the actual or attempted assassinations of individual statesmen. Signs of a similar approach have been evident more recently in Central America.

The demonological approach to foreign policy strengthens another pathological tendency, which is the refusal to acknowledge and cope effectively with a threatening reality. The demonological approach has shifted our attention and concern towards the adherents of Communism—individuals at home and abroad, political movements, foreign governments—and away from the real threat: the power of states, Communist or not. McCarthyism not only provided the most pervasive American example of the demonological approach but was also one of the most extreme examples of this kind of misjudgment: it substituted the largely illusory threat of domestic subversion for the real threat of Russian power.

Finally, it is part of this approach to politics to believe that no problems—however hopeless they may appear—are really insoluble, given well-meaning, well-financed, and competent efforts. I have

---

[1] "Mores of the Present and Future," in *War and Other Essays* (New Haven: Yale University Press, 1911), p. 159.

tried elsewhere to lay bare the intellectual and historical roots of this belief;[2] here I limit myself to pointing out its persistent strength despite much experience to the contrary, such as the Vietnam War and the general decline of American power. This preference for economic solutions to political and military problems is powerfully reinforced by the interests of potential recipients of economic support, who prefer the obviously profitable transfer of economic advantages to painful and risky diplomatic bargaining.

The difference between international politics as it actually is and a rational theory derived from it is like the difference between a photograph and a painted portrait. The photograph shows everything that can be seen by the naked eye; the painted photograph does not show everything that can be seen by the naked eye, but it shows, or at least seeks to show, one thing that the naked eye cannot see: the human essence of the person portrayed.

Political realism contains not only a theoretical but also a normative element. It knows that political reality is replete with contingencies and systemic irrationalities and points to the typical influences they exert upon foreign policy. Yet it shares with all social theory the need, for the sake of theoretical understanding, to stress the rational elements of political reality; for it is these rational elements that make reality intelligible for theory. Political realism presents the theoretical construct of a rational foreign policy which experience can never completely achieve.

At the same time political realism considers a rational foreign policy to be good foreign policy; for only a rational foreign policy minimizes risks and maximizes benefits and, hence, complies both with the moral precept of prudence and the political requirement of success. Political realism wants the photographic picture of the political world to resemble as much as possible its painted portrait. Aware of the inevitable gap between good—that is, rational—foreign policy and foreign policy as it actually is,

political realism maintains not only that theory must focus upon the rational elements of political reality, but also that foreign policy ought to be rational in view of its own moral and practical purposes.

Hence, it is no argument against the theory here presented that actual foreign policy does not or cannot live up to it. That argument misunderstands the intention of this book, which is to present not an indiscriminate description of political reality, but a rational theory of international politics. Far from being invalidated by the fact that, for instance, a perfect balance of power policy will scarcely be found in reality, it assumes that reality, being deficient in this respect, must be understood and evaluated as an approximation to an ideal system of balance of power.

3. *Realism assumes that its key concept of interest defined as power is an objective category which is universally valid, but it does not endow that concept with a meaning that is fixed once and for all.*

The idea of interest is indeed the essence of politics and is unaffected by the circumstances of time and place. Thucydides' statement, born of the experiences of ancient Greece, that "identity of interests is the surest of bonds whether between states or individuals" was taken up in the nineteenth century by Lord Salisbury's remark "the only bond of union that endures" among nations is "the absence of all clashing interests." It was erected into a general principle of government by George Washington:

A small knowledge of human nature will convince us, that, with far the greatest part of mankind, interest is the governing principle; and that almost every man is more or less, under its influence. Motives of public virtue may for a time, or in particular instances, actuate men to the observance of a conduct purely disinterested; but they are not of themselves sufficient to produce persevering conformity to the refined dictates and obligations of social duty. Few men are capable of making a continual sacrifice of all views of private interest, or advantage, to the common good. It is vain to exclaim against the depravity of human nature on this account; the fact is so, the experience of every age and nation has proved it and we must in a great measure, change the constitution of man, before we can make it otherwise.

---

[2] *Scientific Man versus Power Politics* (Chicago: University of Chicago Press, 1946).

No institution, not built on the presumptive truth of these maxims can succeed.[3]

It was echoed and enlarged upon in our century by Max Weber's observation:

> Interests (material and ideal), not ideas, dominate directly the actions of men. Yet the "images of the world" created by these ideas have very often served as switches determining the tracks on which the dynamism of interests kept actions moving.[4]

Yet the kind of interest determining political action in a particular period of history depends upon the political and cultural context within which foreign policy is formulated. The goals that might be pursued by nations in their foreign policy can run the whole gamut of objectives any nation has ever pursued or might possibly pursue.

The same observations apply to the concept of power. Its content and the manner of its use are determined by the political and cultural environment. Power may comprise anything that establishes and maintains the control of man over man. Thus power covers all social relationships which serve that end, from physical violence to the most subtle psychological ties by which one mind controls another. Power covers the domination of man by man, both when it is disciplined by moral ends and controlled by constitutional safeguards, as in Western democracies, and when it is that untamed and barbaric force which finds its laws in nothing but its own strength and its sole justification in its aggrandizement.

Political realism does not assume that the contemporary conditions under which foreign policy operates, with their extreme instability and the ever present threat of large-scale violence, cannot be changed. The balance of power, for instance, is indeed a perennial element of all pluralistic societies, as the authors of *The Federalist* papers well knew; yet it is capable of operating, as it does in the United States, under the conditions of relative stability and peaceful conflict. If the factors that have given rise to these conditions can be duplicated on the international scene, similar conditions of stability and peace will then prevail there, as they have over long stretches of history among certain nations.

What is true of the general character of international relations is also true of the nation state as the ultimate point of reference of contemporary foreign policy. While the realist indeed believes that interest is the perennial standard by which political action must be judged and directed, the contemporary connection between interest and the nation state is a product of history, and is therefore bound to disappear in the course of history. Nothing in the realist position militates against the assumption that the present division of the political world into nation states will be replaced by larger units of a quite different character, more in keeping with the technical potentialities and the moral requirements of the contemporary world.

The realist parts company with other schools of thought before the all-important question of how the contemporary world is to be transformed. The realist is persuaded that this transformation can be achieved only through the workmanlike manipulation of the perennial forces that have shaped the past as they will the future. The realist cannot be persuaded that we can bring about the transformation by confronting a political reality that has its own laws with an abstract ideal that refuses to take those laws into account.

4. *Political realism is aware of the moral significance of political action. It is also aware of the ineluctable tension between the moral command and the requirements of successful political action.*

And it is unwilling to gloss over and obliterate that tension and thus to obfuscate both the moral and the political issue by making it appear as though the stark facts of politics were morally more satisfying than they actually are, and the moral law less exacting that it actually is.

---

[3] *The Writings of George Washington*, edited by John C. Fitzpatrick (Washington: United States Printing Office, 1931–44), Vol. X, p. 363.

[4] Marianne Weber, *Max Weber* (Tuebingen: J.C.B. Mohr, 1926), pp. 347–8. See also Max Weber, *Gesammelte Aufsätze zur Religionssoziologie* (Tuebingen: J.C.B. Mohr, 1920), p. 252.

Realism maintains that universal moral principles cannot be applied to the actions of states in their abstract universal formulation, but that they must be filtered through the concrete circumstances of time and place. The individual may say for himself: *"Fiat justitia, pereat mundus* (Let justice be done, even if the world perish)," but the state has no right to say so in the name of those who are in its care. Both individual and state must judge political action by universal moral principles, such as that of liberty. Yet while the individual has a moral right to sacrifice himself in defense of such a moral principle, the state has no right to let its moral disapprobation of the infringement of liberty get in the way of successful political action, itself inspired by the moral principle of national survival. There can be no political morality without prudence; that is, without consideration of the political consequences of seemingly moral action. Realism, then, considers prudence—the weighing of the consequences of alternative political actions—to be the supreme virtue in politics. Ethics in the abstract judges action by its conformity with the moral law; political ethics judges action by its political consequences. Classical and medieval philosophy knew this, and so did Lincoln when he said:

> I do the very best I know how, the very best I can, and I mean to keep doing so until the end. If the end brings me out all right, what is said against me won't amount to anything. If the end brings me out wrong, ten angels swearing I was right would make no difference.

5. *Political realism refuses to identify the moral aspirations of a particular nation with the moral laws that govern the universe.*

As it distinguishes between truth and opinion, so it distinguishes between truth and idolatry. All nations are tempted—and few have been able to resist the temptation for long—to clothe their own particular aspirations and actions in the moral purposes of the universe. To know that nations are subject to the moral law is one thing, while to pretend to know with certainty what is good and evil in the relations among nations is quite another. There is a world of difference between the belief that all nations stand under the judgment of God, inscrutable to the human

mind, and the blasphemous conviction that God is always on one's side and that what one wills oneself cannot fail to be willed by God also.

The lighthearted equation between a particular nationalism and the counsels of Providence is morally indefensible, for it is that very sin of pride against which the Greek tragedians and the Biblical prophets have warned rulers and ruled. That equation is also politically pernicious, for it is liable to engender the distortion in judgment which, in the blindness of crusading frenzy, destroys nations and civilizations—in the name of moral principle, ideal, or God himself.

On the other hand, it is exactly the concept of interest defined in terms of power that saves us from both that moral excess and that political folly. For if we look at all nations, our own included, as political entities pursuing their respective interests defined in terms of power, we are able to do justice to all of them. And we are able to do justice to all of them in a dual sense: We are able to judge other nations as we judge our own and, having judged them in this fashion, we are then capable of pursuing policies that respect the interests of other nations, while protecting and promoting those of our own. Moderation in policy cannot fail to reflect the moderation of moral judgment.

6. *The difference, then, between political realism and other schools of thought is real, and it is profound.*

However much of the theory of political realism may have been misunderstood and misinterpreted, there is no gainsaying its distinctive intellectual and moral attitude to matters political.

Intellectually, the political realist maintains the autonomy of the political sphere, as the economist, the lawyer, the moralist maintain theirs. He thinks in terms of interest defined as power, as the economist thinks in terms of interest defined as wealth; the lawyer, of the conformity of action with legal rules; the moralist, of the conformity of action with moral principles. The economist asks: "How does this policy affect the wealth of society, or a segment of it?" The lawyer asks: "Is this policy in accord with the rules of the law?" The moralist asks: "Is this policy in accord with moral principles?'' And the political realist asks: ''How does this policy affect the power of the nation?'' (Or of the federal government, of Congress, of the party, of agriculture, as the case may be.)

The political realist is not unaware of the existence and relevance of standards of thought other than political ones. As political realist, he cannot but subordinate these other standards to those of politics. And he parts company with other schools when they impose standards of thought appropriate to other spheres upon the political sphere. It is here that political realism takes issue with the ''legalistic-moralist approach'' to international politics.

IDEALPOLITIK

Stanley Kober

A revolution is sweeping the world—a revolution of democracy. The success of this democratic revolution has shaken Europe to its foundations and shattered the strategic guideposts used to chart American foreign policy for more than 40 years. Groping through this new landscape, foreign policy specialists are struggling to develop policies to encourage democratic change while safeguarding strategic stability.

The failure to anticipate these changes, however, has understandably introduced a note of caution into the American response. The events were unexpected but they should not have been if the policy framework had been correct. Throughout the postwar era, American foreign policy has been dominated by a philosophy of realism, which views international politics as a struggle for power in which the interests of the great powers must be in conflict. This was a natural vision of foreign policy during a time in which then Soviet Foreign Minister Andrei Gromyko declared that "the world outlook and the class goals of the two social systems are opposite and irreconcilable."

It is precisely this "realistic" approach to foreign policy that is now being challenged, however, as Soviet President Mikhail Gorbachev and his allies in the Soviet leadership explicitly repudiate Gromyko's position. "Coexistence," proclaimed Foreign Minister Eduard Shevardnadze in July 1988, "cannot be identified with the class struggle." Instead, it "should have universal interests as a common denominator." The realignment of the Soviet Union's foreign policy has been accompanied by an even more fundamental transformation of its domestic political structure. Indeed, Gorbachev himself has described *perestroika* (restructuring) not as economic reform but as "a legal revolution" designed to keep excessive power from being concentrated in the hands of a few people and to govern society according to the rule of law.

Until November 1989, debate in the West centered on the sincerity of these intentions. However, with the collapse of the Berlin Wall, attention is turning to the survivability of Gorbachev and his reforms, with the attendant question of what the United States and its allies should do. This debate, in turn, is affected by another more fundamental issue: What makes nations adversaries? Are the United States and the Soviet Union doomed by geopolitics to remain enemies? Or does the prospective transformation of the Soviet Union into a parliamentary democracy herald an end to the danger of superpower conflict? The answers should be sought in the competing philosophies of American foreign policy: realism or idealism.

At the end of World War I, President Woodrow Wilson traveled to Europe to help develop a structure assuring that "the war to end wars" would be just that. Wilson's approach consisted of two main parts. First, the Central European empires were dismantled and new states based on the principle of national self-determination were established. Second, Wilson proposed the creation of the League of Nations to handle future threats to international security.

Wilson's ideas were immediately challenged by the great British geopolitician Sir Halford Mackinder. In *Democratic Ideals and Reality*, which was first published in 1919, Mackinder argued that Wilson's democratic idealism might be noble but failed to deal with world realities. "Idealists are the salt of the earth," he wrote condescendingly; but, he warned, "democracy is incompatible with the organization necessary for war against autocracies." Mackinder asserted that "political moralists" like Wilson "refused to reckon with the realities of geography and economics." Mackinder defined these realities in his famous formulation: "Who rules East

Source: Stanley Kober, "Idealpolitik," *Foreign Policy*, no. 79 (Summer 1990), pp. 3–24. Reprinted with permission of Foreign Policy. Copyright 1990 by the Carnegie Endowment for International Peace.

Europe commands the Heartland: Who rules the Heartland commands the World-Island: Who rules the World-Island commands the World.'' Given the importance of Eastern Europe, the prevention of another world war would depend on the establishment of ''a tier of independent states between Germany and Russia.'' The political structure of these states did not concern him; what interested him was the balance of power.

Mackinder challenged not only Wilson, but also another American, Alfred Thayer Mahan. It was Mahan who, in the late nineteenth century, attributed England's preeminence to its reliance on sea power. ''The due use and control of the sea is but one link in the chain of exchange by which wealth accumulates,'' he wrote in 1890, ''but it is the central link.''

Mackinder replied that control of the sea was well and good, but extended naval power would require land bases. Yet this point of disagreement between the geopoliticians of land and sea obscures their more fundamental points of accord. In the first place, Mahan, like Mackinder, was contemptuous of the unmartial spirit of democracy. Second, both were hostile to free trade and the trading classes. Mahan may have praised the use of the sea trade as the source of England's wealth, but it was clearly the control of the sea that captivated him.

Mackinder also believed that economic wealth could not depend on free trade. For Mackinder the classical theories of the division of labor and comparative advantage were not only economically flawed but politically dangerous. Echoing, perhaps unwittingly, Leninist analysis, Mackinder saw the competitive struggle for markets as a major source of war.

To sum up the geopolitical view as defined by Mackinder and Mahan, the strongest country or alliance is the one with direct control over the greatest resources. The benefits of trade outside of one's own zone are illusory because they are bound to lead to vulnerability. The geopolitician is hostile toward business classes and democratic systems of government since they lack martial qualities. Rather, the geopolitician would prefer to have decisions made by people endowed with strategic vision and unaffected by any sectional interests.

POSTWAR REALISM

Mackinder's ''realistic'' critique of Wilson's idealism found an echo in U.S. policy in the late 1940s. Haunted by the failure of democracies to prevent World War II, American political leaders decided to assume the burden of world leadership they had abandoned in the interwar period. ''Soviet pressure against the free institutions of the Western World,'' wrote George Kennan in his famous ''X'' article of 1947, ''is something that can be contained by the adroit and vigilant application of counterforce at a series of constantly shifting geographical and political points, corresponding to the shifts and maneuvers of Soviet policy.'' This definition of containment was purely reactive, however. The United States not only had to respond to the ''shifts and maneuvers of Soviet policy,'' it had to anticipate them. What mechanism could it use for understanding the Kremlin's designs?

According to the political realist, the answer was simple. ''The main signpost that helps political realism to find its way through the landscape of international politics is the concept of interest defined in terms of power,'' wrote Hans Morgenthau, probably the foremost exponent of the realist school. Morgenthau's book, *Politics among Nations: The Struggle for Power and Peace* (1948), helped provide the intellectual basis for America's engagement in power politics. ''Politics, like society in general, is governed by objective laws that have their roots in human nature,'' observed Morgenthau. Since these laws are objective, they are necessarily universal, and consequently it is futile and deceptive to examine foreign policy exclusively by looking at the motives of government officials. Instead, it is assumed that ''statesmen think and act in terms of interest defined as power.'' On this assumption, ''we put ourselves in the position of a statesman who must meet a certain problem of foreign policy under certain circumstances, and we ask ourselves what the rational alternatives are from which a statesman may choose . . . and which of these rational alternatives this particular statesman, acting under these circumstances, is likely to choose.''

Morgenthau placed little emphasis on appeals to ideals as a way of gaining influence in the world. It was only in the preface to his second edition, published in 1954, that he acknowledged, as a result of decolonization, ''the struggle for the minds of men as a new dimension of international politics to be added to the traditional dimensions of diplomacy and war.'' Although Morgenthau acknowledged ''the attractiveness . . . of its political philosophy, political institutions, and political policies'' as one element of a state's power, in the final analysis ''the state has no right to let its moral disapprobation of the infringement of liberty get in the way of successful political action.'' Rather than viewing the clash of ideologies as basic to politics, the realist sees it as an unfortunate intrusion into his relatively stable world. ''This struggle for the minds of men,'' lamented Morgenthau,

> has dealt the final, fatal blow to that social system of international intercourse within which for almost three centuries nations lived together in constant rivalry, yet under the common roof of shared values and universal standards of action. . . . Beneath the ruins of that roof lies buried the mechanism that kept the walls of that house of nations standing: the balance of power.

By acknowledging that the effective functioning of international politics depends on the existence of ''shared values,'' Morgenthau admitted that the ''laws'' of power politics are not so objective after all. Yet if Morgenthau grieved for a world order that was no more, former Secretary of State Henry Kissinger insists that it still exists and is irreplaceable. ''To have stability,'' he wrote in a recent *Washington Post* article, ''an international system must have two components: a balance of power and a generally accepted principle of legitimacy.'' Like Morgenthau, Kissinger believes that the study of policy statements is misguided and bound to lead to error. He wrote in an essay in 1968:

> If we focus our policy discussions on Soviet purposes, we confuse the debate in two ways: Soviet trends are

too ambiguous to offer a reliable guide—it is possible that not even Soviet leaders fully understand the dynamics of their system; it deflects us from articulating the purposes we should pursue, whatever Soviet intentions. . . . Confusing foreign policy with psychotherapy deprives us of criteria by which to judge the political foundations of international order.

Similarly, Kissinger shares Morgenthau's conviction that the realities of power politics compel the subordination of a nation's ideology to more basic interests. ''National security concerns should be in harmony with traditional American values,'' he explained in a 1986 article, but ''this ideal cannot always prevail, imposing the necessity to strike a balance.'' Underlying this view is Kissinger's assessment, expressed at a 1977 lecture at New York University, that ''the United States is now as vulnerable as any other nation.'' Not only is it subject to the danger of nuclear annihilation, but American ''prosperity is to some extent hostage to the decisions on raw materials, prices, and investment in distant countries whose purposes are not necessarily compatible with ours.'' Thus, although ''our morality and our power should not be antithetical,'' in the final analysis ''all serious foreign policy must begin with the need for survival.''

THE NEW IDEALISM

In contrast to geopolitics and realism, idealism has never had a distinct line of philosophical development. The German philosopher Immanuel Kant wrote that the rule of law would result in ''perpetual peace,'' but he provided little guidance on how governments should behave until that day arrives. By contrast, the Manchester school in the nineteenth century, putting its trust in economic self-interest, believed that free trade would make war irrational. Yet the outbreak of World War I demonstrated that governments do not always behave rationally. It is not surprising, therefore, that historian E. H. Carr, in his 1939 volume *The Twenty Years' Crisis, 1919–1939*, described the alternative to realism as utopianism, which he characterized as "the primitive . . . stage of the political sciences."

Viewed in this manner, it is no wonder that the idealist alternative fell into disrepute. Unfortunately, idealism is still seen as a naive philosophy that fails to understand the realities of power politics. Because of the uncompromising moralism with which it is endowed by its opponents, idealism is viewed as leading either to withdrawal from an imperfect world or to unrestrained interventionism to right all the world's wrongs. It is time for a new, more rigorous idealist alternative to realism.

A proper understanding of idealism, therefore, begins with the recognition that ideologies matter, and that the foreign policy of a state is an outgrowth of the values embodied in its domestic institutions. In the idealist view, the structure of a government determines how aggressive it can be. Specifically, dictatorships will be more aggressive than parliamentary democracies, since dictators can undertake military actions on their own initiative without having to obtain prior consent from popularly elected legislatures.

In taking this position, idealists recognize that democracies have behaved aggressively in the past but add that they are also evolving institutions. Democracy embodies strict criteria for majority rule and minority rights. Majority rule means that all the people are entitled to vote, and that those elected are accountable to the voters at frequent and regular intervals. The idealist views a democracy in which women, minorities, or other groups are excluded as more likely to be aggressive, since those making the decisions for war or peace are not accountable to everyone affected. In order to be accountable, representatives must provide the voters with the information they need to exercise their authority properly, and the people must have some mechanism for obtaining this information if it is being improperly withheld.

Minority rights are widely regarded as contradictory to majority rule, but this view is misguided. As recent ethnic conflicts demonstrate, majorities can change over time, and majority rule in the absence of guaranteed minority rights is a prescription for catastrophe. More to the point, however, guarantees of minority rights, which can be enforced only by the voluntary consent of the majority, signify respect for the weak by the strong. This value system of respect for law rather than for power is the best assurance of order and stability, both domestically and internationally.

Thus, the idealist is an unabashed proponent of democracy, seeing democracy as the best guarantee of world peace. While admitting that there is little historical experience of democracies of the sort described, the idealist would point to the relationship between the United States and Canada as instructive. Although these two countries were at war with each other at the beginning of the nineteenth century, they now share the longest undefended border in the world. The idealist would attribute this outcome to their mutual development of democratic institutions and would challenge the realist to explain why, if the balance of power is so important, Canadians do not tremble in fear at the prospect of an American invasion. The realist might reply that although there is an imbalance of power between the United States and Canada, they share an accepted principle of legitimacy. This answer is incomplete, for what is the source of that accepted principle of legitimacy if it is not the democractic values and respect for law both countries share?

In short, if it is democratic values that bring peace, one should say so forthrightly and not pretend that one principle of legitimacy is as good as another so long as it is generally accepted. If the balance of power cannot explain the peaceful U.S.-Canadian relationship, neither can it explain the outbreak of World War II. No geopolitical arrangement achievable at the time could have deterred Adolf Hitler because he saw war as the glorious means for achieving his objective, the occupation and subjugation of lands to the east. "No one will ever again have the confidence of the whole German people as I have," Hitler observed in August 1939. "All these favorable circumstances will no longer prevail in two or three years' time. No one knows how much longer I shall live.'' Whereas normal people are afraid of war, Hitler was afraid he would die before he could start a war.

The cause of World War II, therefore, must be sought not in the geopolitics of Europe, but in the domestic politics of Germany. The question is not how Hitler could have been deterred, because it is impossible to deter an absolute ruler who is seeking war. Rather, the question is how Hitler could have led a reluctant German people into war. Although many factors contributed to the outbreak of World War II, one overlooked cause is the imperfection of the Weimar Constitution. Instead of the American concept of inalienable rights, the Weimar Assembly placed individual rights at the ''service of the collectivity,'' as René Brunet wrote in his 1922 book *The New German Constitution.* ''Individual liberties are no longer an end in themselves, nor do they constitute any longer an independent good,'' he explained. ''They have no value and are not protected except in the measure that they serve for the accomplishment of this social duty.''

Because of this fundamental constitutional defect, Hitler was able to destroy the Weimar democracy and create in its place an instrument of domestic terror and foreign aggression. A democracy that does not have ironclad guarantees of individual rights cannot endure. As Abraham Lincoln observed, ''a majority, held in restraint by constitutional checks and limitations . . . is the only true sovereign of a free people. Whoever rejects it does, out of necessity, fly to anarchy or to despotism.'' Weimar, born of military defeat, had the additional misfortune of being subject to a worldwide economic depression beyond its control. Its political and legal institutions were too new, too fragile, too unprotected to resist Hitler's assault once he came to power.

The outbreak of World War II, therefore, cannot be explained by realism. Indeed, if anything, British Prime Minister Neville Chamberlain followed realist analysis too closely. A realist assumes that because of objective laws of human behavior, all rational people will solve a given problem of foreign policy alike. But this leaves two problems. First, what is the problem of foreign policy the statesman is trying to solve? By defining Hitler's objective as the national self-determination of the German people, Chamberlain and his supporters totally missed the enormity of Hitler's ambition.

Second, what is the definition of rationality? The realist might respond that Hitler was irrational and therefore outside the bounds of realist analysis, but that answer is too glib. Intent on starting a war of expansion, Hitler initiated a massive military buildup while using diplomacy to hide his true intentions. On the eve of war, he reached an agreement with the Soviet Union, his greatest enemy, thereby easing enormously the military challenge immediately confronting him. In other words, Hitler's purposes were certainly irrational, but the purposefulness with which he pursued his objectives cannot be so easily dismissed. And indeed, if Hitler falls outside realist analysis because of his irrationality, how useful is realism as an analytical tool?

Hitler demonstrates the folly of relying on objective laws of human behavior in determining foreign policy. Hitler's methods make perfect sense once one understands his objectives. But to understand those objectives, one would have to look not to his assurances to Chamberlain at Munich, but to statements he made elsewhere and especially to his destruction of Germany's democracy. To the realist such an investigation is meaningless; to the idealist it is of fundamental importance: Hitler's treatment of the Jews and others he disliked foreshadowed how he would behave in the international arena once he was strong enough. If the people of Europe and their leaders had been aware of idealist analysis, they would have readily understood the purpose behind Hitler's military buildup and therefore the danger confronting them.

Idealist analysis provides criteria for assessing whether a military buildup is the result of perceptions of insecurity or the product of a drive for military supremacy to achieve political objectives by the threat or use of arms. The difference is crucial in determining the proper response. If the former, policy should focus on alleviating the political causes of insecurity. In this case, arms control has its greatest effect by building confidence. In the latter case, however, political measures are of limited, if any, use since there is no insecurity to alleviate. On the contrary, policy here should focus on a countervailing arms buildup, both to safeguard one's own security and to convince the arming power that it cannot achieve its objective. Arms control in this case can play a modest role by directing the competition away from the most destabilizing weapons, but it cannot achieve its ultimate objective of building confidence.

Faced with the need to choose between these two causes of an arms race, realism is helpless, since either cause might be rational depending on the policy objectives of a country's leaders. Unwilling to trust policy statements and rejecting the connection between domestic and foreign policy, realists ultimately base their assessments on their own value biases with no independent test. The idealist, on the other hand, insists that policy statements, particularly those designed for domestic officials, are revealing. More to the point, the idealist believes that even if such statements are too ambiguous to be a guide for formulating a response, the values embodied in a country's domestic policy and institutions provide invaluable insight into its purposes in foreign policy.

It is incorrect, therefore, to say that idealism rejects the balance of power. In fact, idealism recognizes that in the face of a military threat, there is no alternative to maintaining a balance, or even a preponderance, of power. What idealism rejects is the idea that international peace is solely the product of a balance of power. For the idealist, a country can have friends as well as interests. The ultimate objective of idealism is to broaden the circle of friendship by fostering the spread of democratic values and institutions. In the meantime, recognizing the dangers of the world as it exists, idealism provides a mechanism for assessing the degree of threat posed by hostile regimes, in particular the threat posed by a military buildup.

But if idealism is more effective than realism in providing timely and accurate warning of military threats, it is also careful not to exaggerate them. For example, the idealist would disagree with Kissinger's assessment that the United States is as vulnerable as any other country. The only credible threat to America's national survival at this time comes from Soviet nuclear weapons; assuming the Kremlin is not suicidal, the United States has more than enough retaliatory power to deter such an attack. Conventional military threats to American interests do not threaten U.S. survival. Perhaps most important, the United States does not have to depend on any other country to assure its security.

Similarly, the idealist would question the idea that the United States is economically vulnerable. While recognizing America's dependence on imports, the idealist believes that so long as the sources of commodities are diversified and market forces are in operation, a cutoff of supplies from one country or a group of countries should be manageable. If further protection is needed, stockpiles of critical goods can be accumulated.

This is not to say that economic sanctions cannot have an effect against relatively small countries, for they ultimately did in Rhodesia and may now be having an effect in South Africa. But these are special cases rather than universal examples. When then President Jimmy Carter embargoed American grain exports to the Soviet Union following the invasion of Afghanistan, Moscow was easily able to find alternative suppliers. Similarly, when tin producers formed a cartel to duplicate the success of the Organization of Petroleum Exporting Countries in the 1970s, the effort collapsed.

In contrast to the realist, the idealist does not believe that U.S. imports of vital commodities pose a security risk so long as proper economic policies are followed. Idealists see American economic security in a vibrant economy producing goods that other people want, rather than in a government-directed policy of import substitution, let alone in military intervention.

This difference in the assessment of American economic vulnerability also extends to policy toward the Soviet Union; underlying the doctrine of containment is the assumption that Soviet expansionism will necessarily increase Soviet power. This assumption reflects the geopolitician's mistaken evaluation of the sources of economic wealth. As the British economic historian Eric Hobsbawm observed in *Industry and Empire* (1969), the imperial expansion that occurred in the late nineteenth century was for Britain "a step back. She exchanged the informal empire over most of the underdeveloped world for the formal empire of a quarter of it, plus the older satellite economies."

For the idealist it is free trade rather than empire that sustains economic growth. One's trade must be protected against attack, but that is different from developing an exclusive economic zone that does not depend upon the goodwill of others. Idealists believe that the wealth of a nation depends not on the extent or characteristics of the territory directly under its control, but as Adam Smith states, "first, [on] the skill, dexterity, and judgment with which its labour is generally applied; and, secondly, [on] the proportion between the number of those who are employed in useful labour, and that of those who are not so employed." Since prosperity "seems to depend more upon the former of those two circumstances than upon the latter," it is important that the labor force of the most advanced country constantly improve its skills so that it can continue to produce innovative goods and services with high added value. Otherwise, it will inevitably fall behind.

Continuing economic prosperity requires a flexible economic system. The problem with empires, as Carlo Cipolla notes in *The Economic Decline of Empires* (1970), is that "all empires seem eventually to develop an intractable resistance to the change needed for the required growth of production. . . . An empire is inevitably characterized by a large number of sclerotic institutions. They hinder change for their very existence." Hobsbawm, assessing the British condition at the time Mahan and Mackinder wrote, agrees with this judgment. "Britain had escaped from the Great Depression (1873–96) . . . not by modernizing her economy, but by exploiting the remaining possibilities of her traditional situation," he wrote. "When the last great

receptacles of cotton goods developed their own textile industries—India, Japan and China—the hour of Lancashire tolled. For not even political control could permanently keep India non-industrial."

Hobsbawm's analysis points to the second fundamental reason why the geopolitical interpretation of the wealth of nations is flawed: Political control over people who resent that control is an unstable basis for continuing economic growth. It is not enough to assert that "who rules the Heartland commands the World-Island." The idealist, mindful of Machiavelli's warning that "princes . . . must first try not to be hated by the mass of the people," will immediately inquire whether that rule is by popular consent or in spite of it. If the latter, it must be a source of economic weakness rather than strength over the long run. Not only will a sullen people be relatively unproductive, but the effort to keep them under control will over time amount to a huge drain on the government's resources.

REVOLUTION IN THE '90s

Viewed in this manner, idealism provides a fundamental challenge to realism and geopolitics. It is no longer possible to dismiss idealists as utopian dreamers who do not understand the harsh reality of power. On the contrary, idealists can respond that it is realists and geopoliticians who have oversimplified the concept of power and misunderstood the lessons of history. The debate between them is of critical importance in formulating policy to respond to the revolutionary changes now confronting the world.

Of all the momentous changes now occurring, the most dramatic is the transformation of the Soviet bloc. It is worth noting that the Soviets have always accepted some principles of idealism. Unlike realists, the Soviets have always stressed the importance of ideology and insisted that it is impossible to understand the foreign policy of a country without appreciating its domestic values and institutions. Similarly, like idealists, the Soviets professed to see the ultimate guarantee of world peace in the domestic structure of states. However, they saw that domestic structure in the communist principles of Karl Marx and V. I. Lenin, rather than in the democratic institutions of Thomas Jefferson and James Madison.

What is so revolutionary about the current changes in the Soviet Union is that they are based on the acknowledgement that the guarantee of world peace lies not in the spread of socialism, but in parliamentary control over war-making power. According to a January 1988 article in *Kommunist*, the theoretical journal of the Soviet Communist party, "there are no politically influential forces in either Western Europe or the U.S." that contemplate "military aggression against socialism." But even if there were, America's democratic institutions would make such large-scale aggression impossible. The article emphasizes that "bourgeois democracy serves as a definite barrier in the path of unleashing such a war. . . . The history of the American intervention in Indochina clearly demonstrated this. . . . The Pentagon now cannot fail to recognize the existence of limits placed on its actions by democratic institutions." By formulating the question of war and peace in this way, the authors posed, albeit implicitly, an extremely profound question: If it is democratic institutions like those in the West that prevent war, then where is the threat to peace? Logically, it must come from those countries without such democratic institutions—countries like the Soviet Union. Astonishing as it may seem, this realization is one of the foundations on which *perestroika* is being built.

"The use of armed forces outside the country without sanction from the Supreme Soviet or the congress is ruled out categorically, once and for all," Gorbachev affirmed in assuming his new powers as president in March 1990. This statement reflects the fundamental nature of the changes taking place in the Soviet Union, which have little, if anything, to do with Marxism-Leninism. Indeed, as the former head of the Soviet Institute of State and Law, Vladimir Kudryavtsev, has forthrightly acknowledged, "Marxists criticized the 'separation of powers' theory which drew a clear dividing line between legisla-

tive and executive power." Now Soviets are recognizing their mistake and embracing the separation of powers and the rule of law. The philosophical basis for these changes can be found in the writings of Kant. "The philosophical foundation of the rule-of-law state was formulated by Kant," Kudryavtsev and Yelena Lukasheva, a doctor of juridical science, flatly stated in a *Kommunist* article following the June–July 1988 19th party conference, which established the rule of law as a major objective of *perestroika*. Soviet officials from Gorbachev on down now routinely refer to Kant, and Shevardnadze has specifically identified Kant's 1795 booklet *Perpetual Peace* as a work deserving special attention.

Perpetual Peace was a major contribution to idealist philosophy. An admirer of the principles behind the American Revolution, Kant saw perpetual peace as a product not of the balance of power, but of republican government. Similarly, he rejected economic mercantilism, which is the foundation of geopolitics, in favor of Adam Smith's promotion of free trade. These themes are now commonplace in the Soviet media.

Viewed from the realist perspective, Gorbachev's actions, particularly in Eastern Europe, are puzzling; viewed from an idealist position, however, they are easily explicable. Since it is commerce rather than control of resources that is the source of wealth, better to abandon the territory where people are resentful of occupation. Free trade will provide more economic benefits than occupation. Nor is there any security risk; Soviet security is, in the final analysis, assured not by the territorial glacis or even by the might of the Soviet armed forces, but by the institutions of Western democracy.

The point is so startling to realists, who emphasize the balance of power, that it deserves elaboration. The Soviets are not deideologizing policy, but rather *re*-ideologizing it on a new basis. The Soviets are not replacing the value-laden system of Marx and Lenin with the value-neutral system of the balance of power, but are instead turning to a new set of values, those of the Enlightenment and especially of Kant.

As Gorbachev told the 19th party conference in words that anticipated the revolutionary changes in Eastern Europe: "A key factor in the new thinking is the concept of freedom of choice. . . . To oppose freedom of choice is to come out against the objective tide of history itself. That is why power politics in all their forms and manifestations are historically obsolescent."

Underlying this shift in the Soviet world view is a reassessment of its domestic value system. "The image of a state," Shevardnadze has proclaimed, "is its attitude to its own citizens, respect for their rights and freedoms and recognition of the sovereignty of the individual." By emphasizing the sovereignty of the individual, Shevardnadze is turning communist philosophy upside down. In addition, he is paying an extraordinary compliment to the principles of the American Revolution. The European tradition has been one of national self-determination. "The basis of all sovereignty lies, essentially, in the Nation," states the French Declaration of the Rights of Man and the Citizen. But the pursuit of national self-determination has proved to be a chimera. What, after all, is a nation? How can it be defined? And the most painful question, which the Soviet Union is now confronting: How can national self-determination be achieved in a multi-ethnic state?

The American principle, on the other hand, is *individual* self-determination, not national self-determination. Americans believe in *e pluribus unum*: one out of many. So long as rights are guaranteed on an individual basis, the concept of a nation is irrelevant. In a multi-ethnic state—and, one is tempted to say, in a multinational world—there can be no other basis for preserving peace.

The changes in Eastern Europe go to the heart of the debate between realism and idealism. Since realists maintain that it is power rather than ideology that matters, they view Gorbachev's changes with suspicion. Realists are concerned that if Gorbachev is successful, the result could be a stronger Soviet Union and thus an even greater threat to the United States. Realists do not see a necessary link between the Soviet Union's domestic changes and its foreign

policy. "*Glasnost* [openness] and *perestroika* represent attempts to modernize the Soviet state," Kissinger wrote in a January 1988 article in the *Washington Post*. "That is an internal Soviet matter, relevant to the democracies only if accompanied by a change in Soviet foreign policy." Indeed, Kissinger worries "whether Americans can be brought to see foreign policy in terms of equilibrium rather than as a struggle between good and evil." In his view, this was the problem with former President Ronald Reagan's policy toward the Soviet Union, which in a few years went from denunciations of an evil empire to an embrace of Gorbachev. "Such an approach," Kissinger stressed in another *Washington Post* article in February 1989, "neglects the realities of power, ambition and national interest."

For the idealist, on the other hand, there are no immutable "realities of power, ambition and national interest." All these must be viewed through the prism of policy, which changes as people change. Policy will be affected by a society's values, which in turn are embodied in its domestic institutions. Thus, the idealist rejects the notion that there is no connection between *perestroika* and Soviet foreign policy. Whereas the realist is in perpetual pursuit of a stabilizing equilibrium—believing, in former President Richard Nixon's words, that "the only time in the history of the world that we have had any extended periods of peace is when there has been balance of power"—the idealist seeks the spread of freedom, which ultimately would eliminate the need for a balance of power.

The difference between the two approaches is manifest in the way their adherents assess current developments in Europe. According to President George Bush, "the enemy is instability." But although instability can be dangerous if it is a prelude to chaos, stability by itself cannot be the highest American value. "Those who won our independence by revolution . . . did not fear political change," Justice Louis Brandeis wrote in 1927. "They did not exalt order at the cost of liberty." Affirming this idealist view, President Vaclav Havel of Czechoslovakia told the American people in February 1990 that "the best guarantee against possible threat or aggressivity is democracy," and, accordingly, he told Congress that the United States should "help the Soviet Union on its irreversible but immensely complicated road to democracy."

Safeguarding and spreading democracy in Eastern Europe means, above all, fostering the demilitarization of the Soviet Union and accelerating the withdrawal of its armed forces from foreign territory. Arguments that Gorbachev's position is too uncertain to be a basis for security decisions are unconvincing because arms control agreements are one of the best ways to bolster Gorbachev's position against hardline rivals. The more the USSR disarms and the more troops it withdraws from Eastern Europe, the more difficult it will be for any regime that might overthrow Gorbachev to reconstitute a significant military threat. In such a situation, moreover, violations of agreements will provide warning of the change in Soviet intentions, thereby further protecting American security.

Thus the current negotiations should focus on ways to accelerate the withdrawal of Soviet forces from Eastern Europe, while two other measures would help demilitarize Soviet society. The first is a mutual East-West ban on conscription. Conscription is the foundation of militarism in the Soviet Union. Eliminating it would not only benefit Western security enormously, but would also represent a diplomatic triumph for Gorbachev because conscription is extremely unpopular in the USSR.

The second step should be assistance designed to foster economic conversion. In this regard, the United States should encourage equity investment by private firms, which has several advantages over loans. First, it would not involve any U.S. government funds. Second, there would be no requirement to pay dividends as there would be to pay debt, so the poor in the USSR would not bear the burden if investments should go bad. Third, it would promote change in the Soviet Union toward a free-market economy. Fourth, it would provide managerial assistance because the firms making investments would want to assure their success. Finally, it would prom-

ise further investment because owners would have a continuing interest in the success of their ventures.

Would the Soviets allow Western investment in areas that might still be sensitive? Recent developments suggest they would. For example, the Votkinsk missile plant, which used to produce SS-20 missiles, is now planning a joint venture with an American firm to produce civilian rockets.

Perhaps the most interesting piece of evidence in this regard is an August 1989 *Wall Street Journal* article by Soviet economist Andrei Kuteinikov stating that "as the most talented people desert the state sector, Soviet co-ops can offer Western partners a highly educated and low-wage labor force. . . . This could turn out to be an intriguing opportunity for many Western industrial companies and venture capitalists, as the most motivated and aggressive scientists leave state labs and factories to launch their own ventures." By providing capital to skilled workers presumably leaving the Soviet defense industry, Western firms would facilitate the process of economic conversion, thereby augmenting Western security while simultaneously providing a financial lift to the struggling Soviet economy.

Two hundred years ago, the Enlightenment produced one of the great eras of human civilization. Its spirit, the spirit of tolerance, was captured by Voltaire: "Every individual who persecutes a man, his brother, because he does not agree with him, is a monster. . . . We should tolerate each other because we are all weak, inconsistent, subject to mutability and to error." This spirit was one of the inspirations for the American form of government. In the words of George Washington, "the Citizens of the United States of America have the right to applaud themselves for having given to mankind examples of an enlarged and liberal policy: a policy worthy of imitation. All possess alike liberty of conscience and immunities of citizenship."

Today, Americans are witnessing the reaffirmation of these principles of the Enlightenment and the power of the American example. For too long Americans have compromised their principles in the name of geopolitics. By doing so, they gave rise to a perception of moral equivalence between the United States and the Soviet Union, which undermined American interests. More to the point, they betrayed their special heritage. "Let us be diverted by none of those sophistical contrivances wherewith we are so industriously plied and belabored," Lincoln urged the American people in 1860 on the eve of their greatest test. "Let us have faith that right makes might, and in that faith, let us, to the end, dare to do our duty as we understand it."

The ultimate objective of American foreign policy, therefore, should not be the establishment of an equilibrium but the spread of freedom. The best way for the United States to do this is by setting an example to the world of the benefits of democracy. Unfortunately, the U.S. obsession with its world role has led it to neglect its domestic problems. American democratic institutions are strong, but they face mounting social problems. With the pressures of the Cold War easing, the United States must turn its attention increasingly to domestic issues in order to strengthen its democracy.

Internationally, U.S. assistance should be guided by two criteria: whether those asking for help share American values and the degree to which they are willing to help themselves. American economic assistance should encourage the development of capitalist institutions as the only means of fostering economic progress. The use of military force needs to be subject to nationwide debate. The successful use of force in Grenada and Panama has obscured its failures in Vietnam and Lebanon. Moreover, the fears generated by the Cold War gave virtually unlimited discretion for the use of force to the president, which may have harmful consequences for democratic government. "Our [Constitutional] Convention," Lincoln once stated, "resolved to so frame the Constitution that no one man should hold the power of this oppression [of war] upon us." Although the world has changed dramatically since Lincoln wrote these words, the Constitution, on this point, has not.

Indeed, a general American debate on the role of the president, the Congress, and the people in foreign policy is long overdue. In recent years, especially, presidents have attempted to claim a virtually exclusive role in the formulation of foreign policy by virtue of their position as commander in chief, even though Alexander Hamilton, in the *Federalist* No. 69, defined the president's powers in this regard as inferior to those of the British monarch. Excessive secrecy, in particular, is bound to erode the foundations of democratic government; the people have a right to know what their government is doing in their name. Claims that matters of foreign policy are too sensitive to be discussed in public must be rejected as incompatible with the American ethos. In Jefferson's words: "It is error alone which needs the support of government. Truth can stand by itself."

The realist perspective has gone unchallenged long enough. Idealism is not naive utopianism but a rigorous approach to the conduct of foreign policy. Moreover, it is idealism that is the great American tradition. As Washington declared in his Farewell Address:

> Observe good faith and justice toward all nations. Cultivate peace and harmony with all. Religion and morality enjoin this conduct. And can it be that good policy does not equally enjoin it? It will be worthy of a free, enlightened, and at no distant period a great nation to give mankind the magnanimous and too novel example of a people always guided by an exalted justice and benevolence. Who can doubt that in the course of time and things the fruits of such a plan would richly repay any temporary advantages which might be lost by a steady adherence to it?

Americans should not fear that the spread of the democratic system created by the founders of their republic could present a threat to their security. They should instead follow Washington's advice and reject the realist's compromises as leading only to those "temporary advantages" of which he spoke. The long-term interests of the United States are fulfilled when it is true to its ideals, thus setting an example for the rest of the world. "We shall be as a City upon a Hill, the Eyes of all people are upon us," John Winthrop proclaimed in 1630. More than 350 years later, our revolutionary world demonstrates that it is the power of America's ideals, and not the might of its armies, that is the real source of U.S. influence in the world.

QUESTIONS FOR DISCUSSION

1. What role should the study of the motivation of statesmen play in analyzing international relations?
2. How should the national interest be defined?
3. How much of realism is descriptive, and how much is prescriptive?
4. To what extent can the realist analysis be used to explain the interdependence of nations?
5. How would a realist analyze current problems in international politics, such as arms control, the Islamic Revolution, and the future of U.S.-Soviet relations?

SUGGESTED READINGS

Carr, E. H. *The Twenty Years' Crisis, 1919–1939: An Introduction to the Study of International Relations*, 2d ed. New York: Harper and Row, 1964.

Frost, Mervyn. *Towards a Normative Theory of International Relations*. Cambridge, England: Cambridge Univ. Press, 1986.

Gellman, Peter. "Hans J. Morgenthau and the Legacy of Political Realism." *Review of International Studies* (Cambridge, England), **14** (Oct. 1988), pp. 247–266.

James, Alan. "The Realism of Realism: The State and the Study of International Relations." *Review of International Studies* (Cambridge, England), **15** (July 1989), pp. 215–229.

Keenes, Ernie. "Paradigms of International Relations: Bringing Politics Back In." *International Journal* (Toronto), **44** (Winter 1988–1989), pp. 41–67.

Kegley, Charles W., Jr. "The Lost Legacy: Idealism in American Foreign Policy." *USA Today* (Magazine), **117** (Mar. 1989), pp. 25–27.

Keohane, Robert O. (ed.). *Neorealism and Its Critics*. New York: Columbia Univ. Press, 1986.

Maghroori, Ray, and Bennett Ramberg (eds.). *Globalism versus Realism: International Relations' Third Debate*. Boulder, Colo.: Westview Press, 1982.

Mansbach, Richard W., and John A. Vasquez. *In Search of Theory: A New Paradigm for Global Politics*. New York: Columbia Univ. Press, 1981.

Smith, Michael Joseph. *Realist Thought from Weber to Kissinger*. Baton Rouge, La.: Louisiana State University Press, 1986.

"Symposium on the New Realism." *International Organization*, **38** (Spring 1984), pp. 225–337.

Vasquez, John A. *the Power of Power Politics: A Critique*. New Brunswick, N.J.: Rutgers Univ. Press, 1982.

Waltz, Kenneth N. *Theory of International Politics*. Reading, Mass.: Addison-Wesley, 1979.

CHAPTER 3

Regional Issues

Some of the most dangerous international issues since the end of World War II have involved regional disputes. At times some of the regional disputes sparked wars, such as the Korean War, the war in Indochina, Arab-Israeli wars, the Iran-Iraq War, and the Persian Gulf War.

Regional wars have for the most part been conducted in third world countries. At the center of conflict were disputes over territory, economics, and political systems. While the cold war between the superpowers raged, the regional disputes usually had a global aspect, with each superpower choosing sides.

And so, sometimes through formal alliance and at other times through less formal acts of friendship, countries engaged in regional conflicts created situations that threatened to escalate into global wars. In Indochina, for example, the Soviet Union backed North Vietnam, while the United States supported South Vietnam. Both superpowers also chose opposing sides in the Korean War, the Arab-Israeli conflict, and the Iran-Iraq War. Each superpower armed its friends, as regional disputes became pawns in the global contest for power and influence.

With the decline of Soviet power in the late 1980s, however, the Soviet Union turned inward and sought to reduce its foreign policy commitments. Instead of conflict between the mighty superpowers, accommodation and mutal interest became the norm. A notable example was the support of the Soviet Union for U.N. action to repel the Iraqi conquest of Kuwait in 1990. That support included cooperation with an international embargo against Iraq as well as the deployment of a strong U.S. military presence in Saudi Arabia and the Persian Gulf. The cooperation between the Soviet Union and the United States on the response to the Iraqi invasion suggested that regional disputes in the post–cold war years would be resolved by the superpowers combining resources.

Superpower cooperation was not limited to third world matters. Since the Soviet Union and Eastern European countries had made efforts to establish more democratic political systems and market economies, Eastern and Western Europe moved toward closer political and economic cooperation, too.

The debates below deal with some of the important regional issues affecting world politics. These debates consider the future of Germany, a common "European House" for Eastern and Western Europe, a Palestinian state, third world debt, and Japan.

GERMANY

The future of Germany has been at the center of the cold war since 1945. When in November 1989, the Berlin Wall came tumbling down, it seemed to many observers that the cold war was collapsing, too.

After its defeat in 1945, Germany was occupied by the victorious Allied Powers—the United States, Great Britain, France, and the Soviet Union—which governed separate sectors in the country and in Berlin, the capital. Within a decade after the war, Germany was formally divided into a pro-West Federal Republic of Germany (West Germany) and a pro-Soviet German Democratic Republic (East Germany). West Germany joined the North Atlantic Treaty Organization (NATO) in 1955, and East Germany then became a charter member of the Warsaw Pact.

West Germany prospered and developed into a thriving democractic country. The East German economy was strong as far as communist countries were concerned but lagged well behind its West German counterpart. The East German political system was dictatorial. Both countries renounced the acquisition of nuclear weapons and were signatories of the Nonproliferation Treaty (1968), the major arms control agreement dealing with the spread of nuclear weapons.

Although German political leaders spoke in terms of eventual reunification, few people in Germany and elsewhere thought that prospects were strong, both because of Western and Eastern fears of a united Germany and because of Soviet security interests. Germany had begun two world wars in the twentieth century, the second of which was the more devastating. The Soviet Union had experienced the most damage of any country in World War II, with deaths estimated at 27 million people.

Jews and others in all nations could never forget the anti-Semitism of Nazi Germany that destroyed 6 million—two-thirds of the Jews of Europe—in what became known as the Holocaust. At least another million non-Jews died in extermination camps and concentration camps as well. West Germany had paid $33 billion in reparations to the State of Israel and to individual victims of Nazism. But with memories of the gas chambers and extermination camps so haunting, many Jews and others swore that such a calamity would never again befall humankind.

Fears of a renascent Nazi Germany increased with the events of 1989 and 1990. The key to the changes was the decision by Soviet leader Mikhail Gorbachev to allow the Eastern European countries to pursue their own courses. Soviet foreign ministry spokesman Gennadi Gerasimov reflected the change when he said in October 1989 that the Brezhnev Doctrine (named in 1968 after Soviet leader Leonid Brezhnev) of military intervention in Eastern Europe to protect communist regimes had been replaced by the Sinatra Doctrine (named for American entertainer Frank Sinatra's hit song "My Way"), which would permit these nations to be independent of the Soviet Union.

Under agreements worked out in 1990, West and East Germany reunited. The new Germany was to remain a member of NATO. Germany agreed to limit the size of its armed forces. Soviet forces would remain in East Germany until 1994. During this period, NATO troops would not be stationed on East German territory. The new Germany committed itself to banning chemical and nuclear weapons from its arsenal. And it accepted the borders set at the end of World War II—a matter of great concern to Poland and Czechoslovakia, which had fears that Germany would reclaim territories it had lost.

Will Germany be a threat to world peace? Michael Lerner, editor and publisher of the Jewish bimonthly journal *Tikkun*, says yes. He contends: (1) The Germans do not deserve reunification because they have not grappled with their past. (2) They do not show a deep awareness of the dangers of nationalism and have not repudiated anti-Semitism. (3) Restrictions on national self-determination are necessary until the German people engage in some sort of public service activities aimed at uprooting and recompensing the evils that they let loose on this world.

Josef Joffe, editor of *Süddeutsche Zeitung*, contends that a united Germany is no threat to world peace. He argues: (1) Reunification has come about peacefully. (2) Democracy is strongly entrenched in Germany. (3) The Federal Republic's political system has worked effectively, with many political institutions similar to those found in the United States. (4) Unified Germany is part of a large community of friendly nations, not resentful neighbors. (5) Rivalry among nations will involve the economic rather than the military arena, and Germany will act peacefully as will its neighbors.

EUROPEAN CONFEDERATION

The events of 1989 and 1990 have had a profound effect on Europe. The cold war divided not only Germany but the rest of Europe as well. Western Europe and Eastern Europe built separate political, military, and economic institutions as the cold war hardened. Although the military alliances of West and East blocs were in balance, the economies of the market-driven Western countries were growing, while the Eastern command economies were in decay.

Gorbachev recognized that for the Soviet Union to prosper, it had to abandon its foreign policy empire, reduce military expenditures, dismantle its command economy, and allow for greater individual freedom. The unification of Germany and the independence of Eastern European countries put Eastern Europe on a course that was now compatible with Western Europe's political and economic institutions, practices, and beliefs.

In November 1990, the Conference on Security and Cooperation (CSCE), a group of thirty-four countries including nearly all the states of Europe, the United States, and Canada, met in Paris and marked the end of the cold war by agreeing to a treaty calling for major reductions of weapons in Europe. It proclaimed the "end of the era of confrontation and division" that followed World War II. It pledged a "steadfast commitment to democracy based on human rights and fundamental freedoms, prosperity through economic liberty and social justice, and equal security for all countries."[1]

---

[1] Quoted in R. W. Apple, Jr., "34 Lands Proclaim a United Europe in Paris Charter," *New York Times*, Nov. 22, 1990, p. A1.

In practical terms, Eastern Europe looked for closer cooperation with Western Europe in economic matters. Western European governments extended loans to Eastern European countries, and multinational corporations provided capital and expertise for new ventures. But some Eastern Europeans sought closer economic and political collaboration with Western Europe through a confederation or closer association with the European Community.

Should Eastern Europe and Western Europe establish unified European political and economic institutions? Former Polish Prime Minister Tadeusz Mazowiecki calls for a confederation of European countries and the establishment of European political institutions. He contends: (1) The upheavals in Central Europe and the Soviet Union create both opportunities and dangers for economic development and political freedom. (2) The Berlin Wall, which symbolized the division of Europe, is now down, so that a European "common home" is possible. (3) A European common home is possible if economic disparities among European countries can be eliminated. (4) The Europe of the year 2000 might be a place where borders and tariffs will be much less of an obstacle than they are today, the contact between creative and scientific communities will be richer, economies will be complementary, differences in living standards will be smaller, international economic exchange will be more substantial, the environment will be cleaner, and progress on disarmament will have been made.

Political commentator Ferry Hoogendijk argues that the idea of one "European House" is unrealistic. He contends: (1) The Russians in particular have little in common with the people of Central and Western Europe. (2) A European House constitutes a danger for the European Community in that the Germans might now be preoccupied by the German issue and use it as an excuse for failing to promote Western integration along the lines of the single European market. (3) Transforming the economic and political systems of Eastern Europe will take a long time. (4) The Soviet Union in particular has too many problems of economic development and political order to participate in a "European House."

PALESTINIAN STATE

A continuing problem in world politics is the inability to reach lasting peace between Israel and its neighbors. The idea of a Jewish state has biblical roots. In modern times, however, it was reflected in the movement known as Zionism that emerged in the late nineteenth century. Zionists believed that the Jews should have their own state in the ancient land of Israel. In response to Zionism and the persecution of Jews in Europe, significant Jewish immigration to Palestine began in the late 1800s. After the defeat of the Ottoman Empire in World War I, Palestine, which had been a part of that empire, came under the British mandate, and Arabs and Jews lived in Palestine under British rule. Nazi persecution of Jews in the 1930s and the Holocaust of the 1940s led to mass migrations of Jews to Palestine. In 1947 the United Nations called for the establishment of both a Jewish state and Arab state. The latter was not created partly because of a war in 1947–1948, which resulted in the territory specified for the Arab state being taken over by Israel, Egypt, and Jordan (the latter two supposedly holding it for eventual return to the Palestinian Arabs). Israel has fought wars with its Arab neighbors in 1947–1948, 1956, 1967, 1973, and 1982.

As a result of the 1967 War, Israel obtained control of the West Bank of the Jordan River with its Arab population and the Old City of Jerusalem—both of which had been under Jordanian rule. It also took the Golan Heights, which had been held by Syria, and the Gaza Strip. Although many proposals were put forward to bring peace between Israel and her neighbors, none was successful until Egypt, under the leadership of Anwar Sadat, and Israel, under the leadership of Menachem Begin, concluded a peace treaty in 1979 with the assistance of President Jimmy Carter. In 1982 tension between Israel and its Arab neighbors was exacerbated when Israeli forces invaded southern Lebanon in an effort to expel Palestinian Liberation Organization (PLO) and Syrian forces. The PLO, established in 1964, is committed to creating a Palestinian homeland.

A Palestinian uprising in the West Bank and Gaza that began in December 1987 added a new dimension to the political instability of the area. The Israelis sought to suppress the uprising, or *intifada* as it is called, which continued in the next few years. Israeli efforts at suppression damaged Israel's overseas support and strengthened forces within Israel calling for a more accommodating position with the Palestinians.

Sparked by a U.S. initiative in 1988, new diplomatic efforts were made for movement in Israeli-Palestinian negotiations. PLO leader Yasir Arafat denounced terrorism and recognized the right of Israel to exist. For its part Israel sought to commence negotiations with Palestinians who were not part of the PLO. But the PLO regarded itself as the representative of the Palestinian people. Negotiations dragged on because of irreconcilable differences and Israeli domestic politics. And when the PLO backed Iraq in its invasion of Kuwait in 1990, movement for negotiations came to a virtual halt.

The central question remains: Would the establishment of a Palestinian state be dangerous to peace? Journalist Michael Widlanski argues that it would. His article reflects the views of a study made by the Institute for Advanced Strategic and Political Studies. He contends: (1) A Palestinian state would rob Israel of strategic assets needed to maintain a credible deterrent to the surrounding states. (2) A Palestinian Arab state would be a hemispheric time bomb and invite the return of hundreds of thousands of Palestinians who would direct their energies against Israel. (3) Solving the "Palestinian agenda" may not end tensions between Israel and its other neighbors.

Ephraim Sneh, an Israeli brigadier general (reserve), argues the Negative. He points out: (1) A bloc of moderate Arab states to Israel's east seeks a peace agreement in the region. (2) Most of the Arab regimes in the region now feel more threatened by Muslim fundamentalism than by Zionism. (3) Even with a Palestinian state, Israel can remain strong militarily, and its military strength would serve as a deterrent against Arab resistance. (4) Demographic trends in Israel, the West Bank, and the Gaza Strip create a paradox for Israel that will not easily be solved:

> In order to preserve Jewish dominance in state institutions, Israel must deprive the Palestinians in the territories of civil rights; while in order to preserve its democratic character, Israel must add 1.7 million Palestinians to the 800,000 Israeli Arabs who are already Israeli citizens and grant them civil rights.

(5) A Palestinian state would not be a threat to Jordan. (6) A Palestinian state can be established conditional on security guarantees for Israel.

THIRD WORLD DEBT

With the rise of new states after World War II, the agenda of world politics turned to economic as well as security considerations. Third world countries possessed important resources that the West needed. The West, moreover, had the capital and managerial skills essential for economic development.

The relationship between third world resources and Western needs became an issue in 1973 when the Arab oil-producing countries announced an embargo of oil shipments to the West. From 1973 on, the Organization of Petroleum Exporting countries instituted constant increases in the price of oil. Oil that sold for $3.02 a barrel in September 1973 rose to $35 a barrel by 1984, although the price has dropped enormously since 1985.

Most of the third world countries are not fortunate enough to be endowed with rich oil deposits. In general third world countries are the poorest in the world. As indicated in Chapter 1, the term "South" is used to refer to these countries because they are located mostly in the southern latitudes. Many third world economies are characterized by low per capita income, low productivity, high illiteracy, high population growth, low status of women, low capital investment, and a predominance of agriculture in their economies. Some countries, such as Bangladesh and Somalia, are so destitute as to be given a separate classification as the "fourth world."

Third world countries have economic development as a primary goal of their policy, both domestic and foreign. In 1974 a number of countries sought help from advanced industrial states, principally in the West. They called for the creation of a New International Economic Order (NIEO). The developing countries made several specific proposals through the NIEO that, if implemented, would help them in their quest for economic development. Among the most important were: (1) preferential access to the markets of the developed countries; (2) commodity agreements that would assure them stable prices for their raw-material exports; (3) the transfer of loans and grants from industrial to developing states through multilateral institutions; (4) larger transfers of technology; and (5) more control of multinational corporations (MNCs) by developing countries.

The developing countries have had limited success in achieving these objectives. A major issue involving developing countries and Western states is the payment of debts incurred by the developing countries that they are finding difficult to repay. In fact, they are finding it difficult to pay the *interest* on the debts.

The problem stems from the rise in oil prices after the October 1973 War in the Middle East. As the price of oil skyrocketed, the United States encouraged OPEC members to invest their money in U.S. financial institutions. When Western banks accumulated extraordinary amounts of money, they were eager to lend that money and lent far more than they should have. When the recession of the late 1970s took hold of the global economy, third world countries were in trouble.

The developing countries have asked for help in dealing with the problem. If they default on repayment, the West, according to some analysts, would probably experience an economic disaster that would be worse than the Great Depression of the 1930s. Other analysts argue that the problem is under control.

The World Bank estimated that the third world debt would reach $1.221 trillion in 1990.[2] Latin American and Caribbean countries are in the most serious condition, owing an estimated $428.6 billion in 1990.[3] The major debtors are Mexico, Argentina, and Brazil. Western governments and banks are reluctant to grant new credit unless old debts are repaid and the economies of the debtor nations are put on a sound footing. Efforts to bring about austerity in developing countries have caused internal social unrest. The economies of developing countries suffered as capital sources were reduced.

A number of proposals have been put forward to deal with the debt crisis. One of the most prominent was offered in 1985 by James Baker when he was U.S. secretary of the treasury. The Baker Plan called for more commercial-bank and multilateral-development-bank lending in Latin American countries and in a few other debtor states in return for growth-oriented policies by the beneficiaries of the plan. The Baker Plan ran into problems, however, when the commercial banks were slow to make loans and when the domestic reforms proved to be limited. In addition, the slow growth in the global economy produced a depression in most commodity prices, resulting in low income for the exports of developing states. Third world countries, moreover, have been hurt by protectionist policies of the developed states.

The Baker Plan was followed in March 1989 by the Brady Plan (named for Nicholas F. Brady who succeeded Baker as Secretary of the Treasury). The Brady Plan called for voluntary reductions by commercial banks of the third world debt through negotiations between creditors and debtors. Brady also indicated that the United States would support greater involvement by the International Monetary Fund, the World Bank, and Japan to provide incentives for the commercial banks to reduce the debt.

The Baker Plan and the Brady Plan were moderate solutions. One of the extreme solutions offered for the debt crisis is for the debtor countries to refuse to pay back some of their debts. Such a solution is debated here by Cuban leader Fidel Castro and British economist Peter T. Bauer.

Is it necessary to forgive third world debt to the West to avoid economic catastrophe? Castro says yes. He argues: (1) The United States is largely responsible for the debt problem of the developing countries through unfavorable trade practices and high interest rates. (2) Debts should be renegotiated, and as a last resort, canceled. (3) The economies of debtor countries would then be restructured, allowing for more trade with the developed states and more business with MNCs. (4) The governments of the developed countries could finance their debt-elimination program by reducing military spending.

Bauer takes the opposing viewpoint. He argues: (1) Debtor countries are capable of paying their debts because they have large liquid assets and large marketable assets. (2) Many billions of dollars lent to the developing countries were unwisely spent by those countries for programs that harmed their economies. (3) By historical standards, neither

---

[2] World Bank, *World Debt Tables, 1990–91: External Debt of Developing Countries: Vol. 1. Analysis and Summary Tables* (Washington, D.C.; World Bank, 1990), p. 12.

[3] Ibid., p. 142.

the total outstanding sovereign debt of the major borrowers nor the interest and principal payments are particularly high. (4) The major debtor governments preside over some of the most prosperous third world economies. (5) Third world governments should have built up foreign-exchange reserves in good times in preparation for hard times. (6) Protectionist politics of developed countries affect other developed countries more than they affect developing countries. The West still offers large markets for the products of third world debtor countries. (7) The repayment of loans by debtor countries would not result in political and social upheaval leading to the coming to power of populist and communist regimes; nor would repayment endanger the Western banking and financial system or mean that the debtor countries would buy less from the West.

JAPAN

When Japan was defeated in World War II, it completely changed its political system and its foreign policy. It had been a dictatorship that pursued expansionist policies, but after 1945, it became a democratic society concerned with economic development rather than imperialism.

Japan accepted a provision in its constitution that limited its military to defensive forces. Devoting only a small percentage of its gross national product to defense, the country seemed so single-minded in its quest for economic development that it was called "Japan, Inc."

Japan prospered. As an island nation with few natural resources, it had always relied heavily on foreign trade. Before World War II, Japan was regarded as a copier of Western products rather than as an innovator. In the decades after the war, Japan became a great innovator, particularly in such fields as electronics and automobile manufacture. Its success in producing high-quality cars made Honda and Toyota popular in the United States. Japanese companies even opened up their own plants in foreign countries, most notably in the United States. Moreover, they bought up American real estate properties and major U.S. companies, such as Columbia Pictures and Firestone Tire.

With its limited military forces, Japan tied its security to the United States. The U.S.-Japan security treaty has now been in effect for more than thirty years, and both countries have benefited.

In the 1980s, however, U.S.-Japanese relations became tenser than they had been in decades. They show strains in the 1990s, as well. Americans have resented the success the Japanese have achieved in producing and selling products abroad. They complain that the Japanese do business easily in the United States but make it difficult for Americans to do business in Japan. They also accuse Japan of unfair practices, such as "dumping" its excess products in the United States at prices so low that American manufacturers cannot compete. As the United States amassed huge trade deficits, some Americans called for greater restrictions on Japanese goods coming into the United States.

Some Japanese, too, have begun to question the strong ties that their country has with the United States. They see the United States blaming the Japanese for economic problems that are not Japan's fault. It is the United States, they say, that perpetuates inefficient enterprises, much spending and little saving, considerable political divisiveness, and a very weak educational system.

The Japanese critics of the U.S.-Japanese relationship ask that it be changed. Should Japan pursue a course that is more independent of the United States? Ishihara Shintarō, a Liberal Democratic member of Japan's House of Representatives, argues that it should. Ishihara is co-author with Sony chairman Morita Akio of *A Japan That Can Say No* (1989), a book highly critical of the United States. Ishihara contends: (1) The U.S.-Japanese relationship, although mutually beneficial, has served the United States more than Japan. (2) Anti-Japanese feeling in the United States is rooted in racial prejudice. (3) Japan was unfairly pressured by the United States in the construction of the FSX military aircraft. (4) U.S. bases in Japan have more to do with U.S. strategy than Japan's safety. (5) The United States is making intrusive and unfair demands on Japan to change its economic practices. (6) U.S. economic problems come about because of the country's own failings rather than because of anything Japan is doing.

Nakanishi Terumasa, a professor at Shizuoka Prefectural University, takes an opposing viewpoint. He contends: (1) Japan has often differed with the United States on key issues. (2) Racism is not the operative factor in U.S. relations with Japan. (3) Japan's ability to use the "high-tech card" would not contribute to Japan's long-term security. (4) It is not possible for anyone to gauge accurately the effectiveness of the U.S. nuclear deterrent in protecting Japan. (5) U.S.-Japanese cooperation should be close even in the post–cold war era because the two nations have mutual interests.

9 Will Germany Be a Threat to World Peace?

YES

Michael Lerner

"No" to German Reunification

NO

Josef Joffe

Reunification II: This Time, No Hobnail Boots

"No" to German Reunification

Michael Lerner

Had the German people, East and West, really engaged in a serious process of denazification, had each German child been required to study the history of anti-Semitism and come to understand how this perverse racism influenced people to vote for Hitler in 1933, and had there been a systematic attempt to uproot the rigid character structures that were encouraged by German cultural and educational norms, I might feel very different as I watch the two Germanies celebrate potential reunification. But when I hear talk of a resurgent German nationalism, when I read about Germans singing World War II songs as they dance on the ruins of the Berlin Wall, I have to question why the American occupiers of Germany seemed to think that fascism (and anti-Semitism) was suddenly not a problem, that the struggle was solely against communism. The sad truth is that in the name of enlisting Germans on our side of the cold war, we in the U.S. never insisted on a serious denazification in West Germany. Conversely, Jews in the Communist Party in Eastern Europe were so anxious to prove their internationalist credentials, and so afraid of appearing self-interested and sectarian, that they never insisted that the East Germans wage a serious campaign against anti-Semitism. No wonder, then, that neo-Nazis are once again popping out of the woodwork in Germany.

It's not that I'm so worried about a new wave of anti-Semitism in Germany—the dangers for that are much greater in Eastern Europe, and anyway the Germans killed so many of us that there just aren't enough remaining alive in that part of Europe for them to get worked up about. Rather, I resist the idea that Germans deserve reunification, that they've served their time and now can forget the past (something that most of them managed to do almost instantaneously in 1945). Judging from the ceremonies at Bitburg honoring the SS dead, and judging from the attempts by German historians to reconceptualize their role in World War II as part of a legitimate struggle to stop Soviet communism, they have a long way to go before the society can or should be treated as though it has the same rights as any other group. It's not a question of how much time has been served, but of how deeply Germans have grappled with their past and how much real change has occurred.

It is Germany's historical amnesia that worries me. The ability to massively repress awareness of a traumatic event, particularly when one is the perpetrator of the trauma, may provide momentary comfort, both for the perpetrator and for observers. "That was just a momentary aberration. We were taken over by some demonic spirit. We weren't really ourselves, it was someone else who was doing all that." But if the source of this behavior is ignored, it will continue to live in the collective unconscious of a people, and once they are no longer under close scrutiny (in this case, once the Soviet Union and the U.S. remove their hundreds of thousands of troops that still occupy Germany), the same problems may pop up again. Already we see neo-Nazi groups from West Germany organizing supporters in a newly liberalized East Germany. And we will see worse unless the Germans are forced to confront and work through their past.

The occasion of reunification could have arrived in a very different spirit. Had they not repressed their past (a repression, we must add, that was encouraged both by the U.S. and the Soviet Union in order to mobilize their respective sides of Germany into being more efficient allies in the cold war), both states might have developed a deep awareness of the dangers of nationalism and solidly repudiated anti-Semitism. The respective populations would have

Source: Michael Lerner, " 'No' to German Reunification," *Tikkun*, 5 (March/April 1990), pp. 6, 121–122. Reprinted with permission from *Tikkun* magazine, a bimonthly Jewish critique of politics, culture, and society. Subscriptions are available for $25/ yr. (6 issues) from 5100 Leona St., Oakland, CA 94619.

approached the issue of reunification with humility and a vision of a new nation that accepted the burden of rectifying wrongs that had been committed in the name of German nationalism. This never took place at all in East Germany; it happened symbolically in West Germany through payment of war reparations to Israel, but not substantively in the consciousness or education of the West German people. Had it happened, we would not see the German Right nostalgically yearning for the good old days of the last Reich. And we would not hear German leftists equating Israeli policy toward the Palestinians (a policy *Tikkun* has consistently opposed) with the Nazis' systematic gassing and cremation of a civilian population. That intelligent and morally sensitive young leftists could make this equation demonstrates how little they have been taught about the Nazis.

But doesn't every group have the right to national self-determination? If the German people want to reunite, what right does anyone have to stop them? Our answer: national self-determination is not an absolute right, but conditional on how it is used. There are some moments when a national group must limit its right, and other moments when it may temporarily lose its right altogether. For example, we believe that Israel is a legitimate expression of the national self-determination of the Jewish people. But we put limits on that right, insisting that it does not include the right to expropriate the land of Palestinians or to prevent Palestinians from exercising their own right to national self-determination in the occupied territories.

In the case of Germany, restrictions on national self-determination must go much further. The virulent form of nationalism that thrived in that society some forty-five years ago brought the world one of its greatest catastrophes, World War II. Tens of millions of people lost their lives in a senseless struggle, and millions of our own people were systematically brutalized, dehumanized, and then annihilated. It is now in the name of this very same German nationalism that we are asked to recognize the right of East and West Germany to reunite. (And possibly next we will be told about Germany's desire to absorb other areas where ethnic Germans live, pre-

cisely the pretext that led to German expansionism in the 1930s.) This is preposterous. German nationalism has no legitimate claim on us and will not until either the entire generation that grew up in Nazi Germany no longer plays any role in German life or until the German people, both in East and West Germany, engage in some set of public service activities aimed at uprooting and recompensing the evils that they let loose on this world. (I'm thinking here of a German peace corps dedicated to fighting racism and anti-Semitism all over the world, a German effort to provide direct economic aid to societies— including the Soviet Union and Israel—in which displaced Jews were resettled, a German educational system that trains its citizens in the skills of combating all forms of totalitarianism and prejudice, a German Church that teaches its members exactly how the Church had collaborated with evil; the list could go on.) A German reunification that comes to us in the name of repairing the damage Germany did would be worthy of consideration. But a German reunification suffused with historical amnesia and fueled by a desire for economic growth and power is a mortal danger to the world.

In short, while recognizing the prima facie claims of any nationalism, we need to distinguish between progressive and destructive nationalism. When national identity is used to satisfy the fundamental needs of a people for community, shared culture, shared ideas, and a shared history, we applaud it. But some nationalisms then become an instrument for the oppression of others. At this point we need to question the validity of that nationalism more closely.

There is a progressive nationalism that emerges from the shared struggle of a people against oppression. The kind of nationalism developed by African-Americans to counter the oppression of a white society embodies elements of humanity that can provide a meaningful and ethical framework for many who remain oppressed. Similarly, there are progressive elements of Jewish nationalism— exemplified in the insistence of Jews to root their history *not* in some glorious superhero founders but in a history of a people that is liberated from slavery . . . —that provide a liberatory framework. To the extent that nationalisms are progressive they enable people to identify with others who are oppressed (as the Torah puts it so clearly, "Do not oppress the stranger; remember that you were strangers in the land of Egypt"). But many nationalisms are not progressive, and as the Israeli experience is beginning to show, even progressive nationalisms can be transformed into mechanisms of oppression.

In the modern world, nationalism is too often an ideology used to allow people to repress awareness of their own pain and alienation in daily life. The need for connectedness and recognition by others is systematically frustrated in the contemporary world. From the moments in early life when alienated parents misrecognize their own children, deny their subjectivity and spontaneity, and project onto them fantasies of who they are (to which the child must conform in order to receive some degree of pseudo-recognition), to an adult life in which human relations are increasingly shaped by the competitive and dominating modes of the marketplace, our human community is increasingly fragmented and emptied of deep connections and ethical wholeness. "The nation" becomes a substitute gratification for the wholeness lacking in one's own immediate life; and instead of struggling to change daily life to make it less fragmented and alienated, people are encouraged to identify with this fantasized national community. Through identification with this larger reality one imagines oneself made whole, fully recognized (as citizen), and accepted into a community whose destiny will provide meaning to one's own fragmented life. But the community exists only in songs, movies, television images, and speeches of politicians—not in how people treat each other or lead their daily lives. So the pain of alienated lives is only momentarily assuaged by the moments of nationalist fantasy, and eventually people suspect that something is still wrong. The solution: to find some "other" (the Jew, the Communist, the Black, the homosexual, the Arab, the Japanese, the Chinese, the capitalist) who is the reason why the nation is not delivering the emotional goodies it was supposed to have in store. The rage that one feels at one's own alienated life can now get externalized in aggression against the other who is allegedly undermining the fantasized community that would otherwise be working well to make life fulfilling and meaningful.

This is the most prevalent way that nationalism functions in the modern world, and I see little reason to encourage it.

Nor is this a moment when we should look favorably on the reemergence of nationalisms throughout Europe. The U.S. helped foster these nationalisms as a way to counter Soviet influence. Yet all too often European nationalisms flourished—even while officially suppressed by the Communists—precisely because they embodied all the vitality of older reactionary fantasies, including anti-Semitism, xenophobia, and religious fundamentalism. These diseases may once again spring to life in a Central and Eastern Europe no longer governed by the Soviet Union. Giving the nod to a reunited Germany, the country that most embodied these tendencies in the recent past, can only encourage the plethora of national groupings that may recreate a Europe so similar to the pre–World War I picture that it dissolves into endless battling between ethnic and religious rivals.

Our point here is not to be unforgiving toward the enemies of the Jews. I would hold any country responsible to the same standard for a similar level of historical outrage in the recent past. For this same reason, I don't recognize any fundamental right for national self-determination of Cambodians under the Khmer Rouge. And I still hope that someday Kissinger and Nixon and others will stand trial for their war crimes against the people of Vietnam, and that they will be sentenced to spend years of their life working to repair the country they did so much to destroy.

I shared the great joy of seeing the Berlin Wall come down—because it symbolized an end to decades of Communist oppression in Eastern Europe—and I rejoice at the surge of democracy that has swept through Europe. There's a new spirit of openness that is shaking even the Soviet Union. South

Africa, too, has recognized the African National Congress, leaving Israel as the one Western-style state unwilling to talk to her enemies (a position that was recently bolstered by the work of Arab terrorists, whose murder of Israeli civilians on a tour bus in Cairo gave aid and comfort to Israeli right-wingers). But much as I welcome the democratization of the world, I also remember that many of the peoples involved were in fact once racists and anti-Semites. The regimes that they are likely to democratically establish may well reflect those sentiments. Sounding the alarm now about German reunification is one way to introduce into the current discussion the notion that all of these resurgent nationalisms have our support only to the extent that they explicitly condemn and struggle against the legacies of anti-Semitism and racism with which they have been identified.

If Germany is allowed to reunite without simultaneously dealing with its past, we will be passing on to history a very unfortunate lesson that will soon come back to haunt us: a people can participate in the worst and most unspeakable crimes, and in a reasonable period of time our collective historical amnesia can be such that this people can return to the collective family of humanity acting as though nothing serious has really happened. If that is the lesson the world learns from Germany, we may see more terrible crimes in the name of nationalism in the years ahead. If it is too late to stop reunification, let it be remembered that liberal Jews sounded the warning.

Reunification II: This Time, No Hobnail Boots

Josef Joffe

In 1871, Germany was unified, and a few years later, *The Times* of London editorialized darkly: "We feel that an enormous power for good or evil has risen up somewhat suddenly in the midst of us, and we watch with interested attention for signs of its character and intention."

On Wednesday, the world will watch "Reunification II"—and as anxiously as 120 years ago. Will the sequel be a repeat performance, starring a restless giant who has become too big for his turf? Will Germany '90 move from strength to arrogance, again bringing grief to Europe and the rest of the world?

The Bismarck-to-Hitler analogy is tempting but misleading. Just compare the opening scenes. In 1871, Germany was unified by "blood and iron"— in a war of aggression launched against France. Today, Germans and French are no longer archenemies but the best of friends. On Wednesday, the loudest sounds to be heard in Berlin will be the whistling of fireworks, not the rumble of artillery. Reunification will be a thoroughly peaceful affair.

Not only is the overture different this time; the stage, script and actors have also changed beyond recognition. Take the lead player. In the Bismarckian Reich, democracy was shouldered aside by a Prussian-dominated state that unleashed an economic revolution while chaining down liberty and dissent. The Kaiser's message to the rising middle classes

was: Go ahead and enrich yourselves, but leave the driving to us.

In the Weimar Republic, born in defeat and disgrace after World War I, democracy never had a chance. Yes, there was a parliamentary regime, but it was ground down in a two-pronged attack by Communists and Nazis who flourished because millions were caught in the maw of the Great Depression. And in 1933, when Hitler came to power, democracy was simply torn to shreds.

After 1945 democracy could at last sink its roots into fertile soil, and in many ways the postwar political miracle in Germany even dwarfed its vaunted economic twin. This time, thanks to generous American help, democracy was not associated with economic misery and humiliation. Instead of reparations, there was Marshall Plan aid; instead of towering tariffs, there was free trade; instead of encirclement, there was NATO [North Atlantic Treaty Organization] and the European Community, extending to the Germans a shelter and a role.

At last, then, German democracy was off to a good start, and today the Cassandras of 1945 have fallen silent. The parties of the extreme right and left have all but vanished, leaving in place a sluggishly centrist regime that is almost boring in its normalcy. The democratic system has weathered every political crisis: neo-Nazis and terrorists, insubordinate generals and rebellious students, large-scale unemployment and mass protests.

In many respects, the political system looks like America writ small. Federalism works, and so does the separation of powers. Compared with the "republican monarchy" that is France, the Federal Republic is a political free-for-all. Nor is there an Official Secrets Act that so hampers the freedom of the press in Britain. State secrets in Bonn last about as long as in Washington—until tomorrow's edition.

The point is not that today's Germans are "good" whereas their grandfathers were thoroughbred authoritarians. The point is that after World War II the stage changed. Flawed as it was in the past, the drama of German history at last could unfold before a benign backdrop. Consider the ugly brew of paranoia and chauvinism that had poisoned the body politic before. The Bismarck Reich, a late arrival in the great power club, was bound to threaten all of its neighbors—and in turn to be threatened by them. The Weimar Republic was a pariah among nations and a target of endless distrust—a perfect breeding ground for the enemies of peace and democracy. It was "us against them" and "Deutschland Uber Alles."

Reunified Germany, by constrast, will be embedded in a larger community, surrounded by friends and not by resentful neighbors. The Federal Republic grew up in security, provided courtesy of the United States, and this cut down the business opportunities of the Pied Pipers. Try as they may, right-wing parties, hawking their message of hate, have never established a foothold in the Federal Parliament.

But, so the skeptics will demur, that wonderful edifice is collapsing before our own eyes. With the Soviet surrender in the Cold War, the Atlantic alliance is fading and the Americans are going home. Won't Germany, finally unshackled from its postwar fetters, again be tempted by sheer strength and the heady lure of aggrandizement?

True, waning dependence equals less deference. Absent the Soviet threat, Bonn-Berlin might be less hesitant to convert economic muscle into political clout. But to argue that Reunification II will turn into a remake of the 1871 original is to ignore how much the script itself has changed.

The rivalry of nations in the democratic-industrial world has moved from the battlefield into the economic arena, and it promises to stay there as long as the marvelous economic community Europeans have built persists. Nobody expects the Germans to invade Alsace again; now they pay for the pleasure of owning the choice plots there, just as the Japanese are buying, not bombing, Pearl Harbor.

Power in Europe (as opposed to Saddam Hussein's neighborhood) is measured not by conquest but by capital surpluses. Not booty and glory define the stakes, but questions such as: "Who determines currency parities?" It so happens that the Bundesbank calls the shots, which understandably grates hard on the French. But worlds separate this contest from the game played out with German

jackboots in Paris 50 years ago. The battle lines are drawn in the balance-of-payments ledgers, and the accounts are settled with dollars and Deutsche marks, not blood and iron. The rivalry is about joint welfare, not this or that province; both sides lose or win together. (American victims of Sony resent cheap VCRs [videocassette recorders] made in Japan, but who would go to war over the privilege of buying worse-quality goods at higher prices?)

Still, might not Bonn-Berlin hanker after nuclear weapons and push for revision of its eastern borders? What for? The new, more civilized and civilianized game of nations offers the largest payoffs to nations such as Germany and Japan. The game has devalued the military chips, delivering power and prestige to those who can back up their bets with investments and loans. Why, then, should they forego their advantage by changing the rules? In the attempt, they would certainly revive the hostile coalitions that proved their undoing in 1945. Also, well-settled democracies are more sensible about such risks than were the Hohenzollerns and Hitlerites.

On Wednesday [October 3, 1990], Bonn Inc. will take over bankrupt Prusso-Marx, a k a [also known as] East Germany. But the remake of 1871 will not be shot with a cast of latter-day Erich von Stroheims. The soundtrack will not be "Deutschland Uber Alles," but Beethoven's "Ode to Joy," Europe's unofficial anthem. Walking alone in the distant past, Germans easily fell for the mesmerizing music of the Pied Pipers. But in the meantime Europe has changed, and so has Germany. Hamburg and Rome, Munich and Marseilles have been listening to the same tune for a long time; adding Dresden and Leipzig should not ruin that score.

QUESTIONS FOR DISCUSSION

1. In what ways are the conditions that produced the unification of Germany in 1871 similar to the conditions that produced the unification of Germany in 1990? In what ways are they different?

2. What implications does Germany's past have for its future foreign policy?

3. What implications does the German economy have for Germany's future foreign policy?

4. How have East and West Germany dealt with anti-Semitism?

5. How long should a nation be held accountable for acts of its past leaders and citizens? What are the reasons for your answer?

SUGGESTED READINGS

Bertram, Christoph. "The German Question." *Foreign Affairs*, **69** (Spring 1990), pp. 45–62.

Grass, Günter. "Don't Reunify Germany." *New York Times*, Jan. 7, 1990, sec. IV, p. 25.

Heibrunn, Jacob. "Who's Afraid of Reunification?" *Freedom at Issue*, no. 114 (May/June 1990), pp. 10–14.

Isaacson, Walter. "Is One Germany Better Than Two?" *Time*, **134** (Nov. 20, 1989), pp. 36, 41.

Mead, Walter Russell. "The Once and Future Reich." *World Policy Journal*, **7** (Fall 1990), pp. 593–638.

Morgan, Roger. "Germany in Europe." *Washington Quarterly*, **13** (Autumn 1990), pp. 147–157.

Nelan, Bruce W. "Anything to Fear?" *Time*, **135** (Mar. 26, 1990), pp. 32–34, 41–42, 47.

Smolowe, J. "This New, New House." *Time*, **135** (May 14, 1990), pp. 26–28.

Stranglin, Douglas. "Finishing What Bismarck Began." *U.S. News and World Report*, **108** (Mar. 5, 1990), pp. 36–37, 40–41.

Szabo, Stephen F. "The German Answer." *SAIS Review*, **10** (Summer/Fall 1990), pp. 41–56.

Warner, Margaret Garrard, and Karen Breslau. "The New Superpower." *Newsweek*, **115** (Feb. 26, 1990), pp. 16–23.

10 Should Eastern Europe and Western Europe Establish Unified European Political and Economic Institutions?

YES

Tadeusz Mazowiecki

Returning to Europe

NO

Ferry Hoogendijk

There Is No "European House"

Returning to Europe

Tadeusz Mazowiecki

Back to Europe! This expression is gaining currency these days in the countries of Central and Eastern Europe. Politicians and economists are speaking of a return. The same applies to members of the cultural world, although it was easier for them to feel they still belonged to Europe: Europe was felt to be their spiritual home, a community of values and traditions. Perhaps the expression ''back to Europe'' is too feeble to describe the process we are experiencing. One should speak rather of a European renaissance, the rebirth of the Europe which virtually ceased to exist after Yalta.

There is also a rebirth of European togetherness and solidarity, which was all too often forgotten in the past. Some, of course, maintained a sense of European community and solidarity. I am thinking of those who publicly voiced their protest against acts of violence, such as the invasions of Hungary in 1956 and of Czechoslovakia in 1968. I am also thinking of all our Western friends who, after the establishment of the state of emergency in 1981, afforded us both moral and material support. At various times throughout these difficult years for us, the personal contacts established in this way helped to create a most valuable network which still subsists and which now offers a priceless foundation for rebuilding the political and economic components of a true community with the other countries of our continent.

The Polish people are acutely aware of belonging to Europe and the European heritage. They are as conscious of this as are the other European peoples situated at the cultural crossroads adjacent to the superpowers, experiencing alternating phases of political existence and non-existence and, hence, feeling the need to strengthen their identity. In all these situations, Europe has always remained a beacon, an object of affection which the Poles felt ready to defend. The idea of being the ''ramparts of Christendom'' and, by the same token, of Europe itself has remained alive in Poland throughout three centuries. Europe is therefore present in the Polish conscience as a value which it is worth living for and sometimes, indeed, dying for.

But at the same time, Poland has borne a grudge against Europe, and this sense of reproach has remained engraved to the present day in our collective consciousness. We continue to regard Europe as an ideal, the home of liberty and the rule of law, and we continue to relate closely to it. But we also continue to feel reproachful because of Yalta, because of the division of Europe and for having been left on the other side of the Iron Curtain.

Today, however, now that the return to Europe, the renaissance of Europe as a single entity, is becoming more and more of a reality, we are wondering more and more frequently what we have to offer, what our contribution can be today to the European treasure house. I believe that we do have a lot to offer. Our contribution to Europe is both our strength and our weakness. We are like someone recovering from a serious illness. For years we have undergone the tremendous pressure of totalitarianism but we have stood firm. However, we are still convalescing. Our economy is still in a critical condition that we are trying to alleviate; the democratic institutions of our state are only just being resuscitated and rebuilt. But we have acquired experience which we shall not forget and which we shall pass on to others.

If we have managed to survive as an entity, we owe this partly to our deep attachment to certain institutions and certain values regarded as the norm in Europe. We owe it to religion and the Church, our attachment to democracy and pluralism, human rights and civil liberties and to the ideal of solidarity. Even when we were unable to give these values their full potential or put them into practice in our public life, we still held them in esteem, we clung to them and struggled for them and therefore we know them

Source: Tadeusz Mazowicki, ''Returning to Europe,'' *European Affairs*, 4 (Spring 1990), pp. 41–43, 46. Reprinted by permission.

and know their value. We know the price of being European, the price of the European heritage which Westerners today have inherited without even having to pay the rights of succession. We can remind them of this price. We, therefore, offer Europe our faith in Europe.

REBUILDING DEMOCRACY

Our country is confronted with the enormous task of reconstituting the rights and the institutions which characterise modern democracies and rebuilding a market economy after an interruption of several decades. Added to this, there is the need to overcome enormous economic problems. We not only have to recreate rights and institutions but, in cases where they were non-existent, we have to start from scratch. Otherwise our two European worlds will never manage to live in harmony.

Poland has already set to work. The government has drafted and enacted numerous laws which provide a legal framework for the independence of the judiciary, for freedom of the press and freedom to organise, for freedom to found political parties, and for local self-government. We are preparing a new Constitution of the Polish Republic, which will become a democratic state subject to the rule of law.

Since the beginning of this year, we have embarked upon a very difficult economic programme, one which aims not only to check inflation but also to establish the foundations for a modern market economy, after the pattern of the institutions which have proved their worth in the highly developed European countries. We intend to continue along this path, successively introducing new elements, among which importance will be attributed to reforming the system of ownership and introducing certain forms of state intervention and social protection within the market economy. We shall gradually develop this system in accordance with our possibilities. We wish our future economic system to combine effective mechanisms for stimulating production with adequate protection for the social groups which require assistance within a free and competitive market economy.

Furthermore, in collaboration with our partners in the CMEA [Council for Mutual Economic Assistance, or COMECON], we have taken far-reaching steps to reform the organisation, which, in our view, should be based on free consent between the states that feel it is in their interest to be members and deal jointly with matters they believe call for concerted measures and action. We have no desire to create closed associations cut off from the rest of the world, not only by frontiers but also by customs barriers. We wish to avoid this so as not to create a Europe where economic walls have replaced the political ones.

GERMANY

Just as the Berlin Wall not so long ago was both the symbol of the divided Europe and a physical barrier splitting Germany into two separate states, so its collapse, while offering an opportunity to unite Europe, at the same time raises the problem of German unification. No people can be denied the right to live within the same state. But the division of Germany resulted from a major disaster caused by the Nazi state which destroyed tens of millions of human lives. It is therefore not at all surprising today if, at the time the prospect is emerging of a reunited German state, the memory of this disaster arouses anxieties which cannot be alleviated even by obviously weighty counterarguments such as the fact that today the situation is different and the Germans themselves are different.

We acknowledge these arguments. But we must understand these anxieties and overcome them by settling the German question with the agreement of all the interested parties and in a manner which, from the outset, will offer a credible sense of security to all those who require it and which above all will guarantee the inviolability of the Western frontier of Poland.

RISKS, CHALLENGES

The upheavals in Central Europe and the Soviet Union are creating unparalleled opportunities but also carry risks. In some countries the supporters of the old regime are no longer in a position to determine the course of events but can still impede it. In others, although they are on the defensive, they have not given up hope, and have not lost the capability, of regaining their former position. If severe symptoms of destabilisation, together with economic chaos, were to persist, these people's chances would increase. They will diminish if the peoples in our region, who at the moment are proving active, can carry through the crucial transformations resolutely but as calmly as possible, and above all if they can resist the temptation to try to achieve everything at once. That approach is often counterproductive.

Another danger is that of Balkanisation of part of the European continent, or of the various countries, because of acute tensions between the peoples or states, tensions whose origins lie in the present as well as the past. If partisan or national interests were to surface and the notion of regional or European interest were to be lost sight of, it would be a major obstacle to establishing healthy cooperation and mutual understanding in this continent of ours.

But the events unfolding in Central and Eastern Europe, although they carry risks, are first and foremost an unbelievable and historic challenge. And although obviously the challenges are mainly for us, the people of Central Europe, they are also a historic challenge and a task for the whole of Europe. The scope is vast. There is room for Western Europeans who see what we are trying to do and believe in our aims. With them it will be easier to narrow the distance between the two Europes. The wall which divided free Europe from enslaved Europe is down. Now we have to fill in the gulf between poor Europe and affluent Europe. If Europe is to be a "common home" whose door is open to all, such great disparities cannot be allowed to continue. A huge job of work awaits us all.

EUROPE 2000

We now need new guidelines to point our endeavours down a common European road, to no one's exclusion and everyone's advantage. It is not easy to chart such a course, for it takes thought and collaboration. But as post-1992 Europe is even now taking shape in Western Europe, we should start thinking in terms of a Europe of the year 2000. To be realistic, what kind of Europe might that be if we unite our efforts?

It will certainly not be a European area with free movement of goods, capital and people, but it might be a Europe where borders and tariffs would be much less of an obstacle, a Europe wholly open to the young. For the fate of our continent depends on what kind of young people we bring up.

It might be a Europe in which contact between the creative and the scientific communities, fostering permeability of national cultures and thereby bringing them closer together, will be richer than it is today.

It will not be a Europe with a common currency, but it might be a Europe in which economies will be complementary and where differences in living standards will be smaller and international economic exchange richer.

It might also be a Europe with a healthy climate, pure water and unpolluted soil, an environmentally clean Europe.

But above all it will have to be a Europe which has made distinct progress towards disarmament, a Europe which will make an impact on the rest of the world as a factor for peace and international coexistence.

By applying our minds, we could find many other spheres of social life which we could arrange better in this last decade of the 20th century. We need but apply ourselves to the task.

EUROPEAN CONFEDERATION

In this continent of ours there are institutions in which a labour of this kind has long-term prospects, because it has already been going on quite a while. One of these institutions is the Council of Europe, one of whose aims is to achieve greater unity among its members for the purpose of safeguarding and realising the ideals and principles which are their common heritage and facilitating their economic and social progress.

Now that events are speeding up in Europe, it is

beginning to be possible for us—states, groups and organisations—to reflect about these matters together, and we can glimpse the possibility of and need for pan-European structures. The time has come to realise the "common home" and the European confederation eminent statesmen have recently proposed. It is time to establish institutions genuinely encompassing all of Europe.

That is why I recently put forward in our parliament a suggestion for a Council of European Cooperation, embracing all signatories to the Final Act of the Conference on Security and Cooperation in Europe [CSCE]. The council would have two functions, firstly to make preparations for summit meetings of the CSCE states, and secondly to examine pan-European problems arising between regular meetings of the CSCE states. This would lend needed impetus to the CSCE process and at the same time facilitate future initiatives concerning our continent and aiming to secure its unity.

Today the whole of Europe is faced with the historic challenge of restoring its unity. Will we be equal to it? That depends on all of us. Let us be capable of recognising a historic juncture and rising to its challenge—cautiously, boldly and clearsightedly.

There Is No "European House"

Ferry Hoogendijk

Successful Western European integration is very appealing to the new regimes in Eastern Europe. Jidi Dienstbier, the Czech Minister for Foreign Affairs, said in Prague: "After the political revolution, Czechoslovakia will fundamentally change its foreign policy, orientate itself towards Europe and play a key role in the unification of Europe." In his speech to the Council of Europe last year, the Soviet leader, Mikhail Gorbachev, said that the United Europe of the 21st century will "be an enormous economic zone spanning an area from the Atlantic Ocean to the Urals."

This might well prove to be the case in economic terms—although a lot will need changing, in particular in the Soviet Union—but in other respects, the Europe that Gorbachev envisages does not and will probably never exist. In our euphoria resulting from the positive developments in Eastern Europe, we should not forget that the Russians in particular have little in common with the people of Central and Western Europe. They took no active part in the spiritual movements (the Renaissance, Humanism) which have heavily influenced Western European society. Philosophers such as Montesquieu, Locke and Hobbes have determined our structures and have created a cultural image which, to the Russians, is quite foreign. In this respect, Western Europe is much more compatible with the United States than with Russia. The "European House," which is being discussed with great enthusiasm, does not exist and—to my mind—is pretty unrealistic. To rephrase this in even stronger terms: it constitutes a danger for the European Community [EC] which we are build-

ing now. Idealists talking about the "European House" clearly overlook the complexities involved in bringing together the 12 such as they are. If we are going to decelerate this process by discussing EC membership for Eastern European countries in the short term, there is the risk of undermining, as opposed to reinforcing, the unity of Europe.

According to a poll conducted by Eurobarometer, EC citizens seem to agree that, in order to deal with the changes in Eastern Europe, the European Community should speed up its own economic, political and monetary integration (70 percent of all those interviewed and 83 percent of those who expressed an opinion). Accelerating integration of the present 12 within the Community is more strongly favoured in the UK [United Kingdom], Portugal, Ireland, France, Italy, Spain and Luxembourg. In West Germany, 62 percent of those interviewed agreed that the process should be speeded up (three out of four who expressed an opinion).

All citizens of the European Community enthusiastically welcomed the changes that have been taking place and would like to see the Western countries, coordinated by the Commission, encourage steps towards democracy (93 percent, EBS = Eurobarometer standard, Oct./Nov. '89). They considered that "the programme for immediate food aid to Poland organised by the Commission" was a "good thing" (84 percent); they also favoured "closer economic cooperation" between the West and Eastern Europe, coordinated and organised by the European Community (84 percent) and they welcomed the implementation of "a joint policy" by the European Community for closing the gap between us and Eastern Europe, i.e., "rapprochement" (78 percent). They agreed that the "Community should take joint action to help European countries carry out their reforms" (86 percent). The risk involved in EC integration results from the fact that the Germans might now be preoccupied by the German issue and use this as an excuse for failing to pursue Western integration along the lines of the single European market.

Irrespective of how successful the economic reforms in Eastern Europe prove to be, even a five-fold

Source: Ferry Hoogendijk, "There Is No 'European House,'" *European Affairs*, 4 (Spring 1990), pp. 36–40. Reprinted with permission.

increase in trade with these countries would not be commensurate with "normal" growth in trade with Western Europe over the next five years. It should be obvious that a continuation of the single market process is essential to the economic well-being of West Germany and Europe.

Various sources, both American and European, have expressed the same wish to see the two Germanys unified within a European or Atlantic context. James Baker, the American Secretary of State, made it plain that the U.S. would not like to see German reunification exceed the "comfortable" tolerance levels of the rest of Western Europe. Mr. Baker emphasised that European institutions such as the EC and NATO [North Atlantic Treaty Organization] should be responsible for ensuring that a unified Germany is firmly anchored in the West.

A poll, organised by Eurobarometer on behalf of the German magazine *Die Bunte*, showed that all 12 countries of the Community favour a possible reunification of the two Germanys. 78 percent of the citizens of the 12 are for German reunification. The percentage in West Germany corresponds exactly with the Community average. Regarding the French, the Italians, the Czechs, the Portuguese and the Spanish, the percentage in favour of German reunification is higher than in West Germany itself!

There are more British than West Germans who would accept a reunited Germany as a member of the EC (UK 82%, Germany 80%, of all those interviewed). In general, three EC citizens out of four agreed that "the Community should prepare for Eastern countries undergoing a process of democratisation to join the Community in the future." As for the West Germans themselves, the 78% in favour of reunification of the present two Germanys dropped to 18% if leaving the European Community were to be imposed as a condition by a referendum in East Germany; fewer than one West German in five is prepared to forego membership in the EC for German unity.

Although four West Germans out of five support economic aid for East Germany, as illustrated in November 1989 by a poll carried out by the Mannheim-based "Forschungsgruppe Wahlen" for the "Zweites Deutsches Fernsehen," less than half of those in favour of reunification are willing to give up part of their present income to assist economic development in East Germany. In other words, two West Germans in three are reluctant to give up a single pfennig for the economic development of East Germany within a reunified Germany.

However, large-scale financial help will be required to back up the economic reforms. Jacques Delors, addressing the European Parliament, estimated that about 19 thousand million ECU [European Currency Units] in the coming 5 years would have to be earmarked for Hungary, Poland, East Germany, Bulgaria, Czechoslovakia and Romania.

Robert D. Hormats, Vice Chairman of Goldman Sachs International, wrote in the *International Herald Tribune* that assistance is a good investment: "Even today with all their problems, Czechoslovakia, East Germany, Hungary and Poland have a combined gross national product which is considerably greater than that of China." At the World Economic Forum in Davos the world's banking and investing elite were reluctant to invest at this stage in Eastern European countries. A U.S. investment banker said: "The spokesman for the new governments were leaders who until a few months ago owed their careers and positions to their commitment to communism. It shows how much still needs to be changed in Eastern Europe. Until then, I think, we will follow what is happening with great interest, but I doubt we will put much money in."

The changes to be made in Eastern Europe (and in the Soviet Union itself) in order to achieve successful reforms are too numerous to have a chance of success in a short time. Eastern Europe is engaged in or preparing for five simultaneous transitions: From central economic planning to reliance upon market forces; from backward, often heavily agrarian economies to modern, competitive ones; from Communist Party domination to multiparty democracy; from trade and financing ties straitjacketed by COMECON [Council for Mutual Economic Assistance, or CMEA] to those that serve their own economic interests; and from regional and international political relationships dictated by Moscow to those shaped by these nations. This is tantamount to expecting a six-month-old baby to learn to walk, eat, go to school and get married all of its own accord!

At the COMECON January meeting, the door to the world economy was opened for everyone to see. So far in Eastern Europe, only Poland has dared to take the painful plunge of moving towards market prices, a mainstay of a restructured economy. However, the transition is not an easy one—there are many problems involved. None of the COMECON countries has any experience regarding free competition. In addition, the Eastern European manufacturers are not used to the high quality standards of the West.

Frans Andriessen, EC Commission member, would like to create a new budget for providing assistance to Eastern Europe. In this way, the EC can help finance the transition of the COMECON system towards a market-oriented trade system. Setting up a development bank for Eastern Europe is a step in the right direction.

However, the Eastern European economic systems will have to gather sufficient momentum in order efficiently to absorb the assistance received. Timing is critical. How long will the population wait for a rosy economic future? If there is not enough bread and meat available on the market, people will get impatient with their political leaders and cut their reforms short.

This is the major dilemma, particularly for Gorbachev himself. He is the architect of this revolution, but he had expected to reform the economy of the Soviet Union under the umbrella and under the control of the Communist Party. The freedom which Gorbachev applauds in the Eastern European countries induced him to go further than he had intended in his own country.

His victory at the February meeting of the Party Central Committee has strengthened his position in the party, but the Russian people are very cynical about all the talks and plans of Gorbachev. The rest of the world is very enthusiastic about the historical meeting of the Central Committee (truly a Third Revolution). *The New York Times* wrote, "The hammer has been separated from the sickle and all who thought this could never happen can rejoice."

But despite all these historical developments it is hard to look at the Soviet Union's future and particularly Gorbachev's future. Liberation, decolonisation and freedom are in themselves good, but you need experience to handle them. Sure, there is time for celebration, but also for caution.

After 70 years of centralisation and suppression you should expect that the Russians will express their happiness about the Kremlin's reform policy. But instead there is scepticism and even fear of anarchy and civil war.

The West should also bear in mind that the current revolution will disrupt the Soviet Union and lead to chaos, which means instability. This is the reason why it is and will continue to be vitally important for the West to retain the alliance between the U.S. and Western Europe.

In addition, it is not yet clear what political form the new Eastern Europe will assume. Dozens of civic groups, parties and forums have just started organising themselves to challenge the Communist parties. "The reform Communists are whistling in the dark," said Zbigniew Brzezinski, the former U.S. national security adviser. "I think they'll be wiped out everywhere in the coming elections."

This has undoubtedly had an impact on the Communist leaders in the Soviet Union itself. The Soviet Union is a patchwork of different peoples who have little or nothing in common with one another. They have been forcibly brought under Moscovite rule by a succession of tsars from Ivan the Great to Alexander III, and subsequently by the Red Army and Stalin.

Gorbachev is forced to apply military force to stop the process of nationalistic separatism. The Baltic states want to get out of the Soviet Union. Armenia and Azerbaijan are hotbeds of widely spreading fires. The Red Army has been active in these areas. In connection with separatism, the role of the army can be defended as being the body which reestablishes law and order. Gorbachev, however, cannot order any military action to be taken against the miners should they repeat their demands for higher wages and better living conditions.

Perestroika has failed and Gorbachev has also failed, said Boris Yeltsin in an interview with

Elsevier. "I foresee an explosive situation. It is the most serious test we are facing," the former Moscow party chief said. Last year, Mr. Yeltsin was elected a member for Moscow to the National Congress of the People's Deputies. This was a head-on attack from Gorbachev's own ranks. The problems for Gorbachev are immense and uniquely diverse. The Soviet Union has to confront a political and economic identity crisis and colonial explosions at the same time. The Soviet Union finds itself in a tricky position: democracy would lead to the destruction of the empire. The dissolution of the Soviet empire is one thing, the dissolution of the Soviet Union is quite another! The dismantling of the Soviet economy has reached its most critical phase. *Perestroika* has to be its saving grace. Gorbachev, however, will never allow the Soviet Union to disintegrate through *glasnost.*

How Gorbachev should face this trial of strength is anybody's guess. Many have started to doubt whether Gorbachev will survive his own politics. In this spirit of pessimism, it is a real relief to see Gorbachev in action, encouraging his people: "We need *perestroika* like we need air." However, we know that the air in the Communist countries is more polluted than anywhere else.

QUESTIONS FOR DISCUSSION

1. What effect would a European common home have on the economic and political systems of Eastern European states?

2. What effect would a European common home have on U.S. foreign policy?
3. What effect would a European common home have on the U.S. economy?
4. What are the chances for the success of political and economic reforms in Eastern Europe?
5. What effect would a European common home have on the European Community?

SUGGESTED READINGS

Brimelow, Peter. "The Dark Side of 1992." *Forbes,* **145** (Jan. 22, 1990), pp. 85–89.

De Michelis, Gianni. "Reaching Out to the East." *Foreign Policy*, no. 79 (Summer 1990), pp. 45–55.

Djilas, Milovan. "A Revolutionary Democratic Vision of Europe." *International Affairs* (Cambridge, England), **66** (Apr. 1990), pp. 265–273.

Reading, Brian. "A Greater European Century?" *Across the Board*, **26** (Dec. 1989), pp. 17–20.

Snyder, Jack. "Averting Anarchy in the New Europe." *International Security*, **14** (Spring 1990), pp. 5–41.

Steel, Ronald. "The Rise of the European Superpower." *New Republic*, **203** (July 2, 1990), pp. 23–25.

Stranglin, Douglas, et al. "Reinventing Europe." *U.S. News and World Report*, **107** (Nov. 27, 1989), pp. 39–43.

Sullivan, Scott. "Big Europe or Little Europe?" *Newsweek*, **115** (Mar. 12, 1990), pp. 38, 40.

von Staden, Berndt. "Nothing Less Than the Whole of Europe Will Do. . . ." *Aussenpolitik* (Hamburg, English ed.), **41** (First Quarter 1990), pp. 24–37.

Wistrich, Ernest. *After 1992: The United States of Europe.* New York: Routledge, 1989.

11 Would the Establishment of a Palestinian State Be Dangerous to Peace?

YES

Michael Widlanski

How Dangerous Would a Palestinian State Be? Very Dangerous

NO

Ephraim Sneh

How Dangerous Would a Palestinian State Be? We Can Live with It

How Dangerous Would a Palestinian State Be?
Very Dangerous

Michael Widlanski

When faced with a perplexing multiple-choice question, the best way to proceed is to eliminate the alternatives that make no sense. In its recent study, *Can Israel Survive a Palestinian State?*, the Institute for Advanced Strategic and Political Studies (IASPS) eliminated one option in the search for possible paths to peace in the Middle East: a Palestinian Arab state west of the Jordan River. With this study my colleagues and I promised no miracle cures for the Arab-Israeli conflict, but we felt that the restoration of some cold analysis to the debate would go a long way toward clarifying the situation. What follows here is a summary of our study and its framework, concentrating on the ramifications for Israel.

In the latter days of the Reagan administration and with the inception of the Bush administration, the Palestinian state option was raised increasingly as a purportedly viable one. The Bush administration's dialogue with the Palestine Liberation Organization further spurred IASPS's interest in the West Bank option.

The framework for the discussion by IASPS was not ideological. We ignored the political and religious aspirations of both Arabs and Jews and considered, instead, the strategic and military consequences of various scenarios. In other words, we bypassed the big moral questions such as: Does Israel have a right to exist? or Should Jews settle on the West Bank? or

What are the legitimate rights of Palestinian Arabs?

IASPS asked a much narrower and more practical question, namely: Is the establishment of a Palestinian Arab state west of the Jordan River likely to bring peace and stability to the Middle East? Our answer was likewise basic: a Palestinian state would destabilize the region to the point of a general Arab-Israeli war. Unconventional weapons would likely be used, and Israel would find itself in mortal peril.

Even a "benign" or "seemingly benign" Palestinian state based on complete Israeli withdrawal from the West Bank, we concluded, would rob Israel of strategic assets needed to maintain a credible deterrent to the surrounding states. In short, a return to an Israel nine miles wide at its waist is an invitation for Arab hard-liners to move militarily against Israel. This assertion was based in part on previously unpublished documentation from the American and Israeli strategic communities, documentation which included the Allon Plan, the Joint Chiefs of Staff Pentagon Plan, and the Ford-Rabin letter.

The Allon Plan, formulated in 1967, represents the strategic thinking of Yigal Allon, the foremost military analyst of the Israeli Labor Party. The formulation by the Pentagon was the judgment of the U.S. Joint Chiefs of Staff as to what constituted "Israel's minimum defense needs." The secret Ford letter of September 1975 sets forth part of America's secret understandings of Israel's defense needs, including Israeli retention of the high ground on the Golan Heights.

Both the Allon Plan and the Pentagon Plan—as well as the Begin Autonomy Plan of Camp David—reject the establishment of a Palestinian Arab state west of the Jordan. This is no accident; a consensus exists between American and Israeli strategic communities on this point. Further corroboration is offered by Professor Eugene V. Rostow, one of the framers of U.N. Resolution 242 and a former under secretary of state in the Johnson administration. In his report, Rostow stresses the idea that the notion of a Palestinian state was specifically addressed and rejected by the framers of Resolution 242, which promises Israel "secure and recognized boundaries"—something incompatible with a Palestinian state west of the Jordan.

Source: Michael Widlanski, "How Dangerous Would a Palestinian State Be? Very Dangerous," *Tikkun*, 5 (July/August 1990), pp. 61–63. Reprinted with permission from *Tikkun* magazine, a bimonthly Jewish critique of politics, culture, and society. Subscriptions are available for $25/yr (6 issues) from 5100 Leona St., Oakland, CA 94619.

The consensus among Israeli citizens is with Rostow. Indeed, newspaper public opinion polls in Israel routinely show that 90 percent of the Israeli population disapproves of a Palestinian state in the occupied territories. There are many reasons for this.

Israel's increased vulnerability alongside a Palestinian state would require that Israel resort to a trip-wire or hair-trigger posture, forcing it to strike in a massive preemptive fashion against even somewhat ambiguous threats. An ideological and strategic first cousin to the trip-wire doomsday scenario is the "massive retaliation" school of thought, espoused in the IASPS study by scholars such as Professor Arnon Soffer, a noted geographer from Haifa University who has written extensively about demographic problems. He once told me, "Israel should pull back from Arab population centers in the West Bank and say, 'If even one Katyusha rocket is fired into an Israeli settlement, we'll destroy you. If even one rocket hits Kfar Sava [an Israeli town near the 1949 Armistice Line], then we'll blast Qalqilya [an Arab town three miles away] into dust and then move in and take it over.'" In both political and strategic terms—let alone the important factor of morality—this massive-retaliation scenario is even less feasible than the so-called "peaceable forced transfer" of Arabs advocated by the extreme Right in Israel.

Both the massive-retaliation school and the automatic-trip-wire approach are simply too rigid, even Strangelovian, and stand in direct opposition to the kind of *flexible response* democratic leaders must exercise in times of crisis. In addition, given the large arsenals of unconventional weapons in the area, there is no assurance that employment of massive retaliation or automatic trip wires might not escalate into a broader conflict involving chemical, biological, or even nuclear devices.

It is no mere coincidence that many of those who favor a total Israeli withdrawal from the West Bank and Gaza conclude that Israel must base its deterrent posture on unconventional weaponry—especially nuclear devices—combined with "smart bombs" such as laser devices, super satellites, permanently airborne spy planes, precision-guided munitions

(FGMs), and so on. But while some or all of these factors can or should play a part in Israel's deterrent posture today and tomorrow, they cannot totally replace the geographical advantages Israel currently enjoys. (Israel cannot, of course, rely only on terrain advantages for its defense.)

Israel must develop its own version of America's strategic "triad." The U.S. triad is built on land-based ICBMs [intercontinental ballistic missiles], submarine-based missiles, and a bomber force designed so that the country is not vulnerable to surprise attack. On a superstrategic level, Israel must have a triad based on strong conventional defense, a stated or unstated unconventional deterrent, and internal unity. Within this superstrategic triad, Israel's conventional defense should rest on several factors:

- qualitative and technological superiority of arms;
- continued edge in manpower and doctrine;
- terrain advantages including retention of Israeli control of high ground on the Golan Heights, and the "natural tank trap" on the West Bank and in the Gaza Strip.

Our study did not rule out some form of territorial compromise, such as the Allon Plan, favored by the Israeli Labor party; nor did it preclude functional compromise agreed to by the Likud, or the divided rule or mixed formulas such as district plans, cantons, mixed Israeli-Jordanian rule, full or partial annexation, federation, confederation, and so forth—*as long as key strategic areas remained under Israeli security control.*

The trouble with a full-fledged Palestinian state extending over the entire West Bank is that it offers Israel no assurance that some Hafez al-Assad or Saddam Hussein might not force a "moderate" PLO [Palestine Liberation Organization]—or even a non-PLO regime—to allow a new Palestinian state to become a base for an Arab war coalition along Israel's most vulnerable frontier, its "Eastern front."

Even if one assumes an unrealistically utopian picture of a docile, newly independent Palestine, one must realize that its location less than fifteen miles from Israel's four major cities and the country's major airport offers an irresistible temptation for hard-line elements inside the Palestinian camp to use relatively low-cost terrorism with crippling effect. Such "rejectionist" groups could create havoc at Ben-Gurion Airport with one or two shoulder-held missiles, and they could have a similar effect on Haifa, an increasingly important port of call for the U.S. Sixth Fleet.

Far from solving Israel's demographic problems, a Palestinian Arab state would itself be a demographic time bomb and invite the return of hundreds of thousands of Palestinians whose energies would then be directed toward pre-1967 Israel. Most of the PLO leadership, one should recall, wants to return to Jaffa (Tel Aviv), Haifa, Lod (the site of Ben-Gurion Airport), Ramle, Majdal (Ashkelon), and Jerusalem—not Nablus, Hebron, and Jenin on the West Bank. Moreover, PLO documents and broadcasts openly invite the support and secessionist tendencies of Israel's own Arab citizens, especially within the Galilee and Negev.

It is only natural that potential Arab foes would try to coax Israel into giving up the high ground on the West Bank and proximate positions in Gaza without a fight. As the strategist B. H. Liddell Hart once observed: "It is . . . more potent, as well as more economical, to disarm the enemy than to attempt his destruction by hard fighting."

It may be argued that Israel has already shown itself able to defeat allied Arab powers from the starting point of the pre-1967 frontiers and therefore need not be afraid of returning territory on the West Bank and Gaza. If attacked, Israel would win as it did in 1967. There are several responses to this argument:

- To deter a war is far better than to fight one.
- In 1967, Israel's geographic inferiority forced it into surprise attack. Such an attack would be impossible today due to the scope and preparedness of Arab forces.
- The Arab states have expanded and upgraded their fighting machines dramatically since 1967 and especially in the last decade. They have multiplied their quantitative edge and closed Israel's qualitative advantages in every respect besides terrain.

Given Israel's limited manpower and monetary resources, the threat to Israel from a Palestinian state may well be insurmountable, particularly if the state were to include the key high ground west of the Jordan River and on the Golan Heights. In effect, Israel would become hostage to the good intentions of the Palestinian state and/or its Arab neighbors, who would be sorely tempted to exploit the strategic areas acquired.

Proponents of the Palestinian-state option defend it as a way of increasing the chances for peace and regional stability. According to this view, the "Palestinian question" is at the core of the Arab-Israeli conflict. Many supporters of the Palestinian-state option contend that the Arab-Israeli conflict itself has really become an Israeli-Palestinian conflict which, if solved by the creation of a Palestinian Arab state, would be defused. Many Arab states, it is claimed, are leaning solidly toward making peace with Israel, and solving the symbolically important "Palestinian problem" would clear the way for a general Arab-Israeli settlement.

But if this supposition is false, then there is no strategic justification for a Palestinian state. If several Arab states' hostility to Israel has no connection to the "Palestinian question," then fulfilling some Palestinian aspirations will not necessarily lead to a lessening of Arab-Israeli tensions. In other words, creating a Palestinian state may not end tensions between Israel and its other neighbors.

Indeed, if someone were to demonstrate that creating a Palestinian state would both weaken Israel and fail to end the Arab-Israeli conflict, then it would be foolish for Israel to support such a position. Moreover, if creating a Palestinian state were actually to encourage more aggressive Arab behavior against Israel, as well as increased conflict and regional instability, then it would be both strategically and morally absurd to advance the creation of such a state.

Our study, I believe, demonstrated the negative effect a Palestinian state would have on the region. The strategic argument has given way to a moral one because the practical claims for a two-state solution are unfounded.

How Dangerous Would a Palestinian State Be?
We Can Live With It

Ephraim Sneh

In my former job as head of the Civil Administration on the West Bank, I frequently had the opportunity to brief visiting foreign delegations. On one such occasion, I remarked to a leading American foreign policy analyst that, unless there is movement toward territorial compromise, Israeli troops will have to patrol the streets of Hebron for the next one hundred years. His off-the-cuff reply was ''So what?''

I was reminded of this incident upon reading the recent report issued by the Institute for Advanced Strategic and Political Studies [IASPS] and summarized in *Tikkun* by its principal author, Michael Widlanski. This acceptance of the inevitability of the status quo is the hallmark of the analysis presented by IASPS. Not surprisingly, the same visiting American foreign-policy analyst I refer to above is also a contributor to the IASPS report.

The IASPS report claims to be an in-depth academic study of the consequences a Palestinian state would have for Israel's security. But the characterization of its authors as objective, neutral, nonpartisan academic scholars who professionally analyze a strategic problem is a deception. The Israeli contributors (with one exception) belong to the right wing of the Israeli political spectrum. An effort was made to bring together almost all the Israeli reserve generals who oppose the formula of ''territories for peace''; there are not too many of them, so it was easy to get them together. The civilians in the group,

both Israelis and Americans, are well known for their right-wing convictions. They are of course entitled to express their opinions about Israel's security, but the IASPS report is not a study; it is a propaganda brochure, skillfully presented on glossy paper with striking maps and illustrations.

What is absent from the maps of the IASPS report is the population of the territories it describes. For Widlanski and his contributors, the West Bank and Gaza Strip are merely staging grounds for Arab troops, launching sites for missiles, hiding places for terrorists, geography without demography. The fact that 1.7 million Palestinians live there, and that these are human beings with personal and national aspirations, is negligible.

So much for the obvious. The IASPS team also ignores recent developments in the Middle East, the role of Egypt in the peace process, and changes in the attitudes of the Palestinians themselves. Widlanski and colleagues believe Arabs only when they make threats, not when they speak moderately. Not surprisingly, the report is full of deceptions and distorted presentation of facts:

- The Allon Plan is mentioned in the report as an example of defense doctrine opposing Palestinian sovereignty west of the Jordan River. In fact, the spirit of the Allon Plan is ''maximum security for Israel with minimum control over the Palestinian population.'' The Allon Plan provided for Israeli strategic positions in the Jordan River Valley while also providing sovereignty to the Palestinian population on most of the West Bank, not necessarily with geographical linkage to Jordan.

  Allon wrote his plan a few weeks after Israel's victory in June 1967 and did not include Jewish settlements on the populated parts of the West Bank as part of his conception. The one hundred settlements built by the Likud government between 1977 and 1984 have made the Allon Plan inapplicable and impractical. The principles and spirit of the plan, however, remain the cornerstone of the Labor party doctrine regarding territorial solution, and they are a far cry from the conclusions reached by the IASPS ''study.''

- Widlanski emphasizes the threat of an Arab coali-

Source: Ephraim Sneh, ''How Dangerous Would a Palestinian State Be? We Can Live with It,'' *Tikkun*, 5 (July/August 1990), pp. 63–65. Reprinted with permission from *Tikkun* magazine, a bimonthly Jewish critique of politics, culture, and society. Subscriptions are available for $25/yr. (6 issues) from 5100 Leona St., Oakland, CA 94619.

tion on Israel's "Eastern Front." Yes, this is a serious potential threat. But what exists now is a bloc of moderate Arab states that seek a peace agreement in the region. The extremist militant Syria is isolated today in the Arab world. What may help Syria break its isolation and build an anti-Israel coalition amongst other states is a continuation of the status quo that prolongs the Israeli-Palestinian conflict. Iraq, with its military potential, is a regional counterbalance to Syria, especially as a backing to Jordan against its northern militant neighbor. But, if an anti-Israel coalition forms as a result of the stalemated peace process, Iraq will join as a very powerful partner. In the wars of 1967 and 1973, Iraq did not form the aggressive coalition but joined it during the war. Israeli intransigence—what Widlanski and the IASPS report so vehemently advocate—is the prescription for the unification of the Arab world against Israel.

- Widlanski ignores the changes that have occurred in the region in the last decade. In that time, most of the Arab regimes have come to the conclusion that the ideology which threatens their existence is not Zionism, but Muslim fundamentalism, inspired by Iran. Of the four Arab states which share borders with Israel, Egypt signed a peace treaty with Israel, and Jordan reached an agreement with Israel about the initiation of negotiations (the Hussein-Peres Agreement signed in London in April of 1987). It was Shamir who rejected this agreement and blocked its adoption by Israel.

The third state, Lebanon, is not a state any more, but a state of mind. Still, if only as an historical footnote, it, too, signed a peace treaty with Israel in May 1983. Now Israel successfully uses the southern part of Lebanon as a security zone and will continue to do so as long as terrorist organizations take advantage of the chaos which prevails in that country.

The fourth state, Syria, with which Israel has the shortest border, still opposes any peace process, and waits for the failure of the current process in order to regain leadership in the Arab world. Widlanski's recommendation to keep the

Israeli-Palestinian conflict unresolved just because Israel's neighbors maintain their animosity toward Israel ignores the strategies of the actual actors involved.

- Widlanski speaks of "massive retaliation" theories which are used by those in Israel who favor territorial compromise. They adopt "Strangelovian" approaches, he says, to counteract the vulnerability of a smaller Israel. To substantiate his claim, Widlanski quotes a distinguished Israeli geographer—a geographer, and not a political leader or strategic thinker. Widlanski's selective quotation does not represent any strategic school of thought in Israel.

It is more accurate and honest to say that those in Israel who advocate the formula of "territories for peace" strongly insist that even in conditions of peace, Israel must maintain its military superiority. Even when the prophecy of Isaiah becomes a reality, we would prefer Israel as the wolf and not the lamb.

The distance between Kfar Sava and Qalqilya is the same as that between Qalqilya and Kfar Sava, and the distance between Ashkelon and Gaza is the same as between Gaza and Ashkelon. This means that the densely populated Palestinian towns are as exposed to Israel's military strength as Israeli towns may be to terrorist attackers. Israel can rely on this sort of deterrence.

- One of the illustrations in the IASPS report shows a terrorist hidden behind a bush as he launches a shoulder missile at a 747 airliner landing at Ben-Gurion Airport. This is a concrete threat, often repeated to American Jews who use the international airport on their visits to Israel. The implication of such an image is, "If we give back the West Bank, you will be unable to safely land at Ben-Gurion Airport."

Interestingly, there is another international airport in Israel, the Eilat Airport, which has been in use for three decades and which lies only one mile from the border with Jordan. Hundreds of Israelis and tourists use it daily and not a single missile has ever been launched from Jordan at one of the aircraft landing or taking off. Are the Arabs in this area pro-Israeli? No. What matters is not the technical ability to shoot missiles, but who controls the other side of the border. A responsible government that cares for its own vital interests has an incentive to prevent such an attack and can do so effectively.

- The report minimizes the demographic problem and Widlanski entirely ignores three factors which may shift Israel's demographic balance: the birth rate of the Palestinians on the West Bank and in the Gaza Strip is one of the highest in the Middle East; there is a permanent stream of Jewish emigration from Israel, mainly to the U.S. (between 1980 and 1987 the number of immigrants exceeded the number of emigrants by only two thousand people); and the emigration of Palestinians from the territories to Jordan and the Gulf States—an important factor in the slowdown of Arab population growth in the seventies and early eighties—has ceased. Due to the outcome of the Iran-Iraq War and the economic crisis in Jordan, these countries can no longer offer jobs to Palestinians who come from the outside. Even if the immigration from the Soviet Union manages to maintain the Jewish majority between the Jordan River and the Mediterranean, an Arab minority of 40 percent means a bi-national state. In order to preserve Jewish dominance in state institutions, Israel must deprive the Palestinians in the territories of civil rights; while in order to preserve its democratic character, Israel must add 1.7 million Palestinians to the 800,000 Israeli Arabs who are already Israeli citizens and grant them civil rights. Widlanski offers no solution to this existential paradox.

- Widlanski speaks about the danger that a Palestinian state poses to Jordan, though once again he ignores the facts. More than 1.5 million Palestinians live in Jordan, approximately two-thirds of its population. The Palestinians there are fully integrated into Jordanian society. At the same time, there are family ties, shared economic interests, and other connections of the like between this Palestinian community and the Palestinian community in the occupied territories. It is unrealistic

to assume that after permanent arrangements have been achieved, these two communities can be totally separated. It is also unrealistic to believe that the Hashemite kingdom can restore its control on the West Bank and in the Gaza Strip. Eventually the practical arrangement will have to be a confederation of the East Bank, the West Bank, and the Gaza Strip. Some initial understandings already exist between the PLO and Jordan on this matter, though what really endangers Jordan's stability is the radicalization inspired by the intifada.

Nothing is more important to us, the Israelis, than ensuring Israel's security within the framework of a peace agreement. It must be clearly said that no peace agreement will be achieved that does not provide Israel with satisfactory security guarantees while also satisfying Palestinian aspirations for sovereignty.

The IASPS report correctly describes the vulnerability of Israel's population, mainly concentrated within the narrow coastal plain. Israel must not be exposed to attack by troops deployed along its border from the West Bank, as almost happened in 1967. The IDF (Israel Defense Force) is composed mainly of reserve units, which are ready for battle only after a process of mobilization. To avoid a surprise attack, Israel will need sufficient early-warning capability.

No Israeli leader will sign a peace agreement that does not satisfy the country's security needs. What are the essential guarantees necessary to ensure Israel's security? The West Bank and Gaza Strip have to be totally demilitarized so that they cannot serve as a springboard for a military offensive against Israel by standing Arab armies, or as a base for terrorist raids on Israel by extremist Palestinian organizations. This demilitarization would be, of course, a part of the peace treaty. Deployment of military forces by Arab states would not be allowed, and only Palestinian policemen would be authorized to carry light weapons.

Verification of this demilitarization would involve Israeli control over a strip along the Jordan River, as well as the establishment of a few early-warning installations if and where airborne systems are not sufficient. The Israeli military presence along the Jordan River Valley would prevent any infiltration by terrorists and arms smugglers since there are no airports or harbors on the West Bank. The only route of infiltration, then, is through the Jordan River, while the Jordan River Valley is a natural obstacle with few points where a regular army might cross. The Israeli presence along the Jordan River Valley would be substantial enough to contain any attack from the eastern side of the Jordan River. Of course, Israel would have the right to reinforce its troops there in case of imminent confrontation. It should also be remembered that in the valley area the Palestinian population is very small, so it is likely that the friction would be kept to a minimum.

The verification of Gaza Strip demilitarization would be much easier. The Israeli navy could easily prevent any military use of the Mediterranean coast, while the army could protect the land borders. Egypt, meanwhile, could efficiently control the Strip's southern border.

Although providing these guarantees to Israel stands in contrast to absolute Palestinian sovereignty, this is the character of the compromise: the meeting point of the two parties' demands is where Palestinian sovereignty might endanger Israel's security. A detailed study of this issue by prominent Israeli military commentator Ze'ev Schiff has recently been published by the Washington Institute for Near East Policy ("Security for Peace: Israel's Minimal Security Requirements in Negotiations with the Palestinians").

Schiff's study stands in direct contrast to Widlanski's report, which is riddled with anxiety and projected dangers that seem justified when only the military aspects of Israeli-Arab relations are discussed. But one has to remember that peace—not only war—has a momentum and dynamic of its own. Coexistence and open borders for trade and tourism may create incentives for both peoples to live in peace. Building common economic interests, for example, should be an integral part of a projected Israeli-Arab peace.

The IASPS report is titled: "Can Israel Survive a Palestinian State?" But the question Israel faces now would be a more fitting topic for the next report from Widlanski and his colleagues: "Can Israel Survive the Status Quo?"

QUESTIONS FOR DISCUSSION

1. What strategic areas are crucial for Israel in protecting its security?
2. What effect would the creation of a Palestinian state have on the relations between Israel and its neighbors?
3. Would the creation of a Palestinian state make the use of nonconventional weapons in the region more or less likely? What are the reasons for your answer?
4. How would security guarantees for Israel be implemented once a Palestinian state were established?
5. Under what regional political conditions could a Palestinian state be established?

SUGGESTED READINGS

Abed, George T. "The Economic Viability of a Palestinian State." *Journal of Palestine Studies*, **19** (Winter 1990), pp. 3–28.

Ahmed, Hisham H. "Palestinian State Formation: Means and Ends." *American-Arab Affairs*, no. 33 (Summer 1990), pp. 10–34.

Bickerton, Ian J., and Carla L. Klausner. *A Concise History of the Arab-Israeli Conflict.* Englewood Cliffs, N.J.: Prentice-Hall, 1991.

Friedman, Thomas L. *From Beirut to Jerusalem.* New York: Farrar, Straus, Giroux, 1989.

Khalaf, Salah. "Lowering the Sword." *Foreign Policy*, no. 78 (Spring 1990), pp. 91–112.

Norton, Augustus Richard, and Martin H. Greenberg. *The International Relations of the Palestine Liberation Organization.* Carbondale, Ill.: Southern Illinois University Press, 1989.

Oddie, D. A. P. "Vision of a Palestinian State alongside Israel." *RUSI Journal* (London), **135** (Summer 1990), pp. 31–36.

Peretz, Don. "The Intifada and Middle East Peace." *Survival* (London), **32** (Sept./Oct. 1990), pp. 387–401.

Quigley, John. *Palestine and Israel: A Challenge to Justice*. Durham, N.C.: Duke Univ. Press, 1990.

Rubin, Barry. "Reshaping the Middle East." *Foreign Affairs*, **69** (Summer 1990), pp. 131–146.

Schiff, Ze'ev, and Ehud Ya'ari. *Intifada: The Palestine Uprising—Israel's Third Front*. New York: Simon and Schuster, 1990.

Yorke, Valerie. "Imagining a Palestinian State: An International Security Plan." *International Affairs* (Cambridge, England), **66** (Jan. 1990), pp. 115–136.

Would debtor nations also cut defense spending?

Yes, if there were plans for economic amnesty and international détente.

Isn't this proposal utopian?

If it is somewhat utopian, President Reagan's idea—that saving the U.S. economy will save the world economy—is not only a fantasy, but also an elegant lie. The fantasy is his belief that he is the author of a Roosevelt-style economic recovery plan that will save the U.S. from a crisis more profound than that of the 1930s. He expects the American economy to grow by more than 6 per cent per year while inflation stays at 4 per cent. Increased production and stable prices are any administrator's dream, but that dream is as unreal as the mirage of an oasis in the desert.

America's recovery is a facade because the difference between what Washington takes in and what it spends is massive. The public debt, expressed in treasury notes sold to finance this debt, is headed for the $2-trillion mark. This sum is beyond imagination; it sounds like science fiction.

My economic advisers say the U.S. government, technically, is already the world's largest debtor. It owes almost as much as the third world owes. The greatest power in the universe owes its soul to the banks, both at home and abroad.

Is it true that the U.S. "owns the world's mint"?

Yes. The U.S. can print dollars without any domestic backing to them. Richard Nixon set this scheme into action in 1972 by cutting the dollar's link to gold—because the gold standard relied on a metal of which the Soviet Union was the world's largest producer. Now the manager of the world's economy is the U.S. Federal Reserve System, America's central bank, which dictates monetary policy. It decrees rates of inflation, unemployment, and dissatisfaction around the world—because the market in the Socialist orbit also reacts to the vagaries of uncontrolled capitalism.

Who financed the military adventure in Vietnam?

Who is financing the U.S. deficit? Can you imagine the advantages of a war without taxes, a deficit without taxes, the conquest of outer space without taxes, Star Wars without taxes? Wouldn't it be wonderful to govern without paying the bills?

How about Reagan's recent spending cuts?

They are a sham. The gains from cutbacks in education, health, and welfare are not nearly enough to compensate for the rising cost of arms and military research. Reagan's 1980 military budget was $136 billion. Today it is $292 billion, and it will be about $314 billion next year. In half a decade it has more than doubled. During those years the interest on exported capital more than doubled and relative prices for imported goods and services fell by half.

Is the U.S. exporting revolution?

Yes, because it is exporting inflation, recession, rebellion, and subversion. And in its campaign to destabilize both its enemies and its allies, the U.S. is using the IMF and its austerity policies.

Where is the risk in the West's system?

In the illusion of impunity. The material that this magic model is made of will wear out. The huge public debt will not be eliminated by decree, and the trade deficit, which is growing by almost $13 billion per month, is leading to retaliatory protectionism. It is magnificent propaganda for the cause of Socialism.

In foreign trade the capitalists impose barriers and charge their fellow capitalists duty while making speeches in defense of free trade. They ascribe blame for everything that goes wrong in the world to their ideological adversaries—who now are held responsible for the arms race. That race has been transferred into an economic and technological frontier because it is paid for by the debtors.

The next victims may be the Japanese, who do not make missiles or bombs. They work hard, achieving the world's second largest gross national product on an island that was pulverized by President Truman's atomic bombs. They are in the vanguard when it comes to new management techniques, and compete well in the high-technology race.

Japan is a showwindow for the capitalist system. But how long will the Japanese go unpunished when they have a trade surplus of $50 billion a year with the U.S., a surplus built on hard work and efficiency? The 30 million unemployed on both sides of the North Atlantic are out of work because of Japan and not because of the administrative obsolescence of the industrialized economies, now being masked by moves into robotics.

Will capitalism succumb to its own excesses?

No. I still believe in the rationality of organized societies. Crises generate ideas. For good or for bad, things have to change. It is the law of history.

The *Titanic* of the world financial system, believed to be unsinkable, will sink. On that day, we will stop paying the illegitimate part of our debts and negotiate the honest repayment of the rest, with rates and terms adjusted to the abilities of some 120 debtors around the world. The project is simple: Reestablish conditions as they were before 1979.

For more than a century banks loaned money at 6 per cent. In 1978 the West, still reeling from the oil-price shock, still had interest rates below the inflation rate in the credit-exporting nations. Why not rescue capitalism by reestablishing the rules of capitalism?

To take advantage of the coming disaster it will be necessary to tie debt service to trade balances. Repayments will have to depend not only on the value of exports but also on the formation of a trade reserve, because the debtor will have to be able to afford essential imports. Luxuries will not enter into the calculation of this reserve.

Should we pray for the "Titanic" to sink?

No. We should avoid it. Prevention is much cheaper than cure. But the alarm bells have been ringing since 1982 and we have seen no change.

Accounts Receivable

Peter T. Bauer

The realities of the so-called debt crisis are often ignored, possibly because powerful political and commercial interests both in the West and in the third world have a stake in overlooking them. Third world debtors could readily meet their obligations, but they would be foolish to do so as long as they are not being pressed. The decision by Citicorp bank to write off $3 billion in foreign loans relieves the pressure further.

Third world debt is sovereign debt, owed or guaranteed by governments. The debtors can always pay, since governments can tax their citizens. They also generally have substantial marketable assets, and they can requisition the assets of their citizens. The sovereign debtor cannot be taken to courts. Payment depends on the government's willingness, which depends on the political and economic consequences of the decision. Governments try to avoid the political and economic costs until the consequences of default outweigh them. The most important adverse consequence would be the failure to secure further external finance, which could result in economic breakdown. In the current climate, such an outcome is improbable. Debtors feel little incentive to pay.

The statistics bandied about on third world debt sound frightening. But the figures of hundreds of billions of dollars are misleading. It is rarely made clear whether the figures are gross or net—that is, whether they allow for the financial assets of the debtors, let alone for other marketable assets. And it is often left unspecified what debts are being discussed. Some statistics refer to debt to the banks; others include debts to Western governments and international organizations such as the International Development Association (IDA). These are unindexed loans of 50-year maturity with ten-year grace periods at zero interest. Although termed loans, they are effectively grants. Yet they are included in third world debt. Debts owed to Western governments are usually subsidized loans under foreign aid programs. They are often scaled down or written off by the creditors cum donors.

The assets of the debtors are rarely mentioned in polite international society—even large liquid assets that in many cases run into billions of dollars. Petroleos de Venezuela, the Venezuelan state oil monopoly, was recently reported to have billions of dollars in financial assets held in the United States. The government of Peru, an intransigent debtor, recently refused to pay a few million dollars of interest on its external debts. Its foreign reserves are about $1.2 billion.

Liquid reserves aside, the major debtors also have large marketable assets. In 1983 Pemex, the state-owned Mexican oil monopoly, earned $5.3 billion. It is widely believed that if it were managed privately the earnings would have been much larger. But even at $5.3 billion the capital value of Pemex could then be conservatively valued at between $35 billion and $40 billion. The sovereign debt of Mexico was around $80 billion. The sale or pledge of part of Pemex might well have averted the Mexican debt crisis; it would have shown the readiness of the government to meet its obligations.

It is often argued that the sale or pledging of debtors' assets in response to demands by creditors would infringe on national sovereignty. But why should the use of assets to honor obligations arising from borrowing have this effect? In both world wars the British government pledged some of its own securities and requisitioned those of its citizens for sale without this being regarded as infringement of its sovereignty.

Another issue rarely mentioned in polite society is the disposition of the many billions borrowed by the third world debtors. . . . Many governments have spent hugely on prestige projects, on unviable indus-

Source: Peter T. Bauer, "Accounts Receivable," *New Republic,* **196** (June 15, 1987), pp. 10–12. Reprinted with permission.

trialization, on politically motivated subsidies, and on other undertakings designed to keep the rulers in power.

Debtor governments typically restrict the inflow of equity capital, and reserve for themselves or their nationals a large part of the equity in large parts of their economies. For instance, Brazil, Mexico, Ethiopia, Ghana, Nigeria, and Tanzania—all debtor nations—ban foreign participation in much or all of the economy. These restrictions are maintained or even extended amid rescheduling negotiations and the pleas of debtors about their inability to pay. The restrictions have promoted reliance on bank finance and official foreign aid. They also obstruct the enterprise, know-how, and skills that usually accompany the inflow of equity.

World Bank statistics suggest strongly that, as a percentage of GNP [gross national product], neither the total outstanding sovereign debt of the major borrowers nor the interest and principal payments are particularly high by historical standards. In 1983 the GNP of the major third world debtors was more than three times their sovereign debt, without allowing for reserves. Interest on the debt was about 2.3 percent of GNP and total debt service about 3.9 percent. As a percentage of export earnings, interest payments were about 12.9 percent and total debt service about 22 percent. Most of these ratios are significantly lower than they were, say, for Canada and Argentina on the eve of World War I, when these countries were first-class debtors.

The major debtor governments often preside over some of the most prosperous third world economies. According to World Bank statistics, the income per capita of Mexico in 1984 was over $2,000, that of Brazil over $1,700, and that of Venezuela over $3,400. In 1985, often cited as a critical year for Brazil, the largest third world debtor, automobile sales totaled about a million units, a near all-time record. In the same year both the earnings and the dividend of Petrobras, the state-controlled oil monopoly, were almost certainly all-time highs. The cost of the construction of Abuja, the new capital of Nigeria, being built from scratch, exceeds the total

sovereign debt of that country. The same is almost certainly true for Brasilia in Brazil and for Dodoma in Tanzania. Such countries don't have to resort to anything remotely resembling policies of austerity to pay their debts. They could simply sell state-owned or -controlled companies, reduce the more extravagant forms of public spending, lift restrictions on the inflow of equity capital, and adopt more market-oriented policies.

It is sometimes argued that adverse external changes warrant substantial concessions to the debtors, and even additional transfers. It is obviously improvident to assume a country will never encounter economic setbacks. But a prudent government would accumulate foreign-exchange reserves in good times to meet its commitments in bad times. Much current discussion implies that third world governments can be expected to behave like children with no thought for tomorrow. The possibility of setting aside reserves in prosperity is rarely mentioned. The major debtors, including Mexico, Brazil, and Venezuela, among others, enjoyed sustained prosperity from 1945 through 1980. But in contrast with Hong Kong and Taiwan, for example, they did not set aside reserves for less favorable times.

The fact is, the diversity of third world debtors makes the deterioration of the world economy a moot point. Mexico, Venezuela, and Nigeria are large oil exporters; Brazil is a large importer. A fall in oil prices damages the former and benefits the latter. By choosing particular years, commodities, and countries, it can always be suggested that the terms of trade of debtors have deteriorated. In the 1970s the rise in oil prices was used as an argument for more aid, more lending, and debt write-offs for less developed countries; in the 1980s the decline in oil prices is used to support the same argument.

Another frequently cited problem is the imposition of import restrictions by Western nations. Without doubt, these adversely affect many less developed nations. But they do not have a significant effect on the debtor countries. South Korea, Taiwan, and Hong Kong are far more affected by such restrictions than debtors such as Mexico, Venezuela, Brazil, and Nigeria. Yet they have grown rapidly in recent years. The truth is the West still offers huge markets for the third world debtors. The debtors are affected far more by domestic policies (i.e., wasteful public spending and state monopolies) than by such external factors as import restrictions or changes in rates of growth in the West.

Three additional arguments are often heard favoring large concessions to debtors and the transfer of additional funds to the third world. First, it is said that attempts to make the debtors pay would result in a political and social upheaval that would create populist or Communist governments hostile to the West. Second, it is said that without major concessions, the plight of the debtors would endanger the Western banking and financial system. Third, it is claimed that without such concessions and transfers the third world would buy less from the West, risking our own exports and jobs. None of these carries particular weight.

The emergence of populist, Communist, or other governments hostile to the West does not depend on the level of income or its rate of change. This is evident from experience in the Far East, the Middle East, and Africa. Moreover, the notion that concessions and transfers to third world debtors are necessary to avert political changes damaging to the West opens the door to indefinite blackmail by third world governments abroad and by commercial banks at home.

If the banks' solvency is threatened by the third world debts, how can they declare large profits and pay substantial dividends? If their capital base is insufficient, should they not strengthen it by reducing their dividends and calling for more capital instead of lending more to third world debtors? And if it is necessary to rescue banks with taxpayers' money, why not do it directly rather than send the money through third world governments that are unlikely to use the funds to service their debts?

Even default by third world debtors would not threaten the Western financial system. Western governments can ensure that bank losses will not endanger the depositors (as distinct from the stockholders or the management) of any bank—let alone the financial system. The Western governments could insist that the banks build up their capital base by reducing dividends and seeking new capital. The governments could also purchase loans at market value and/or take over some of the banks and sell them as going concerns after writing down the balance sheets.

The most influential proposals currently under discussion for solving the debt crisis involve increased lending by the World Bank and the International Monetary Fund (IMF) to the most heavily indebted countries, combined with more lending by the commercial banks. Related proposals involve more foreign aid, and outright cancellation or scaling down of third world debts. The Baker plan, for example, envisages increased lending by the World Bank, by the IMF, and by the banks, and more market-oriented policies by the debtors. The plan provides for additional resources on favorable terms to debtors who have not met their obligations—that is, who have defaulted. This means preferential treatment of the improvident, incompetent, and dishonest governments over those more scrupulous in meeting their contractual obligations.

Such a policy does little to promote conduct helpful to economic development. Instead, it only further politicizes life in the third world and arouses the indignation of those third world governments, like Colombia, that do meet their obligations. Preferential treatment of third world debtor governments will also arouse the indignation of many debtors at home. Why should foreign debtor governments be treated leniently and even receive additional funds when domestic farmers and homeowners have to surrender their assets, which may be the source of their livelihood?

It is unlikely that the beneficiaries of such concessions and transfers would alter their policies in a more market-oriented direction without direct pressure. They may make cosmetic changes, especially in macroeconomic policies. But they will not dismantle the public sector, reduce major categories of public spending, or abandon major state controls.

Why should they? Their policies, which have been supported for decades by official Western aid, accord with their own interests. They will modify them only if continued pursuit promises to result in economic breakdown threatening their political survival.

The dominant view of the debt problem reflects the activities and opinions of powerful interest groups. These include: major banks that wish to avoid or postpone overt losses on their portfolios, and to continue their profitable activities with the least risk; the World Bank and the IMF, which seek to expand their roles at a time when the grounds for their existence are increasingly questionable; third world governments that understandably press for more resources to keep themselves in power, reinforce their grip over their subjects, and persist in their policies; and the aid lobbies, which welcome the most widely canvassed proposals because they envisage further transfer of resources from the West to third world governments. Moreover, transfers to the major debtors pave the way for further transfers.

The likely outcome of the current discussions is the continued rescheduling and scaling down of existing debts and the injection of more funds into the third world, especially third world governments. This will encourage those who disregard their obligations. It will increase the moral hazard of lending to third world governments. It will expand the role of the World Bank and the IMF and lead to a further waste of resources.

QUESTIONS FOR DISCUSSION

1. Who is responsible for the debt accumulation of developing states?
2. What would be the consequences to Western economies if Castro's plan were adopted?
3. What would be the consequences to developing countries if Castro's plan were adopted?
4. What should be the policy of Western governments toward commercial banks if debtor countries refuse to pay their debts?

5. What are the political strengths and weaknesses of the borrowers and of the lenders in achieving their objectives?

SUGGESTED READINGS

Bogdanowicz-Bindert, Christine A. (ed.). *Solving the Global Debt Crisis: Strategies and Controversies from Key Stakeholders.* New York: Harper and Row, 1989.

Bulow, Jeremy, and Kenneth Rogoff. "Cleaning up Third World Debt without Getting Taken to the Cleaners." *Journal of Economic Perspectives*, **4** (Winter 1990), pp. 31–42.

Clausen, A. W. "Beyond the Lost Decade: Prospects for the Third World." *Vital Speeches of the Day*, **56** (Mar. 15, 1990), pp. 344–347.

Felix, David. "Latin America's Debt Crisis." *World Policy Journal*, **7** (Fall 1990), pp. 733–771.

Henriot, Peter J. "Forgive Us Our Debts. . . ." *America*, **161** (Dec. 9, 1989), pp. 420–422, 424.

Maktouf, Lotfi. "Some Reflections on Debt-for-Equity Conversions." *International Lawyer*, **23** (Spring 1989), pp. 909–919.

Roberts, Paul Craig. "Up from Mercantilism: Solving the Latin Debt Mess." *National Interest*, no. 20 (Summer 1990), pp. 63–70.

Sachs, Jeffrey D. "A Strategy for Efficient Debt Reduction." *Journal of Economic Perspectives*, **4** (Winter 1990), pp. 19–29.

Sjaastad, Larry A. "Debtor Nations Have Never Had It So Good." *Wall Street Journal*, Mar. 9, 1989, p. A16.

U.S. Cong., Senate. *The Impact of Third World Debt on U.S. Trade.* Hearing before the Committee on Banking, Housing, and Urban Affairs, 101st Cong., 1st Sess., 1989.

———. *New Approaches to the Third World Debt Problem.* Hearings before the Subcommittee on International Finance Policy of the Committee on Banking, Housing, and Urban Affairs, 101st Cong., 1st Sess., 1989.

———. *Third World Debt Strategy.* Hearing before the Subcommittee on International Finance and Monetary Policy of the Committee on Banking, Housing, and Urban Affairs, 101st Cong., 2d Sess., 1990.

Vogel, Frank. "Ten Steps to Debt Relief." *International Economy*, **4** (Oct./Nov. 1990), pp. 84–87.

13 Should Japan Pursue a Course That Is More Independent of the United States?

YES

Ishihara Shintarō

Learning to Say No to America

NO

Nakanishi Terumasa

Saying Yes to the Japan–U.S. Partnership

Learning to Say No to America

Ishihara Shintarō

The name Heisei that was given to the new era when the Shōwa emperor died may be indicative of the role Japan will play in world history in the future. The two classical sources that inspired this name, "Make things smooth (*hei*) on earth, and all will be well (*sei*) in heaven" and "If there is peace (*hei*) at home, all will be well (*sei*) abroad," seem to offer a clear description of the shape of the new civilization that is now emerging, one in which Japan's stability and development will be closely tied to that of the world as a whole.

This is probably the first time the Japanese have had a role to play in world history. I think that we are capable of performing this role and that indeed it is our responsibility to do so. Still, it is certainly not something Japan can do by itself. Our country will definitely need the cooperation and understanding of many other countries, and I see the United States as an indispensable partner for us.

In times of peace, the relations between countries do not change suddenly, but still there comes a point in periods of transition when people can see that a change has occurred—presuming, that is, that they have a proper view of history and are sensitive to its undulations. As has been said time and again, the study of history can be instructive for nations and individuals in such periods of transition, offering sound principles to guide their judgment about what course to follow and what methods to adopt. But what is past is past; though we should of course heed

Source: Ishihara Shintarō, "Learning to Say No to America," *Japan Echo*, 17 (Spring 1990), pp. 29–35. Translated from "No wa no de aru," in Bungei Shunju, November 1989, pp. 94–111; abridged by about one-third. Reprinted by permission.

the lessons of yesteryear, we should pay even more attention to the signs of the future. That, I would say, is the true message of history. I get the feeling that much of the current strain in relations between Japan and the United States results from failure on both sides to read this message correctly.

THE SETTING OF THE CONTROVERSY

We are certainly living in interesting times. The modern civilization that prevailed for such a long period is finally at an end, and we are witnessing the birth of a new civilization to replace it. And though the twentieth century might be labeled the age of ideology, its closing years have unmistakably demonstrated the failure of communism. Finally we are seeing the resolution of ideological strife to which the human race has been subjecting itself.

Liberated from the mental shackles of ideology, people will probably seek new ways to compete with each other. This competition, whatever specific form it may take, is sure to revolve around the new system of advanced technology that has transformed civilization. Merely acquiring this technology will not be sufficient; people will have to be clever in putting it to use. They will have to come up with ideas for new products and devise ways to manufacture them reliably and efficiently.

If the next century brings a shift in the focus of competition from the military arena to the economic playing ground, production processes are bound to be seen as a form of high technology to be protected by patent. Managerial techniques, including ways of handling interpersonal relations, will also be key competitive tools. Managers will have to be ready to discard the customs and thinking of the past and subject themselves to the harsh criterion of efficiency.

Japan and the United States, it seems to me, are likely to be the leading actors in the new civilization, to judge from their existing abilities and potential in various areas that are likely to be crucial in the age to come. Some people would add Europe, the Soviet

Union, and China to the list, envisioning a five-pole world, but I disagree. It remains to be seen how successful the European Community will be in its 1992 market-integration program, and for the Soviet Union and China I would suggest that a decline in global status is inevitable.

The Pacific basin, across which Japan and the United States face each other, and the countries of East and Southeast Asia, the region with which Japan is most intimately linked, should come to have far more significance and value for the world than they do now. And for the sake of the world under this new global order, the Japan-U.S. relationship will in some respects have to be a more productive one than it is today. This is my basic view of the world of the future and of the Japan-U.S. relationship in that world.

Relations between Japan and the United States are now troubled. Both sides are responsible for this strain—Japan certainly is not solely to blame.

People suggest that *"No" to ieru Nihon* (A Japan That Can Say No; Tokyo: Kōbunsha, 1989), the book that I coauthored with Sony Chairman Morita Akio last year, has caused a storm of negative reaction in the United States. But looking into the matter, I find that the uproar seems to be greater in Japan. If my observation is correct, then we are witnessing a typically Japanese case of reacting with excessive inferiority toward anything and everything American. Be that as it may, requests for translation rights have come in from the United States and a number of other countries. The implication is that, however one may judge the book, this is the first time that this sort of message to Americans has come out of Japan.

I myself have not read any of the foreign comments on the book except for a review in the *New York Times*, which struck me as fairly balanced, although on some points I would have liked to offer a rebuttal or clarify my position. But according to the Japanese press, the work has provoked violent reactions in many quarters. Most common, apparently, are claims that its message is arrogant. The major complaints seem to be with my suggestion that racial

prejudice underlies the American criticism of Japan and with Morita's finding fault in a country to which he sells so many of his products.

AN UNAUTHORIZED TRANSLATION

As I see it, there is not a single part of what Morita says that is mistaken, although the Americans may not like hearing it. As for my own points, I will attempt to make myself clearer in what follows. First, however, I wish to lodge a sharp protest against the circulation of an English translation that neither Morita nor I approved. I had suggested having the book translated, believing that it could contribute to better Japan-U.S. relations, and a synopsis in English was sent to some American publishers. But then somebody made a complete translation without permission. It was passed out in the U.S. Congress, of all places, where the people who read it have been raising a ruckus. I do not know who was responsible for the translation—some say the Department of State, others the Pentagon—but clearly its subsequent unauthorized circulation is an act of piracy. It would be one thing if one or two copies had been made for reference purposes, but when they are handed out in volume to members of Congress and used as a source material for political criticism, the matter is serious.

I grant that in some of the passages I was responsible for, I did not express myself very well. If I had been involved in the preparation of an authorized translation to be presented to Americans, I would have expanded the potentially misleading parts to make them more comprehensible. Consider, for example, the semiconductors for use in fifth-generation computers, pivotal components that are now produced only in Japan. In the book, I discussed them as follows:

> Without using computer chips made in Japan, the United States will be hard put to guarantee the precision of its nuclear weapons (which will be even more advanced in the future). No matter what kind of military buildup the United States attempts, if Japan ceases

to sell it chips, the United States will be totally hamstrung.

The global military balance could be completely turned on its head if, just as a hypothesis, Japan decided to sell its computer chips to the Soviet Union instead of to the United States.[1]

I still think this is the case. The well-known Department of Defense report on Japanese electronics, which I cited in the book, makes much the same point. And I doubt that any American company is capable of profitably producing today's 1-megabit chips. Consider also the case of the FSX, Japan's next-generation support fighter, which Japan was planning to develop on its own but now, at the insistence of the United States, is to be handled as a joint Japan-U.S. project.[2] Not content with just preventing Japanese development, the U.S. side has been tacking unilateral new conditions onto the memorandum of understanding between the U.S. and Japanese governments. But even as they limit Japan's role in the project, the Americans unabashedly inform us that our country is to supply the computer chips for the plane.

I grant that it is provocative to talk about a possible Japanese refusal to sell semiconductors to the United States, especially when you consider that Japan may be the only country capable of producing the next models with 4-megabit and higher integration. To hint that Japan might instead send such chips in the Soviet direction seems inflammatory even to me. A couple of years back, just after Congress adopted a one-sided semiconductor resolution, I tried out this line at a gathering of political friends and acquaintances in Washington, and for a minute my listeners were too stunned to speak.

But I had a reason for applying shock therapy on that occasion. The sentiment in Washington toward Japan was particularly poisonous, and legislators and lobbyists were feeling really pleased with themselves, bragging that they had finally dealt Japan a blow. In this charged atmosphere, even my friends in and around Congress were using fairly hysterical language toward me. The remark that particularly annoyed me was one to the effect that a power shift was underway and that it might decisively alter the Japan-U.S. relationship.

This line of thought is nothing new to us in Japan, but I decided to ask for further explanation. Now that U.S.-Soviet relations have taken a sudden turn for the better, I was told, the Japan-U.S. partnership might even be scrapped. To push the point, I asked with a laugh, "Do you mean to tell me that the Americans and the Russians will reawaken to their shared identity as whites?" The reply to this was a nod of assent.

THE UNCOMFORTABLE ISSUE OF PREJUDICE

My comments in the book on the racial prejudice of Americans have also been controversial. People do not care to be reminded of their faults, particularly the ones that they have succeeded in banishing from their consciousness. I may have violated a taboo in this respect, but I ventured to do so because the matter bears on an extremely important bilateral relationship.

At the same gathering in Washington, one of my friends in Congress remarked that I was always so provocative in my remarks, unlike most Japanese, and he asked if I had some special reason. "As a matter of fact," I parried, "an American soldier once hit me for no good reason when I was a kid."

Of course I was joking, though something like that actually did happen. It was a year after the end of World War II; I was in my second year of middle school, living in Zushi, not far from Tokyo. It was a quiet town, but because the old Imperial Navy had had a large ammunition depot nearby, we saw a lot of American soldiers. The townspeople behaved with great deference to their new overlords, promptly

---

[1] The English version of this passage is from "A Clear Yes or No: Frankness for the Sake of the Future," an earlier translation of this article that appeared in *Bungei Shunjū Digest*, pilot issue (January 1990), pp. 8–17 (quotation on pp. 10–11).—Ed.

[2] See Ishihara Shintarō, "From Bad to Worse in the FSX Project," in *Japan Echo*, vol. **16**, no. 4 (Autumn 1989).

clearing the way for them whenever they walked down the street. This was apparently amusing to the young Americans, but it was irritating to me. One day on my way home from school I found myself approaching three soldiers who were sucking popsicles as they walked along. Pretending not to see them, I continued straight ahead, passing right beside them. As I did, the one closest to me—who probably thought I was being fresh—suddenly hit me on the cheek with his popsicle!

Seeing how deeply disturbed my friend was by this tale, I hastened to remind him that I did not take it seriously. But he still seemed unsatisfied, observing that even if the incident no longer bothered me, I would probably never forget it. A little later he brought up the matter again, asking if the soldiers had been blacks. No, I replied, two had blond hair and the third was a redhead. But his question, I thought, was very revealing.

AN OUTDATED VIEW OF THE WORLD

I do not deny that modern civilization is largely, if not entirely, the creation of white Europeans. But Japan already had a culture and civilization that ranked among the world's best before this modern civilization was born. This explains why our country was quick to recognize the need to modernize itself in the nineteenth century when it was fully exposed to this civilization for the first time. It also explains why Japan was successful in its modernization despite the handicap of its relatively late start. The other countries inhabited by colored people were colonized by the whites. None proceeded down the road of modernization as far as did Japan, which even acquired colonies of its own. The Japanese, in fact, are the only colored people to have played the role of the colonial oppressor in modern history.

In the many countries that were not ready for modernization and that came to be ruled as colonies, the native colored peoples were in a position close to that of serfs in the Middle Ages. Not surprisingly, the white masters were strongly convinced of their superiority and looked down on the natives with disdain.

This sort of prejudice is not a good thing, of course, but the fact that such feelings occurred is only natural.

Recently, however, some of these putatively inferior colored people, the Japanese, have been overtaking the white world's achievements in several areas of high technology, which forms the nucleus of the emerging postmodern civilization. Seen from the white people's perspective of history, this is hardly a pleasing development. Indeed, it may even seem beyond reason. Quite a few whites probably think that the modern civilization born in Europe is still alive and well. This is a matter of individual historical judgment. But in my view this civilization, if not already over, is clearly approaching its end. My message is that there is no point continuing to carry the psychological baggage of an age that is receding into the past.

Americans, however, probably think that a Japanese person has no cause to be talking to them like this. And they seem to consider it arrogant of me to even mention their racial prejudice. I would be worse than arrogant if I were lecturing them about a fault they did not have, but can they really say there is no contempt and disdain for colored peoples in the hearts of America's whites? No Japanese who has lived in the United States for three years or longer would deny the existence of such prejudice. More to the point, try asking nonwhite U.S. citizens, like blacks, Asians, Hispanics, and native Americans. They would laugh at the very suggestion that the prejudice is not there.

The fortunes of various peoples and countries have risen and fallen over the course of history. Nothing comes of clinging to the status quo of the past. When today's Americans talk about a power shift, the players they have in mind are their own country, the Soviet Union, and perhaps Europe. They relegate Japan to a subordinate status in the shadow of these leading actors. But that worldview is outdated. Also, they seem to think that the Japanese have no global political ideals. But that is true only of the politicians and bureaucrats currently in power. They need to be made aware that a new type of Japanese is coming on the scene.

Japan's new technology is bringing the new Japanese into being. One of the ideas that have come from their ranks concerns the high-temperature superconductors that Japan alone seems serious about developing. If Japan were to patent the whole production process along with the perfected superconductors, it would be in a position to control the global economy. The person who first suggested this possibility was neither an economist nor a bureaucrat but a young electrical engineer. Superconductors and other such high-tech devices offer enormous potential for creating a new civilization, including its economic system. Yet most Japanese, let alone Americans, are unaware that Japan has already brought much of this potential close to where it can be put to use.

THE FSX ISSUE: AMERICA'S OUTRAGEOUS DEMANDS

In their dealings with Japan, Americans are arrogant and unreasonable in a way that they would never be in their relations with any other industrially advanced nation. I can only judge that this difference is a reflection of their racial prejudice.

Even as Japan was being forced to give ground on the FSX project, members of Congress latched onto a new issue to give further force to their demagogy. Taking aim at Mitsubishi Heavy Industries, the main Japanese contractor for the FSX, they accused it of cooperating in the construction of a poison gas plant in Libya, a country that Americans love to hate. These lawmakers were actually seeking an excuse to derail the joint development project for the new plane, despite its great advantages for the U.S. side. In fact the charge was groundless, as the astounded State and Defense departments determined after hastily arranged investigations. At that point one would have expected an apology for the false accusation, but that was not to be. Far from saying they were sorry, Congress members actually demanded that Mitsubishi promise never in the future to aid Libya in questionable construction projects. It is like calling a man a thief and then, when you find he is

innocent, telling him that he looks shifty anyway and demanding that he swear never to rob in the future.

Japan's initial decision to develop the FSX domestically was based on the reasoning that though the price of the fighter might be somewhat high, the country would benefit from having what would be one of the world's top-performing planes for years to come, a fighter that would greatly enhance Japan's deterrent power and self-defense capability. At first the Americans laughed the idea off, saying that Japan could not possibly build such a jet, but then they discovered to their great surprise that it indeed had the ability and might even come up with a truly awesome plane. Promptly shifting tactics, they called for codevelopment based on an existing U.S. fighter. The plane thus produced will be far inferior to the model Japan was planning on, but Tokyo eventually accepted it under heavy U.S. pressure. For the administration of President Ronald Reagan, this was a major diplomatic victory.

But then the next Republican administration took office, and a bunch of legislators who had not done their homework and knew nothing about Japan's technological situation began saying that the project was an American giveaway. The Japanese and American administrations were both embarrassed by this, but the congressional opponents only got louder, and eventually some bureaucrats started spouting the same line. Finally the negotiations had to be opened again—virtually un unprecedented move in a case where two countries have already finalized a memorandum of understanding—and Tokyo had to respond to a set of new conditions laid down by Congress. The American demands were spelled out in the renegotiated accord, but when the Japanese side asked for some modifications in exchange, the U.S. negotiators offered only their verbal agreement, citing the difficulty of getting Congress to accept the changes in writing. Is this any way to conduct diplomacy? The partner that insisted on it is bad enough, but our own ignominious acquiescence is worse.

According to the new agreement, (1) all the technology developed in the project is to be handed over to the United States free of charge, (2) Japan must pay patent and licensing fees for all the U.S. technology it receives, (3) the United States will place various restrictions on the technology it supplies and will not offer all the technology Japan requests, (4) the United States may use the technology it gets from Japan as it sees fit, and (5) Japan cannot apply the technology it gets from the United States to any use outside the FSX project. As surprising as it may seem to people who know little about such affairs, Japan was unable to say no to even one of these unequal conditions. And as the project progresses, it will be supplying for free much of the technology that the United States needs for the ATF, the advanced tactical fighter that the Pentagon is preparing to develop.

Actually what Congress would have preferred is for the Japanese to purchase American planes ''off the shelf.'' Japan, we were told, should content itself with some old F-15s or F-16s, since buying them would lessen the bilateral trade imbalance. Basically it seems that the Americans want Japan to be a vassal to the United States, at least in defense. Since they are finding it very hard to control Japan economically, they are determined to hold on to the reins in the vital area of national security.

I am quite aware of all the help Japan has received from the United States in the past. But I question whether the Americans can really claim they are still doing us a big favor by protecting us. Probably almost no experts in the Defense Agency think that today's Japan is being protected by the United States. The Japan-U.S. Security Treaty will naturally continue to be essential for some time to come, but the footing on which it is based has clearly altered.

As anyone in the U.S. military will admit, the gigantic U.S. bases being maintained in Japan have more to do with America's own global strategy than Japan's safety. Nothing could be stranger than the annually increasing appropriations in Japan's defense budget to help the United States defray the cost of stationing its troops here. If the importance of the bases to each side could be translated into monetary figures, the United States would probably come out

owing Japan money. But despite the break they are getting on the use of their facilities in this country, the Americans swat us down whenever we attempt to use our own technology to enhance an independent defense capability.

CONFRONTING STRUCTURAL IMPEDIMENTS HONESTLY

The real feelings of the fading superpower can be glimpsed in ''Containing Japan,'' an article by the American journalist James Fallows in the May 1989 *Atlantic*. In one passage, for instance, Fallows states that ''unless Japan is contained, . . . several things that matter to America will be jeopardized,'' and the first item in his endangered list is ''America's own authority to carry out its foreign policy and advance its ideals.'' In another passage Fallows demonstrates a good grasp of the real reason for the U.S. bases in Japan by stating that the ''leading power'' should ''explore space, improve its schools, maintain its military bases in Japan so that Japan doesn't build its own army, and so on.'' In short, U.S. troops are here to keep the country in line.

These are fine-sounding words, but the ideals Fallows would have America advance are not absolute values—except to Americans. To other peoples, U.S. displays of authority are on occasion an eyesore. At the end of the essay he declares, ''But we do have the right to defend our interests and our values, and they are not identical to Japan's.'' In that case we Japanese should certainly be defending *our* values, even when we come up against the United States.

Fallows suggests that it is up to a leading power like the United States to undertake the exploration of space. Though I would not insist on a role for Japan that would extend as far as projects like sending a rocket to Neptune, I would like to see our country launch more high-capability satellites for a variety of tasks. In ways both open and covert, however, Washington is blocking a Japanese plan for a surveillance satellite far more advanced than the ones we now have. American restraining pressure is being applied in many other areas as well, particularly those with a bearing on U.S. security strategy. Under these circumstances it strikes me as a trifle hypocritical for the Americans to call Japan an ''equal partner.''

Now a new round of Japan-U.S. negotiations has begun. Labeled the structural impediments initiative, it might be seen as a pretext for an impatient America to haul Japan over the coals for the good of the world. Actually, though, I am hopeful about these talks. Some say they represent unwarranted meddling in Japan's internal affairs, but I disagree. It all depends on our stance. When the Americans make demands of us, we should respond in kind.

The U.S. negotiators have placed six items on the agenda. One is Japan's distribution system, which is certainly irrational. I, like a great many other Japanese, would be delighted to see it streamlined. The imbalance between investment and saving and the high price of land will also be discussed, but since both are essentially issues of internal resource allocation, it will probably be difficult to hammer out an agreement.

Eliminating exclusionist business practices is another American goal. In some cases this will turn into a debate over differing values born of different cultures. Take the case of the corporate raider T. Boone Pickens, who acquired a block of shares in a supplier of Toyota Motor, came to Japan with a set of demands, found that he could not get his way, and then, as often happens, went to Congress with his complaints. Though I do not want to go into the details of the case here, I would point out that there is no reason for Japan to accede to American demands that business operations here, including the treatment of stockholders, be conducted as they are in the United States. The unfortunate results that American-style practices can produce were pointed out quite aptly by Morita in our book.

I can understand the American frustration with Japan's corporate groups, which are also on the agenda. Though their formation can be defended as another example of a Japanese response in a specific historical setting, the details of the group relationships should be made public. If they are not, Japan can be justifiably accused of a form of insider trading.

Yet another issue is price formation. The underlying problem here is not a difference in customs so much as a different approach to human relations. The Japanese take a longer-range view of pricing than Americans, frequently setting prices low today in order to ensure the prosperity of a business partner tomorrow. Any attempt to switch immediately to perfectly rational pricing decisions would run into knotty problems. But there is no defense for the sort of pricing that makes some Japanese-produced goods more expensive at home than abroad. This is an insult to domestic consumers. The Fair Trade Commission, meanwhile, nest of bureaucrats that it is, has not been applying the Antimonopoly Law as strictly as it should. The foreign complaint that the Japanese business world is ridden with cartels is, I believe, on target.

Foreign pressure is often quite welcome. Take the case of the entry of Motorola into the Japanese market for cellular phones. There are a lot of problems with Japanese-made cellular phones. The lack of sufficient competition from abroad in this field has left consumers with substandard products.

The root of this problem is the Ministry of Posts and Telecommunications, which clings to the antiquated notion that the airwaves are something to be lent to the lowly by those on high. Basically the ministry seems to think that it is better to hold airwave frequencies in reserve than to open them to the common people for their own use in emergencies and other situations. The ministry's handling of Motorola's bid to sell car phones in Japan was particularly inept. In a temporizing move, it opened the door a crack but excluded the Tokyo market, where the users are overwhelmingly concentrated. The deal was so blatantly unfair that the officials concerned must have known from the beginning that it would cause problems. I wonder what earthly sort of national interest they thought they were protecting.

CHARTING A JAPANESE FUTURE

To Americans I would say one more thing. The greatest problem is not the strength of the Japanese economy but the weakness of the U.S. competitive position. American attempts to treat the problem only through changes on the Japanese side will thus not have the intended results. In fact, to judge from past experience, Japan's concessions in areas where change is truly justified will make the Japanese economy stronger than before. If that is what the Americans really want, then fine. But I doubt that this will really do. What I really hope is that the bilateral talks on trade will provide Americans with an opportunity to take a hard look at their own failings and lead to their country's recovery as a strong economic power. This will make it possible for the United States to achieve its full potential in the area of high technology, where its contribution is needed in the building of the new civilization to come.

Americans and others are too ready to presume that any Japanese view of history or world affairs that differs from their own is no more than a revival of the wartime Greater East Asian Co-Prosperity Sphere or an attempt to justify Japan's military actions in the 1930s. This shows a lack of imagination on their part. There is no need for us to let ourselves be blocked from following our own will, accepting our own responsibilities, and exercising our own rights in the human affairs that concern us in the years to come.

It should come as a pleasure for us Japanese, who alone have experienced the tragedy of a nuclear holocaust and who have pledged never to use nuclear weapons, to find that we are attaining a position where we can render the superpowers' nuclear warheads harmless by holding back the semiconduc-tors they depend on. What could be a more fitting revenge for Hiroshima? To the fine words carved into the memorial cenotaph there, ''We will never repeat this error,'' can finally be added the phrase, ''nor will we allow others to repeat it.''

Let me say again, Japan can and should uphold its own political ideals. There is no need for our country to follow the United States slavishly or get our ideals spoon-fed to us by the Americans. I hardly think that possessing ideals of our own means being over-confident or lapsing into an arrogant, dangerous sort of nationalism.

Even if what Japan seeks to accomplish for the world in the Heisei era runs counter to the United States' antiquated global strategy, we must have the will to go through with it. To stick to this course, we must say no quite firmly when necessary. It is also obvious, however, that we cannot afford suddenly to lose our ties with America. For the sake of the more cooperative and mature relationship that should exist between our two countries, we must say yes equally clearly when that is the appropriate response. At times this will require a determination on the part of our political leaders to say no to the Japanese people.

The time has come for the people in both countries to make a dispassionate assessment of whether they are allowing old prejudices to linger in their hearts and clinging too tenaciously to outdated concepts and systems. Today we must put together a new framework of bilateral cooperation. If we fail in this task, we may allow the best future for the world to slip through our fingers.

Saying Yes to the Japan-U.S. Partnership

Nakanishi Terumasa

Reviewing Japanese books is not usually enjoyable. Most authors seldom stray far from that which is obviously true or possibly correct, winding up with vague conclusions. In this respect, *"No" to ieru Nihon* (A Japan That Can Say No; Tokyo: Kōbunsha, 1989), coauthored by Sony Chairman Morita Akio and the politician Ishihara Shintarō, gives the critic plenty to dig into. The parts by Ishihara in particular are crammed full of statements that are false or objectionable.

SLIPSHOD WRITING AND POOR TIMING

When I finished reading the book, my first reaction was to sigh deeply at the sloppiness of the presentation and to wonder how long Japan's authors would be allowed to get away with slipshod treatments of weighty matters of state. Here, for example, is how Ishihara describes the functioning of a multiple independently targeted reentry vehicle [MIRV]: "When it senses the approach of an interceptor missile, the warhead splits into eight or nine pieces, each carrying a hydrogen bomb. Some of the nine are decoys, designed to lure the interceptor away, and they end up being shot down." For a man who stresses the importance of technology to the modern military, this passage reveals a lack of knowledge about his own subject matter. MIRVs do not "sense" the approach of an interceptor and immediately release their warheads. If they had that sort of capability, the whole idea of America's "Star Wars" strategic defense initiative would have never been possible.

Elsewhere Ishihara argues that high technology was a major factor behind the December 1978 decision to normalize diplomatic relations between the United States and China. In this passage he relates in some detail how the United States, which had taken satellite photographs of China's handling of the Sino-Vietnamese conflict, dispatched its secret emissary Henry Kissinger to show the photos to the Chinese leaders, who were so impressed with America's tremendous high-tech power that they decided to normalize relations. The problem here is not simply that he mistakes historical periods, confusing the Sino-Vietnamese conflict, which was just then beginning, with the earlier Sino-Soviet clashes (even though he refers to them shortly thereafter). He also mixes up the place of Kissinger and the Vietnam War in the sequence of events that led eventually to the normalization of U.S.-China relations. He evidently has a very faulty grasp of even recent relations of cause and effect in the strategic environment surrounding Japan.

My intention is not to pick faults. Given the heavy demands placed on today's politicians, we should perhaps be tolerant of minor mistakes regarding the details of technology and history. The tendency in the Japanese publishing industry not to make a fuss over such inaccuracies is probably a contributing factor. But we must not let discussions of this nature be reduced to the level of uninformed banter. Because one of Ishihara's central objectives in the book is to demonstrate the great import of technology in Japan's strategic and diplomatic choices, moreover, errors concerning technology assume a nature of fatal flaws. When dealing with Americans, at least, any bid to say no and drive a hard bargain backed up by such a faulty grasp of the facts will be preempted by a barrage of American nos to the Japanese perception of the situation. When the rumored official English version of this book is published, these and other defects should be corrected.

Leaving aside points of this sort, two things can be said about the book as a whole. First, while agreeing that Japan must learn to say no to the United

Source: Nakanishi Terumasa, "Saying Yes to the Japan-U.S. Partnership," *Japan Echo*, 17 (Spring 1990), pp. 36–42. Translated from "'Seiki no ayamachi' o sakeru tame ni," in Chūō Kōron, December 1989, pp. 90–100; slightly abridged. Reprinted by permission.

States, Morita and Ishihara frequently disagree on other matters, even on the policy Japan should take toward the United States, the main theme of the book.

Second, the publication of the book seems to have been badly timed. Its appearance in January 1989, at the start of a new administration in the United States, came at a time when Washington was groping toward a new Japan policy to deal with such issues as the FSX, the next-generation support fighter for Japan's Air Self-Defense Force. A month before, moreover, Soviet leader Mikhail Gorbachev had announced a unilateral reduction of Soviet armed forces, and it was becoming evident that the cold war was drawing to a close. It was also evident that America's enormous trade deficit with Japan was not about to contract quickly, and there was little doubt that Washington would soon be lashing out at Japan for ''unfair trade,'' using the Super 301 provision of the Omnibus Trade Act of 1988. In such a context, the Japan-U.S. relationship was obviously entering a difficult period, and one wonders if the two men had thought through the book's likely impact on it. Perhaps they reasoned that at such a critical juncture, Japan needed to assert itself more than ever. In terms of political judgment, however, one can only question this sense of timing of these two prominent figures.

The Uruguay round of talks under the General Agreement on Tariffs and Trade is now heading toward its scheduled conclusion in December 1990. At stake in these talks is the continued vitality of the free-trade system, an issue of far more import than Japan's emergence as a leader in an ultramodern civilization. Ishihara, it seems to me, appreciates this. His decision to make a forthright statement of his controversial convictions at this time was taken, I believe, in full knowledge that he would be harshly criticized. With open eyes, he made himself a ''prisoner of conscience.'' We should accordingly question not his timing so much as the content of the convictions he expressed.

In what follows, I will examine Ishihara's position as expressed in the book and in recent magazine articles, excluding Morita's stance from the discussion. It is not my intention to deal with his ambitions as a politician who, as leader of a group—albeit a small one—within the ruling Liberal Democratic Party [LDP], hopes to become prime minister and shape Japan's policy to his liking. Here I wish to address his views as one thinker to another, offering my own thoughts on his perception of the course Japan should take in international society.

ISHIHARA'S THESIS IN THREE POINTS

Ishihara's arguments can be condensed into three general points. The first is that in negotiations with the United States, Japan must not make unnecessary concessions. This is a perfectly reasonable stance, and it deserves recognition as such. There has long been something fundamentally unsound in the posture that some Japanese, trade negotiators in particular, have adopted at the bargaining table. Many other people have made similar complaints, but the dramatic way this point is made in Ishihara's book may be valuable.

In Ishihara's hands, however, this very natural assertion that Japan must not always say yes takes on a meaning above and beyond that of an open exchange of views among equals. To many Japanese, who have been led by distorted media reports to feel irritated toward the United States, the position Ishihara has adopted is a compelling one. But in endorsing his position on trade issues, these people get drawn into a stance where they seem also to endorse his position on the Japan-U.S. Security Treaty, defense, and Japan's future role in the global community—all areas where Ishihara holds unorthodox views. The first person to find himself allied with Ishihara in this way was Morita. He really should have said no to Ishihara before saying it to the United States.

Actually Japan has already said no to American requests on many occasions, and some of its refusals have been in dangerous areas. For example, during the recent strife in the Persian Gulf, Japan rejected an American plan for the protection of Japanese oil tankers. From the standpoint of political relations between two allied countries, that kind of decision to go it alone is a risky affront to the other ally. One problem is that the Japanese press failed to inform the public about the matter in an appropriate manner, but even more problematic is the fact that few people in the government or the LDP seem to realize how dangerous such decisions can be.

The second point in Ishihara's thesis is the charge of racial discrimination in the attitudes and policies white Americans have adopted toward colored Japanese. This argument, together with the third point discussed below, is developed only crudely, and one is led to suspect that Ishihara thrusts it forward simply to be provocative. In any event, no Japanese can be unaware that prejudice against them indeed exists in the West and that it is one of the factors underlying today's disputes. Naturally Westerners are also aware of this prejudice, as can be seen in the rebuttals to the late Theodore White's well-known article "The Danger from Japan," carried four years ago in the *New York Times Magazine.*

Yet charges and countercharges of racism have no place in serious policy debate. To use them is to take a cheap shot at an embarrassing weakness in the adversary's armor while ignoring the same weakness in one's own armor. We must not forget that the Japanese themselves, with their love of theories about how unique their country is, are prone to feelings of racial superiority, making them easy targets of criticism. Indeed, the world is even coming to believe that the real racists are the Japanese.

In 1929 British Prime Minister Stanley Baldwin vented his ire at Americans after several years of vigorous confrontations over oil rights, calling them beavers who were using the power of money to eat into the natural resources of the British Empire. This, mind you, was between two countries with the same racial heritage. But today, when Japanese companies are doing the same thing to American companies in the oil fields of the Gulf of Mexico, they are being extended free access to a truly vital resource—despite the racial difference between Japan and the United States. Racism hardly seems to be the operative factor behind this American behavior.

Ishihara's third point involves a view of civilization in which technology is the prime mover. Re-

cently a number of Japanese have proposed similar theories featuring the role of technology in the evolution of history. In Ishihara's scheme, the supremacy of the white race was based on the technological superiority attained in the European cultural sphere. Now that Japan is taking the lead in various high-tech areas, accordingly, it has the potential to take over leadership in the formation of an ultramodern civilization. Apart from the unstated implication of Japan's exclusive supremacy, there is little to note in this somewhat simplistic theory of the preeminence of technology. It is the sort of thesis that any amateur philosopher might espouse. I am disturbed, however, by the emphasis placed on material things in the unfolding of history and international relations. Just when the historical materialism of the left is finally on the wane in Japan and elsewhere around the world, here we have a new doctrine of materialism advanced from the right.

In Ishihara's view Japan holds a "high-tech card" that it should be playing while it has the chance, perhaps not for as long as a century but at least over the next several decades. In this respect he is strongly displeased with Japan's decision not to use the card in the FSX project, which is to be implemented in cooperation with the United States instead of as a domestic Japanese project. Surely he is correct in stressing the need for a long-range defense strategy, but a single plane with limited uses is not enough for that. In the end one gets the impression that he lacks a strategic view and simply assumes that if Japan were to play its high-tech card, somehow or other it would gain ascendancy in an ultramodern civilization. But would possessing the ability to produce a fighter really make a great contribution to Japan's long-term security? Would it be in the interests of Japan's national strategy? Those who answer in the affirmative are lacking in strategic sense.

THE ILLUSORY SOVIET CARD

I am critical of former Prime Minister Nakasone Yasuhiro's political leadership in many respects, but I applaud his 1983 decision to supply military technology to the United States. On one level this involved a unilateral concession, but on a higher level it promises a great return. Skilled statecraft requires the vision to perceive both levels.

Prior to the United States' entry into World War II, Britain gave it both radar technology, on which hung the fate of the war against Germany, and the equally important code-breaking technology it had acquired. This was a sound move even though the desired repayment—America's direct intervention in the fighting—might not have been obtained had Japan not attacked Pearl Harbor. In the maintenance of alliances, high prices must be paid. Similarly, when the Soviet Union shot down a Korean Air Lines plane in 1983, Japan gave the United States the information it had secretly collected on the incident. Even Congress was pleased by this, and it expressed its pleasure with a vote of thanks. Anyone who has a rudimentary understanding of strategy should know that such exchanges of technology and intelligence are vital to any alliance. Cooperation in a mutual security setup cannot be measured simply by the scale of defense spending as a percentage of gross national product.

Joint weapons development within an alliance has always been a thorny issue. The history of the North Atlantic Treaty Organization is full of instances in which one country or another has had to make painful concessions. The United States has on many occasions discouraged the attempts of its European allies to achieve greater capabilities in military technology. This sort of contention is inevitable in an alliance made up of countries at similar levels of technological advancement. If we look at the FSX flap in this light, we can see that it cropped up at a time when Japan was surging forward in the economic, technological, and military spheres. Washington and Tokyo suddenly found themselves facing each other as equals, and neither knew how to treat the other. Americans felt that Japan should go on buying off-the-shelf U.S. planes or participating in joint projects, but some Japanese felt that a grown-up country should make its planes by itself.

If Japan indeed has the capability to develop and manufacture a high-performance fighter, the deci-

sion to go ahead with a codevelopment setup should have been presented to the public as a major concession on Japan's part, one in which Japan was doing its bit in "burden sharing" and giving America a "free ride." If Japan's leaders simply lack the ability to turn this kind of decision to the country's diplomatic advantage, perhaps the Dutch journalist Karel van Wolferen is correct in claiming that the Japanese "System" has nobody in charge. In that case Japan must make the fostering of more competent leaders a top priority in its long-range strategy. In any event, the combination of politicians incapable of leadership and technonationalists incapable of strategic thinking is not good news for Japan's prospects in the twenty-first century, much less for its hopes of bringing an ultramodern civilization into being.

Ishihara seems to believe that Japan can duck American demands by playing its "Soviet card"— the threat to sell high-tech devices to the Soviet Union—but this card will be hard to use now that Washington and Moscow are forging cooperative relations. It may be that Ishihara raises this point solely to reassure the Japanese that their country has solid grounds for taking a stance independent of the United States, but if he is serious, he has misread the Soviet situation. Even if Moscow would love to get its hands on Japanese technology, it would not consummate any deal that might jeopardize U.S.-Soviet relations. And even if we accept the proposition that American and West European technology is no longer as good as Japan's, it is easily sufficient for Soviet needs.

From Moscow's perspective, Japan is hardly trustworthy. Moscow has fought Japan three times in the twentieth century: the Russo-Japanese War of 1904–5, the Siberian Intervention of 1918–22, and World War II. Aware as it is of Japan's past ambitions, it would approach any offer of Japanese technology with wariness. Perhaps the Soviet leaders might have welcomed a deal when their policy toward Japan was geared toward separating it from the United States, but they are unlikely to be so receptive now that this policy has lost most of its meaning. The Soviet thirst for Japan's high-tech expertise will be no more than a secondary motive.

BEYOND THE COLD-WAR FRAMEWORK

Ishihara's stance on the Japan-U.S. Security Treaty is unclear. In his controversial book he contends that ''Japan no longer needs help in defense; we can manage with our own strength and wits'' and ''at the present time Japan does not necessarily need the Security Treaty; we are fully capable of maintaining the status quo by ourselves.'' But in a more recent magazine article, he writes that ''the Japan-U.S. Security Treaty will naturally continue to be essential for some time to come.''[1] I can only imagine that like a vacillating adolescent, he cannot make up his mind.

In other respects his assertions are arbitrary and biased. In the book, for instance, he states that ''the Japanese are deluding themselves in their belief that the American nuclear umbrella is protecting them,'' and in the article he opines that ''probably almost no experts in the Defense Agency think that today's Japan is being protected by the United States.'' In fact, the effectiveness of the U.S. nuclear deterrent cannot be accurately gauged by anyone. To reach a conclusion, one would have to be privy to the discussions within the leadership circles of the Soviet Union, China, and even North Korea, which is reportedly developing its own nuclear capability. As to the Defense Agency experts, probably almost none concur with Ishihara's views.

He does make a timely remark, however, in calling for a fundamental rethinking of the mutual security setup. Particularly over the last year, people in a variety of quarters have been saying much the same thing. Consider, for example, a recent book on diplomacy by University of Tokyo Professor Asai Motofumi.[2] Writing from the leftist stance, Asai proposes that the three nonnuclear principles of not producing, possessing, or permitting the introduction of nuclear weapons be enthroned in Japanese law.

He wants Japan to scrap the Security Treaty in favor of a neutral course, although whether this is to be armed or unarmed neutrality is not clear.

On three points this leftist treatise and Ishihara's rightist arguments reach a strange harmony. First, both see Japan as an oppressed country that the United States has manipulated at will ever since World War II. Second, both agree that Japan's future course lies not in continued subservience to the West but in teaming up with other Asian countries. Third, as a concomitant of the first two points, the security arrangements with the United States should be terminated or at least modified. Arguments of this sort are now triggering reactions across the Pacific, where some Americans are saying that if Japan really wants to set its own course, it should be given a free hand. Thus the Japan-U.S. alliance is under an unexpected attack from three quarters.

These Americans and the Japanese who are calling for scrapping or revising the Security Treaty are in agreement in a number of areas. Both consider postwar Japan to be a country that the United States has largely shaped. The problem with their analysis is that it is based on an overly rigid view of the postwar context. Presuming that the mutual security arrangements were meaningful only as long as Japan was a weak country in a cold-war setting, these people fail to see the great latent potential the Japan-U.S. alliance still has for the future.

George Kennan, the father of the containment policy toward the Soviet Union, was one of the chief architects of the old framework. Through his work at the U.S. Department of State and his consultations with General Douglas MacArthur, commander of the occupation forces in Japan, he helped to shape a long-term U.S. strategy in which Japan's role was to act as a helper in the execution of the cold war. But subsequent developments have made that strategy obsolete. As Kennan stated in testimony before the U.S. Senate in May 1989, the time has come to put the cold war behind us.

The United States and Japan now need a second Kennan to move their bilateral relationship to a new track. The American views on the appropriate track seem to be split down the middle. Some people

---

[1] The article from which this is quoted, in *Bungei Shunjū,* November 1989, is translated in this issue of *Japan Echo,* pp. 29–35.—Ed.

[2] Asai Motofumi, *Nihon gaikō—hansei to tenkan* (Rethinking and Reorienting Japan's Foreign Policy) (Tokyo: Iwanami Shoten, 1989).

suggest that the Japanese are a breed apart and that America should give up expecting Japan to play by the same rules as other countries. Others, following the Kennan tradition, are seeking to construct a new cooperative framework with the two countries' global roles foremost in mind. The former camp is not mistaken in seeing the Japanese as different from Americans; it has long been apparent that the societies of Japan and the United States diverge in various ways. The error lies in the conclusion that because of the differences, Japanese and Americans will never play by the same rules. Ever since the second half of the nineteenth century Americans have been confident that Japan can be encouraged to change itself, but now that confidence appears to be receding. If so, perhaps the United States really is in decline. The Americans who are carrying forward their nation's tradition of spiritual vitality are those who are trying to put the Japan-U.S. partnership on a new footing of cooperation.

A SCENARIO OF GLOBAL DISASTER

In 1960 John F. Kennedy argued in *The Strategy of Peace* that the real struggle in Asia was between China and India, claiming that the outcome of this struggle would determine which country would become the model for Asia's future development. Today, 30 years later, it is not these countries but Japan that has become the Asian model. After long years of endeavor, Japan has attained its national goal, and just at that point the cold war is drawing to a close. The key question now is whether the Japanese, as they put the old Japan-U.S. relationship behind them, will make a clear commitment to cooperation with the United States in global leadership, as some Americans are proposing. The current friction between the two countries is taking place in the absence of a clear vision of the future. On one side are worried Americans, whose preoccupation with Japan's ascending star has caused them to fear a reversal of positions; on the other side are puzzled Japanese, who are interested only in the present and cannot understand why they are being bashed for doing what they have always done. The time has

come for an active debate in Japan on the future of the partnership across the Pacific. Only when Japan clarifies its intentions can the friction be eased.

As I see it, Japan should make three things clear to the world. It should first explain why and how it will be continuing to cooperate closely with the United States in defense and other fields even after the cold war is over. It should next state its resolve to carry through with the construction and opening of a new society. Third, it should unveil the features of the new nationalism it will be espousing in the years to come.

In making a commitment to this three-legged stance, Japan will have to complete several unfinished tasks. As yet the concepts of individualism and liberty are not deeply rooted in Japanese society—except perhaps for the liberty of laissez-faire economics. This lack must be called to people's attention and remedied. The formulation and acceptance of new concepts of social justice may also be necessary. From a long-range perspective, the current upheaval in Japan's political system, which has been rocked by the Recruit influence-peddling scandal and the unpopular consumption tax, together with the East-West thaw and the exacerbation of Japan-U.S. friction, may provide a great opportunity for initiating changes in Japanese society and its relations with the United States.

Security will remain at the heart of the Japan-U.S. relationship. The Soviet threat should diminish in the long run, but China will continue to present problems for Japan, as has always been the case in the past. To see China simply as a threat would naturally be mistaken. We must realize, however, that there is a clear military imbalance between the two countries marked by, for instance, China's nuclear capability. This imbalance, which was long overshadowed by the Soviet threat, has not been unsettling because of Japan's alliance with the United States.

The strategic balance between Japan, with its American backing, and its Chinese neighbor is a prerequisite for exchange in other fields. It also plays a key role in maintaining the stability in other East and Southeast Asian countries. Partly as the product of chance and partly by design, the Japan-U.S. alliance is thus a vital component of the complicated strategic balance in an Asian region where there is a confrontation between the two Koreas, animosity between China and Vietnam, and a delicate relationship between China and Taiwan. This alliance is a cornerstone that cannot be removed without causing the entire structure to crumble.

Sudden changes in the strategic picture in Asia are not desirable for the United States either. As a Pacific rim nation, it would be dealt a tremendous strategic and economic blow by turbulence in the region, and its position as the leading global power might even be undermined. Were Japan left to fend for itself, the only result would be a traumatic realignment of Asian countries that could bring about a fundamental deterioration in global politics. Loss of the cooperative ties between Japan and the United States, which between them produce 40 percent of the world's GNP [gross national product] and have a dominant position in technology and international finance, could turn global politics into an arena where disorderly competition and distrust reign supreme, possibly even causing humankind to plunge into another costly and lengthy world war. Today, with the cold war finally ending, even the thought of such a future is horrifying. If it comes about due to an American rejection of a partnership with Japan, this will be a second ''mistake of the century'' to follow the 1919 vote in the U.S. Congress rejecting membership in the League of Nations.

The world's people sincerely desire continued cooperation between Japan and the United States. In the November 12, 1987, edition of the *International Herald Tribune*, Singapore's Prime Minister Lee Kuan Yew predicted a disastrous outcome for the world if the Japanese, having decided that cooperation with Americans in economic and security affairs no longer made sense, embarked on a military buildup. In its February 25, 1989, edition, the *Economist* made a similar point, stating that ''this is precisely the time when America must work out with Japan how best to move from the post-1945 world to the post-1980s one. . . . Japan's partnership with America, odd as it seems, offers one of the world's greatest hopes of harnessing strength with strength for the interests of free markets and democracy.''

JAPAN'S OEDIPUS COMPLEX

A Japan that is to fulfill a global role must not only accept the costs entailed but also behave in a responsible manner, for which it will need to foster a healthy form of nationalism. The so-called burden sharing being required of Japan is also referred to as ''responsibility sharing,'' a term that implies increased authority as well as additional obligations. With this authority in their hands, the Japanese must commit themselves to a nationalism with an internationalist character. Simply stepping up international cooperation in such forms as economic aid to developing countries will not be enough; people must come to see themselves not just as Japanese but as individuals with a broader identity. Now that Japan is entering a new era under a new emperor, Japanese nationalism must be rebaptized as internationalism.

Thus far in the postwar period the role of national symbolism has assumed more significance than is usual. Because the global community and Japan's own political world have been split into antagonistic camps, nobody in Japan or overseas has been greatly disturbed by excessively fervent displays of Japanese nationalism. The rise of Japan's power and the intensification of economic friction make some Japanese inclined to parade their nationalism forward even more assertively than before, but the former magnanimity toward such attitudes is wearing thin. With the end of the cold war and the defeat of communism drawing near, the global community no longer has any reason to be tolerant of the old Japanese nationalism. Just as the Japan Socialist Party, the leader of the opposition, is being pressed to accept the Self-Defense Forces and the Security Treaty, the conservative LDP is being forced to abandon its narrow nationalistic thinking.

In some of his writings Ishihara makes sound comments about nationalistic sentiments. Consider, for example, this passage: ''Forming a partnership does not mean becoming a vassal. Japan's culture and customs may place it in the minority, but this is no reason for being subservient or allowing the culture and customs to wither away'' (*Sapio*, October 12, 1989). But his conclusion in *A Japan That Can Say No* seems immature: ''I get the feeling that the Japanese people's worldview will change if on important matters they stand up and say no to the United States. I believe that when they gain awareness of the no they have delivered, their entry into the concentric circle of the world community as adult Japanese will become possible for the first time.''

Saying no, Ishihara seems to think, takes desperate courage and yet must be done if one is to mature into adulthood. To fail this test, he exhorts us, would be to lose all hope. It sounds just like a teenage son trying to attain adulthood by rebelling against his father. Ishihara's thesis, we might say, is an international version of the Oedipus complex. Once Japan, the son, has asserted itself on one issue or another, it can break free of its tangled emotions toward its American father.

Perhaps it is only natural that many older Japanese are now struggling to see the United States not as an absolute figure but as one among a number of countries. Surely, however, there is a better way than rebellion to a mature outlook. It may be true that since no countries are permanent enemies and none are eternal allies, all that lasts is national interests, but as long as Japan's interests coincide with American interests, the two countries should cooperate to the fullest extent. The Japanese will not grow up by banding together to deliver a collective no. Only through a dispassionate and thoroughgoing debate on where Japan's true interests lie can individual Japanese develop mature views and create an adult Japan.

QUESTIONS FOR DISCUSSION

1. What are the reasons for the U.S.-Japan Security Treaty?

2. What effect will the end of the cold war have on Japan's security interests?

3. Will Japan replace the Soviet Union as the rival of the United States? What are the reasons for your answer?

4. What steps should be taken to improve U.S.-Japan relations?

5. Will these steps be taken? What are the reasons for your answer?

SUGGESTED READINGS

Akaha, Tsuneo. ''Japan's Security Policy after US Hegemony.'' *Millennium* (London), **18** (winter 1989), pp. 435–454.

Drifte, Reinhard. *Japan's Foreign Policy.* New York: Council on Foreign Relations Press, 1990.

Haber, Deborah L. ''The Death of Hegemony: Why 'Pax Nipponica' Is Impossible.'' *Asian Survey*, **30** (Sept. 1990), pp. 892–907.

Ikle, Fred Charles, and Terumasa Nakanishi. ''Japan's Grand Strategy.'' *Foreign Affairs*, **69** (Summer 1990), pp. 81–95.

Islam, Shafiqul. ''Capitalism in Conflict.'' *Foreign Affairs*, **69** (Fall 1990), pp. 172–182.

Ito, Kan. ''Trans-Pacific Anger.'' *Foreign Policy*, no. 78 (Spring 1990), pp. 131–152.

Krugman Paul. ''Japan Is Not Our Nemesis.'' *New Perspectives Quarterly*, **7** (Summer 1990), pp. 41–45.

Trezise, Philip H. ''Japan, the Enemy?'' *Brookings Review*, **8** (Winter 1989–90), pp. 3–13.

von Wolferen, Karel. ''Darkness at Sunrise.'' *New Perspectives Quarterly*, **7** (Summer 1990), pp. 18–21.

Zinsmeister, Karl. ''Shadows on the Rising Sun.'' *American Enterprise*, **1** (May/June 1990), pp. 52–61.

CHAPTER 4

Instruments of Power

Even when the objectives of a state's foreign policy are clear, there are often differing views among policymakers about what instruments of foreign policy should be used. Faced with the problem of an Iraqi invasion and conquest of Kuwait in 1990, President George Bush had to decide *how* to meet the challenge.

Proposals put forward included launching an immediate air attack of military installations and other strategic targets, rallying the United Nations to take action, implementing an economic embargo, and accepting the new status in the Persian Gulf as a *fait accompli.* Bush chose to get U.N. support for an economic embargo and later received U.N. authorization to use military force if necessary to get Iraq out of Kuwait. In 1991, U.S. and allied forces conducted war against Iraq, forcing it to withdraw from Kuwait.

Debates in Chapter 4 focus on the use of military and economic levers of power. Issues include the future of war in developed societies, the wisdom of retaining U.S. forces in Europe in the post–cold war era, and the effectiveness of economic sanctions.

THE FUTURE OF WAR IN DEVELOPED SOCIETIES

After wars have taken a heavy toll in life and property, they often produce hopes that the subsequent peace will begin a future that will not repeat the mistakes of the past. After World War I, Woodrow Wilson's appeal for the establishment of a League of Nations was made in such a spirit. After World War II, it was hoped that the wartime alliance of the major powers, including most notably the United States and the Soviet Union, would continue and that the United Nations would usher in an era of peace and cooperation.

But the League of Nations was a most imperfect institution—weakened at its outset by the failure of the United States to join. Nationalism, fascism, and a global economic crisis produced the conditions that brought on World War II. After that war the failure of the Soviet Union and the United States to cooperate precipitated the cold war.

With the collapse of the Soviet empire, as reflected in the tearing down of the Berlin Wall in 1989, the democratization of many Eastern European countries, and the obvious failure of communism as a driving force in world politics, there was a new optimism that peace and political stability could be brought at least to the developed world. Eastern Europe rejected its command economies, which failed to produce the kinds of material goods in abundance in the West and in some Asian countries that had strong capitalist economies. Eastern Europe sought to restructure its economies in a market-oriented way and replaced one-party communist governments with free elections, a free press, and other democratic processes.

Debate 14 reflects the kinds of questions that are being asked in the post–cold war atmosphere: Is war among developed countries likely to diminish?

Political scientist John Mueller contends that war among developed countries is becoming obsolete. He argues: (1) War is not something that is somehow required by the human condition, by the structure of international affairs, or by the forces of history. Rather, war can disappear. (2) The idea that war should be used to resolve conflicts has increasingly been discredited and abandoned in the developed world. (3) Other time-honored institutions—dueling and slavery—became obsolescent, and war can have a similar fate. (4) Since 1800, the experience of once-warlike countries like Holland, Switzerland, and Sweden dropping out of the war system shows that war is not inherent in human nature. (5) The rise of an organized peace movement—particularly after World War I—made peace advocates a pronounced majority in the developed world and destroyed war romanticism. (6) The cold war never brought the East and West close to major war. (7) The kinds of wars involving developed countries since World War II—wars of colonialism and wars of national liberation—are declining in frequency and relevance. (7) The demise of the cold war will lead to a reduction in arms, an expansion of international trade, and interdependence. (8) War—even within the developed world—has not become impossible, but it has become less likely.

Political scientist John J. Mearsheimer suggests that in this period of transition and uncertainty we are likely to miss the cold war. Of course we will not miss the hot wars, international crises, domestic turmoil, and xenophobia generated by the cold war, but he nonetheless contends: (1) The cold war brought order out of the anarchy of international relations. (2) The forty-five years following the end of the cold war will be more violent than the forty-five years of the cold war. (3) The conditions that produced peace in the cold war—bipolarity, an equal balance of military power, and superpower predominance in nuclear weapons—will diminish in the future and thus threaten peace. (4) Scenarios for a peaceful future—based on the notions that war is obsolete, prosperity is the path to peace, and democracies love peace—are wrong.

NATO AND THE UNITED STATES

The North Atlantic Treaty Organization (NATO) was formed in April 1949 because of a fear by its original signatories—Belgium, Canada, Denmark, France, Iceland, Italy, Luxembourg, the Netherlands, Norway, Portugal, the United Kingdom, and the United

States—that the Soviet Union posed a major threat to their security. Its central provision is Article 5, which states: "The Parties agree that an armed attack against one or more of them in Europe or North America shall be considered an attack against them all."[1]

NATO is a grand alliance, but it is different from earlier alliances. The grand alliances of the past—those that put down Napoleon, Kaiser Wilhelm, and Adolf Hitler—were formed after an act of aggression had occurred. The purpose of NATO is twofold: deterrence and defense. The very act of forming a peacetime alliance, it was believed, would serve to deter aggression by the Soviet Union. If deterrence failed, however, the alliance would be politically united and militarily strong so as to protect its members from a Soviet victory.

Certain factors underlay the formation of NATO. These involved the supremacy of the United States as a nuclear power, the fear of Soviet policies, and the economic condition of the Europeans. First, in April 1949, the United States had a monopoly of nuclear weapons. It could carry these weapons to the Soviet Union itself by relying on its air bases in Western Europe and Africa. NATO members could believe that the U.S. nuclear forces offered a credible deterrent to Soviet aggression.

Second, it seemed to NATO members that the Soviet Union in particular and communism in general posed a threat to Western security. The post–World War II period was characterized by such apparent threats as a civil war in Greece, communist political strength in France and Italy, a Soviet-inspired communist takeover of Czechoslovakia in 1948, and a blockade of Allied surface routes to Berlin in 1948.

Third, Western Europe was devastated by World War II. It depended on the United States for its economic support. The Marshall Plan of 1947, in which the United States committed nearly $15 billion of economic aid to its Western European allies, was a reflection of that economic bond.

In the four decades since NATO came into existence, there have been many changes in the conditions underlying NATO and in the character of the alliance itself. Most important, no longer does the United States possess a monopoly of nuclear weapons. Even after it lost that monopoly in 1949, the United States maintained a superiority of nuclear weapons that extended into the 1960s. During the Cuban missile crisis of 1962 the Soviet Union had about seventy long-range missiles that took ten hours to fuel, so they were easily vulnerable to a U.S. attack before they could be launched. Even as late as the October 1973 War in the Middle East the United States had a superiority of about 8 to 1 in nuclear warheads. The United States had maintained through this period a superiority in theater nuclear forces as well.

Starting in the 1960s, however, the Soviet Union began a massive nuclear program. In the 1970s it reached nuclear parity with the United States in strategic and tactical weapons. In the first years of his administration, President Ronald Reagan stated that the Soviet Union had superiority in nuclear weapons, although that contention was challenged by a number of observers. In the later years of his administration the president and his supporters took pride in their efforts to modernize the defense establishment,

---

[1] *North Atlantic Treaty*, Apr. 4, 1949, in Henry Steele Commager and Milton Cantor (eds.), *Documents of American History*, 10th ed. (Englewood Cliffs, N.J.: Prentice Hall, 1988), II, 549.

and there was no repetition of comments about Soviet military superiority. Whatever the exact relationship between Soviet and U.S. nuclear capabilities, the rising Soviet military strength led to changed military relationships and political uncertainties.

Since the 1950s the Soviets have engaged in various peace offensives. Soviet leader Nikita Khrushchev became identified with a policy of "peaceful coexistence." Khrushchev's successor Leonid Brezhnev advocated a policy of détente. The current Soviet leader Mikhail Gorbachev engaged in a fundamental restructuring of Soviet foreign policy, seeking improved relations with the West.

In the 1980s the Western European economy experienced continuing improvement. Western Europeans rid themselves of their African and Asian colonies, which had become indefensible and economically debilitating. The establishment of the European Economic Community served to strengthen the economies of Western European countries. Trade between Western Europe and Eastern Europe increased. No longer was Western Europe as dependent on the United States as it had been immediately after World War II, so Western European countries could more readily pursue an independent course in foreign policy.

There were changes in the organization of NATO as well. Its membership grew. Greece and Turkey joined the alliance in 1952, and the Federal Republic of Germany in 1955. West German entrance into NATO was the immediate cause of the establishment of the Soviet equivalent alliance defense organization—the Warsaw Pact. In 1982 Spain became the sixteenth member of NATO.

Even before the events of 1989, strains appeared in the alliance on economic and military matters. U.S. critics complained that the United States was bearing too much of a burden in deploying hundreds of thousands of its troops in Europe. They called for a reduction in U.S. forces and a greater European commitment to defense. Some Europeans sought to eliminate nuclear weapons from Europe. The West Germans were particularly active in the antinuclear movement because they recognized that a ground war between NATO and the Warsaw Pact would take place on German soil and destroy their country.

But disagreements among the members of NATO became obsolete once the cold war ended. With the unification of Germany, the establishment of democracies in the countries of Eastern Europe, the dismantling of the Warsaw Pact, and the actual and anticipated reduction of Soviet forces in Eastern Europe, the future of NATO became uncertain.

Some people argued that NATO was needed because the Soviet Union was still a strong military power and could reverse its current course. Others contended that NATO still had a role to play, although it was now more political than military. Still others thought that NATO could be disbanded and replaced by an all-European security alliance.

Debate 15 deals with one central aspect of the future of NATO: Should U.S. forces withdraw from Europe? *Defense Monitor*, a publication of the Center for Defense Information, argues that the stationing of U.S. forces in Europe is no longer needed. It contends: (1) The cold war is over, and it is time to bring U.S. forces home. (2) The United States bears too much of the burden for defending Europe. (3) The NATO Treaty imposes no legal obligation for the United States to station troops in Europe. (4)

Europeans can afford to provide for their own security. (5) A less militarized Europe is a better alternative to NATO. (6) The Warsaw Pact remains a military alliance in name only. (7) The Soviet Union is demilitarizing. (8) The presence of U.S. forces in Germany impedes progress in arms control and is a source of potential hostility by the German people.

International relations specialist Robert McGeehan argues that the United States should retain its forces in NATO. He contends: (1) The threat to the West comes from the Soviet Union and not the Warsaw Pact. The Soviets retain their ability to cause trouble in the West through blackmail, coercion, and intimidation. (2) Western Europe needs U.S. military power to defend against a Soviet threat. (3) NATO can perform new missions in peaceful security cooperation and in so doing serve the interests of all of Europe. (4) The Soviet military establishment is perfecting its weapons and increasing its firepower. (5) The Soviet leadership may resume the cold war. (6) The continued presence of U.S. forces in Europe will strengthen stability on that continent.

ECONOMIC SANCTIONS

Economic sanctions are an instrument of foreign policy that have been imposed by international institutions as well as states. The League of Nations implemented economic sanctions against Italy after it invaded Ethiopia in 1935. In 1965, 1966, and 1968 the Security Council of the United Nations invoked economic sanctions on Rhodesia in condemnation of that country's white rule.

During wartime, trade between belligerent forces usually stops. Sanctions, however, have been imposed when countries are not directly at war with each other. Arab nations attempted to boycott companies in Western countries dealing with Israel in an effort to undermine Israel's economy. The United States has a boycott on trade with Castro's Cuba. It also imposed severe restrictions on trade with South Africa in an effort to force the white South African government to allow greater freedom to the nonwhite majority.

Three notable recent efforts at imposing sanctions came in the Carter, Reagan, and Bush administrations. After the Soviet Union sent troops into Afghanistan in 1979, President Jimmy Carter imposed a partial grain embargo on the Soviet Union. The Soviet Union was able to break the embargo by purchasing grain from other countries.

Ronald Reagan tried to stop the sale of equipment from the West to the Soviet Union that would have helped to build a gas pipeline between the Soviet Union and Western Europe. He was as unsuccessful in his efforts at embargo as his predecessor had been.

In 1990, George Bush engineered U.N. Security Council decisions adopting economic sanctions against Iraq because of its invasion of Kuwait. The blockade successfully stopped the exports of oil from Iraq. It achieved a great measure of success in stopping the flow of both military and nonmilitary goods to that Middle East country, although some supplies were getting through overland. While some argued that the economic sanctions should be given additional time to force Iraq to withdraw from Kuwait, Bush and other coalition leaders decided in January 1991 to pursue military operations. The military option brought defeat to Iraq in six weeks.

Writer Gregory A. Fossedal makes the case for economic sanctions. He contends: (1) The Arab oil embargo in 1973–1974 was clearly a political and economic success. (2)

Economic sanctions helped defeat Nazi Germany in World War II. (3) Economic sanctions can be effective if the country imposing the sanctions suffers less than the country targeted for the sanctions. (4) In practice, markets are often not fungible. A targeted country may experience increased costs and difficulties in production if it has to switch to new suppliers. (5) Although economic sanctions hurt the people of a targeted country, in some cases this pain can cause the people to inflict pain on their government.

Economist Bruce Bartlett argues against economic sanctions. He contends: (1) There is little historical evidence that economic sanctions have achieved their purpose. (2) More often than not, sanctions result in the targeted country becoming more self-sufficient and more determined to continue its policies. (3) Trade sanctions are more likely to alter trade patterns than to inflict serious damage on the targeted country. (4) Economic sanctions often have adverse economic consequences on the country employing the sanctions.

14 Is War among Developed Nations Likely to Diminish?

YES

John Mueller

The Obsolescence of Major War

NO

John J. Mearsheimer

Why We Will Soon Miss the Cold War

The Obsolescence of Major War

John Mueller

INTRODUCTORY REMARKS

In discussing the causes of international war, commentators have often found it useful to group theories into what they term levels of analysis. In his classic work, *Man, the State and War*, Kenneth N. Waltz organizes the theories according to whether the cause of war is found in the nature of man, in the nature of the state, or in the nature of the international state system. More recently Jack Levy, partly setting the issue of human nature to one side, organizes the theories according to whether they stress the systemic level, the nature of state and society, or the decisionmaking process.[1]

In various ways, these level-of-analysis approaches direct attention away from war itself and toward concerns which may influence the incidence of war. However, war should not be visualized as a sort of recurring outcome that is determined by other conditions, but rather as a phenomenon that has its own qualities and appeals. And over time these appeals can change. In this view, war is merely an idea, an institution, like dueling or slavery, that has been grafted onto human existence. Unlike breathing, eating, or sex, war is not something that is somehow required by the human condition, by the structure of international affairs, or by the forces of history.

Accordingly, war can shrivel up and disappear; and this may come about without any notable change or improvement on any of the level-of-analysis categories. Specifically, war can die out without changing human nature, without modifying the nature of the state or the nation-state, without changing the international system, without creating an effective world government or system of international law, and without improving the competence or moral capacity of political leaders. It can also go away without expanding international trade, interdependence, or communication; without fabricating an effective moral or practical equivalent; without enveloping the earth in democracy or prosperity; without devising ingenious agreements to restrict arms or the arms industry; without reducing the world's considerable store of hate, selfishness, nationalism, and racism; without increasing the amount of love, justice, harmony, cooperation, good will, or inner peace in the world; without establishing security communities; and without doing anything whatever about nuclear weapons.

Not only *can* such a development take place: it *has* been taking place for a century or more, at least within the developed world, once a cauldron of international and civil war. Conflicts of interest are inevitable and continue to persist within the developed world. But the notion that war should be used to resolve them has increasingly been discredited and abandoned there. War is apparently becoming obsolete, at least in the developed world: in an area where war was once often casually seen as beneficial, noble, and glorious, or at least as necessary or inevitable, the conviction has now become widespread that war would be intolerably costly, unwise, futile, and debased.[2]

Some of this may be suggested by the remarkable

Source: John Mueller, "The Obsolescence of Major War," *Bulletin of Peace Proposals,* **21** (Sept. 1990), pp. 321–328. Reprinted by permission.

[1] Kenneth N. Waltz, *Man, the State and War* (New York: Columbia University Press, 1959); Jack S. Levy, "The Causes of War: A Review of Theories and Evidence," in Philip E. Tetlock, Jo L. Husbands, Robert Jervis, Paul C. Stern and Charles Tilly, eds., *Behavior, Society, and Nuclear War*, vol. 1 (New York: Oxford University Press, 1989), pp. 209–333. See also J. David Singer, "The Levels of Analysis Problem in International Relations," in Klaus Knorr and Sydney Verba, eds., *The International System* (Princeton, N.J.: Princeton University Press, 1961), pp. 77–92; and James N. Rosenau, "Pretheories and Theories of Foreign Policy," in R. B. Farrell, ed., *Approaches to Comparative and International Politics* (Evanston, Ill.: Northwestern University Press, 1966), pp. 27–92.

[2] For a further development of these arguments, see John Mueller, *Retreat from Doomsday: The Obsolescence of Major War* (New York: Basic Books, 1989).

developments in the Cold War in the late 1980s. The dangers of a major war in the developed world clearly declined remarkably, yet this can hardly be attributed to an improvement in human nature, to the demise of the nation-state, to the rise of a world government, or to a notable improvement in the competence of political leaders.

TWO ANALOGIES: DUELING AND SLAVERY

It may not be obvious that an accepted, time-honored institution which serves an urgent social purpose can become obsolescent and then die out because many people come to find it obnoxious. But the argument here is that something like that has indeed been happening to war in the developed world. To illustrate the dynamic, it will be helpful briefly to assess two analogies: the processes by which the once-perennial institutions of dueling and slavery have all but vanished from the face of the earth.

Dueling

In some important respects, war in the developed world may be following the example of another violent method for settling disputes, dueling. Up until a century ago dueling was common practice in Europe and the U.S.A. among a certain class of young and youngish men who liked to classify themselves as gentlemen.[3] Men of the social set that once dueled still exist, they still get insulted, and they are still concerned about their self-respect and their standing among their peers. But they no longer duel. However, they do not avoid dueling today because they evaluate the option and reject it on cost-benefit grounds. Rather, the option never percolates into

their consciousness as something that is available. That is, a form of violence famed and fabeled for centuries has now sunk from thought as a viable, conscious possibility.

The Prussian strategist, Carl von Clausewitz, opens his famous 1832 book, *On War*, by observing that "War is nothing but a duel on a larger scale."[4] If war, like dueling, comes to be viewed as thoroughly undesirable, even ridiculous, policy, and if it can no longer promise gains, or if potential combatants come no longer to value the things it can gain for them, then war can fade away as a coherent possibility even if a truly viable substitute or "moral equivalent" for it were never formulated. Like dueling, it could become unfashionable and then obsolete.

Slavery

From the dawn of prehistory until about 1788 slavery, like war, could be found just about everywhere in one form or another, and it flourished in every age.[5] Around 1788, however, the anti-slavery forces began to argue that the institution was repulsive, immoral, and uncivilized: and this sentiment gradually picked up adherents. Remarkably, at exactly the time that the anti-slavery movement was taking flight, the Atlantic slave economy, as Seymour Drescher notes, "was entering what was probably the most dynamic and profitable period in its existence."[6]

Thus the abolitionists were up against an institu-

[3] For other observations of the analogy between war and dueling, see Bernard Brodie, *War and Politics* (New York: Macmillan, 1973), p. 275; Norman Angell, *The Great Illusion* (London: Heinemann, 1914), pp. 202–203; G. P. Gooch, *History of Our Time, 1885–1911* (London: Williams and Norgate, 1911), p. 249; J. E. Cairnes, "International Law," *Fortnightly Review*, vol. **2** (1 November 1865), p. 650 n.

[4] Carl von Clausewitz, *On War* [1832] (Princeton, N.J.: Princeton University Press, 1976), p. 75.

[5] See Orlando Patterson, *Slavery and Social Death: A Comparative Study* (Cambridge, Mass.: Harvard University Press, 1982); Stanley Engerman, "Slavery and Emancipation in Comparative Perspectives: A Look at Some Recent Debates," *Journal of Economic History*, vol. **46**, no. 2 (June 1986), pp. 318–339. For another comparison of the institutions of war and slavery, see James Lee Ray, "The Abolition of Slavery and the End of International War," *International Organization*, vol. **43**, no. 3 (Summer, 1989), pp. 405–439.

[6] Seymour Drescher, *Capitalism and Antislavery: British Mobilization in Comparative Perspectives* (New York: Oxford University Press, 1987), p. 4. See also David Eltis, *Economic Growth and the Ending of the Transatlantic Slave Trade* (New York: Oxford University Press, 1987); Engerman "Slavery and Emancipation," pp. 322–333, 339.

tion that was viable, profitable, and expanding, and moreover one that had been uncritically accepted for thousands—perhaps millions—of years as a natural and inevitable part of human existence. To counter this powerful and time-honored institution, the abolitionists' principal weapon was a novel argument: it had recently occurred to them, they said, that slavery was no longer the way people ought to do things.

As it happened, this was an idea whose time had come. The abolition of slavery required legislative battles, international pressures, economic travail, and, in the United States, a cataclysmic war (but it did *not* require the fabrication of a functional equivalent or the formation of an effective supranational authority). Within a century slavery, and most similar institutions like serfdom, had been all but eradicated from the face of the globe. Slavery became controversial and then obsolete.

War

Dueling and slavery no longer exist as effective institutions; they have largely faded from human experience except as something we read about in books. While their re-establishment is not impossible, they show after a century of neglect no signs of revival. Other once-popular, even once-admirable, institutions in the developed world have been, or are being, eliminated because at some point they began to seem repulsive, immoral, and uncivilized: bear-baiting, bareknuckle fighting, freak shows, casual torture, wanton cruelty to animals, burning heretics, flogging, vendetta, deforming corsetting, laughing at the insane, the death penalty for minor crimes, eunuchism, public cigarette smoking.

War may well be in the process of joining this list of recently-discovered sins and vices. War is not, of course, the same as dueling or slavery. Like war, dueling is an institution for settling disputes; but it was something of a social affectation and it usually involved only matters of ''honor,'' not ones of physical gain. Like war, slavery was nearly universal and an apparently inevitable part of human existence, but it could be eliminated area by area: a country that

abolished slavery did not have to worry about what other countries were doing, while a country that would like to abolish war must continue to be concerned about those that have kept it in their repertory.

On the other hand, war has against it not only substantial psychic costs, but also obvious and widespread physical ones. Dueling brought death and destruction but, at least in the first instance, only to a few people who had specifically volunteered to participate. And while slavery may have brought moral destruction, it generally was a considerable economic success.

In some respects then, the fact that war has outlived dueling and slavery is curious. But there are signs that, at least in the developed world, it too has begun to succumb to obsolescence.

TRENDS AGAINST WAR BEFORE 1914

There were a number of trends away from war in the developed world before World War I. Two of these deserve special emphasis.

The Hollandization Phenomenon

As early as 1800 a few once-warlike countries in Europe, like Holland, Switzerland, and Sweden, quietly began to drop out of the war system. While war was still generally accepted as a natural and inevitable phenomenon, these countries found solace (and prosperity) in policies that stressed peace. People who argue that war is inherent in nature and those who see war as a recurring, cyclic phenomenon need to supply an explanation for these countries. Switzerland, for example, has avoided all international war for nearly 200 years. If war is inherent in human nature or if war is some sort of cyclic inevitability, surely the Swiss ought to be roaring for a fight by now.

The Rise of an Organized Peace Movement

While there have been individual war opponents throughout history, the existence of organized groups devoted to abolishing war from the human condition is quite new. The institution of war came under truly organized and concentrated attack only after 1815, and this peace movement did not develop real momentum until the end of the century.[7]

War opponents stressed various arguments against war. Some, like the Quakers, were opposed to war primarily because they found it immoral. Others stressed arguments that were essentially aesthetic: war, they concluded was repulsive, barbaric, and uncivilized. Still others, such as the British liberals, stressed the futility of war: particularly from an economic standpoint, they argued, even the winners of war were worse off than if they had pursued a policy of peace. These protesters were joined by socialists and others who had concluded that war was a capitalistic device in which the working class was used as cannon fodder. Among their activities, the various elements of the anti-war movement were devoted to exploring alternatives to war such as arbitration and international law and organization, and to developing mechanisms, like disarmament, that might reduce its frequency or consequences.

Peace advocates were a noisy gadfly minority by 1900, and they had established a sense of momentum. Their arguments were inescapable, but, for the most part they were rejected and derided by the majority which still held to the traditional view that war was noble, natural, thrilling, progressive, manly, redemptive, and beneficial.[8] Up until 1914, as Michael Howard has observed, war "was almost universally considered an acceptable, perhaps an inevitable and for many people a desirable way of settling international differences."[9]

THE IMPACT OF WORLD WAR I

The holocaust of World War I turned peace advocates into a pronounced majority in the developed

world and destroyed war romanticism. As Arnold Toynbee points out, this war marked the end of a "span of five thousand years during which war had been one of mankind's master institutions." Or, as Evan Luard observes, "the First World War transformed traditional attitudes toward war. For the first time there was an almost universal sense that the deliberate launching of a war could now no longer be justified."[10]

World War I was, of course, horrible. But horror was not invented in 1914. History had already had its Carthages, its Jerichos, its wars of 30 years, of 100 years. Seen in historic context, in fact, World War I does not seem to have been all that unusual in its duration, destructiveness, grimness, political pointlessness, economic consequences, breadth, or intensity. However, it does seem to be unique in that it was the first major war to be preceded by substantial organized anti-war agitation, and in that, for Europeans, it followed an unprecedentedly peaceful century during which Europeans had begun, perhaps unknowingly, to appreciate the virtues of peace.[11]

Obviously, this change of attitude was not enough to prevent the wars that have taken place since 1918. But the notion that the institution of war, particularly war in the developed world, was repulsive, uncivilized, immoral, and futile—voiced only by minorities before 1914—was an idea whose time had come. It is one that has permeated most of the developed world ever since.

WORLD WAR II

It is possible that enough war spirit still lingered, particularly in Germany, for another war in Europe to be necessary to extinguish it there. But analysis of opinion in the interwar period suggests that war was viewed with about as much horror in Germany as

[7] For a useful history, see A. C. F. Beales, *The History of Peace: A Short Account of the Organized Movements for International Peace* (New York: Dial, 1931).

[8] For an excellent discussion, see Roland N. Stromberg, *Redemption by War: The Intellectuals and 1914* (Lawrence, Kans.: Regents Press of Kansas, 1982).

[9] Michael Howard, *The Causes of Wars and Other Essays* (Cambridge, Mass.: Harvard University Press, 1984), p. 9.

[10] Arnold J. Toynbee, *Experiences* (New York: Oxford University Press, 1969), p. 214; Evan Luard, *War in International Society* (New Haven, Conn.: Yale University Press, 1986), p. 365.

[11] For a further development of this argument, see John Mueller, "Changing Attitudes Toward War: The Impact of the First World War," *British Journal of Political Science*, **21** (January 1991), pp. 1–28.

any place on the continent.[12] To a remarkable degree, major war returned to Europe only because of the astoundingly successful machinations of Adolf Hitler, virtually the last European who was willing to risk major war. As Gerhard Weinberg has put it: "Whether any other German leader would indeed have taken the plunge is surely doubtful, and the very warnings Hitler received from some of his generals can only have reinforced his belief in his personal role as the one man able, willing, and even eager to lead Germany and drag the world into war."[13] That is, after World War I a war in Europe could only be brought about through the maniacally dedicated manipulations of an exceptionally lucky and spectacularly skilled entrepreneur; before World War I, any dimwit—e.g., Kaiser Wilhelm—could get into one.

The war in Asia was, of course, developed out of the expansionary policies of distant Japan, a country which neither participated substantially in World War I nor learned its lessons. In World War II, Japan got the message most Europeans had received from World War I.

THE COLD WAR, THE LONG PEACE, AND NUCLEAR WEAPONS

Since 1945 major war has been mostly likely to develop from the Cold War that has dominated postwar international history. The hostility of the era mostly derives from the Soviet Union's ideological—even romantic—affection for revolution and for revolutionary war. While this ideology is expansionistic in some respects, it has never visualized major war in the Hitler mode as a remotely sensible tactic.[14]

East and West have never been close to major war, and it seems unlikely that nuclear weapons have been important determinants of this—insofar as a military deterrent has been necessary, the fear of escalation to a war like World War I or II supplies it. Even allowing considerably for stupidity, ineptness, miscalculation, and self-deception, a large war, nuclear or otherwise, has never been remotely in the interest of the essentially-contented, risk-averse, escalation-anticipating countries that have dominated world affairs since 1945. This is not to deny that nuclear war is appalling to contemplate and mind-concentratingly dramatic, particularly in the speed with which it could bring about massive destruction. Nor is it to deny that decisionmakers, both in times of crisis and in times of non-crisis, are well aware of how cataclysmic a nuclear war could be. It is simply to stress that the horror of repeating World War II is not all that much less impressive or dramatic, and that leaders essentially content with the status quo will strive to avoid anything that they feel could lead to either calamity. A jump from a fiftieth-floor window is probably quite a bit more horrible to contemplate than a jump from a fifth-floor one, but anyone who finds life even minimally satisfying is extremely unlikely to do either.[15]

In general the wars that have involved developed countries since World War II have been of two kinds, both of them declining in frequency and relevance. One of these concerns lingering colonial responsibilities and readjustments. Thus the Dutch got involved in (but did not start) a war in Indonesia, the French in Indochina and Algeria, the British in Malaya and the Falklands.

The other kind relates to the Cold War contest between East and West. The communists have generally sought to avoid major war, not so much because they necessarily find such wars to be immoral, repulsive, or uncivilized, but because they find them

---

[12] For a discussion of the antipathy felt by the German people toward war in the 1930s, see Ian Kershaw, *The "Hitler Myth"* (Oxford: Oxford University Press, 1987), pp. 122–147, 229, 241; Marlis G. Steinert, *Hitler's War and the Germans: Public Mood and Attitude During the Second World War* (Athens, Ohio: Ohio University Press, 1977), pp. 40–41, 315, 341.

[13] Gerhard Weinberg, *The Foreign Policy of Hitler's Germany* (Chicago: University of Chicago Press, 1980), p. 664.

[14] For a valuable discussion, see Frederic S. Burin, "The Communist Doctrine of the Inevitability of War," *American Political Science Review*, vol. **57**, no. 2 (June 1963), pp. 334–54.

[15] For a further development of this argument, see John Mueller, "The Essential Irrelevance of Nuclear Weapons: Stability in the Postwar World," *International Security*, vol. **13**, no. 2 (Fall 1988), pp. 55–79.

futile—dangerous, potentially counter-productive, wildly and absurdly adventurous. However, for decades after 1945 they retained a dutiful affection for what they came to call wars of national liberation—smaller wars around the world designed to further the progressive cause of world revolution. The West has seen this threat as visceral and as one that must be countered even at the cost of war if necessary. Wars fought in this context, such as those in Korea and Vietnam, have essentially been seen to be preventive—if communism is countered there, it will not have to be countered later, on more vital, closer turf.

The lesson learned (perhaps overlearned) from the Hitler experience is that aggressive threats must be dealt with by those who abhor war when the threats are still comparatively small and distant; to allow the aggressive force to succeed only brings nearer the day when a larger war must be fought. Thus some countries which abhor war have felt it necessary to wage them in order to prevent wider wars.

CONSEQUENCES OF THE DEMISE OF THE COLD WAR

Because of economic crisis and persistent ideological failure, it now appears that the Cold War has ended as the Soviet Union, following the lead of its former ideological soulmate, China, abandons its quest for ideological expansion, questing instead after prosperity and a quiet, normal international situation. Unless some new form of conflict emerges, war participation by developed countries is likely to continue its decline.

As tensions lapse between the two sides in what used to be known as the Cold War, there is a natural tendency for the arms that backed that tension, and in a sense measured it, to atrophy. Both sides have begun what might be called a negative arms race. Formal arms negotiations will probably be only slow and pedantify this natural process, and might best be abandoned at this point. It may also be time to confederate the East-West alliances (rather than allowing them to fragment) with the combined organiza-

tion serving to regulate the remarkable changes going on in Europe.[16]

The demise of the Cold War should also facilitate further expansion of international trade and interdependence. Trade and interdependence may not lead inexorably to peace, but peace does seem to lead to trade, interdependence, and economic growth—or, at any rate, it facilitates them. That is, peace ought to be seen not as a dependent but rather as an independent variable in such considerations. The 1992 economic unity of Europe and the building of a long-envisioned Channel tunnel are the consequences of peace, not its cause.

Left alone, enterprising business people will naturally explore the possibilities of investing in other countries or selling their products there. Averse to disastrous surprises, they are more likely to invest if they are confident that peace will prevail. But for trade to flourish, governments must stay out of the way not only by eschewing war, but also by eschewing measures which unnaturally inhibit trade.

Furthermore, if nations no longer find it sensible to use force or the threat of force in their dealings with one another, it may be neither necessary nor particularly desirable to create an entrenched international government or police force (as opposed to ad hoc arrangements and devices designed to meet specific problems). Indeed, an effective international government could be detrimental to economic growth since, like domestic governments, it could be manipulated to reward the inefficient, coddle the incompetent, and plague the innovative.

WAR IN THE THIRD WORLD

War has not, of course, become fully obsolete. While major war—war among developed countries—seems to be going out of style, war obviously continues to flourish elsewhere. The demise of the Cold War suggests that the United States and the Soviet Union, in particular, are likely to involve themselves

---

[16] On these two policy proposals, see John Mueller, ''A New Concert of Europe,'' *Foreign Policy*, Winter 1989–90, pp. 3–16.

less in these wars. Moreover, it is possible that the catastrophic Iran-Iraq war will sober people in the Third World about that kind of war. And it does seem that much of the romance has gone out of the concept of violent revolution as Third World countries increasingly turn to the drab, difficult, and unromantic task of economic development.

Thus it is possible that the developed world's aversion to war may eventually infect the rest of the world as well (international war, in fact, has been quite rare in Latin America for a century). But this development is not certain, nor is its pace predictable. As slavery continued to persist in Brazil even after it had been abolished elsewhere, the existence of war in some parts of the world does not refute the observation that it is vanishing, or has vanished, in other parts.

IMPERFECT PEACE

War, even war within the developed world, has not become impossible—nor could it ever do so. When it has seemed necessary, even countries like the United States and Britain, which were among the first to become thoroughly disillusioned with war, have been able to fight wars and to use military force—often with high morale and substantial public support, at least at first. The ability to make war and the knowledge about how to do so can never be fully expunged—nor, for that matter, can the ability or knowledge to institute slavery, eunuchism, crucifixion, or human sacrifice. War is declining as an institution not because it has ceased to be possible or fascinating, but because peoples and leaders in the developed world—where war was once endemic—

have increasingly found war to be disgusting, ridiculous, and unwise.

The view presented in this article is based upon the premise that, in some important respects, war is often taken too seriously. War, it seems, is merely an idea. It is not a trick of fate, a thunderbolt from hell, a natural calamity, or a desperate plot contrivance dreamed up by some sadistic puppeteer on high. If war begins in the minds of men, as the UNESCO [United Nations Educational, Scientific, and Cultural Organization] charter insists, it can end there as well. Over the centuries, war opponents have been trying to bring this about by discrediting war as an idea: the argument here is that they have been substantially successful at doing so. The long peace since World War II is less a product of recent weaponry than the culmination of a substantial historical process. For the last two or three centuries, major war has gradually moved toward terminal disrepute because of its perceived repulsiveness and futility.

It could also be argued that, to a considerable degree, people have tended to take *peace* too seriously as well. Peace is merely what emerges when the institution of war is neglected. It does not mean that the world suddenly becomes immersed in those qualities with which the word ''peace'' is constantly being associated: love, justice, harmony, cooperation, brotherhood, good will. People still remain contentious and there still remain substantial conflicts of interest. The difference is only that they no longer resort to force to resolve their conflicts, any more than young men today resort to formal dueling to resolve their quarrels. A world at peace would not be perfect, but it would be notably better than the alternative.

Why We Will Soon Miss the Cold War

John J. Mearsheimer

Peace: it's wonderful. I like it as much as the next man, and have no wish to be willfully gloomy at a moment when optimism about the future shape of the world abounds. Nevertheless, my thesis in this essay is that we are likely soon to regret the passing of the Cold War.

To be sure, no one will miss such by-products of the Cold War as the Korean and Vietnam conflicts. No one will want to replay the U-2 affair, the Cuban missile crisis, or the building of the Berlin Wall. And no one will want to revisit the domestic Cold War, with its purges and loyalty oaths, its xenophobia and stifling of dissent. We will not wake up one day to discover fresh wisdom in the collected fulminations of John Foster Dulles.

We may, however, wake up one day lamenting the loss of the order that the Cold War gave to the anarchy of international relations. For untamed anarchy is what Europe knew in the forty-five years of this century before the Cold War, and untamed anarchy—Hobbes's war of all against all—is a prime cause of armed conflict. Those who think that armed conflicts among the European states are now out of the question, that the two world wars burned all the war out of Europe, are projecting unwarranted optimism onto the future. The theories of peace that implicitly undergird this optimism are notably shallow constructs. They stand up to neither logical nor historical analysis. You would not want to bet the farm on their prophetic accuracy.

The world is about to conduct a vast test of the theories of war and peace put forward by social scientists, who never dreamed that their ideas would be tested by the world-historic events announced almost daily in newspaper headlines. This social scientist is willing to put his theoretical cards on the table as he ventures predictions about the future of Europe. In the process, I hope to put alternative theories of war and peace under as much intellectual pressure as I can muster. My argument is that the prospect of major crises, even wars, in Europe is likely to increase dramatically now that the Cold War is receding into history. The next forty-five years in Europe are not likely to be so violent as the forty-five years before the Cold War, but they are likely to be substantially more violent than the past forty-five years, the era that we may someday look back upon not as the Cold War but as the Long Peace, in John Lewis Gaddis's phrase.

This pessimistic conclusion rests on the general argument that the distribution and character of military power among states are the root causes of war and peace. Specifically, the peace in Europe since 1945—precarious at first, but increasingly robust over time—has flowed from three factors: the bipolar distribution of military power on the Continent; the rough military equality between the polar powers, the United States and the Soviet Union; and the ritualistically deplored fact that each of these superpowers is armed with a large nuclear arsenal.

We don't yet know the entire shape of the new Europe. But we do know some things. We know, for example, that the new Europe will involve a return to the multipolar distribution of power that characterized the European state system from its founding, with the Peace of Westphalia, in 1648, until 1945. We know that this multipolar European state system was plagued by war from first to last. We know that from 1900 to 1945 some 50 million Europeans were killed in wars that were caused in great part by the instability of this state system. We also know that since 1945 only some 15,000 Europeans have been killed in wars: roughly 10,000 Hungarians and Russians, in what we might call the Russo-Hungarian War of October and November, 1956, and somewhere between 1,500 and 5,000 Greeks and Turks, in the July and August, 1974, war on Cyprus.

Source: John J. Mearsheimer, "Why We Will Soon Miss the Cold War," *Atlantic,* **266** (August 1990), pp. 35–37, 40–42, 44–47, 50. Reprinted by permission.

The point is clear: Europe is reverting to a state system that created powerful incentives for aggression in the past. If you believe (as the Realist school of international-relations theory, to which I belong, believes) that the prospects for international peace are not markedly influenced by the domestic political character of states—that it is the character of the state system, not the character of the individual units composing it, that drives states toward war—then it is difficult to share in the widespread elation of the moment about the future of Europe. Last year was repeatedly compared to 1789, the year the French Revolution began, as the Year of Freedom, and so it was. Forgotten in the general exaltation was that the hope-filled events of 1789 signaled the start of an era of war and conquest.

A "HARD" THEORY OF PEACE

What caused the era of violence in Europe before 1945, and why has the postwar era, the period of the Cold War, been so much more peaceful? The two world wars before 1945 had myriad particular and unrepeatable causes, but to the student of international relations seeking to establish generalizations about the behavior of states in the past which might illuminate their behavior in the future, two fundamental causes stand out. These are the multipolar distribution of power in Europe, and the imbalances of strength that often developed among the great powers as they jostled for supremacy or advantage.

There is something elementary about the geometry of power in international relations, and so its importance is easy to overlook. "Bipolarity" and "multipolarity" are ungainly but necessary coinages. The Cold War, with two superpowers serving to anchor rival alliances of clearly inferior powers, is our model of bipolarity. Europe in 1914, with France, Germany, Great Britain, Austria-Hungary, and Russia positioned as great powers, is our model of multipolarity.

If the example of 1914 is convincing enough evidence that multipolar systems are the more dangerous geometry of power, then perhaps I should rest my case. Alas for theoretical elegance, there are no empirical studies providing conclusive support for this proposition. From its beginnings until 1945 the European state system was multipolar, so this history is barren of comparisons that would reveal the differing effects of the two systems. Earlier history, to be sure, does furnish scattered examples of bipolar systems, including some—Athens and Sparta, Rome and Carthage—that were warlike. But this history is inconclusive, because it is incomplete. Lacking a comprehensive survey of history, we can't do much more than offer examples—now on this, now on that side of the debate. As a result, the case made here rests chiefly on deduction.

Deductively, a bipolar system is more peaceful for the simple reason that under it only two major powers are in contention. Moreover, those great powers generally demand allegiance from minor powers in the system, which is likely to produce rigid alliance structures. The smaller states are then secure from each other as well as from attack by the rival great power. Consequently (to make a Dick-and-Jane point with a well-worn social-science term), a bipolar system has only one dyad across which war might break out. A multipolar system is much more fluid and has many such dyads. Therefore, other things being equal, war is statistically more likely in a multipolar system than it is in a bipolar one. Admittedly, wars in a multipolar world that involve only minor powers or only one major power are not likely to be as devastating as a conflict between two major powers. But small wars always have the potential to widen into big wars.

Also, deterrence is difficult to maintain in a multipolar state system, because power imbalances are commonplace, and when power asymmetries develop, the strong become hard to deter. Two great powers can join together to attack a third state, as Germany and the Soviet Union did in 1939, when they ganged up on Poland. Furthermore, a major power might simply bully a weaker power in a one-on-one encounter, using its superior strength to coerce or defeat the minor state. Germany's actions against Czechoslovakia in the late 1930s provide a good example of this sort of behavior. Ganging up and bullying are largely unknown in a bipolar system, since with only two great powers dominating center stage, it is impossible to produce the power asymmetries that result in ganging up and bullying.

There is a second reason that deterrence is more problematic under multipolarity. The resolve of opposing states and also the size and strength of opposing coalitions are hard to calculate in this geometry of power, because the shape of the international order tends to remain in flux, owing to the tendency of coalitions to gain and lose partners. This can lead aggressors to conclude falsely that they can coerce others by bluffing war, or even achieve outright victory on the battlefield. For example, Germany was not certain before 1914 that Britain would oppose it if it reached for Continental hegemony, and Germany completely failed to foresee that the United States would eventually move to contain it. In 1939 Germany hoped that France and Britain would stand aside as it conquered Poland, and again failed to foresee the eventual American entry into the war. As a result, Germany exaggerated its prospects for success, which undermined deterrence by encouraging German adventurism.

The prospects for peace, however, are not simply a function of the number of great powers in the system. They are also affected by the relative military strength of those major states. Bipolar and multipolar systems both are likely to be more peaceful when power is distributed equally in them. Power inequalities invite war, because they increase an aggressor's prospects for victory on the battlefield. Most of the general wars that have tormented Europe over the past five centuries have involved one particularly powerful state against the other major powers in the system. This pattern characterized the wars that grew from the attempts at hegemony by Charles V, Philip II, Louis XIV, Revolutionary and Napoleonic France, Wilhelmine Germany, and Nazi Germany. Hence the size of the gap in military power between the two leading states in the system is a key determinant of stability. Small gaps foster peace; larger gaps promote war.

Nuclear weapons seem to be in almost everybody's bad book, but the fact is that they are a powerful force for peace. Deterrence is most likely to hold when the costs and risks of going to war are unambiguously stark. The more horrible the prospect of war, the less likely war is. Deterrence is also more robust when conquest is more difficult. Potential aggressor states are given pause by the patent futility of attempts at expansion.

Nuclear weapons favor peace on both counts. They are weapons of mass destruction, and would produce horrendous devastation if used in any numbers. Moreover, they are more useful for self-defense than for aggression. If both sides' nuclear arsenals are secure from attack, creating an arrangement of mutual assured destruction, neither side can employ these weapons to gain a meaningful military advantage. International conflicts then become tests of pure will. Who would dare to use these weapons of unimaginable destructive power? Defenders have the advantage here, because defenders usually value their freedom more than aggressors value new conquests.

Nuclear weapons further bolster peace by moving power relations among states toward equality. States that possess nuclear deterrents can stand up to one another, even if their nuclear arsenals vary greatly in size, as long as both sides have an assured destruction capability. In addition, mutual assured destruction helps alleviate the vexed problem of miscalculation by leaving little doubt about the relative power of states.

No discussion of the causes of peace in the twentieth century would be complete without a word on nationalism. With "nationalism" as a synonym for "love of country" I have no quarrel. But hypernationalism, the belief that other nations or nation-states are both inferior and threatening, is perhaps the single greatest domestic threat to peace, although it is still not a leading force in world politics. Hypernationalism arose in the past among European states because most of them were nation-states—states composed mainly of people from a single ethnic group—that existed in an anarchic world, under constant threat from other states. In such a system people who love their own nation can easily come to be contemptuous of the nationalities inhabiting opposing states. The problem is worsened when domestic elites demonize a rival nation to drum up support for national-security policy.

Hypernationalism finds its most fertile soil under military systems relying on mass armies. These require sacrifices to sustain, and the state is tempted to appeal to nationalist sentiments to mobilize its citizens to make them. The quickening of hypernationalism is least likely when states can rely on small professional armies, or on complex high-technology military organizations that operate without vast manpower. For this reason, nuclear weapons work to dampen nationalism, because they shift the basis of military power away from mass armies and toward smaller, high-technology organizations.

Hypernationalism declined sharply in Europe after 1945, not only because of the nuclear revolution but also because the postwar occupation forces kept it down. Moreover, the European states, no longer providing their own security, lacked an incentive to whip up nationalism to bolster public support for national defense. But the decisive change came in the shift of the prime locus of European politics to the United States and the Soviet Union—two states made up of peoples of many different ethnic origins which had not exhibited nationalism of the virulent type found in Europe. This welcome absence of hypernationalism has been further helped by the greater stability of the postwar order. With less expectation of war, neither superpower felt compelled to mobilize its citizens for war.

Bipolarity, an equal balance of military power, and nuclear weapons—these, then, are the key elements of my explanation for the Long Peace.

Many thoughtful people have found the bipolar system in Europe odious and have sought to end it by dismantling the Soviet empire in Eastern Europe and diminishing Soviet military power. Many have also lamented the military equality obtaining between the superpowers; some have decried the indecisive stalemate it produced, recommending instead a search for military superiority; others have lamented the investment of hundreds of billions of dollars to deter a war that never happened, proving not that the investment, though expensive, paid off, but rather that it was wasted. As for nuclear weapons, well, they are a certifiable Bad Thing. The odium attached to these props of the postwar order has kept many in the West from recognizing a hard truth: they have kept the peace.

But so much for the past. What will keep the peace in the future? Specifically, what new order is likely to emerge if NATO [North Atlantic Treaty Organization] and the Warsaw Pact dissolve, which they will do if the Cold War is really over, and the Soviets withdraw from Eastern Europe and the Americans quit Western Europe, taking their nuclear weapons with them—and should we welcome or fear it?

One dimension of the new European order is certain: it will be multipolar. Germany, France, Britain, and perhaps Italy will assume major-power status. The Soviet Union will decline from superpower status, not only because its military is sure to shrink in size but also because moving forces out of Eastern Europe will make it more difficult for the Soviets to project power onto the Continent. They will, of course, remain a major European power. The resulting four- or five-power system will suffer the problems endemic to multipolar systems—and will therefore be prone to instability. The other two dimensions—the distribution of power among the major states and the distribution of nuclear weapons—are less certain. Indeed, who gets nuclear weapons is likely to be the most problematic question facing the new Europe. Three scenarios of the nuclear future in Europe are possible.

THE "EUROPE WITHOUT NUCLEAR WEAPONS" SCENARIO

Many Europeans (and some Americans) seek to eliminate nuclear weapons from Europe altogether. Fashioning this nuclear-free Europe would require that Britain, France, and the Soviet Union rid themselves of these talismans of their sovereignty—an improbable eventuality, to say the least. Those who wish for it nevertheless believe that it would be the most peaceful arrangement possible. In fact a nuclear-free Europe has the distinction of being the most dangerous among the envisionable post–Cold

War orders. The pacifying effects of nuclear weapons—the caution they generate, the security they provide, the rough equality they impose, and the clarity of the relative power they create—would be lost. Peace would then depend on the other dimensions of the new order—the number of poles and the distribution of power among them. The geometry of power in Europe would look much as it did between the world wars—a design for tension, crisis, and possibly even war.

The Soviet Union and a unified Germany would likely be the most powerful states in a nuclear-free Europe. A band of small independent states in Eastern Europe would lie between them. These minor Eastern European powers would be likely to fear the Soviets as much as the Germans, and thus would probably not be disposed to cooperate with the Soviets to deter possible German aggression. In fact, this very problem arose in the 1930s, and the past forty-five years of Soviet occupation have surely done little to mitigate Eastern European fears of a Soviet military presence. Thus scenarios in which Germany uses force against Poland, Czechoslovakia, or even Austria enter the realm of the possible in a nuclear-free Europe.

Then, too, the Soviet withdrawal from Eastern Europe hardly guarantees a permanent exit. Indeed, the Russian presence in Eastern Europe has surged and ebbed repeatedly over the past few centuries. In a grave warning, a member of President Mikhail Gorbachev's negotiating team at the recent Washington summit said, ''You have the same explosive mixture you had in Germany in the 1930s. The humiliation of a great power. Economic troubles. The rise of nationalism. You should not underestimate the danger.''

Conflicts between Eastern European states might also threaten the stability of the new European order. Serious tensions already exist between Hungary and Romania over Romania's treatment of the Hungarian minority in Transylvania, a formerly Hungarian region that still contains roughly two million ethnic Hungarians. Absent the Soviet occupation of Eastern Europe, Romania and Hungary might have gone to war over this issue by now, and it might bring them

to war in the future. This is not the only potential danger spot in Eastern Europe as the Soviet empire crumbles. The Polish-German border could be a source of trouble. Poland and Czechoslovakia have a border dispute. If the Soviets allow some of their republics to achieve independence, the Poles and the Romanians may lay claim to territory now in Soviet hands which once belonged to them. Looking farther south, civil war in Yugoslavia is a distinct possibility. Yugoslavia and Albania might come to blows over Kosovo, a region of Yugoslavia harboring a nationalistic Albanian majority. Bulgaria has its own quarrel with Yugoslavia over Macedonia, while Turkey resents Bulgaria's treatment of its Turkish minority. The danger that these bitter ethnic and border disputes will erupt into war in a supposedly Edenic nuclear-free Europe is enough to make one nostalgic for the Cold War.

Warfare in Eastern Europe would cause great suffering to Eastern Europeans. It also might widen to include the major powers, especially if disorder created fluid politics that offered opportunities for expanded influence, or threatened defeat for states friendly to one or another of the major powers. During the Cold War both superpowers were drawn into Third World conflicts across the globe, often in distant areas of little strategic importance. Eastern Europe is directly adjacent to both the Soviet Union and Germany, and it has considerable economic and strategic importance. Thus trouble in Eastern Europe would offer even greater temptations to these powers than past conflicts in the Third World offered to the superpowers. Furthermore, Eastern European states would have a strong incentive to drag the major powers into their local conflicts, because the results of such conflicts would be largely determined by the relative success of each party in finding external allies.

It is difficult to predict the precise balance of conventional military power that will emerge in post–Cold War Europe. The Soviet Union might recover its strength soon after withdrawing from Eastern Europe. In that case Soviet power would outmatch German power. But centrifugal national forces might pull the Soviet Union apart, leaving no remnant state that is the equal of a unified Germany. Finally, and probably most likely, Germany and the Soviet Union might emerge as powers of roughly equal strength. The first two geometries of power, with their marked military inequality between the two leading countries, would be especially worrisome, although there would be cause for concern even if Soviet and German power were balanced.

A non-nuclear Europe, to round out this catalogue of dangers, would likely be especially disturbed by hypernationalism, since security in such an order would rest on mass armies, which, as we have seen, often cannot be maintained without a mobilized public. The problem would probably be most acute in Eastern Europe, with its uncertain borders and irredentist minority groups. But there is also potential for trouble in Germany. The Germans have generally done an admirable job of combating hypernationalism over the past forty-five years, and of confronting the dark side of their past. Nevertheless, a portent like the recent call of some prominent Germans for a return to greater nationalism in historical education is disquieting.

For all these reasons, it is perhaps just as well that a nuclear-free Europe, much as it may be longed for by so many Europeans, does not appear to be in the cards.

THE "CURRENT OWNERSHIP" SCENARIO

Under this scenario Britain, France, and the Soviet Union retain their nuclear weapons, but no new nuclear powers emerge in Europe. This vision of a nuclear-free zone in Central Europe, with nuclear weapons remaining on the flanks of the Continent, is also popular in Europe, but it, too, has doubtful prospects.

Germany will prevent it over the long run. The Germans are not likely to be willing to rely on the Poles or the Czechs to provide their forward defense against a possible direct Soviet conventional attack on their homeland. Nor are the Germans likely to trust the Soviet Union to refrain for all time from nuclear blackmail against a non-nuclear Germany. Hence they will eventually look to nuclear weapons

as the surest means of security, just as NATO has done.

The small states of Eastern Europe will also have strong incentives to acquire nuclear weapons. Without them they would be open to nuclear blackmail by the Soviet Union, or by Germany if proliferation stopped there. Even if those major powers did not have nuclear arsenals, no Eastern European state could match German or Soviet conventional strength.

Clearly, then, a scenario in which current ownership continues, without proliferation, seems very unlikely.

THE "NUCLEAR PROLIFERATION" SCENARIO

The most probable scenario in the wake of the Cold War is further nuclear proliferation in Europe. This outcome is laden with dangers, but it also might just provide the best hope for maintaining stability on the Continent. Everything depends on how proliferation is managed. Mismanaged proliferation could produce disaster; well-managed proliferation could produce an order nearly as stable as that of the Long Peace.

The dangers that could arise from mismanaged proliferation are both profound and numerous. There is the danger that the proliferation process itself could give one of the existing nuclear powers a strong incentive to stop a non-nuclear neighbor from joining the club, much as Israel used force to stop Iraq from acquiring a nuclear capability. There is the danger that an unstable nuclear competition would emerge among the new nuclear states. They might lack the resources to make their nuclear forces invulnerable, which could create first-strike fears and incentives—a recipe for disaster in a crisis. Finally, there is the danger that by increasing the number of fingers on the nuclear trigger, proliferation would increase the risk that nuclear weapons would be fired by accident or captured by terrorists or used by madmen.

These and other dangers of proliferation can be lessened if the current nuclear powers take the right steps. To forestall preventive attacks, they can extend security guarantees. To help the new nuclear powers secure their deterrents, they can provide technical assistance. And they can help to socialize nascent nuclear societies to understand the lethal character of the forces they are acquiring. This kind of well-managed proliferation could help bolster peace.

Proliferation should ideally stop with Germany. It has a large economic base, and so could afford to sustain a secure nuclear force. Moreover, Germany would no doubt feel insecure without nuclear weapons, and if it felt insecure its impressive conventional strength would give it a significant capacity to disturb the tranquility of Europe. But if the broader spread of nuclear weapons proves impossible to prevent without taking extreme steps, the current nuclear powers should let proliferation occur in Eastern Europe while doing all they can to channel it in safe directions.

However, I am pessimistic that proliferation can be well managed. The members of the nuclear club are likely to resist proliferation, but they cannot easily manage this tricky process while at the same time resisting it—and they will have several motives to resist. The established nuclear powers will be exceedingly chary of helping the new nuclear powers build secure deterrents, simply because it goes against the grain of state behavior to share military secrets with other states. After all, knowledge of sensitive military technology could be turned against the donor state if that technology were passed on to adversaries. Furthermore, proliferation in Europe will undermine the legitimacy of the 1968 Nuclear Non-Proliferation Treaty, and this could open the floodgates of proliferation worldwide. The current nuclear powers will not want that to happen, and so they will probably spend their energy trying to thwart proliferation, rather than seeking to manage it.

The best time for proliferation to occur would be during a period of relative international calm. Proliferation in the midst of a crisis would obviously be dangerous, since states in conflict with an emerging nuclear power would then have a powerful incentive to interrupt the process by force. However, the opposition to proliferation by citizens of the potential nuclear powers would be so vociferous, and the external resistance from the nuclear club would be so great, that it might take a crisis to make those powers willing to pay the domestic and international costs of building a nuclear force. All of which means that proliferation is likely to occur under international conditions that virtually ensure it will be mismanaged.

IS WAR OBSOLETE?

Many students of European politics will reject my pessimistic analysis of post–Cold War Europe. They will say that a multipolar Europe, with or without nuclear weapons, will be no less peaceful than the present order. Three specific scenarios for a peaceful future have been advanced, each of which rests on a well-known theory of international relations. However, each of these ''soft'' theories of peace is flawed.

Under the first optimistic scenario, a non-nuclear Europe would remain peaceful because Europeans recognize that even a conventional war would be horrific. Sobered by history, national leaders will take care to avoid war. This scenario rests on the ''obsolescence of war'' theory, which posits that modern conventional war had become so deadly by 1945 as to be unthinkable as an instrument of statecraft. War is yesterday's nightmare.

The fact that the Second World War occurred casts doubt on this theory: if any war could have persuaded Europeans to forswear conventional war, it should have been the First World War, with its vast casualties. The key flaw in this theory is the assumption that all conventional wars will be long and bloody wars of attrition. Proponents ignore the evidence of several wars since 1945, as well as several campaign-ending battles of the Second World War, that it is still possible to gain a quick and decisive victory on the conventional battlefield and avoid the devastation of a protracted conflict. Conventional wars can be won rather cheaply; nuclear war cannot be, because neither side can escape devastation by the other, regardless of what happens on the battlefield. Thus the incentives to avoid war are of another order of intensity in a nuclear world than they are in a conventional world.

There are several other flaws in this scenario. There is no systematic evidence demonstrating that Europeans believe war is obsolete. The Romanians and the Hungarians don't seem to have gotten the message. However, even if it were widely believed in Europe that war is no longer thinkable, attitudes could change. Public opinion on national-security issues is notoriously fickle and responsive to manipulation by elites as well as to changes in the international environment. An end to the Cold War, as we have seen, will be accompanied by a sea change in the geometry of power in Europe, which will surely alter European thinking about questions of war and peace. Is it not possible, for example, that German thinking about the benefits of controlling Eastern Europe will change markedly once American forces are withdrawn from Central Europe and the Germans are left to provide for their own security? Is it not possible that they would countenance a conventional war against a substantially weaker Eastern European state to enhance their position vis-à-vis the Soviet Union? Finally, only one country need decide that war is thinkable to make war possible.

IS PROSPERITY THE PATH TO PEACE?

Proponents of the second optimistic scenario base their optimism about the future of Europe on the unified European market coming in 1992—the realization of the dream of the European Community [EC]. A strong EC, they argue, ensures that the European economy will remain open and prosperous, which will keep the European states cooperating with one another. Prosperity will make for peace. The threat of an aggressive Germany will be removed by enclosing the newly unified German state in the benign embrace of the EC. Even Eastern Europe and the Soviet Union can eventually be brought into the EC. Peace and prosperity will then extend their sway from the Atlantic to the Urals.

This scenario is based on the theory of economic liberalism, which assumes that states are primarily motivated by the desire to achieve prosperity and that leaders place the material welfare of their publics above all other considerations, including security. Stability flows not from military power but from the creation of a liberal economic order.

A liberal economic order works in several ways to enhance peace and dampen conflict. In the first place, it requires significant political cooperation to make the trading system work—make states richer. The more prosperous states grow, the greater their incentive for further political cooperation. A benevolent spiral relationship sets in between political cooperation and prosperity. Second, a liberal economic order fosters economic interdependence, a situation in which states are mutually vulnerable in the economic realm. When interdependence is high, the theory holds, there is less temptation to cheat or behave aggressively toward other states, because all states can retaliate economically. Finally, some theorists argue, an international institution like the EC will, with ever-increasing political cooperation, become so powerful that it will take on a life of its own, eventually evolving into a superstate. In short, Mrs. Thatcher's presentiments about the EC are absolutely right.

This theory has one grave flaw: the main assumption underpinning it is wrong. States are not primarily motivated by the desire to achieve prosperity. Although economic calculations are hardly trivial to them, states operate in both an international political and an international economic environment, and the former dominates the latter when the two systems come into conflict. Survival in an anarchic international political system is the highest goal a state can have.

Proponents of economic liberalism largely ignore the effects of anarchy on state behavior and concentrate instead on economic motives. When this omission is corrected, however, their arguments collapse for two reasons.

Competition for security makes it difficult for states to cooperate, which, according to the theory of economic liberalism, they must do. When security is scarce, states become more concerned about relative than about absolute gains. They ask of an exchange not "Will both of us gain?" but "Who will gain more?" They reject even cooperation that will yield an absolute economic gain if the other state will gain more, from fear that the other might convert its gain to military strength, and then use this strength to win by coercion in later rounds. Cooperation is much easier to achieve if states worry only about absolute gains. The goal, then, is simply to ensure that the overall economic pie is expanding and that each state is getting at least some part of the increase. However, anarchy guarantees that security will often be scarce; this heightens states' concerns about relative gains, which makes cooperation difficult unless the pie can be finely sliced to reflect, and thus not disturb, the current balance of power.

Interdependence, moreover, is as likely to lead to conflict as to cooperation, because states will struggle to escape the vulnerability that interdependence creates, in order to bolster their national security. In time of crisis or war, states that depend on others for critical economic supplies will fear cutoff or blackmail; they may well respond by trying to seize the source of supply by force of arms. There are numerous historical examples of states' pursuing aggressive military policies for the purpose of achieving economic autarky. One thinks of both Japan and Germany during the interwar period. And one recalls that during the Arab oil embargo of the early 1970s there was much talk in America about using military force to seize Arab oil fields.

In twentieth-century Europe two periods saw a liberal economic order with high levels of interdependence. According to the theory of economic liberalism, stability should have obtained during those periods. It did not.

The first case clearly contradicts the economic liberals. The years from 1890 to 1914 were probably the time of greatest economic interdependence in Europe's history. Yet those years of prosperity were all the time making hideously for the First World War.

The second case covers the Cold War years, during which there has been much interdependence among the EC states, and relations among them have been very peaceful. This case, not surprisingly, is the centerpiece of the economic liberals' argument.

We certainly see a correlation in this period between interdependence and stability, but that does not mean that interdependence has caused cooperation among the Western democracies. More likely the Cold War was the prime cause of cooperation among the Western democracies, and the main reason that intra-EC relations have flourished.

A powerful and potentially dangerous Soviet Union forced the Western democracies to band together to meet a common threat. This threat muted concerns about relative gains arising from economic cooperation among the EC states by giving each Western democracy a vested interest in seeing its alliance partners grow powerful. Each increment of power helped deter the Soviets. Moreover, they all had a powerful incentive to avoid conflict with one another while the Soviet Union loomed to the East, ready to harvest the grain of Western quarrels.

In addition, America's hegemonic position in NATO, the military counterpart to the EC, mitigated the effects of anarchy on the Western democracies and induced cooperation among them. America not only provided protection against the Soviet threat; it also guaranteed that no EC state would aggress against another. For example, France did not have to fear Germany as it re-armed, because the American presence in Germany meant that the Germans were contained. With the United States serving as a night watchman, fears about relative gains among the Western European states were mitigated, and furthermore, those states were willing to allow their economies to become tightly interdependent.

Take away the present Soviet threat to Western Europe, send the American forces home, and relations among the EC states will be fundamentally altered. Without a common Soviet threat or an American night watchman, Western European states will do what they did for centuries before the onset of the Cold War—look upon one another with abiding suspicion. Consequently, they will worry about imbalances in gains and about the loss of autonomy that results from cooperation. Cooperation in this new order will be more difficult than it was during the Cold War. Conflict will be more likely.

In sum, there are good reasons for being skeptical about the claim that a more powerful EC can provide the basis for peace in a multipolar Europe.

DO DEMOCRACIES REALLY LOVE PEACE?

Under the third scenario war is avoided because many European states have become democratic since the early twentieth century, and liberal democracies simply do not fight one another. At a minimum, the presence of liberal democracies in Western Europe renders that half of Europe free from armed conflict. At a maximum, democracy spreads to Eastern Europe and the Soviet Union, bolstering peace. The idea that peace is cognate with democracy is a vision of international relations shared by both liberals and neoconservatives.

This scenario rests on the ''peace-loving democracies'' theory. Two arguments are made for it.

First, some claim that authoritarian leaders are more likely to go to war than leaders of democracies, because authoritarian leaders are not accountable to their publics, which carry the main burdens of war. In a democracy the citizenry, which pays the price of war, has a greater say in what the government does. The people, so the argument goes, are more hesitant to start trouble, because it is they who must pay the bloody price; hence the greater their power, the fewer wars.

The second argument rests on the claim that the citizens of liberal democracies respect popular democratic rights—those of their countrymen, and those of people in other states. They view democratic governments as more legitimate than others, and so are loath to impose a foreign regime on a democratic state by force. Thus an inhibition on war missing from other international relationships is introduced when two democracies face each other.

The first of these arguments is flawed because it is not possible to sustain the claim that the people in a democracy are especially sensitive to the costs of war and therefore less willing than authoritarian leaders to fight wars. In fact the historical record shows that democracies are every bit as likely to fight wars as are authoritarian states, though admittedly, thus far, not with other democracies.

Furthermore, mass publics, whether in a democracy or not, can become deeply imbued with nationalistic or religious fervor, making them prone to support aggression and quite indifferent to costs. The widespread public support in post-Revolutionary France for Napoleon's wars is just one example of this phenomenon. At the same time, authoritarian leaders are often fearful of going to war, because war tends to unleash democratic forces that can undermine the regime. In short, war can impose high costs on authoritarian leaders as well as on their citizenry.

The second argument, which emphasizes the transnational respect for democratic rights among democracies, rests on a secondary factor that is generally overridden by other factors such as nationalism and religious fundamentalism. Moreover, there is another problem with the argument. The possibility always exists that a democracy, especially the kind of fledgling democracy emerging in Eastern Europe, will revert to an authoritarian state. This threat of backsliding means that one democratic state can never be sure that another democratic state will not turn on it sometime in the future. Liberal democracies must therefore worry about relative power among themselves, which is tantamount to saying that each has an incentive to consider aggression against another to forestall trouble. Lamentably, it is not possible for even liberal democracies to transcend anarchy.

Problems with the deductive logic aside, at first glance the historical record seems to offer strong support for the theory of peace-loving democracies. It appears that no liberal democracies have ever fought against each other. Evidentiary problems, however, leave the issue in doubt.

First, democracies have been few in number over the past two centuries, and thus there have not been many cases in which two democracies were in a position to fight with each other. Three prominent cases are usually cited: Britain and the United States (1832 to the present); Britain and France (1832–1849; 1871–1940); and the Western democracies since 1945.

Second, there are other persuasive explanations for why war did not occur in those three cases, and these competing explanations must be ruled out before the theory of peace-loving democracies can be accepted. Whereas relations between the British and the Americans during the nineteenth century were hardly blissful, in the twentieth century they have been quite harmonious, and thus fit closely with the theory's expectations. That harmony, however, can easily be explained by common threats that forced Britain and the United States to work together—a serious German threat in the first part of the century, and later a Soviet threat. The same basic argument applies to relations between France and Britain. Although they were not on the best of terms during most of the nineteenth century, their relations improved significantly around the turn of the century, with the rise of Germany. Finally, as noted above, the Soviet threat goes far in explaining the absence of war among the Western democracies since 1945.

Third, several democracies have come close to fighting each other, suggesting that the absence of war may be due simply to chance. France and Britain approached war during the Fashoda crisis of 1898. France and Weimar Germany might have come to blows over the Rhineland during the 1920s. The United States has clashed with a number of elected governments in the Third World during the Cold War, including the Allende regime in Chile and the Arbenz regime in Guatemala.

Last, some would classify Wilhelmine Germany as a democracy, or at least a quasi-democracy; if so, the First World War becomes a war among democracies.

While the spread of democracy across Europe has great potential benefits for human rights, it will not guarantee peaceful relations among the states of post–Cold War Europe. Most Americans will find this argument counterintuitive. They see the United States as fundamentally peace-loving, and they as-

cribe this peacefulness to its democratic character. From this they generalize that democracies are more peaceful than authoritarian states, which leads them to conclude that the complete democratization of Europe would largely eliminate the threat of war. This view of international politics is likely to be repudiated by the events of the coming years.

MISSING THE COLD WAR

The implications of my analysis are straightforward, if paradoxical. Developments that threaten to end the Cold War are dangerous. The West has an interest in maintaining peace in Europe. It therefore has an interest in maintaining the Cold War order, and hence has an interest in continuing the Cold War confrontation. The Cold War antagonism could be continued at lower levels of East-West tension than have prevailed in the past, but a complete end to the Cold War would create more problems than it would solve.

The fate of the Cold War is mainly in the hands of the Soviet Union. The Soviet Union is the only superpower that can seriously threaten to overrun Europe, and the Soviet threat provides the glue that holds NATO together. Take away that offensive threat and the United States is likely to abandon the Continent; the defensive alliance it has headed for forty years may well then disintegrate, bringing an end to the bipolar order that has kept the peace of Europe for the past forty-five years.

There is little the Americans or the West Europeans can do to perpetuate the Cold War.

For one thing, domestic politics preclude it. Western leaders obviously cannot base national-security policy on the need to maintain forces in Central Europe simply to keep the Soviets there. The idea of deploying large numbers of troops in order to bait the Soviets into an order-keeping competition would be dismissed as bizarre, and contrary to the general belief that ending the Cold War and removing the Soviet yoke from Eastern Europe would make the world safer and better.

For another, the idea of propping up a declining rival runs counter to the basic behavior of states.

States are principally concerned about their relative power in the system—hence they look for opportunities to take advantage of one another. If anything, they prefer to see adversaries decline, and invariably do whatever they can to speed up the process and maximize the distance of the fall. States, in other words, do not ask which distribution of power best facilitates stability and then do everything possible to build or maintain such an order. Instead, each pursues the narrower aim of maximizing its power advantage over potential adversaries. The particular international order that results is simply a by-product of that competition.

Consider, for example, the origins of the Cold War order in Europe. No state intended to create it. In fact the United States and the Soviet Union each worked hard in the early years of the Cold War to undermine the other's position in Europe, which would have ended the bipolar order on the Continent. The remarkably stable system that emerged in Europe in the late 1940s was the unintended consequence of an intense competition between the superpowers.

Moreover, even if the Americans and the West Europeans wanted to help the Soviets maintain their status as a superpower, it is not apparent that they could do so. The Soviet Union is leaving Eastern Europe and cutting its military forces largely because its economy is floundering badly. The Soviets don't know how to fix their economy themselves, and there is little that Western governments can do to help them. The West can and should avoid doing malicious mischief to the Soviet economy, but at this juncture it is difficult to see how the West can have a significant positive influence.

The fact that the West cannot sustain the Cold War does not mean that the United States should make no attempt to preserve the current order. It should do what it can to avert a complete mutual withdrawal from Europe. For instance, the American negotiating position at the conventional-arms-control talks should aim toward large mutual force reductions but should not contemplate complete mutual withdrawal. The Soviets may opt to withdraw all

their forces unilaterally anyway; if so, there is little the United States can do to stop them.

Should complete Soviet withdrawal from Eastern Europe prove unavoidable, the West would confront the question of how to maintain peace in a multipolar Europe. Three policy prescriptions are in order.

First, the United States should encourage the limited and carefully managed proliferation of nuclear weapons in Europe. The best hope for avoiding war in post–Cold War Europe is nuclear deterrence; hence some nuclear proliferation is necessary, to compensate for the withdrawal of the Soviet and American nuclear arsenals from Central Europe. Ideally, as I have argued, nuclear weapons would spread to Germany but to no other state.

Second, Britain and the United States, as well as the Continental states, will have to counter any emerging aggressor actively and efficiently, in order to offset the ganging up and bullying that are sure to arise in post–Cold War Europe. Balancing in a multipolar system, however, is usually a problem-ridden enterprise, because of either geography or the problems of coordination. Britain and the United States, physically separated from the Continent, may conclude that they have little interest in what happens there. That would be abandoning their responsibilities and, more important, their interests. Both states failed to counter Germany before the two world wars, making war more likely. It is essential for peace in Europe that they not repeat their past mistakes.

Both states must maintain military forces that can be deployed against Continental states that threaten to start a war. To do this they must persuade their citizens to support a policy of continued Continental commitment. This will be more difficult than it once was, because its principal purpose will be to preserve peace, rather than to prevent an imminent hegemony, and the prevention of hegemony is a simpler goal to explain publicly. Furthermore, this prescription asks both countries to take on an unaccustomed task, given that it is the basic nature of states to focus on maximizing relative power, not on bolstering stability. Nevertheless, the British and the Americans have a real stake in peace, especially since there is the risk that a European war might involve the large-scale use of nuclear weapons. Therefore, it should be possible for their governments to lead their publics to recognize this interest and support policies that protect it.

The Soviet Union may eventually return to its past expansionism and threaten to upset the status quo. If so, we are back to the Cold War. However, if the Soviets adhere to status-quo policies, Soviet power could play a key role in countering Germany and in maintaining order in Eastern Europe. It is important in those cases where the Soviets are acting in a balancing capacity that the United States cooperate with its former adversary and not let residual distrust from the Cold War obtrude.

Third, a concerted effort should be made to keep hypernationalism at bay, especially in Eastern Europe. Nationalism has been contained during the Cold War, but it is likely to re-emerge once Soviet and American forces leave the heart of Europe. It will be a force for trouble unless curbed. The teaching of honest national history is especially important, since the teaching of false, chauvinist history is the main vehicle for spreading hypernationalism. States that teach a dishonestly self-exculpating or self-glorifying history should be publicly criticized and sanctioned.

None of these tasks will be easy. In fact, I expect that the bulk of my prescriptions will not be followed; most run contrary to important strains of domestic American and European opinion, and to the basic nature of state behavior. And even if they are followed, peace in Europe will not be guaranteed. If the Cold War is truly behind us, therefore, the stability of the past forty-five years is not likely to be seen again in the coming decades.

QUESTIONS FOR DISCUSSION

1. What causes war?
2. What forces for peace did the cold war produce? What forces for war?
3. To what extent are the conditions that cause war absent in Europe in the post–cold war era? What are the reasons for your answer?
4. Do democracies favor peace? What evidence do you have for your answer?
5. What impact does a peace movement have on war?

SUGGESTED READINGS

Angell, Sir Norman. *The Great Illusion: A Study of the Relation of Military Power in Nations to Their Economic and Social Advantage.* New York: Garland, 1972. Published in 1909 under the title *Europe's Political Illusion.*

Blainey, Geoffrey. *The Causes of War*, 3d ed. New York: Free Press, 1988.

Brown, Seyom. *The Causes and Prevention of War.* New York: St. Martin's Press, 1987.

Domke, William K. *War and the Changing Global System.* New Haven, Conn.: Yale Univ. Press, 1988.

Kaysen, Carl. "Is War Obsolete?" *International Security,* **14** (Spring 1990), pp. 42–64.

Luard, Evan. *War in International Society: A Study in International Sociology.* New Haven, Conn.: Yale Univ. Press, 1986.

Mueller, John. *Retreat from Doomsday: The Obsolescence of Major War.* New York: Basic Books, 1989.

U.S. Cong., House of Representatives. *U.S. Power in a Changing World: Proceedings of a Seminar Held by the Congressional Research Service, September 19–20, 1989.* Report prepared for the Subcommittee on International Economic Policy and Trade of the Committee on Foreign Affairs, 101st Cong., 2d Sess., 1990.

Waltz, Kenneth N. *Man, the State and War: A Theoretical Analysis.* New York: Columbia Univ. Press, 1959.

15 Should U.S. Forces Withdraw from Europe?

YES

Defense Monitor

U.S. Armed Forces in Europe: From Burden Sharing to Burden Shedding

NO

Robert McGeehan

The United States and NATO after the Cold War

U.S. Armed Forces in Europe: From Burden Sharing to Burden Shedding

Defense Monitor

Within the past year the foundations of East-West relations have been transformed. The possibility of a Soviet-led attack on Western Europe has almost vanished. Eastern Europe is embracing liberalization and democracy. The Berlin Wall is being reduced to rubble and sold as souvenirs as East and West Germany rush toward unification. Western Europe is uniting to form a single economy.

The path is open to new, cooperative security arrangements in Europe. Secretary of State James Baker has called for ''a new architecture for a new era.'' President Bush has stated it is time ''to move beyond the era of containment.'' Yet movement by the U.S. so far has been minimal. It would appear that the Bush Administration intends to preserve the existing architecture.

It is clinging to a military alliance, the North Atlantic Treaty Organization (NATO), that is fast becoming a relic of the Cold War. It insists that U.S. troops should remain in Western Europe even if all Soviet troops leave Eastern Europe.

The U.S. still spends an estimated $160–$170 billion each year preparing for war in Europe, more than all the European members of the NATO alliance combined. This is enough money to eliminate the annual federal budget deficit that weakens the U.S. economy. Or it could house every homeless American, provide adequate drug treatment, and rebuild crumbling roads and bridges.

The Cold War has ended. When a war ends, troops should come home. The NATO alliance and the stationing of U.S. military forces in Europe are old medicine for a malady that no longer exists. There remains an opportunity to go far beyond the Bush Administration's proposals. In the new security climate of the 1990s the U.S. can significantly reduce its military burdens. Europe is the best place to begin.

U.S. MILITARY PROTECTORATE

The U.S. stations about 336,000 troops in Europe—more than 65 percent of all U.S. overseas troops. The majority of these troops remain on alert near the now superfluous border between East and West Germany. There are more than 246,000 U.S. soldiers in West Germany alone—almost 50 percent of all U.S. overseas troops.

There are 25,000 more U.S. soldiers stationed in Europe than there are soldiers in the entire armed forces of the United Kingdom. There are 110,000 more U.S. soldiers in West Germany than there are East German troops in East Germany.

Europe is host to 70 percent of all U.S. overseas military installations. Sixty percent—224 bases—are in West Germany. The U.S. also has military installations in Belgium (2), Greece (4), Greenland (2), Iceland (1), Italy (10), the Netherlands (2), Portugal (1), Spain (6), Turkey (7), and the United Kingdom (19). It has intelligence gathering facilities [in] Norway.

About 28 percent of all U.S. Army servicemen and women and a quarter of the U.S. Air Force's 36 active tactical air wings (one air wing typically consisting of 72 combat aircraft) are stationed in Europe. The entire Atlantic Fleet, about half of all active U.S. naval forces, is committed to support NATO forces in a European war.

According to the Pentagon *the U.S. contributes 46 percent of NATO ground forces combat strength, 63 percent of naval force tonnage, 46 percent of tactical air force combat aircraft, and 88 percent of tactical fixed-wing naval combat aircraft.*

In the event of war additional air, ground, and naval forces based in the U.S. would be sent to Europe. The Pentagon's goal is to reinforce Europe with the equivalent of 10 U.S. divisions within 10

Source: ''U.S. Armed Forces in Europe: From Burden Sharing to Burden Shedding,'' *Defense Monitor*, **19**, no. 4 (1990). Reprinted by permission.

days of a decision to mobilize NATO forces. The ultimate number of U.S. troops sent to fight in Europe would be determined by the scale and length of the war.

The Pentagon also pre-positions some 544,000 tons of weapons and equipment in Europe. West Germany stores approximately 70 percent of U.S. war materiel that is in place and ready for use by reinforcement troops. Pre-positioned materiel is also stored in Belgium, the Netherlands, and Norway.

Some 150,000 civilian employees of the Pentagon plus 296,000 dependents raise the total military-related American presence in Europe to more than 750,000 individuals. To support their needs there is a large, expensive support infrastructure in Europe, including housing, schools, day care centers, medical care facilities, and morale and welfare facilities.

TACTICAL NUCLEAR FORCES

The U.S. stations more than 3,700 tactical nuclear weapons in seven European countries: Belgium, Greece, Italy, the Netherlands, Turkey, the United Kingdom, and West Germany. Other than the U.S., only France and the United Kingdom among NATO countries possess nuclear weapons, with about 500 and 300 nuclear weapons respectively.

The alliance military strategy of ''flexible response'' is based upon the assumption that if the West began to lose a conventional war in Europe it would have to resort to the use of nuclear weapons. While the Soviets have vowed not to be the first to use nuclear weapons, flexible response has dictated a NATO ''first use'' nuclear weapons policy.

NATO plans to use nuclear weapons in Europe, never very credible, are now obsolete. The 1990 ''Joint Military Net Assessment'' of the U.S. Joint Chiefs of Staff states, ''The probability that NATO would need to resort to the use of nonstrategic nuclear forces is assessed to decrease with elimination [under a CFE (Conventional Forces in Europe) treaty] of conventional force asymmetries.''

In any event U.S. Lance missiles and nuclear artillery shells (some of which have been discovered to be potentially unsafe) currently in West Germany are capable only of reaching Eastern Europe, which

U.S. PREPARATIONS FOR WAR IN EUROPE

Cost	$160–$170 Billion Annually[a]
Bases	278
Troops	336,000
Civilian Employees/Dependents	450,000
Main Battle Tanks	6,000
Armored Combat Vehicles	6,100
Artillery	2,232
Combat Aircraft	700
Major Surface Warships	115
Tactical Nuclear Weapons	3,740

U.S.-Based Reinforcements:

6 Army Divisions (approx. 275,000–288,000 troops)

37 Tactical Fighter Squadrons (approx. 112,000 troops)

1 Marine Expeditionary Brigade (approx. 15,000 troops)

[a] The Pentagon has disclosed that about 60 percent of the total annual U.S. military budget is devoted to preparations for war in Europe. This includes both European-deployed U.S. troops and all planned reinforcements and both direct costs, such as pay and operations, and indirect costs, such as U.S.-based training and logistics support and research, development, and production of new weapons and equipment for fighting in Europe. This does not include strategic nuclear forces for the U.S. ''nuclear umbrella'' that covers Europe under the doctrine of ''extended deterrence.''

Chart prepared by the Center for Defense Information   Sources: DOD, CBO, BASIC, IISS, CDI

Defense Secretary Richard Cheney has acknowledged is no longer "a target rich environment."

Still the Bush Administration has requested over $118 million for fiscal year 1991 for the Short-Range Attack Missile-Tactical (SRAM-T), a nuclear-armed air-to-surface missile. According to the Pentagon SRAM-Ts will have a range of about 250 miles and carry 10- and 100-kiloton warheads. Initial plans are to build 450 SRAM-Ts for possible deployment on U.S. F-15E, F-16, and F-111 aircraft and British Tornado aircraft at air bases throughout Western Europe.

The SRAM-T is both unnecessary and a potential political liability for the U.S. While it is designed to strike targets in the Soviet Union by evading Soviet air defenses in Eastern Europe, it seems only a matter of time until the Soviets will be forced to remove these air defenses. Meanwhile, with anti-nuclear sentiment on the rise in Europe, deploying new nuclear weapons could damage U.S. relations not only with the Soviet Union, but also with Western Europe.

TROOP CEILINGS. . . .

The Bush Administration has proposed a ceiling of 195,000 each on U.S. and Soviet ground and air force personnel in Central Europe. Reductions would be implemented under a Conventional Forces in Europe treaty. The U.S. would be permitted to station 30,000 additional troops outside of Central Europe for a total of 225,000 troops in all of Europe, excluding naval forces. This would require the withdrawal of some 80,000 U.S. troops.

. . . AND FLOORS

Undersecretary of Defense for Policy Paul Wolfowitz told Congress in early 1990, "We also see the necessity now of underlining the permanence of some level of U.S. forces in Europe—a 'floor' force level—that will remain even after the very large reductions we expect to make from current levels."

After the December 1989 Malta summit President Bush declared, "Even after all the planned reductions in Soviet forces are complete, even if our current arms control proposals are agreed to and implemented . . . militarily significant U.S. forces must remain on the other side of the Atlantic for as long as our allies want and need them."

Adding the more than 35,000 U.S. Navy and Marine Corps personnel excluded from the CFE talks, the U.S. would still have more than 260,000 troops in Europe after a CFE treaty.

Growing support for deeper reductions, however, may force the Bush Administration to abandon or lower its troop floor. Former Defense Secretaries James Schlesinger and Harold Brown and Senator Sam Nunn (D-Ga.), chairman of the Senate Armed Services Committee, have proposed a residual U.S. military force in Europe of 75,000 to 100,000 troops.

AT THE CREATION

The stationing of U.S. troops in Europe and the establishment of the NATO military alliance were responses to specific conditions after World War II. Western Europe lay in ruins. The Soviet Union was perceived as threatening. The Western allies occupied Germany and would eventually oversee its rearmament. Neither the presence of U.S. military forces in Europe nor the NATO alliance, however, was intended to be permanent.

During the 1949 Senate hearings on the NATO treaty, Senator Bourke Hickenlooper asked Secretary of State Dean Acheson whether the U.S. would "be expected to send substantial numbers of troops [to Europe] as a more or less permanent contribution to the development of [Western Europe's] capacity to resist." Acheson responded, "The answer to that question is a clear and absolute 'no.' "

In fact, *nothing in the NATO treaty requires the U.S. to station a single soldier, sailor, or airman in Europe or even to come to the aid of an alliance member.*

General Dwight Eisenhower, the first Supreme Allied Commander in Europe, wrote in 1951, "If in ten years, all American troops stationed in Europe for national defense purposes have not been returned to the United States, then this whole project will have failed.''

Nevertheless, U.S. troops remained in Europe, ostensibly to ''couple'' European defense with U.S. strategic nuclear weapons and to serve as a ''tripwire'' to ensure that any attack against Western Europe would automatically result in U.S. military involvement.

Today, however, the conditions that underlay the NATO alliance's founding and the stationing of U.S. troops in Europe no longer apply. Western Europe is strong. The ''Soviet threat'' has diminished. Germany has no aggressive military ambitions.

EUROPEAN RESPONSIBILITY

For decades the U.S. has been carrying burdens and taking risks that belong to Europe. American leaders have long regarded U.S. military efforts on behalf of Western Europe's defense as serving important U.S. interests. Now, with pressing economic and social needs at home, many people are questioning whether this remains true.

To some, the alliance strategy of ''collective defense'' has meant that the U.S. defends while Europe collects. Continuing U.S. military contributions to Western Europe have freed local funds to build strong economies and advanced social welfare and educational programs in NATO nations.

Europe has long since recovered from the ravages of World War II. In 1988 the combined gross national products [GNPs] of the European members of the NATO alliance exceeded the GNP of the U.S. by about $74 billion, and if NATO member Canada is included, by $550 billion. The U.S. share of the collective GNP of the NATO allies fell from 70 percent in 1950 to about 47 percent in 1988.

Today the nations of Western Europe have the money, manpower, and technology to forge whatever military forces they deem necessary for their security. The combined population of European NATO nations exceeds that of the U.S. by 130 million. The armed forces of these nations total more than 3 million troops. It is in U.S. interests to insist that the Europeans now accept full responsibility for their

own defense as a corollary of their political and economic strength and independence.

Former West German Chancellor Helmut Schmidt has argued that the combined forces of France and Germany alone are capable of defending Western Europe without the aid of U.S. forces. France has pledged its commitment to the conventional defense of Germany. Since 1987 the countries have shared a joint defense council to coordinate military policies, have maintained a joint brigade of 4,200 soldiers, and have collaborated in military exercises and a helicopter program.

France and the United Kingdom could also expand military cooperation. In 1988 they concluded an agreement providing for British use of French lines of transportation (ports, airports, railways, and highways) in time of war. French Defense Minister Jean-Pierre Chevenement has stated that nuclear deterrence in Europe could be assured with French and British nuclear forces on one side and a reduced Soviet arsenal on the other.

ALTERNATIVES TO NATO

President Bush has stated ''NATO will continue to be vital to America's place in Europe.'' *While the Bush Administration continues to see Western security almost exclusively in the framework of the NATO alliance, leaders in Europe have begun to carve a new identity and future for the continent.* The new Europe favors security arrangements that are less militarized and less expensive than NATO.

Czechoslovakian President Vaclav Havel stated in early 1990, ''We want to belong to a Europe that is a friendly community of independent states, a stable Europe, a Europe that does not need protection from superpowers because it is capable of defending itself by constructing its own security system.'' Instead of engineering efforts to forestall NATO's obsolescence, the U.S. could best enhance its role within Europe by supporting these aspirations.

A new European security order could assume a number of forms. The 12-nation European Community is considering establishing a common defense policy and appears poised to assume a broader role in security matters. West German Foreign Minister Hans-Dietrich Genscher has proposed establishing a European conflict management center and an arms limitations verification center.

While the NATO alliance represents the past, the 35-nation Conference on Security and Cooperation in Europe (CSCE) perhaps best symbolizes Europe's future. Since 1975 the CSCE has served as a forum for improving East-West relations through confidence- and security-building measures addressing economic, environmental, human rights, and security affairs (including exchanges of military data and advance notification of training activities).

Czechoslovakia has proposed establishing a European Security Commission to give the CSCE a permanent secretariat. Comprised of all members of the NATO and Warsaw Pact alliances plus all other European countries except Albania (which recently applied for membership), the CSCE can preserve Europe's security link to the U.S. without NATO's cold war connotations and confrontational edge.

"A DEAD LETTER"

The Warsaw Pact remains a military alliance in name only. [Editor's Note: The Warsaw Pact was disbanded in 1991.] Its top policymaking group of Communist Party officials has been disbanded. Czechoslovakia, Hungary, and Poland have stated that they must approve any use of their military forces outside their national territories.

The Soviet Union would first have to fight its way through Eastern Europe before attacking NATO nations. But faced with crushing economic problems and a military plagued by low morale, ethnic strife, insubordination, and desertion, the Soviets are in no condition for a war.

Richard Perle, Assistant Secretary of Defense under the Reagan Administration, told Congress in early 1990, "It is simply no longer possible to imagine a cohesive Warsaw Pact, led by Soviet troops, forcing its way through the center of Europe in a massive invasion of NATO territory." Former Defense Secretary Frank Carlucci stated, "*The Warsaw Pact is a dead letter, and the canonical threat of*

Soviet and East European hordes pouring into the central plains of Europe has disappeared."

SOVIET DEMILITARIZATION

Unilateral actions by the Soviet Union lie at the center of the fundamental realignments that have taken place in Eastern Europe. The Soviet military is undergoing a significant overhaul of its force structure, doctrine, and policies.

President Gorbachev has spelled out a criterion of defensive sufficiency. He has pledged to cut Soviet annual military expenditure by 14.2 percent and weapons production by 19.5 percent by the end of 1991. U.S. intelligence has acknowledged that Soviet military spending and tank production have declined sharply.

At the United Nations in December 1988, Gorbachev announced that within two years the Soviet Union would unilaterally cut 500,000 troops and 50,000 tanks and withdraw from Eastern Europe 10,000 troops, 5,000 tanks (later increased to 5,300), 8,500 artillery weapons, and 800 combat aircraft.

In early 1990 CIA [Central Intelligence Agency] Director William Webster told Congress that the Soviets had already withdrawn about 2,700 tanks from East Germany and Czechoslovakia. Assault landing formations and units and river-crossing forces have also been withdrawn. In addition the Soviet navy has scaled back its presence in the Mediterranean Sea and is emphasizing defensive operations.

The Soviets have begun to reconfigure their military forces in accordance with the idea of "nonoffensive defense." Weapons and forces best suited for offensive operations, such as heavy tanks, strike aircraft, and river-crossing formations and units, are being removed from the front lines. Less-threatening, defensive equipment incapable of capturing and holding territory will be emphasized instead, such as mine fields, air defense weapons, and tank barriers.

The Soviets have offered to withdraw all of their troops from Eastern Europe by 1995 if all U.S. and allied foreign troops are removed from Western

Europe. They are already withdrawing all 73,500 Soviet troops from Czechoslovakia and 49,700 troops from Hungary, aiming to complete the pullout by the end of June 1991.

WARNING TIME

In the past the NATO alliance operated under the assumption that it could expect as little as 14 days of advance warning before a Soviet-led attack on Western Europe, or perhaps no warning if the Soviets launched a so-called ''standing-start'' or ''bolt-out-of-the-blue'' attack. Such overly pessimistic assumptions drove NATO nations to keep their forces at a constant high level of readiness.

With the unilateral cuts in Soviet military forces and the collapse of the Warsaw Pact, however, the readiness of Western military forces can be substantially lowered. There is no military requirement that justifies maintaining U.S. troops in Europe.

GERMAN UNIFICATION

As German unification fast becomes a reality, fears of a strong Germany have resurfaced. Negotiations among the two Germanys and the four occupying powers (the U.S., the Soviet Union, France, and the United Kingdom) under the so-called ''two-plus-four'' formula will attempt to iron out questions about how to fit and ''contain'' a unified Germany within Europe.

The Soviets prefer a Germany that is neutral, nonaligned, and without nuclear weapons. They argue that if Germany remains a member of the NATO alliance, like France, it should not be part of NATO's integrated military command. In addition they have called for special limits on the size of a unified Germany's armed forces.

The U.S. and other NATO nations, however, want Germany to remain within the alliance with U.S. troops and nuclear weapons, albeit with no NATO troops stationed in what is presently East Germany. In a development that once would have been inconceivable, West Germany has indicated a willingness to pay the cost of maintaining Soviet troops in East Germany for a transitional period in exchange for Soviet acceptance of a unified Germany within NATO.

Insistence on continued NATO membership for Germany, against Soviet objections, places at risk promising progress in arms reductions. The continued presence of U.S. troops in West Germany supports Soviet arguments for keeping its troops in East Germany. Prominent Soviet Politburo member Alexander Yakovlev declared recently, ''Soviet troops will not leave a reunified Germany if the military units of the Western countries remain there.''

A unified Germany is unlikely to be a military threat in the near future. Aware that its strength lies in its vibrant export economy, Germany currently has no aggressive military ambitions. It will remain an active, central participant in peaceful European affairs through its membership in the European Community and the CSCE. It will also be preoccupied with the tasks of unification and the many internal problems in East Germany.

Concerns about German unification should not be exploited to justify the continuation of the NATO alliance and the presence of U.S. troops in Europe. Germany is unlikely to tolerate foreign troops on its soil forever. Opinion polls in West Germany have revealed that as much as 70 percent of the German public favors the departure of all U.S. troops.

NEW ''ENEMIES''

Where once U.S. military and political leaders talked of ''vital interests'' and the ''Soviet threat,'' there is now ''instability,'' ''unpredictability,'' and ''uncertainty.'' These are the new watchwords the Bush Administration uses to justify a continued role for the NATO alliance and U.S. military forces in Europe.

When President Bush was asked ''Who is the enemy?'' he responded, ''The enemy is unpredictability. The enemy is instability.'' In his view U.S. military forces must remain in Europe to hold historical antagonisms and unresolved territorial conflicts in check. U.S. forces would contain Germany and guard against the possibility of a reversal of current Soviet policy.

CIA Director William Webster, however, advised Congress recently, *"even if a hardline regime were able to retain power in Moscow, it would have little incentive to engage in major confrontations with the United States.* New leaders would be largely preoccupied with the country's urgent domestic problems, and would be unlikely to indulge in a major buildup . . . [a successor regime] would be unlikely, in addition, to seek a broad reversal of the changes that have occurred in Eastern Europe, or to try to revive the Warsaw Pact."

Jeane Kirkpatrick, Ambassador to the United Nations under the Reagan Administration, wrote recently that the U.S. "should not be overly worried about instability" and "should face the fact it does not and cannot control these events." President Havel of Czechoslovakia told Congress in early 1990 that "American soldiers shouldn't have to be separated from their mothers just because Europe is incapable of being a guarantor of world peace."

It is not the responsibility of the U.S. to be the guarantor of European stability. The unspoken danger of the Bush Administration's position is that U.S. troops could eventually become embroiled in conflicts in which it has no justifiable military role and which the American public would be unlikely to support.

"IRRITATIONS"

No longer held hostage to their need for U.S. military protection, the European hosts are growing increasingly weary of their military guests. Former Defense Secretary James Schlesinger testified recently, *"there is . . . a high degree of irritation with the American forces that has been dwarfed in the past by fears of the Soviet Union. As the fears of the Soviet Union have diminished, the attention to the irritations will grow."*

This may be particularly true in West Germany, a country the size of Oregon where about 1,000 U.S. Army training maneuvers are conducted off-base each year. These maneuvers produce millions of dollars of damage to roads and fields as well as noise and traffic delays. As many as 580,000 NATO combat aircraft training flights each year plus more than 130 crashes of NATO aircraft in the last 10 years also contribute to growing public complaints.

General John Vessey, Jr., former Chairman of the Joint Chiefs of Staff, said in 1987, "If you multiply the population of Oregon by 20, give each person a car, arm one million of them, bring in another half-million armed foreigners, put 50,000 armed vehicles and 100,000 wheeled vehicles on the roads and put a couple-thousand jets in the air, then at least the Oregonians would know what the Germans put up with."

COMPETITIVE DISARMAMENT

Recognizing that it is now possible to obtain adequate military security at a greatly reduced cost, Europe, both East and West, is unilaterally drawing down its military spending and armed forces in response to domestic considerations. The U.S. has abandoned its past insistence that NATO nations increase their military spending by 3 percent annually, a target most governments never met. *Military reductions by West European nations should occur in addition to and not in place of U.S. military cuts.*

Belgium has announced plans to withdraw its 25,000 troops stationed in West Germany. The Netherlands plans to withdraw 750 of its 5,000 troops in West Germany by 1992 and reduce the number of F-16 jet fighters it assigns to NATO from 162 to 144. West Germany plans to reduce its armed forces by 20 percent by 1995 and has decided against extending conscription service from 15 to 18 months. Greece has reduced its conscription service by one month. Italy has cut its annual number of conscripts by 20,000 and is considering disbanding as many as 20 battalions.

The Netherlands has canceled plans to modernize its Leopard 1 main battle tanks and to purchase 50 anti-tank helicopters. The United Kingdom has deferred plans to replace its Chieftain tanks. Canada has canceled plans to build additional CP-140 maritime patrol aircraft, CF-18 jet fighters, and night vision equipment and has deferred plans to replace Leopard 1 tanks and upgrade avionics systems for CF-5 fighters. Only the U.S. and Canada among eight participating countries have not withdrawn from a NATO program to build a new navy frigate.

The nations of Eastern Europe are also hurrying to shed their military burdens. Bulgaria has cut its military spending by 12 percent and is reducing its number of tanks by 30 percent and armored troop carriers and combat vehicles by 10–30 percent. Czechoslovakia is destroying 850 tanks, 51 combat aircraft, and 165 armored vehicles and plans to reduce the size of its army by 20,000 by the end of 1990 and 40,000 by the end of 1991.

East Germany plans to cut its military spending by 10 percent by the end of 1990. Desertions and the collapse of its military draft have reduced the size of the East German army from 173,000 to 135,000 troops. The government plans to further cut the army's size to 70,000 over the next three years. Hungary meanwhile plans to cut military manpower and artillery by 40 percent and tanks by 50 percent, while Poland has stated that it will only maintain the armed forces necessary to defend its territory.

MISSING THE BOAT

Far-reaching, irreversible changes in the Soviet Union and Europe are pulling the rug out from under Cold War policies. It does not make sense for the U.S. to continue to protect a strong Western Europe from a weakened, much less threatening Soviet Union. It is unnatural and unnecessary to maintain so many troops abroad over so long a period of time.

Rather than substituting new nuclear weapons for existing tactical nuclear weapons, President Bush should call for the elimination of all nuclear weapons in Europe. The U.S. should join the Soviet Union in pledging not to be the first to use nuclear weapons.

U.S. troops in Europe have outlived their purpose and are wearing out their welcome. It is in American interests to withdraw all U.S. military forces in Europe by 1995 and place European security where it belongs—in European hands. Any nation that lags behind the rapid changes taking place in the world risks being left behind altogether.

CONCLUSIONS

- The military forces of the Warsaw Pact, including the Soviet Union, lack the capability to launch a successful surprise attack against Western Europe.

- West European nations have the money, manpower, and technology to maintain the modest military forces necessary for the foreseeable future.

- There is no military requirement which justifies stationing U.S. troops in Europe. The return of all U.S. military forces from Europe could be completed by 1995.

- NATO plans to use nuclear weapons in Europe are obsolete. No military justification now exists for the 3,700 U.S. tactical nuclear weapons in Europe.

- The U.S. military role in Europe is rapidly diminishing as the NATO alliance becomes increasingly irrelevant.

The United States and NATO after the Cold War

Robert McGeehan

Does an alliance need a threat? Paul-Henri Spaak, the former Belgian statesman and NATO [North Atlantic Treaty Organization] Secretary General, once remarked that there should be a statue of Josef Stalin in every NATO capital city, as a reminder of our debt to the Soviet dictator for providing the cement to bind together the Atlantic Alliance. To-day, thinking about NATO's military future is not unlike considering what to do with armed forces after winning a war,[1] and some wonder whether the United States will disarm after the Cold War as it has after every other war, with the same disastrous results.[2]

An alliance relies on a shared definition of mutual interest to deter, or if necessary to defend against, an identified adversary. The United States favours maintaining Western strength through NATO even as the Cold War fades away, but the practical problem will be to make operational match declaratory policy. History is not rich in *political alliances* whose enemies have ceased to threaten. While a process of transition can justify the extension of an alliance during a period of change from hostility to cooperation, can there be a future for NATO without a perceived threat of conflict or the potential for a future crisis to justify the sacrifices connected with keeping up its defence forces?

The significance of the debilitation of the Warsaw Treaty Organisation (WTO) should be appraised carefully in the wake of changes in the East. The threat to NATO security has never been from the WTO as an organisation, or from its individual members. The only important question concerns the capabilities and intentions of the USSR: what *is* the Soviet threat? The answer, still not fully appreciated by critics of deterrence even after four decades of East-West stability, is that in addition to armed aggression (perhaps never a likely possibility) there have always been the threats of blackmail, coercion and intimidation—practices which Moscow has demonstrated are well within its options, even under new leadership.[3]

There has been a remarkably consistent coincidence of both interests and values across the Atlantic since the later 1940s. The NATO Alliance has had to meet internal as well as external challenges, but differences within have always been managed without real loss of Western cohesion. The fundamental conviction remains that U.S. security is inseparable from that of Western Europe, whether or not the Cold War has ended.

The Soviet threat is not one of ideology but of military power facing a Western Europe whose local defence capability is still fragmented without assured prospects of cohesion. North America and Europe still, in these circumstances, need each other. They will continue to do so as long as the international system is strategically bipolar, until lower conventional force level agreements have been reached and implemented and until a stable balance has been assured and tested over time.

In the meanwhile, the challenge of the Nineties will not be the risk that the U.S. commitment will diminish, but that the form it takes will not produce the proper mix of military and political ingredients.

Source: Robert McGeehan, "The United States and NATO after the Cold War," *NATO Review,* **38** (Feb. 1990), pp. 7–13. Reprinted by permission.
    [1] Robert O'Neill, "Shaping NATO for the Nineties," *The Times* [London], 27 December 1989.
    [2] Richard Perle, *European Wireless File,* U.S. Information Service, London, 1 December 1989.

    [3] An example is Soviet Defense Minister Dmitri Yazov's threat that the USSR will violate the INF [intermediate-range nuclear force] treaty and resume production of SS-23 missiles if NATO proceeds to modernize SNF [short-range nuclear forces] in Europe. *The Times* [London], 29 July 1989.

This possibility has been implicit in the shifts of Western public and governmental opinion for several years, but only with the liberation currently taking place in Eastern and Central Europe has a reappraisal of the Warsaw Treaty Organisation been a realistic endeavour. Even so, conclusions vary, both between and within NATO governments.

A WATERSHED YEAR

On 3 December 1989, it was proclaimed at the Malta summit meeting of the leaders of the superpowers that the ''epoch of Cold War'' had ended. Mikhail Gorbachev expressed his commitment to deepening and extending East-West détente and cooperation, and George Bush pledged to work for results which would go beyond policies of containment and produce a Europe ''whole and free.''

While these signals of willingness to enhance stability were being transmitted, however, other factors imposed a more complex reality. New fears arose from the upheavals in Eastern and Central Europe; from uncertainties about the control of disruptive elements within the USSR; and, in many quarters, from the apprehensions about the suddenly topical subject of German reunification. Thus in addition to the old problems of maintaining the US commitment to NATO,[4] new ones appeared to make salient the question of whether an enormously successful military organisation could be shaped into a more political alliance as what seemed to be its principal *raison d'étre* appeared to recede.

While this analysis focuses on the United States and NATO, America's involvement has always been related to developments in Eastern and Central Europe. The convulsions within the Warsaw Pact states are unprecedented in their occurrence and unpredictable in their consequences. So rapid and unexpected have been the scope and pace of change that events have run beyond the expectations of even the experts, of whom there are virtually none any longer.

Scholars of Warsaw Pact affairs anticipated that Gorbachev's willingness to free East and Central European countries from past restraints could bring the relative destabilization of the whole area,[5] but it can be fairly said that no one could have guessed that in early 1990 the only old-fashioned Communist regime left would be Albania. At the beginning of 1989, NATO leaders had called for sweeping changes in East Europe; by the year's end, many urged caution as kaleidoscopic variations suggested that events might, in some places, become uncontrollable. Most noticeably, critics of President Bush's supposed timidity and indecisiveness about mounting bold responses to alleged opportunities were praising the wisdom of his prudence.

AN EVOLVING ASSESSMENT

George Bush is, by his own design, a cautious person; he is, in many ways, a timely American answer to the atmospherically dynamic offensive of *Gorbacharm*. When the new administration first assumed office in January of last year, it was thought that the Reagan Administration had set in motion processes between the super-powers which, even if ultimately desirable, were proceeding too quickly—arms control generally and questions concerning nuclear weapons in particular. With these factors in mind, President Bush announced a broad ''strategic review'' of U.S. policies. This was not only to take stock of the East-West relationship, but also, discreetly, to create some distance from the trends inherited from his predecessor. The exercise paid off both in its original purposes and in setting the stage for the very successful 40th anniversary NATO summit meeting of 29–30 May when a feared crisis was avoided.[6]

Washington's caution persisted until the latter

---

[4] See James Schlesinger, ''Preserving the American Commitment,'' *NATO Review*, Vol. **37**, No. 1, February 1989.

[5] Otto Pick, ''Perestroika and the Warsaw Pact,'' *NATO Review*, Vol. **36**, No. 5, October 1988.

[6] See Henning Wegener, ''The Management of Change: NATO's Anniversary Summit,'' *NATO Review*, Vol. **37**, No. 3, June 1989 and Documentation section in this issue.

part of 1989, when a more receptive attitude towards Soviet policies was manifested, beginning with meetings in late September between Secretary of State James Baker and Foreign Minister Eduard Shevardnadze. When President Bush and Chairman Gorbachev met at Malta in early December, a new age of East-West relations was said to be at hand, and shortly thereafter, Secretary Baker, in an address in Berlin, outlined a blueprint for the ''new era'' in Europe.[7] He called for creative arrangements and a new architecture to reflect developments in East Europe while retaining old foundations and structures which remain valuable, especially NATO, since North America's security is still linked to Europe's.

Secretary Baker went on to discuss new missions for the Alliance which would reflect the changing balance between the decreasing military component of the Cold War years and the increasingly political role for NATO in Europe's new security structure. ''Arms control agreements, confidence-building measures and other political consultative arrangements'' will become more important, he said, and NATO will be the forum for Western cooperation in matters of East-West agreements. In serving as a model of peaceful security cooperation, the Alliance would serve not only its own interests but those of Eastern and Central Europe and the Soviet Union.

The Secretary's vision cannot be faulted for lack of optimism, nor can any sensible observer want to disband the Atlantic Alliance regardless of whether the Warsaw Pact remains intact—if only because of the need to insure that an organisation is available to keep what Paul Nitze called ''the bottom line on defence.''[8] Towards its end, the Baker speech touched on another problem inseparable from the U.S. involvement in postwar European history, the reunification of the Germanys.

---

[7] Official text published by U.S. Information Service, London, 13 December 1989.

[8] *International Herald Tribune*, 3 January 1990.

THE GERMAN CONUNDRUM

The United States has been central to the security of the Federal Republic since its inception. The NATO allies, for their part, have consistently pledged to work for German unity, although this was easier to embrace when its chances of realization seemed remote. Today, even though it arose too rapidly for some, the German question is very much on the agenda and it involves the future of the U.S. commitment.

There is no agreement so far on any coordinated approach to the reunification question, and until elections are held in March [1990] in the German Democratic Republic, the intensity of support for reunification there cannot really be known. United States policy is that whatever arrangements are made must, in Secretary Baker's words in Berlin, ''satisfy the aspirations of the German people and meet the legitimate concerns of Germany's neighbours.'' On 13 February, Secretary Baker reached agreement in Ottawa with his British, French and Soviet counterparts for ''two-plus-four'' meetings of Foreign Ministers, that is, from the two Germanys and the four powers that have certain legal rights and responsibilities with respect to Germany. These meetings will, in the words of the statement issued in Ottawa ''discuss external aspects of the establishment of German unity, including the issues of security of the neighbouring states.'' Whether all these aspirations can be reconciled may be open to doubt, as may the other U.S. preferences—that reunification should be gradual; not involve any change of borders incompatible with the Helsinki Final Act; occur in a context of Germany's continued commitment to NATO and an increasingly integrated European Community; and that there be due regard to the legal role and responsibilities of the wartime allied powers. Such a formula would seem to contain too many vetoes and imply endless negotiating delays. It remains to be seen whether it will survive massive nationalistic emotions, and whether deteriorating conditions in the GDR [German Democratic Republic] can be controlled sufficiently to avoid its effective collapse.

To these points must be added others whose implications are quite different. Some observers, for example, have argued that the military forces of both Germanys should be dramatically reduced and that all foreign troops should be withdrawn from both Germanys by the end of this decade. Should the latter be done, this would surely threaten the Atlantic Alliance; among the least persuasive scenarios for a post–Cold War NATO is that which posits an American commitment to European defence without U.S. troops in Germany.

As long as the Soviet Union clearly opposed German reunification, the question remained very uncertain. But agreement on the ''two-plus-four'' approach and the statement of Chairman Gorbachev on 21 February in his Pravda interview that the two Germanys had a ''right to unity'' open up many new possibilities. The East German leadership was calling in early February for a united and neutral German state, notwithstanding the unqualified commitment by the Federal Republic to remain part of the Alliance. NATO Secretary General Manfred Wörner, speaking in Hamburg on 8 February, maintained that there is no acceptable alternative to a reunified Germany anchored in the Atlantic Alliance. He went on to suggest that ''special arrangements'' could be devised to take account of Soviet security interests, giving as possibilities ''a special military status for the territory of the GDR or perhaps an agreement not to extend military integration to that territory.''

REMAINING THREAT

Recent NATO analysis has suggested that it would be premature to conclude that Soviet military preparations have fundamentally changed. Both nuclear and conventional weapons have been modernized and upgraded for increased firepower, and in spite of some evidence that overall spending has been reduced, the stated defence budget is thought to be misleading—with actual spending perhaps double the amount Chairman Gorbachev has admitted.

These reminders that Soviet intentions are not always as benign as they might seem have been underlined by U.S. Defense Intelligence Agency assessments which show that even though some Soviet troops have been withdrawn from Eastern Europe, large forward-based stockpiles of fuel and ammunition are being maintained which belie Moscow's willingness to alter its offensive capabilities. NATO cannot yet assume a surprise attack of some sort is completely out of the question; it is hoped the current Vienna CFE [Conventional Forces in Europe] negotiations will clarify this situation, but until they do the contradictions will remain.[9] In addition, Soviet military force plans anticipate the effects of a CFE agreement, and through selection of the oldest equipment for elimination a ''leaner but meaner'' capability could result.[10]

Along with the Soviet picture, U.S.-NATO relations are bound to change as the 1990s compel a redefinition of the prudent minimum necessary for Western defence. If the CFE process produces the expected reductions towards parity, smaller forces at equal levels will mean a structural shift away from the former pattern of massive Soviet forces facing an inferior NATO defence. In the new configuration, NATO forces would remain vital as an insurance policy against sudden change. If their nuclear capabilities are kept, not for reasons of balancing formerly numerically superior Soviet forces, but for deterrence, coupling will remain guaranteed between the U.S. and Europe.[11]

THE GORBACHEV FACTOR

Another consideration concerns the political future of the individual without whom current changes would not be taking place. While Mikhail Gorbachev

---

[9] *The Times* and *International Herald Tribune*, both 12 January 1990; see also ''Soviet Strength No Less Despite Force Cuts,'' *Janes Defence Weekly*, Vol. **12**, No. 15, 14 October 1989, p. 785.

[10] *Jane's Defence Weekly*, Vol. **13**, No. 1, 6 January 1990, p. 13.

[11] Francois Heisbourg, ''Defending Europe without Uncle Sam,'' *The Independent*, 28 December 1989.

has shown great flexibility in his ability to shift course, sometimes at the expense of contradicting his previous positions, he remains a gambler and an opportunist rather than a visionary leader or a chess-playing strategist. Even before the recent ''Z'' article in *Daedalus*,[12] critics were pointing out that as long as the East European countries were being allowed to move away from Communist systems while this was not permitted within the USSR, this contradiction was bound to generate strong political demands and widespread instability.

This is compounded by Gorbachev's stubborn efforts to reform Communism rather than getting rid of it. The chaotic failure of *perestroika* could bring either the fall of the Soviet leader or his transformation into a frustrated and angry authoritarian in whose hands the reins of power are already concentrated. It may be too pessimistic to conclude that the resumption of the Cold War could ensue from such developments, but unless domestic conditions improve, the reappearance of an intensified Soviet military threat could hang on the weakening thread of Gorbachev's fortunes. For now, his amazing willingness to permit change favours, on balance, Western interests as well as democratic values.

The Bush-Gorbachev rapport, which the Malta summit enhanced, is a positive factor. American sensitivity in signalling that no attempt would be made to exploit the unrest in Eastern and Central Europe to the detriment of Soviet interests is clear. Outside powers cannot ''help'' Gorbachev very much, but it is undoubtedly to NATO's benefit that he has redefined Soviet national security interests. He has decided, correctly, that a nuclear super-power does not need old-fashioned buffer zones for security, especially if the cost of maintaining them is high and if the potential adversary is as patently non-aggressive as is NATO.

It must be recalled, notwithstanding these changes, that nothing the Soviet leader has done in the least suggests that he contemplates making his country the world's first ex-super-power. He has won the trust of the West by not using force when his predecessors would have done so, perhaps at some risk—but if his long-range aim was to influence the mixture of anti-Americanism, anti-nuclear feeling and semi-neutralism in parts of Western Europe so as to influence NATO governments in his direction, then Gorbachev has done remarkably well.[13]

NATO is not being dismantled, and for the time being it is useful to Moscow to keep the Warsaw Pact alive as a balancing factor. Nuclear weapons are not being totally eliminated, as the Soviet leader has repeatedly demanded, indeed they could now be considered more necessary for Soviet security with the buffer zone in tatters and with German re-unification a short-term prospect. For the latter reason as well, the Soviet wish to get U.S. troops out of Europe must be somewhat reduced. In sum, compared to his predecessors, Gorbachev's policies are militarily more clever, politically shrewder and economically cheaper; if he could achieve domestically what he has gained abroad, his murky prospects would be infinitely improved. Yet he continues to spin on a log with no end in sight. Domestic failure may not be mitigated by foreign success: his great victory in the West of exorcising the ghost of those unerected statues and gaining with a smile what decades of intimidation by his predecessors have failed to bring, could still turn to dust as forces unleashed abroad consume him at home.

THE ATLANTIC PROPOSALS

The United States has explicitly promised that an American military presence will remain in Western Europe for as long as it is needed and wanted. Financial pressures and budgetary constraints will bring lower force levels, but no unilateral step will be

---

[12] See *International Herald Tribune*, 5 January 1990, for a summary of the ''Z'' thesis, and related article by William Safire.

[13] As *The Economist* quite presciently wondered only a few months after Gorbachev came to power. *The Economist*, 12 October 1985.

taken without consultation, especially in the light of encouraging progress at the CFE talks. The Pentagon has stated that the risk of war is as low as it has ever been in the postwar period, although senior U.S. officials do not believe that either Gorbachev's good intentions or further democratic developments in Eastern Europe are irreversible. Even without the reimposition of Soviet control, Eastern Europe is showing disturbing signs of Balkanization and the revival of ethnic rivalries and nationalistic animosities. While most in the West wish the Soviet leader well, as Defense Secretary Dick Cheney has said, ''we can't base our strategy on what fate may have in store for one man.''[14]

In view of all these factors, the United States will remain committed to a strong NATO including a major U.S. force, whose presence, moreover, will not be tied solely to the Soviet military presence in East Europe.[15] The super-powers are bound to compete even if the Cold War has ended, and an assured American presence will continue to afford stability to Europe's changing balance of power as the allies search for a viable new Atlanticism to meet the evolving political conditions of the 1990s.

QUESTIONS FOR DISCUSSION

1. What would be the consequences of a U.S. withdrawal of military forces from Europe?

2. Can the cold war be resumed? What are the reasons for your answer?
3. What are the prospects for NATO in the post–cold war age?
4. Under what conditions should U.S. troops be withdrawn from Europe?
5. What are the security alternatives to NATO?

SUGGESTED READINGS

Bandow, Doug, and Ted Galen Carpenter. ''Preserving an Obsolete NATO.'' *Cato Policy Report*, **12** (Sept./Oct. 1990), pp. 1, 10–12.

Callaghan, Thomas A., Jr. ''NATO at Forty.'' *Defense and Diplomacy*, **7** (Apr. 1989), pp. 19–29.

Carpenter, Ted Galen (ed.). *NATO at 40: Confronting a Changing World.* Washington, D.C.: Cato Institute, 1990.

Cortieier, Peter. ''*Quo Vadis* NATO?'' *Survival* (London), **32** (Mar./Apr. 1990), pp. 141–156.

Gottfried, Kurt, and Paul Bracken (eds.). *Reforging European Security: From Confrontation to Cooperation.* Boulder, Colo.: Westview Press, 1991.

''NATO at 40.'' *CRS Review*, **10** (Apr./May 1990), pp. 1–27.

Nunn, Sam. ''Challenges to NATO in the 1990s.'' *Survival* (London), **32** (Jan./Feb. 1990), pp. 3–13.

Riding, Alan. ''The New Europe.'' *New York Times*, Nov. 20, 1990, p. A14.

Sharp, Jane (ed.). *Europe after an American Withdrawal: Economic and Military Issues.* Oxford, England: Oxford Univ. Press, 1990.

U.S. Cong., Senate. *The Future of NATO.* Hearing before the Committee on Foreign Relations, 101st Cong., 2d Sess., 1990.

Worner, Manfred. ''NATO Celebrates Its Fortieth Anniversary.'' *NATO's Sixteen Nations* (Brussels), **34**, special ed. (1989), pp. 16–19, 22.

---

[14] *European Wireless File*, U.S. Information Service, London, 19 December 1989.

[15] Following an initiative by President Bush, agreement has been reached on even deeper U.S. and Soviet troop cuts, down to 195,000 on each side for forces stationed in Central and Eastern Europe.

16 Are Economic Sanctions an Effective Instrument of Foreign Policy?

YES

Gregory A. Fossedal

Sanctions for Beginners

NO

Bruce Bartlett

What's Wrong with Trade Sanctions?

Sanctions for Beginners

Gregory A. Fossedal

This much can be said for economic sanctions: they produce bipartisan behavior. Members of both political parties issue passionate, hypocritical, and often contradictory statements about them. Both Republican and Democratic administrations use them on some countries, dismiss them as ineffective against others. Thus George Ball, a chief spokesman for the Kennedy administration's program of sanctions against Cuba, wrote a cover article for *The New York Times Magazine* three years ago denouncing Ronald Reagan's cutoff of technology for the Soviet gas pipeline as "catastrophe." In one week in December 1982, Daniel Patrick Moynihan called for sanctions against the pipeline, then, days later, told the "Today" show that the sanctions would "have little impact" and complained that "the United States should have gone to the United Nations" first. Ronald Reagan, who believes sanctions would only hurt blacks in South Africa, has continued them against Cuba (where they only hurt Castro?) and enacted them against Nicaragua.

This is a great misfortune for U.S. foreign policy. The United States alone produces perhaps twice as much as the Soviet Union and the entire Warsaw Pact. Add in Japan and Western Europe, and the Western democracies control two-thirds to three-quarters of the world's output. When intelligent people cannot agree whether Sanction A will produce result X—or whether it will produce result Y, Z, or even the precise opposite of X—a potentially effective tool sits unused, or worse, is used ineptly.

Do sanctions work? As with many such issues, the question hinges on what we mean by "work."

Consider, for example, the Arab oil embargo against the United States and some of Europe. On one level, the embargo was a colossal failure. Few people in the United States froze to death or had to quit their jobs because they could no longer drive cars. Nor did the embargo succeed in its professed objective of forcing Israel to withdraw from lands occupied in the 1967 war.

Yet the Arab oil embargo was clearly a political and economic success. Gas lines and unemployment fueled by the energy crisis helped bring down three consecutive presidents: Nixon, Ford, and Carter. Many European countries, far more dependent on Arab oil than the United States was, became anti-Israel in rhetoric and policy. In the Middle East, PLO [Palestine Liberation Organization] sympathizers such as Assad and Qaddafi were strengthened by the demonstration of radical Arab muscle, while "moderate" leaders faced greater pressures at home—and saw a weaker U.S. and Western Europe available to help them resist those pressures. All of these developments had something to do with the growing economic clout of the oil producers, brought on in part by the embargo.

Historically, the Arab embargo is no isolated example. Economic pressure against Germany and Japan first helped bring America into World War II—the "hinge of fate" as Churchill called it—and then helped win it. And even though such countries as Switzerland continued trading with Nazi Germany well into 1945, the Allies' sanctions, coordinated by Dean Acheson, helped deprive Hitler of supplies (petroleum, ball bearings, iron ore, and some industrial diamonds) that might have substantially lengthened the war.

In spite of these and other successes, "sanction" remains a dirty word, a foreign policy lever regarded with suspicion by liberals and conservatives alike. One reason is that nobody has studied the issue very systematically. Of two prominent books that examine sanctions, one, by Robin Renwick, is well-written and thoughtful but modest in scope, evaluating only half a dozen sanction episodes. The other, by

Source: Gregory A. Fossedal, "Sanctions for Beginners," *New Republic*, **193** (Oct. 21, 1985), pp. 18–21. Reprinted by permission.

Gary Hufbauer and Jeffrey Schott, is extremely broad, with case abstracts of 83 sanctions in this century and dozens of footnotes in each case study. But it consists largely of paste-and-clip assessments taken from other sources, and attempts to establish ludicrously precise estimates such as "per capita" harm of sanctions "as a share of domestic GNP [gross national product]."

Perhaps the chief problem, though, is three understandable, but damaging, conceptual errors.

The first involves a misapplication of free trade theory. Free trade theory argues (correctly, in my view) that all nations benefit from free trade, concentrating on production of goods in which they enjoy the greatest comparative advantage. Notice, however, what this theory does not argue: that all countries gain equally from free trade. Yet this is precisely what some analysts twist it to mean when they argue that a cutoff of, say, U.S. computer technology will hurt the U.S. by damaging its computer industry. Of course this is a cost of the sanction. The question for policymakers is whether the U.S. will suffer more from this lost revenue than the country we wish to punish will suffer from losing our computers. On these relative costs, free trade doctrine is silent.

Consider a simple two-family economy involving Smith and Jones. Smith trades Jones bananas that grow in his backyard—which, by the way, are Jones's favorite fruit. In exchange, Jones gives Smith insulin, which Smith needs to survive. Both families gain; both are happy. One day, Jones sees Mr. Smith beating Mrs. Smith. After repeated efforts to persuade Smith to cease this human rights violation, Jones decides to go the sanction route, cutting off all insulin trade to Smith. Smith retaliates by refusing to sell any bananas to Jones, forcing him to give up his favorite fruit and survive on wild nuts. Both families, in line with free trade theory, will suffer. But Smith may die, and Mr. Jones's sanctions have a good chance of working.

The second error is the notion that the "fungible market" will render any trade sanction useless: the old someone-else-will-sell-it-to-them-anyway argument. Though this contradicts argument one, it is often raised in the same breath. The problem is that

there are few fungible markets. In practice, even the most "fungible" commodities—including grain, oil, and gold—may be dominated by a small number of producers who can greatly influence the market price. Then too, people who talk about a fungible "market" often misunderstand the nature of a market, ignoring subtle costs and differences in production. Under the Carter embargo, the Soviets were able to buy much more "grain" from Argentina and Canada. But they could not make up critical shortfalls in feed-quality grains—thus suffering a drastic meat shortage in 1979 and 1980 that helped spark the Solidarity uprising in Poland, according to an economic analysis performed by the Department of Agriculture. In our Smith-Jones analogy, it is as if Smith can buy insulin elsewhere—but only by walking several miles each morning, giving up more bananas, and dealing with a factory that often shuts down.

A final confusion in the sanction debate is a political one—perhaps the most difficult of all to address. Many oppose a given sanction because it is bound to inflict pain largely on the people of a country rather than on their elites. Ronald Reagan complains that sanctions against South Africa will "mostly damage the people we want to help"; Senator Patrick Leahy, questioning Reagan's pipeline action, objected that it would "hurt the Poles" in Poland. Whether a sanction really works may come down to whether this pain on the people will in turn cause them to inflict pain on the government. The countries where sanctions are most likely to work politically, then, are the countries on which we are least likely to impose sanctions. Ultimately, "this argument would imply that sanctions should be used only against democratic states," as Harvard's Nick Eberstadt puts it.

The criterion of Reagan and Leahy is too narrow. What is needed to evaluate a sanction's efficacy is a close look at Smith: What sort of adversary is he? What sort of pressures is he subject to? It seems to me we can consider the world in terms of four different types of "Smiths": strong enemies, weak enemies, strong friends, and weak friends. Looking at these four different groups, one finds that economic pressure has achieved notable policy results against all four. But the potential for success is particularly great against the kind of smaller, quasi-allies mentioned above—including South Africa.

SANCTIONS AGAINST THE SOVIETS

Probably the toughest sanction imposed against the Soviets in recent years was the much-maligned Carter grain embargo. . . . During the years the Carter embargo remained in force, the Department of Agriculture study estimates, the Soviets lost more than six million tons of grain.

Some concede that the Carter embargo was successful economically, but not politically. The embargo was a response to the Soviet invasion of Afghanistan; on this level, it failed. But surely Afghanistan is no worse off than it would have been without some sanctions. And it is arguably much better off, thanks to the weak Soviet economy and the economic pressure caused by the deteriorating situation of other Soviet allies around the globe, from Ethiopia to Angola to Nicaragua. Major sanctions against the Soviets, in response to major offenses such as the invasion of country, are never likely to produce an overt capitulation. "It is not within the power of the West to bring the Soviet economy to its knees," as Richard Pipes said in January 1983. "What one can and ought to strive for is compelling the Soviet regime to bear the consequences of its own priorities."

SANCTIONS AGAINST ALLIES

The most notable example of U.S. sanctions against Western Europe came in the 1956 Suez crisis. One can argue about whether the objective of the sanctions was wise. One cannot argue about their impact: the British and French rapidly withdrew from the Sinai in response to U.S. restrictions on oil deliveries and trade credits to France and Britain. In a general sense, it stands to reason that sanctions against allies are likely to have more impact; allies generally conduct more trade and are more dependent on their friends.

The most recent example is Reagan's cutoff of U.S. technology for the Soviet-European gas pipeline. By denying export licenses, Reagan sought to block the transfer of critical turbines from General Electric and other high-technology items needed for the pipeline. When the allies pressured their own companies to ignore the ban, the U.S. threatened to revoke trade privileges for firms that disobeyed. There were several economic repercussions. First, the completion of the pipeline was delayed by at least one year, and arguably two years. During that time some governments, notably the Dutch, realized that Soviet demands for subsidized credit of about 8.67 percent, combined with a "floor price" for gas purchases in the midst of declining world energy prices, made the pipeline a poor deal anyway. France and Italy negotiated an escape clause allowing them to wriggle out of payment for 20 percent of the contracted shipments. (Gordon Crovitz outlined these economic impacts in a series of articles from 1982 to 1984 in *The Wall Street Journal*.) Judging the political effects of all this on the Western alliance is a subjective business, but on the whole, the exercise was a plus.

Reagan's sanctions produced no long-term fissure in the alliance. If anything, they contributed to a matrix of useful pressures that have led France, Britain, and Germany to policies more supportive of the United States. In Germany the pipeline fiasco was part of a broad reaction against *Ostpolitik* that helped bring to power the Kohl government. Since the deal, French president Mitterrand has become arguably the staunchest ally the U.S. has on most foreign policy questions. Reagan's stand showed that he was willing to run risks, to bear criticism from Europe, in pursuit of a longer-run effort to make the Soviets bear a higher cost for repression in Eastern Europe and elsewhere.

Another example is the case of Turkey, the object of U.S. and then European sanctions from 1974 to 1978 and 1981 to 1982. Such sanctions do not appear to have satisfied the lust of the Turks for Cyprus. But they have arguably helped contain that lust. And Europe's 1981 cutoff of Organization for Economic Development credits and other assistance has led to visible movement toward complete democracy. As a result, the West enjoys an ally that is more democratic, and thus more strong and more stable, than it was several years ago.

SANCTIONS AGAINST SMALL ENEMIES

Perhaps the most attractive target for sanctions is the small, pesky foe: Cuba, Vietnam, Nicaragua. After all, though these countries are weak economically, their Marxist-military governments may wreak havoc among their neighbors. What's more, despite their size, they are no pushover militarily. A stiff package of sanctions is often seen as the best way to keep the heat on.

Economically, such sanctions have a good record. The U.S. embargo of Cuba was begun in 1960 under Eisenhower and extended beyond sugar to all Cuban goods by President Kennedy in 1962. It has, in the words of Harvard's Robin Renwick, helped to "increase the costs to the Soviet Union of support for the Cuban economy." By one estimate that subsidy is on the order of five [million] dollars per day—greater, as a share of the Soviet economy, than the costs to the U.S. of supporting Vietnam in 1973. We can never be precisely sure where these increased costs will be reflected in altered behavior. But it is plausible to speculate that wavering Soviet-Cuban support for Angola and Nicaragua reflects in part the thinning of resources imposed by 20 years of pressure. Though generally pessimistic about the effectiveness of sanctions, Hufbauer and Schott credit them with helping to weaken the economies of both North Korea and Vietnam.

Politically, the effect of sanctions on such small but resilient enemies is more doubtful. Indeed, economic sanctions may hasten their growing ties with the Soviets. In the case of a popular leader like Castro, sanctions may provide a common external enemy, useful in whipping up domestic support. They may raise anti-American leaders to greater status. Still, in these cases, the question of whether economic pressure produces some directly tangible result resembles the somewhat artificial distinction between "military aid," which involves sending

someone guns, and "humanitarian aid," which involves sending them butter, so they can cut their own spending on butter and buy more guns. Even if sanctions against a Vietnam or Cuba fail to topple a regime and temporarily strengthen it, in the long run they lessen its ability to spread trouble elsewhere.

SANCTIONS AGAINST SMALL ALLIES

These offer perhaps the most potent impact. Consider the Smith and Jones paradigm: the small ally often relies on the United States for the economic or moral equivalent of insulin. This may sound harsh, but it is a recognition of reality. If U.S. leaders keep this reality in mind as they shape foreign policy, the result will not be cruel but beneficial to America and its neighbors.

From 1975 to 1977, U.S. economic pressure deterred both South Korea and Taiwan from building nuclear reprocessing plants. Swift and decisive sanctions by Gerald Ford have prevented both countries from joining the club of nuclear-armed nations. Beginning in 1977, and ending with the suspension of U.S. military aid in 1979, Jimmy Carter's withdrawal of support from Nicaragua helped bring down the already rickety Somoza regime. One can argue about the wisdom of these sanctions, since they brought to power a government arguably no more humane than Somoza's. On the other hand, various economic pressures on Brazil, Argentina, and El Salvador, initiated during the Carter administration, helped convince those countries of the need to improve on human rights. Today all three have held, by Latin standards, impressively peaceful and honest elections.

The potential effectiveness of economic pressure is being demonstrated today as the West begins to apply sanctions against South Africa. The program, first approved in both houses of Congress, and then largely co-opted by the administration, seeks to abolish the sale of gold Krugerrands in the United States, cut off future credit from U.S. banks, and ban further computer sales. Sheer numbers suggest the effect could be significant. South Africa sold more than

$600 million worth of Krugerrands in the United States in 1984, almost 40 percent of the country's coin exchange. Computer sales from the United States were valued at $184 million, about 70 percent of South Africa's total purchase of such equipment. U.S. loans in the last several years have run between $300 million and $600 million per annum. Altogether these items total more than one billion dollars, or about one percent of South Africa's gross national product. And they hardly exhaust the possibility for sanctions. If the Western allies are serious, they might add diamonds to the list of contraband, a much larger export item.

Of course, critics argued, Germany and Britain conduct more trade with South Africa, and might well be induced to fill the U.S. gap. But if this were a certainty, the prospect of sanctions would hardly have provoked such opposition from U.S. supporters of South Africa and from the South African government itself. The old argument that a number of countries must cooperate in a sanction misses the more important question of how you get them to cooperate. First French and then U.S. sanctions have made it harder for other Western governments to blink at apartheid. Last week Britain joined the other Common Market countries in applying sanctions.

Adding to the potential impact will be the growing moral stench of apartheid among Westerners, and the presence of a democratic movement within South Africa. Freedom fighters have already produced successful boycotts of white stores and closed down vital mines and transportation industries with peaceful work stoppages. Black consumers in South Africa, according to *The Wall Street Journal*'s Steve Mufson, control about 47 percent of the total buying power in the country. Boycotts have already imposed a 30 percent loss of business on average on largely white-owned stores. Foreign investment capital, fearing just such developments, has begun to flee.

Obviously, the hope is that such confrontations, even economic ones, can yet be avoided if the Botha government sees them as a clear possibility and acts to avoid them. But what if it does not? Or what if it is already so weakened that militant black rebels spurn even genuine reforms? The reluctance of conservatives to use sanctions against countries like South Africa—or the even closer calls of Chile and the Philippines—derives, it seems to me, from precisely this fear. It is not the fear that sanctions will not work. It is a fear that they will "work," producing another Nicaragua or Iran.

Even so, there are some pragmatic reasons for Reaganites to support Reagan's de facto policy of "constructive disengagement," as William Safire calls it. For one would think, if a Ronald Reagan will not step in to prevent the emergence of a Soviet client state in South Africa, who would? Pushing the moment to its crisis may be dangerous, but it may be more dangerous not to. In the sweep of history, apartheid is bound to change, and probably in a dramatic spurt rather than, as the human heart would prefer but the human mind can seldom engineer, in some gradual and predictable fashion.

What seems obvious is true. America's vast economic resources are a powerful tool. Like any tool, they are often misused, applied ineptly on behalf of right purposes, or used skillfully on behalf of bad ones. But where sanctions are used ineptly, it does not mean that sanctions cannot work. As the world now stands, many other levers are either in moral disrepute (say, covert action) or unusable (nuclear weapons) or ineffective (propping up friendly dictators). The United States may need its economic powers of persuasion more than ever.

What's Wrong with Trade Sanctions?

Bruce Bartlett

Under pressure from a majority of Congress, Pres. Reagan recently instituted a program of economic sanctions against South Africa to protest that country's racial policies. Although there is no question that the South African government's apartheid regime is abhorrent, before rushing into sanctions we ought to give serious thought to whether they will work. There is little historical evidence that sanctions have ever achieved their purpose; recent examples of such nonsuccess include the U.S. embargo on grain shipments to the Soviet Union in 1981 and U.S. sanctions against Nicaragua in 1985. More often than not, sanctions end up making the target country more self-sufficient and strengthening its resolve to continue its policies. In the case of South Africa, the result may be a strengthening of apartheid, rather than its demise.

The first recorded case of trade sanctions occurred in 432 B.C., when the Athenian leader Pericles imposed sanctions on Megara. Megara appealed to Sparta for aid, resulting in the Peloponnesian War. An early example of U.S. trade sanctions occurred in 1807 when Pres. Thomas Jefferson embargoed all U.S. trade with Europe to protest British attacks on U.S. merchant ships. As with later trade sanctions, this effort also proved to be a complete failure. In modern times, sanctions have been used a great many times in both major and minor efforts to change government behavior. Almost universally, they have failed.

A particularly dramatic failure was the Roosevelt Administration's program of economic sanctions against Japan in the late 1930's and early 1940's. U.S. sanctions against Japan were first instituted in 1938, following the *Panay* sinking. Private companies were urged to halt shipping goods to Japan and banks were discouraged from extending credits to Japan. In this effort, the Administration was continually pressed by businessmen who wished to exclude Japanese goods from the U.S. market. U.S. sanctions were extended in 1940 to a mandatory embargo on the export of arms, munitions, aviation fuel, and other items deemed useful to Japan's war effort. They culminated in Roosevelt's July 25, 1941, order freezing all Japanese assets in the U.S., thereby effectively shutting off all trade between the two countries. The major impact of this action on Japan was the immediate loss of virtually all oil imports. At that time, 80 percent of Japan's oil came from the U.S.

Historians agree that the freeze order was the final straw causing Japan to attack Pearl Harbor. Robert J. C. Butow, in *Tojo and the Coming of War*, said the order produced feelings in Japan "similar to those that grip a man when a noose is placed around his neck." William L. Langer and S. Everett Gleason, in *The Undeclared War, 1940–1941*, indicated that the freeze order "was probably the crucial step in the entire course of Japanese-American relations before Pearl Harbor." In "The Case against Sanctions," *New York Times Magazine*, Sept. 12, 1982, former Under Secretary of State George W. Ball concluded from this episode that economic sanctions are more likely to strengthen aggressive tendencies than to compel greater docility:

> One has only to recall the effect of the so-called ABCD [American-British-Chinese-Dutch] encirclement of prewar Japan, and particularly the American embargo on oil exports to Tokyo. Not only did the latter action play into the hands of the aggressive Japanese military clique, it provided a decisive argument for seizing the oil-rich Dutch East Indies and attacking Pearl Harbor.

Recently, Gary Hufbauer and Jeffrey J. Schott of the Institute for International Economics studied 103

Source: Bruce Bartlett, "What's Wrong with Trade Sanctions?" *USA Today Magazine*, **114** (May 1986), pp. 22–25. Copyright © 1986 by the Society for the Advancement of Education.

episodes of trade sanctions since World War I. They concluded that sanctions are seldom successful, even under a loose definition of "success," except against small countries and only when the goals are modest. Moreover, since 1973, the proportion of cases in which sanctions have achieved any success has fallen from almost half to about one-quarter. "In most cases," according to Hufbauer and Schott, "sanctions do not contribute very much to the achievement of foreign policy goals. . . . We conclude that sanctions are a decreasingly useful policy instrument."

This negative view of trade sanctions is widely shared by those who have studied them. Robert Gilpin of Princeton University notes that the theory behind sanctions is that they cause a split between the leadership and the masses of the people, "but in almost all cases, it's been just the opposite. What you have is really a rallying-around-the-flag response in these countries." Margaret Doxey of Trent University says, "One may conclude that economic sanctions should not be seen as a useful, peaceful weapon of pressure which can be readily employed at low cost." Secretary of State George Shultz stated in 1982, "As a general proposition, I think the use of trade sanctions as an instrument of diplomacy is a bad idea. . . . Our using it here, there and elsewhere to try to affect some other country's behavior . . . basically has not worked."

An example of the failure of trade sanctions is the case of Rhodesia, one that most clearly corresponds to the South African situation. An embargo sponsored by the U.N. against Rhodesia ran from 1965 to 1975. On Nov. 11, 1965, Rhodesian Prime Minister Ian Smith issued a unilateral declaration of independence from Great Britain, setting up a government controlled by Rhodesia's white minority. Great Britain immediately announced the imposition of sanctions, including the freezing of Rhodesian assets. Shortly thereafter, the U.N. passed a resolution urging member states to withhold recognition of the new regime, break economic relations, and embargo oil exports. Eventually, the sanctions were broadened, culminating in a 1968 U.N. resolution requiring mandatory sanctions against Rhodesia.

Although the Smith regime was ultimately thrown out in 1979, it does not appear that the economic sanctions contributed much to that result. In a 1981 study for the Harvard Center for International Affairs, Robin Renwick, head of the Rhodesian Department of the British Foreign Office, reported that, between 1965 and 1974, Rhodesia's real output increased six percent per year "despite the depressing effect of sanctions"; the value of exports more than doubled between 1968 and 1974 and continued to rise afterward, although much more slowly.

Hufbauer and Schott calculate that the annual cost of economic sanctions to Rhodesia was just $130,000,000 per year. This figure is only slightly higher than the $100,000,000 annual cost to its neighboring countries, Zambia and Mozambique, which lost trade and had to bear the increased costs of acquiring goods and raw materials elsewhere. Great Britain also sustained heavy costs in airlifting oil to Zambia and maintaining a naval blockade against the Rhodesian port of Beira. Hufbauer and Schott conclude that the per capita cost of the embargo was just $29 per year for each Rhodesian.

The embargo did have important effects on the Rhodesian economy, of course. According to Renwick, however, it led mainly to Rhodesia becoming more self-sufficient: "In the decade from 1965 to 1975, the Rhodesian economy was transformed from virtually total dependence on the importation of manufactured goods in exchange for raw materials to a remarkable degree of self-sufficiency in most areas except oil and industrial plant and machinery." Renwick concluded that "sanctions against Rhodesia did exert some pressure for a negotiated solution, though the pressure was never irresistible and they did so at the considerable political cost of tending to consolidate rather than diminish white support for the regime."

EVADING SANCTIONS

Trade sanctions, especially when they unilaterally are imposed by only one country or a small group of countries, are more likely to alter trade patterns than to inflict serious damage on the target nation. The

U.S. embargo on grain shipments to the Soviet Union is instructive in this regard. In the end, the Soviets imported only one percent less grain than pre-embargo forecasts had predicted, and U.S. grain exports were about the same as pre-embargo estimates. What happened, according to economist Clifton B. Luttrell of the Federal Reserve Bank of St. Louis, was that ''large quantities of U.S. grain were shipped to nations which normally purchase grain from other sources, thereby permitting these sources to supply grain to the Soviet Union.'' Similarly, Congress' Office of Technology Assessment found that the costs of the grain embargo to the U.S. economy ''were at least as great as those which developed on the U.S.S.R., and that the Soviet Union seems to have succeeded in replacing the United States as its principal agricultural supplier.''

This failure was recognized by Pres. Reagan, and it contributed to his decision to rescind the grain embargo in 1981. He stated later:

> In the Spring of 1981, I lifted the grain embargo imposed by the previous administration because it was not having the desired effect of seriously penalizing the U.S.S.R. for its brutal invasion and occupation of Afghanistan. Instead, alternative suppliers of this widely available commodity stepped in to make up for the grain which would have been normally supplied by U.S. farmers.

Other methods of evading sanctions include substituting other products—if steel is not available, for example, one might make do with aluminum—and obtaining embargoed goods through third parties. As *Time* magazine observed in January, 1980, ''There are too many middlemen for supplies to be effectively shut off—they can simply be routed through friendly countries.''

The magnitude of the problem is probably best shown by the consistent ability of the Soviet Union to obtain U.S. technology, which, we may assume, is far more closely guarded than shipments of nonstrategic materials we may wish to keep out of another country's hands simply for political reasons. The fact is, with an open economy like ours, it is almost impossible to keep the Soviets from obtaining much of the technology they desire. Moreover, the U.S. is not the only place where many strategic materials can be obtained, and most of our allies are far more lax about protecting such material than we are. It is more and more frequently the case that, when the U.S. embargoes the export of goods to the Soviet Union or any other country, there is another nation willing and able to provide similar goods. As Donald M. Kendall, chairman of PepsiCo, put it in 1984,

> We are no longer the sole or predominate supplier of equipment and technology in the world marketplace. As we have witnessed so many times in the past, unilateral U.S. actions to control the transfer of our equipment and technology have generally contributed to the export sales of our trading competitors rather than a denial of such items to the Soviet Union.

Consider the U.S. embargo on pipeline equipment to the Soviet Union in 1981–82. The U.S. embargoed the sale of equipment the Soviets intended to use for the construction of a 2,000-mile natural gas pipeline. It immediately became apparent that much of this equipment could simply be supplied by foreign subsidiaries of U.S. companies. Although the Reagan Administration attempted to control these exports as well, it was generally unsuccessful. ''As a result,'' one assessment found, ''it appears that the sanctions neither thwarted nor appreciably delayed construction of the Yamal pipeline.'' However, the pipeline embargo fiasco did sow deep seeds of discord within the Western alliance and further contributed to foreign perception of the U.S. as an unreliable trading partner, thereby costing us sales throughout the world.

In spite of this, many American conservatives continue to push for sanctions against the Soviet Union. However, they would do well to consider the possibility that such actions will strengthen, rather than weaken, the Soviets' aggressive tendencies. As George Ball argues,

> American sanctions are more likely to strengthen the aggressive tendencies in Soviet policy than to impel the leadership toward greater docility and arms reduction. If, as some in the Administration would wish, the

Western allies were to try through collective action to impose economic hardship on the Russians, the most likely effect would be to strengthen the military's hand in shaping Soviet policy. That would only heighten the danger of military adventurism.

Similarly, many conservatives applauded Pres. Reagan's imposition of trade sanctions against Nicaragua on May 1, 1985, despite evidence that sanctions are unlikely to cause the Nicaraguan government to alter its policies. Nevertheless, conservatives argued that sanctions were an important symbolic action. "I'd always opposed sanctions before," said Sen. Lloyd Bentsen (D.-Tex.), "but this time I thought at least sanctions would be an overt action we could take." Sen. Nancy L. Kassebaum (R.-Kans.) said, "I never believed sanctions will make a lot of difference. I just felt it was important to take an action that could be legally done and would show we're not going to carry on business as usual with the Sandinistas."

Perhaps the principal reason that sanctions will not have a major impact on Nicaragua is that no other nation in the world has participated in the embargo. Typical was the response of an Italian government official: "We are not going to participate in the boycott. We are not going to cut aid to a country that could otherwise go toward the Eastern bloc. We don't think the boycott is the way to put pressure on Nicaragua."

Nor were the sanctions really intended to be effective. From the beginning, the Reagan Administration gave wide latitude to companies with contracts for delivery to Nicaragua to honor those contracts. The sanctions were not accompanied by other diplomatic efforts, such as breaking relations, which would have buttressed the embargo effort. In any case, U.S. trade with Nicaragua is not very significant, the Sandinistas apparently having anticipated U.S. sanctions some years ago and reduced their dependence on U.S. trade accordingly.

Moreover, such trade is not heavily made up of what one might call essential commodities. According to the Commerce Department, U.S. exports to Nicaragua consist largely of insecticides, organic chemicals, paper products, hydrocarbons, vegetable oils, and animal fats and oils—hardly the sorts of things Nicaragua would have difficulty replacing on the open market. From the very beginning, therefore, the efficacy of the embargo was questioned by many commentators, including some conservatives such as William F. Buckley, Jr.

Six months after sanctions were imposed, *The New York Times* reported that "the embargo on United States trade with Nicaragua . . . has yet to result in more than a ripple in Nicaraguan economic activity." Canada and several European nations have replaced the U.S. as major buyers of Nicaraguan exports, and Nicaragua seems to have had no trouble getting the spare parts it cannot obtain from U.S. companies. Furthermore, the sanctions do seem to have pushed the Sandinistas even closer to Moscow; the Soviet Union promptly promised to supply practically all of Nicaragua's oil needs.

WILL SANCTIONS WORK IN SOUTH AFRICA?

Unfortunately, many of the people who point out the weaknesses of sanctions against Nicaragua and the Soviet Union reverse themselves on the question of sanctions against South Africa. When the Nicaragua sanctions were applied, for example, Rep. Don Bonker (D.-Wash.) said, "I fear that, when all is said and done, we will see as we have in the past that such actions are not effective when they are applied unilaterally." Rep. Michael D. Barnes (D.-Md.) called the sanctions against Nicaragua "ludicrous." Earlier, on the floor of Congress, Rep. Paul Simon (D.-Ill.) had criticized the embargo on grain shipments to the Soviet Union: "First, generally, the country that imposed the embargo shot themselves in the foot. And second, an embargo can be effective only if you have a monopoly on the product." Nevertheless, Bonker, Barnes, and Simon, along with many other Congressmen who in the past had voiced opposition to sanctions, supported sanctions against South Africa.

In any case, no matter how tight the sanctions eventually become against South Africa, they are unlikely to deny that country any essential commodities. As one South African economist recently put it, ''Given time, we can probably replace whatever we can't import''—a prediction that has some historical basis. Before the U.N. arms embargo was imposed in the early 1960's, South Africa was 60% dependent on foreign arms. Now, it is 90% self-sufficient, in many cases producing weapons under license from such countries as France and Israel. Similarly, South Africa has dealt with the embargo on oil exports by developing a synthetic fuels industry that manufactures oil and gas from abundant supplies of available coal.

Moreover, just because the U.S. honors an embargo does not mean that other countries will. As a 1984 Commerce Department report pointed out, past U.S. sanctions against South Africa led Europe and Japan to increase their marketing effort there, turning U.S. restrictions into strong selling points for their own manufacturers. The report also noted that U.S. controls have furthered South Africa's determination to achieve economic self-sufficiency and independence from any one foreign supplier. Thus, the U.S. share of South Africa's imports has fallen from over 19% in 1977 to a current level of less than 16%. Even more dramatically, South Africa has reduced the share of its imports from the European Common Market from about 53% in 1978 to about 38% today. These reductions are part of a significant overall reduction in South Africa's total imports, from $21,000,000,000 in 1981 to about $15,000,000,000 in 1984, thereby making South Africa less vulnerable to foreign trade embargoes.

Ironically, another important reason South Africa is unlikely to suffer too much from U.S. sanctions is because so many black African nations are expected to continue trading with it. Although no black African state will admit to trading with South Africa, many already do trade with it for simple economic reasons—whatever they may think of apartheid, South Africa is their best source of many commodities, credit, and services. For most African countries, to adhere strictly to an embargo on trade with South Africa would impose a far more severe burden on them than on South Africa. Indeed, there is evidence that the U.S. could also suffer badly from an all-encompassing trade embargo, owing to South Africa's position as a supplier of many critical strategic materials. According to a recent Commerce Department report, the U.S. obtains 61% of its cobalt, 55% of its chromium, 49% of its platinum, 44% of its vanadium, and 39% of its manganese from South Africa.

The more self-sufficient South Africa becomes, the less dependent it will be on any single country to supply it with goods, the less leverage the U.S. will have on the South African government, and the more strongly that government will be able to resist demands to end apartheid. As *The Economist* pointed out in August, 1985, ''The assumption that isolation would cause the Afrikaner electorate to alter its current policy of controlled political change in any fundamental way has no evidence to support it. The more sweeping the economic sanctions, the more self-sufficient South African industry would set out to become, and the more protectionist the government would be towards it.''

Hence, it has been a longstanding principle of U.S. policy not to push South Africa too far, lest it make the South African government even more intransigent. As early as 1963, the U.S. Ambassador to the U.N. Adlai E. Stevenson, spoke out against an arms embargo against South Africa: ''The application of sanctions in this situation is not likely to bring about the practical result that we seek. . . . Punitive measures would only provoke intransigence and harden the existing situation.'' More recently, in June, 1985, former Deputy Secretary of State Kenneth W. Dam told Congress, ''Sanctions . . . would be counterproductive: they are more likely to strengthen resistance to change than to strengthen the forces of reform.''

Why, then, is there such a clamor to impose sanctions on South Africa? The answer, as former Secretary of Defense James R. Schlesinger remarked with regard to the embargo on grain shipments to the Soviet Union, is that sanctions ''appeal to Americans because they seem to be a substitute for the stiffer measures that may be required.'' In short, they are a way of making ourselves feel that we are doing something substantive about a serious problem without really doing anything at all.

The problem is that we are paying a heavy price for invoking this "feel good" policy over and over again, currently for 11 different countries, Libya being the latest example. First, there is the question of effectiveness. Trade sanctions rarely achieve their purpose because the goods controlled are generally available from our trading partners. Clearly, the 25-year U.S. embargo on trade with Cuba has done little to curb that country's aggressive tendencies.

There are also the effects U.S. trade sanctions have on our own economy to consider. Because controls are often applied to preexisting contracts and foreign affiliates of U.S. firms, the President's Commission on Industrial Competitiveness noted in 1983, "we have created a reputation for American industry as an unreliable supplier." A recent report by the U.S. International Trade Commission shows that past agricultural embargoes have substantially reduced the U.S. market-share of major commodities and have given the U.S. a reputation as an unreliable trading partner. The President's Commission on Industrial Competitiveness concluded that foreign policy controls are costing the U.S. $4,700,000,000 per year in lost sales. Other studies confirm these huge losses, which are contributing to the growing U.S. trade deficit. Even the modest sanctions being imposed on South Africa are bound to add to the perception of U.S. unreliability and will possibly cost us billions of dollars more.

This does not suggest a do-nothing policy. It simply argues against the use of trade sanctions as an instrument of foreign policy. They seldom accomplish their purpose, but they do often exacerbate the problems they were supposed to correct, make the U.S. appear to be an unreliable trading partner, and cost us foreign sales in areas unrelated to the embargo—all of which translates into reduced exports and increasing unemployment.

Sanctions are hardly in keeping with the U.S.'s historic role as an international leader in the effort to preserve and extend free trade. This commitment to open world markets is worth preserving, even if it costs us an occasional chance to "punish" a government we disapprove of. Trade should not be viewed as a favor that a beneficent America bestows on other nations, but, rather, as a thoroughly practical policy that leads to international prosperity and a reduction in tensions. In any case, it is not the responsibility of the U.S. to punish Nicaragua for its moves toward totalitarianism or to punish South Africa for its racist policies, however much we deplore them.

QUESTIONS FOR DISCUSSION

1. What criteria should be used in evaluating whether economic sanctions have been successful?
2. Under what conditions should economic sanctions be used?
3. What are the alternatives to trade sanctions as a means of influencing a country's behavior? Are these alternatives less satisfactory than sanctions?
4. If sanctions are ineffective, why do states impose them? If they are effective, why don't states impose them more often?
5. What lessons can be learned from the sanctions against Iraq in 1990–1991?

SUGGESTED READINGS

Carter, Barry E. *International Economic Sanctions: Improving the Haphazard U.S. Legal Regime.* Cambridge, England: Cambridge Univ. Press, 1988.

Daoudi, M. S., and M. S. Dajani. *Economic Sanctions: Ideals and Experience.* London: Routledge and Kegan Paul, 1983.

Doxey, Margaret P. *International Sanctions in Contemporary Perspective.* New York: St. Martin's Press, 1987.

Ellings, Richard J. *Embargoes and World Power: Lessons from American Foreign Policy.* Boulder, Colo.: Westview Press, 1985.

Elliott, Kimberly Ann. ". . . And Sanctions Can Do the Trick." *New York Times*, Aug. 3, 1990, p. A27.

Hufbauer, Gary Clyde, Jeffrey J. Schott, and Kimberly Ann Elliott. *Economic Sanctions Reconsidered.* Washington, D.C.: Institute for International Economics, 1990.

Losman, Donald L. *International Economic Sanctions: The Cases of Cuba, Israel, and Rhodesia.* Albuquerque, N.M.: Univ. of New Mexico Press, 1979.

Marsh, Pearl-Alice. ''The Case for Economic Sanctions against South Africa.'' *World and I*, **5** (Feb. 1990), pp. 594–603.

Nossal, Kim Richard. ''International Sanctions as International Punishment.'' *International Organization*, **43** (Spring 1989), pp. 301–322.

Phillips, James A. ''Can the Embargo on Iraq Succeed?'' Backgrounder 789. Washington, D.C.: Heritage Foundation, 1990.

Shepherd, George W., Jr. (ed.). *Effective Sanctions on South Africa: The Cutting Edge of Economic Intervention*. New York: Praeger, 1990.

CHAPTER 5

Constraints on War

For practical and ethical reasons, states have sought to constrain the use of force through disarmament and arms control agreements, international law, diplomacy, and moral considerations. In the nineteenth and twentieth centuries in particular, states set up restrictions in the law of war—a practice that continues to the present. Military forces are not legally permitted, for example, to torture prisoners or deliberately harm innocent civilians, and the use of certain weapons in war has been made illegal.

Disarmament and arms control agreements have limited the kinds of weapons that can be employed. Disarmament is the abolition or reduction of armaments and armed forces; arms control is the regulation of armaments for the purpose of promoting stable relationships among potential adversaries. An example of disarmament is the Allied effort through the Versailles Treaty to reduce sharply the armed forces of Germany after World War I. An example of arms control is the agreement by the Soviet Union and the United States in 1972 to limit the number of antiballistic missile installations to two each.

International law, like arms control, may serve as a constraint on power. International law, developed in the past four centuries to regulate state behavior in a predictable and orderly manner, consists of principles and rules that states and other international entities feel bound to observe. Some of the essential areas of international law deal with the protection of diplomats, jurisdiction in disputes involving nationals of different countries, maritime law, and peaceful settlement of disputes.

Diplomacy is the art of peaceful negotiations among states. Diplomatic efforts involve government-to-government interactions in both state and multinational forums.

Moral considerations may limit the use of force. The British felt constrained to allow peaceful protests against British colonial rule in India rather than to execute independence activists. Evidence indicates that in the Cuban missile crisis of 1962 John Kennedy chose to quarantine Cuba by United States naval forces rather than to bomb Cuban missile sites because of moral considerations for Cuban lives.

The debates in Chapter 5 consider four topics involving constraints on war: the relevancy of international law, the influence of arms control, the control of nuclear proliferation, and the banning of chemical weapons.

INTERNATIONAL LAW

Unlike domestic law, international law has no overriding central authority that can enforce it. States, however, often feel bound to follow international law because it provides rules in an interdependent world.

When matters of vital concern to states arise, international law is less likely to be followed. When U.S. hostages were taken at the American Embassy in Teheran in 1979, for example, the United States went before the International Court of Justice in an effort to force the Iranian government to release the hostages. The Iranian revolutionary government refused to recognize the court's decision calling for the release of the hostages. When the United States was accused by Nicaragua of providing assistance to antigovernment rebels in mining Nicaraguan waters, the United States announced in 1984 that it would not recognize the authority of the International Court of Justice to deal with any matters concerning United States–Nicaragua relations for two years.

Is international law relevant to world politics? International lawyer John A. Perkins makes a case for its relevance. He argues: (1) International law remains as relevant to resolving conflicts among nations today as it has in the past. (2) International law is of great value in dealing with foreign intervention in the internal affairs of countries, arms control agreements, and the maintenance of the balance of power. (3) It is wrong to regard the preservation of international law as hostile to the national interest. (4) International law has developed more fully since the end of World War II than during other comparable periods.

Legal scholar Robert H. Bork challenges the relevancy of international law. He contends: (1) The principles of international law are often contradictory. (2) The major difficulty of international law is that it converts what are essentially problems of international morality, as defined by a particular political community, into arguments about law that are largely drained of morality. (3) International law will not tame the desires of aggressors; instead it imposes costs disproportionately on liberal, democractic nations. (4) There can be no authentic rule of law among nations until nations have a common political morality or are under a common sovereignty.

ARMS CONTROL

The regulation of armaments has been on the agenda of nations for centuries, but the nuclear age has made the subject more vital than ever. The world became a more dangerous place in the 1980s because of the increase in both nuclear and conventional weapons.

States have raised the level of defense expenditures for many reasons. (1) Foremost is the uncertainty of living in an international system in which states feel that they alone must provide for their security. (2) The character of technology is so rapidly changing that states must keep up with research and development of new weapons systems so as not to lose the advantages of their existing arsenals. (3) States have formed strategic doctrines that have required ever larger numbers of nuclear weapons. (4) States have been encouraged to increase defense spending by bureaucratic agencies charged with providing security and by interest groups that benefit from a big military establishment. In this regard, some observers point to a military-industrial complex composed of military officers who favor war for their promotion, politicians who support military action for their popularity and reelection, and private firms that depend on defense contracts.

The attempt to control nuclear weapons has involved not only the United States and the Soviet Union but other countries as well. The earliest effort to regulate nuclear weapons was the Baruch Plan, which called for the establishment of an international atomic agency with broad powers to inspect and monitor weapons systems and production facilities in all countries in the world.

The Soviet Union rejected this plan and called instead for the United States to turn over its weapons to an international agency. It insisted, however, that there be no compulsory inspection system. Neither the United States nor the Soviet Union trusted each other, and no substantial progress was made on arms control for years.

There have, however, been arms control successes, and these have taken different forms: test ban treaties, geographical disengagement, and nonproliferation.

With the widespread recognition that nuclear tests in the atmosphere posed dangers to health, a movement emerged in the 1950s to end the testing of nuclear weapons. In 1963 the United States, the Soviet Union, and other nations concluded the Partial Test Ban Treaty (PTBT, sometimes called the Limited Test Ban Treaty), which prohibits nuclear weapons tests or any other nuclear explosions in the atmosphere, in outer space, and under water. Underground tests were not covered by this agreement. Efforts to bring about a comprehensive test ban treaty in which all nuclear tests would be forbidden have been unsuccessful. The Soviet Union and the United States signed a Threshold Test Ban Treaty (1974), which establishes a nuclear ''threshold'' by prohibiting tests having a yield exceeding 150 kilotons, and a Partial Nuclear Explosion Treaty (1976), which permits nuclear explosions for digging canals and in other nonmilitary projects, but these treaties were never ratified by the United States.

In addition to test bans, a geographical approach to arms control was adopted in the postwar period. The principle of geographic disengagement places certain regions off limits for the storage or testing of nuclear weapons. The Antarctica Treaty (1961) prohibits nuclear explosions and the disposal of radioactive wastes in Antarctica. The Outer Space Treaty (1972) mandates that no signatory place nuclear or any other weapons of mass destruction in orbit around the earth, install them on the moon or any other celestial body, or otherwise station them in outer space. The Seabed Treaty (1972) prohibits parties from emplacing nuclear weapons or other weapons of mass destruction on the seabed and the ocean floor beyond a twelve-mile coastal zone. The Treaty for the Prohibition of Nuclear Weapons in Latin America (1967), known as the Treaty of Tlatelolco, prevents the introduction of nuclear weapons into areas of Latin America hitherto free from them.

Some arms control proposals with a geographical approach have been put forward that have not been adopted. In 1958 the Polish foreign minister, Adam Rapacki, suggested that Central Europe become a denuclearized zone. Other advocates of arms control have suggested nuclear-free zones for the Middle East and for Africa.

Another approach to arms control deals with nonproliferation, the topic of Debate 19.

Arms control is popular in many countries, and many international arms control agreements have been concluded. In spite of its popular appeal, a lingering question remains: Do arms control agreements serve as a constraint on war? The Arms Control Association argues that arms control is beneficial to the cause of peace. It contends: (1) Arms control can promote military stability and predictability, consequently strengthening the security of participating parties. (2) It can reduce the risk of nuclear war or military confrontation in a crisis. (3) It can prevent or slow down the proliferation of nuclear weapons to other nations. (4) It can improve political relations. (5) It can reduce the destructiveness of war should nuclear war break out. (6) It can reduce the economic burden of military forces.

Historian Michael Howard contends that arms control is based on four illusions. He takes issue with those who argue that: (1) Arms races build up to war; arms reductions logically lead to peace. (2) Arms reductions would make war less destructive if it came. (3) The application of science and technology to the development of weapon systems is in itself a threat to peace and should be inhibited. (4) Arms control provides an alternative to armament as a means of ensuring international security. Howard concludes that armaments are about deterrence and arms control about reassurance. In his view security is achieved by a synthesis of the two.

NONPROLIFERATION TREATY

Because nuclear-weapons states (NWS) and nonnuclear-weapons states (NNWS) were concerned about the proliferation of nuclear weapons, the Nonproliferation Treaty (NPT) was concluded in 1968. It has three goals: (1) to prevent the further spread of nuclear explosives. (2) to foster the peaceful uses of nuclear energy, and (3) to encourage good-faith negotiations to end the nuclear arms race. The principal terms of the treaty require the NNWS that ratified the treaty not to produce nuclear weapons. The NPT also had as a major objective a commitment by the NWS to reduce their nuclear-weapons arsenals, and the United States and the Soviet Union consequently agreed to enter into negotiations on the matter.

The NPT had many loopholes. Not all states signed or ratified the treaty although today 140 countries have accepted it. The most notable nonsignatories are Argentina, Brazil, India, Israel, Pakistan, and South Africa. The treaty did not cover peaceful nuclear explosions, nor did it prevent building everything necessary for a nuclear weapon except the last pin. States, moreover, could withdraw from the treaty with three-months' notice if they found that extraordinary events jeopardized their supreme interests.

Still, both NWS and NNWS have heeded its provisions. Spurred on by the pressure of the small powers, voices for arms control within the United States and the Soviet Union, and a realization that nuclear forces were becoming so large that the security of both sides was threatened, the two superpowers entered into negotiations to limit the size of their strategic nuclear forces.

They have concluded a number of arms control agreements, including the Strategic Arms Limitation Treaty of 1972, which set limits for strategic weapons to which the superpowers would adhere. Since the Reagan administration, the superpowers have engaged in the Strategic Arms Reduction Talks (START). In July 1991, the two countries reached agreement on a START treaty.

The NPT is designed to control vertical nuclear proliferation (the strengthening of nuclear weapons arsenals by the states already possessing nuclear weapons), and horizontal nuclear proliferation (the spread of nuclear weapons to countries that do not have them). Progress of the superpowers in controlling vertical nuclear proliferation, which continued since the United States and the Soviet Union acquired nuclear weapons, has been slow. As mentioned in Chapter 1, NWS in addition to the superpowers include France, Great Britain, and the People's Republic of China. India tested a nuclear warhead in 1974 that it described as a peaceful nuclear explosion. Israel is believed to have nuclear weapons. Pakistan and South Africa are thought to be close to producing such weapons. Iraq sought nuclear weapons, too. A number of other countries have the technology and know-how to develop and produce such weapons, and some may be quietly moving in that direction—a process that one commentator, Leonard S. Spector, refers to as the "silent spread."[1]

Governments decided to build nuclear weapons primarily because of security concerns, bureaucratic pressures, and economic interests. Some governments felt that in the final analysis they could rely only on their own military forces to protect vital interests. Particularly as intercontinental delivery systems became available in abundance to the superpowers, the leaders of many other countries believed that security guarantees by the superpowers had lost their credibility.

Bureaucratic pressures encouraged states to become NWS. Once a government organization was formed that was concerned with nuclear energy, it seemed natural for it to expand its interests to include a nuclear-weapons field.

Economic forces played a role, too, as economic interests benefit from weapons development and production. Moreover nuclear energy is also a vital source of energy for many energy-hungry countries. The same technology that is designed to produce enriched uranium and plutonium necessary to build nuclear weapons also serves peaceful nuclear-energy needs. As the price of oil soared after 1973, countries relied more and more on nuclear energy as a way to become less dependent on the Organization of Petroleum Exporting Countries (OPEC).

Even before 1973, however, countries had sought nuclear reactors for their energy programs. Although many of these reactors were supposed to be under international inspection so that no enriched uranium or plutonium could be diverted for military purposes, there was much doubt about the effectiveness of inspection measures to prevent such diversion. Business organizations in France, the Federal Republic of Germany, and the United States sought contracts in other countries to build nuclear reprocessing plants in NNWS such as Brazil and South Korea. Although ostensibly for nonmilitary purposes, the plants could produce weapons-grade material.

---

[1] Leonard S. Spector, "Silent Spread," *Foreign Policy*, no. 58 (Spring 1985), pp. 53–78.

Both superpowers helped NNWS to become NWS. The United States shared its information with Great Britain. The "special relationship" of close historic collaboration between Great Britain and the United States served to irritate leaders of other countries allied to the United States—most notably France. For a short time, moreover, the Soviet Union aided China in its efforts to become a NWS.

Is the Nonproliferation Treaty effective? Former U.S. arms control negotiator Lewis A. Dunn argues that the NPT should be retained. He contends: (1) The treaty has helped prevent the spread of nuclear weapons. (2) It has provided a framework for peaceful nuclear use. (3) Much progress has been made in international arms control agreements. (4) The NPT reflects a carefully negotiated balancing of obligations between non-nuclear-weapons states and the nuclear-weapons states and, consequently, should be neither terminated nor amended.

Political scientist Ashok Kapur calls for a scuttling of the treaty. He contends: (1) The treaty's beneficiaries are the five major nuclear powers. (2) Would-be nuclear-weapons states—Israel, India, Argentina, and others—are on the rise in regional and international influence and have not been impeded by the NPT. (3) The NPT ignores the major factors for the proliferation of nuclear weapons: the costs of modern arms, strategic needs for nuclear arms or a nuclear-weapons option, and unwillingness to accept permanent technological and legal inferiority. (4) The treaty contains irreparable defects: (a) it appeared too late since some nations were already on the nuclear path; (b) the superpowers never seriously intended to disarm; (c) the treaty has too many loopholes on its list of suspect items; (d) there is no enforcement mechanism in the treaty or in the hands of the International Atomic Energy Agency. (5) Staying outside the NPT does not appear to diminish a country's security.

CHEMICAL WEAPONS TREATY

When more than 400,000 U.S. forces were deployed in the Persian Gulf for possible use against Iraq in 1990, one of the principal concerns of Americans was that the Iraqis would use chemical weapons and so cause enormous loss of American life. Iraq had in fact used chemical weapons in the 1980s—against a "human wave" assault by its Iranian enemies in the Iran-Iraq War and against its own Kurdish population. That use was effective in achieving Iraqi goals.

There was little doubt that Iraqi leader Saddam Hussein would use such weapons if he had to. In fact, the fears that chemical weapons will be used have become a major concern for those decision makers involved in national security matters. By 1991, some estimates indicate that thirteen countries have chemical weapons, including Iran, Iraq, Syria, Israel, Ethiopia, and Libya.

Although attention today is focused on third world chemical weapon states, the use of modern chemical weapons originated with Europeans. During World War I, chlorine and mustard gas killed nearly 100,000 people and injured almost 1 million more. After the war, European powers stockpiled chemical weapons, fearing that they would be used again. In World War II, however, they were not used in Europe, although there were some reports that Japan used chemical weapons against China.

Attempts to impose legal controls on chemical weapons originated nearly a century ago. The Hague Declaration of 1899 prohibited projectiles designed to diffuse poison gas. When using chemical weapons in World War I, Germany contended that it had complied with the declaration because it released chlorine from cylinders and not projectiles. In 1925, many countries adopted the Geneva Protocol, which banned the use of poisonous gas and biological weapons. The protocol did not ban the manufacture and stockpiling of such weapons, however.

Because of the use of chemical weapons in the Middle East and because of the increasing number of countries producing these weapons today, some countries have sought to ban chemical weapons completely—not only actual use but manufacturing and stockpiling as well. These countries met in Paris in 1989 to work out a convention that would be acceptable to most countries.

Other countries do not want a ban. They claim they need the weapons because hostile countries already have such weapons. Still others point to the problems of verification and inspection, which are far more difficult than for nuclear weapons.

Some commentators regard chemical weapons as legitimate, especially for small powers that cannot afford to build a nuclear arsenal. To these countries chemical weapons are "the poor man's atom bomb," for they are relatively cheap to produce. These observers say that chemical weapons are no less indiscriminate than nuclear weapons and offer security to those states that otherwise could not afford it.

Should chemical weapons be banned? George Shultz, secretary of state in the Reagan administration, argues that a treaty banning chemical weapons should be adopted. Speaking at the Conference on the Prohibition of Chemical Weapons in 1989, he contends: (1) Chemical weapons are so devastating to civilian and military targets that they should be banned. (2) In recent years the international norms against chemical weapons use have begun to erode in practice. (3) New technology and the ability of some states to produce ballistic missiles make chemical warfare even more dangerous. (4) Although there are verification problems in dealing with chemical weapons, the world community should take steps to assure not only that such weapons be banned but also that the proliferation of the weapons to other states and terrorist groups be stopped.

Frank J. Gaffney, Jr., director of the Center for Security Policy, argues that chemical weapons cannot be abolished. He contends: (1) There is no certain way to distinguish between legitimate facilities producing a range of chemical products for civilian use and those producing weapons. (2) The industrialized world's companies, banks, and governments are fostering the spread throughout the developing world of indigenous infrastructures with the inherent capability to produce chemical weapons. (3) A plant producing commercial chemical products could readily be converted to the production of chemical weapons. (4) It is difficult to get international agreement that a given activity is related to chemical weapons manufacture. (5) Chemical weapons are a fact of life since they can be produced cheaply and easily. (6) Because of the factors mentioned, a treaty banning production and stockpiling of chemical weapons is futile. Gaffney favors the imposition of sanctions on countries that sell or buy such weapons rather than a treaty ban.

17 Is International Law Relevant to World Politics?

YES

John A. Perkins

The Relevance of International Law

NO

Robert H. Bork

The Limits of "International Law"

The Relevance of International Law

John A. Perkins

Professor Oscar Schachter of Columbia University School of Law, in addressing a convocation at Pace University School of Law, said of the concepts of just war and human rights that these conceptions have a prominent place in international law as well as in other thought:

> They are, above all, ideas that have powerfully influenced human conduct and continue to do so. Countless persons have died in wars proclaimed as just. Many others have given their lives in the cause of human rights which they considered more important than life itself. No, these are not academic topics, abstract as they seem and however learned the discussions about them. They are ideas that almost certainly will have an impact on your own lives (even more, I venture to suggest, than product liability or corporate buy-outs). The United States has been in four major wars during my life; in each one, ideas of justice and human rights were used to justify the wars and their human sacrifices. I am far from sure that they will be the last wars in which one or both of these ideas will have an impact.

International law, in dealing with the conduct of nations and relations between them, addresses just such issues in many contexts. It addresses issues involving the most deeply felt aspirations and passionately held rights of peoples. It addresses issues that are involved in areas of dangerous conflict between nations. In this sense no kind of law could be more relevant. However, the notion that international law has any realistic role in dealing with issues of serious contention between nations has been out of favor since the Iron Curtain and the Cold War

numbed the hopes and aspirations that marked the end of World War II. It may fairly and cogently be contended that the failure to look to international law exacerbated and prolonged those troubled times. That is not an issue to be dealt with here. Rather the focus here is on the present and the future.

We are again in a period of dramatic change in international relations, requiring even those for whom there was nothing beyond the Cold War to look anew at the insights of international experience reflected in international law. If new occasions teach new duties, as James Russell Lowell wrote, so also they may reteach old lessons.

NEW CONTEXTS FOR OLD ISSUES

International law brings clearly into focus a role that all law plays, the resolution of conflict according to rules that can be accepted as justifiable by all concerned. It has been well said that: "International law, like law in general, has the object of assuring the coexistence of different interests which are worthy of legal protection." (Palmas Island Arbitration, quoted in Sir Hersh Lauterpacht's classic book, *The Function of Law in the International Community*, 1933.) Events are demonstrating in several contexts the continuing validity of this role of law in the resolution of conflict.

If the prospect for resolving some of the world's persistent regional conflicts seems to be upon us, what has become the basis of that resolution? Where interests of the superpowers are perceived to be in conflict, in Afghanistan, in Angola, and in Nicaragua, the key to resolution, *mirabile dictu*, turns out to be withdrawal of all external forces and reciprocal abstention from military involvement or supply of arms to any of the parties to the internal conflict. For international lawyers this is not news. It is the principle of nonintervention as it is coming to be understood.

A primary rationale of the internal law prohibition against intervention by force or other coercion is, of course, to protect the right of the people to self-determination. As a rule of reciprocal restraint it is also a recognition of the fact that if intervention on

Source: John A. Perkins, "The Relevance of International Law," *Boston Bar Journal*, **34** (January/February 1990), pp. 4–7. Reprinted by permission.

behalf of one side is permitted, intervention on the other side is inevitable, resulting in an escalation of action, response, and counterresponse that risks confrontation between the superpowers in local contests everywhere. Aid to a government for other purposes may be entirely legitimate. Where self-determination implications are not involved it is not intervention and is permitted, but in the emerging international law something approaching a consensus exists that in cases of genuine civil conflict third states may not legally supply arms to either side, except, within limitations governing countermeasures, to redress a violation by another state.

Faced with the unwinding of interventions that have already occurred, it becomes clear that implementation of the rule of nonintervention will often require something more than withdrawal. If withdrawal, even reciprocal withdrawal where action and response by competing outside states is involved, allows either side in the local conflict to preserve an advantage gained from the involvement of outsiders, the result may be to vindicate the offense rather than to nullify it. This is apparent in the conflicts in Afghanistan, Angola, and Nicaragua, and the concerns seem implicit in U.S. policy as well as in United Nations actions. In these circumstances implementation of the rule of nonintervention requires an opportunity for a free, open and controlling act of self-determination.

Nowhere is this process complete, but the political logic of law is reflected in events. In Central America the agreement of the Central American presidents of August 7, 1987, expanded by their further agreement in February 1989, reflects in part this need for an unequivocal act of self-determination in its focus on the conduct of the elections to be held in Nicaragua on February 25, 1990. (*New York Times*, Feb. 16, 1989, A14.) The importance attached to the election as a matter of international concern is evidenced in the arrangements already made and activated for monitoring of the entire election process by observer teams established by the United Nations and the Organization of American States. (*New York Times*, Oct. 2, 1989, A10.)

The ideas inherent in the principle of nonintervention have been at the root of the historic role of United States leadership in world affairs. The rule of nonintervention is a rule to protect the political independence of states against domination and coercion by force or other means. Our commitment to this aspiration of all peoples has been and continues to be the foundation for active, effective U.S. leadership.

International law is also coming to the fore in another context. The prospect of significant progress in negotiating further reductions in nuclear and nonnuclear arms brings concerns of international law into focus. Arms control, we begin to understand, is not simply a matter of working out highly complex and technical limitations on highly complex and technical weaponry to balance overkill on both sides and to avoid a breakaway arms race. The significant reductions in long range missiles and in conventional weapons now under negotiation and, indeed, the further reductions to levels of minimum deterrence, which both sides are trying to think through, require a return to issues that have always been the focus of international law. In a world of independent nation states, how can the peace be maintained?

Without an acceptance of the fundamental rules of international law as binding, how can the major powers carry forward the process of arms reduction to a point where arms no longer threaten the extinction of the human race? The rules limiting the use of force, asserting the right of self-determination of all peoples and the sovereign equality of states, prohibiting acts to coerce states in the exercise of their sovereignty are the essence of the order, which has to be the premise for a nuclear-safe world.

Arms reduction brings these issues into focus in several ways. Nuclear arms have provided a kind of umbrella, albeit at unacceptable risk, against direct warfare between major powers. Minimum deterrence is by definition intended to provide sufficient deterrence to continue this umbrella, but if it reduces the penalty for an unsuccessful first strike, it may also increase the acceptability of taking the risk. Moreover, with the nuclear powers possessing drastically reduced stocks of nuclear weapons, the problem of nuclear proliferation takes on a new face.

The risk of a lesser power that has nuclear weapons holding others hostage in a mad scheme of defiance looms. For these and other reasons, successful nuclear arms negotiations to bring arms to minimum deterrence levels will have to put a higher than ever priority on a world in which the order of international law will be assured.

On still another issue events have brought new perspectives on the role of international law. Governments rightly recognize that considerations of national security dictate a concern to protect a global and regional balance of power. Perhaps the high cost and frustration of the U.S. experience in Vietnam and the Soviet adventure in Afghanistan are stimulating second thoughts on how this works.

The political climate in which major powers could with impunity dominate subservient peoples for their own strategic advantage began to change after World War I. After World War II irreversible forces were put in motion reflected in the United Nations Charter. Within ten years after the unanimous adoption in 1960 of General Assembly Resolution 1514, calling for implementation of a right to independence for so-called non-self-governing territories, the colonial era was all but ended, overwhelming even the resistance of powerful, reluctant colonial powers.

In the post–World War II political and legal environment, balance of power as a concept took on a new meaning, and protecting the balance of power called for a new geopolitical strategy. A balance of power was as essential as ever; ultimately the freedom of all nations may depend on it. But the ancient game assuring, often manipulating, the balance of power through the domination of others became a route that the realities of world politics almost always precluded as a viable, achievable option.

In this new environment the strategy for assuring a balance of power was in fact turned on its head. The balance of power was effectively protected not by attempted domination of countries believed to be essential components of one's own side of the balance but by protecting the independence of countries. In the real world, even for the superpowers themselves, protection against hegemonic designs of other superpowers lies in the secure independence of states.

Many years ago Eugene V. Rostow attempted to define the balance of power for post–World War II conditions in these terms:

> I should put it this way: equilibrium, and therefore the possibility of detente, requires mutual understanding that neither side should attempt to change the frontiers of the system by force or by the threat of force. For such attempts, unlike certain other forms of change, threaten the general world equilibrium, and therefore risk a confrontation between great powers and world war.

A policy to maintain a balance of power has to be one of preserving it against change by force or the threat of force, or, I would add, any other coercive interference with the right of self-determination.

Even for the Soviets, who no doubt once thought they could act effectively against world opinion and against the aspirations of peoples within the Communist bloc for real independence, the strategy of protecting power through domination is now unraveling in Eastern Europe. It is a process they even abet, perhaps in the light of a belated understanding of the kind of role effective leadership calls for in the world today. The fragility of the order they once constructed is, in any event, a timely reminder of the geopolitical cogency of the international order upon which international law is founded.

HOW WE GOT TO PRINCIPLES

That the generalized principles of international law are highly relevent to the concerns and interests of states should not be surprising, for paradoxical as it may seem, principles of international law arise not out of ivory tower theories but out of the assertions of states, often in the formulation of foreign policy positions in terms designed to gain acquiescence by others. The formation of international law has been a process of such assertion and acquiescence, leading to reiteration and reformulation in other situations over time, gaining in the process moral force and power as emerging law and finally general acceptance as binding law.

Two examples will illustrate. No doubt the term "self-determination" was unknown to President Monroe, but the Monroe Doctrine was more than a naked assertion that the United States would consider any attempt by European powers to "extend their system to any portion of this hemisphere as dangerous to our peace and safety." Principled grounds were stated for the U.S. to assert its power, declaring:

> With the existing colonies or dependencies of any European power we have not interfered and shall not interfere. But with the governments who have declared their independence and maintained it, and whose independence we have, on great consideration and on just principles, acknowledged, we could not view any interposition for the purpose of oppressing them or controlling in any other manner their destiny, by any European power, in any other light than as the manifestation of an unfriendly disposition toward the United States.

The corollary to the right of self-determination is a principle of nonintervention. In fortifying the position of President Cleveland in demanding under the Monroe Doctrine that Britain agree to arbitrate its dispute with Venezuela over the boundary between British Guiana and Venezuela, Secretary Olney carefully delineated the limitations of the Monroe Doctrine to Britain's foreign minister, Lord Salisbury, stating:

> It does not establish any general protectorate by the United States over other American states. It does not relieve any American state from its obligations as fixed by international law nor prevent any European power directly interested from enforcing such obligations or from inflicting merited punishment for the breach of them. It does not contemplate any interference in the internal affairs of any American states. It does not justify any attempt on our part to change the established form of government of any American state or to prevent the people of such state from altering that form according to their own will and pleasure. The rule in question has but a single purpose and object. It is that no European power or combination of European powers shall forcibly deprive an American state of the right and power of self-government and of shaping for itself its own political fortunes and destinies.

> That the rule thus defined has been the accepted public law of this country since its promulgation can not fairly be denied.

If the United States later waffled on these limitations in the era of gunboat diplomacy, as it clearly did, the need to reiterate the rhetoric of nonintervention persisted. Indeed, the concerns raised by our aberrations only served to create pressures that led the U.S. finally to accept an unequivocally stated nonintervention norm by binding treaty in the Montevideo Convention of 1933.

In a similar way the legal prohibition in Article 2(4) of the United Nations Charter against the "threat or use of force against the territorial integrity or political independence of any state, or in any other manner inconsistent with the Purposes of the United Nations" and the earlier renunciation of war "as an instrument of national policy" in the Kellogg-Briand Pact of 1928 grew out of painful experience. World War I and World War II demonstrated that sooner or later the use of force as an instrument of national policy by a major power is likely to so endanger the world's balance and the kind of world in which free institutions can prosper as to involve even a reluctant United States in war.

Our stake in a legal regime for the limitation of force is no less today, when the use of force has the potential to escalate into a nuclear disaster. Our stake is in a legal regime that not only limits the use of force but also permits the use of force under law, limited by law and in support of law, to address an offender's violation when other effective recourse is not available.

WHY LAWYERS HAVE A ROLE

If law is to serve its role of providing the fabric for a just and peaceful international order, there will need to be a deeper understanding of the functioning of law than now exists. The lack of this understanding is evident in many ways.

There is widespread skepticism about the role of law in international affairs. We read it and hear it in various forms. Some see law only as imposing restraints against interest and not as itself an objective of policy. Some, seeing international law as lacking the enforcement systems available for domestic law, treat it as no more than lofty aspirations for a nonexistent ideal world. There has been almost a cult of ''sophisticated'' thinking that looks to short-term calculations of risk or advantage as all that matters. It is a mind-set that focuses on the wisdom that nations have only interests, that results are what count.

Irving Kristol expressed some of this in an article in the *New York Times Magazine* (June 14, 1987, volume 31, at page 53), trumpeting:

> In the area of foreign policy, the spectrum of discourse has shifted so decisively to the right that whole portions of the liberal vocabulary have, to all intents and purposes, been forgotten. Who today looks on the United Nations and other such international organizations as reliable instruments of American foreign policy? Who seriously declaims on the virtues of ''international law'' among a ''world community of nations'' as a relevant solution to American foreign-policy problems? The entire outlook once designated as ''liberal internationalism'' is a shambles, even NATO coming under critical scrutiny. Our State Department is still committed to its outlook, but everyone else now talks about our ''national interest.'' It is the conception of our ''national interest'' that sets the terms for all our debates on foreign policy.

From the low estate to which one might conclude international law has fallen it might seem that it is law, not war, that is to be renounced as an instrument of national policy.

For the point is that international law is in the national interest. Cold War chills provided reason for some solemn soul-searching as to whether the effort to build a world order under law could succeed. There is no reason for that soul searching to lead to the dead-end conclusion that international law is inane and irrelevant. Rather, it should lead to understanding that international law has to be viable for the kind of world that it has to confront. This is the age of Angola, Ethiopia, Afghanistan, El Salvador, Nicaragua, Lebanon, and Grenada. Realism dictates that in a world made up of separate nation-states we must be prepared to face the omnipresent risk, if not

the crisis reality, that some states will be prepared to advance what they perceive to be their strategic advantage however they think they can. International law has to be viable for that kind of world.

Many of those who reject international law as softheaded have a concept of international law and how it works that does not grant much to the statesmen and practical-minded men and women in and out of government who have devoted their efforts to build a safer, more just world under law. No, the way to international law is *not* by unilateral disarmament. No, international law does *not* mean giving up effective means of dealing with violations by self-defense and other self-help measures under law, when other effective recourse is not available. No, international law does *not* require the U.S. to rest its national security on the moral power of a good example, or on the willingness of the nations of the world to accept the compulsory jurisdiction of the International Court of Justice or to abide by its judgments. We can protect ourselves as we go forward, while even now, as pointed out in the first section of this paper, international law provides the key for solutions or at least for progress on immediate pressing issues.

A more serious problem for the future than extremist rhetoric about international law is concern that the foreign-policy decision-making process is being impaired by an unrealistic and unnecessary dichotomy separating the disciplines of international law and international relations, with the result that important policy insights reflected in emerging international law are overlooked or even excluded.

International lawyers are addressing policy issues highly relevant to foreign policy, but by and large this thinking is not brought to bear in the shaping of day to day, country by country, area by area foreign-policy decisions. Important foreign-policy perspectives of international law are being ignored in much of foreign-policy decision-making.

At the same time international relations has developed as an almost separate discipline, built on a concentration on specifics, especially the specifics of arms and defense policy, political and economic developments, current policies of governments, friends, and enemies. Expertise is measured by the monitoring of events and developments in detail, and international law is shunned as a discipline unrelated to the hard choices that have to be made. There seems to be an underlying assumption that a scientific expertise for decision-making has to disregard the policy insights and perspectives of international law.

This dichotomy is perhaps itself a product of the era of Cold War. It has been a time in which the public dialogue on foreign policy has been concentrated on ideology, while in the back rooms the focus is on realpolitik. The urgent task of building the foundations for a survivable, peaceful world seems to be quietly elbowed off the public agenda.

Facing a future of unparalleled risk, it is unacceptable to set aside the long-standing effort to build an international order under law. We cannot afford to ignore policy insights of international law capable of getting us beyond a world of irreconcilable conflict, a world held back from war only by a precarious nuclear standoff.

Despite the apparent low estate of law in international affairs, the years since World War II have in fact been years of greater development in international law than has ever occurred in a comparable period of time. And now extraordinary developments in Soviet policy in unwinding the policies of the Cold War and pressing in significant ways for strengthening the principles and institutions of international law bring us to opportunities we cannot afford to neglect.

If it is ironic that the articulation of this opportunity comes from Mr. Gorbachev, it is nonetheless a time for U.S. leadership, and it is a time for lawyers to become a part of the process of returning the United States to its historic role in moving the world toward an order built on the rule of law.

We have only to recall the roles, among others, of Elihu Root, Charles Evans Hughes, Frank B. Kellogg, and Henry L. Stimson to recognize the important role American lawyers have played in advancing the rule of law. It is a role that American lawyers must once again take up in earnest. For it is lawyers first and foremost who understand the problem solving, conflict resolving, peace building capacities of law. It is lawyers who best understand that only equal justice under law can bring order and peace to the world.

THE LIMITS OF "INTERNATIONAL LAW"

Robert H. Bork

On October 25, 1983, armed forces of the United States invaded Grenada. President Reagan at once stated that our purpose was not only to protect Americans there but to "help in the restoration of democratic institutions" in a country where "a brutal group of leftist thugs violently seized power." Both the President and Secretary of State George P. Shultz said the operation was fully consistent with international law.

Senator Daniel Patrick Moynihan disagreed: "I don't know that you restore democracy at the point of a bayonet." He said we had clearly violated international law. (Moynihan is the public official who most persistently invokes this law and his views deserve attention.) Soon, Harvard law professor Abram Chayes, who had served as legal adviser to the State Department in the Kennedy administration, wrote in the *New York Times* that among international law experts there existed "remarkably broad agreement that the United States' invasion was a flagrant violation of international law." On the same page, Eugene V. Rostow, a professor and former dean of the Yale Law School, wrote that "the American and allied campaign in Grenada is legitimized by classic precedents in international law, notably the Cuban missile crisis of 1962."

The American public, to the degree that it paid any attention, must have been quite mystified. High public officials and an undefined group of "experts in international law" were bitterly divided over the legality of what the United States had done. The pattern is familiar. Whenever an American President uses or subsidizes force against another country, the halls of Congress resound and the pages of newspapers sizzle with pronouncements by his political opponents (and his allies) that he is (and is not) a lawbreaker. Some months later articles arguing both sides appear in scholarly journals. Since the public is assured that there is a law of nations but have no idea what it is, they are almost certain to come away with the impression that, according to a substantial segment of informed opinion, the United States is a habitual lawbreaker. Indeed, the U.S. appears to be a recidivist. That is no small matter. People who deliberately break known laws are immoral. So it must be with nations. Or must it? The word "law" is a capacious one and before we accept a sense of guilt it would be well to inquire further.

What, exactly, is international law? Is it law at all? What purposes does it serve?

In some of its branches, it is law in a conventional sense. If two nations dispute fishing rights in the sea under a treaty, they may submit the matter to an international tribunal and agree to abide by the decision. In addition, there are international conventions, some of long standing, that govern the treatment of prisoners of war, of diplomats, of the rights of neutrals, etc. But that is not the kind of international law about which politicians and scholars grow passionate.

In its grandest (or most grandiose) form, international law is about the use or support of armed force against another nation. Concerning that subject, there are a great many statements of principle that *purport* to be law. They may be found, for example, in the Charter of the United Nations, in the Charter of the Organization of American States, in any number of bilateral and multilateral treaties, and in custom. The rules of customary law, indeed, supposedly derived from the actual practices of nations, are said to be just as binding as any charter.

Most people find this rather perplexing. Nations regularly act in ways that, we are assured by politicians and scholars, constitute clear violations of international law . . . and nothing happens. No police

Source: Robert H. Bork, "The Limits of International Law," *National Interest*, no. 18 (Winter 1989/1990), pp. 3–10. Reprinted with the permission of *The National Interest* © Winter 1989/90, no. 18, *The National Interest*, Washington, D.C.

force goes into action, no grand jury indicts, no petit jury sits, no verdict is announced by a court or, if one is, the convicted party ignores it. Articles and books gradually appear contending vociferously, and sometimes learnedly, that there was, or that there was not, a law violation. What can it mean to say that rules like that are in some sense, in any sense, "law"?

Senator Moynihan has no doubts on that subject: "International law *exists*. It is not an option. It is a fact." Others are less sure; and it is not merely laymen who feel unease. Treatises on international law commonly open by addressing the question whether the subject contains much that can properly be called "law." Most writers seem a touch defensive, but they assure the reader that there is "law" there. Yet the explanations themselves tend to be more than a trifle elusive and often romantic. A very prominent international lawyer, Philip Jessup, once offered an argument better than most:

> The layman and the common lawyer who find it difficult to fit international law into their concept of "law" . . . usually are alike in asserting that there isn't any international law. They forget that law has many meanings. There is the law of gravity, the Sherman Anti-Trust law, the law of supply and demand, international law.

The passage confuses rather than clarifies. The law of gravity describes a force in the natural universe. The law of supply and demand is an observation about human behavior in markets. One who attempts levitation or tries to purchase more than anyone is willing to sell at a particular price would not be called a law violator. The Sherman Act is a rule made by a legislature with conceded political authority and is enforced by courts through damages, fines, and even imprisonment. The fact that all of these things are called "laws" demonstrates only that the word has been applied to things that have little or nothing in common.

Professor Michael Reisman of Yale notes that "Law is perforce a system of authorized coercion, and it can neither be conceived of nor operate without a supportive political system or power process.

In the absence of a centralization of authoritative force and an effective monopoly over who can use it to maintain community order and values, individual actors must look to their own resources." Jessup recognized this problem but tried nonetheless to edge international law closer to the Sherman Act:

> In most cases the layman is impressed by the reality of breaches of international law and is not sufficiently aware of the reality of reliance upon it. He does not pause to wonder why foreign offices bother to maintain legal staffs, which are an expense and sometimes a hindrance to the execution of policy.

But the existence of legal staffs poring over issues of international law proves little about a law relating to international violence. Thousands of mundane commercial and political matters arise in international settings, where the meaning of "international law" is itself not a focus of controversy. But so long as there purports to be international law *about the use of force*, the most cynical and predatory government will employ a legal staff to engage in international "shystering" as the need arises. Jessup finally resorted to the argument that, since people called international lawyers are doing something, what they are doing must be international law:

> Impotent to restrain a great nation which has no decent respect for the opinion of mankind, failing in its severest test of serving as a substitute for war, international law plods on its way, followed automatically in routine affairs, invoked, flouted, codified, flouted again but yet again invoked. The Legal Adviser of the United States Department of State still sits at his desk . . . in Washington and his counterparts sit at Downing Street, the Quai d'Orsay and the Wilhelmstrasse. It is not their task to frame policies. But can one say that the international law with which they deal has no reality?

In January of 1940, when Jessup's article appeared, one might have been inclined to say precisely that. One might have said it scores or hundreds of times since. The Soviets used force to crush movements toward freedom in Hungary, Czechoslovakia, and East Germany, and to seize Afghanistan. But it is not just a great power such as the Soviet Union that is immune to the blandishments of international law.

Cuba and Nicaragua have armed and supported insurgency movements attempting to destroy democratic governments in Central America. China overran Tibet, India seized the Portuguese colony of Goa. The least one can say is that, in such cases, whatever reality this wraith called international law possesses is not visible to the non-expert.

This is not to deny that the *idea* of international law has real-world effects. It does. To see what those effects are, it is helpful to examine a pair of recent instances in which actions of the United States raised issues of international law. Two of the most spectacular such examples were the invasion of Grenada and our support of contra forces fighting the Sandinista regime in Nicaragua. The relevant facts cannot reasonably be disputed in either case.

The Nicaraguan revolution that deposed the dictator Anastasio Somoza in 1979 was made by a broad coalition, including the church, organized labor, professional and business groups, and peasants. Cuba, however, armed and advised the Marxist-Leninist Sandinistas who gradually removed democrats from positions of power, suppressed civil, political, and religious rights, and built a powerful army with arms and assistance from the Soviets and their allies. Nicaragua itself began supporting armed insurgencies designed to overthrow other democractic regimes. El Salvador was a particular target.

Alarmed, the United States began to support the Nicaraguan insurgency of the contras and to take other actions, such as the mining of harbors. Nicaragua struck back, using, among other tactics, international law. When the U.S. learned in the spring of 1984 that Nicaragua would file a claim in the International Court of Justice [ICJ] (or World Court), a body established by the Charter of the United Nations as the U.N.'s "principal judicial organ" and composed of judges from various nations, our government suspended its acceptance of the ICJ's jurisdiction as to disputes with any Central American state. The Court nevertheless decided that it retained jurisdiction and the United States then announced that it would not participate further because the dispute involved "an inherently political problem that is not appropriate for judicial resolution." The U.S. then terminated its qualified 1946 acceptance of the Court's compulsory jurisdiction.

This was hardly novel. At the time, only 47 of the 162 nations entitled to accept that compulsory jurisdiction did so—and nine of the fifteen judges on the ICJ came from nations that did not! The Court proceeded to hear only Nicaragua because the U.S. was absent and El Salvador's petition to intervene had been denied—although the ICJ's own statute gave El Salvador that right. At that point, it should have been obvious to anyone what the outcome of the case would be.

In the event, the fears of the United States were realized. The case proceeded in an odd way. Assuming that it had any jurisdiction to begin with, the ICJ clearly had none under the treaties invoked by Nicaragua—the Charters of the United Nations and the Organization of the American States—because the U.S. had long before excepted issues arising under multilateral treaties unless *all* signatories were present. The Court claimed, nonetheless, that it could apply customary international law to the dispute. It found these principles binding despite their incorporation in provisions of the treaties that could not be applied. Customary international law is supposed to reflect the actual practices of nations, but the principles the Court applied were distinguished more for their continual violation by nations than for being followed. They were, moreover, principles hotly disputed among the scholars of international law. Despite these difficulties which, perhaps separately but certainly in combination, would seem to be insuperable, the Court went forward, making law as it went.

The ultimate difficulty with the ICJ's performance, however, was that the principles it fashioned turned out to be one-sided, wooden, and wholly unsuited to the realities of international conflict. The Court decided that merely arming rebels, even in combination with providing military advice and sanctuary for rebel leaders, does not constitute an "armed attack" and that only such an attack brings the issue of individual or collective self-defense into play.

Having found that Nicaragua had not engaged in an armed attack against El Salvador, according to the ICJ's definition, there was no reason whatever for the Court to go on to address the United States' claim that it was exercising the well-established right of collective self-defense. But the Court chose to do so and found this defense legally insufficient for a very odd reason:

> [I]t is the State which is the victim of an armed attack which must form and declare the view that it has been so attacked. There is no rule in customary international law permitting another State to exercise the right of collective self-defence on the basis of its own assessment of the situation.

This was an entirely new procedural requirement, and it means that, even if El Salvador was under attack by Nicaragua and the entire world knew it, if El Salvador, for understandable reasons of prudence, did not wish to make a formal declaration of that fact, the United States could not respond by doing to Nicaragua what that country was doing to El Salvador. The ruling was triply odd since El Salvador had asked the U.S. to assist in its defense, President Duarte had repeatedly mentioned the Nicaraguan attack in press conferences, and El Salvador's rejected petition to intervene in the Court's proceedings had declared the existence of an attack.

It is customary for even those scholars who have pointed out the manifold deficiencies of the ICJ's performance—in its assumption of jurisdiction, its fact-finding, and its legal argument—to deny that they see bias or incompetence. But one must wonder whether an international tribunal can ever be entirely free of the foreign policy interests of the nations whose jurists sit on the tribunal. The ICJ judges, moreover, are elected by the U.N.'s General Assembly and Security Council, often after a highly political process. In explaining the U.S. decision to terminate our acceptance of the Court's jurisdiction, Abraham D. Sofaer, the legal adviser to the State Department, said: "One reasonably may expect at least some judges to be sensitive to the impact of their decisions on their standing with the U.N. majority." He continued, in rampant understatement, that

the U.N. "majority often opposes the United States on important international questions." It did so on the question of our conduct with respect to Nicaragua.

Every lawyer with a national practice knows that if his corporate client is sued by a local plaintiff in certain state courts, the client is likely to have to eat what the bar calls "home cookin'." The lawyers for the commissioner of baseball were recently reminded of that. So, it would appear, was the United States in the International Court of Justice.

But there appears to have been more to the matter than a politically-inspired but perhaps aberrational decision. As Professor Reisman points out, the

> international law-making process has itself undergone change and has subtly, but steadily, sought to change international law with regard to certain unilateral uses of force. While it has not totally succeeded, it has accomplished enough to have made expectations of who and how the law is made and what the law *is* less certain than in the past.

This has much to do with the change in the nature of the U.N. General Assembly as many new nations were admitted. The Assembly began to operate on the assumption that what was said there was international law or evidence of it. These were largely have-not nations and they want an international law that implements their desires. The result, as Reisman says, is the inversion of many established rules about the use of force. The decision in *Nicaragua v. United States* is a case in point.

In any event, the entire episode of *Nicaragua v. United States* had a distinctly odd feel for those who fall into the category of what Jessup called the "common lawyer." No court of the United States would entertain a suit challenging the legality of our actions with respect to Nicaragua. Various radical groups tried to litigate our involvement there and elsewhere in Central America, but were not successful. Our courts, under one legal rubric or another, essentially agreed that this was an inherently political dispute, not fit for judicial resolution.

As much could be said for all disputes about the use of force by one nation against another—but that is exactly my point about international law. We have not entrusted matters so gravely affecting our national interests, security, and foreign policy to American judges. Yet many argue that we should entrust such matters to a Court sitting on another continent, made up predominantly of jurists from foreign nations, and elected by an international body dominated on such issues by Communist bloc and Third World nations. Perhaps the administration's objection to the proceedings should have been couched differently: "This is an inherently political problem which we are unwilling to submit to political judgment outside the American political process."

The U.S., of course, refused to honor the judgment of the ICJ by paying damages to Nicaragua. But that does not mean that no harm was done. Even before the Court's decision, Carlos Arguello, Nicaragua's ambassador to the Netherlands who filed the case in the ICJ, announced that a decision against the United States would "be a serious political and moral blow to them." And so it proved. That was true in the U.S. as well as abroad. International law scholarship, along with the rest of the American academic community, was partially politicized and for every professor who criticized the Court's opinion another castigated the United States.

Thus, Herbert W. Briggs, an emeritus professor at Cornell, wrote in the *American Journal of International Law* that "An administration in Washington that takes satisfaction in invading Grenada, hijacking foreign planes in the Mediterranean, bombing people in Libya and attempting to overthrow foreign governments is unlikely to regard making the United States of America a fugitive from justice, dodging a Court decision, as a serious matter. In each case, the end is supposed to justify the means." The fact that the Mediterranean hijacking brought to justice in Italy PLO [Palestine Liberation Organization] terrorists who had themselves hijacked the cruise ship *Achille Lauro* and murdered an American, or that the bombing of Libya was designed to (and did) deter Qaddafi's support of international terrorism—all this was deemed irrelevant. To which one can only reply that if the U.S. is a fugitive from justice for rejecting the jurisdiction of a biased court over matters vital to

its security, then a large majority of the world's nations are in flight.

Except that there was no judgment by the World Court, much the same situation arose when the United States invaded Grenada. Grenada, a recently independent small island nation, had its government overthrown in a coup by Maurice Bishop and his revolutionary party in 1979. Developments followed much the same pattern seen earlier in Cuba and later in Nicaragua: the end to elections, freedom of the press, other political freedoms, and habeas corpus. A large number of political prisoners were held and the new regime engaged in rapid and heavy militarization with the assistance of arms and advisers from the Soviet Union, Cuba, and other nations of the Communist bloc. Grenada's neighbors, the other six island nations of the Organization of Eastern Caribbean States [OECS], were alarmed, since Grenada's military forces exceeded all of theirs combined and seemed to have no possible purpose other than to support subversion in order to overthrow their democractic governments.

Factions existed within the Grenadan ruling party, however, and on October 13, 1983, Bishop was arrested and subsequently murdered, along with three of his cabinet and certain union leaders. It is thought that this coup may have been the work of even more hard-line Marxist-Leninists, but, in any case, chaos followed as no group seemed in control. Rioting, looting, demonstrations, shootings, and a round-the-clock curfew on the civilian population, enforced by threats to shoot on sight, left the island without a real government. The other nations of the OECS expressed serious concern, and the United States was concerned as well, for there were about one thousand Americans on the island, many of them medical students. As Richard Cheney, then a member of the congressional mission that later investigated, wrote: "Cut off from the outside world, dependent on the People's Revolutionary Army for food and water, and confined to their quarters on pain of death, they were, the State Department employee [who had been trying without success to arrange their evacuation] believed, already hostages."

The OECS member nations, along with Barbados

and Jamaica, met and decided to take military action, provided the United States would assist the effort, since their own military forces were meager. The U.S. agreed, and on October 25 the OECS mission, supported by Barbados and Jamaica, but consisting almost entirely of U.S. forces, invaded. When the fighting was over, a CBS News poll found that 91 percent of Grenadans were glad the U.S. troops had come. By December 15, U.S. armed forces had left the island, order had been restored, American and Grenadan lives very probably saved, and plans were underway for free elections so that the people of Grenada could choose their own government. One would have thought that outside the Communist bloc the American action would have been joyfully received.

One would have been quite wrong. Already, early in November, the U.N. General Assembly voted to condemn the action as a violation of international law. The majority was larger than that which had condemned the Soviet invasion of Afghanistan! The vote had been taken, moreover, without even allowing the nations of the OECS and the United States to present their case. Yet once more many of the U.S. international law academics responded in their own political fashion. No less than nine professors of international law, including Professor Chayes, signed a short article finding the U.S. "in egregious violation of international law" and stating that the lack of the "imprimatur" of the Organization of the American States [OAS] would "raise serious doubts concerning the international legitimacy of any successor government." That the government ousted was a Communist dictatorship and that its successor would be freely chosen by the Grenadan people apparently raised no question in the professors' minds about the legitimacy of the former or the asserted doubtful legitimacy of the latter. The professors were not alone, of course. A number of politicians, along with Senator Moynihan, announced a U.S. violation of international law.

What are we to think about these pronouncements? Did the U.S. violate international law so that we are right to condemn the Reagan administration's international lawlessness? Are there known rules that lead reasonable people to firm conclusions about our actions in Nicaragua and Grenada? Or about Soviet and other nations' behavior around the world?

If there are such rules that lead to firm conclusions, this fact is well hidden. The *American Journal of International Law* ran separate symposia on the Grenada invasion and our support of the Nicaraguan contras. The various experts took almost every position imaginable, from the assertion that the United States is a dangerous international outlaw to the contention that everything done exemplified our devotion to the rule of law. Some arguments, such as those by Professor John Norton Moore of the University of Virginia Law School, in defense of our action, seemed to me far more persuasive than others, but I quickly realized that I was judging not on grounds that might be called "legal" but rather on political and moral considerations. The "law" itself seemed infinitely flexible and indeterminate.

This is due to a contradiction at the heart of the subject. Moynihan states the contradiction without seeming to realize that it is fatal to his idea that there is a solid body of law to which the United States must adhere:

> Manifestly, we cannot hold the rest of the world to a good many of the propositions relating to their internal conduct that we wrote into covenants and charters and declarations with such earnestness in the first half of this century. An ancient doctrine (going back at least to Grotius) is *rebus sic stantibus*, which denotes "a tacit condition, said to attach to all treaties, that they shall cease to be obligatory as soon as the state of facts and conditions upon which they were founded has substantially changed" (*Black's Law Dictionary*). For all that Chapter II of the charter of the Organization of American States requires of members "the effective exercises of representative democracy," this is not going to be the political norm of this hemisphere or this world during the foreseeable future. It had once looked that way; it no longer does. Circumstances have changed. What has not changed—what the United States must strive to make clear has not changed—is the first rule of international law: *Pacta sunt servanda*, agreements must be kept.

But if the condition upon which the United States agreed to the OAS Charter—that the members would be democracies—has changed, why does not *rebus sic stantibus* relieve us of the obligation to keep the rest of the agreement? Moynihan's argument lacks all coherence.

The major difficulty with international law is that it converts what are essentially problems of international morality, as defined by a particular political community, into arguments about law that are largely drained of morality. I once listened to a professor of international law defend the United States' actions in Grenada. The argument seemed tortured and artificial, the most important considerations omitted. When he had done, I asked whether three factors that most Americans deemed relevant counted in international law. (1) The Grenadan government consisted of a minority that seized control by violence and maintained it by terror. (2) It was a Marxist-Leninist regime and represented a further advance in this hemisphere of a power that threatens freedom and democracy throughout the world. (3) Finally, the people of Grenada were ecstatic at being relieved of tyranny and the ever-present threat of violence. The expert replied, somewhat sadly, that these considerations had no weight in international law.

A moment's reflection makes it clear that, in the real world, they could not. In order to be international, rules about the use of force between nations must be acceptable to regimes that operate on different—often contradictory—moral premises. The rules themselves must not express a preference for freedom over tyranny or for elections over domestic violence as the means of coming to power. This moral equivalence is embodied in international charters. The charters must be neutral and the easiest neutral principle is: No force. The fact that the principle will not be observed by those who simply see international law as another foreign policy instrument does not affect the matter.

But even the principle of neutrality is now being altered to the disadvantage of the United States and other democracies. The U.N. General Assembly, as Reisman notes, has begun to redefine the unlawful use of force so that those whom the General Assembly chooses to regard as struggling for "freedom and independence" may legally attack their own government, another nation may legally provide bases from which the attacks are launched—but the targeted state behaves illegally if it then attacks those bases! This reverses the older rule to the benefit, primarily, of Communist insurgencies supported by nations in the Communist bloc and to the detriment of the United States when it aids the nation under attack.

It might be said that we must accept moral equivalence in international law in order to have rules that are acceptable to, and therefore may deter, Communist bloc nations and others from the use of armed force. The notion that it is worth keeping alive this idea of law in the power relations of nations because eventually that idea may tame the drives of aggressors is a bit like preaching the ideal of the rule of law to the Medellin cartel in the hope that one day the drug lords will be worn down by the rhetoric of idealism and submit to the law of Colombia. Even if one might hope that the aspiration of international law might one day lessen the amount of aggression in the world, there is the present reality that it does not, and that it imposes costs disproportionately on liberal, democratic nations.

The major cost is that, by eliminating morality from its calculus, international law actually makes moral action appear immoral. It can hardly be doubted that, in the American view, it would be a moral act to help a people overthrow a dictatorship that had replaced a democratic government by force, and to restore democracy and freedom to such people. Yet when our leaders act for such moral reasons, they are forced into contrived explanations. The implausibility of such explanations then reverses the moral stance of the parties.

International law thus serves, both internationally and domestically, as a basis for a rhetoric of recrimination directed at the United States. Those who disapprove of a President's actions on the merits, but who fear they may prove popular, can transform the dispute from one about substance to one about legality. The President can be painted as a lawbreaker and perhaps drawn into a legalistic defense of his actions. The effect is to raise doubts and lower American morale. The Soviets and other nations have no such problem.

As currently defined, then, international law about the use of force is not even a piety; it is a net loss for Western democracies. Senator Moynihan, speaking of international relations in Woodrow Wilson's time, said, approvingly, that "the idea of law persisted, even when it did not prevail." That is precisely the problem. Since it does not prevail, the persistence of the idea that it exists can be pernicious. There can be no authentic rule of law among nations until nations have a common political morality or are under a common sovereignty. A glance at the real world suggests we have a while to wait.

QUESTIONS FOR DISCUSSION

1. What criteria should be used in evaluating whether international law exists?
2. What criteria should a state use to determine whether it will resolve its disputes with another country through international law?
3. What effect does U.S. compliance with international law have on the behavior of other states in resolving their disputes through international law?
4. What areas of public policy are more conducive to resolving conflicts through international law than national security matters?
5. What are the similarities and differences between domestic law and international law with respect to enforcement of judicial decisions and power over conflicting parties?
6. How will the end of the cold war affect international law?

SUGGESTED READINGS

Boyle, Francis Anthony. *World Politics and International Law*. Durham, N.C.: Duke Univ. Press, 1985.

Bozeman, Adda B. "Does International Law Have a Future?" *New York Law School Journal of International and Comparative Law*, **6** (Winter 1985), pp. 289–299.

Coll, Alberto R. "The Limits of Global Consciousness and Legal Absolutism: Protecting International Law from Some of Its Best Friends." *Harvard International Law Journal*, **27** (Spring 1986), pp. 599–620.

D'Amato, Anthony. "Is International Law Really 'Law'?" *Northwestern University Law Review*, **79** (Dec. 1984/Feb. 1985), pp. 1293–1314.

Falk, Richard. *Revitalizing International Law*. Ames, Iowa: Iowa State Univ. Press, 1989.

Fawcett, James. *Law and Power in International Relations*. London: Faber and Faber, 1982.

Moynihan, Daniel Patrick. *On the Law of Nations*. Cambridge, Mass.: Harvard University Press, 1990.

Quigley, John. "Law for a World Community." *Syracuse Journal of International Law and Commerce*, **16** (Fall 1989), pp. 1–38.

Slomanson, William R. *Fundamental Perspectives on International Law*. St Paul, Minn.: West, 1990.

U.S. Cong., House of Representatives. *U.S. Decision to Withdraw from the International Court of Justice*. Hearing before the Subcommittee on Human Rights and International Organizations of the Foreign Affairs Committee, 99th Cong., 1st Sess., 1985.

18 Do Arms Control Agreements Serve as a Constraint on War?

YES

Arms Control Association

Arms Control

NO

Michael Howard

Illusions That Fuel Pressure for Arms Control

Arms Control

Arms Control Association

Arms control seeks to reduce the risk of war by limiting or reducing the threat from potential adversaries rather than relying solely on unilateral military responses to perceived or anticipated changes in the military threat. Arms control is not in conflict with, or a substitute for, military preparedness, but seeks to complement it by providing increased security at lower and less dangerous levels.

Ideally, one might hope to eliminate the threat of nuclear war by agreeing to ban nuclear weapons entirely. The ultimate goal of a nuclear-free world has had much support since the end of World War II. Most recently, Reagan and Gorbachev independently proclaimed this goal, which had been advocated 25 years earlier by President John Kennedy and General Secretary Nikita Khrushchev.

In a nuclear-disarmed world, however, even a small number of illegal nuclear weapons could provide an enormous military advantage. Confirming that all nuclear weapons have been dismantled and no new ones fabricated would appear to be a nearly impossible task. Consequently, so long as nations continue to have deepseated differences, to entertain territorial ambitions, and to seek military advantage over their adversaries, complete nuclear disarmament will remain a distant goal. Until there have been fundamental changes in international relations, the best that can be done is to reduce to the lowest possible level the chances that nuclear weapons will ever be used.

The concept of arms control today encompasses a wide range of existing agreements and concrete pro-

posals designed to constrain and manage the nuclear and general military confrontation. Through such agreements, nations can pursue a number of important goals that improve their security interests without waiting to resolve the ultimate question of whether, or on what time schedule, nuclear weapons will be eliminated. These immediate goals include: increased stability and predictability in the overall military relationship by limitations and reductions in the level of nuclear confrontation; enhanced military stability in times of crisis; prevention of the spread of nuclear weapons to additional nations; improvement in the political environment; decreases in the potential consequences of nuclear war; and reductions in the cost of military preparedness.

MILITARY STABILITY AND PREDICTABILITY

Limiting and reducing the level of the nuclear confrontation between the superpowers is a central goal of arms control. Such quantitative constraints lower the risks of nuclear war by stabilizing the military relationship and greatly improving the predictability of the future threat. The experience of the past 40 years has demonstrated that the nuclear military competition in itself contributes significantly to the political tension between the two sides.

In the absence of arms control agreements, the United States and Soviet Union have both built weapons in part to maintain what they perceive to be a favorable military balance with their principal adversary. Whenever an increase in threatening Soviet weapons has been observed, military and political pressures for an increase in U.S. weapons have inevitably grown. The same dynamic has operated within the Soviet Union. This "action-reaction" cycle has been a major factor in the continuing arms race.

Uncertainties about the future also stimulate the cycle of action and reaction. Because new weapons take many years to build, each side must plan not only against today's threat but against tomorrow's as well. Given the mistrust of the other side's intentions, each superpower has tended to assume the worst about the military capabilities and future plans

Source: Arms Control Association, *Arms Control and National Security: An Introduction* (Washington, D.C.: Arms Control Association, 1989), pp. 10–15. Reprinted by permission.

of the other side. Such "worst-case analyses" create pressure to build ever larger or more sophisticated military forces, contributing to the arms competition.

Arms control can greatly reduce these real and imagined pressures to build new forces. When both sides agree to limit or reduce specific military forces in a verifiable manner, the predictability of the military relationship can be dramatically improved. Agreements can constrain the evolving threat each side must plan its military forces to meet. Improved predictability contributes directly to the longer term stability of the military relationship since both sides can have greater confidence that there will not be sudden military developments that will drastically undermine their security. As a result, pressures to build up new forces can be significantly decreased.

Past agreements have done a great deal to improve the predictability of the U.S.-Soviet relationship. The Antiballistic Missile (ABM) Treaty of 1972, which effectively limits the testing and development of ballistic missile defenses, has so far prevented the deployment of nationwide ballistic missile defensive systems. Because of the adversarial nature of the U.S.-Soviet relationship, such defensive systems would not only stimulate an arms race in space-based weapons, but would also increase pressures to deploy more and better offensive systems to overcome these defenses. Agreements through the Strategic Arms Limitation Talks, known as SALT I and SALT II, limited the number of missile launchers each side could build. Rather than having to project the largest number of missiles the other country could build in 10 years, the military could plan on the basis of the limits set in the agreement, thereby decreasing the requirement for future forces.

The Strategic Arms Reduction Talks (START) treaty which is now being negotiated would take this process a step further and create agreed ceilings at a significantly reduced level. This agreement would commit the sides to a verifiable program of phased reductions and reverse the strategic nuclear buildup that has dominated the U.S.-Soviet strategic relationship since World War II. The agreed reductions would not only decrease the perceived threat but would improve the predictability of the resulting relationship.

The complete elimination of specific categories of nuclear activities is a particularly effective way of enhancing the predictability of future developments and creating greater arms race stability. Such bans increase the ability of the parties to foresee the evolution of an adversary's forces in a more restricted context and greatly reduce pressures to pursue matching or reactive military programs. The Intermediate-range Nuclear Forces (INF) Treaty, for example, has eliminated the entire class of intermediate-range missiles which were perceived as being particularly threatening by both the Soviet Union and the NATO [North Atlantic Treaty Organization] allies of the United States.

In sum, the more confidence the major powers have that their adversaries are not seeking to develop new quantitative or qualitative military threats, the less pressure there will be to maintain or increase the pace of military competition. If pursued prudently with due concern for national security interests, such a stable military environment encourages the reduction of political tensions that might otherwise increase the possibility of military confrontations and the risk of war.

CRISIS STABILITY

Reducing the risk of nuclear war in a crisis or military confrontation involving the superpowers is a central objective of arms control, as it is also of unilateral national security policy. A nuclear war could result from a major crisis or military conflict involving the two superpowers. Such a confrontation might begin as a conventional war in Europe or Asia or as a war between allies of the two superpowers in the Third World. There is general agreement that this scenario is far more likely than a calculated surprise or "bolt from the blue" attack that once preoccupied many military strategists.

The world has come closest to the brink in those rare cases when crises between the superpowers have led to direct confrontation, as in the Cuban missile crisis of 1962. . . . So far, political leaders on both sides have recognized that a nuclear conflict is totally unacceptable and have drawn back from the brink. Nevertheless, a future crisis that might somehow lead to the direct engagement of U.S. and Soviet conventional military forces would pose the terrible risk that the fighting would escalate to nuclear war.

The less incentive each side has to launch a nuclear strike in such a crisis, the less likely it will be that large-scale nuclear war will break out. Real or perceived vulnerability of nuclear forces might create such an incentive to strike. In a severe crisis, in which political leaders concluded that nuclear war was very likely, there could be tremendous pressure to launch a nuclear "first strike" if political leaders thought the damage to their own country would be reduced by attacking and destroying as much as possible of the other side's forces before they could be launched. The pressures would be greatest, and the danger of nuclear war worst, if both sides' nuclear forces were vulnerable to attack. Then each side might believe it was threatened by an imminent preemptive attack by the other side and hope that its own preemptive attack would be successful. In this case, it might decide to strike first before its own weapons were destroyed, in the hope of preventing, or at least blunting, the other side's retaliation. In the tension of such a crisis, even if it were recognized that both sides would probably be destroyed as viable societies, firing first may seem preferable to firing second or not at all. In short, the pressure to "use them or lose them" would create a hair-trigger situation.

Fortunately, a substantial fraction of the nuclear forces of both superpowers are essentially invulnerable to attack. The leaders of both sides know that, even if an attack could destroy a large number of the other side's forces in a first blow, the surviving forces could carry out a devastating retaliation. The inability to escape this state of mutual deterrence minimizes any rational incentive to preempt in a crisis. If mutual deterrence persists even in crises, the strategic relationship is referred to as "stable." Anything that undermines mutual deterrence is referred to as "destabilizing."

To improve crisis stability, the superpowers can agree to reduce reliance on particularly dangerous weapons, such as those that are both vulnerable to attack and capable of attacking other missiles. Land-based missiles in fixed silos, for example, are becoming increasingly vulnerable to attack as missile accuracy improves, and those armed with multiple warheads (so-called multiple independently targetable reentry vehicles, or MIRVs) could each theoretically destroy several missiles on the other side, giving an advantage to the side that strikes first.

For this reason, the SALT I and SALT II agreements allowed within specified limits replacement of vulnerable land-based missiles by relatively invulnerable submarine-launched weapons, and the START treaty now being negotiated would cut in half the number of heavy SS-18 intercontinental ballistic missiles (ICBMs), the most accurate and threatening missiles in the Soviet arsenal. Similarly, the ABM Treaty banned the construction of nationwide missile defenses since such a defense would work better against a ragged and disorganized retaliation than against an all-out first strike, giving an advantage to whoever strikes the first blow in a crisis.

Over the long term, the United States and the Soviet Union have both sought to improve the survivability of their strategic forces and now appear to be moving toward adopting even more survivable systems. Arms control can play a vital role in this continuing process by ensuring that systems that are survivable today will still be survivable tomorrow.

Arms control can also reduce the risk of conventional war escalating to nuclear war by lowering overall reliance on nuclear weapons for other than basic deterrence. With many thousands of nuclear weapons available, the military forces and strategies of both the United States and the Soviet Union have become heavily dependent on employing nuclear weapons in case of an actual military confrontation. From long-range missiles to short-range artillery, nuclear weapons have spread throughout military forces, greatly increasing the number of different situations in which such weapons might plausibly be used. Moreover, with so many nuclear weapons available, military doctrines and plans designed to attempt to fight a war with such weapons have become ever more sophisticated. By scaling back the number of nuclear weapons, particularly those likely to be on the front lines during future crises, arms control can help to reduce reliance on nuclear "warfighting" strategies, and thereby make it less likely that nuclear weapons would be used in future military engagements.

Arms control can play a similar role in reducing the risk of conventional war by limiting each side's capability to launch surprise offensive attacks. This might be done by limiting offense-oriented forces such as tanks, by pulling back forces capable of offensive action from the front lines, or by confidence-building measures that could provide greater warning of a conventional attack. As the risk of conventional war is diminished, so too would be the prospect that such a war between the superpowers would escalate to nuclear war. Some very limited measures of this kind have already been agreed upon. The current talks on Conventional Armed Forces in Europe (CFE) are intended to go further in scaling back the European military confrontation.

PREVENTING PROLIFERATION

In the future, the greatest risks of initiating nuclear war may lie not with the actions of the superpowers and their allies, but with other countries that gain access to nuclear weapons and other high-technology armaments. One of the highest priority objectives of arms control is to stop or reverse the spread, or "proliferation," of nuclear weapons to additional nations beyond the five that have a demonstrated capability (the United States, the Soviet Union, the United Kingdom, France, and China). This effort is complicated by the fact that a few nations (Israel, India, Pakistan, South Africa) have probably secretly developed the ability to produce nuclear weapons and may have already produced some nuclear weapons.

The more nations that possess nuclear weapons, the greater the chance that a future conflict somewhere in the world could lead to their use. Regional nuclear war could escalate to involve the superpowers. There is even the possibility that a rogue nuclear nation might make nuclear weapons available to terrorists or attempt to spark a "catalytic" nuclear war between the superpowers. The nations of the world clearly share a common interest in preventing the spread of nuclear weapons to countries that have unstable governments or could easily become engaged in regional military conflicts. In an attempt to contain this threat, the Nonproliferation Treaty (NPT) and a complex of other agreements and arrangements have been negotiated.

Other high-technology armaments are also spreading as the international arms market includes ever more sophisticated weapons. In recent years, new negotiations and arrangements have begun to try to stem the spread of chemical weapons. The use of chemical and biological weapons in warfare is banned by the Geneva Protocol of 1925, and the production and stockpiling of biological weapons were banned by the Biological Warfare Convention of 1972. The United Nations Disarmament Conference in Geneva is trying to negotiate a global ban on possession of chemical weapons. Similarly, increased attention is being given to the prevention of the proliferation of ballistic missiles, which could be used to deliver weapons of mass destruction without warning against adversaries. Initially, these efforts have included formal and informal understandings among potential missile technology suppliers.

Arms control can also play a role in improving regional security. For example, the nations of Latin America in 1967 agreed in the Treaty of Tlatelolco to make all of Latin America a nuclear-free zone. Many ceasefire agreements in regional wars—such as the Arab-Israeli ceasefire in 1973—include measures to pull back threatening military forces, or other arms control measures.

IMPROVING POLITICAL RELATIONS

Political tensions between countries clearly contribute to the development of crises and the risk of war. In general, a successful arms control regime builds confidence between adversaries and contributes to the reduction of political tensions and distrust. Over the years, progress in arms control has been a central element in improved relations between the United States and the Soviet Union; and at the same time the relaxation of tensions has generally improved the climate for arms control as well. The U.S.-Soviet relationship improved dramatically from the days of President Reagan's speech labelling the Soviet Union as the "evil empire" to the Moscow summit of 1988 when Reagan and Gorbachev walked arm in arm through Moscow's Red Square. It is difficult to know to what extent this change resulted from the successful negotiation of an INF Treaty or made that treaty possible.

There is little question, however, that the completion of the INF Treaty, with the actual destruction of hundreds of missiles under the watchful eyes of inspectors on each side, and a prospective agreement of more far-reaching reductions in strategic arsenals, will help to decrease tensions over the next several years, perhaps creating a new "glasnost" in U.S.-Soviet military relations.

REDUCING THE CONSEQUENCES

The reduction of the potential destructiveness of nuclear war is a long-range goal of arms control. At present, however, the nuclear arsenals of the United States and the Soviet Union are so large and the heavily urbanized societies of the world so vulnerable, that even reductions far deeper than those contemplated under a START Treaty would not prevent global devastation from an all-out nuclear war.

In the longer term, extremely drastic cuts in nuclear forces could reduce the number of likely direct casualties in the event of a nuclear war and would certainly reduce the global impact of such a conflict. But so long as there are even hundreds of deliverable nuclear weapons, each tens of times more powerful than the one that destroyed Hiroshima, a nuclear war would remain an unprecedented catastrophe for humanity.

REDUCING THE COST

In addition to improving security, arms control can help reduce the economic burden of military forces. Throughout the world, but particularly in the United States and the Soviet Union, staggering sums are allocated to military budgets, diverting resources from other important national priorities. Both the United States and the Soviet Union now face budgetary problems that are forcing them to rethink the size and composition of their military forces. This has clearly been a major consideration in Gorbachev's intense interest in arms control. His concern was underscored by his announcement in December 1988 of unilateral cutbacks in the size of the Soviet army.

Nuclear arms control agreements have already saved many billions of dollars, particularly by avoiding military competitions that might otherwise have taken place. Former Secretary of Defense Harold Brown has estimated that the ultimate cost of the kind of continuous competition between offensive missiles and defensive weapons that could develop were it not for the ABM Treaty and the SALT agreements could reach over $100 billion a year. Specifically, the ABM Treaty has so far prevented the deployment of nationwide strategic defensive systems, which according to former Secretaries of Defense Harold Brown and James Schlesinger could ultimately cost as much as a trillion dollars. Moreover, by reducing existing forces, a START Treaty could save many billions of dollars over present expenditures for strategic systems.

Even far-reaching nuclear arms control agreements will not result in radical reductions in the military budget, since less than 20 percent of the U.S. military budget is allocated to strategic forces. Indeed, in the short term, some of the savings from nuclear arms control would likely be invested in modernization of conventional forces rather than in the civilian economy.

If major progress can also be made in negotiations to reduce conventional forces, much larger savings could result. In the longer term, a successful arms control regime coupled with improved U.S.-Soviet relations and reduced worldwide tensions should result in truly deep cuts in U.S. and Soviet military budgets. While attention has focused on the potential for reduction in the military budgets of the superpowers and their allies, the reallocation of resources from military to other pressing societal priorities is particularly needed in many areas of the developing world.

Illusions That Fuel Pressure for Arms Control

Michael Howard

Four illusions lie behind the past and current pressures for arms control. The first illusion is that the danger of war is in direct ratio to the number of weapons that exist in the world; so, conversely, the fewer weapons nations have, the less likely they are to fight.

Arms races build up to war, or so it is alleged; arms reductions, therefore, logically lead to peace. I do not want to labor again the points that I and others far better qualified have made over the past 10 years about arms races. Some wars have been preceded by intensive armaments competitions; others—and the great majority over the past 150 years—have not. Some arms competitions have made a considerable contribution to the international tensions that culminated in war; others have simply died away. Wars can break out between fully armed nations, partially armed nations, or nations with virtually no arms at all. When they do occur, it is for a very simple reason: one side or the other, or more often both, believes that it can win. That belief is based on a perception of the ratio of strength between the adversaries—economic potential and social cohesion as well as military capability. Such a perception of imbalance can occur as much between lightly armed states as between heavily armed ones. Arms increases or arms reductions may be valuable in conveying messages of intent, and affect the international atmosphere accordingly, but the size of inventories is in itself indifferent. A diplomatic revolution such as the Anglo-French entente of 1904 or the Sino-American rapprochement 70 years later, and the former adversary's armed forces suddenly become a powerful guarantee of peace. Arms reductions, therefore, may be a welcome indicator of the ebbing of international tensions but, unless the basic source of those tensions is removed, they are as likely to exacerbate as to alleviate the situation, creating new uncertainties, new suspicions, new fears of imbalance and threat.

READINESS TO ENDURE

The second illusion is that arms reductions would make war less destructive if it came. The destructiveness of war is not to be measured by the number of weapons, even the number of nuclear weapons, held in the arsenals of the belligerent states at the outset of hostilities. By the end of 1914, the belligerent powers of Europe had virtually exhausted the stocks of ammunition they had accumulated before the outbreak of war, but they fought on for four more increasingly ghastly years. The United States entered both World Wars minimally armed. The destructiveness of a war is determined not so much by the capacity of belligerents to inflict punishment as by their readiness to endure it. The nuclear arsenals of the superpowers today could be reduced by a factor of a hundred without affecting their capacity to destroy one another, and probably the rest of the world as well. But even if those reduced arsenals were used as selectively and discriminately as the advocates of nuclear-war fighting suggest, the length of the war, and the destruction it caused would be determined not by the number of weapons available for use, but by the readiness of the belligerents to endure punishment in the hope of ultimate victory. A few missiles directed against carefully selected targets might cause the moral collapse of one belligerent, or indeed both; or they might fight on as grimly among their radioactive ruins as did the Russians in the ruins of Stalingrad or the Germans in the ruins of Berlin. A knowledge of the continuing capacity of the adversary to inflict further destruction could be a far greater incentive to peaceful accommodation than the realization that he had shot his nuclear bolt and that war could now be pursued by more traditional means.

The third illusion is that the application of science

Source: Michael Howard, "Illusions That Fuel Pressure for Arms Control," *Atlantic Community Quarterly*, **24** (Summer 1986), pp. 119–121. Reprinted by permission.

and technology to the development of weapons systems is in itself a threat to peace and should be inhibited. Part of the rhetoric of disarmament is that the superpowers are crazily building up arsenals of ever-larger and more-destructive weapons. In fact, for the past 25 years, they have been replacing their large and destructive weapons with small and discriminating ones as fast as their technological resources have permitted them to do so. The Americans have eliminated some 8,000 warheads from their arsenal over the past two decades and withdrawn 2,000 tactical nuclear warheads from their forces in Europe. The actual payload, or deliverable explosive capacity, of their bombs and missiles today is barely half what it was 20 years ago. Technology has made possible precisely the kind of build-down that many arms-control specialists advocate, and the fact must be faced that this has only been rendered possible by a continuation of nuclear testing.

Now, I must admit that I am probably in a minority of one on the question of nuclear testing. The original objections that led to the Test Ban Treaty of 1963 still seem to me entirely valid: tests must not be conducted in such a way as to provide a hazard to the environment. But the object of replacing large and dirty weapons with small, clean, and controllable ones seems to me both militarily and morally unobjectionable. I do not believe that they would make it easier to contemplate the initiation of nuclear war, but they certainly make it easier to escape from the appalling alternatives of genocide (accompanied by suicide) or surrender. To halt the development of nuclear weapons at a point of maximum lethality and uncontrollability would not, it seems to me, make very much sense. Had all nuclear tests been abandoned 30 years ago, nuclear stockpiles would still consist of the vulnerable, inaccurate, and hideously destructive weaponry of that era, and it is not self-evident that the world would be more peaceful or secure as a result.

LACK OF FRANKNESS IN POLITICIANS

Finally, there is the illusion that arms control, however one may interpret that concept, provides an alternative, and a preferable alternative, to armament as a means of ensuring international security. In fact, the two activities are totally interdependent. Security is a subjective condition, a state of mind. It is based upon two elements: first, the assumption that no one wishes to attack us; and second, the belief that, even if they have the will and capability to do so, they will be deterred by our evident capacity to resist. Of those two elements, the first is, of course, by far the most important: security based simply on military deterrence is a very poor second-best to security based on mutual confidence, and provides by itself a totally inadequate framework for world order. Armaments may, and should ensure that, if a potential adversary has the will to attack us, he will be deterred from doing so. But arms control should ensure that, if he does not have the will, he will not be led to develop it through a misperception of our own intentions.

States acquire arms from the day of their creation to transmit to the world the message that they belong to that species of *méchant animal*, which will, if attacked, defend itself. They need also to transmit the simultaneous message that their arms contribute no threat to the security of their neighbors—and that is what arms control is all about. Finally, in the nuclear age they need to make it clear to their own peoples that their weapons constitute no threat to the survival of their own society, a message that is not always transmitted as clearly as one would wish. If I may summarize in a highly simplistic manner, I would say that armaments are about deterrence and arms control about reassurance. Security is achieved by a synthesis of the two.

This skeptical analysis is not the kind of thing that is usually said in public lectures on this kind of topic. But I suspect that anyone involved in government, irrespective of their nationality, would quietly agree with much of it. Nevertheless, they would probably say, the illusion that arms reductions would in themselves make peace more secure and that total disarmament would make it perpetual is so deeply rooted and so widespread as to constitute an ineluctable political fact that has to be accommodated into our policy. It is, as it were, a Platonic "noble lie": governments themselves may not believe it, but it is an aspiration to be encouraged and not discouraged—and anyhow, no Western politician dares confront his or her electorate and tell them frankly that they are wrong. Governments must be seen to be striving to attain the heavenly city of disarmament. Even if the goal is unattainable, the object is a noble one, and the very process of trying to reach it will be a civilizing and pacifying influence on international behavior.

QUESTIONS FOR DISCUSSION

1. What criteria should be used in evaluating whether arms control agreements are successful?
2. What advantages and disadvantages do democracies possess in arms control negotiations with dictatorships?
3. What is the relationship between arms races and war?
4. What role does technological innovation play in arms control?
5. What is the relationship between arms control agreements and military expenditures?

SUGGESTED READINGS

Codevilla, Angelo. "The Abuse of Arms Control." *Global Affairs*, **5** (Summer/Fall 1990), pp. 36–46.

Craig, Paul P., and John A. Jungerman. *Nuclear Arms Race: Technology and Society*, 2d ed. New York: McGraw-Hill, 1990.

Eden, Lynn, and Steven E. Miller (eds.). *Nuclear Arguments: The Major Debates on Strategic Weapons and Arms Control*. Ithaca, N.Y.: Cornell Univ. Press, 1989.

Fetter, Steve. *Toward a Comprehensive Test Ban*. Cambridge, Mass.: Ballanger, 1988.

Goodby, James E. "Can Arms Control Survive Peace?" *Washington Quarterly*, **13** (Autumn 1990), pp. 93–101.

Gray, Colin S. "Does Verification Really Matter? Facing Political Facts about Arms Control Compliance." *Strategic Review*, **18** (Spring 1990), pp. 32–52.

————. "Nuclear Delusions: Six Arms Control Fallacies." *Policy Review*, no. 37 (Summer 1986), pp. 48–53.

"Has Arms Control Worked?" *Bulletin of the Atomic Scientists*, **45** (May 1989), special sec., pp. 26–45.

Klare, Michael T. "An Arms Control Agenda for the Third World." *Arms Control Today*, **20** (Apr. 1990), pp. 8–12.

Nitze, Paul H., with Ann M. Smith and Steven L. Rearden. *From Hiroshima to Glasnost: At the Center of Decision—A Memoir*. New York: G. Weidenfeld, 1989.

Nye, Joseph S., Jr. "Arms Control after the Cold War." *Foreign Affairs*, **68** (Winter 1989–90), pp. 42–64.

"Policy Focus: Arms Control Verification Reconsidered." *International Security*, **14** (Spring 1990), pp. 140–184.

Schwartz, William A., and Charles Derber. *The Nuclear Seduction: Why the Arms Race Doesn't Matter—And What Does*. Berkeley, Calif.: Univ. of California Press, 1990.

Tsipis, Kosta. *New Technologies, Defense Policy, and Arms Control*. New York: Harper and Row, 1989.

19 Is the Nonproliferation Treaty Effective?

YES

Lewis A. Dunn

It Ain't Broke—Don't Fix It

NO

Ashok Kapur

Dump the Treaty

It Ain't Broke—Don't Fix It

Lewis A. Dunn

In 1995, the parties of the Nuclear Non-Proliferation Treaty (NPT) will assemble to decide ''whether the Treaty shall continue in force indefinitely, or shall be extended for an additional fixed period or periods.'' The prospect of this 1995 extension conference has led already to proposals to reform, strengthen, expand, or even abolish the NPT. The Fourth Review Conference, which will be held this summer [1990] will set the tone, if not shape the agenda, for 1995.

The proposals for change need to be set against the treaty's record of substantial contributions to the security of its parties. Different schemes should also be evaluated in terms of the motives of their proponents as well as the high risks of attempting to amend the treaty. In other words, since the treaty isn't broken, don't fix it.

The Nuclear Non-Proliferation Treaty has three goals: to prevent the further spread of nuclear weapons; to promote the peaceful uses of nuclear energy under safeguards against misuse; and to encourage nuclear disarmament, the cessation of the nuclear arms race, and general and complete disarmament. How well has it worked?

■ *An essential nonproliferation bulwark.*

Under Article I of the treaty, the states that possess nuclear weapons have pledged not to assist other states to acquire them. Few doubt that this pledge has been met, despite occasional unintended breakdowns of nuclear export controls. Nor is there any reason to question the continued commitment of virtually all of the non-nuclear-weapons states which are party to the treaty not to manufacture or acquire nuclear weapons, as stipulated by Article II. This commitment has signaled their peaceful intentions and has helped to avert suspicions that could lead their neighbors to think about nuclear weapons. It has strengthened a global norm of nuclear nonproliferation.

The treaty has helped prevent the spread of nuclear weapons in other ways. Under Article III, parties which are nuclear suppliers promise to require safeguards on their nuclear exports, and implicitly, all treaty parties are obliged not to assist other countries to acquire nuclear weapons. This has been the primary legal foundation of international efforts to control nuclear exports. Despite occasional breakdowns, these obligations have been honored. The treaty has made it time-consuming, costly, and difficult to acquire the materials, facilities, and components needed to make nuclear weapons.

The NPT has indirectly restricted the political freedom of action even of non-party states that might be contemplating acquiring nuclear weapons. Above all, the treaty symbolizes international opposition to the further spread of nuclear weapons and a growing belief in the illegitimacy of these weapons. The acquisition of nuclear weapons is now likely to meet with condemnation, not praise. This changed milieu has contributed significantly to the reluctance of countries today—as opposed to two or three decades ago—to seek nuclear weapons openly. Since the treaty entered into force in 1970, not one additional country has openly acquired and deployed a nuclear arsenal. This has enhanced the security of all the NPT's parties.

■ *A framework for peaceful nuclear use.*

Many developed countries have assisted developing countries which are party to the treaty to gain access to the benefits of the peaceful atom. The International Atomic Energy Agency (IAEA) has also provided extensive technical assistance, with support from NPT developed countries.

IAEA safeguards have not impeded peaceful nuclear cooperation. Instead, their widespread acceptance has been an essential precondition for cooperation, reassuring nuclear suppliers that exports would

Source: Lewis A Dunn, ''It Ain't Broke—Don't Fix It,'' *Bulletin of the Atomic Scientists,* **46** (July/August 1990), pp. 19–20. Reprinted by permission of the *Bulletin of the Atomic Scientists* © 1990 Educational Foundation for Nuclear Science, 6042 S. Kimbark Ave., Chicago, IL 60637.

only be used for peaceful purposes and giving non-weapons states an effective means to demonstrate their peaceful intentions.

But not all NPT nuclear supplier states require their non-party customers to accept IAEA safeguards on all peaceful nuclear activities ("full-scope safeguards"). This has weakened the NPT regime and discriminates between NPT parties, whose nuclear imports are strictly controlled, and non-parties. The 1985 review conference called for "effective steps" toward agreement to require full-scope safeguards.

■ *The arms control and disarmament imperative.*
It is not surprising that this was the most troublesome substantive issue at earlier review conferences. But with changing East-West political relations, the arms control logjam has finally begun to break up. The 1987 Intermediate-Range Nuclear Forces (INF) Treaty is being implemented. By the time of the conference, there is likely to be a framework START agreement beginning the reduction of U.S. and Soviet strategic offensive nuclear forces, and probably a treaty by the end of the year. An agreement markedly reducing conventional forces in Europe will be in sight by the time of the conference. A multilateral ban on chemical weapons will be in the offing. Negotiated cuts of short-range nuclear forces are ahead as well. These accomplishments will be a substantial step toward meeting the NPT's arms control and disarmament goals, contributing to the security of the treaty's parties.

A comprehensive ban on nuclear testing is conspicuously absent from this set of important arms control and disarmament advances. The preamble to the NPT does recall the determination of the parties to the Partial Test Ban Treaty "to seek to achieve the discontinuance of all test explosions of nuclear weapons for all time and to continue negotiations to this end." But careful reading of the negotiating record of the Non-Proliferation Treaty does not support the view that a ban on all nuclear testing is the sole litmus test of progress in meeting the treaty's disarmament goals, or the key to its long-term vitality. Other measures—further nuclear force reductions and stability measures, a global chemical weapons ban, new arms control initiatives for conflict-prone regions—hold out much greater prospect of enhancing global peace and security.

Some states that are not party to the treaty are proposing not to extend the NPT in 1995 but to replace it with a new, nondiscriminatory system of comprehensive global nuclear and conventional disarmament. It is hard not to conclude that the disguised motive behind such proposals is to destroy the NPT. Given regional and global political realities, such a replacement system has no chance of coming into being. And without the NPT, non-party states could more easily pursue nuclear weapons ambitions.

Other proposals to amend the NPT seem motivated by a desire to use the treaty to pursue a particular disarmament goal, for example, a comprehensive nuclear test ban or a cutoff of nuclear materials production. Using the NPT to pull the disarmament cart, however, puts at risk the treaty's substantial contribution to global security. It is highly unlikely that the three signatory nuclear weapons states will agree to amend the treaty and bind themselves to undertake specified nuclear disarmament steps, especially under duress.

Other proposals to amend or reform the NPT are said to be motivated by a desire to improve its effectiveness by closing loopholes, to tighten the obligations of nuclear weapons states, and to strengthen its appeal to non-party states. They range from requiring full-scope safeguards to delineating specific nuclear disarmament objectives.

But once the amendment process begins, it will be virtually impossible to stop until all of the treaty's basic provisions have been reopened. The NPT reflects a carefully negotiated balancing of obligations—between non-nuclear and nuclear weapons states, developing and developed countries, nuclear suppliers and recipients, and among the non-weapons states themselves. Attempting to amend the balance in all probability would undermine support for the old one but fail to reach a new consensus. As for critical non-parties—Pakistan, India, Israel, Argentina, and Brazil—the most important reason why they have not joined the NPT is that they want to retain the nuclear weapons option.

There are some problems with the treaty's implementation, and these will be addressed at the review conference. North Korea's foot-dragging in bringing its nuclear research and reprocessing facilities under safeguards, and Iraq's apparent efforts to acquire nuclear-weapons-related materials and components are at odds with the spirit if not yet the letter of their treaty obligations. Other issues such as "negative security assurances" have a legitimate place on the agenda. . . .

The Nuclear Non-Proliferation Treaty works. It makes an essential contribution to global peace and security. No single initiative is the key to the treaty's successful extension in 1995. Nor should we pursue possibly well-intentioned but no doubt dangerous proposals to fix the treaty. Instead, the United States and other parties to the treaty need to rededicate themselves to making even greater progress toward the treaty's basic goals: preventing nuclear proliferation, fostering the peaceful uses of nuclear energy, and negotiating arms control and disarmament. That is the best way to strengthen the NPT.

Dump the Treaty

Ashok Kapur

The Nuclear Non-Proliferation Treaty [NPT] is the Berlin Wall of nuclear affairs. Although its downfall is not imminent, the system of atomic apartheid embodied in the treaty has been unravelling for some time. In a modern and open world where walls are crumbling, the NPT is an anachronism. It is in force in a technical sense but without force as a regulatory regime among those determined to defy it. The regime works best where it is needed least, and it does not work at all where it is needed most.

In order to survive, a regime must have power to enforce discipline, and it must possess the consent of its constituents. Without consent, it is vulnerable to circumvention and opposition. The NPT has the consent of the five major nuclear powers because it accommodates their interests. But it lacks the consent of the outer ring of emerging nuclear powers, which are also regional leaders. These states are treated as outlaws by the NPT.

The NPT was conceived at a time when the superpowers headed two blocs and seemed to be able to call the shots. The review conferences, however, have taken place in a changing context. The superpowers are on the decline, and unless they can compromise with lesser powers and persuade them to cooperate, their capacity to maintain the NPT regime is limited. On the other hand, the most determined of the would-be nuclear-weapons states—Israel, India, Argentina, South Africa, and others—are on the rise in regional and international influence. Most of them recognized the utility of

Source: Ashok Kapur, ''Dump the Treaty,'' *Bulletin of the Atomic Scientists*, **46** (July/August 1990), pp. 21–22. Reprinted by permission of the *Bulletin of the Atomic Scientists* © 1990 Educational Foundation for Nuclear Science, 6042 S. Kimbark Ave., Chicago, IL 60637.

nuclear weapons in the 1940s and chose to pursue that path before the treaty was created. During the life of the regime, they have become dedicated to acquiring nuclear weapons.

Lectures about the NPT and international security are of no avail because they do not demonstrate to skeptical policymakers how the treaty really helps security in these states. Unfortunately, few of the dedicated opponents of proliferation are acquainted with the political cultures, decisionmaking styles, and the mix of incentives and disincentives behind the drive to acquire nuclear weapons in each of the ''hard-core'' cases. The proliferators and the treaty supporters are in different worlds.

The intellectual foundations of the NPT have always been weak, yet as long as the superpowers and their cohorts were in charge, the mistaken notions did not matter. But now the false bases of the treaty must be addressed if the treaty is to be amended or even abolished in favor of a new strategy on nonproliferation. Otherwise, the NPT debate is likely to remain an exercise in propaganda and counter-propaganda, a murky story of vague allegations and denials.

The idea for the treaty emerged in the 1960s in response to the fear, expressed especially by President John F. Kennedy and his brother Robert, that irresponsible and unstable leaders in the Third World were likely to gain nuclear arms and stumble into a nuclear war. But this perception is a sign of ethnocentric and racist thinking. There are no accidental wars. Not even ''crazy'' leaders like Muammar Khadaffi fight wars without some calculation and deliberation, whether for good reasons or bad.

The states most determined to acquire nuclear weapons are motivated by an interplay among three factors: the costs of modern arms, strategic needs for nuclear arms or a nuclear-weapons option, and unwillingness to accept permanent technological and legal inferiority. The NPT regime, however, is insensitive to these three factors. Under the treaty, a country is either pure or sinful; there is no middle way.

NPT review conferences and U.N. [United Nations] speeches tout the NPT and International

Atomic Energy Agency (IAEA) as pillars of international security. This is mere rhetoric. The NPT and IAEA contribute only marginally, if at all, to international and regional security. No country relies on the regime for its security. The superpowers rely on arms, coercive diplomacy, and the capability to intervene. The Indians, Israelis, and others do likewise. Many NPT parties, such as Canada, rely on military alliance arrangements as well as national defense. Even small states like Sweden and Switzerland have chosen armed, not disarmed, neutrality.

The NPT regime suffers from awesome defects which cannot be remedied in today's world. One is that its net was cast much too late. By the 1960s, India, Israel, South Africa, and Argentina were already on the nuclear path, driven by a concern to use science for development and security. Another is that when the treaty was being negotiated, from 1961 to 1968, and when it came into effect in 1970, the established U.S. policy was not to rely on disarmament for security. Article VI, the promise to disarm, was wool pulled over the eyes of naive utopians in the Third World to get them to sign the treaty. The superpowers never seriously intended to disarm. The so-called bargain between the treaty principals and the parties that do not possess nuclear arms was always subject to changed circumstances. Since world circumstances continually change, in this view, the time will never be ripe for disarmament.

The superpowers now point to the Intermediate-Range Nuclear Forces Treaty and the strategic arms negotiations as evidence that they have been negotiating in good faith. But even with recent progress, they have more arms now than they did in 1970, and their commitment to modernizing arms is not likely to change.

The NPT regime's elaborate institutional and legal network is impressive on paper. Besides the treaty's provisions, there are lists of suspect items prepared and updated periodically by the London Nuclear Suppliers Group; IAEA safeguards rules, also upgraded periodically; national nuclear export regulations; and nuclear-weapons-free zones in Latin America and the South Pacific. But these are riddled with loopholes which cannot be filled.

There is no enforcement mechanism in the treaty or in the hands of the IAEA. For example, France gave Pakistan blueprints for a reprocessing plant in the 1970s, under an agreement which included the IAEA. But the agency was not able to determine the status of the supply and safeguards arrangement because it had to depend on reports from the two governments, and these were not forthcoming. After Canada supplied heavy water to Romania and concerns were expressed in 1986 about what it would be used for, the IAEA could do little to reassure the world but issue vague statements. Israel did not think much of the NPT and IAEA safeguards when it attacked a safeguarded reactor in Iraq in 1981. When China was widely seen as having supplied vital test data to Pakistan in the mid-1980s, the IAEA and the United States looked the other way.

The foreign policy and commercial interests of important powers and their allies take precedence over non-proliferation. The NPT operates in a context in which there is neither a consensus against proliferation nor one for disarmament.

Staying outside the NPT does not appear to diminish a country's security. Canada applied sanctions against India after it detonated a nuclear device in 1974, and the Indian nuclear program suffered a temporary setback. But in the long run, the sanctions stimulated proliferation. The incident showed that contracts meant nothing and reinforced the Indian nationalist drive to secure nuclear autonomy. Today, Indian scientists associated with the nuclear program are in high political positions. South Africa suffered a loss in the world uranium market, but still did not feel compelled to join the treaty. Israel and Pakistan, two U.S. allies, went ahead with their nuclear programs and paid no price.

Indeed, there are advantages in not joining the NPT. The hold-out countries remain objects of international attention and have opportunities to bargain.

What should be done? In reassessing the treaty's future we must recognize that its provisions have been circumvented in a major way not only by non-member states but by states such as France and China, which claim to believe in nonproliferation, and by activities within the jurisdiction of the NPT states. Moreover, the NPT appears to be irrelevant to the massive restructuring of global and regional power relations that is currently under way. It has not served as a confidence-building measure. It has not deterred slow and incremental proliferation in Israel, India, Pakistan, South Africa, Argentina, Brazil, Iraq, Taiwan, and South Korea. Western attempts to model control of chemical arms and ballistic missiles on the NPT scheme have gone nowhere. The NPT has not produced disarmament.

The world nuclear order is in a state of flux. Changing power relations are driving a dozen or so secondary nuclear powers to continue their quest for nuclear weapons. As long as the power-bloc leaders continue to lose their international authority, and new power centers continue to grow in important regions of the world, incremental nuclear proliferation is irreversible. The NPT will remain irrelevant.

The NPT cannot pull the disarmament cart, or even the antiproliferation cart. It cannot pull the foreign policy cart, the regional security cart, or the international security cart. A crippled donkey cannot pull any kind of cart, no matter how hard it is beaten. Perhaps it is time to retire the tired, overworked donkey.

QUESTIONS FOR DISCUSSION

1. What are the factors that lead to a country's decision to build nuclear weapons?
2. What effect would horizontal proliferation have on war?
3. What states have benefited the most from the Non-proliferation Treaty? What states have benefited the least? Why?
4. Why has horizontal proliferation not been more pervasive?
5. What criteria should be used to evaluate the number of countries that will have nuclear weapons by the year 2000?
6. Why have some states refused to sign the Non-proliferation Treaty?

SUGGESTED READINGS

Bellany, Ian, Coit D. Blacker, and Joseph Gallacher (eds.). *The Nuclear Non-Proliferation Treaty*. London: Frank Cass, 1985.

Dhanapala, Jayantha. "Disappointment in the Third World." *Bulletin of the Atomic Scientists*, **46** (July/Aug. 1990), pp. 30–31.

Dunn, Lewis A. "Four Decades of Nuclear Non-proliferation: Some Lessons from Wins, Losses, and Draws." *Washington Quarterly*, **13** (Summer 1990), pp. 5–18.

Goldblat, Jozef. "Nuclear Non-Proliferation: A Balance Sheet of Conflicting Trends." *Bulletin of Peace Proposals*, **20** (Dec. 1989), pp. 369–398.

Graham, Thomas, Jr. "The Duration of the Nuclear Non-Proliferation Treaty: Sudden Death or New Lease on Life?" *Virginia Journal of International Law*, **29** (Spring 1989), pp. 661–677.

Kaiser, Karl. "Non-Proliferation and Nuclear Deterrence." *Survival* (London), **31** (Mar./Apr. 1989), pp. 123–136.

Lomas, Peter, and Harald Muller (eds.). *Western Europe and the Future of the Non-Proliferation Treaty*. Brussels: Centre for European Policy Studies, 1989.

Nolan, Janne. "Ballistic Missiles in the Third World: The Limits of Nonproliferation." *Arms Control Today*, **19** (Nov. 1989), pp. 9–14.

Sanders, Ben. "Non-Proliferation Treaty: A Broken Record?" *Bulletin of the Atomic Scientists*, **46** (July/Aug. 1990), pp. 15–18.

Smith, Gerard C., and Helena Cobban. "A Blind Eye to Nuclear Proliferation." *Foreign Affairs*, **68** (Summer 1989), pp. 53–70.

Spector, Leonard S. "The New Nuclear Nations." *Social Education*, **54** (Mar. 1990), pp. 143–145, 150.

———. *The Undeclared Bomb*. Cambridge, Mass.: Ballinger, 1988.

U.S. Cong., Senate. *Nuclear and Missile Proliferation*. Hearing before the Committee on Governmental Affairs, 100th Cong., 1st Sess., 1989.

Van Doren, Charles N. "Prognosis for the Fourth NPT Review Conference." *Arms Control Today*, **20** (June 1990), pp. 18–21.

20   Should Chemical Weapons Be Banned?

YES

George Shultz

Ban Chemical Weapons

NO

Frank J. Gaffney, Jr.

Forget about Banning Chemical Weapons

Ban Chemical Weapons

George Shultz

As we begin our consideration of the compelling challenge that chemical weapons pose to world security, I have the privilege of conveying to you a message from the President of the United States, Ronald Reagan. It reads:

Distinguished Delegates:

Less than three months ago, I called on the Parties to the Geneva Protocol and other concerned countries to convene a conference for the purpose of restoring respect for the international norms against the illegal use of chemical weapons. Today, thanks to the initiative of President Mitterrand and the French Government, representatives of more than 100 nations are gathered in Paris to reaffirm their commitment to the goal of putting an end to the proliferation of these dreaded weapons and preventing their use.

Your presence underlines the deep concern and alarm shared by all countries of the world over the dangerous spread and resurgent use of one of humanity's most dreaded and dreadful forms of warfare. It demonstrates as well that you share a desire to take the necessary actions to ensure that such weapons are not used again.

The Geneva Protocol of 1925 remains an invaluable and necessary compact, but its objectives can only be achieved if nations comply. Rededication to the objectives of the Geneva Protocol is not just a question of law, but an important step toward securing a safer future for mankind. It is my hope that the participants in the Paris Conference will take that important step.

The Government and people of the United States send our prayers and best wishes for the success of the vital effort you are undertaking.

Source: George Shultz, address to Conference on the Prohibition of Chemical Weapons, January 7, 1989, *Department of State Bulletin*, **89** (Mar. 1989), pp. 4–6.

Indeed, we are brought here today by a horror that has cast a pall over mankind for nearly 100 years—the threat and use of chemical and biological weapons.

History records that on the eve of this troubled century—one that would prove to be burdened with a variety of manmade horrors—the participants in the First Hague Peace Conference of 1899 were moved to condemn chemical weapons. Already, the vicious effects of such weaponry could be anticipated, even though our predecessors of 90 years ago had not yet experienced their destructiveness.

But the warnings of The Hague Gas Declaration [of 1899] were not heeded. And, in 1915, in Flanders Fields near Ypres—only 200 kilometers from where we now sit—chemical weapons were first unleashed on a large scale in war. In the First World War, over 1 million people, both soldiers and civilians, suffered casualties from chemical weapons—a grim harbinger of the hundreds-of-thousands yet to die by this scourge.

The fate of the survivors scarcely was better than that of those who immediately succumbed. An eyewitness later described them:

Faces, arms, hands were a shiny gray-black. With mouths open and lead-glazed eyes, they were all swaying backwards and forwards trying to get their breaths, struggling, struggling for life.

In the Great War, the deadly chemical clouds swept over western and eastern fronts alike, acknowledging no boundaries and uniting in horror and shared suffering many of the nations and governments represented here today. This destruction conferred no military advantage. It simply made the deadlock of conflict that much more devastating—so terrible that the world community finally was moved to act.

That action came quickly, and culminated in the 1925 Geneva conference, where the major nations of the world—the U.S. Government among them—crafted an agreement which outlawed the use in war of chemical and biological weapons. The work of the conference had effect for six decades. To be sure, these legal and moral barriers erected in Geneva were tragically breached in the 1930s and 1940s. Therefore, Franklin Roosevelt was correct when he said that it was ''the general opinion of civilized mankind'' that chemical weapons should be outlawed.

HAVE WE FORGOTTEN THE LESSONS OF HISTORY?

That opinion remains valid. Yet, in recent years, the international norms against chemical weapons use have begun to erode in practice—first in the Middle East and, most recently, in regional conflicts from Southeast Asia, to Afghanistan, to the Persian Gulf.

And even if peace should come to these strife-ridden areas—and we hope and pray and work for the day that it does—this horrific legacy of chemical weapons use quite literally will harm them for years to come. As the 1970 World Health Organization report on the effects of the possible use of chemical and biological weapons on civilian population groups concluded: ''Chemical and biological weapons pose a special threat to civilians. Large-scale use of chemical and biological weapons could cause lasting changes of an unpredictable nature in man's environment.

The consequences of past chemical weapons use still plagues Europe today. Unexploded chemical munitions from World War I continue to release their aging—yet lethal—contents into the waters where they were dumped. North Sea fishermen and bathers in coastal areas still suffer mustard gas burns from sunken and deteriorating chemical munitions. Similarly, unexploded chemical munitions now littering the waters of the Shatt al Arab will threaten human life and the environment for decades to come.

So like the contaminated battlefields of Europe, the residue of more recent chemical weapons use in other strife-ridden parts of the world—unexploded chemical munitions, people maimed for life, a poisoned environment—will be reminders for generations of those vicious conflicts.

Must it take a fresh shock of human tragedy— must more places like Flanders Fields earn their place in the history books through the particular ghastliness of their destruction—before governments work together to restore respect for the international norms against chemical weapons use? Ninety years ago, our predecessors at The Hague conference only could imagine the horrifying destructive potential of chemical weaponry. Today we have witnessed its devastating capability. We cannot claim now that we have not seen, that we do not know. But have we the will, the courage, and the vision to act on the collective conscience of mankind and control this proliferating threat to civilization?

We cannot delay. Time is not on our side. Technology is not stagnant. Ever more lethal and insidious chemical weapons are being developed— weapons which defeat defenses and are devastating in their effects. The ability to produce such weapons is rapidly spreading—and with it the technology to produce ballistic missiles as delivery vehicles.

None of us can escape the consequences of chemical warfare. Its resurgence has placed an additional burden on international organizations and specialized agencies that already are overwhelmed with the victims of war in hospitals and refugee camps. Victims of chemical warfare rarely have proper protective equipment or medical facilities. A number of governments represented here have generously treated victims at considerable expense in their specialized medical institutions. Out of fear more and more countries are heavily investing in protective equipment for their forces and in some cases for their civilian population. We must be alarmed that we have reached the point where some countries are prudently making special protective suits for children. Each of us now must consider the security of our embassies from chemical attack.

Moreover, we face the even more grotesque specter of the proliferation of biological weapons. Nations are developing, producing, and stockpiling ever more deadly and resistant strains of disease in violation of the 1972 Biological and Toxin Weapons Convention. It is no hyperbole to state that the mere existence of these weapons poses one of the most serious threats to the survival of mankind.

Isn't it grimly ironic that these new and deadly

threats have arisen to haunt us at the very time we have begun to make progress in controlling and reducing nuclear arms? A nightmare for all, of course, would be the combination of ballistic missiles, chemical warheads, and biological weapons in the hands of governments with histories of the conduct of terrorist violence.

Terrorists' access to chemical and biological agents is another growing threat to the international community. There are no insurmountable technical obstacles that would prevent terrorist groups from using chemical weapons. With the inhibitions against employing such weapons now weakened through recent use—and with targets for conventional terrorist attacks becoming better protected—terrorist groups could be tempted to shift, without warning, to use of chemical weapons for dramatic political and media attention. The threat is a real one. Some governments which have been known to sponsor terrorism now have sizable chemical weapons capabilities.

At stake in all of this is not just the violation of codes of international conduct but civilization itself. If we tolerate the breakdown of barriers against the use of chemical and biological weapons, such agents of mass destruction may come to be seen as both advantageous and legitimate in pursuit of national security interests—as just another "weapon of choice." Countries that use chemical weapons in violation of international law are wrong—and they know it. We must not legitimize, by our acquiescence, a practice that will threaten all civilized societies.

WHAT ACTION MUST WE TAKE?

President Reagan, in a speech to the U.N. General Assembly, proposed this conference. Let us recall his words.

> . . . poison gas, chemical warfare—the terror of it; the horror of it. . . . It is incumbent upon all civilized nations to ban, once and for all . . . the use of chemical and gas warfare.

The international community must act now on several fronts to eradicate the threat of chemical weapons, prevent their illegal use, and staunch their dangerous proliferation. Even as we push forward in the Geneva negotiations to ban the development, production, acquisition, stockpiling, retention, or transfer of chemical weapons, each of us now must take steps to strengthen our political commitment to expose the threat and control the spread and use of these hideous weapons.

My government never has underestimated the difficulties—chief among them, verification—that must be overcome in pursuit of this urgent objective. When Vice President Bush, on behalf of President Reagan, tabled the 1984 draft treaty in Geneva, he said that a comprehensive ban on chemical weapons cannot work unless states are prepared to "commit themselves to a new but absolutely necessary degree of openness"—"a new way of doing business." But however formidable the challenge, the world community should not underestimate the United States' determination to overcome those problems and put an effective treaty into force.

Recently, President-elect Bush has declared that one of his highest priorities will be to deal with what he appropriately calls "this terrible scourge." He has said that he wants to be remembered as the President who—working with our allies, the Soviet Union, and other nations—brought about the elimination of chemical warfare and chemical weapons.

The world community needs to band together and rededicate itself—forcefully and effectively—to the purposes and principles of the 1925 Geneva protocol. No country should face the threat of chemical weapons alone, for no country is immune to it. We must be prepared to exercise statesmanship, to cooperate, and to exact enforcement.

We, therefore, call on this conference to support the following steps immediately.

• Every nation must undertake the political commitment to comply with the international norms relating to chemical weapons use.

- Nations which have not done so should accede to the 1925 Geneva protocol.
- The U.N. Secretary General's ability to investigate promptly allegations of illegal use of chemical weapons in armed conflict should be reinforced and enhanced.

There is still more that we must do, both at this conference and after it.

We should consider procedures for humanitarian assistance to victims of chemical weapons attack. We need to bolster support for the measures embodied in the U.N. Charter should there be any future illegal use of chemical weapons—and here I have Chapter 7 sanctions expressly in mind. As President-elect Bush has said:

> . . . the nations guilty of chemical warfare must pay a price. They must know that violation of the ban against the use of such weapons carries a heavy penalty. Not just a fine or a minor sanction that can be ignored.

There is an urgent need for steps to achieve greater international restraint in the export of chemical weapons-related technologies, chemicals, and weaponry. Since 1985 the United States has cooperated with 18 other nations to coordinate efforts to control international trade in chemical weapons-related commerce. We should explore possibilities for more effective means to control the transfer of chemical weapons precursors, technology, and weapons without impeding legitimate commerce and peaceful pursuits that will benefit mankind.

Finally, I also urge you to join me in committing our governments not only to prevent the use of chemical weapons in armed conflict but also to prevent the spread of chemical weapons to terrorist groups.

The problem of chemical weapons proliferation is as difficult as it is dangerous. The challenge it poses to world security is so urgent that international efforts in this area should not be made contingent on other difficult arms control issues, such as nuclear proliferation. And if we are to deal with the chemical weapons threat effectively in all its respects, we must see the problem for what it is.

Chemical weapons proliferation is *not* an issue between the developed and developing world. It is *not* a matter of some nations trying to maintain a monopoly on chemical weapons by making it impossible for other nations to obtain them. All countries have everything to gain by keeping their focus on the real issue: preventing these weapons from spreading and being used, even as we devote ourselves to ridding the world of those which already exist.

For our part, the United States has participated actively in the negotiations at the Conference on Disarmament since 1971. We are committed to success in these negotiations, and we will stay at the table for however long it takes. We will abide by the 1925 Geneva protocol and all other provisions of international law related to the use of chemical weapons, including the 1949 Geneva conventions. We urge every country here—indeed, every country in the world—to make a similar pledge.

A GLOBAL EFFORT IS NEEDED

We all owe a debt of gratitude to the Government of France and to President Mitterrand for assembling the world community here in Paris in answer to President Reagan's call at the U.N. General Assembly. Together, we must meet the challenge posed by chemical weaponry. It is a global challenge. And it is grievously apt that these weapons were first used during the first worldwide war in human history. But as experience, stretching back almost a century to The Hague Gas Declaration teaches us, sweeping statements of principle are not a substitute for concrete deeds. We all have an obligation to take action.

The resumption in the past 25 years of chemical warfare is a dangerous step backward for mankind, for reason, for civilization. President-elect Bush has called the outbreak of chemical warfare and ballistic missile proliferation ''sharp reminders of how easily the nations can turn from the high road and head for the abyss.'' And he has declared it his ''solemn mission'' to work with the international community ''to stop it and stop it now!''

Now is the time for us all to stand up and face our responsibilities squarely. Together, let us get on with the task of fulfilling our solemn moral and legal obligations.

We must, quite simply, reaffirm the international norms against chemical weapons and raise them higher. Unless we summon the political will and establish rigorous and reliable international means of vigilance and restraint, we will condemn ourselves to repeat tragic experience. We already have witnessed one century-long cycle of international concern, followed by violence, tragedy, outrage, and then, alas, complacency.

I am haunted by a poem written in 1916 by the great American poet Carl Sandburg—in his time a European war correspondent. It is called ''Grass,'' and it ends with these stark and bitter lines:

> Pile the bodies high . . . at Ypres and Verdun.
> Shovel them under and let me work.
> Two years, ten years, and passengers ask the conductor:
> What place is this?
> Where are we now?
> I am the grass.
> Let me work.

I say to you now, let *us* instead work to ensure that we never forget the victims of chemical warfare. Let each and every one of us work to ensure that neither the passage of time nor the exigencies of the moment ever again obscure the responsibilities we have to all mankind.

Forget about Banning Chemical Weapons

Frank J. Gaffney, Jr.

INTRODUCTION

Mr. Chairman, members of the Committee, it is a particular pleasure for me to appear before a joint hearing of the Committee and its Permanent Subcommittee. These distinguished panels of the Senate were the locus of my first employment with the United States government nearly 13 years ago. I have always had fond memories of my time with the PSI's [Permanent Subcommittee on Investigations] then-Chairman, Sen. Henry M. Jackson ["Scoop"], and I can honestly say that there is no more appropriate venue for my testimony on chemical weapons than this one.

This is so for several reasons: First, it was Sen. Jackson who taught me much of the practical limitations of arms control, especially in the area of verification and enforcement of compliance—two subjects to which I will return momentarily.

Second, Sen. Jackson shaped my early thinking about the nature of—and the vital need for—deterrence in the world in which we live. Scoop understood that the world was not always as we would like it to be. I learned from him that we should seek to improve it where we could but that the United States must be able, where necessary, to deter military aggression and other forms of violence. This required the maintenance of our own, effective military forces and, if possible, close collaboration with key allies.

Third, it was during my service with Sen. Jackson that I became concerned about the problem of chemical weapons (CW). At that time, the United States had, for most of a decade, observed a unilateral moratorium on the production of chemical munitions. Evidence was mounting that the existing U.S. stockpile of chemical weapons was increasingly obsolete and—to an alarming degree—comprised of leaking weapons likely to prove more dangerous to American personnel than to our adversaries.

Sen. Jackson was concerned in the late 1970's about the very considerable offensive and defensive CW capabilities of the Soviet Union. He understood that the unilateral U.S. disarmament that would, in effect, result from our continued failure to modernize America's chemical arsenal could invite lethal chemical attacks against us and our allies.

RESTORING AMERICA'S CHEMICAL DETERRENT

Gradually, a bipartisan coalition formed in the Senate—thanks not only to Scoop's leadership, but also to the work of the distinguished co-chairmen of this hearing, Senators Glenn and Nunn, and then-Senator John Tower. By the early 1980's, a majority in the Senate believed that production of a safer form of chemical weapon—known as binaries—was essential if the United States were to retain a credible CW deterrent. Eventually, and belatedly, the House of Representatives followed suit.

The legislative struggle to overcome the inertia of America's unilateral moratorium on chemical weapons production is one of the great parliamentary sagas of our time. I am proud to have played a small part in it as a member of the Senate staff.

Interestingly, it took not only years of effort and great courage on the part of many members of Congress; it also required the then–Vice President, George Bush, to cast the decisive tie-breaking vote for chemical modernization on no fewer than three different occasions. This pivotal role is often cited as

Source: Frank J. Gaffney, Jr., testimony, U.S. Congress, Senate, *Global Spread of Chemical and Biological Weapons*, Hearings before the Committee on Governmental Affairs and Its Permanent Subcommittee on Investigations, 101st Cong., 1st Sess., 1989, pp. 337–347.

the catalyst for President Bush's intense personal determination to negotiate a ban on all chemical weapons.

Late in 1987, the United States finally resumed the production of chemical munitions, clearing the way to replace the existing inventory on a less than one-for-one basis. As a consequence, *we have begun to restore to the U.S. arsenal the single, proven deterrent to chemical aggression—a reliable and effective chemical retaliatory capability.*

The prescience of President Reagan in requesting this capability, and that of the Congress in ultimately approving it, is now clearer than ever. Not only does the Soviet Union retain its formidable capacity for conducting chemical warfare; today a growing number of Third World nations are obtaining the means to produce and use lethal chemical agents—the subject of these hearings.

THE LESSONS OF THE LIBYAN PLANT

The much publicized Libyan chemical weapons plant at Rabta is but the most recent—if among the most frightening—of the emerging CW programs in developing countries. While Qaddafi's potential to employ toxic chemical weapons in pursuit of his own aggressive aims (or on behalf of the international terrorists he supports) is grounds for ample concern, at least as troubling should be what the Rabta facility suggests about CW proliferation more broadly.

- First, this plant illustrates the point that there is simply no certain way to distinguish between legitimate facilities producing a range of chemical products for civilian use (e.g., fertilizers, pesticides, pharmaceuticals, etc.) and those producing weapons. The catastrophe at Bhopal, India, reveals just how lethal can be the products of some such facilities—even when used for civilian purposes.

- Consequently, the industrialized world's companies, banks and, yes, even governments are—knowingly or not—fostering the spread throughout the developing world of indigenous infrastructures with the inherent capability to produce chemical weapons. West Germany's assistance to the building and fitting out of Libya's Rabta complex is an infamous, but hardly unique, example of the phenomenon. The sources of chemical technology appear to be either indifferent to the potential for misuse—as the German exporters seemed to be—or they are willing to overlook it in the interest of making a sale.

- Even if one were able to determine on a given day—or, for that matter, over a period of time—that a plant was engaged in the manufacture of commercial chemical products, there is no known means of ensuring that its equipment will not be put to CW-related uses shortly thereafter. It was for precisely this reason that the United States properly declined when Qaddafi proposed to allay our concerns about the Rabta facility by offering an on-site inspection of it.

- The Rabta plant is, if anything, *more obviously associated with military activities* than one would expect to observe at facilities that were either engaged in covert manufacture of chemical weapons or being held in reserve against the day when such manufacture was deemed necessary. Its reported 40-foot earthen wall, rings of air defenses and other security measures are fairly compelling, albeit circumstantial, evidence of the purposes to which it will be put.

- It has, nevertheless, proven remarkably difficult to obtain allied—to say nothing of neutrals'—endorsements of the U.S. assessment of the Rabta complex. Perhaps the governments in question are unpersuaded because such a finding would be inconvenient for their relations with the Libyans—possibly exposing them or their citizens to increased threat of Libyan-sponsored terrorism. Or it may be that their acknowledgement of the facts might oblige them to take some responsibility for resolving the problem (e.g., sanctions or endorsement of military action).

- Whatever the reason, the fact is that—*even in the absence of a treaty banning production of chemical weapons*—it is excruciatingly difficult to get international agreement that a given activity is related to chemical weapons manufacture. We must expect that, should a treaty outlawing chemical weapons ever be achieved, persuading others that a given country (the Soviet Union, for example) is violating the agreement will become still more difficult.

- It is far from clear what the Libyans could now do—should they wish to do so—to persuade the United States that they have completely eliminated their incipient CW capability. Just as the Libyans were reported several weeks ago to be spiriting lethal precursors away from the Rabta facility, so too they could secretly relocate (or try to procure anew) the equipment needed to combine them with other agents to produce toxic agents for weapons. The termination of chemical warfare-related activities is likely to be as difficult to verify as their conduct.

These considerations serve to make two points: First, *chemical weapons proliferation is a fact of international life*. Such weapons can be manufactured cheaply; there is neither a need for expensive, dedicated facilities (as with nuclear weapons plants) nor for great technical sophistication. Countries around the world are availing themselves of the ability—actual or potential—to produce lethal chemical agents.

The reasons for their doing so are diverse: Some regard it as the easiest route to obtaining weapons of mass destruction—the poor man's atom bomb. Of these, some fancy CW's offensive potential, as vividly demonstrated in the effective use made of toxic chemical weapons by Iraq in its war with Iran. Many of the others see possession of CW as a feasible means of checkmating an adversary's nuclear arsenal.

Then there is the somewhat special case of a nation like Libya. Its purpose in acquiring a chemical weapons manufacturing capability appears motivated, at least in part, by the desire to add CW to the gruesome tools of the trade of the world-wide terrorist groups it sponsors.

A second point is that *the aforementioned factors make any effort to respond to CW proliferation by negotiating a ban on the production and stockpiling of chemical weapons dangerously futile*. It is simply not possible today to prevent countries with modern commercial chemical industries from also having thereby the ability to produce chemical weapons. There is no verification system known today *or in prospect* that will be able unfailingly to detect lethal chemical agent production and storage.

What is more, as the technology for manufacturing chemical products advances, the few signatures that today do provide important indications of CW activity are likely to disappear. Devices are already available on the commercial market that can manufacture lethal chemical agents (and, for that matter, toxin and biological weapons) without *specialized or dedicated facilities*. In fact, such agents can, with this technology, be produced *virtually anywhere*. There is no practicable verification scheme for dealing with such technical developments.

THE UNITED STATES GOVERNMENT'S 1987 REASSESSMENT

Considerations such as these in 1987 prompted *every involved agency of the United States government to recommend that the formal U.S. position seeking a global ban on chemical weapons be abandoned*. It would be hard to overstate the significance of this recommendation.

After all, the United States had been committed publicly to such a ban since Secretary of State George Shultz took it upon himself—without formal coordination or Cabinet approval—to announce that we would table a treaty for a global CW ban in a speech given in Stockholm in January, 1984. Moreover, Vice President George Bush in April 1984 personally tabled a U.S. text for a draft treaty prohibiting CW production and stockpiling that the U.S. government hastily put together following the Shultz announcement. That draft treaty called for developing the most rigorous verification regime ever designed—one that would provide for inspection of suspect sites "anywhere, anytime."

Given this highly visible and forward-leaning

public position on a CW ban, it was nearly inconceivable in 1987 that the United States government could actually *change its mind*. Not only would there be the considerable diplomatic embarrassment entailed in abandoning a position advanced at the highest levels; America's allies were virtually unanimous in their enthusiasm for a ban. It was also argued that the modest program for modernizing the U.S. inventory of chemical weapons would be halted if Congress saw a backing away from the concomitant effort to prohibit CW.

It was, nonetheless, a reflection of the perceived infeasibility of a ban on chemical weapons—*and the real risks that would accrue to the United States were it to enter into an unverifiable one*—that prompted the 1987 interagency consensus in favor of a change of U.S. CW arms control policy. But for the intervention of representatives of then–Vice President Bush who objected to the proposed change, I believe the United States government would have disavowed its own goal of negotiating a ''global,'' ''verifiable'' chemical weapons ban in favor of more modest limitations.

PROBLEMS WITH THE CURRENT ADMINISTRATION POSITION

Instead of putting aside the illusion of such a CW ban, the United States is today moving forward inexorably—in part thanks to the new impetus provided by the recent international conference in Paris—toward its negotiation. In fact, anything that will emerge from the Geneva negotiations is unlikely to be either ''global'' or ''verifiable.''

A Less Than ''Global'' Ban

As it may well prove impossible to get every nation to subscribe to the ban, the U.S. position is that the United States will enroll so long as *some* substantial number of other countries (e.g., sixty) do so. On the face of it, this means that America could enter into an agreement requiring it to eliminate *all of its CW capability* while many other nations are under *no* such obligation.

We are assured that, before the United States becomes a signatory, others like the Soviet Union, Iraq and Libya must agree to sign up. But this approach begs several questions: What if nations suspected of having CW are *not* among the signatories—will the United States still disarm? Even if non-signatories did not have a chemical weapons capability at the moment of U.S. signature, do we believe they will not obtain one subsequently? What would we do if they did?

A Less Than ''Verifiable'' Ban

As a practical matter, there is no such thing as a verifiable ban on chemical weapons. Short of true omniscience, in any arms control agreement involving closed, totalitarian societies, there is always some degree of verification uncertainty. What invariably occurs is a two-step process that erodes the value of any agreement reached.

First, the negotiators arrive at a lowest-common-denominator solution; they establish the degree of intrusive inspections and other monitoring arrangements that every signatory can accept. Inevitably, this outcome falls far short of what is required to verify even less daunting arms control agreements than a global CW ban.

Next comes the overselling of the treaty's verification provisions. Executive branch officials troop to the Senate to attest to the verifiability of provisions they know to be deficient in important respects. They rationalize that, as long as the treaty can be ''effectively,'' or ''sufficiently'' or ''adequately'' or ''reasonably'' verified, that is enough. In any event, it is the best they could get. In the end, they are betting that a party to the treaty will not cheat. The theory usually is that, even though such a party can be reasonably sure that its cheating would not be detected, it will, nonetheless, be deterred from doing so by the threat that other signatories' will take unpalatable retaliatory steps.

COMPLIANCE AND NON-COMPLIANCE

Regrettably, as the recent Paris conference illustrated so well, there is no reason whatsoever for believing that collective enforcement of compliance will occur. Indeed, the conferees found themselves unable even to *mention* countries (such as Iraq) clearly guilty of violating the existing international arms control agreement on chemical weapons—the 1925 Geneva convention banning their first use.

It is hard to imagine that the nations of the world will be more willing to take punitive measures when the result of a violation is not the wholesale murder of innocent civilians, brutally documented by television, but simply the existence of a building suspected of manufacturing illegal agents. If anything, the quarrels over the exact nature of the Libyan plant at Rabta augur ill for even reaching consensus positions on the facts concerning such facilities.

BIOLOGICAL WEAPONS

This question of verification, compliance and enforcement is not, unfortunately, an idle one. *There is already on the books a global ban on easily produced, cheap weapons of mass destruction—the 1972 prohibition on biological weapons* (BW).

Like that being sought for CW, the Biological Weapons Convention is utterly unverifiable; its framers, however, understood it to be so and simply dispensed with any effort to draft verification provisions. Like the proposed CW ban, it is supposed to prevent any nation from obtaining and stockpiling quantities of the prohibited substances. And, as will surely be the case with any future ban on chemical weapons, it is being violated by at least several of its signatories (e.g., the Soviet Union and Iraq). Yet, the United States remains in total compliance with its commitments under the Biological Weapons Convention.

This compliance extends not only to the literal obligation not to produce and possess *offensive* biological weapons; the United States today has *essentially no capability* to *defend* against biological attack by others. Understandably, the U.S. military has—in the aftermath of a solemn international agreement that is supposed to eliminate all BW weapons—accorded the biological warfare threat a low budgetary and doctrinal priority.

Unfortunately, the combination of this country's utter defenselessness against BW and its lack of an in-kind deterrent to biological weapons use against the United States could invite such use. At a minimum, it provides a powerful incentive to an adversary to exploit the inadequacies of the existing international convention banning biological weapons and attendant U.S. (and, more generally, Western) vulnerabilities.

A similar situation to that we face in the biological weapons area would almost certainly arise in the aftermath of a ban on the production and stockpiling of chemical weapons: The United States would faithfully comply with its terms. Its retaliatory stockpile and associated production base would be quickly rendered unusable and, in due course, would be eliminated. The United States would not only submit to whatever monitoring and inspection regime were agreed; it would also ensure through domestic laws and regulations that no inadvertent circumvention occurs.

Perhaps most sinister of all, the United States would almost certainly succumb over time to the temptation to dispense with *defensive CW training and preparations.* In fact, as hearings in the Armed Services Committee have repeatedly shown, *even in the face of a massive—and growing threat—U.S. CW defenses are already exceedingly modest.* How much less capable they will become when there is not supposed to be any CW threat can only be surmised.

CONCLUSIONS AND RECOMMENDATIONS
Forget about Banning Chemical Weapons

For these reasons, *I strongly recommend to the Committee and the Subcommittee that you regard the Bush Administration's pursuit of a global, verifiable ban on chemical weapons with great skepticism. The President must be encouraged to abandon this potentially dangerous goal.*

Ironically, those in the Administration responsible for fulfilling President Bush's oft-stated commitment to such a ban know better. Some senior officials have privately expressed to me their view that the ban is ill-advised; their hope is that, eventually, they will be able to disabuse the President of his illusions.

In the meantime—at least in the absence of vigorous Congressional scrutiny—these officials appear unwilling to admit that the ''emperor has no clothes.'' As a result, the United States lurches inexorably onward toward a dangerous, unverifiable chemical weapons ban.

I believe the United States cannot afford to engage in such hypocrisy. It is irresponsible to pay lip service to an objective whose accomplishment we know would be highly dangerous. American participation in a chemical weapons ban is—and will under all foreseeable circumstances remain—simply a formula for unilateral U.S. chemical disarmament. It is beneath us as a nation and, in any event, a delusion to believe that we can prevent this outcome by simply dragging our feet in the negotiations over some technical point of verification or another.

There are, of course, those who advocate a CW ban even though they understand that it might result in our complete disarmament *without effecting a perfect ban world-wide*. They tend to argue that it would be worth our while to give up our deterrent if that is the necessary price for dissuading even *some* nations around the world from acquiring chemical weapons. Such individuals frequently assert that whatever risks arise from other nations not being so dissuaded (i.e., those that choose to possess quantities of chemical weapons), can be fully offset by the deterrent value of our nuclear arsenal.

Scoop Jackson, for one, would have been appalled at the naivete and dangerous caprice involved in such statements. He would have given short shrift to the notion that, under present circumstances, we can responsibly enter into a CW ban in the hope of offering a model that others may or may not choose to follow. This would be particularly true given the verification uncertainties with which such a ban is fraught. Sen. Jackson also recognized the real limitations on threatening the use of nuclear weapons to deter less than wholesale conventional or nuclear aggression. I hope those who serve in the Senate today will be as wise.

Indeed, Congress can—and, in my view, must— play an instrumental role by demanding honest appraisals of the prospects for a global, verifiable ban

from Administration spokesmen. Halting the United States' headlong pursuit of a dangerous CW ban— and challenging the wishful thinking that motivates it—will require no less courage than Congress exhibited in approving the binary program some years ago. And yet, the risks to U.S. and allied security of doing otherwise are no less great than those that prompted the prudent, earlier action.

Pursue Other Measures for Curbing CW Proliferation

This is not to say that we are unable to take—or should refrain from taking—steps to slow the proliferation of chemical weapons. I strongly support economic sanctions as a means of imposing real penalties on those who would sell or buy CW-related capabilities. I commend Senators Pell, Dole and Helms for their leadership in this regard.

Obviously, if the United States hopes to prevail upon the other advanced industrial nations to give up lucrative sales of CW-related materials to developing nations, we must observe a consistent standard ourselves. On that point, I hope that the Bush Administration and the Congress will act to reverse an ill-considered decision taken in the last days of the Reagan Administration. This decision would permit two American firms, Honeywell and Bailey Controls, to provide the Soviet Union with the technology and equipment to manufacture under joint ventures automated controls that lend themselves to more efficient CW (and nuclear) weapons production.

I would strongly urge, as well, that the Congress look carefully at the means whereby countries like Libya obtain the financing by which they can buy chemical weapons-related facilities. It seems quite likely that allied banks and companies have made such procurements possible through their credit arrangements with and/or deposits in the Libyan Arab Foreign Bank. Swift action aimed at denying the Libyans such sources of revenue could have a dramatic effect on their ability to proceed with a CW program.

Finally, I hope the Congress will recognize that

the threat of chemical agents coming into the hands of state sponsors of terrorism like Libya is a sufficient menace as to warrant physical destruction of the site, if the preceding techniques prove ineffective.

Maintain the U.S. CW Deterrent

In the end, however, Mr. Chairman, *I do not believe the United States can prevent Libya—or other nations so disposed—from obtaining the capability to manufacture chemical weapons through an arms control agreement.* The effect of such an accord may be to slow proliferation marginally or—more likely—to make evidence of proliferation harder to come by. What it will assuredly do, however, is to prevent the United States from retaining the ability to deter chemical attacks against it and its allies by threatening credible, in-kind retaliation.

Based upon my thirteen years of professional experience in this field, starting with my service to this Committee, I must tell you such an outcome would entail unacceptable risks for U.S. national security and should be avoided at all costs. Unless and until a better, more reliable approach to preventing the use of chemical weapons against U.S. and allied personnel can be found, I believe the United States must maintain its own, modest but effective chemical retaliatory capability.

QUESTIONS FOR DISCUSSION

1. Is there a moral difference between using chemical weapons and using nuclear weapons? What are the reasons for your answer?
2. Compare the verification problems for nuclear weapons and for chemical weapons.
3. Why have states been reluctant to use chemical weapons?
4. Are chemical weapons more or less likely to be used in warfare now that the cold war is over? What are the reasons for your answer?

5. Does the acquisition of chemical weapons by third world nations make war more or less likely? What are the reasons for your answer?

SUGGESTED READINGS

Budensiek, Lt. Mark D. "A New Chemical Convention: Can It Assure the End of Chemical Weapon Proliferation?" *Stanford Journal of International Law*, **25** (Spring 1989), pp. 647–679.

Douglass, Joseph D., Jr. "Beyond Nuclear War." *Journal of Social, Political and Economic Studies*, **15** (Summer 1990), pp. 141–156.

Dunn, Lewis A. "Chemical Weapons Arms Control." *Survival* (London), **31** (May/June 1989), pp. 209–224.

Goldberg, Andrew C., and Debra van Opstal. "The Poor Man's Bomb." *World and I*, **4** (Apr. 1989), pp. 141–145.

Jones, David T. "Eliminating Chemical Weapons: Less Than Meets the Eye." *Washington Quarterly*, **12** (Spring 1989), pp. 83–92.

Klare, Michael T. "An Arms Control Agenda for the Third World." *Arms Control Today*, **20** (Apr. 1990), pp. 8–12.

Low, Susan McKiernan. "Controlling the Proliferation of Chemical Weapons: Can the Genie Be Put Back in the Bottle?" *Houston Journal of International Law*, **12** (Fall 1989), pp. 77–123.

Miller, A. J. "Towards Armageddon: The Proliferation of Unconventional Weapons and Ballistic Missiles in the Middle East." *Journal of Strategic Studies* (London), **12** (Dec. 1989), pp. 387–404.

U.S. Cong., Senate. *Chemical and Biological Weapons Proliferation.* Hearing before the Subcommittee on International Finance and Monetary Policy of the Committee on Banking, Housing, and Urban Affairs, 101st Cong., 1st Sess., 1989.

———. *Chemical and Biological Weapons Threat: The Urgent Need for Remedies.* Hearings before the Committee on Foreign Relations, 101st Cong., 1st Sess., 1989.

Weekly, Terry M. "Proliferation of Chemical Warfare: Challenge to Traditional Restraints." *Parameters*, **19** (Dec. 1989), pp. 51–66.

Zanders, Jean Pascal. "Chemical Weapons: Beyond Emotional Concerns." *Bulletin of Peace Proposals*, **21** (Mar. 1990), pp. 87–98.

CHAPTER 6

The Future World Order

The world has experienced cataclysmic war and depression in the twentieth century. It has also known peace and prosperity. What will the future world order be? Political leaders, scholars, and writers disagree. Some are optimistic and others pessimistic.

Some of the more optimistic visions of the future are reflected in the readings of this book. The view that states will decline in importance as greater interdependence among nations requires cooperation rather than conflict is one optimistic vision. Other observers foresee rising standards of living as the benefits of science and technology become available to all the people of the world. This view is in keeping with nineteenth-century liberal and Marxist belief that industrial society will usher in an age of unprecedented abundance of goods so that real improvement in the quality of life will be experienced everywhere.

Today pessimistic visions of the future are more common. Essential themes of this pessimistic outlook are also reflected in the readings in this book: the danger of nuclear war, the prevalence of widespread poverty among the masses of people in the third and fourth worlds, and the persistence of nationalism.

The debates in Chapter 6 deal with three issues crucial to the future world order: the problem of terrorism, the impact of population growth on peace and prosperity, and the level of U.S. military commitments abroad in the post–cold war era.

TERRORISM

The use of armed power by one state to fight wars against the armed forces of another country constitutes a traditional application of force in international politics. The post–World War II period, however, has been characterized not only by conventional warfare but also by a different form of force: terrorism.

Terrorism lacks a precise definition. The term ''terror'' was first used in a political sense during the French Revolution. The Terror referred to the period between June 1793 and July 1794 in which a dictatorship promoted terror through its policies of political repression. The uncontrolled use of coercion by a government against its people continues to be a practice of governments. Josef Stalin and Adolf Hitler in the 1930s are modern examples of political leaders who engaged in terror against their own peoples. Pol Pot, the communist leader of Cambodia in the 1970s, is a more recent example, responsible for liquidating millions of his own people.

"Terrorism" has another principal meaning: the use of violence by substate actors against civilians and political figures for the purpose of ending a regime's rule and establishing a new government. Terrorism in this sense is a form of unconventional war. Because nongovernmental terrorists are militarily weak, they cannot hope for success by confronting government forces in set battles. Rather they must engage in activities that are unexpected, secret, and newsworthy.

Terrorist actions became global and particularly prominent in the 1970s and 1980s. They involved the hijacking of aircraft, assassination of political leaders, bombing of government buildings, and kidnapping of business leaders who work in multinational corporations. Organizations such as the Black September movement and the Irish Republican Army (IRA) have engaged in major terrorist plots. The actions of these organizations are diverse.

In 1972, for example, nine members of Black September, an organization committed to the creation of a Palestinian state, entered the grounds of the Olympic Games in Munich and held Israeli athletes as hostages. In the end some Israeli hostages were murdered, and the terrorist squad got away in airplanes that took them out of the Federal Republic of Germany and into a friendly Arab country.

In 1979 the IRA, which seeks to unite Northern Ireland with the Republic of Ireland, was responsible for the assassination of Lord Mountbatten, British Queen Elizabeth's uncle. To draw attention to its cause, it has placed bombs in British cities in locations where ordinary citizens congregate.

The Symbionese Liberation Army, a U.S.-based organization of revolutionaries, kidnapped heiress Patricia Hearst in 1974 and held her hostage at the same time that it made public threats about killing her. The revolutionaries forced Hearst's father, publisher William Randolph Hearst, to provide funds for distributing food to people living in poor neighborhoods. While under terrorist control, Patricia Hearst engaged in illegal activities alongside the group's members.

These terrorists and others have received media publicity of their exploits. This publicity gives exposure to their causes at the same time that it creates fear among people everywhere. Terrorists rely on such acts as kidnapping, hijacking of aircraft, assassinations, and the sporadic use of explosives against people and property because they lack sufficient military strength to engage enemy armed forces in direct combat.

The world has learned to live with terrorism. Although governments have improved surveillance, detection, and other antiterrorist techniques, terrorist acts continue. Will terrorism end if solutions are found for its root causes? Anthropologist William O. Beeman argues the Affirmative. He contends: (1) In general, terrorism can be seen as a form of social pathology arising in communities that find themselves under extreme pressure. (2) Lebanese Shiites and Palestinians are two communities that fit into this category. (3) Even the removal from power of Libyan leader Muammar Qaddafi, who is often accused of sponsoring terrorism, will not make terrorism go away. (4) To deal with terrorism one must come to terms with the root cause—the underlying community malaise that stems from injustice. Beeman advocates a global forum addressing the real grievances of the communities from which terrorism is arising.

Expressing an opposing view, syndicated columnist Charles Krauthammer argues: (1) There is no correlation between ostensible root causes of terrorism and acts of terrorism. (2) Many of the demands of terrorists to deal with root causes cannot be achieved—at least in the short run. (3) The root cause idea is dangerous for it leads to despair, because root causes cannot be changed, or to moral ambivalence, because legitimacy necessarily accrues to those who fight with root cause on their side. (4) Many of the terrorist groups in the Middle East will be satisfied only with the destruction of Israel. The people in the Middle East who engage in terror do not want peace, and those who want peace are not engaged in terror.

POPULATION GROWTH

More than five billion people inhabit our planet. Many countries—particularly in the third world—are experiencing rapid population growth. Is rapid population growth a threat to economic development and world peace?

Predictions of economic decline based on population go back at least to Thomas Malthus, an eighteenth-century economist. Malthus believed that population was increasing more rapidly than food supplies and suggested that famines, wars, plagues, earthquakes, floods, and other disasters were essential interactions between people and the environment.

Neo-Malthusians of the twentieth century use computers and mathematical models to come to similar conclusions. In 1972 the Club of Rome sponsored *The Limits to Growth*, a study that predicted a global disaster if economic growth and population growth were not sharply reduced. Some pessimists of the twentieth century have also pointed to ecological disasters ahead.

In 1977 President Jimmy Carter asked the U.S. Department of State and the Council on Environmental Quality to analyze economic and environmental trends as the world heads toward the year 2000. The major conclusion of the report—*The Global 2000 Report*—issued in 1980, is that if present trends continue, ''the world in 2000 will be more crowded, more polluted, less stable ecologically, and more vulnerable to disruption than the world we live in now.'' In the view of the analysts, people will be poorer in 2000 than they are today.[1]

Is rapid population growth a threat to economic development and world peace? Scientists Paul R. Ehrlich and Anne H. Ehrlich see population growth as a global disaster. They contend: (1) Global population growth is still out of control except for a slowdown due to fertility reductions in China, the industrialized West, and a few other

---

[1] Council on Environmental Quality and the Department of State, *The Global 2000 Report to the President of the United States: Entering the 21st Century*, vol. 1: *The Summary Report* (Washington, D.C.: Government Printing Office, 1980), p. 1.

developing nations. (2) Halting population growth in less-developed nations will be much harder than in industrialized nations. (3) Rates of population growth will not decline with industrialization. (4) Overpopulation has an adverse impact on the planet's environment. (5) Richer industrial nations should assist developing nations in their programs to limit population growth.

Writer Karl Zinsmeister argues that the increasing size of the world's population is not a great problem. He contends: (1) The dire predictions made about population wars and famines generated because of high population have proven false. (2) Since the mid-1970s, the less-developed world has moved three-fifths of the way toward a fertility rate that yields zero population growth. (3) The standard of living of third world countries has been rapidly improving during the last few decades. (4) Social scientists have determined: (a) the growth of large cities in the third world cannot be attributed to population growth; (b) population growth has had almost nothing to do with the famines of recent decades. (5) Density of population has no consequences for economic development and standard of living. (6) Socioeconomic development ought to be the centerpiece of population policy, since population growth declines with greater economic development.

UNITED STATES FOREIGN POLICY

With the demise of the cold war, world politics itself is undergoing a vast change. To many observers, recent changes in the communist world have been so thorough that it would be difficult to reverse course even if Mikhail Gorbachev, the architect of the new Soviet foreign policy, lost power.

The Soviet Union has taken obvious steps to signal a real change in its foreign policy. It accepted the unification of Germany, the demise of the Warsaw Pact, and the establishment of democratic regimes in Eastern Europe. It allowed greater political freedom in the Soviet Union than Soviet citizens had ever experienced. It sought improved relations with the West.

Because of its domestic problems, the Soviet Union has also recognized that its ability to play a strong role in world politics is limited. The Soviet economy cannot provide everyday consumer needs on any scale close to that in developed, capitalist economies. Moreover, ethnic disputes are resulting in bloodshed, and independence movements are asserting themselves in every Soviet republic.

To some extent, the new Soviet role in world politics may be presaged in its behavior when Iraq invaded Kuwait in 1990. Moscow did not attempt to support Iraq, its former client state. Although Soviet policy differed from that of the United States, Moscow supported the United States and other major powers in condemning Iraqi action. The Soviet Union did not use its veto power in the U.N. Security Council to prevent the coalition forces led by the United States from taking economic and military action against Iraq. Although Soviet leaders tried to salvage something for Iraq through negotiations, they never stood in the way of U.S.-led forces.

Recognizing that world politics was entering a new phase, President George Bush spoke of a new international order. He never spelled out in detail what this world order would look like except to say that global politics would no longer be dominated by the Soviet-U.S. rivalry.

With the end of the cold war, new debate in the United States centers on the U.S. role in the new international order. Some seek a sharp reduction in U.S. military power, with a "peace dividend" diverted to pressing domestic needs such as education, health, and housing. Others favor a return to neo-isolationism and a reduction of overseas commitments. Still others hope that the United States will continue to play a strong role in world politics. Some urge that the United States be at the forefront in promoting democracy around the world. And some argue for a Pax America (American Peace), world peace wrought by the superior power of a single state in the way Great Britain dominated in the nineteenth century (Pax Britannica).

Should the United States sharply reduce its military commitments abroad in the post–cold war era? *Defense Monitor*, a publication of the Center for Defense Information, says that it should. It contends: (1) U.S. military forces based in foreign countries do not contribute to the defense of the United States. (2) The United States is not bound by treaties to use its military forces to defend other countries. (3) The world has changed significantly with the collapse of communism in East Europe. (4) Other countries are capable of providing their own defenses. (5) The world does not need the United States to be global policeman. (6) Military forces in the United States can respond quickly to crises anywhere in the world. (7) Military forces do not assure economic access and political influence. (8) U.S. military forces are not needed to deter German and Japanese disarmament. (9) U.S. forces are wearing out their welcome. (10) Withdrawing and demobilizing U.S. forces will save tens of billions of dollars.

Midge Decter, a writer and former executive director of the Committee for the Free World, takes an opposing viewpoint. Speaking at the conservative think-tank Heritage Foundation several weeks before the United States engaged in combat operations against Iraq in January 1991, she contends: (1) Since the United States is the richest and most powerful country in the world, it cannot withdraw from the affairs of other countries. (2) Although the United States should not intervene in every international crisis, it will have to intervene in some of the most important, especially those that threaten the peace and security of international neighborhoods and, ultimately, of the United States. (3) U.S. foreign policy for the future could be exercised under a principle of Pax Americana in which the United States will be both powerfully armed and defended.

21 Will Terrorism End If Solutions Are Found for Its Root Causes?

YES

William O. Beeman

Terrorism: Community Based or State Supported?

NO

Charles Krauthammer

Terror and Peace: The "Root Cause" Fallacy

Terrorism: Community Based or State Supported?

William O. Beeman

A new report from the Rand Corporation points out that terrorist activity is increasing at 12 to 15 percent per year. Moreover, terrorism is likely to continue to increase. It is becoming institutionalized, according to the report, and soon may become a normal feature of human life if measures are not taken to curtail it.

This news cannot be greeted with much joy in a world already surfeited with news reports of terrorist activities everywhere. The hijackings of TWA flight 847 and the Italian cruise ship *Achille Lauro*, combined with bombings and suicide missions in Europe, India and the Middle East, have made many think that the world has gone mad in recent years.

More disturbing was the fact that the governments of the world seem to have no effective way to deal with terrorists. Threats to ''retaliate'' or ''send a message'' to terrorists issued from Washington and other world capitals turn out to be largely empty rhetoric; terrorism continues unabated. The Rand Corporation report was notably lacking in suggestions for controlling terrorism.

Anthropological research on disaffected communities provides a great deal of understanding about the dynamics of terrorism, however. From an anthropological standpoint terrorism is not a normal form of human behavior, but it is definitely predictable, arising under clearly defined conditions. Because of the extreme nature of those conditions, it is unfortunately clear that eliminating terrorism is neither easy nor quick.

Source: William O. Beeman, ''Terrorism: Community Based or State Supported?'' *American-Arab Affairs*, no. 16 (Spring 1986), pp. 29–36. Reprinted by permission.

As a working definition, terrorism may be described as:

1. illegal acts of violence
2. carried out against defenseless targets
3. in order to achieve political goals
4. perceived as unaddressable in any other fashion.

The most important insight we have about terrorism is that it is community based. In general, terrorism can be seen as a form of social pathology arising in communities which find themselves under extreme pressure. Anthropologist Colin Turnbull described such a community in his book, *The Mountain People*. The people described therein, the Ik, were forced from their extensive homelands into a minuscule territory, deprived of their natural livelihood, and made dependent on central governmental charity. They soon turned violent and paranoid.

The Ik, a relatively small and powerless community, were unable to strike out at the forces that oppressed them, so they directed random violence against their own people. Terrorism is violence turned outward, often directed against targets other than those causing the perceived oppression of the community from which it arises. It is likewise a form of social violence manifested by peoples who feel they have no other recourse in dealing with their social difficulties. It is an outgrowth of the social dynamics of particular communities where individuals feel themselves to be beleaguered and ignored both at home and by the international community.

When they feel themselves under siege, community members begin to tolerate more extreme behavior in the name of community causes. The surest sign of imminent terrorist activity coming out of a community is unwillingness of community leaders to condemn extreme elements in the community for fear of losing overall community support.

We may speak of such communities as ''terrorist-generating communities.'' The Sikh community in India, Catholics in Northern Ireland, Shiites in Lebanon and Palestinians throughout the Middle East are good examples. These communities feel, rightly or wrongly, that they have exhausted every channel in getting their needs met. No one cares about them, and thus violent force will give a sense of movement to their cause, galvanizing internal support, and attracting international attention to it. Because community causes are righteous, indeed often religious, the terrorist acts of community members are not condemned by the community.

LEBANESE SHIITES AND PALESTINIANS— TWO TERRORIST-GENERATING COMMUNITIES

One of the best examples of a terrorist-generating community in recent years is the Shiite community in southern Lebanon. The Shiites are the largest ethnic community in Lebanon, but they have historically been the poorest and most disadvantaged community. The government of Lebanon has been dominated for over 50 years by the Maronite Christian community, which is the third largest community in that country. The Christians have done little to improve the lot of the Shiites and have actively opposed giving them greater governmental power.

The Shiites' plight has been a festering sore to the community, unrecognized by the outside world. Their dissatisfaction was aggravated by the presence of Palestinians in refugee camps in Lebanon who competed with them for jobs.

The revolution of 1978–79 in Iran showed the Shiites that armed opposition to a central government could result in successful revolution. When the United States, Israel and other Western powers lent support to the Christian government, extremist elements in the Shiite community began terrorist attacks and kidnappings in the name of Islamic resistance to illegitimate outside powers. Shiite leaders such as Nabih Berri were powerless to condemn these acts, for fear of being toppled from their own positions as heads of the community. If the new accords between Shiite, Sunni and Christian communities in Lebanon hold, and the Shiites do accede to power, terrorist actions from that community will cease.

Palestinian terrorism is another clear case in point. Here again, the Palestinian community fits the definition of a terrorist-generating community very well. Hundreds of thousands of Palestinians who lived in areas near Haifa, Jaffa, Jerusalem, Beersheba, and the Galilee region left their homelands after they fell under Jewish control during and following the war with Israel in 1948. No autonomous Palestinian homeland was ever established, and the Palestinians were prevented from returning to their original homes by the State of Israel. In the 1967 war between Israel and its Arab neighbors, another group of Palestinians fled from the West Bank to other Arab nations. Though not officially classified as refugees, these individuals have also been displaced from their homeland.

As a refugee people with no land of their own since 1948, Palestinians have had to rely on the goodwill of host nations. Sadly they have also been exploited by those nations. This has led to bitterness and frustration which has often spilled over into violence.

The most disturbing aspect of life for Palestinians is the knowledge that they are not wanted in their host countries and are being used by host governments for their own purposes.

King Hussein of Jordan needs the Palestinians as diplomatic partners to regain the West Bank territories lost in the 1967 war. Militarily he knows that he cannot stand up to Israel. Therefore he must pursue a negotiated solution if he hopes to obtain any concessions from the Israelis. In a negotiated solution, however, his claims of sovereignty over the West Bank are not persuasive if pursued without participation of the Palestinians who live there.

Palestinians have ambiguous feelings toward the King. It is clear that he must work constantly to retain Palestinian support. "King Hussein is not our leader," says Mohammad Hamid, a young Palestinian shopkeeper in Jerusalem. "But he is King of Jordan so we are dependent on him, and he is useful to us too." "King Hussein is not always doing his homework on the West Bank," claims one former Palestinian official now in exile in Amman. "He needs to spread more money on the West Bank and shore up his support. Otherwise the Palestinians may split with him later."

Part of the Palestinian discomfort stems from

Hussein's purge and expulsion of the PLO [Palestine Liberation Organization] in 1970, an act that has bad memories for Palestinians even today. A young girl in a West Bank vocational training school said, "We do not like the King. He murdered our people in 1970." When reminded that she was only three or four years old when this occurred, she replied, "Still we can never forget what happened."

Despite continual statements of support for the Palestinian cause, Hafez Assad of Syria seems to be using the Palestinians to further his government's influence in the region and in the Arab world at large. He dreams one day of uniting the entire region as "Greater Syria." To this end, factionalism and rivalry assure greater power for a strong, unified Syrian presence.

Syria promotes and supports dissident factions of the Palestine Liberation Organization, particularly those led by Arafat rival Colonel Abu Musa, for two purposes: to put direct pressure on the governments of Lebanon and Jordan without having to expend any direct Syrian military effort, and to assure that the PLO itself remains divided. If the West Bank is regained, the presence of strong rival factions assures that the Palestinians will have a difficult time re-establishing themselves in any unified fashion.

Assad's government uses other Palestinians in their regular military forces. All Palestinians in Syria must serve in the Syrian armed forces in a special division—the Palestinian Liberation Army [PLA]. Sohail Hamid, director of GAPAR, the Syrian agency charged with refugee affairs, claims that all officers of the PLA are Palestinian themselves, a statement denied by foreign diplomats in Damascus. What seems clear is that if there is a military confrontation between Syria and Israel over the Golan Heights or other territory, the Palestinian forces will be at the fore.

In Lebanon, the Palestinians are despised by the population and the Lebanese government. Their existence in Lebanon is a supercharged emotional issue. Consequently they have been used for twenty years by rival political factions to beat up on each other.

Their political role has now become that of universal scapegoats, at the bottom of every heap. According to U.N. officials serving in Lebanon, they are barely employable, obtaining only the most menial labor. They receive few social services and almost no military protection from the Lebanese central government. Moreover they are constantly under attack from every military force in the region. Because the Lebanese will not or cannot protect them, their sole defense is the PLO. Paradoxically, the stronger the PLO presence in Palestinian areas, the more likely those areas are to be attacked.

The strongest independent military forces in Lebanon are the Shiite Amal, and the Christian Phalangists, both of whom regularly attack the PLO, killing vast numbers of innocent Palestinians in the process. The central government tacitly supports this. As long as the Palestinians are the principal target of Shiite wrath, the Christian government buys itself more time. Phalangist attacks against Palestinians likewise prevent more divisive struggles between Christians and other Moslems.

Israel currently exploits Palestinians living in the West Bank and Gaza. The Palestinians constitute a huge pool of cheap skilled labor for Israeli agriculture and industry, and Israel apparently wants the labor situation to remain at this level. Unskilled labor is hired at approximately 5,000 shekels ($5.00) per day, well below market rate. Moreover, Israel's economic politics in the West Bank are guaranteeing that most laborers will continue to be employed at that rate as day laborers.

Palestinians have not been allowed to develop or expand their own industries, banks, hospitals or educational institutions. This leaves many thousands of educated young people with only three choices: remain unemployed, take menial jobs at minimal wages or go abroad to find work. If young men go to Jordan, the easiest labor market for them, they are liable for military service. After serving in the Jordanian army the Israelis will not let them return to Israel. The end result is masses of college and technical-school graduates either sitting at home, or hoeing tomatoes on Israeli kibbutzim.

Nor has agriculture been allowed to develop, despite the fact that West Bank land is extremely productive. Palestinians are convinced that the Israelis want their land, and want to drive them off of it. Since cultivated land cannot be declared "state land" and appropriated for settlement, the Israeli government has tried to prevent new cultivation whenever possible. "Anyone wanting to plant anything must get a permit," claims former mayor Abu Bassam Shakka of Nablus. "They can even prevent me from planting in my own garden."

All of this bodes ill for negotiations for a Palestinian homeland. Israel clearly wants to maintain land under its control, and possibly the people as well as a continuing economic resource. King Hussein wants to use those same people as a political resource to regain sovereignty over that same land. Hafez Assad sees continued turmoil in the area as working to his government's advantage.

Even the best of the Palestinians' "friends" seem unwilling to provide support for Palestinians in their current situation in terms of basic social support services. Moreover, all of the states in which Palestinians reside are bent on making political capital of their situation. Under these circumstances it is not surprising that a significant number of Palestinians still feel that armed struggle is the only way they are going to obtain anything for themselves.

"STATE SPONSORED TERRORISM" AND MUAMMAR QADDAFI

Many Americans, and indeed others in the world, reject the notion that terrorism could have any legitimate ideological base. The position of Secretary of State George Shultz, and indeed a good portion of the Reagan administration, is that there would be no terrorism if there were no support from state governments, such as Iran, Syria or Libya.

Of course the basic theme expressed in this discussion directly contradicts this notion. If terrorism is indeed community based, then state sponsorship of it is somewhat irrelevant. To explore this proposition more fully, let us examine the case of Colonel Muammar Qaddafi, targeted by the U.S. government as one of the chief causes, if not the chief cause, for terrorism in the world today. If terrorism is seen as stemming primarily from disaffected communities, how dangerous is Qaddafi?

First, what kind of support is Libya providing to terrorists?

Evidence shows that Libya has at times provided broad support to many revolutionary groups, including the Provisional Wing of the Irish Republican Army, Muslim insurgents in the Philippines, the Japanese Red Army, and several dissident factions of Palestinians. Libya also supports a number of political and religious groups throughout the world. Some of the groups supported by Libya have committed terrorist acts. The nature of Libyan support has been financial. Occasionally leaders of revolutionary groups, such as Palestinian leader Abu Nidal, have found sanctuary in Libya.

Libya has also provided highly ephemeral, short-term "workshops" on terrorism. The U.S. administration has made it seem that there are established terrorist training camps in Libya, but even administration officials when questioned closely admit that "training" in Libya has been ad hoc, sporadic and temporary. There have also been relatively few such operations. The Cubans, for example, have done much more, much more systematically.

Terrorist acts have also been undertaken by Libyans themselves but only against other Libyans who oppose Qaddafi's regime. One such terrorist attack was foiled in April 1985 in London. Another took place in the United States and was the only act of 23 terrorist incidents taking place in the United States that involved a Libyan.

Second, if Libya stopped all support for groups that commit terrorist acts, would terrorism stop or be significantly impaired?

Undoubtedly terrorist groups would be impaired in their operations if Libya stopped giving them any financial or logistic support, but they would probably neither cease to exist, nor would they stop terrorist tactics. If Libya stops giving them money, they will obtain it elsewhere, from other nations, from even more outrageous criminal acts such as smuggling, gun-running for other groups, or kidnapping. Failing that, they will slow down their activities, committing acts with less frequency but with just as much fervor. Nothing will stop terrorism until the perceived grievances of the communities from which terrorists emerge are addressed.

Third, what effect do U.S. sanctions have on Qaddafi?

U.S. threats and sanctions have had exactly the opposite effect on Colonel Qaddafi that the Reagan administration would wish. They have given him greater political strength. Qaddafi is considered a loner and a maverick in the Arab world. He considers himself the heir to Gamal Abdul Nasser's pan-Arab doctrines, and aspires to leadership of the entire Arab world. In his ambition he is often viewed with great skepticism, even ridicule, among Arab leaders. Moreover, in the past two years he has lost popularity with his own people due to quixotic economic and trade restrictions imposed by him. The Soviet Union, though counting him as an ally, views him as an unguided missile—unpredictable and a little mad.

In the Arab world, however, there is a saying: Me against my brother, my brother and I against our cousins. By attacking Qaddafi through military exercises of the kind carried out in the Gulf of Sidra in 1981, 1983 and March 1986, the United States has caused the entire Arab world to rally around him in opposition to us. Forty-five Arab prime ministers meeting in Fez voted unanimously to support Libya after Reagan's speech attacking him early in 1986. The Soviet Union has vowed to break any U.S. blockade of Libya. The Libyan people have also rallied to his support, when last month they were grumbling about his regime. Nothing he could have done would have given him as strong a political boost as President Reagan's continual invective against him.

Fourth, does Qaddafi constitute a terrorist threat to the United States?

Qaddafi knows a bargain when he sees it. As long as he can continue to score political points by issuing empty threats, he will do so. He will become a real threat to the United States if and only if America actually attacks Libya. At that point, his honor would be at stake, and he would find many, many people willing to carry out his threat of attacking targets within the United States itself.

Americans do not properly appreciate the power of revenge in the Middle East. Avenging a wrong takes priority over many other considerations in life. To "make one's name good" is of utmost importance, even if it means destroying one's entire material well-being. The United States must not make the mistake of starting a cycle of revenge, when what is desired is to create a deterrent.

Finally, what should the United States do about Qaddafi?

The truth is, attacking Qaddafi economically, militarily and verbally is useless if the United States truly wishes to stop terrorism. A "victory" over Qaddafi has the quality of the U.S. "victory" in Grenada—a lot of flash, proving nothing and accomplishing very little.

Even if the United States wipes Libya off the map with the Sixth Fleet, terrorism will not stop. Colonel Qaddafi is indeed a reprehensible character for feeding and encouraging community terrorist pathology, but he did not create it, and attacking him will not make it go away.

DEALING WITH TERRORISM—NO QUICK FIX

Terrorist-generating communities are not a very new phenomenon, nor are they restricted to the Middle East or the developing world. The Sons of Liberty, from the American Revolution, has been used as a case study of a terrorist organization by no less an organization than the U.S. Central Intelligence Agency. The French Canadian separatist movement and linguistic chauvinists in Belgium have also used terrorist tactics in recent years. Some inner-city violence in the United States might also qualify as terrorist in nature.

Even Israeli officials who are most strident in

their criticism of terrorist tactics must remember that the establishment of the State of Israel in 1948 was preceded by terrorist acts against British administrative and military facilities. Former Prime Minister Menachem Begin was under order of arrest by British officials for committing terrorist acts.

Because the acts are based in the community, attacking individual terrorists is futile. Individuals who are arrested or executed become martyrs to the basic community cause, and are quickly replaced by others inspired by their "heroism." Thus "getting tough" with terrorists is directly counterproductive.

There are probably no short-term "quick-fix" solutions to terrorism. Trying to deal with the surface phenomena of terrorist activity without treating the underlying community malaise will only create temporary cessation in terrorist activity. Some measures can be taken to lessen the force of terrorist attacks, however.

1. To forestall terrorist attacks against their citizens, the United States and other nations should avoid making public statements in support of the groups which terrorists feel are oppressing them. The United States quickly learned in Lebanon that direct support expressed for the Christian minority government there increased attacks against American installations.

2. Attempts should be made to limit publicity given to terrorist acts. One of the rewards of terrorism is international attention for the community causes espoused by the terrorists. Limiting publicity for the terrorist acts denies terrorists those rewards. Of course with a free press, news blackouts are not practical or desirable, but avoidance of the sensationalism and emotionalism in reporting terrorist actions would do a great deal in making those actions seem less important. We need far fewer television and newspaper interviews focusing on weeping relatives of hijack victims.

3. Encourage addressing of real grievances of the communities from which terrorism is arising. These communities feel trapped and at the end of their resources. The media, religious organiza-

tions and world governments should work to establish platforms where communities that feel themselves under siege like the Sikhs, Shiites and Northern Irish Catholics can air their grievances before the world without having to throw bombs to be heard. It is pathetic and tragic to see young men and women willing to risk their lives and the lives of innocent victims for twenty minutes of television time.

There is no such platform at present anywhere. (The World Court only deals with disputes between states, not with grievances of individual communities within those states.) In the absence of any institutionalized structure for dealing with these problems, such organizations as Amnesty International, the International Human Rights Commission and the Nobel Prize Committee (through granting the Peace Prize to significant leaders in these communities) have provided virtually the only peaceful vehicles for publicizing these communities' grievances.

An example of the power of an international platform for the airing of grievances can be seen in the case of South Africa. International press attention, aided by the powerful presence of Bishop Desmond Tutu, has resulted in extraordinary political and economic pressure against the government of South Africa which will surely result in the eventual lessening of the evils of apartheid in that nation. But for every South Africa, there are hundreds of other beleaguered communities that may turn into terrorist-generating communities in the near future. Among them are the Tamil minority in Sri Lanka, the Native American populations in Latin America— even European groups, such as the Bretons in France and Croatians in Yugoslavia.

Most nations and international agencies are reluctant to provide a stage for the airing of these grievances because to do so would constitute "interference in the internal affairs of another nation." However, terrorism is becoming such a profound international problem that these "internal matters" are creating tragedy for people everywhere. A global forum would give responsible leaders of communities under siege a platform for presenting their message to the world in a non-violent manner.

Mere airing of grievances will be useless if some action is not taken to show that nonterrorist approaches to settling community grievances can be effective. Palestinian and Shiite leaders favoring negotiation of their difficulties have had little to offer their communities in terms of results, leaving the public open to the arguments of extremists.

Of course individual terrorists must be pursued and convicted, but it must be recognized that their crimes, as reprehensible as they are, are crimes of conscience not undertaken for personal gain. Merely arresting and executing them will do little to stop terrorism as long as the communities they come from see themselves as frustrated and under attack.

Terror and Peace:
The "Root Cause" Fallacy

Charles Krauthammer

The idea of "root causes" has great political attraction. Some years ago in the U.S., it dominated debate on policy toward El Salvador. It was argued that the Administration's hopes for a military solution were futile because the real causes of the insurrection were poverty, misery and hunger.

Well, yes. Revolutions do need misery to feed on. (There are exceptions. Occasionally there are revolutions of the comfortable, as in the 1960s in the U.S. and France. Such facsimiles, however, are invariably short-lived and harmless.) But these conditions, while obviously a necessary cause of revolution, are not sufficient. If they were, there would be revolution everywhere and always, since, aside from in a few countries in very modern times, poverty is the common condition of mankind.

But revolution is neither ubiquitous nor permanent. We need, therefore, something beyond poverty and misery to explain why there is revolt in some places and not others. This takes us out of the realm of what is usually meant by root causes, to culture, history, revolutionary leadership, foreign sponsorship and other presumably contingent causes.

That some causes and not others are accorded the honorific "root" has consequences. The first is to confer some special legitimacy on one set of grievances and thus on the revolutionary action that is taken in its name.

A second consequence emerges from a peculiar property of root causes: on close examination they turn out to be, as a matter of practice or policy, insoluble. There is no conceivable American policy that will solve the problem of poverty in Central America. (Not that poverty can never be ameliorated. It can. But not by a simple act of political will. In the West, for example, the conquest of mass poverty was the product of two centuries of painful industrialization.) The term "root" tends to be assigned to the most intractable of conditions. Except in the mind of the revolutionary, that is. The idea of root causes is therefore an invitation to surrender—to the resistant reality of misery or to the revolutionary who alone offers the promise of instant redemption.

Thus the danger of the root cause idea. It is offered as an analytic tool to understand an unpleasant reality: revolutionary violence. But whether intended or not, the logic of the root cause argument suggests one of two attitudes toward the unpleasantness: (1) despair, because root causes cannot be changed, or (2) moral ambivalence, because legitimacy necessarily accrues to those who fight with root cause on their side. One must not find oneself "on the wrong side of history."

That does not mean that revolutionary violence can never be justified. It is hard to argue, for example, that South African blacks may not take up arms for their freedom. It means only that an appeal to root causes is not automatic justification. The Philippine Islands are replete with root causes as deep and difficult as any others in the world. Appeal to these causes, however, is not enough to justify either the ends (Communist) or the means (brutal and terroristic) of the New People's Army.

Three years ago, Senator Christopher Dodd delivered a nationally televised speech on behalf of the Democratic Party opposing proposed aid to the government of El Salvador. "If Central America were not racked with poverty . . . hunger . . . injustice," argued Dodd, "there would be no revolution." That is the premise. And the conclusion? "Unless those oppressive conditions change"—Can they? Can the U.S. will them to?—"the region will continue to seethe with revolution." The choice? Either "to move with the tide of history" or "stand against it."

Today that argument is hardly heard anymore in the Central American context. Something happened. The Salvadoran guerrillas are in retreat, and yet, mirabile dictu, root causes remain. The tides have changed, while poverty and misery endure. As for Nicaragua, those most habituated to the use of the root cause argument are *contra* opponents. They are hardly likely to invoke it to explain—i.e., legitimize—the *contra* cause.

One place where the root cause idea does survive is the Middle East. The issue is terrorism, and the argument is familiar: Isn't the best way to fight terror to go after the root causes? Counter-terrorism, embargoes, threats and, finally, air raids treat only symptoms. Band-Aids on a wound. (The metaphors mix.) Why not attack the root causes? In the context of the Middle East, that means "solving the Palestinian problem." Accommodation between Israel and the Palestinians. The way out of the nightmare. Jews and Arabs living together in historic Palestine. An end to war. Peace as the cure for terror.

It is an honorable dream. And it is based on a clear logic: since much of the terrorism in the Middle East is committed either by Palestinians or by others acting in their name, why not solve the terrorism problem by solving their problem?

Unfortunately—unfortunately for Palestinians, Israelis and assorted innocents who wander into the crossfire—the logic fails. To understand why, one must start by asking, Who are the terrorists? The major sponsors of Middle East terror are Iran, Syria and Libya. And its major practitioners are Islamic fundamentalists, pro-Syrian nationalists and Palestinian extremists. These groups and states are distinguished not just by their choice of means but by the nature of their end. And their end is not peace with Israel. It is peace with no Israel.

The various terror groups have different versions of the end of days, but none include a Jewish state. The *Achille Lauro* hijackers, for example, issued a communiqué in Cyprus saying they had planned to land at "Ashdod harbor in occupied Palestine." Ashdod is not in the West Bank or Gaza. It is within pre-1967 Israel. If you consider Ashdod "occupied," every inch of Israel is occupied.

For such people, the only peaceful solution to the Middle East problem is a peace of the grave, a Zionist grave. Any settlement short of that will leave the terrorists unappeased. It will not solve the terrorists' problem. It thus does not solve the terrorism problem.

Indeed, it aggravates it. Any movement toward a negotiated peace that permits any part of Palestine to remain occupied is considered a threat. Negotiations are thus a spur, not a deterrent, to terror. Whenever a "peace scare" breaks out, terrorism *increases*, as King Hussein of Jordan is well aware. During the time he was trying to arrange for joint Jordanian-Palestinian negotiations with Israel, his diplomats in Ankara, Bucharest and Madrid were assassinated. The talks are off now, and Jordanians abroad are enjoying a rare respite from attack.

Last July [1985] Prime Minister Peres of Israel flew to Morocco for peace talks with King Hassan II, and before anyone knew the contents of the negotiations, Syria broke off diplomatic relations with Morocco and the PLO [Palestine Liberation Organization] declared it would oppose to the end *any* outcome. Some interested observers of this overture were candid and clear about the relationship between terrorism and peace, even a hint of peace: "Now," Royal Air Maroc stewards told a *New York Times* correspondent, "we will have to start worrying about hijackings and terrorist attacks."

The fundamental fact of the Middle East today is that those who engage in terror do not want peace, and those who want peace are not engaged in terror. Those who make the slightest move to eliminate the vaunted root cause of terror—i.e., those who genuinely seek a compromise solution to the Israeli-Palestinian problem—get shot. The latest victim is the mayor of Nablus, whose crime was to take over responsibility for fixing potholes. That was too much accommodation with the Zionist entity, as the rejectionists like to refer to Israel.

Issam Sartawi, the one PLO leader who advocated exactly the kind of solution Americans like to dream about, a Palestinian state living side by side with Israel, was also murdered, shot dead in Portugal in 1983. Not too many Palestinians have since risen to take up his cause. It is truer to say that terrorism is a root cause of the continuing Arab-Israeli conflict than vice versa.

Syria has little sympathy for *either* half of the peace envisioned in the West. Syria not only rejects the existence of an Israeli state, it has little use for a Palestinian state. Syria and its favorite Lebanese terror group, the Syrian Socialist Nationalist Party [SSNP], have a different vision. An Associated Press dispatch summarizes it nicely: "The secular SSNP seeks the merger of Lebanon, Syria, Jordan, pre-Israel Palestine, Iraq, Kuwait and Cyprus"—Cyprus!—"into a Greater Syria."

Abu Nidal, a Palestinian who was the author of last December's [1985] Vienna and Rome airport massacres and may also be linked to the Karachi airport attack, concurs. "Syria for us is the mother country." he says. "For 2,000 years the Palestinians have not lived in an independent territory. Palestine of the future must be incorporated within Syrian territory."

Such people—and these are the people going around spraying airliners and synagogues with bullets—will not retire even if Israel makes the most extreme concession and gives up the West Bank in favor of a Palestinian state. What Abu Nidal and Abu Abbas and indeed every Palestinian guerrilla group demand as a right is not a Hebron vineyard but downtown Tel Aviv. Even a radical West Bank solution will leave all of today's major terror groups and their sponsoring states aggrieved and in the field.

And even if peace were attainable, terrorism would outlive peace for another reason: the Arab-Israeli dispute is not the sole—the root—cause of terror in the Middle East. There are at least two other fundamental causes of instability, war and murder. One is the anti-Western, antimodern, antisecularist movement that is sweeping the Islamic world and has already wholly captured Iran. As Daniel Moynihan has said of the United Nations, the anti-Zionist campaign there is but the leading edge of a larger anti-Western campaign. Israel, as the most vulnerable Western outpost, becomes the most convenient target. Israeli territory, however, turns out to be well guarded, and thus a dangerous and inconve-

nient target for terrorists to attack. So the imperialist demon is confronted at other, easier points: European planes, ships, discos—wherever Westerners, preferably Americans, preferably civilians, are to be found.

Anti-Western terrorism—from the seizure of American hostages in Tehran to the blowing up of Western embassies in Kuwait to the killing of American G.I.s in Germany—is not primarily concerned with Israel. It is concerned with expelling an alien and corrupting West from the Islamic world. The Ayatollah has had much to say on the subject.

The other great fuel for Middle East terrorism is also anti-Western, but modern and secular, and is thus often at war with Islamic fundamentalism (sometimes quite literally, as in 1982 when President Assad of Syria killed an estimated 30,000 of his own people in putting down the Muslim Brotherhood revolt in Hama). Principally, however, this form of terrorism is at war with the West or, more precisely, with Western influence in the Middle East. This anti-Western strain is nationalist. The grievance is that after centuries of ascendancy, the Arab world has in modern times been subordinated by the West, first by naked colonialism, now by the more subtle devices of political, cultural and economic neocolonialism. This complaint echoes "anti-imperialist" sentiments felt in other parts of the third world. And, as with anti-imperialism elsewhere, the issue is not Israel. Eradicate Israel and you have not eradicated the grievance.

Nor the terrorism. Grievances, after all, need not result in terror. Many groups have grievances. Occasionally, a few issue in terror. In the Middle East, however, the resort to terror is ubiquitous. Think only of the numberless atrocities of the Lebanese civil war, now twelve years old. Revolutionary violence in the Middle East, whether Palestinian, Islamic or pan-Arab in objective, routinely turns to terror as an extension of war by other means. First, because terrorism as an instrument suits those who are otherwise not equipped to challenge superior power in direct military confrontation. Terrorism thus becomes a kind of appropriate technology for the warfare of the weak. But terrorism must not only fit the struggle; it must fit the political culture. "To speak of solving the problems of terrorism is an illusion," argues the West German Middle East expert Helmut Hubel. "Over the past three centuries, terrorism has been regarded as a legitimate instrument of policy and is part of Middle Eastern political culture."

The proof of this proposition is that in the Middle East terror is not merely an instrument of the weak against the powerful Western enemy. It is an endemic feature of local politics. In fact, most of the terror practiced in the Middle East is not anti-Israel or even anti-West but intra-Arab and intra-Muslim. It is a way for Syria to check Jordan, for Iran to subvert Iraq (and vice versa), for Lebanese factions to deal with one another, and for Libya to tame its enemies everywhere.

To see the Palestinian issue as the all-encompassing root cause of terrorism is not just a misperception. It is a danger. To await the messianic resolution of the Palestinian issue (messianic because the terrorists reject any imaginable compromise) is to invite dangerous despair and passivity. It is to neglect those things that can be done to restrain terrorism by way of this-worldly means, such as political, economic and military pressure. The U.S. air raid on Libya was followed by months of relative quiet. With Karachi and Istanbul the respite is over. Perhaps a new wave of terror is about to begin. To expect that after 20 years of passivity, a single act of American retaliation should have put a permanent end to terrorism is absurd. Only the steady, unwavering application of all forms of pressure against terrorists and their more easily found sponsors will have any lasting effect.

There are men around who, in the name of some cause, take machine guns onto airplanes and into synagogues and kill as many as they can. One of the overriding obligations of the age is to use every available means to hunt down today's machine gunners and deter tomorrow's. The pursuit of peace is also an obligation. But it is an entirely different enterprise.

QUESTIONS FOR DISCUSSION

1. What are the causes of terrorism?
2. What effect would the removal of state sponsorship of terrorism have on terrorism?
3. What similarities and/or differences exist between American Revolutionary heroes and Palestinian guerrillas?
4. What are the strengths and weaknesses of democracies in dealing with terrorism?
5. What effect would the establishment of a Palestinian state have on acts of terrorism?

SUGGESTED READINGS

Alexander, Yonah. "The Terrorist Network." *Defense and Diplomacy*, **7** (Sept. 1989), pp. 36–41, 70.

Cetron, Marvin J. "The Growing Threat of Terrorism." *Futurist*, **23** (July/Aug. 1989), pp. 20–24.

Decter, Moshe. "Terrorism: The Fallacy of 'Root Causes.'" *Midstream*, **33** (Mar. 1987), pp. 8–10.

Hanle, Donald J. *Terrorism: The Newest Face of Warfare.* Washington, D.C.: Pergamon-Brassey's, 1989.

Kennedy, Moorhead. "The Root Causes of Terrorism." *Humanist*, **46** (Sept./Oct. 1986), pp. 5–9.

Kupperman, Robert, and Jeff Kamen. *Final Warning: Averting Disaster in the Age of Terrorism.* New York: Doubleday, 1989.

Phillips, Robert L. "The Roots of Terrorism." *Christian Century*, **103** (Apr. 9, 1986), pp. 355–357.

Scheuer, Jeffrey. "Moral Dimensions of Terrorism." *Fletcher Forum of World Affairs*, **14** (Winter 1990), pp. 145–160.

Sederberg, Peter C. *Terrorist Myths: Illusion, Rhetoric, and Reality.* Englewood Cliffs, N.J.: Prentice-Hall, 1989.

Wilkinson, Paul. "The Future of Terrorism." *Futures* (Guildford, England), **20** (Oct. 1988), pp. 493–504.

22 Is Rapid Population Growth a Threat to Economic Development and World Peace?

YES

Paul R. Ehrlich and Anne H. Ehrlich

Why Isn't Everyone as Scared as We Are?

NO

Karl Zinsmeister

Supply-Side Demography

Why Isn't Everyone as Scared as We Are?

Paul R. Ehrlich and Anne H. Ehrlich

In the early 1930s, when we were born, the world population was just 2 billion; now it is more than two and a half times as large and still growing rapidly.[1] The population of the United States is increasing much more slowly than the world average, but it has more than doubled in only six decades—from 120 million in 1928 to 250 million in 1990.[2] Such a huge population expansion within two or three generations can by itself account for a great many changes in the social and economic institutions of a society. It also is very frightening to those of us who spend our lives trying to keep track of the implications of the population explosion.

A SLOW START

One of the toughest things for a population biologist to reconcile is the contrast between his or her recognition that civilization is in imminent serious jeopardy and the modest level of concern that population issues generate among the public and even among elected officials.

Much of the reason for this discrepancy lies in the slow development of the problem. People aren't scared because they evolved biologically and culturally to respond to short-term "fires" and to tune out long-term "trends" over which they had no control.[3] Only if we do what doesn't come naturally—if we determinedly focus on what seem to be gradual or nearly imperceptible changes—can the outlines of our predicament be perceived clearly enough to be frightening.

Consider the *very* slow-motion origins of our predicament. It seems reasonable to define humanity as having first appeared some four million years ago in the form of australopithecines, small-brained upright creatures like "Lucy."[4] Of course, we don't know the size of this first human population, but it's likely that there were never more than 125,000 australopithecines at any given time.

Our own species, *Homo sapiens*,[5] evolved a few hundred thousand years ago. Some ten thousand years ago, when agriculture was invented, probably no more than five million people inhabited Earth—fewer than now live in the San Francisco Bay Area. Even at the time of Christ, two thousand years ago, the entire human population was roughly the size of the population of the United States today; by 1650 there were only 500 million people, and in 1850 only a little over a billion. Since there are now well past 5

Source: Paul R. Ehrlich and Anne H. Ehrlich, *The Population Explosion* (New York: Simon & Schuster, 1990), pp. 13–23. Copyright © 1990 by Paul R. Ehrlich and Anne H. Ehrlich. Reprinted by permission of Simon & Schuster, Inc.

[1] The world population in 1990 is about 5.3 billion. Most demographic information in this book, unless otherwise noted, is from *1989 World Population Data Sheet*, issued by the Population Reference Bureau (PRB), 777 Fourteenth St. NW, Suite 800, Washington, D.C. 20005. In some cases, as above, we have made simple extrapolations for the 1990 figures. Besides the fine annual data sheet, PRB produces several very useful publications on population issues.

[2] Note that the U.S. population was growing much faster before then, spurred by substantial numbers of immigrants. It *quadrupled* in the 6 decades before 1928, turning a post–Civil War society largely restricted to the eastern half of the nation into a cosmopolitan world power spanning the continent.

[3] This evolutionary blind spot is discussed at length in R. Ornstein and P. Ehrlich, *New World/New Mind* (Doubleday, New York, 1988).

[4] D. Johanson and M. Edey, *Lucy: The Beginnings of Mankind* (Simon and Schuster, New York, 1981). While there is still controversy over details of human history, there is no dispute that an erect, small-brained hominid something like Lucy was one of our ancestors. This exciting book beautifully presents the view of human origins of one outstanding group of scientists. For more on the controversies and on other discoveries, see R. Lewin's excellent *Bones of Contention* (Simon and Schuster, New York, 1987).

[5] Note that we are considering *Homo sapiens* as the latest human species and are applying the term "human" to all hominids since the australopithecines (just as the term "ape" is applied to several species). Some people would restrict the term "human" to *Homo sapiens*.

billion people, the vast majority of the population explosion has taken place in less than a tenth of one percent of the history of *Homo sapiens*.

This is a remarkable change in the abundance of a single species. After an unhurried pace of growth over most of our history, expansion of the population accelerated during the Industrial Revolution and really shot up after 1950. Since mid-century, the human population has been growing at annual rates ranging from about 1.7 to 2.1 percent per year, doubling in forty years or less. Some groups have grown significantly faster; the population of the African nation of Kenya was estimated to be increasing by over 4 percent annually during the 1980s—a rate that if continued would double the nation's population in only seventeen years.[6] That rate did continue for over a decade, and only recently has shown slight signs of slowing. Meanwhile, other nations, such as those of northern Europe, have grown much more slowly in recent decades.

But even the highest growth rates are still *slow-motion changes compared to events we easily notice and react to*. A car swerving at us on the highway is avoided by actions taking a few seconds. The Alaskan oil spill caused great public indignation, but faded from the media and the consciousness of most people in a few months. America's participation in World War II spanned less than four years. During the last four years, even Kenya's population grew by only about 16 percent—a change hardly perceptible locally, let alone from a distance. In four years, the world population expands only a little more than 7 percent. Who could notice that? Precipitous as the population explosion has been in historical terms, it is occurring at a snail's pace in an individual's perception. It is not an event, it is a trend that must be

analyzed in order for its significance to be appreciated.

EXPONENTIAL GROWTH

The time it takes a population to double in size is a dramatic way to picture rates of population growth, one that most of us can understand more readily than percentage growth rates. Human populations have often grown in a pattern described as "exponential."[7] Exponential growth occurs in bank accounts when interest is left to accumulate and itself earns interest. Exponential growth occurs in populations because children, the analogue of interest, remain in the population and themselves have children.[8]

A key feature of exponential growth is that it often seems to start slowly and finish fast. A classic example used to illustrate this is the pond weed that doubles each day the amount of pond surface covered and is projected to cover the entire pond in thirty days. The question is, how much of the pond will be covered in twenty-nine days? The answer, of course, is that just half of the pond will be covered in twenty-nine days. The weed will then double once more and cover the entire pond the next day. As this example

---

[6] When annual growth rates are under 5 percent, a working estimate of the number of years required to double the population at the rate can be obtained by simply dividing the percentage rate into 70. Thus, with Kenya's growth rate of 4.1 percent, the estimate of doubling time is 70/4.1 = 17.1 years. A recent decline in Kenya's birthrate was reported in J. Perlez, "Birth Control Making Inroads in Populous Kenya," *New York Times*, Sept. 10, 1989, but the population still has a doubling rate of less than 20 years.

[7] Exponential growth occurs when the increase in population size in a given period is a *constant* percentage of the size at the beginning of the period. Thus a population growing at 2 percent annually or a bank account growing at 6 percent annually will be growing exponentially. Exponential growth does not have to be fast; it can go on at very low rates or, if the rate is negative, can be exponential shrinkage.

Saying a population is "growing exponentially" has almost come to mean "growing very fast," but that interpretation is erroneous. True exponential growth is rarely seen in human populations today, since the percentage rate of growth has been changing. In most cases, the growth rate has been gradually declining since the late 1960s. Nevertheless, it is useful to be aware of the exponential model, since it is implied every time we project a population size into the future with qualifying statements such as "if that rate continues."

[8] For mathematical details on exponential growth, see P. R. Ehrlich, A. H. Ehrlich, and J. P. Holdren, *Ecoscience: Population, Resources, Environment* (Freeman, San Francisco, 1977), pp. 100–104. The term "exponential" comes from the presence in the equation for growth of a constant, *e*, the base of natural logarithms, raised to a power (exponent) that is a variable (the growth rate multiplied by the time that rate will be in effect).

indicates, exponential growth contains the potential for big surprises.[9]

The limits to human population growth are more difficult to perceive than those restricting the pond weed's growth. Nonetheless, like the pond weed, human populations grow in a pattern that is essentially exponential, so we must be alert to the treacherous properties of that sort of growth. The key point to remember is that *a long history of exponential growth in no way implies a long future of exponential growth.* What begins in slow motion may eventually overwhelm us in a flash.

The last decade or two has seen a slight slackening in the human population growth rate—a slackening that has been prematurely heralded as an ''end to the population explosion.'' The slowdown has been only from a peak annual growth rate of perhaps 2.1 percent in the early 1960s to about 1.8 percent in 1990. To put this change in perspective, the population's doubling time has been extended from thirty-three years to thirty-nine. Indeed, the world population *did* double in the thirty-seven years from 1950 to 1987. But even if birthrates continue to fall, the world population will continue to expand (assuming that death rates don't rise), although at a slowly slackening rate, for about another century. Demographers think that growth will not end before the population has reached 10 billion or more.[10]

So, even though birthrates have declined somewhat, *Homo sapiens* is a long way from ending its population explosion or avoiding its consequences. In fact, the biggest jump, from 5 to 10 billion in well under a century, is still ahead. But this does not mean that growth couldn't be ended sooner, with a much smaller population size, if we—all of the world's nations—made up our minds to do it. The trouble is, many of the world's leaders and perhaps most of the world's people still don't believe that there are compelling reasons to do so. They are even less aware that if humanity fails to act, *nature may end the population explosion for us*—in very unpleasant ways—well before 10 billion is reached.

Those unpleasant ways are beginning to be perceptible. Humanity in the 1990s will be confronted by more and more intransigent environmental problems, global problems dwarfing those that worried us in the late 1960s. Perhaps the most serious is that of global warming, a problem caused in large part by population growth and overpopulation. It is not clear whether the severe drought in North America, the Soviet Union, and China in 1988 was the result of the slowly rising surface temperature of Earth, but it is precisely the kind of event that climatological models predict as more and more likely with continued global warming.[11] In addition to more frequent and more severe crop failures, projected consequences of the warming include coastal flooding, desertification, the creation of as many as 300 million environmental refugees,[12] alteration of patterns of disease, water shortages, general stress on natural ecosystems, and synergistic interactions among all these factors.[13]

Continued population growth and the drive for development in already badly overpopulated poor

---

[9] The potential for surprise in repeated doublings can be underlined with another example. Suppose you set up an aquarium with appropriate life-support systems to maintain 1,000 guppies, but no more. If that number is exceeded, crowding will make the fishes susceptible to ''ich,'' a parasitic disease that will kill most of the guppies. You then begin the population with a pair of sex-crazed guppies. Suppose that the fishes reproduce fast enough to double their population size every month. For eight months everything is fine, as the population grows $2{\rightarrow}4{\rightarrow}8{\rightarrow}16{\rightarrow}32{\rightarrow}64{\rightarrow}128{\rightarrow}256{\rightarrow}512$. Then within the ninth month the guppy population surges through the fatal 1,000 barrier, the aquarium becomes overcrowded, and most of the fishes perish. In fact, the last 100 guppies appear in less than five days—about 2 percent of the population's history.

[10] Note that ''doubling times'' represent what would happen if the growth rates of the moment continued unchanged into the future. Demographic projections include changes in growth rates, usually caused by reductions in birthrates and/or *declines* in death rates (demographers classically don't consider rises in death rates

in their global projections). Projections therefore often show the population taking more, and occasionally less, time to double than was indicated by the ''doubling time'' of a recent year.

[11] For a fine discussion of climate models, see S. H. Schneider, *Global Warming* (Sierra Club Books, San Francisco, 1989).

[12] ''Eco-Refugees Warning,'' *New Scientist*, June 10, 1989.

[13] Synergisms occur when the joint impact of two (or more) factors is greater than the sum of their separate impacts.

nations will make it *exceedingly* difficult to slow the greenhouse warming—and impossible to stop or reverse it—in this generation at least. And, even if the warming should miraculously not occur, contrary to accepted projections,[14] human numbers are on a collision course with massive famines anyway.

MAKING THE POPULATION CONNECTION

Global warming, acid rain, depletion of the ozone layer, vulnerability to epidemics, and exhaustion of soils and groundwater are all, as we shall see, related to population size. They are also clear and present dangers to the persistence of civilization. Crop failures due to global warming alone might result in the premature deaths of a billion or more people in the next few decades, and the AIDS [acquired immune deficiency syndrome] epidemic could slaughter hundreds of millions. Together these would constitute a harsh ''population control'' program provided by nature in the face of humanity's refusal to put into place a gentler program of its own.

We shouldn't delude ourselves: the population explosion will come to an end before very long. The only remaining question is whether it will be halted through the humane method of birth control, or by nature wiping out the surplus. We realize that religious and cultural opposition to birth control exists throughout the world; but we believe that people simply don't understand the choice that such opposition implies. Today, anyone opposing birth control is unknowingly voting to have the human population size controlled by a massive increase in early deaths.

Of course, the environmental crisis isn't caused just by expanding human numbers. Burgeoning consumption among the rich and increasing dependence on ecologically unsound technologies to supply that consumption also play major parts. This allows some environmentalists to dodge the population issue by emphasizing the problem of malign technologies. And social commentators can avoid commenting on the problem of too many people by focusing on the serious maldistribution of affluence.

But scientists studying humanity's deepening predicament recognize that a major factor contributing to it is rapidly worsening overpopulation. The Club of Earth, a group whose members all belong to both the U.S. National Academy of Sciences and the American Academy of Arts and Sciences, released a statement in September 1988 that said in part:

> Arresting global population growth should be second in importance only to avoiding nuclear war on humanity's agenda. Overpopulation and rapid population growth are intimately connected with most aspects of the current human predicament, including rapid depletion of nonrenewable resources, deterioration of the environment (including rapid climate change), and increasing international tensions.[15]

When three prestigious scientific organizations cosponsored an international scientific forum, ''Global Change,'' in Washington in 1989, there was general agreement among the speakers that population growth was a substantial contributor toward prospective catastrophe. Newspaper coverage was limited, and while the population component was mentioned in *The New York Times*'s article,[16] the point that population limitations will be essential to resolving the predicament was lost. The coverage of

---

[14] See S. H. Schneider, *Global Warming*, and the extensive references therein.

[15] Statement released Sept. 3, 1988, at the Pugwash Conference on Global Problems and Common Security, at Dagomys, near Sochi, USSR. The signatories were Jared Diamond, UCLA; Paul Ehrlich, Stanford; Thomas Eisner, Cornell; G. Evelyn Hutchinson, Yale; Gene E. Likens, Institute of Ecosystem Studies; Ernst Mayr, Harvard; Charles D. Michener, University of Kansas; Harold A. Mooney, Stanford; Ruth Patrick, Academy of Natural Sciences, Philadelphia; Peter H. Raven, Missouri Botanical Garden; and Edward O. Wilson, Harvard.

The National Academy of Sciences and the American Academy of Arts and Sciences are the top honorary organizations for American scientists and scholars, respectively. Hutchinson, Patrick, and Wilson also are laureates of the Tyler Prize, the most distinguished international award in ecology.

[16] May 4, 1989, by Philip Shabecoff, a fine environmental reporter. In general, the *Times* coverage of the environment is excellent. But even this best of American newspapers reflects the public's lack of understanding of the urgency of the population situation.

environmental issues in the media has been generally excellent in the last few years, but there is still a long way to go to get adequate coverage of the intimately connected population problem.

Even though the media occasionally give coverage to population issues, some people never get the word. In November 1988, Pope John Paul II reaffirmed the Catholic Church's ban on contraception. The occasion was the twentieth anniversary of Pope Paul's anti-birth-control encyclical, *Humanae Vitae*.

Fortunately, the majority of Catholics in the industrial world pay little attention to the encyclical or the Church's official ban on all practical means of birth control. One need only note that Catholic Italy at present has the smallest average completed family size (1.3 children per couple) of any nation. Until contraception and then abortion were legalized there in the 1970s, the Italian birth rate was kept low by an appalling rate of illegal abortion.

The bishops who assembled to celebrate the anniversary defended the encyclical by announcing that "the world's food resources theoretically could feed 40 billion people."[17] In one sense they were right. It's "theoretically possible" to feed 40 billion people—in the same sense that it's theoretically possible for your favorite major-league baseball team to win every single game for fifty straight seasons, or for you to play Russian roulette ten thousand times in a row with five out of six chambers loaded without blowing your brains out.

One might also ask whether feeding 40 billion people is a worthwhile goal for humanity, even if it could be reached. Is any purpose served in turning Earth, in essence, into a gigantic human feedlot? Putting aside the near-certainty that such a miracle couldn't be sustained, what would happen to the *quality* of life?

We wish to emphasize that the population problem is in no sense a "Catholic problem," as some would claim. Around the world, Catholic reproductive performance is much the same as that of non-Catholics in similar cultures and with similar eco-

nomic status. Nevertheless, the *political* position of the Vatican, traceable in no small part to the extreme conservatism of Pope John Paul II, is an important barrier to solving the population problem.[18] Non-Catholics should be very careful not to confuse Catholics or Catholicism with the Vatican—most American Catholics don't. Furthermore, the Church's position on contraception is distressing to many millions of Catholics, who feel it morally imperative to follow their own consciences in their personal lives and disregard the Vatican's teachings on this subject.

Nor is unwillingness to face the severity of the population problem limited to the Vatican. It's built into our genes and our culture. That's one reason many otherwise bright and humane people behave like fools when confronted with demographic issues. Thus, an economist specializing in mail-order marketing can sell the thesis that the human population could increase essentially forever because people are the "ultimate resource,"[19] and a journalist can urge more population growth in the United States so that we can have a bigger army![20] Even some environmentalists are taken in by the frequent assertion that

---

[17] *Washington Post*, Nov. 19, 1988, p. C-15.

[18] Italy is a not freak case. Catholic France has an average completed family size of 1.8 children, the same as Britain and Norway; Catholic Spain, with less than half the per-capita GNP of Protestant Denmark, has the same completed family size of 1.8 children. We are equating "completed family size" here with the *total fertility rate*, the average number of children a woman would bear in her lifetime, assuming that current age-specific birth and death rates remained unchanged during her childbearing years—roughly 15–49. In the United States, a Catholic woman is more likely to seek abortion than a non-Catholic woman (probably because she is likelier to use less-effective contraception). By 1980, Catholic and non-Catholic women in the U.S. (except Hispanic women, for whom cultural factors are strong) had virtually identical family sizes. (W.D. Mosher, "Fertility and Family Planning in the United States: Insights from the National Survey of Family Growth," *Family Planning Perspectives*, vol. **20**, no. 5, pp. 202–17, Sept./Oct. 1988.) On the role of the Vatican, see, for instance, Stephen D. Mumford, "The Vatican and Population Growth Control: Why an American Confrontation?," *The Humanist*, September/October 1983, and Penny Lernoux, "The Papal Spiderweb," *The Nation*, April 10 and 17, 1989.

[19] J. Simon, *The Ultimate Resource* (Princeton Univ. Press, Princeton, N.J., 1981).

[20] B. Wattenberg, *The Birth Dearth* (Pharos Books, New York, 1987).

"there is no population problem, only a problem of distribution." The statement is usually made in a context of a plan for conquering hunger, as if food shortage were the only consequence of overpopulation.

But even in that narrow context, the assertion is wrong. Suppose food *were* distributed equally. If everyone in the world ate as Americans do, less than half the *present* world population could be fed on the record harvests of 1985 and 1986.[21] Of course, everyone doesn't have to eat like Americans. About a third of the world grain harvest—the staples of the human feeding base—is fed to animals to produce eggs, milk, and meat for American-style diets. Wouldn't feeding that grain directly to people solve the problem? If everyone were willing to eat an essentially vegetarian diet, that additional grain would allow perhaps a billion more people to be fed with 1986 production.

Would such radical changes solve the world food problem? Only in the *very* short term. The additional billion people are slated to be with us by the end of the century. Moreover, by the late 1980s, humanity already seemed to be encountering trouble maintaining the production levels of the mid-1980s, let alone keeping up with population growth. The world grain harvest in 1988 was some 10 percent *below* that of 1986. And there is little sign that the rich are about to give up eating animal products.

So there is no reasonable way that the hunger problem can be called "only" one of distribution, even though redistribution of food resources would greatly alleviate hunger today. Unfortunately, an important truth, that maldistribution is a cause of hunger now, has been used as a way to avoid a more important truth—that overpopulation is critical today and may well make the distribution question moot tomorrow.

The food problem, however, attracts little immediate concern among well-fed Americans, who have

no reason to be aware of its severity or extent. But other evidence that could make everyone face up to the seriousness of the population dilemma is now all around us, since problems to which overpopulation and population growth make major contributions are worsening at a rapid rate. They often appear on the evening news, although the population connection is almost never made.

Consider the television pictures of barges loaded with garbage wandering like The Flying Dutchman across the seas, and news stories about "no room at the dump."[22] They are showing the results of the interaction between too many affluent people and the environmentally destructive technologies that support that affluence. Growing opportunities to swim in a mixture of sewage and medical debris off American beaches can be traced to the same source. Starving people in sub-Saharan Africa are victims of drought, defective agricultural policies, and an overpopulation of both people and domestic animals—with warfare often dealing the final blow. All of the above are symptoms of humanity's massive and growing negative impact on Earth's life-support systems.

RECOGNIZING THE POPULATION PROBLEM

The average person, even the average scientist, seldom makes the connection between such seemingly disparate events and the population problem, and thus remains unworried. To a degree, this failure to put the pieces together is due to a taboo against frank discussion of the population crisis in many quarters, a taboo generated partly by pressures from the Catholic hierarchy and partly by other groups who are afraid that dealing with population issues will produce socially damaging results.

Many people on the political left are concerned that focusing on overpopulation will divert attention from crucial problems of social justice (which certainly need to be addressed *in addition* to the popula-

[21] R. W. Kates, R. S. Chen, T. E. Downing, J. X. Kasperson, E. Messer, S. R. Millman, *The Hunger Report: 1988* (The Alan Shawn Feinstein World Hunger Program, Brown University, Providence, R.I., 1988). The data on distribution in this paragraph are from this source.

[22] The name of a series of reports on KRON-TV's news programs, San Francisco, the week of May 8, 1989.

tion problem). Often those on the political right fear that dealing with overpopulation will encourage abortion (it need not) or that halting growth will severely damage the economy (it could, if not handled properly). And people of varied political persuasions who are unfamiliar with the magnitude of the population problem believe in a variety of far-fetched technological fixes—such as colonizing outer space—that they think will allow the need for regulating the size of the human population to be avoided forever.[23]

Even the National Academy of Sciences avoided mentioning controlling human numbers in its advice to President Bush on how to deal with global environmental change. Although Academy members who are familiar with the issue are well aware of the critical population component of that change, it was feared that all of the Academy's advice would be ignored if recommendations were included about a subject taboo in the Bush administration. That strategy might have been correct, considering Bush's expressed views on abortion and considering the administration's weak appointments in many environmentally sensitive positions. After all, the Office of Management and Budget even tried to suppress an expert evaluation of the potential seriousness of global warming by altering the congressional testimony of a top NASA [National Aeronautics and Space Administration] scientist, James Hansen, to conform with the administration's less urgent view of the problem.[24]

All of us naturally lean toward the taboo against dealing with population growth. The roots of our aversion to limiting the size of the human population are as deep and pervasive as the roots of human sexual behavior. Through billions of years of evolution, outreproducing other members of your population was the name of the game. It is the very basis of natural selection, the driving force of the evolutionary process.[25] Nonetheless, the taboo must be uprooted and discarded.

OVERCOMING THE TABOO

There is no more time to waste; in fact, there wasn't in 1968 when *The Population Bomb* was published. Human inaction has already condemned hundreds of millions more people to premature deaths from hunger and disease. The population connection must be made in the public mind. Action to end the population explosion *humanely* and start a gradual population *decline* must become a top item on the human agenda: the human birthrate must be lowered to slightly below the human death rate as soon as possible. There still may be time to limit the scope of the impending catastrophe, but not *much* time. Ending the population explosion by controlling births is necessarily a slow process. Only nature's cruel way of solving the problem is likely to be swift.

Of course, if we do wake up and succeed in controlling our population size, that will still leave us with all the other thorny problems to solve. Limiting human numbers will not alone end warfare, environmental deterioration, poverty, racism, religious prejudice, or sexism; it will just buy us the opportunity to do so. As the old saying goes, whatever your cause, it's a lost cause without population control.[26]

America and other rich nations have a clear choice today. They can continue to ignore the population problem and their own massive contributions to it. Then they will be trapped in a downward spiral that may well lead to the end of civilization in a few decades. More frequent droughts, more damaged crops and famines, more dying forests, more smog,

[23] For an amusing analysis of the ''outer-space'' fairy tale, see Garrett Hardin's classic essay ''Interstellar Migration and the Population Problem,'' *Journal of Heredity*, vol. **50**, pp. 68–70 (1959), reprinted in G. Hardin, ed., *Stalking the Wild Taboo*, 2nd ed. (William Kaufmann, Los Altos, Calif., 1978). Note that some things have changed; to keep the population of Earth from growing today, we would have to export to space 95 million people annually!

[24] This story received broad coverage in both electronic and print media; for instance, *New York Times*, May 8, 1989.

[25] For a discussion of natural selection and evolution written for nonspecialists, see P. R. Ehrlich, *The Machinery of Nature* (Simon and Schuster, New York, 1986).

[26] . . . ''population control'' does not require coercion, only attention to the needs of society.

more international conflicts, more epidemics, more gridlock, more drugs, more crime, more sewage swimming, and other extreme unpleasantness will mark our course. It is a route already traveled by too many of our less fortunate fellow human beings.

Or we can change our collective minds and take the measures necessary to lower global birthrates dramatically. People can learn to treat growth as the cancerlike disease it is and move toward a sustainable society. The rich can make helping the poor an urgent goal, instead of seeking more wealth and useless military advantage over one another. Then humanity might have a chance to manage all those other seemingly intractable problems. It is a challenging prospect, but at least it will give our species a shot at creating a decent future for itself. More immediately and concretely, taking action now will give our children and their children the possibility of decent lives.

Supply-Side Demography

Karl Zinsmeister

For more than two decades, population control groups have waged a powerful political and philosophical campaign to advance the proposition that a continued rise in human numbers is one of the world's gravest problems. Popular concern took root in 1968, when Professor Paul Ehrlich wrote a best-selling book in which he described population growth as a "bomb," and claimed that during the 1970s it would "explode," causing hundreds of millions of deaths, leading to war and violence, and destroying the planet's ability to support life.

An equally apocalyptic view was expressed five years later by Robert McNamara, then president of the World Bank:

> The greatest single obstacle to the economic and social advancement of the majority of the peoples in the underdeveloped world is rampant population growth. . . . The threat of unmanageable population pressures is very much like the threat of nuclear war. . . . Both threats can and will have catastrophic consequences unless they are dealt with rapidly.

A large international apparatus of population control groups has promoted the idea that we are in the midst of a runaway crisis. Population growth, these groups maintain, is a major cause of poverty, starvation, pollution, unemployment, and political tension today; extreme measures are called for. The United Nations and the World Bank have made population control a central part of their work. Public opinion has also been strongly influenced. Polls show that much of the public in the Western world believes mankind is darkly threatened by current population growth. Indeed, this view has become so strong that until very recently it was considered intellectual heresy to question it publicly.

But in the last few years that has begun to change as an expanding revisionist school of population studies has taken root. Research by economists, demographers, and social historians has shown that much of the alleged harm from population growth has turned out to be nonexistent and that population change has often been used as a scapegoat for problems that actually have other sources. Revisionists point out that it is not slowed population growth that brings social prosperity, but rather social prosperity that brings slower population rise. The result: A great, new population debate is now underway.

What brought about this turnaround? Why is it that the last decade's conventional wisdom has suddenly been called into question? Three reasons stand out.

First, there was the shock of reality itself. As new data on population growth and its effects came in over the last decade or so, it was clear that the dire predictions of the "population explosionists" had failed, and failed utterly, to come true. There were no population wars in the 1970s. There were famines but they were not population famines. The exponential growth and predicted calamities just didn't take place. On the contrary, there were many pleasant surprises.

For instance, Paul Ehrlich wrote in 1968 that it was a "fantasy" to think that India—which he cites as a paradigm of overpopulation—could feed itself anytime in the near future, "if ever." One participant at the Second International Conference on the War on Hunger in 1968 argued that India's 1967–68 grain production of approximately 95 million tons represented the maximum possible level. Yet today India's annual grain production is over 150 million tons, and the country has become a net *exporter* of food. The fact that the quality of life has improved so markedly and so rapidly even in India—which, until recently, was referred to as an international "basket case"—suggests that those who argue that produc-

Source: Karl Zinsmeister, "Supply-Side Demography," *National Interest,* no. 19 (Spring 1990), pp. 68–75. Reprinted with the permission of *The National Interest.* © Spring 1990, no. 19, *The National Interest,* Washington, D.C.

tion can never keep up with growing numbers of people do not appreciate how quickly new technology and improved economic structures can convert formerly ''redundant'' people into productive resources.

Another fact the traditional population theorists did not fathom was how fast the world was changing demographically when they made their dire predictions. As recently as 1970, women of the less developed world were bearing an average of 6 children each. Today, that average is down to 3.7 children. When you consider that about 2.2 children would produce *stable* populations in the less developed countries (that is, each generation merely replacing its parents, with a small factor for childhood mortality, etc.) then this remarkable fact can be seen: *In just the last fifteen years or so, the less developed world moved three-fifths of the way toward a fertility rate that yields ''zero population growth.''*

So great was the change, it now appears, that the official United Nations' estimates of world population in the year 2000, put together at the end of the 1960s, will be more than 20 percent too high.

To be sure, it should be noted that the less developed countries did not all share equally in the fertility fall. Fertility in Asia dropped very rapidly, while in parts of Africa it has remained high. But, after all, it was in Asia (with 2.8 billion people, almost 60 percent of the world's total) that the population problem was supposed to be the worst. Africa, the partial exception to the worldwide downward fertility trend, is still a relatively sparsely inhabited continent with a total of 550 million residents and low overall population density, even excluding desert areas.

Another factual development often overlooked by population alarmists is that, contrary to popular claims, the standard of living in most of the Third World has been rapidly improving, not declining, during the last few decades—the very decades when population was growing fastest. The Third World infant mortality rate has fallen from 125 deaths per 1,000 births in 1960, to 69 in 1986; life expectancy at birth has risen incredibly—from 42 years to 61 years; adult literacy rates in the Third World doubled in 20 years; the number of physicians per 100,000

people went up 2.5 times; and the calorie supply per capita rose from just 87 percent of healthy daily requirements to 102 percent. The claim that rapid population growth vetoes social progress runs head-on into strong countervailing evidence from the last 25 years.

The second major factor that led many to question the prevailing orthodoxy was the serious human rights violations that followed in the wake of the population control alarms of the 1960s and 1970s.

In 1976 the Indian government declared, ''Where a state legislature . . . decides that the time is ripe and it is necessary to pass legislation for compulsory sterilization, it may do so.'' In the six months following that ruling, over six million Indians were sterilized, many thousands forcibly. That episode inspired such fierce resistance among Indians that the government of Indira Gandhi was eventually brought down.

Even before the government issued this public justification, coercion in the name of population control had been rife in India. The distinguished demographer Richard Easterlin reports that when he was a member of a United Nations Family Planning Mission to India in 1969, program administrators in Bombay told him how strong-arm tactics were used in the slum districts to assure that government vasectomy targets were met. When he expressed concern at this, a surprised official answered, ''Surely, the end justifies the means.''

Indian authorities were not the only ones who held this view. In November 1976—after the forced sterilization program had already been unveiled—World Bank president Robert McNamara paid a personal visit to the Indian family planning minister ''to congratulate him for the Indian Government's political will and determination in popularizing family planning.''

An even more massive campaign of intimidation and violence in the name of population control has been, and to a considerable extent continues to be, conducted in China. In the early 1980s reports began to reach the West that the Chinese government was exerting enormous and often brutal pressure on couples to limit their family size to one child. After a graphic series of articles was published by the *Washington Post* in January 1985, American authorities could no longer ignore the evidence. Upon returning from a four-year assignment in China, when he was finally free to publish his findings without risking expulsion, correspondent Michael Weisskopf filed his report:

> What emerges from more than 200 interviews spaced over three years with officials, doctors, peasants and workers in almost two-thirds of China's 29 local jurisdictions is the story of an all-out government siege against ancient family traditions and . . . reproductive habits. . . .
>
> Nowhere is this dark side of family planning more evident than in Dongguan . . . in southern China. Here, abortion posses scoured the countryside in the spring of 1981, rounding up women in rice paddies and thatched-roof houses. Expectant mothers, including many in their last trimester, were trussed, handcuffed, herded into hog cages and delivered by the truckload to the operating tables of rural clinics. . . .
>
> Any mother who becomes pregnant again without receiving official authorization after having one child is required to have an abortion, and the incidence of such operations is stunning—53 million from 1979 to 1984, according to the Ministry of Public Health. . . .
>
> Nor is the timing of abortion usually a factor. Many are performed in the last trimester of pregnancy—100,000 in Guangdong last year, or 20 percent of the province's total abortions—and some as late as the ninth month. . . .
>
> In the Inner Mongolian capital of Hohhot . . . hospital doctors practice what amounts to infanticide by a different name. . . . After inducing labor . . . doctors routinely smash the baby's skull with forceps as it emerges from the womb. In some cases . . . newborns are killed by injecting formaldehyde into the soft spot of the head. . . .
>
> China's family-planning work is backed by the full organizational might of the Communist Party, which extends its influence to every factor, neighborhood and village. Every Chinese belongs to a "unit"—workplace or rural governing body—and every unit has a birth control committee headed by party officials.
>
> Few unauthorized pregnancies can elude the tight supervision of birth control activists, a phalanx of female members of the party . . . who are deputized by local officials to monitor the reproductive lives of Chinese couples. . . .
>
> They keep detailed records of every woman's menstrual cycle, checking to make sure of regularity. . . .
>
> A positive test spells trouble for any woman who already has a child. She is urged to have an abortion, offered a cash bonus and time off from work as a reward. If she refuses, the pressure mounts.
>
> First come the tactics of persuasion played out in what is known euphemistically as "heart-to-heart chats."
>
> If she holds her ground, the talks intensify. . . . Now the pregnant woman is criticized for resisting and warned of the penalty for unauthorized birth, which varies from place to place but can include loss of farmland, fines of up to $1,000, firing from factory jobs, public censure and the denial of land, medical benefits, grain rations and educational opportunities for the unplanned child. . . .
>
> Meanwhile, the meetings go on, often all the way up to the point of delivery. Where talking fails, force often prevails.

The Indian and Chinese programs are extreme examples of the human rights violations carried out in the name of population control in a number of countries. What is worse, international authorities of the population control movement have presented, and continue to present, rationalizations and apologies for harsh measures of these sorts. In 1983, the United Nations awarded its first U.N. medal for family planning achievement. Its joint winners: the heads of the Chinese and Indian programs.

American population control groups continue to praise the Chinese program. They fought to overturn Congress's 1985 decision to end U.S. foreign aid to the United Nations' Family Planning Agency (UNFPA) because of UNFPA's close collaboration in the Chinese brutality. In late 1989, a foreign aid bill restoring UNFPA funds was passed, only to be vetoed by President Bush.

The sad fact is that it is not merely officials of totalitarian governments who are willing to see these delicate family decisions transferred from the private to the public realm. Traditionally, international family planning efforts supported by the United States aimed to do only one thing: extend human choice by bringing modern supplies and services to persons who wanted but could not afford them. Few persons would object to such an effort. Recently, however, important parts of the international family planning apparatus have begun to veer dangerously *beyond* voluntary family planning, toward social control and coercion. In a widely cited 1984 report, the population division of the World Bank—an institution which is completely dependent upon American sponsorship—presented a mainstream rationalization for taking the voluntary family-planning movement a step further, into active efforts by national governments to suppress reproduction through financial, political, and social pressures. "Ensuring that people have only as many children as they want . . . might not be enough," the World Bank report asserted. Where "privately desired" child-bearing exceeds the "socially desired" level, it claimed, government ought to step in. Readers with a sense for *realpolitik* will detect in this logic a chilling door-opening for massive state intrusion into the most sensitive of human prerogatives.

In addition to the problem of making such fundamental decisions for people without their consent, there is a deeper philosophical issue. The argument is often made by advocates of state-dictated population control that the life of certain Asian or African or Latin American peasants is miserable, and that we who understand cannot allow them to perpetuate their misery. Population revisionists, on the other hand, start with the belief that there is dignity and potential in every human life, that even an existence considered deprived by modern standards can carry great meaning and pleasure. Population revisionists believe it is very dangerous to construct a generalized, systematic argument the bottom line of which is that humans are economic, social, and ecological nuisances—in short that people are a kind of pollution.

So, sharp changes in demographic conditions as well as worrisome human rights trends helped spark some of the new thinking on population. But proba-

bly even more important in reshaping the debate has been a third factor: the influence of new research and empirical analysis on the actual results of population growth. Over the last decade the prevailing shibboleths about alleged economic and social ill-effects have been examined, one by one. Most of them have been found wanting.

For instance, it was claimed in the 1960s that the presence of children in a society would depress savings and investment. It was also argued that population growth would have major negative effects—slowing income growth, increasing unemployment, and deterring technological innovation. None of these assertions has proven true.

When the population scare was in full bloom, it was claimed that population growth reduced educational attainment—which turned out to be absolutely false. Population rise was said to be responsible for the growth of Third World mega-cities. In truth, the rural to urban shift has been shown to spring primarily from other sources. It was asserted that population was the major cause of world hunger. But population level has had almost nothing to do with the famines of recent decades. Experts agree that those famines have been, almost without exception, the result of civil strife, of political and economic disruptions.

Through most of the 1970s those who saw population as a problem insisted that less was always better. After all, more people meant more mouths to feed, more feet to shoe, more schools to build. More people, in short, meant more trouble.

Plenty of activists still think that way. But many scientists have changed their minds, believing it is a mistake to talk of population as an undifferentiated global problem. What matters is not some abstract total number of people in existence, but where they are and how they are living. There are certain countries with ample population and others with too few people.

It does not matter to the people of Zaire—which suffers underdevelopment partly because in many parts of the country there are not enough people to support an efficient infrastructure—that there are 97 million people in Nigeria. Zaire has certain needs and Nigeria has certain needs, and it is nonsense to lump them together under the simple heading of "overpopulated Africa."

Related to this is another insight of the new demographic thinking: The number of people which a given area can "support" is subject to constant change, and is related to the way those people are economically and socially organized. There are 120 million people jammed onto the rocky islands of Japan. Yet, because of their well-structured and highly-productive society, they are among the richest and longest-lived people in the world. If you had asked the Algonquian Indians who inhabited the island of Manhattan in the 1700s how many people they thought it could support, they might have told you it was already full. Holland—which few people would describe as being unable to support its population—has a population density of 354 people per square kilometer; India, which we are told is one of the most overpopulated nations in the world today, contains 228 people per square kilometer.

There are many other such interesting contrasts. The United States is the richest nation in the world, and is sparsely populated with 25 people per square kilometer. West Germany is the second richest nation, and is densely populated—246 people per square kilometer. South Korea is even more densely populated—409 citizens per square kilometer—yet it is also one of the fastest-growing countries on earth. A very slow-growing and very poor nation is Bolivia—thinly populated with just 6 persons per square kilometer. The poorest nation in the world is Ethiopia. It is also one of the more sparesely populated—35 Ethiopians per square kilometer.

In other words, there are dozens of lightly populated countries that are poor, dirty, and hungry. And there are plenty of countries with large, dense populations that are prosperous and attractive. This is not to argue that density is an advantage, but rather that the number of people is not the critical variable in determining these things.

There is no such thing as a "proper" number of people—economic success can be achieved in both sparsely and densely populated countries. Revi-sionist demographers like to point out that each baby comes equipped not only with a mouth, but also with two hands and a brain. People not only consume, they produce—food, capital, even resources. The trick is to organize society so that each person will be an asset and not a burden. In a country whose economy is a mess even one additional baby can be an economic liability. But if the country is structured in such a way as to allow that child to labor and think creatively, he becomes an asset.

In short, people are a valuable resource. The fundamental insight of a diverse group of revisionist scholars—including Simon Kuznets, Colin Clark, P. T. Bauer, Ester Boserup, Albert Hirschman, Julian Simon, Richard Easterlin, and others—was in building up a body of thought that emphasizes the creative potential of individual humans and demonstrates their productive capacities when living in well-organized societies. Because these thinkers have emphasized production more than consumption, human supply more than human demand, their school might rightly be called "supply-side demography."

Within the citadels of population alarmism at the United Nations, the World Bank, and elsewhere, resistance to these new insights continues to be strong. But the monolithic character of the population debate has thankfully passed. One of the first public airings of the insights of supply-side demography took place at the World Population Conference sponsored by the United Nations and held in Mexico City in 1984. Under the leadership of James Buckley and Ben Wattenberg, the American delegation introduced several revisionist declarations into the conference report. The main one was a plank suggesting that in Third World efforts to moderate population growth, economic development ought to be given equal emphasis with family planning. Economic growth is, of course, desirable in its own right. But the more direct, often overlooked, effect of economic growth on population is its vital role in bringing about the very social transformations which ultimately reduce high birth levels. Improvements in income, education, and health, and the changes in cultural mores and living patterns that economic development brings—like improved female status, more urbanization, and so forth—all act powerfully to suppress fertility.

That is the position Indira Gandhi came around to late in her life. In 1984 Mrs. Gandhi stated:

> The very best way of inducing people to have smaller families is more development. Where we have highly industrialized areas or much better education or even much better agriculture, we find automatically families tend to grow smaller.

To put the idea in shorthand, one might say that economic growth is itself the equivalent of a powerful contraceptive.

Not only is development the best way of producing smaller families, it may be the *only* fully effective way, short of coercion. To see why this is the case, consider that surveys throughout the developing world show that when women are asked what number of children they consider ideal, what number they would *like* to have in their lifetime, how many they *desire*, the answers average approximately four children per woman. That would of course double the population every generation (two parents yielding four children).

Such an answer is not terribly surprising. After all, roughly three-quarters of the people of the developing world still live in rural settings—in villages where hands are needed for agricultural labor, where social practices tend to be traditional, where values change slowly. For a variety of reasons, most families in the Third World still *want* relatively large families. And that is rational behavior.

Consider specifically the case of Africa. The World Fertility Survey canvassed ten nations there. It showed that African women want families even *larger* than their already high current average of over six children. It is absurd, then, to argue that high world fertility is just a result of unmet demand for modern contraception. In many places such demand is limited or nonexistent because Third World families view children as social and economic assets.

It should not be assumed from any of this that revisionist demographers are opposed to family planning programs. In fact, most would argue that access to products that allow individuals to control the number and timing of their offspring is one of technology's great liberating gifts to this century. But while contraception is a family right, revisionists would argue, it is *not* a national duty. Too many governments—under pressure from the international population control apparatus—are setting up programs which pressure families about childbearing choices, on the false grounds that unless certain nationwide fertility goals and timetables are met, social progress will be unattainable.

In truth, that formulation is exactly reversed. Fertility levels reflect a society's level of development and proceed apace with it. Small families are a symptom, not a cause, of socio-economic advancement. Former Population Association of America president Richard Easterlin has written that "Family planning programs may be a misuse of scarce public funds early in the development process" because cultural modernization must take place before birth desires will decline significantly and demand for contraception will root. There is no shortcut. A society that is backward in every other way cannot be jumped to an advanced demographic stage. (Absent force, that is.) Attempts to push new reproductive attitudes onto a society faster than its social and economic standing allow it to assimilate such changes only brings on instability.

It follows from all this that socio-economic development ought to be the centerpiece of population policy. And if rapid social and economic progress is the goal, as the U.S. delegation at Mexico City asserted, then the institution of free markets ought to be the favored instrument. (In the period since 1984 even the opinions of world communist leaders have been added to the economic history of the West in making that case.)

The influence of this global move toward market-based economics on population policy can be seen in a landmark report by the U.S. National Academy of Sciences. In 1986 the academy released the results of a major two-year study by some of the world's leading experts on population and economic development. The summary report was a committee document, and as such contained plenty of the usual genuflections to the previous generation of scholarship. Nonetheless, it surprised those who had taken the pessimistic view of population trends as an obvious truth. It suggested that while slower population growth might be helpful in some developing countries, the economic, resource, and environmental benefits would usually be very modest.

The critical insight of the academy scholars is the fundamental premise of revisionists and supply-side demographers, namely that in most nations, the crucial variable in determining future development will be the structure of the country's economic and political institutions, not the number of people. The "key" factor, the academy wrote, is the "mediating role that human behavior and human institutions play in the relation between population growth and economic processes."

The academy particularly emphasized the importance of free markets in achieving this development. They suggested that national leaders interested in directing their people down the path to both further development and continued decline in birthrates ought to stop ignoring the new lessons on the importance of socio-economic reform, and to start freeing up their economies.

As a hard-headed scientific document which challenged many of the longstanding assumptions of population policy, the academy report caused a considerable stir in the demographic community. One leading authority, Dr. Allen Kelley of Duke University, described the report as representing "a watershed. . . . It retreats very substantially from many previous assessments which concluded that population growth exerted a strong negative impact on development." "We have before us," he concluded, "a strong revisionist interpretation."

Revisionist demographers accept that population growth must eventually end. That will happen as a matter of course, they believe, in an organic natural process that occurs as a society matures, modernizes, and the incentives for very large families disappear. A society need not wait until it is rich for this to happen. Even modest levels of development bring steep drops in birthrates. Assuring that contraceptive availability matches private demand in the interim is a reasonable undertaking for governments and interested parties. But to force fertility preferences will inevitably lead to unhappy results. No intellectual justification can be claimed to exist for intrusions on family and individual sovereignty when it comes to questions of family size.

It is now possible to leave behind the erroneous belief that population growth is a catastrophic, uncontrollable horror. The obvious, long-neglected truth is that in addition to consuming and making demands on society, people also produce. It is not governments, corporations, banks, or even natural resources that produce wealth, but people availed of efficient and open economic systems—witness the Japanese, the Swiss, the Taiwanese.

What prevents most developing countries from providing for their growing populations is not a lack of family planning programs or a paucity of physical resources or a shortage of Western aid. Rather it is a defective economy and government. Individuals concerned for the welfare of people in poor countries around the globe ought to focus not on raw numbers, but on the institutions that prevent citizens from exercising their creative and productive potential.

QUESTIONS FOR DISCUSSION

1. What criteria should be used to evaluate whether the economic condition of third world countries is getting better or worse?
2. Which third world countries have achieved the best records of economic development? Which have the worst records? What are the lessons that can be learned from such an analysis?
3. What effect does population growth have on economic development?
4. What effect does population growth have on renewable resources?
5. On the basis of your predictions about the global economy, what steps should current policymakers take concerning population growth?

SUGGESTED READINGS

Bauer, Peter T. "Population Scares." *Commentary*, **84** (Nov. 1987), pp. 39–42.

Berreby, Davis. "The Numbers Game." *Discover*, **11** (Apr. 1990), pp. 42–43, 46–49.

Brown, Lester R. "Feeding Six Billion." *World Watch*, **2** (Sept. 1989), pp. 32–40.

Demeny, Paul. "World Population Trends." *Current History*, **88** (Jan. 1989), pp. 17–19, 58–59, 64.

Fornos, Werner, "Gaining People, Losing Ground." *Humanist*, **50** (May/June 1990), pp. 5–6.

Hall, Ray. *World Population Trends*. Cambridge, England: Cambridge Univ. Press, 1989.

Hardin, Garrett. "There Is No Global Population Problem." *Humanist*, **49** (July/Aug. 1989), pp. 11–13, 32.

"The Population Explosion." *Amicus Journal*, **12** (Winter 1990), pp. 22, 24–33.

"Population Patrol." *Progressive*, **54** (Sept. 1990), pp. 18–28.

Preston, Samuel H. (ed.). "World Population: Approaching the Year 2000." *Annals of the American Academy of Political Science*, **510** (July 1990), entire issue.

Raven, Peter H. "A World in Crisis." *USA Today Magazine*, **117** (May 1989), pp. 48–50.

Simon, Julian Lincoln. *Theory of Population and Economic Growth*. Oxford, England: Blackwell, 1986.

———— and Herman Kahn (eds.). *The Resourceful Earth: A Response to Global 2000*. Oxford, England: B. Blackwell, 1984.

Tierney, John. "Betting the Planet." *New York Times Magazine*, Dec. 2, 1990, pp. 52–53, 74, 76, 78, 80–81.

Wattenberg, Ben, and Karl Zinsmeister (eds.). *Are World Population Trends a Problem?* Washington, D.C.: American Enterprise Institute for Public Policy Research, 1985.

23 Should the United States Sharply Reduce Its Military Commitments Abroad in the Post-Cold War Era?

YES

Defense Monitor

The U.S. as the World's Policeman? Ten Reasons to Find a Different Role

NO

Midge Decter

Shaping a Foreign Policy Agenda for the 1990s

The U.S. as the World's Policeman? Ten Reasons to Find a Different Role

Defense Monitor

Under the Bush Administration, the United States appears to be expanding the role it has long performed as global policeman. President Bush's vision of a "new world order" seems to mean that the U.S. military's mission is shifting from "fighting communism" to capturing drug lords and stopping dictators. It is shifting from defending half the world against the other half to defending the entire world against new "threats" sometimes identified by the Pentagon simply as "instability, uncertainty, and unpredictability."

Since August 1990, President Bush has assembled a military force of about 460,000 U.S. troops in the Middle East to do battle with Iraq and Saddam Hussein. After the war in the Persian Gulf ends, the Bush Administration may seek to maintain American military personnel in Saudi Arabia or on the territory of other countries in the Middle East on a long-term basis. These forces would join almost half a million U.S. troops—one quarter of all active-duty American men and women in uniform—already stationed on military bases in foreign countries and aboard ships in distant waters.

With the U.S. military buildup in the Persian Gulf, *40 percent of all active-duty American military personnel currently are deployed outside the U.S. and its territorial waters.* Prior to the Gulf conflict, 435,000 U.S. troops already were assigned to 395 major military bases in 35 foreign countries. Accompanying them were more than 168,000 civilian Pentagon employees and 400,000 family dependents.

Another 47,000 U.S. Navy and Marine Corps personnel were stationed aboard ships in foreign waters and 10,000 U.S. troops were stationed at 20 military bases on the American overseas territorial possessions of Guam, Johnston Atoll, the Marshall Islands, Midway Island, Puerto Rico, the Virgin Islands, and Wake Island.

Altogether, today more than a million American military personnel and civilian Pentagon employees are stationed abroad. Prior to World War II, the U.S. maintained only a handful of military installations in foreign countries. When troops were dispatched overseas they generally were returned home in short order. The first permanent U.S. bases in foreign countries were established in Cuba and in the Philippines following the Spanish-American War in 1898.

After World War II, America adopted a strategy of "forward defense" to contain perceived Soviet expansionism by establishing "front lines" at outposts far from U.S. shores. Today the danger posed by the Soviet Union has receded. The containment mission upon which forward defense rested has essentially disappeared. Yet the Bush Administration is busy finding new rationales to keep American troops stationed in distant corners of the world in perpetuity.

In the 1980s the U.S. annually spent about $160–$170 billion to defend countries in Europe, $30–$40 billion to defend countries in Asia, and $20–$40 billion to protect U.S. access to Persian Gulf oil. This included the costs of pay, operations, maintenance, training, and support for American military forces based in foreign countries and for all planned reinforcements from the U.S., plus the costs of the research, development, and production of weapons and other equipment used by these forces.

Future U.S. military spending must be weighed against growing nonmilitary threats to American security not included in Pentagon "threat scenarios." These include a deepening budget crunch, trade deficits, a $3 trillion national debt, inadequate health care, drug problems, homelessness, deteriorating highways and bridges, a $500 billion savings-and-loan bailout, and perhaps as much as $300 billion worth of damage to the enviroment from operations

Source: Defense Monitor, "The U.S. as the World's Policeman? Ten Reasons to Find A Different Role," *Defense Monitor,* **20** (Jan. 1991), pp. 1–7. Reprinted by permission of The Center for Defense Information, Washington, DC.

at Pentagon bases and Department of Energy nuclear weapons plants.

In the post–Cold War world the U.S. should now be able to meet critical domestic needs while still satisfying all essential security requirements. It can reduce its annual military budget to two-thirds or less of its present size. It can cut its nuclear forces by three-quarters and its conventional forces by one-half. *The U.S. can safely reduce by almost a million the number of its active-duty military personnel. These reductions should begin with troops in Europe, Japan, South Korea, and the Philippines.*

The closure of obsolete military bases in foreign countries should precede any additional base closings in California, Alabama, Texas, and other places in the U.S. In 1990 the Pentagon announced plans to withdraw 40,000 American troops from Europe over the next year and 14,000–15,000 troops from Asia over 3 years. It plans either to end or to cut back operations at 150 sites in 10 foreign countries.

But according to Representative Patricia Schroeder (D.- Colo.), the "150 sites" include "gas stations on the autobahn, isolated housing units, athletic fields, and sites which have long ago been cited for closure." Only a few are major military bases slated for complete closure. One of those, Torrejon Air Base, is closing because in 1988 Spain refused to renew the U.S. lease. Rather than bring home the 5,000 U.S. airmen and 72 F-16 warplanes stationed at Torrejon, the Bush Administration wants to relocate them in Crotone, Italy, after constructing a new base so extravagant that some have called it "our little Italian theme park."

The U.S. is moving too slowly to reduce old military burdens in Europe and Asia, while in the Persian Gulf it has taken on new burdens not yet fully defined. The Bush Administration has yet to forge a new American security policy and to restructure U.S. military forces in a way that acknowledges the tremendous changes in the world.

There are at least 10 good reasons why the U.S. should begin gradually to reduce its foreign military involvements, close down its costly foreign bases, and withdraw and demobilize all U.S. troops in foreign countries by the year 2000.

Reason 1: *U.S. Military Forces Based in Foreign Countries Do Not Contribute to the Defense of the U.S.*

There is no national consensus about what constitute the "vital interests" of the U.S. There is also no consensus about how to protect them. Interests change with time and politics, but most people would agree that America does not have interests everywhere in the world and that some interests matter more than others.

According to General Wallace Nutting, former Commander-in-Chief of the U.S. Readiness Command, "We today do not have a single soldier, airman, or sailor solely dedicated to the security mission within the United States." In fact, about 70 percent of America's annual military spending and most of its military forces—even those based in the U.S.—are intended to further U.S. capabilities for fighting nonnuclear, "conventional" wars in foreign countries.

Many things said to be vital interests cost more to defend than they are worth. While America's industries, living standards, and military power remain all too dependent upon oil, *any hardship suffered by the U.S. from losing access to Persian Gulf oil or from an increase in the price of oil seems negligible when compared with the devastating costs of war.*

Persian Gulf oil is much less important to the U.S. than it is to Europe and Japan. Japan imports 99 percent of the oil it consumes, 70 percent coming from Gulf countries. The U.S., on the other hand, imports 46 percent of the oil it uses. Only 24 percent of U.S. oil imports and 8.5 percent of total U.S. energy supplies come from the Persian Gulf. Iraqi and Kuwaiti oil together account for just 7.5 percent of all U.S. oil imports.

A country willing to spend almost $300 billion each year for its military certainly could endure the far smaller economic costs of a cutoff of the supply of less than a quarter of its foreign oil. If the U.S. spent only half as much money on domestic energy conservation and diversification efforts as it does on military forces to fight for oil, the nation would be far more secure in terms of energy resources.

Interests that were defined in the context of the

Cold War—particularly containment of communism—are now overdue for reevaluation. *Those interests precious enough to be deemed "vital interests" should have a direct, immediate, and substantial connection with America's physical survival.* First and foremost the U.S. should defend its own territory and the immediate approaches to its territory.

Reason 2: *The U.S. Is Not Bound By Treaties to Use Its Military Forces to Defend Other Countries*

Two hundred years ago George Washington admonished his countrymen to "steer clear of permanent alliances." Thomas Jefferson spoke of "peace, commerce, and honest friendship with all nations, entangling alliances with none." For most of America's history their advice was heeded. Since World War II, however, the U.S. has signed military treaties with 43 countries.

Nevertheless, *not one U.S. defense treaty with other countries commits America to military action in the event of an attack on its treaty partners. Nor does any treaty require the U.S. to station its armed forces on another country's territory.*

The North Atlantic Treaty, signed in 1949, states that an attack against one or more alliance member "shall be considered an attack against them all." Each alliance member, however, retains the right to decide "individually and in concert with the other parties *such action as it deems necessary* [emphasis added], including the use of armed force."

The original U.S.-Japan Security Treaty, signed in 1951, stated that "the U.S. is presently willing to maintain forces in and about Japan," but "in the expectation, however, that Japan will itself increasingly assume responsibility for its own defense against direct and indirect aggression." Similarly, the revised treaty in effect today does not commit a single U.S. soldier, sailor, airman, or Marine to defend Japan.

America always has possessed the freedom to bring home its military forces in foreign countries whenever it chooses. It need not secure the blessing or permission of host governments or enter into drawn-out negotiations before closing obsolete bases and withdrawing troops.

Reason 3: *The World Has Changed Significantly*

The existing U.S. military force structure, with its forward deployment of troops and weapons in foreign countries and waters, was designed to meet the perceived threats of a very different world. Over the past few years some startling changes have taken place.

Communism in Eastern Europe has collapsed. East and West Germany have united. As a military organization the Warsaw Pact is defunct. It is expected that Soviet military forces will empty out of Czechoslovakia and Hungary completely by mid-1991, Poland perhaps by 1992, and Germany by 1994. The Soviets also are reducing their forces in Asia and have declared their intention to withdraw all of their foreign-based troops by the year 2000.

Just how much the world has changed is perhaps most evident in Germany's agreement to pay the Soviet Union several billion dollars a year to subsidize—until they depart—the 600,000 Soviet troops and dependents remaining in what used to be East Germany. In Asia, meanwhile, the Soviet Union may return several islands to Japan which it has occupied since World War II. Relations between North and South Korea are improving to the point where federation before the end of the century seems possible.

In today's world *national power has become more complex. It is defined as much by economic, social, and political components as by military power.* Today military power generally is less practical, less usable, and less translatable into political or economic advantage. Increasingly, economic leadership is the true measure of a nation's strength. While governments in the Soviet Union, Europe, and Japan appear to have recognized this, U.S. officials lag behind.

America can ill afford to continue to postpone putting its economic house in order. It needs an economy that is innovative, that is dynamic, and that is doing the kinds of things people now see Japan doing. If the economic challenge goes unmet, then our security is threatened. The American way of life can be endangered by economic weakness just as surely as by a Soviet attack. In fact, *economic vulnerability now is a much greater threat to the U.S. than Soviet aggression.*

Reason 4: *Other Countries Are Capable of Providing Their Own Defenses*

The countries hosting U.S. troops are more than capable of providing for themselves whatever military forces they deem necessary. Europe and Japan have long since recovered from the ravages of World War II. If anything, the ongoing U.S. military subsidy only acts as an incentive for host countries to be militarily weak, perpetuates a dependent relationship, and suggests that the security of these countries means more to the U.S. than it does to them.

Today the European members of the NATO [North Atlantic Treaty Organization] military alliance have a collective gross national product (GNP) greater than that of the U.S. and at least two times greater than that of the Soviet Union. Yet *America spends more on NATO defenses than the other 15 alliance members combined.*

America's European NATO allies collectively have more than 3 million active-duty troops drawn from a combined population of almost 400 million. If needed, between them there are 87 million males aged 15–49 available for military service. Excluding Britain and Iceland, neither of which has compulsory military service, about 2.6 million males in the remaining 12 European NATO countries reach draft age annually.

Beyond questions of manpower sufficiency, France, Britain, Germany and Italy—powerful industrial countries that are among the world's 10 leading exporters of weapons—are capable of manufacturing in mass quantity all of the weapons necessary to satisfy their own security requirements. France and Britain also possess sizable stocks of nuclear weapons.

Germany, the world's leading exporter of goods, hosted 240,000 U.S. troops before President Bush reassigned some units to the Persian Gulf. Yet a unified Germany has a population of 78 million and a military force that currently numbers almost 600,000 troops (to be reduced to 370,000 troops by the end of 1994). If needed, Germany now has 17 million males aged 15–49 available for military service. Every year about 418,000 German males reach military age.

Japan, although it faces no military threats, hosted 47,000 U.S. troops before President Bush ordered some of the Marines in Okinawa to the Persian Gulf. It is the world's second-ranking economic power with a GNP of $2.8 trillion. It has a population of almost 124 million and more than 27 million males aged 15–49 available for military service. About a million Japanese males reach draft age annually.

South Korea remains host to 41,000 U.S. troops even though the Pentagon admitted in testimony to Congress that "South Korean forces are capable of defending themselves against any threat from the North that does not involve either the Soviet Union or the People's Republic of China." South Korea's population of 43 million is twice that of North Korea. Its economy is 10 times larger. It has more than 8 million males aged 15–49 available for military service. Every year about 445,000 South Korean males reach military age.

The Philippines, confronting only internal threats from the rebel New People's Army, remains host to 13,000 U.S. troops. It has a population of 66 million, of which more than 11 million are males aged 15–49 available for military service. About 685,000 Filipino males reach draft age yearly.

Reason 5: *The World Does Not Need the U.S. to Be Global Policeman*

The Bush Administration maintains that American troops must remain in allied countries as their security blanket, preparing not only to meet every known threat and enemy, but also to meet the "unforeseeable," and as yet unidentified, threats and enemies that may or may not materialize in the future. It cautions that the U.S. must guard against a possible reversal of policy in the Soviet Union and serve as a stabilizing force in the face of potential "volatility" and "turbulence" from ethnic, nationality, and religious conflicts and separatist movements.

CIA [Central Intelligence Agency] Director William Webster, however, advised Congress in early 1990 that "even if a hardline regime were able to retain power in Moscow, it would have little incentive to engage in major confrontations with the United States." Defense Secretary Richard Cheney acknowledged, "The threat of a sudden attack by Soviet forces in Europe has basically evaporated." And General Colin Powell, chairman of the Joint Chiefs of Staff, stated, "In the Pacific it is unlikely that the Soviets would initiate hostilities which threaten our interests."

With the November 1990 signing of the Conventional Forces in Europe (CFE) Treaty, the Soviet Union has agreed to destroy tens of thousands of its tanks, armored combat vehicles, artillery weapons, and combat aircraft. In the future *the U.S. may have as much as 2 years warning in which to dispatch military forces to Europe in the unlikely event that the Soviet military decided to prepare to fight its way through Eastern Europe to attack Western Europe.*

Many uncertainties and potential instabilities in the world are either peripheral or irrelevant to U.S. security and thus do not warrant American military involvement. If Romania and Hungary were to go to war over the disputed territory of Transylvania, for example, or if hostilities between Croatia and Serbia were to lead to civil war in Yugoslavia, in neither case would vital American interests be threatened.

The U.N. Security Council, with its multinational peace-keeping forces, or the strengthened dispute resolution mechanisms of the Conference on Security and Cooperation in Europe (CSCE), including the newly-established Center for the Prevention of Conflict, are better suited to intervene in such situations than are U.S. troops.

Increasingly, the leading concerns of nations in Western Europe are drugs, unemployment, environmental degradation, and the potential mass immigration of people from Eastern Europe and elsewhere— hardly problems that can be prevented or resolved

with U.S. military forces. *Military might is a blunt instrument good at destroying things and killing people, but not at resolving complex political, ethnic, religious, and historical disputes.*

It is not in America's interest to be the world's "911 number." If the U.S. withdraws its forward-based military forces, the world is not going to come apart and America's security is not going to suffer. Since the peak years of the 1960s when it had bases in or special access arrangements with more than 60 countries, the U.S. has pulled military forces out of a number of countries. In no case has this led to a lasting decline in security.

Reason 6: *Military Forces in the U.S. Can Respond Quickly to Crises Anywhere in the World*

At one time the U.S. needed bases abroad in order to supply coal, food, water, and supplies to Navy ships and their crews. In the early years of the Cold War it needed airfields for American nuclear bombers that lacked sufficient range to reach the Soviet Union from bases in the U.S. But today, while foreign bases may continue to be convenient to the U.S. in some cases, they are not vital to American security.

With in-flight refueling, modern U.S. Air Force strategic bombers can reach targets anywhere in the world within hours. Intercontinental ballistic missiles (ICBMs) can devastate the Soviet Union within half an hour. "Over-the-horizon" satellite communications have greatly diminished the need for radio relay stations.

The U.S. Navy has 56 underway replenishment ships to supply warships in distant waters with fuel, ammunition, and other stores. It has 41 maintenance logistics ships to provide repairs when necessary. Nuclear propulsion, by increasing the global reach of ships and submarines, has decreased the importance to the U.S. of having naval refueling facilities in other countries.

In the future there are likely to be increasingly fewer instances in which it would be in American interests to intervene militarily in foreign countries. But if deemed necessary, the U.S. can quickly dispatch armed forces to any place in the world from bases in California, North Carolina, and many other American locations. *There is no military requirement to have U.S. troops and weapons in place in foreign countries.*

Modern long-range transport aircraft, aerial refueling tankers, and strategic sealift ships have largely eliminated the need for overseas staging facilities. Currently the U.S. Air Force has 110 C-5 and 250 C-141 long-range cargo aircraft. It plans to build 120 new C-17 cargo aircraft. It has 591 KC-135 tanker aircraft for in-flight refueling. The U.S. Navy has 69 active sealift ships.

For additional air- and sealift the U.S. can rely on 504 commercial aircraft in its Civil Reserve Air Fleet, 242 reserve ships (93 Ready Reserve Force ships and 149 National Defense Reserve Fleet ships), and 318 U.S.-flag and effectively U.S.-controlled ships.

The Bush Administration's military buildup in the Persian Gulf has demonstrated impressive airlift and sealift capabilities. As of mid-January 1991 the U.S. Transportation Command was employing 212 ships and had moved 3.4 million measurement tons (136 million cubic feet) of cargo to Saudi Arabia, 7,000 miles from the closest U.S. shores. The Military Airlift Command had completed 10,000 missions in which it delivered over 371,000 personnel and 346,000 tons of cargo.

The U.S. airlifted more personnel and equipment in the first 3 weeks of the Persian Gulf buildup than it moved in the first 3 months of the Korean War. By the sixth week the U.S. already had moved by air the equivalent of what was delivered during the entire 65 weeks of the 1948–49 Berlin Airlift.

Reason 7: *Military Forces Do Not Assure Economic Access and Political Influence*

Some argue that it is in the interest of the U.S. to keep military forces abroad because their presence in foreign countries enhances America's "status," guarantees the U.S. a voice in the affairs of the host countries, and reassures American companies conducting business in other countries. Total two-way American trade with Europe exceeds $200 billion annually, with East Asia $300 billion.

Having military forces abroad, however, contributes little if anything to America's economic access and political influence around the world. On the contrary, *by continuing to relieve major economic competitors such as Germany and Japan of the military burden of providing their own defenses, the U.S. weakens its own security by placing unnecessary strains on its economy.*

At the present the U.S. still has the largest economy in the world. By virtue of this fact, it will have economic access, troops or no troops. As for providing security for businesses, a recent survey of multinational corporations operating in the Philippines revealed that the presence of American military bases ranked only tenth in their decision to invest there.

There is little recent evidence that having U.S. military forces in foreign countries translates into political influence. During the 1973 Yom Kippur war in the Middle East the U.S. was denied access to facilities and airspace over Western Europe in order to resupply Israel with weapons. In the early 1980s America's European allies refused to accede to Reagan Administration wishes that construction of a natural gas pipeline to the Soviet Union be stopped.

After the 1985 hijacking of the *Achille Lauro* cruise ship, Italian and American troops squared off against each other over the issue of custody of suspected terrorist Muhammad Abbas. European governments denied overflight rights for the Reagan Administration's bombing of Libya in 1986. Throughout the 1980s the Europeans also disagreed with U.S. policies toward Central America.

In the future it would be unwise for the U.S. to rely on its military power to influence other countries, whether friends or adversaries. America's foreign military bases increasingly are a drain on, rather than a contributor to, its national power. *It is in the interest of the U.S. to remain actively involved in the world's affairs, but primarily through economic and diplomatic efforts with much less reliance on military strength.*

Reason 8: *U.S. Military Forces Are Not Needed to Deter German and Japanese Rearmament*

The reason for stationing U.S. military forces in Europe and in Asia sometimes has been expressed as follows: "to keep the Soviets out, the Americans in, and the Germans and Japanese down." Pointing to the last objective, some argue that withdrawing U.S. military forces would leave "power vacuums" that would encourage former World War II villains Germany and Japan to rearm even more than they already have, making neighboring countries apprehensive and resulting in regional instability.

Even while American troops have been stationed on their soil both countries, with U.S. encouragement, have amassed powerful militaries. Continuing to keep U.S. troops in Germany and Japan will not prevent these countries from exercising their sovereign right to further add to their armed forces if they so choose. On the other hand, it should be recognized that *German and Japanese citizens today have thoroughly rejected militarism and aggression.*

For the foreseeable future, battles involving Germany and Japan and other countries will remain in the global marketplace. What possible advantage could these economic juggernauts acquire through military means that cannot be satisfied without loss of blood through their powerful economies?

Initial concerns of the Soviet Union, Poland, and other countries about German unification have since lessened. In signing the so-called "Treaty on the Final Settlement With Respect to Germany" in September 1990, Germany agreed to reduce the size of its armed forces to 370,000 troops within 3–4 years and to refrain from building and stockpiling nuclear, chemical, or biological weapons. The Treaty also formally settled the Oder-Niesse boundary question with Poland by confirming the current border.

Japan, still harboring painful memories of Hiro-

shima and Nagasaki, is a country imbued with strong peaceful tendencies. The overwhelmingly negative reaction of Japanese citizens thwarted their government's plan to assign just a few hundred soldiers to noncombat duties in the Persian Gulf. Ryoji Onodero, an official of the Japan Defense Agency, recently stated that "Japan does not want to take over from the U.S. as world policeman." Japan's new 5-year defense plan envisions annual military spending increases of only about 3 percent, considerably below the 5.4 percent yearly increases of the previous 5-year plan.

Reason 9: *U.S. Forces Are Wearing Out Their Welcome*

Anti-American sentiment is on the rise in many of the places where U.S. military forces are stationed. The State Department recently cautioned Americans in the Philippines about "possible imminent terrorist bombing" by rebel guerrillas. Similarly, in South Korea the continued presence of U.S. forces has strengthened opposition groups and placed Americans at risk.

In Germany, many citizens have demanded reductions in destructive military training on their country's land and in its airspace. U.S. and other NATO forces already have been forced to limit the amount of realistic training they conduct to minimize citizen complaints regarding noise, environmental damage, and safety.

Support for U.S. bases and forces has declined in other countries as well. *Increasingly, American military forces abroad are regarded as an infringement upon sovereignty. They have outlived their usefulness and overstayed their welcome.*

Some host governments, given the choice, would prefer that the U.S. military remain in their countries. Through money spent and foreign nationals employed, American bases are a boon to host country economies. In addition, base rights agreements often entail quid pro quo transactions in the form of economic and military aid.

In the Philippines, U.S. bases create about 70,000 jobs. In Germany, they are the thirteenth largest employer. American troops, civilian Pentagon employees, and their dependents pump about $7-$9 billion into Germany's economy each year. When they leave, numerous enterprises, including apartments, bars, restaurants, and brothels, will be affected. But *the purpose of the U.S. military should be to defend the U.S., not to stimulate the economies of other countries.*

Reason 10: *Withdrawing and Demobilizing U.S. Forces Will Save Tens of Billions of Dollars*

It costs more to operate military bases in expensive environments like Europe and Japan than in the U.S. As the value of the dollar drops, maintaining foreign bases becomes even more expensive. A dollar, worth 3.5 German marks in 1987, today is worth only 1.6 marks. *Withdrawing and demobilizing American military personnel and civilian Pentagon employees stationed in Europe and in Asia would go a long way toward resolving America's budget problems.*

In 1988 the U.S. spent $3.5 billion to construct and repair bases in foreign countries, $2.7 billion to employ 120,000 foreign nationals, $1.3 billion for overseas cost-of-living differentials and supplements, $12.5 billion for base operation support costs, and $500 million for financing currency fluctuations.

With their supermarkets, shopping malls, split-level homes, swimming pools, schools, day care centers, bowling alleys, barber shops, bars, and barbeque pits, America's foreign bases could be Anytown, USA. As such, they are enormously expensive to sustain. It costs the Pentagon about a billion dollars alone each year to operate 271 schools for 150,000 American children at foreign bases in 19 countries.

In 1988 the Pentagon spent $1.3 billion on travel costs for permanent change-of-station moves to foreign bases. Every month that year the Pentagon flew about 12,000 U.S. troops and 10,000 dependents between the U.S. and Germany. It costs American taxpayers about $4,000 for the Pentagon to relocate an enlisted soldier and family to Germany. It costs $13,000 to relocate an officer.

Every year the Penatagon transports 750 million pounds of household effects to foreign bases at a cost of about half a billion dollars. In accordance with the so-called "buy American" rule, it stocks overseas commissaries and PXs with American-made goods at a cost of about $250 million annually. To pet owners, the Pentagon supplies 432,000 cases of cat and dog food. It provides American-brewed Miller, Coors, and Budweiser to soldiers stationed in beer-rich Germany.

In 1989 the Army shipped almost 50,000 cars to Europe at a cost of $1,000 per car—the shipping cost sometimes exceeding the value of the car. The total amount spent on delivering service members' cars equaled what was spent on transporting ammunition!

WHITHER THE U.S.?

The Pentagon's "forward defense" strategy of stationing U.S. military forces in foreign countries and in distant waters is now obsolete. America far too long has borne the burden of defending other countries that now are more than capable of defending themselves.

The U.S. has a choice. It can adapt to a changing world and begin drastically to reduce its military burdens by closing its foreign military bases and bringing troops home. We can choose to pay greater attention to crucial nonmilitary determinants of the nation's security—social, political, economic, and environmental components. Or, the U.S. can further strain its economy and weaken its security by continuing and expanding its role as the world's policeman.

Shaping a Foreign Policy Agenda for the 1990s

Midge Decter

I want to talk about other groups who are participating in this great new debate about foreign policy. To begin with, there are those whom I would call without the least bit of disrespect intended, but for the sake of brevity, the Endowment for Democracy Party.

These are the people who say we must consolidate our ideological and political winnings and push forward in a campaign to bring the blessings of democracy and the free market. (Have you ever noticed how funny it is that even to this day people are a little bit inhibited about using the word "capitalism"? So now we talk about the free market.) We must continue the effort to bring democracy to those ever-growing masses of people who are clamoring for it.

On the other side there are the isolationists, whose classic formulation from as far back as the country's founding has let us perfect ourselves and let our impact on the world, if any, be that of a model for envy and emulation.

And there are radical libertarians who are prepared to say that the rights of government should be so circumscribed as to make impossible any commitment beyond the literal defense of the country's own territory.

UNGRATEFUL ALLIES

And somewhere along this spectrum, representing what I suspect is the largest constituency at this moment, are the party of the "Fed Up." Call them for short, the Pat Buchanan Party. Their view is one that no matter how much you disagree with it, it cannot fail to touch the nervous system and pluck the heartstrings. For more than 40 years, runs this argument, we pursued a policy which enabled our allies—not to speak of our World War II enemies—to get on their feet and then prosper mightily. And all the while as they depended on us to defend them, they hamstrung us, undermined our policies, in some cases like Nicaragua, supported our enemies outright—and above all, subjected us to a continuing moral attack.

And now, more than a quarter of a million of our boys and girls are being forced to suffer the heat and tedium of Saudi Arabia, forbidden, as it were, to show their faces or fly their flag, in order to protect the supply of oil and the economies of these allies.

Meanwhile, with the always honorable exception of Margaret Thatcher—and let us now hope of Prime Minister Major—they wring their hands in uncertainty as to how far they feel we should go in dealing with Saddam Hussein.

Who can read the newspapers, at least some part of each week, without finding some reason or some occasion to say "the hell with the whole lot of them"? Emotion, however, is not a policy, nor does it even give guidance to it.

The fear of nuclear weapons is no doubt a perfectly legitimate emotion. One of the prominent policy suggestions it gave rise to, however, that the world would be a safer place if the United States had no nuclear weapons, does not even qualify as legitimate nonsense.

It will be objected that I have left out of this list so far the position, everybody's favorite in this town, of the hard headed, the national interest school—those who say that all foreign policy decisions are properly made only on the basis of a realistic calculation of the country's interests.

The people who assume this position naturally believe themselves, and are able to behave as if they are, wiser, more worldly, more sophisticated than those who over the years earned for themselves the designation of anti-communist ideologues, like Senator Wallop and like a few other people in this room.

Source: Midge Decter, "Shaping a Foreign Policy Agenda for the 1990s," *Heritage Lectures* No. 296 (1990), pp. 6–10. Reprinted by permission.

CIRCULAR POSITION

There is a problem with the position of hard headedness however, and that is quite simply that it is entirely circular. For how can you hard headedly say what is the national interest at any given moment—especially should it be a moment of crisis—without some prior notion of what your belief is about and what your ambitions for the country are? And in addition, how you read the real and moral nature of the world?

For someone like me, who takes none of the positions I have just described, though I feel great emotional sympathy for all of them at different times—it seems that the first thing that has to be said on the subject of America's role in the world is that when you are the richest and most powerful nation on earth—and despite the best efforts of many of our social philosophers, educators and policy bureaucrats, we are still, and are likely to remain, the richest and most powerful nation on earth—when you are that, it is pure fantasy to imagine that there is such an option for you as withdrawal from the affairs of other countries.

There is no such thing as "non intervention." If you decide to sit out some crisis, that is as much a form of intervention as sending troops. And in some cases, that can in the long run be even more dangerous.

If the 20th century has not taught the United States that lesson over and over in at least five different ways, then we are as a nation doomed forever to be casting around like a blind creature.

The question therefore, is not should we or shouldn't we intervene—but how. Now obviously there have been and will continue to be many crises in the world where it makes no sense for us to mix in. We might at any given moment differ about which these are or should be and why.

PRUDENT ANSWERS

That is what is called among serious people, trying to arrive at a wise application of a policy. Should we try to help settle civil wars in Rwanda and Liberia? The prudent answer, at least for now, would seem to be

no. And there are some conflicts—and I would say the Israeli-Palestinian conflict is one of those—for which there is simply nothing to be done by anyone but sit tight and wait for history to erode what are some of the key heated-up issues.

There are few assertions more specious, however, than the declaration that because we cannot or should not intervene in this place or that place at any given time, the obvious conclusion is that we must not intervene at all.

Indeed, this kind of argument is not only specious, it's rather cheaply specious. Given the consequentiality of American conduct in the world, whether we will it or not—how should we understand that role now that 40-plus years of the organizing principle for American foreign policy is coming apart?

Quite simply, history—or, if you will, fate—has ordained that we must play a key role in keeping international law and order; we must because there is no one else to do it.

I don't, in this auditorium of all places, have to say that the United Nations as an instrumentality for maintaining international comity has for almost the very first moment of its existence if not before that, been a farce.

WORST POLICY

History may decide that the very worst policy of George Bush, in fact, is that he gave a new shot of energy to the United Nations.

And no more than on the streets of Washington or New York City can criminal conduct in the international arena be controlled without the belief that the authorities have power and are prepared to wield it.

It is always to be hoped that the power and the readiness to use it will by themselves act as a deterrent. Often they do; we tend to forget that.

Sometimes, on the other hand, they don't. Then what? We can choose to ignore criminal acts. Again, if it is necessary to spell out the point in answer to those who say we cannot be the world's policeman, let me say that the criminal acts of which I speak are those that threaten the peace and security of whole neighborhoods in the world and ultimately, if not immediately, our own neighborhood.

These crimes against the international order: we can ignore them, we can tell lies about them, we can deny to ourselves that they are taking place. Actually, we along with our Western allies at different times, have done all of these things—ignore, deny or just plain lie.

We and our allies have done these things in particular because, as the late C. P. Snow once put it: "There is that in democratic peoples which hates the bearing of arms. It is a virtue and a dangerous weakness."

And whenever we have denied or deceived ourselves, we have paid dearly. "Hitler had a legitimate right to a bit of *Lebensraum,*" said our forbears in the 1930s. "Let him have the Rhineland, and later the Sudetenland, and he will be satisfied."

BLOODY COSTS

There are many examples of this kind of highly costly sloth and self-deception. To be sure, none so bloody or scarifying in outline as the British and French failure to deter a still weak Hitler in the 1930s. I don't have to belabor the point.

As for our presence in the Persian Gulf, if I felt I knew with any degree of certainty just what the Bush Administration has in mind there—and I don't think Mr. Bush himself knows any more by now—it would be easier to discuss this in such a context.

But one thing is certain; we are there because a crime has been committed, a crime of the kind I described. Not only the invasion and rape of a small oil-rich kingdom on the Persian Gulf, but the threat of disruption to a whole already badly battered system of nations.

In a region vitally important both to the peace and the economic welfare of the world, it is being said constantly by the isolationists, the libertarians, and the fed up that we, the United States of America, have no serious interest there, that if our allies, for instance, need oil, let them see to their own problem, and so on and so on.

All very appealing and very tempting things to believe. But oil is an issue for the entire world economy, and that includes us—and that means women and children all over the world, in poor countries as well as rich ones. Never, never again should we let anybody make the remark that our troops are in Saudi Arabia to make the world safe for gas guzzlers.

There is nothing more cynical that anyone can say than that.

And there is another problem here. The invasion of Kuwait was an act for which we as Americans bear some indeterminate but not small amount of responsibility. Did not the American ambassador, certainly speaking for the United States Department of State (for ambassadors, after all, do not say such things on their own), tell Saddam Hussein that the United States would take no interest in the matter of an Iraqi invasion of Kuwait?

This assurance of our nonintervention was a highly consequential factor. How could it be otherwise? There is indeed no more poignant evidence that for the U.S. nonintervention is a mirage than the role we played in inciting the invasion of Kuwait.

So we have no choice but to play for now the central role in channeling the tides of world order. What we do have a choice about however, is whether to play this role on purpose or inadvertently.

Iraq is the perfect example of playing it inadvertently, and we may not yet get out of it without a serious loss of life. I freely admit that without the organizing principle of anti-communism and the so-called "Royale Politique" notwithstanding, it was anti-communism that held our policy together—and that brought its most notable successes, I might point out.

PAX AMERICANA

Without this principle, it will not be so easy to formulate an encompassing doctrine. Nevertheless, I for one am prepared to say that such a doctrine when it arrives, will bear a powerful resemblance to something called "Pax Americana."

I know that term is one that is usually uttered only with a sneer; let me remind you, so was the term "free world" always spoken with a sneer.

This role will require us to be powerfully armed, a requirement about which we are already going to have a bitter political battle, but that will, if we are going to live in an even minimally peaceful world, may be more urgent than ever now.

Part of being powerfully armed is of course, being powerfully defended, a requirement receding further and further from us every day. I was recently at a meeting where people were speaking and cheering about SDI [Strategic Defense Initative, or "Star Wars"], and my heart was breaking because SDI was sailing off into the sunset before our very eyes.

We cannot have the wisdom to know at every moment what to do, and we will make mistakes of course—but these mistakes will not be fatal, as long as we are prepared to acknowledge the real weight of our responsibility. And one thing more. Let us carry the burden of that responsibility with confidence, and this not only refers to Congress, this refers to all of us. All of us who attempt to influence public opinion.

Pax Americana will not be some dark imperialist conspiracy; the further we carry the force of the American political culture and spread the influence of American political institutions, a better place the world will be.

Russians know that, Ukrainians know that, Poles know that. Why don't we know it? Once again, the main job of convincing people about the legitimacy of American aims will be here at home—and that job is up to us.

QUESTIONS FOR DISCUSSION

1. Do U.S. forces abroad strengthen or weaken U.S. security? What are the reasons for your answer?

2. What relevance does U.S. action in the Persian Gulf in 1990–1991 have on your answer to Question 1?
3. What effect would a return to U.S. isolationism have on the foreign and defense policy of its allies?
4. What effect would a return to U.S. isolationism have on the foreign and defense policy of its adversaries?
5. Would the world be a better place if the United States sought to implant American political culture and spread the influence of American political institutions to other countries? What are the reasons for your answer?

SUGGESTED READINGS

Buchanan, Patrick J. "America First—and Second, and Third." *National Interest*, no. 19 (Spring 1990), pp. 77–82.

Gershman, Carl. "Freedom Remains the Touchstone." *National Interest*, no. 19 (Spring 1990), pp. 83–86.

Goldberg, Andrew C. "Challenges to the Post–Cold War Balance of Power." *Washington Quarterly*, **14** (Winter 1991), pp. 51–60.

Kennedy, Paul M. *The Rise and Fall of the Great Powers: Economic Change and Military Conflict from 1500 to 2000.* New York: Random House, 1987.

Krauthammer, Charles. "Universal Dominion: Toward a Unipolar World." *National Interest*, no. 18 (Winter 1989–90), pp. 46–49.

Kristol, Irving. "In Search of Our National Interest." *Wall Street Journal*, June 7, 1990, p. A14.

Manes, Charles William. "America without the Cold War." *Foreign Policy*, no. 78 (Spring 1990), pp. 3–25.

Muravchik, Joshua. "At Last, Pax Americana." *New York Times*, Jan. 24, 1991, p. A23.

Nye, Joseph S., Jr. "The U.S.: Managing Global Responsibilities." *World and I*, **6** (Jan. 1991), pp. 20–23, 25–27.

Ravenal, Earl C. "The Case for Adjustment." *Foreign Policy*, no. 81 (Winter 1990–91), pp. 3–19.